Development Windows

Development Windows

Essays in Honour of Prof. V.M. Rao

Editors

R.S. Deshpande, K.V. Raju,
S.M. Jharwal and D. Rajsekhar

ACADEMIC FOUNDATION
NEW DELHI

www.academicfoundation.com

First published in 2011
by

ACADEMIC FOUNDATION
4772-73 / 23 Bharat Ram Road, (23 Ansari Road),
Darya Ganj, New Delhi - 110 002 (India).
Phones : 23245001 / 02 / 03 / 04.
Fax : +91-11-23245005.
E-mail : books@academicfoundation.com
www. academicfoundation.com

Cataloging in Publication Data--DK
Courtesy: D.K. Agencies (P) Ltd. <docinfo@dkagencies.com>

Development windows : essays in honour of Prof. V.M. Rao / editors, R.S. Deshpande, K.V. Raju, S.M. Jharwal and D. Rajsekhar.
p. cm.
ISBN 13: 9788171888085
ISBN 10: 8171888089

1. Economic development--India. 2. Poverty--India. 3. Agriculture--Economic aspects--India. 4. India--Economic policy. I. Rao, V. M. (Vidyananda Mohan), 1931- II. Deshpande, R. S. III. Jharwal, S. M. (Sanwar M.)

DDC 338.954 22

Typeset by Italics India, New Delhi.
Printed and bound in India.

Contents

Section II
Agricultural Development

Section III
Irrigation

Section IV
Poverty

Section V
Governance

List of Tables and Figures

Tables

Figures

About the Editors/ Contributors

Editors:

R.S. Deshpande is Director, Institute for Social and Economic Change (ISEC), Bangalore. Earlier, he worked as Professor and Head of the Agricultural Development and Rural Transformation Centre, ISEC and as Registrar at Gokhale Institute of Politics and Economics, Pune. His publications include two volumes in the *State of the Farmer: A Millennium Study, Watershed Management, Where Water Seeps, Glimpses of Indian Agriculture, Tenancy Reforms and Contract Farming.* He has published extensively and has worked as Consultant to World Bank, DFID, and Land Equity, Australia. He has served on many policy bodies of the Government of India and the Government of Karnataka.

K.V. Raju is Adviser to the Chief Minister, Government of Karnataka, and worked as Professor and Head in the Centre for Ecological Economics and Natural Resources of ISEC, Bangalore. He has published extensively on irrigation reforms, irrigation policy, regional agricultural development, and natural resource economics. He has a large number of articles in international and national journals to his credit. Prof. Raju has been policy adviser to many State and cCentral bodies as well as worked at international organisations like IFPRI.

S.M. Jharwal is the Chairman of National Pharmaceutical Pricing Authority, Government of India. Earlier, he has served as the Principal Advisor in the Ministry of Agriculture, Member Secretary (CACP), Advisor (Telecom) and Director (PDS) in the Central government. An academician in the administrative setup, he has published work to his credit on public distribution system, issues in Indian agriculture, telecom and many other aspects of Indian economy. He worked as Member and Chairman of many committees and working groups set up by Government of India and possesses a rare combination of administrative and academic experience.

D. Rajasekhar is Professor and Head of the Centre for Decentralisation and Development of ISEC, Bangalore. He has published on poverty, non-governmental organisations, watershed development, and social security. Dr. Rajasekhar specialises in decentralisation and development as well as role of local organisations and microfinance. He has been helping several State and Central government policy bodies and has a rich research experience behind him.

Contributors:

S.S. Acharya, Chairman, Institute of Rural Management (IRM), Jairpur and Former Chairman, Commission for Agricultural Costs and Prices (CACP), Government of India, New Delhi.

Lalith Achoth, Professor, Department of Agricultural Economics, College of Agriculture, University of Agricultural Sciences (UAS), Bangalore.

M.G. Chandrakanth, Professor, Department of Agricultural Economics, College of Agriculture, University of Agricultural Sciences (UAS), Bangalore.

H. Chandrashekhar, Associate Professor, Department of Agricultural Economics, College of Agriculture, University of Agricultural Sciences (UAS), Bangalore.

Samar K. Datta, Professor, Centre for Management in Agriculture (CMA), Indian Institute of Management (IIM), Ahmedabad.

Saurabh C. Datta, Researcher, Centre for Management in Agriculture (CMA), Indian Institute of Management (IIM), Ahmedabad.

Sudarshan Iyengar, Vice-Chancellor, Gujarat Vidyapith, Ahmedabad.

R.L. Jogi, Project Associate, Institute of Development Studies (IDS), Jaipur.

Gopal K. Kadekodi, Hon. Professor, Centre for Multi-Disciplinary Development Research (CMDR), Dharwad.

K.P. Kannan, Professor, Centre for Development Studies (CDS), Trivandrum.

G.K. Karanth, Professor and Head, Centre for Study of Social Change and Development, ISEC, Bangalore.

Jos Mooij, Visiting Fellow, Centre for Economic and Social Studies (CESS), Hyderabad.

N.A. Mujumdar, Editor, *Indian Journal of Agricultural Economics*, Mumbai.

P.S. Srikantha Murthy, Assistant Professor, Department of Agricultural Economics, College of Agriculture, University of Agricultural Sciences (UAS), Bangalore.

Dilip M. Nachane, Director, Indira Gandhi Institute of Development Research (IGIDR), Mumbai.

M.V. Nadkarni, Chairman, Board of Governing Members CMDR, Dharwad and Hon. Visiting Professor at ISEC, Bangalore.

N. Nagaraj, Professor, Department of Agricultural Economics, College of Agriculture, University of Agricultural Sciences (UAS), Bangalore.

Rahul Nilakantan, Researcher, Centre for Management in Agriculture (CMA), Indian Institute of Management (IIM), Ahmedabad.

R. Parthasarathy, Professor, Centre for Environmental Planning and Technology (CEPT) University, Ahmedabad.

R. Radhakrishna, Chairman, National Statistical Commission, Government of India, New Delhi.

V. Ramaswamy, Associate Professor, Centre for Study of Social Change and Development, ISEC, Bangalore.

N. Rashmi, Junior Research Fellow, Department of Agricultural Economics, College of Agriculture, University of Agricultural Sciences (UAS), Bangalore.

V. Ratna Reddy, Formerly Professor, Centre for Economic and Social Studies (CESS), Hyderabad.

Jyothis Sathyapalan, Associate Professor, Centre for Economic and Social Studies (CESS), Hyderabad.

Khalil Shah, Researcher at Institute for Social and Economic Change, Bangalore.

A. Vaidyanathan, Emeritus Professor, Madras Institute of Development Studies (MIDS), Chennai.

V.S. Vyas, Emeritus Professor, Institute for Development Studies (IDS), Jaipur.

Vinod Vyasulu, Director, Centre for Budget and Policy Studies, Bangalore.

Preface

Over the years, development as a concept has acquired many connotations both in theoretical and empirical knowledge base. It is utilised differently across all the social science disciplines, rightfully has been receiving attention in every sphere. As a result, development over years acquired a complex but interdisciplinary character. It has got analytically richer through positive interactions with the society, either through interventions or protests against such interventions. Therefore, when one needs to have a look at the issues in development, there are different windows that give only glimpses of individual components, leaving the interpretation of the entirety to the researchers/readers. This compendium of essays in honour of Professor V.M. Rao, is an attempt to open such windows, through which the development thinkers have viewed and interpreted diverse components of development. Actually, these windows cover many of those academic pursuits of Professor Rao during his writings and encompass new issues that he would like to and may investigate. All these essays are skillfully drafted by his admirers and colleagues and therefore, have one theme in common, that is, the fraternity of development thinkers reinforcing interdisciplinary perspectives.

This volume deals with various aspects of development, touching many a milestone that have been achieved over in these decades with some the important ones including: agricultural policy, globalisation, development of irrigation, participatory irrigation management system, and so on. Professor Rao has contemplated upon quite a few of these in his unique style. The essays are thus planned and organised to give a cohesive reading in providing those crucial features of development in India and reflect upon many of these aspects in an innovative manner.

The volume begins with a study of Indian economy from macrohistorical perspective by the in-depth thinkers like Professor

Nachane and Professor Nadkarni. There are a few current problems in India's economic development that need attention based on the understanding of microrealities. In this volume, while Kadekodi analyses the measurement of quality of life, Kannan exemplifies the Kerala model of development. The environmental interface with development is discussed by K.V. Raju. Issues in agricultural development are dwelled upon by Mujumdar, Acharya and Deshpande from three different angles. The discussion includes terms of the policy, diversification, irrigation and market imperfections. The need for a consistent long-term and regionally diversified agricultural policy is also argued here. Vaidyanathan reviews researches carried out in the area of irrigation packing in his lifetime experience. While Reddy and Parthasarathy take up some interesting case studies. Groundwater irrigation raises many questions in the context of hard-rock regions of the country and Chandrakanth brings in a fresh methodology to amortisation of wells in a hyperbolic trend. All these issues have been the themes pursued by Professor Rao himself in diverse ways and at different times providing innovative ideas on each of the themes.

As many of us know, Professor Rao's interest in poverty and conditions of the poor is unparallel. It is a great tribute to the work of Professor Rao that the best among the academics have preferred to write on this issue in this volume. Professor Vyas's analysis of poverty alleviation programmes touches on those finer issues. Similarly, Professor Radhakrishna elaborates on the debate pertaining to food security and poverty. In a similar vein, the environmental angle of poverty is taken up by Sudarshan Iyengar and Jyothis, whereas Jos Mooij looks at the issue of poverty in the context of children and human face of reforms. All these essays put together provide a panoramic view of the poverty debate.

The essays presented in this volume provide some of the interesting facets of development being pursued by the authors with outstanding insights in their respective areas. Almost every essay discusses one or the other aspect dealt with by Professor Rao throughout his academic writings, and open to the readers those windows of development through which one can see the various nuances of those microfacets. I feel honoured and humbled in writing this 'Preface' to this insightful volume, and join the editors and contributors in felicitating a great scholar and a very good human being. I am sure this volume will provide for a good reading to readers and students of development as a discipline.

— Abhijit Sen

Member
Planning Commission
Government of India

Acknowledgements

Professor V.M. Rao is known for his simplicity and excellence in research to all his admirers. A few years back we had decided to bring out this festschrift in honour of Prof. Rao. There were a lot of problems that had to be gone through, and getting the papers, revising them and finally putting the volume together was a big but pleasant task. All the authors cooperated with the editors and had given their inputs. We must record our gratitude to all of them. The volume could come out due to the untiring work by Mr. Khalil, Mithila and Neelkantha. They helped us to get the proofs corrected and finally see the manuscript through the publisher. Mr. Mohankumar did the word processing of the entire volume and corrected quite a few drafts over time. We must also mention the help received from our friend Mr. Sanu Kapila, of Academic Foundation who readily agreed to publish this volume out and did his best. We derived lot of help from the Institute for Social and Economic Change (ISEC) and therefore must record our gratitude to the authorities of ISEC.

— Editors

1 Development Windows

An Introduction

R.S. Deshpande, S.M. Jharwal and Khalil Shah

Development is a complex and multifaceted phenomenon; therefore, it is not surprising that the definition of development is embroiled in various controversies over time. This controversy reached a crescendo when Dudley Seers wrote the famous essay on the "Birth, Life and Death of Development Economics" after the Manchester Conference. The debate on the demise of development economics and the obituary notes that followed created more controversies than solving them. But the subject withstood all the critics and stayed afresh, adding many new areas for discussions. One needs to view development from Chenery's full length evaluation of the discipline, including many of the authors of recent understanding of development from the perspective of civil society. The debate did not confine itself to economists and economics *per se*, but it spilled over to development sociology and political development, transcending the make-believe borders of various disciplines in social sciences and acquiring the status of an interdisciplinary theory.

Understanding about development has evolved differently across various disciplines drawing on theories prevailing in the individual disciplines. Naturally, the process of understanding development has its own roots in the accepted process of wisdom and training of the elaborator. An economist's understanding is largely influenced by the variables that facilitate and dominate their understanding of growth with distribution. It may be argued that the relative pre-occupation of its practitioners in utilising the mathematical rigour to understand and construct models of their choice with a view to define and describe development, generally loses the track in terms of human concern.

Economists, by the sheer adoptability to such tools, partially distanced themselves from other disciplines. In the process, social generality and simplicity essential for codifying their basic theoretical constructs, got blurred. On the one hand, this has enhanced the span of the discipline but on the other, has created imaginary walls and debates over misunderstandings. This state of affairs is likely to grow worse if the mutual understanding is unclear.

In other social science disciplines, development is understood from various perspectives. Sociologists are more focused on the family and society as the crux of development and focus on human, natural, cultural, technological and organisational issues in the context of change. Political scientists view the concept from the viewpoint of democracy and its institutions. The discipline is oriented towards the development of institutions of governance and the interface between humans and such institutions.

Our intention here is to provide only a partial peep through these windows. These windows are chosen, keeping in view the academic interests and research areas frequented by Prof. Rao, through his writings. We have chosen five areas so as to give effect to this view and carefully selected the authors having close affinity and academic interactions with Prof. Rao primarily with a view to developing an integrated framework. These five areas include: aggregate economic development, agricultural development, irrigation development, poverty and issues related to governance.

The section on aggregate economic development begins with Prof. Nachane's strong argument on the study of Indian economics. Following historical treatises by many economists from India and their views on Indian economy, Prof. Nachane forcefully stresses the necessity of understanding and highlights the nuances of Indian economics as an independent branch of knowledge. Even though it sounds traditional, this intense and logically argued viewpoint emerges out of vast teaching and research experience. Indianness in terms of economic thinking is fast disappearing and getting readily replaced by the fashionable models that hides more than they reveal. He illustrates how neoclassical prescriptions have little theoretical or empirical relevance to the Indian context. This is closely followed by Prof. Nadkarni's Hindu approach to development. Prof.

Nadkarni is more concerned with developing the indigenous way of thinking and method of analysis, than devoting the entire treatise to a religious discourse. He wades through various scriptures to bring home the basic economic concepts as perceived and historically developed in India. These two essays provide the most needed push to answer some of the intricate analytical questions relating to appropriate methodology for understanding Indian economic issues.

Kadekodi, Kannan and Raju follow the customary pattern of addressing the current problems of Indian economic development. While Kadekodi deals with the measurement of the quality of life, Kannan illustrates the Kerala model of development. Raju adds the most needed environmental dimension to the analysis of development in the Indian context. Kadekodi discusses an emerging dimension of village development citing Ralegaon Siddhi as a case in point. He concludes that the integration of societal and individual rankings is still prompted by normative considerations rather than perceptions of people. True, but it will be a long time before this could happen. Prof. Kannan's Kerala model of development of course holds out a promise in terms of learning a new process. It is quite promising to generalise this so as to make it broadly applicable, in that one can plug the regional specificities for obtaining a suitable version. Environment, in all our development models, is taken as given and rarely receives any specific treatment. Raju not only argues for the legitimate place environment deserves but also provides empirical evidences to highlight the imminent problems.

The second section is in tandem with the initial argument and is contributed by Mujumdar, Acharya and Jogi, and Deshpande and Raju. In the first essay of this section, Mujumdar draws on his rich experience in providing an overview of agricultural development. He argues that an agenda in terms of the policy leads, is urgently needed in the context of cotemporary changes that are unaccompanied by any social security. His sharp views on the probable bottlenecks have to be seriously considered. Diversification of agriculture under the present friendly market environment attracts the attention of Acharya and Jogi. After establishing empirical evidence about the pace of diversification, they underscore the need for enhancing infrastructure. The recent changes in the market policy have been heralded. Deshpande and Raju visit the policy-making in Indian agriculture and conclude that the policy must evolve as a bottom-up approach.

Irrigation has an important role in India's agricultural development, and Prof. Rao has worked consistently on two themes, *viz.*: i) linking irrigation with development and ii) looking at the land deprived of this vital resource. Vaidyanathan reviews research carried on in the areas of irrigation packing his lifetime experience. In this essay, he underscores the importance of institutions and the need for interdisciplinary approach to the study of institutions. The issue of connecting natural resources to irrigation and the management through people's participation are visited by Reddy and Parthasarathy. While Reddy takes up the case of irrigation tanks from Andhra Pradesh, Parthasarthy reviews the Participatory Irrigation Management (PIM) system in Gujarat. Reddy emphasises the revival of traditional water management institutions and structures with Parthasarathy also upholding the experience of PIM. Irrigation based on groundwater involves many issues, and out of these myriad questions, Chandrakanth and Rashmi visit the use of hyperbolic discounting, keeping in view the natural behaviour of the resource. Invariably in the literature on groundwater, only a linear discounting is employed, ignoring completely the behaviour of groundwater economy. Keeping in view the hyperbolic behaviour of the variables, this essay provides an innovative approach demonstrating its the utility.

The fourth section contains a few interesting works concerning poverty. The section opens with Prof. Vyas's analysis of the poverty alleviation programmes followed by the piquant analysis of food security by Prof. Radhakrishna. Prof. Vyas draws seven important lessons in the context of poverty alleviation programmes besides discussing a sustainable policy framework. He leaves it to the policy makers to draw inferences from the questions he has addressed in the paper. Prof. Radhakrishna writes on food security from the point of an analyst engaged for many years in this area of research. The essay is not only an analytical feast but also has potential policy relevance. Linkages between poverty and environment are analysed by Iyengar and Sathyapalan, whereas Mooij looks at the issue of poverty in the context of concern for children and human face of reforms. Wage mix between contractual and kind wages is dealt by Prof. Datta, Nilakantan and Datta using Datta,

Nugent and Tisher (DNT) model to provide explanation about the risk in wage markets. This has its own influence on perpetuation of poverty. Deshpande and Raju provide a framework for poverty monitoring in order to frame policies aimed at eradicating poverty. All these essays put together should satisfy any policy maker for drawing appropriate lessons in terms of framing policies for alleviation of poverty.

Good governance is the key to most of the issues pertaining to delivery of development. Annual budget is the main tool for incorporating online corrections in financial governance. There are many issues that crop up every year after the budget, and as the year draws to a close these die down to be resurrected during the next season. Prof. Vyasulu elaborates on these most important issues in the context of a medium term fiscal policy. We have been always concerned with allocations but rarely do we discuss the outcomes. He brings under the scanner our concerns related to transparency, accountability and citizen partnership. Finally, he highlights the importance of citizens' partnership in the allocations and achievements of development. Prof. Karanth and Ramaswamy look at the same subject from a sociologist's perspective. Although they have located their argument in participative research process, the paper focuses on the theme of participation from the society's perspective.

We do not want to claim that this volume covers every aspect of the development scenario. It is neither possible nor can be attempted so easily. However, in the context of honouring Prof. V.M. Rao, our attempt here is to present these different facets pursued by the authors having outstanding insights in their respective areas. Considering analytical abilities and the philosophy followed by Prof. Rao throughout his writings, this being a small part of the universe of development, we therefore decided to have a look through several windows. Each of these windows gives us some glimpses of different facets of development from the vantage point of the authors. When one looks out through these windows at the world of development, the panoramic view (though fragmented) from diverse angles gives a picture of seemingly continuum of development. The intention of this volume is to create that most needed panorama with an excellent collage of this view through different windows which are Prof. Rao's favourites.

2 V.M. Rao

An Academic Travelogue

R.S. Deshpande, K.V. Raju, S.M. Jharwal and M.G. Chandrakanth

2.1 Sketch of a Noble Researcher

Generally, a biography describes a travelogue in the active life of an individual but personalities are made more through their work and the events during their life; therefore, their work assumes prime space in the life of such individuals. As one views the past from today's window, these tend to be of interest only to a few select groups or the inner circle of an individual. In that context, an academic biography is different in its content, approach and sustainability of interest. Writing an academic biography is certainly a much more difficult and sensitive task, but that provides an opportunity to understand the personality of an individual from his or her life-long academic pursuits. It undoubtedly involves the viewpoint of the writer about the work of a person and hence, cannot be a really truthful representation of the original ideas. Even with this major bottleneck, we undertook the difficult task of writing an academic biography of Prof. V.M. Rao to understand the path he tracked. Though he has passed through many junctions, very painstakingly he kept himself on to the track of his choice. Prof. Rao's academic contribution combines high calibre intellect, astonishing creativity, analytical acumen and an in-depth understanding of society for the benefit of social science researchers. Prof. VM, as is well known, is simplicity incarnate and his works covers a large span specifically in agriculture and rural

We must put on record here that the choice of studies and the interpretation of views expressed are solely the responsibility of the authors and Prof. V.M. Rao holds no responsibility for these. If we have misinterpreted him (of course, inadvertently), we apologise for the mistakes and request the readers to consult his original work as well.

development. VM has always been an unpretentious worker with great human qualities to understand the nuances in the complex field of economics. His approach towards understanding the problem and analysing has been extremely scholarly but without the laces of paraphernalia and methodological jargons. His demonstration of astuteness in describing facts in a simple manner is accomplished in such an easy way that the reader is rarely allowed second thinking. He mastered that art of simplifying the complex abstruseness, and his employment of methodology always stood as his asset with the preference to write on a reverse spin. His dealing with difficult statistical problems like decomposition of Gini ratio is as simple as interpreting the field data from a small village on the periphery of Bangalore. Thus, his authority on the interpretation is unparallel, as also his capability of getting into crevices of issues in question. An intellectual of great height, he always kept himself in a low profile with which anyone else with that capability would have boasted.

This academic biography of Prof. Rao is a modest attempt to understand his personality through his works. We are not very sure, if we have done justice to collate a picture on the vast canvas of masterly strokes provided by Prof. Rao, but we have tried to gave a full and sincere try to it. We neither claim nor would like to give any impression that this piece deals with all the works of Prof. Rao and its many facets, but the effort is to cater to the interest of academics. At some stages, this write-up may seem close to a review of Prof. Rao's work which has neither been our intention nor goal. We cherish this opportunity provided to recapitulate the academic personality of Prof. Rao and have approached the work of Prof. Rao, more by the subjects handled by him rather than by chronology of his work.

2.2 Agricultural Economy of India

2.2.1 Pace and Pattern of Growth

Agriculture sector of India witnessed many changes during post-Independence period. Prof. Rao wrote about the stagnation in agricultural sector and the growth performance before Independence. In his article on pace and pattern of growth in agricultural production in

India, in the monumental volume edited by Prof. Dantwala, he presented a long-term review of the growth of India's agriculture. He demonstrated that the performance of agriculture in post-Independence (before eighties) had been impressive owing to its distinct sources of growth and it can be viewed through two broad phases—first, community development phase and second, Green Revolution phase. In the first phase, severe complacency was noted followed by some growth in the productivity of food grains and non-food grains. The high growth rate of non-food grains was due to increase in area and favourable market conditions. The second phase witnessed a marked increase in growth rate of area, production and productivity due to technological change in crop varieties operating and increased use of modern inputs like fertilisers. The effect of green revolution apparently reflected in improvement of productivity of food grains though there was uneven growth across states, crops and years.

Prof. V.M. Rao brought forth that growth of agriculture depends on the right combination of promotional policies. If agriculture growth picks up and surpasses the past trends, there would be adequate food grains as well as opportunities for diversification of crops beyond food grains. Thus, rainfed area as well as the eastern region could be the major thrusts and these could be brought under the following phase of green revolution. These regions would be slower in pace with modest impact but their contribution to development would be extending the base of agricultural growth to depressed rural regions with meagre economic opportunities outside agriculture. We should remember that these findings were noted in early eighties and eventually became the theme in the policy that followed and currently being pursued in systematic and strategic manner.

Prof. Rao considered stability in production and prices as crucial for confidence building among farmers for investment and adoption of technological change. There are differences in the sources of instability. But the instability has been generally cost-based and weather-based. Some researchers found that in the phase of technological change, increase in input prices was the major source of instability in the production whereas, some others referred to droughts and widespread failure of rainfall. Prof. Rao, however, explained that the process of adoption and focus on vulnerable areas could ease the problem. While he appreciated and decomposed the variability in its components, his emphasis was on the implications. India has remarkable performance in agricultural production and production-oriented policies but however, it did not provide adequate strategy for growth with social justice for vulnerables. His emphasis on welfare-centred development was apparent from the very beginning and later became a crucial issue during economic reforms process.

After a few decades while analysing the phase of liberalisation in India and its impact on the agricultural sector, he revisited the issue with a new perspective. Arguing that India has to go a long way before its human development can match even those of the more advanced Asian countries, India should build a strong complementary relationship between economic growth and human development. He attempted to find, if agricultural growth has been pro-poor in breaking through constraints and barriers that hold them BPL. The findings are from village level studies conducted in the periphery of Bangalore. Agricultural growth remained slow and was confined to limited areas and crops. In this context, policy remained unmoved and the economy suffered from severe strains on resources, infrastructure and environment. These led to regional disparities of acute form. He emphasised change in the regional focus while making it strongly pro-poor. We shall have to wait for the results of regionally-focused policy frame.

2.2.2 Food Security: A Prominent Issue

Food security for the poor has always remained high on the research agenda of Prof. Rao. It is partially due to acute food insecurity during the years when he started his academic career. His latest work also deals with a similar issue that endorses his commitment. When access to food was a crucial issue as against availability, he wrote incicisively analysing the nuances and the paradoxical situations prevailing. There were transportation barriers to access amidst plenty, resulting in to shortages. Prof. Rao found that the narrow base of economic growth in general and agriculture growth in particular were causing the problem. He pointed out that even green revolution was confined to a few areas and largely to two crops. This, along with centralised nature of the public distribution system, led to lack of access to food to the poor. On the basis of this, he favoured broadening the policy front and the base of growth process to support rainfed farming, which has the largest density of poor.

Considering the available historical evidence with regard to problems of food security, he voiced his concern about the problem of food insecurity, hunger and malnutrition at national and international level which are evoked only in the wake of famines. Though much of the help is provided by altruistic, generous individuals and international aid agencies, it could do little to avoid increasingly growing famines in developing countries. The very failure in dealing with the problem of food security is the result of the inability of the national authorities in coping with famines and eliminating factors responsible which led to their recurrence. Prof. Rao brought out paradoxical conditions in which international programmes ended up in deteriorating national food security systems rather than improving these. The relief-oriented operations followed a more fire-fighting approach without creating enabling situations. International interventions were activated only when a chain of disasters caused distress and it was common with them to depart from the scene once they could manage to relieve from the problem temporarily and the glare of publicity shifted to other promising locales.

In the book on "Studies in Rural Poverty" published by the International Fund for Agricultural Development, he analysed the issues on food security and the risk of famines. Tracing the weaknesses of the food security system to the absence of broad based and participatory agricultural growth programs, he writes "...where hunger is due to drought, disaster or strife, the emergency need to be dealt with through food aids and similar programmes. But immediate relief is not a long-term solution to hunger, since hunger is rooted in a structural factor, *viz.*, poverty. The poor too often have neither the means to produce food nor to buy it...to overcome chronic hunger, various long term and complementary steps have to be taken". The core of the book is on production, supply, distribution, poverty and the policy environment at the national and international levels. Here he concludes that the elites in developing countries who wield authorities and control resources for their narrow interests are the responsible persons for famines and resultant widespread human distress. An incisive observation and the situation have remained unchanged even after 50 years of Independence.

During the late sixties and early seventies, *Second India* studies were initiated and Prof. Rao did his monumental work on assessing the capacity to meet increasing food requirements of the growing population. The study focused on the prevailing patterns of food consumption by different classes of population. The data showed that an average Indian used to spend about one rupee per day to meet different needs of which food used to claim a little over 70 paise during the seventies. In rural area, food grains accounted for two-thirds of expenditure on food with little amount spent on items of 'other foods' like milk, meat, etc. In urban areas, expenditure on 'other foods' formed around 50 per cent of expenditure incurred on food. It is here that he proposed a gradual shift of the column of poor upwards to deal with poverty. He concluded that with a proper set of policies relating access to food, India could find a solution to her food problem and that came to be realistic during the decades of eighties and thereon.

2.2.3 Drought-prone Areas and Drylands: The Major Footprints

Since Independence, though India managed reducing the incidence of poverty through initiating several anti-poverty programmes and production-oriented strategies of green revolution, there is still a significant proportion of the population in the country living under precarious poverty and these are located largely in rainfed areas. Development of rainfed agriculture is one of the favourite themes of Prof. Rao and after substantial initial work, he chose this theme for his presidential address of the Indian Society of Agricultural Economics in 1991 at Hyderabad. Here he enlisted the barriers to growth in the dryland communities. Recently, he shifted to the usage 'rainfed areas' instead of 'drylands'. Dryland agriculture in Karnataka had experienced contrasting phases of a modest growth followed by nearly a decade of stagnation. The presidential address makes use of the Cost Cultivation Reports of the Government of Karnataka to analyse the growth potential of the new dryland technology and characteristics of the market environment.

He showed how the robust growth was prompted by structural characteristics of Karnataka's new technology and how the policy environment contributed to that. Next, he took a close look at these characteristics covering traditional dryland, new dryland and irrigated technologies. Here he looked at the gross returns per hectare across the crops for segregating them into three groups of crops and three tiers of technologies. He derived inferences on quality of growth. Further, he related this to the cost-price balance reflecting the nature of market in which dryland agriculture operates.

In the same context, he argued that the existing Public Distribution System (PDS) has become unwieldy and unsustainable and it is time to review this in the context of Panchayat Raj Institutions (PRI). He identified two important flaws in the present food security system. First, the problems of the relatively better-off sections of farmers received more attention in policymaking than the deprived peers. Second, while drought-prone areas urgently needed investment and infrastructure, the emphasis in policies remained on ad hoc relief measures rather than on any intentions to change the existing structures. With the help of illustrative data from two drought-prone districts in Karnataka, he showed how the PDS works in drought-prone areas. While Chitradurga district showed a slightly higher percentage share of PDS grains to total consumption of food grains than that of Bijapur district, it was well below 20 per cent in both districts. Even during peak drought season, the PDS could not meet even 20 per cent of the consumption needs and hence, he lamented that PDS can hardly be regarded as a major factor in providing food security in drought–prone areas. Thus, he advocated the need for an alternative system based on local staples consumed by the poor. There should be a watchdog body to ensure that the system covers all eligible households and when a disaster strikes, all tiers of the government should get together to handle the crisis. There is already some evidence now that by targeting the PDS, the share of PDS in their total food grain basket has increased over the years. We feel that his policy suggestions are contributing towards this.

2.2.3.1 Technology for Dryland Agriculture: Experience in Karnataka

It is a well known fact that dryland areas are generally backward in rural infrastructure and amenities. There is a persuasive evidence that the growth-oriented technologies are entering slowly in dryland agriculture and the process of realising the full potential of new dryland technologies is likely to be slow. This may change the situation in the long run.

2.2.3.2 Development Opportunities in Dryland Agriculture

In an illustrative case study from Karnataka dealing with technological intervention, Prof. Rao showed that concerted efforts for yield improvement through diffusion of technology and supply of inputs have been effective in the dryland areas even under chronic drought-prone environment. The dryland technology is broad-based and widespread compared to green revolution technology in terms of distribution of income benefits, income generation, crop diversification, easy adoption under varied socio-economic conditions, is environment-friendly and accessible to poor. But its spread is constrained due to the incidence of frequent droughts. He expressed the need for designing multi-sectoral approach with broad framework that meets micro level requirements by considering peculiarities of agro-climatic zones and compatible with development objectives. He suggested active government support for building participatory institutions and organisations for mobilisation of financial resources.

2.2.3.3 Change Processes in Dryland Communities

Planning process is a continuum comprising interactions between 'planners', and 'beneficiary groups'. Prof. Rao distinguished three broad groups of 'planners' by their distinctive roles in planning process—'policy makers' who formulate policies and priorities, 'researchers' who add new economic analysis, and 'village-level personnel' who help the beneficiary groups to become productive. He elaborated the planning process as a component of broader change in dryland communities. Here it was brought out that dryland farmers have a favourable attitude towards change and modernisation. He drew attention to the effectiveness of policies in relation to investment, conservation and upgradation of principal resource base and policy framework to make dryland agriculture drought-proof. He illustrated how rural communities in India adjust to the stress and strains of development process and how they could be helped to participate in development process and policy lead that needs to be taken further.

2.2.3.4 *Illustrative Profiles from Drought-prone Villages*

Rural transition and urbanisation are complex processes. At one point, Prof. Rao examined the difficulties created by the process of urbanisation in rural diversification. He presented the profiles of the drought-prone areas of Karnataka and Andhra Pradesh. The profiles illustrate how the household data routinely collected in rural investigations could be used for conducting an analysis to understand the developmental role of agriculture and rural diversification. Villages in Karnataka are benefited from agriculture diversification towards sericulture, dairy and vegetables. Farmers face even a prolonged drought without overt distress and dependence on wage labour. However, sustainability of these activities is at stake due to over-extraction of groundwater. The villages in Andhra Pradesh showed a significant vulnerability to droughts with signs of distress like sale of assets and need to economise on food. He pointed out that, a sustained improvement in agriculture is feasible only when land and water resources are properly conserved and utilised, and when adequate employment opportunities are generated with local resources via diversification. In the predominant small farm economy this gives a good policy platform.

2.2.4 Returns to Family Labour on Small Farms in India

The existence of disguised unemployment in traditional agriculture is widely believed and was the focal point of discussion during sixties and seventies. Considering studies on cross-sectional data which suffers from multicollinearity among variables and time series data which are less helpful due to their scanty and lack of comparability nature for estimation of marginal product of labour, he expressed the need for devising alternative test for verification of hypothesis in Indian context. Through this analysis, he presented an alternative test for estimation of returns to family labour on small farms of India using data from *Studies in Economics of Farm Management* (SEFM). His hypothesis was that if there is a widespread disguised unemployment in agriculture, family labour on small farms would be the most affected. The test is based on the classification of samples of small farms covered by SEFM on the basis of residual returns to family labour. He used residual return very innovatively as the balance after deducting actual and imputed costs from total revenue and is compared with its opportunity cost at the going wage rate. Using a four-fold classification of samples of small farms for comparison of returns to family labour with its imputed value at going wage rate, he juxtaposed the family labour across these groups to conclude about the hypothesised innovative test. From this test, Rao observed that in relation to both the cost accounting and sample surveys of small farms, only one-third of samples indicated existence of disguised unemployment, certainly a different finding than what was believed.

2.2.5 Inequality of Farm Incomes

Pranab Bardhan's findings on inequality in the distribution of farm business income in agriculture had raised a number of questions regarding the informativeness of the concentration ratio and its analytical utility in monitoring changes in land and income distribution. Prof. Rao places limitations and usefulness of the concentration ratio for Bardhan and researchers in the field of farm income distribution. Rao employed decomposition of the Gini concentration ratio to prove that there is no simple interpretation of the ratio, but one needs to look beneath for the facts.

Considering its informative contents and utility in monitoring the changes in income distribution, the intermediate values of concentration ratio usually pose difficulties in interpretation of two or more values pertaining to two different time periods. In such circumstances, the concentration ratio provides no clues regarding the features of distribution depending on the absolute values of the relevant variable, such as the portion of the population below the poverty line etc. He argued that it is even less communicative in the assessment of changing distribution of land and income in a given community over time through diverse mode especially brought by changing ownership of land, changing government policies and other factors like migration, inheritance, break-up of joint families. Further, in addition to this, the assessment of changing distribution of income by researchers and policy makers would be seen more on these modes of changes and causative factors rather than only on decreasing or increasing value of concentration ratios. Prof. Rao suggested that researchers should adopt certain ground rules while making use of concentration ratio to ensure a fuller and incisive analysis of the data. For this, Prof. Rao propounded two rules—the first rule relates to situations in which data are available only on size-distribution of land/income with no further details in respect of members comprising the distribution. The second rule relates to analyses of inequality from field-material collected in village surveys and farm investigations. Such analysis is more appropriate to understand better the dynamics of changing land/income distribution and factors affecting them in agriculture. This is another high point in his innovative approach.

2.2.6 Marginalisation Process in Agriculture: Indicators, Outlook and Policy Implications

Marginalisation process in agriculture is a theme he pursued consistently and he suggested way back that this process will get intensified over time. He argued that policy environment, markets and modernised agriculture bypass the poor rather than work towards their development and this leads to marginalisation. There has been downward movement of cultivators towards smallholdings, weak viability and eventual landlessness. Marginalisation is due to three provocations. First, urban India and large industries have received far more policy attention than rural resources. Second, agricultural growth strategy and policies have benefited limited regions, crops, and farmer groups leading to dualism in rural India. Third, due to unfavourable policy thrust for rural people, there is an institutional vacuum at the ground level. His recent work showed some policy leads and one of the links he established here is with the farm sector distress.

2.2.7 Agricultural Growth and Farmer Distress: Tentative Perspectives from Karnataka

Causes of farmers' distress are many and varied. It has become a volcanic force capable of sweeping away political parties and political regimes which are not friendly to farmers. Dr. Rao presented Karnataka's case to understand farmers' distress, its nature and sources. A large part of Karnataka's agriculture is located in drought-prone areas. Despite this handicap, farmers are shifting towards commercial crops. The policy regime helped this pattern of growth but has fallen far short of providing the required infrastructure for growth and modernisation of agriculture. The policy regime, along with the drought-prone environment fuelled victimisation of agricultural producers. The resultant suicides among farmers, according to Rao were more due to the non-caring policy regime along with in-built non-viability of their profession.

2.3 Land Issues

2.3.1 Land Transfers in Rural Communities: Some Findings in a *Ryotwari* Region

Prof. Rao's one of the initial and sustained interest (as a young researcher) has been land issues and function of land market. He took up that during the wee years of land reforms. His initial analysis of local issues began with a field view of land transfers in a *ryotwari* region. He analysed the process and the factors contributing to the concentration of land ownership with the help of the findings from the *ryotwari* areas of Maharashtra and Gujarat states that formed the part of the erstwhile Bombay state. This was the region that pioneered tenancy reforms with its tillers' day legislation. However, the policy makers' contention is that unregulated land market is leading to concentration of landownership. Prof. Rao used the data on distribution of the landownership in the selected villages on the eve of implementing tillers' day legislation and the land market data in the preceding decade. The analysis of changes in concentration ratio (Gini coefficient) using the cross-section of cultivators indicated the growing concentration of the land ownership in the hands of large owners pushing the small owners down the ladder to become the tenant cultivator. He identified the motivating factors behind the increase of these land acquisitions to enlarge the farms rather than to remain on land as renters. This gives rise to an implication that problems arise more from the growing scarcity of land in relation to cultivators' demand than just from unequal distribution of the land ownership and hence the need for measures other than mere redistribution.

2.3.2 Land Reforms Experiences: Perspective for Strategy and Programmes

Prof. Rao's understanding of the land reform process is well demonstrated through his works. He observed increasing marginalisation of landholdings in the face of reforms, and at the same time the falling re-distributional potential. Recognising clearly the first task of structured land reforms, he emphasised on strengthening the capacity and willingness of the government machinery in order to improve the capabilities of the rural poor.

Considering implementation of land reforms, he contended that the fallout of land reforms has been a large failure in terms of reaching down to the poor because of dominant rural groups having decisive influence on formulation and implementation. For the success of land reforms, he took strong view of designing a cohesive development strategy capable of integrating growth with equity and poverty reduction, and emphasised on a point that the priority task for the reform process is to improve poor peoples' access to common lands on which they depend for their livelihood. In the case of stagnated agriculture, increasing casualisation and employment in unorganised activities, he suggested that land reforms are to be implemented as a component of package measures and the process should be so designed as to meet the requirements of different subgroups of labour communities and the poor. He concluded that the ultimate goal of land reforms and other structural reforms is to promote the emergence of a viable and modernised peasantry consisting of small farmers besides, facilitation of the entry of landless into the peasant sector or other self-employment sectors in the context of growing and technologically resilient agriculture.

2.3.3 Inequality in Ownership of Land—Nature, Extent and Redistributive Implications

While dealing with the land issues, Prof. Rao was aware of the fact that land is one of the scarce factors of production having the potential to increase inequality in the society because of ownership pattern and productivity. Recognising the need of highlighting the dimensions of inequality in terms of ownership pattern, cultivation practices and leasing activities, Prof. Rao came with a few approaches for measuring inequality and exploitation. To measure the excessive skewed ownership pattern in the community, Prof. Rao contended that shortened and summarised version of the lost units is more useful than the concentration ratio. However, the method is inconvenient for the classification of inequality in case of a single or both the deficient and excessive ownership pattern exists. Prof. Rao suggested that classification of the property in a community be based on sets of norms where tolerance interval is not too low or not too high and while doing so, forces operating in the community in the past must be taken into account.

2.3.4 Structural Features of Village Lease Markets

In a chapter in *Evaluation of Land Reforms in Western India* edited by M.L. Dantwala and C.H. Shah, Prof. Rao dealt with the analysis of structure of village lease market at the micro level. The first section commences with 'Market'. The analysis brings out different methods of leasing land across India. There is a separate discussion on lessors and lessees. The type of principal participants, socio-economic factors and interest rates in the market are the main factors that help in shaping the lease market. He talked of three stages with regards to the lease market in India: a) Type of the lease market, b) Form of lease market, and c) Nature of integration of the lease market. These features are explained with the help of computational devices. The second section relates to 'Result of Analysis' to show diversity of participants in the lease market. However, the legislation policy of total termination (1956-1957 to 1964-65) might prove to be a disproportionately strong measure in addressing the problem of exploitative lease relationship. Finally, he warned that this policy might possibly lead us towards inefficient use of leased land by the tenants besides, the undesirability of non-functional ownership. His warning a few decades back is turning out to be a reality now.

2.3.5 Perspectives on Redistribution of Land

This study was based on assumptions of dynamic agricultural economy and associated technological change and diversification. The two reasons for the failure of the redistribution are 'soft democracy' and 'non-feasibility' hypotheses. The soft democracy relates to 'regimentation' and 'domination by vested interest'.

In an economy subject to development and technological change, objectives of land reforms have to be scaled down in addition to having policies in place for ensuring supply of inputs to cultivators, especially small farmers, discouraging capital-intensive mechanism, minimum price support for ensuring minimum profitability; and for this, the scope for redistribution of the land must be assessed in terms of community-wise distribution of the cultivated land rather than the region-wise distribution of land ownership in order to achieve twin objectives of equitable distribution and elimination of absentee ownership. According to Rao, for the redistribution process to be successful, feasibility studies at the village level are to be considered as the basis.

2.3.6 Land Reforms: The Next Phase

Prof. Rao revisited land reforms from an altogether fresh viewpoint. Here, he took into account the changes and failures to look at the new phase of reforms. In the work *Land Reforms: The Next Phase*, he laid emphasis on land as a productive resource rather than an asset *per se*. He opined that for land reforms to be effective, the process of agricultural modernisation and policies for improving land productivity should go hand in hand with the land reform process. Besides, he expressed the need to establish harmony and commonality of interests between the large and medium cultivators on the one hand, and the small, marginal cultivators and the landless labourers who lack adequate and assured access to land, on the other. He suggested that tenancy system allows for the flexibility to overcome the constraint of limited scope for redistribution and prevents emergence of dominant landowners in the next phase of land reforms.

2.4 Agricultural Price Policy

2.4.1 Fixing Agricultural Prices: Issues and Experiences

Agricultural price policy has been one of the consistent themes of analysis by Prof. Rao. He analysed the issue from a ringside view, as a member of the Commission for Agricultural Costs and Prices. Analysing the masterly contribution by A.S. Kahlon and D.S. Tyagi (1989) on "Agricultural Price Policy in India", he explained how agricultural prices generated anxiety in the mid 60s and how agricultural prices institutionally fixed by the state had little influence. He also showed how agricultural prices' issues flared up in the wake of emergence of farmers' organisations. He dealt with emerging issues through: i. Price fixation, ii. Crop-wise experiences, and iii. Agriculture-non-agriculture terms of trade. He provided an effective formulation for reorientation and adjustment of the price policy in the context of the present economic system. He modestly wrote, "...what we present is an illustrative formulation based on an 'optimistic' characterisation, more to a provoke discussion than as a prescription".

2.4.2 Government Intervention in Agriculture: A Review of Studies in Developing Countries

This review article relates to the study of *The Political Economy of Agricultural Pricing* (John Hopkins University Press, Baltimore, USA), consisting of five volumes, concerning government intervention issues in republic of Korea, Malaysia, Pakistan, Sri Lanka, Brazil, Argentina, Ghana and Zambia. Prof. Rao brought out the obvious and inherent differences in the development situations in developing countries and their policy needs. The review article highlighted the fact that the government interventions which are appropriate in a particular country depend on the development space the country has accommodated in its strategy of development and the extent to which dominant lobbies influence the government in adopting interventionist approach towards agriculture.

2.4.3 The Making of Agricultural Price Policy: A Review of CACP Reports

The article on review of CACP (Commission for Agricultural Costs and Prices) Reports is his masterly piece on the development of price policy spanning over five sections. In the first section, Prof. Rao explained the evolution of agricultural price policy over a period of time, sketching a clear picture of operations and nuances related to CACP recommendations. Achieving self-sufficiency in food grains is analysed as one of the major objectives of price policy in the second section. The issue of minimum support price (MSP) is the central point in this analysis. Here, he gave a detailed account of how the procurement price was allotted to wheat from 1967 to 1978 and its trend at the same period as against food security. He raised the issue of MSP as, "Have the large increases in the MSP for wheat made in the current and the preceding seasons raised it to a level difficult to sustain in future? There are some signals which should cause anxiety". He offered suggestions to solve anxiety in the announcement of price for the wheat crop to reduce dependence on the PDS for superior cereals and the need for a serious thought on the part of the government and public agencies. In the third section, he explained the major problems involved in price policy formulation of sugarcane, jute, cotton and oilseeds, concerning quality, quantity, trends and market. Waiting for the winds of change to blow about centres around the fourth section concerning the basic elements in the agricultural price policy. Systemic reforms are dealt with in the fifth section. Removing discrimination between organised and unorganised groups, execution of support operations for all the areas and all the time, decentralisation of PDS in the villages, establishment of nodal agencies and prevention of present lobbies were also covered. His views on price policy became quite pertinent in the context of the liberalisation process.

2.5 Liberalisation and New Economic Policy

The process of liberalisation began in India during early nineties but the seeds for the process were sown way back from the 1982, with the slight liberalisation in the industrial sector. This took a clear shape with the budgets—in mid eighties. It was clear from the beginning that this change in the development thinking will have some impact on rural India in general and agricultural sector in particular. Prof. Rao took this issue from its beginning and his focus remained on the impact on rural areas and participation of these regions in the process of liberalisation.

2.5.1 Planning For Liberalisation: ACRP in the Changing Context

With the initiation of economic reforms, India entered the new phase of economic development witnessing widespread changes in the agricultural economy, particularly in the remarkably performing green revolution areas. The course of growth caused sharp differences, both intra-sectoral and inter-sectoral differences between a considerably viable growth-oriented industry and neglected areas in Indian agricultural sector. Understanding the gravity of the situation, Prof. Rao emphasised on the need for restructuring India's agricultural planning based on similar agro-climatic characteristics. Prof. Rao recognised the importance of agro-climatic regional planning (ACRP), which he felt essential in the transitory process for its corrective, regulatory and promotional interventions to ensure the resulting benefits of liberalisation to reach the poor and deprived sections. He provided suggestions to ACRP to help agriculture in adjusting to the process of reforms and making more effective use of the opportunities in the transitory process. While looking into the performance of the green revolution areas, he argued that promotional measures and removal of restrictions create a favourable environment for green revolution areas in a liberalised regime with a larger role for the markets. In addition to this, sub-sectors like horticulture and floriculture, which are in embryonic state, he believed, would receive a big thrust by the modern corporate sector. Hence, Prof. Rao called for proactive promotional and regulatory policies without hurting the pace of growth, in favour of small and marginal farmers and backward regions. He emphasised on the two-way coordination and communication between national policy makers and state level units, and between state level units and regional and zonal level representative bodies for ensuring the needs of each state, sub-region and formulisation of effective strategies at the national level to achieve steady and equitable growth across the states. He also laid stress on the formulation of plans in tandem with state government's regional development strategies that would help and encourage collaboration between implementing agencies—both state and ACRP units.

2.5.2 Policy Research for Liberalised Agriculture: Some Illustrative Research Areas

Prof. Rao highlighted the fact that in the wake of liberalisation of agriculture, the rural economy did not receive the needed attention. He focused on the problems involved in terms of adjustment of the liberalised markets to changes in the rural economy and how research could help the process of such adjustments. He cited a number of issues and questions relating to food security as well as commercialisation contending that researchers need to play a vital role in analysing the direct, indirect and the link effects of different policies towards providing safety nets to vulnerable groups that are likely to get affected due to the liberalisation process.

2.5.3 Agriculture and Liberalisation: Some Implications for Development Policies

Prof. Rao regarded that liberalisation is an appropriate development strategy for Indian economy. At the same time, Prof. Rao did not support a complete withdrawal of the state from the economy, but shifts the focus of government's policies and concerns from helping and subsidising the organised sector which are now capable for operating on their own. Rural and agriculture sector still remains unorganised and backward and therefore, needs strong support. He argued that only such a strategy of liberalisation will promote broad-based agricultural growth and enable backward areas and the poor to participate in the growth process and share benefits that will reduce the risk of crisis and widening income gap. With this backdrop, he suggested that liberalisation of the economy to be carried forward with a continued role of the state to help backward regions/sectors get integrated with market-led mainstream economy. Without government's effective role, problems faced by the unorganised sector would further worsen over time.

In order to achieve three per cent growth rate in agriculture, considering the wide diversity of physical and socio-economic conditions, Prof. Rao argued for the policies required to be formulated to help the growth process. He emphasised on three sub-sectors, which needed diverse policy regimes. The first sub-sector consisted of agro-based activities, where private entities have a definite role. He argued that liberalisation of this sub-sector would encourage private entities to take to production and marketing of horticulture, floriculture and fishery products. Simultaneously, vertical linkage will also help in modernising Indian farming and for enclave growth by creating more employment opportunities within the sector. Hence, he suggested that such viable sub-sectors need to be freed from excessive legal restrictions. Prof. Rao categorised other two sub-sectors in agriculture under the "crops under green revolution" and crops in the most backward agriculture. All major crops showed upward trends during the post-Independence period. However, sharp contrasts were observed in production, productivity and extension of irrigation. Prof. Rao brought out the major handicap of the third sub-sector of agriculture, which according to him are dispersed small producers who find it difficult to cope with volatile, unpredictable and often depressed markets.

For promoting broad-based and pro-poor agricultural growth, he supported development strategies which were based on participation by local people, voluntary organisations and their co-ordination with administrative mechanism at the grassroot level through the *panchayat* institution. In order to accelerate the transition process in the backward regions, Prof. Rao emphasised on the need of a strong policy support in terms of infrastructural development, improvement in institutional services, large-scale public investments and administrative reforms in the forefront for avoiding co-ordination failure.

The question of farmers withstanding the process of liberalisation worried Prof. Rao and he wrote about their role in the market economy. Considering the trends in the wholesale price index (WPI) (with monthly changes in prices of commodities), he highlighted the difficulties farmers are likely to face in commodity markets. He looked into governmental interventions to help farmers, and the scope of such interventions in the light of liberalisation. From careful observation he opined that though liberalisation gives stimulus to agriculture through increases in value addition and exports, adverse factors are needed to be tackled. Prof. Rao made a point that welfare gains obtained by farmers from intervening measures of the government depend on the interaction between relatively competitive markets and markets for manufactured products and exports which are protected.

2.5.4 Coping with Liberalisation: The Next Phase in Anti-Poverty Strategy

Prof. Rao, here, outlines the role of anti-poverty strategies in the liberalised economy with an overview of nature and performance since Independence. He argued that laying a firm foundation for anti-poverty strategy to equip the poor with adequate resources and making them self-reliant is crucial. The backward regions, dryland areas and fallow and wastelands which are bypassed policies have potential for growth. There is scope for anti-poverty strategies for promoting agriculture growth and improving living conditions in these regions. He highlighted four policies as critical in achieving the objectives: (i) direct or indirect support measures, (ii) public investment, (iii) incentives through regulatory, promotional measures, and (iv) deregulation and efforts towards strengthening PRIs. He further argued that these are very crucial in utilising existing resources at the grassroot level and linking them with markets so as to achieve dignity of human life.

2.5.5 Farmers in Market Economy: Would Farmers Gain through Liberalisation?

Prof. Rao presented prospects for economic reforms considering its impact on the poor and symbolised a shift in India's development strategy to redefine roles of government, market, PRIs and voluntary organisations. Prof. Rao through this approach analysed economic reforms in isolation and categorised strategies to distinguish its impact on the poor. He has shown that the procurement and distribution of food by PDS centres through government departments increased the transaction cost of operations. This benefited green revolution farmers but sidelined the poor who could not afford, either due to costly food, income constraints or malpractices at food distribution centres. Thus, he highlighted that support-based strategies can provide relief to the poor only in distress but fail to make them productive members of the society. A fair degree of scepticism on the longevity of the process exists that the decision-making processes are leaning in favour of poor like the empowerment-based strategy where emphasis is on people's participation in development programmes through *panchayats* and voluntary groups.

2.5.6 Where Reforms do not Reach: Rural Poor in the Bangalore Neighbourhood

From his experience in rural neighborhood of Bangalore city, Karnataka, Prof. Rao showed that access of rural poor to growth is weak even with a favourable area. Most of the policies towards poor are populist aiming at winning over the electorate. The policies focus on relief and subsidy rather than their integration with mainstream society. Rural poor with some informal education, have access to urban informal sector. But urban informal sector keeps the poor at the periphery allowing only a modest proportion to trickle down. New strategy of economic development relates to empowerment of poor through participation in decision-making process and implementation of programmes at the grassroot level through *panchayat* institutions. Even though PRIs have failed in providing favourable results in a dual society for the poor, we cannot deny the emergence of political mobilisation of the poor. Empowerment is a long-term strategy that demands patience and perseverance and moves at a slow pace. However, rise in aspirations of the poor for better standard of living and higher share in government programmes along with a rise in power to influence election results, are signals for their better future through PRIs.

2.6 Poverty, Nutrition and Income Inequality

2.6.1 Poor as a Social Stratum: Economic Criteria for Studying Poverty

Prof. Rao is known for his in-depth understanding of issues pertaining to poverty and the best testimony for this could be found in his latest book on "Poverty Reduction in An Elite Driven Democracy". When the debate on poverty in India among the stalwarts was heating up in EPW, he participated in his unique style. He approached poverty from the angle of expenditure on non-food consumption pattern. He argued that poor are to be identified distinctly from other classes with a clear distinction between current expenditure and other expenditure. The poor as a social stratum have inadequate income for current needs and hence lack resources for future needs and goods. Using consumer expenditure data from the 28th round of NSSO with 12 categories to represent both current and future consumption, he found that percentage of consumption expenditure decreases after a certain level. However, decisions of the poor are constrained by time and intensity of other needs. He also demonstrated that the proportion of expenditure spent on food items declined at an income level even below the poverty line. This indicates that diversification of expenditure away from food begins to gain strength even before the attainment of calorific norm. Prof. Rao's contribution highlights that the decisions of the poor on food spending are based on starvation prevention rather than nutritional food.

2.6.2 Calorie Norm Controversy

"Nutritious food is a key actor for good health". Thus, the need for population-specific norms in terms of nutrition requirement varies across states. The need for population specific measures is due to differences in per capita daily intake of calories in the three uppermost expenditure classes accounting for 10 to 20 per cent of states' population. The population-specific norms help in avoiding technical controversy of nutritious food in the study of poverty.

2.6.3 Growth, Modernisation and Poverty: The Emerging Institutional Issues in Indian Agriculture

Self-help groups (SHGs), Panchayat Raj Institutions (PRIs) and mainstream institutions pave the way for polity and economy. SHGs, PRIs and MSIs should form an interlinked chain providing an institutional environment for sustainable agriculture growth. Formation of SHGs depends on government support, NGO initiative or local leadership. If these three change agents pool their resources, SHGs would have a stronger foundation for growth and viability. The policy regime of Central and state governments and their interventions in the economy are a crucial determinant for healthy institutions. Major changes in the policy regime and government interventions to make environment institution-friendly are suggested.

2.6.4 Income Barrier in Reaching Food to the Poor

While writing on reaching food to the poor, Prof. Rao raised fundamental questions hitherto ignored in research on food and policy formulation. Most researchers have used calorie requirements as a standard measure of poverty to draw the income line below the poverty and to obtain minimum food needs. Indicators based on this measure show a staggering proportion of population below the poverty line. Questions such as how such large proportion of population live without their minimum food needs being met over time, what is the adequacy of direct interventions to raise their purchasing power or reach food to the poor, bothered Prof. Rao. Towards an answer, he suggests to consider decision-making by the poor in relation to allocation of income for different needs. Here, he made two propositions regarding expenditure on food by the poor. First, there is a positive income effect on the food consumption expenditure. This has always been implicitly assumed in most research, literature and policy formulations. Realistic proposition is that relationship between food consumption and income would not work readily and mechanically because decisions by policy makers and poor are taken from different perspectives. According to him, decisions by those who have been living long at the subsistence level or in its close vicinity would be different from those who never knew extreme deprivation and how it shapes human behaviour. This section of policy makers tend to believe that given the rise in income, the poor increase expenditure on nutritional food rather than diversify their spending on other needs. However, ground realities do not reflect what policy makers or economic theories want them to behave.

2.6.5 Eradicating Poverty: Some Missing Policy Dimension

The anti-poverty strategy in India is in the process of shifting its focus from poverty line to a broader concept of poverty, but its capabilities seldom match the ambitious goals. This paper highlights weak aspects of the present strategy after describing a hardcore poverty situation. Extremely backward villages fail to attract attention of policy makers and better-off villages manage to attract attention and monopolise the development. Villages in the periphery, remain backward due to factors *inter alia*, small size, adverse location, poor resource base, low caste status and prolonged neglect by policy makers. Planning for neglected communities would have to be innovative, paying attention to specific features of each case. The poor can move along the economic route if they have access to assets, training and skill. Here, government should offer a sustained support. The support from the present anti–poverty strategy is too modest. Alternatively, route for upward mobility is to get together to form groups operating on political arena. Here, the initial push has to come from activists. The activists willing to help the poor are neither many nor are fully committed to the welfare of the poor. Thus, future prospect for the poor is mixed and uncertain. The hindmost suffer the worst and these are the weaker sections of the society.

2.6.6 Beyond Quantification of Poverty: Emerging Issues in Poverty Reduction

Prof. Rao classified three phases of poverty reduction in India. In the first phase, two types of reforms were advocated. First, agrarian reforms and second, reforms in delivery systems to reach basic needs to the poor. While progress has been achieved in building delivery system, agrarian reforms had limited impact and some even went against the poor. Thus, the first phase of poverty reduction could not complete its full course and the foundation remained weak for the next phase. The next phase of reforms included mechanism to improve quality and accountability of delivery system, promotion of local organisations to manage natural resources and enhanced opportunities for the poor in local governance. The upper layers benefited more from the institutional reforms of the second phase than the poor. The third phase was identified as empowerment of poor. Empowerment of the poor provides them with the capacity for upward mobility and for mobilising themselves by demanding the rights.

2.6.7 The Elusive Goal of Empowerment: A Review of the Emerging Phase in Poverty Reduction

Empowerment of the poor has been a major objective component in poverty reduction programmes and planning strategies of India. However, nature of such programmes witnessed many changes over the years. In this paper, Prof. Rao examined thoroughly the transition of anti-poverty strategy from poverty ratio to current phase of multiple deprivations like power, dignity and justice and pointed out weaknesses in strategies and blocks obstructing progress. Considering employment, food and land security, human development, access to resources and decision-making power, Prof. Rao argued that if empowerment of the poor is the aim of poverty reduction, anti-poverty strategy should work for progress of the poor from the perspective of acceptance of poverty as their fate, to actively seek and work for empowerment. Concurrently, he also emphasised on needed efforts for improvement in living conditions and credible prospects for a better future of the poor. Besides, mainstream society should have enough space and opportunities to accommodate the poor with access to viable income-yielding activities. Prof. Rao proved that there is a continuing and flagrant violation of these conditions from the very beginning of India's efforts to poverty reduction.

2.6.8 Choosing Among the Equals: Beneficiary Selection for Anti-Poverty Programmes

The BPL criteria to identify poor suffers from political clout in the selection of beneficiaries and hence with misidentification. To overcome this problem to some extent, Prof. Rao proposed a method of choosing beneficiaries, capturing local acquaintances of decentralisation and categorising poor as very poor, poor and not so poor. Here, the very poor group consisted of households who have neither skills nor assets and require steady support. Prof. Rao highlighted that the poor possess skills but require financial support, whereas the 'not so poor' are known as upwardly mobile households but categorised as poor only due to their caste. Thus, to identify different categories, Prof. Rao proposed an index based on 10 characteristics such as landholding, ownership of consumer durables, indebtedness, literacy and so on. By applying this method to

Karnataka state, he found that BPL criteria include 'not so poor' category as poor, and hence lead to misidentification. Thus, he suggested replacement of BPL criteria with the new method and backed it up by empowering to PRIs for the selection of poor.

2.6.9 Development of the Scheduled Castes: A Systemic View

Prof. Rao's keynote address at the National Workshop on "Economic Development of the Scheduled Castes with Special reference to Agricultural Landless Labourers" focused on the position of scheduled caste and tribes in agriculture and in politics. There are no two opinions about the high concentration of poverty among scheduled castes in India and the 'Dalit' concept emerged out of such debate on poverty and social exclusion. He showed the evidence of existing disparity in the performance of scheduled castes along political and economic considerations. Prof. Rao suggested that with the development programmes transferred to the PRIs, the developmental personnel at district and lower levels should be brought under PRIs by controlling corruption, competitive politics and creating powerful pressure for allocating funds to developmental programmes. He argued that the basis of social exclusion is the unequal access of social groups to agricultural land and a major structural weakness of the rural economy is the stagnancy of production and service activities outside agriculture. Thus, those lacking adequate access to land are left with few development opportunities to turn to. This could be due to continuing dependence on agriculture, the root cause of persistence of perceptions and attitudes, rural isolation and non-percolation. He concluded that, "The untouchability practices and the overt coercion and exploitation of the scheduled caste may diminish, not their marginalisation in the society and their inability to have access to the mainstream growth and development process". Will that mean poverty will continue to haunt them? We shall wait for him to write!

2.6.10 Survey of Drinking Habit and Socio-economic Conditions in Vidarbha and Maharashtra

The report represents findings of a survey of four villages in Vidharbha and Marathwada which were prior to 1st April 1959. These were incorporated in the Bombay state after reorganisation of the state in 1956. The aspects investigated by survey are the magnitude of alcoholism and the economic conditions of the alcoholics' families, such as income, standard of living, indebtedness. The report contained analysis of duration of drinking habit, preference for different types of drinks, frequency and intensity of drinking. Also, it presented a comprehensive comparison of the economic conditions of drinking and non-drinking families with data on value of property, magnitude of indebtedness and standard of living as reflected in the pattern of household expenditure. The report concludes that drinking habit in the rural areas of Vidharbha and Marathwada prevails extensively among lower strata of society.

2.6.11 Towards Human Development

Human development has always been built in the thinking and analytical process of Prof. Rao. He looked at the facets of human development whenever he analysed the issue of poverty or labour. Further, he specifically addressed the issue by viewing the process and status of human development parameters in his recent 'Rampure endowment lecture' delivered in 1999, and which later appeared in the *Indian Journal of Labour Economics*. He postulated that in the land of Gandhi, how can a poor household be raised above the poverty line by just providing enough food to meet the calorie norm and argued for inclusion of human liberty and dignity as important components. He analysed the picture across states and that of Karnataka so as to bring out the weak spots in the path of human development.

2.7 Labour and Wages

2.7.1 Technical Constraints in Programmes for Farm Employment

Issues pertaining to labour and wages attracted attention of Prof. Rao right from the beginning of his career. The quest for the determinants of employment elasticity in agriculture was answered with some unique results in the work he jointly published with G. Ahmed. While analysing the technical constraints for farm employment, he concluded that the size of the farm may not have a significant impact on the employment elasticity as much as the change in crop pattern. Therefore, it is the crop combination in the long run that decides the labour absorption in farm sector.

2.7.2 Labour Requirement in Indian Agriculture in 1981

Keeping with the argument developed earlier, he analysed the labour requirement across the regions, to raise questions regarding surplus labour and labour requirements. The objective was to compare the size of agricultural labour force and problems due to surplus labour. He studied the balance between labour requirements and size of labour with the help of determinants such as national income, income-elasticity of demand for farm products and labour ratio in agriculture. He concluded that the rise of labour ratio as well as surplus labour could only be checked with developmental programmes and progress of technology in the farm sector. In the end, he shared concern about agriculture labour wage earnings.

2.7.3 Minimum Wages in Agriculture: Implementation

In his work on minimum wages, Prof. Rao emphasised on whether legislation approach is desirable for implementation of minimum wages. The literature survey on poverty indicated that this approach is not useful for 'sweated labour'. The instrument of minimum wages needs to be considered in a positive manner to find conditions and modes of implementation to make the instrument effective. The then "Twenty-Point programme" of the GoI illustrated the success of legislature in the implementation of socio-economic programmes. At the other end, legislature is not enough for the implementation of minimum wage. While implementing the minimum wages, there should be good atmosphere in output of farm products. Prof. Rao suggested the need for improvement in collection, compilation and quick availability of quality data on wages while examining the Minimum Wage Survey conducted by the Central ministry of labour for determining change/increase in wages in the states and union territories in 1970-1980. He reiterated that minimum wages are not a total substitute for developmental reforms and that patience and determination are crucial for policy makers to overcome this limitation.

2.8 Perspectives on Rural Development

2.8.1 Relevance of Nehru's Perspective for Rural Upliftment

In this article on Nehru's perspective (1989), Prof. Rao highlighted the fact that Nehru could look decades ahead in charting the path of development for poor and disadvantaged when Indian society was entering a new phase of development. Nehru's perspective and sense of priorities in rural development could be more relevant than before in the face of various challenges. Rural development cannot address directly the problems of particular categories of rural people and of rural resources without considering village communities comprising the 'problem' people using the 'problem' resources. What promotes or weakens the community and which of its components are manipulable through planning are crucial for strengthening the planning system with insight into the role of human resources in development and requirements of problem-specific programmes for integrated rural development. A strategy for integrated development needs to examine not only sectors, resources and space, but also village communities. In his writing, he analysed the planning system in India and suggested to unlearn the old modes of functioning and devise new modes to cope with requirements of development planning in changing circumstances. The need to reach planning to district and *panchayat* levels is recognised by all. Achieving this two-way consistency between the macro and micro plans has always posed a limitation that needs considerable experimentation and trial to develop pragmatic procedures. While devolving responsibility of micro plans, rural people progressively seek active role in the formulation of macro plan in the strategies and programmes. He advocated a cautious approach. Thus, involving rural people in planning would mean giving them a much better say than now in the overall policies and priorities in development. This implies that relationships among rural people and their representatives, and the officials and administration, will have to be more balanced to allow genuine thinking for working together.

2.8.2 Rural Development

Prof. Rao carried intensive work in Tumkur district of Karnataka addressing various dimensions and perspectives that led to constraints in rural development. Although focused on one district, the issues raised could be generalised to rural situations in other parts of India. Rural underdevelopment is a consequence of a strong growth-oriented larger economy. In the Indian context, a close rapport between the poor and modest growth-oriented strategies could emerge gradually in the course of building an expanded and broad-based cadre of personnel supported by adequate political commitment at the top for the target groups. The politicisation of rural masses is an additional factor helping this process with inclusion of lower strata in development and a greater readiness on the part of target groups to stand for their rights. There is a persistent feeling that rural development ought to receive higher priority and larger resources than it has received till now in the development plans. There are active endeavours to evolve a decentralised pattern of organisation for formulating and implementing rural development programmes.

For this, he advocated a perceptible increase in the contribution of non-agricultural activities to rural growth. There should be adequate opportunities for rural landless and poor in non-agricultural sector to compensate for their handicaps in benefiting from agricultural growth. These should be complemented by decentralisation of planning and administration and building of participatory mechanisms for providing greater say for rural people in the decisions and policies that influence them.

2.8.3 Village Studies from the Economic Perspective: Some Priority Issues and Themes

The purpose of the paper was to make systematic enumeration of themes relating to villages viewed as micro-level economic system. Prof. Rao argued that absence of substantive diversification in the rural economy may induce policy makers to provide relief and support rather than providing them with a strong foundation. He saw the emergence of younger, better educated leaders in villages, which was a good sign of rural development. The leased market and migration of farmers show the level of development of rural villages. Hence, while selecting the priority themes for the "Economic Studies of Villages", he included interaction between village and large economy, percolation of development in the rural space, stratification of rural communities, rural attitudes and behaviours to cover comprehensive aspects of rural life.

2.8.4 Intra-rural Employment Variations between Types of Villages

Looking through his glasses, the field view of the nature of rural underemployment (1981), rural economic activities between types of villages are extremely interesting and offer relevant insights. In his usual style, he analysed the groups of villages. He, in his study on rural underemployment, found that the outpost villages are large and have a relatively diversified economy, while for land based villages focal points are small in size and almost wholly agricultural in activity. He argued that small and declining villages have a lot to lose and little to gain when growth and development occur in the larger economy. The group of villages with weak economic base has irrigation on par with district average, with low man-land and agricultural worker-land ratios as compared to the ratio in other types of villages.

2.8.5 Migration

Migration is the typical negative response hardly conducive to rural growth and development. Capacity of village community to respond to land constraint depends on opportunities for intensive cultivation or for non-agricultural activities. Prof. Rao argued that intensive margin villages provide positive response for intensive cultivation due to technical research output in dry farming. A pervasive factor inhibiting rural non-agricultural activities is the non-viability of the dispersed and household mode of production in the context of growing integration of agriculture and rural people with the markets of the larger economy.

2.8.6 Manifestation of Poverty Issues

Mapping the Periphery: The Poor Communities in the Southern States (2000), analyses development of rural poor, scheduled castes, scheduled tribes, backward castes and religious minorities and compares them with upper strata. While bringing out differences in development status among the rural poor and the gap that exists between them, Prof. Rao suggested that mapping succession of periods would aid in understanding the changing economic conditions, which help policy makers and administrators prioritise anti-poverty programmes in a more effective manner than depending completely on the same procedures of measuring poverty. However, for ensuring broad-based development and empowerment of the poor, he emphasised on the need for providing the principal role to PRIs in the entire exercise for a secure foundation.

2.8.7 Hurdles in Rural Development

In *Barriers to Development* (1983), Prof. Rao identifies several factors which hinder even spread of development across a district or a block. He opined that lack of local level planning and support of information-cum-monitoring system, cause uneven percolation of development components providing clues to underlying factors. Local level planning by itself is no answer to problems of slow and uneven rural development. Hence, according to him rural development needs a complementary set of infrastructural, institutional and organisational changes capable of activating human factor in development process.

Through his field observations, Prof. Rao suggested some noticeable drop in certain indicators of development as one moves from local village to villages in its neighbourhood. He clearly noticed the underlying reason of non-percolation of development in a fact that those who lacked assets were having a weak economic base and hence, remained below the threshold of viability despite being located in focal villages. Besides this, he also highlighted the functioning of social exclusion process due to their low caste status, an additional handicap suffered by poor households belonging to lower castes. Some important observations made by him included: a) while households in focal villages have a number of features typical of the urban way of living, this was not true to the same extent in the adjoining villages, b) compared to the isolated villages, adjoining villages to urban areas had convincingly better performance in production assets, modern inputs and access to institutional finance.

2.8.8 Rural Areas Lack Required Socio-economic Infrastructure Facilities

In his paper "Spatial Aspects of Integrated Rural Development" (1979), Prof. Rao showed that many of the villages in the district are not viable for providing necessary socio-economic infrastructure facilities, thus indicating that many villages do not satisfy population threshold criterion required for balanced regional development. Hence, he suggested cluster approach to focus on binding concerns in rural development. Besides, he emphasised that this needs to be with the human and social task of putting the rural communities back to their feet.

2.8.9 Lack of Basic Amenities

In this paper (considering Tumkur), Prof. Rao focused on availability of basic amenities as the most crucial factor for rural development programmes since the basic amenities touch all sections of the population and can be a powerful instrument in building community identity. He argued that providing a minimum degree of inhabitability to villages should deserve high priority. It is obvious that roads and other links among the neighbouring villages are an important component of the amenities.

2.8.10 Poor Micro-level Research and Planning

In his article "Rural Development and the Village—Perspectives for Planning for Development" (1980) Prof. Rao argued that effective planning for rural development needs grouping of villages into clusters capable of serving as 'unit areas of development'. Identifying key issues, he opined that there is little attention paid to micro-level village level research on rural development since planners assume that once a general spatial plan is implemented for a *taluk,* a small sized village will pose no further problems and this is the limitation. There is a linkage between spatial perspective and perspective of village studies and both approaches are important and relevant in their own manner for planning for rural development.

2.8.11 Limits of State Intervention

In this paper, Prof. Rao argued that growth, development and modernisation do not automatically reach and percolate evenly within local level rural economies. Market and vested interest forces from larger economy build rural–based groups belonging to upper strata having enough purchasing power and hence, lack the right kind of links and rapport with the rural mass who haven't. Further, state interventions lack strategy and design for development in terms of activating human factor in the rural economy. Prof. Rao reminds the policy makers and administrators for having understanding of these situations before any intervention to be made for socio-economic integration among neighbouring villages for emergence of viable rural communities. In the process, he suggested that revitalising *panchayats* and co-operatives and drawing latent capacities of rural people are crucial for working together and for the success of intervention. This needs a design to strengthen the position of local-level rural economies for bringing changes for rural development.

2.8.12 Unskilled Rural Development Personnel

Village based personnel need to be expanded in number and made more broad based and dispersed beyond the large size villages. This requires a fresh approach to building up personnel. This involves a distinct departure from the prevailing system of selection, recruitment where the recruited urban people are reluctant to move to villages. The bias is due to wilful discrimination by policy makers against poorer tracts. Tracts with better economic base offer more opportunities for industry rural development personnel and also are more articulate in attracting attention of policy makers towards infrastructural and development needs. Two-thirds of development personnel are located in large sized villages as compared to less than half of rural population belonging to these villages. Physical proximity itself does not help in building rapport with a body of people as rapport involves other crucial dimensions such as similarity of status, interests and a sense of identification with people with whom rapport is sought.

2.8.13 On Programmes

The history of rural India traverses through a maze of various programmes. The success and failure of the objectives are largely judged by the programmes alone. Prof. Rao critically examined the ongoing anti-poverty programmes like IRDP and Rural Diversification (1987). Considering the number of beneficiaries, acceptability and impact criteria, IRDP in Karnataka can be regarded as reasonably effective. Land linked schemes form the major component of IRDP activities. Village industries and service schemes are small in number but absorb households with these activities as their traditional occupation and not categories like landless labourers whose need for self-employment opportunities are far more pressing. As a consequence, impact of IRDP in terms of diversification of rural economy remains modest. The enduring benefits of the programme reach a few households having a land base and only the poor relatively close to poverty line, manage to cross it.

2.8.14 Cluster Approach to Solve Problems

'Clustering of villages' is a catch-all to overcome non-geographical distances separating them. Here the initiative rests with policy maker and progress can be visualised in terms of time bound programmes and quantitative targets. The social and economic process in which the individual villages begin to perceive themselves as a part of a larger and viable community is crucial. Prof. Rao emphasises that the social change is neither controlled by policy maker nor shaped by his own actions. The best point to move towards 'clustering of villages' is the provision for basic amenities. Planning for utilisation of human resources is crucial for the policy maker to build community identity. Giving support price for unskilled labour is an employment guarantee for local works for a firm grip on problems of rural poverty, inequity and social distance. Here there is a large meeting ground between 'clustering of villages' and spatial plans. Literacy is equally important for elimination of mass illiteracy.

He explained that what happens to the process beyond this point, depends on how local people carry this movement forward. Success of village clustering is measured by the extent to which it passes to hands of local people as it involves deeper issues in rural development rather than issues of viable size of a settlement for a particular amenity or service. It refers to subservience of villages to external decisions, their lack of capacity and initiative in organising development activities in their area of habitation, and their inability to participate in the processes of change and modernisation. Effectiveness of a cluster as a grassroot unit depends not on the size of the population brought together but on the degree of integration among the constituent villages and social groups, quality of local leadership and capacity of rural institutions to include rural weak and poor into their folds. Understanding the villages as a community of people and as a part of a rural neighbourhood is the key factor in planning for development.

2.8.15 Rural Diversification and the Strategy for Rural Employment

At the Round table Employment Policies seminar held in Poona, March 1980, Prof. Rao's paper deals with the conditions of poor people in Indian economy and how they are exploited by the elite. A few strategies are mentioned to overcome this such as a fuller use of agricultural land, increasing agricultural production with the help of green revolution and adding new lines of production creating new opportunities in rural area. Prof. Rao provides field experience of Tumkur district with reference to rural diversification as strategy for rural employment. The strategy needs to shift its focus from 'rural works' to 'rural factories'.

2.8.16 Issues in Decentralised Planning

Presently, decentralised planning is in the preliminary stage of experimentation. Prof. Rao's interest in decentralisation could be traced in his writings from mid-eighties. This paper on "Decentralised Planning—Priority Economic Issues" (1993) highlights issues of developing decentralised planning to a functioning operational system. The issues are planning for growth, planning for minimum needs and promotion of participation in planning. According to Rao, Indian approach to rural development has relied on short-term perspectives and low-cost strategies. This is reflected in the primary emphasis on relief and support rather than on complementing growth and participation. A consequence of this approach is seen in methodologies for formulation of decentralised plans which have remained inadequate for growth, needs and participation. Beyond the initial phase, effectiveness of decentralised planning depends on mobilisation of rural elite and middle strata. Rao participated effectively in the process of decentralised planning during mid-nineties.

Effective planning for rural development needs grouping of villages into clusters capable of serving as 'unit areas of development'. This offers scope for bringing neighbouring villages to share common amenities, to constitute *panchayats* and co-operatives and conglomerating villages for improving rural environment conducive for economic growth, rural diversification and emergence of viable rural institutions. Mega projects could involve the local community and its development in a well thought-out plan. Options may be like pursuing on a conscious policy of drawing their workers and subordinate staff from the surrounding areas which would help in their overall development, and combating threat of pollution by transparent policy of educating local people about problems of pollution seeking their co-operation in solving them. Another initiative is to pursue collectively through their consortium of a representative body for provision of infrastructure and amenities and institutional arrangements for training and imparting skills.

He emphasised that local level plans need an informative and probing monitoring system than is provided by the mundane programme-wise statistics on physical norms, expenditure incurred, beneficiaries covered. It should be possible to set up a simple and practicable information system, to be operated as a part of implementation of the local-level plans based on a combined observation of programme-wise data and household data over a cross-section of selected villages of different types identified in the area.

2.9 Shaping Agricultural Economists

Prof. Rao's contribution in shaping agricultural economists is unique. The Indian Society of Agricultural Economics completed its 50 years as a national institution in 1989 and contributed significantly to the development of human capital in agricultural economics. Most of the leading agricultural economists of the country owe their status to their publications in this reputed journal. Prof. Rao had been associated with the Journal of the Society for a long time in various capacities as a Member of the Editorial Board and its Chairman later. He took this opportunity to view in retrospect the role played by the Indian Society of

Agricultural Economics in the development and professionalism of agriculture economics in India. The journal brought out by the society provided a much-needed channel for communication of results of research and exchange of views at the academic level. There can be no second opinion that the journal achieved international standards due to dedication of Prof. M.L. Dantwala, Dr. V.M. Jakhade, Dr. N.A. Mujumdar and Prof. Sundaram. Prof. V.M. Rao's contribution to the journal's recognition is substantial.

One of the important initiatives undertaken by Prof. Rao was to investigate into the rejected papers by the journal. This work was undertaken as a part of initiative of the society to help young researchers to locate their missed steps. This speaks of Prof. Rao, who always remained concerned and continues to show a great deal of interest in the work being done by the young researchers. The journal receives several articles and naturally many of them are rejected though they may be of reasonable quality. The newcomers to the field and young scholars are normally the victims who are not equipped to bring the article to the level of quality publication. Prof. Rao's analysis provided a clue to hold a workshop for the authors of such papers to discuss with them to bring their research paper to an acceptable level. These workshops have been quite successful. Many of the authors, who attended such workshops, improved their articles in quality and these were then found to be fit for publication in the journal. This small recommendation to the ISAE made a great difference in the academic life of many young authors.

List of Professor Rao's Publication

Books/Monographs

1. 1962, Desai. M.B. and V.M. Rao. *Survey of Drink Habit and Socio-Economic Conditions in Vidarbha and Marathwada*. Bombay: University of Bombay.

2. 1967, Rao, V.M. *Notes on Estimation of Farm Production Function* (Mimeographed-Prepared for submission to the Planning Commission), New Delhi: Government of India.

3. 1967, Rao, V.M. Theory of Producer Behaviour in Agriculture (Mimeographed; prepared for the Refresher Course in Pune), Mumbai: Indian Society of Agricultural Economics.

4. 1975, Rao, V.M. *Food: Second India Study*. New Delhi: Macmillan Publication.

5. 1977, Rao, V.M. *The Teaching of Economics: Methods and Techniques: Volume-I*. New Delhi: Allied Publishers.

6. 1978, Rao, V.M. *Village in Tumkur: A Preliminary Perspective* (Mimeographed: presented to the UNAPDI-ISEC Workshop on Population Planning and Area Development), Bangalore: Institute for Social and Economic Change.

7. 1980, Rao, V.M. *Rural Development and the Village: Perspectives for Planning for Development*. New Delhi: Sterling Publishers.

8. 1984, Rao, V.M., G.H. Peiris and S. Tilakaratne. *Planning for Rural Development: The Experience of the District Integrated Rural Development Programme of Sri Lanka*. Bangkok, Thailand: International Labour Organisation (ARTEP).

9. 1985, Rao, V.M. *Rural Development: Policies, Programmes and Constraints: Proceedings of an ILO Seminar held in Sri Lanka, Bangkok*. Thailand: International Labour Organisation (ARTEP).

10. 1989, Abdul Aziz and V.M. Rao. *Poverty Alleviation in India: Programmes and Action* (ed.). New Delhi: Ashish Publishing House.

11. 1998, Rao, V.M. *The Poor in a Hostile Society: Glimpses of Changing Poverty Scenario in India* (eds.), New Delhi: Vikas Publications.

12. 2000, Rao, V.M. and P.D. Jeromi. *Modernising Indian Agriculture: Priority Tasks and Critical Policies*. Study No. 21, Development Research Group, Department of Economic Analysis and Policy, Mumbai: Reserve Bank of India.

13. 2004, Rao, V.M. *Rainfed Agriculture: State of the Indian Farmer- A Millennium Study*, Volume 10, New Delhi: Academic Foundation and Ministry of Agriculture, Government of India.

14. 2004, Deshpande, R.S. and V.M. Rao. *Coarse Cereals in a Drought-Prone Region: A Study in Karnataka Monographs* No. 2, Bangalore: Institute for Social and Economic Change.

Published Research Papers/Articles/Chapters in Edited Books

P1. 1960, Rao, V.M. and S.H. Deshpande. "Agriculture in Maharashtra", in *Problems of Maharashtra* (eds.). Bombay: The Indian Committee for Cultural Freedom.

P2. 1961, Rao, V.M. "A note on government expenditure and physical achievements in the community projects of Bombay deccan", *Journal of the University of Bombay*, January, Bombay.

P3. 1963, Rao, V.M. "Labour requirements in Indian agriculture", *Indian Journal of Agricultural Economics* 15(2), April-June.

P4. 1965, Rao, V.M. "Farm management data and analysis of costs, returns and efficiency in agriculture", *Journal of the University of Bombay*, January.

P5. 1966, Rao, V.M. "Return to family labour on small farms in India", *Indian Journal of Agricultural Economics* 21(1), January-March.

P6. 1966, Rao, V.M. "A note on changes in crop pattern in Bombay deccan", *Indian Journal of Agricultural Economics* 21(3), July-September.

P7. 1966, Rao, V.M. and G. Ahmed. "The technical constraints in the programmes or farm employment", *Artha Vijnana* 8(1), March.

P8. 1968, Rao, V.M., N.S. Shetty and S.A. Shetty. "Final and revised crop estimates: An analysis of discrepancies", *Economic and Political Weekly* 3(43): A39-A46, October 26.

P9. 1969, Rao, V.M. "Two decompositions of concentration ratio", *Journal of Royal Statistical Society* 132(3): 418-425.

P10. 1971, Rao, V.M. "Inequality in ownership of land-nature, extent and redistributive implications", in M.L. Dantwala and C.H. Shah (Eds.), *Evaluation of Land Reforms in Western India*, Bombay: Department of Economics, University of Bombay.

P11. 1971, Rao, V.M. "Structural features of villages lease markets", in M.L. Dantwala and C.H. Shah (eds.), *Evaluation of Land Reforms in Western India*. Bombay: Department of Economics, University of Bombay.

P12. 1972, Rao, V.M. "Land transfers in rural communities—Some findings in a ryotwari region", *Economic and Political Weekly* 7(40): A133-144, (September 30).

P13. 1974, Rao, V.M. "Two perspectives on redistribution of land", *Economic and Political Weekly* 9(13): A2-A10, (March 30).

P14. 1974, Rao, V.M. and M.C. Sayyed. "Crop production and productivity in Maharashtra during the period 1955-56 to 1968-69", in S.H. Deshpande (ed.), *Economy of Maharashtra*, Joag Felicitation Volume, Poona: Samaj Probodhan Sanstha.

P15. 1974, M.L. Dantwala and V.M. Rao. "Inequality of farm incomes: A comment", *Economic and Political Weekly* 9(20): 801-803. (May, 18).

P16. 1974, Rao, V.M. "Village lease markets for agricultural land: Some approaches for analysis", *Economic and Political Weekly* 9(26): A55-A62, June 30.

P17. 1976, Rao, V.M. "Agricultural labour market in India", *YOJANA* (Marathi) 4(12-13), January.

P18. 1977, Rao, V.M. "Minimum wages in agriculture: Implementation", in S.D. Punekar and Others (eds.), *Economic Revolution in India*. Bombay: Himalaya Publishing House.

P19. 1978, Rao, V.M. "Linking irrigation with development: Some policy issues", *Economic and Political Weekly* 13(14, 24): 993-997, June 17.

P20. 1978, Rao, V.M. "Perspective plan-goal, targets and strategy", in VKRV Rao (ed.), *Planning in Perspective: Policy Choices in Planning for Karnataka* (1973-74 to 1988-89). New Delhi: Allied Publishers.

P21. 1979, Rao, V.M. "Linking irrigation with development: Some policy issues", in M.V. Nadkarni *et al.*, (eds). *Impact of Irrigation: Canal, Well and Tank Irrigation in Karnataka*, Bombay: Himalaya Publishing House.

P22. 1979, Rao, V.M. "Spatial aspects of integrated rural development in pigmy", *Economic Review of Syndicate Bank* 24(10-11), May-June.

P23. 1979, Rao, V.M. "Spatial aspects of integrated rural development", in G. Thimmaiah (ed.), *Studies in Rural Development*. Allahabad: Chugh Publications.

P24. 1979, Rao, V.M. "Economic theory: A rational framework for rural India", *The Economic Times*, October 1.

P25. Rao, V.M. "The cluster approach to rural analysis and planning", in C.H. Hanumantha Rao and P.C. Joshi (eds), *Reflections on Economic Development and Social Change—Essays in Honour of VKRV Rao*. New Delhi: Allied Publishers.

P26. 1979, Rao, V.M. and M. Vivekananda. "Food: Problems and policy priorities", in C.H. Shah (ed.), *Agricultural Development of India—Policy and Problems*. Bombay: Orient Longman.

P27. 1980, Rao, V.M. "Income barrier in reaching food to the poor", COMMERCE, December 13.

P28. 1981, Rao, V.M. "Nature of rural underdevelopment: A field view", *Economic and Political Weekly* 16(41): 1655-1666. October 10.

P29. 1982, Rao, V.M. "Rural development personnel: Location, status and development characteristics", *Economic and Political Weekly* 17(42): 1691-1696, October 16.

P30. 1982, Rao, V.M. and M. Vivekananda "Calorie norm controversy", *Economic and Political Weekly* 17(7): 254-255, February 13.

P31. 1982, Rao, V.M. and M. Vivekananda. "The poor as a social stratum: Some economic criteria for studying poverty", *Economic and Political Weekly* 17(27): 1107-1112, July 3.

P32. 1982, Rao, V.M. "Problems of relevance in social science research: Some illustrations from agricultural economic research in India", in Institute of Economic Growth (ed.), *Relevance in Social Science Research - A Colloquium*. New Delhi: Vikas Publishing House.

P33. 1983, Rao, V.M. "Rural diversification and the strategy for rural employment", in Austin Robinson, P.R. Brahmananda and L.K. Deshpande (ed.), *Employment Policy in a Developing Country - A Case Study of India*. London: Macmillan.

P34. 1983, Rao, V.M. "Barriers in rural development", *Economic and Political Weekly* 18(27), July 2.

P35. 1983, Rao, V.M. "The distant neighbours—A fuller view of the clusters and their villages", in Abdul Aziz (ed.), *Studies in Block Planning*. New Delhi: Concept Publishing Company.

P36. 1983, Rao, V.M. "Information system for rural plan implementation: A proposal", Submitted to the Working Group for Preparing Guidelines for District-level Planning, New Delhi: Planning Commission.

P37. 1984, Rao, V.M. and M.G. Chandrakanth. "Resources at the margin: Tank irrigation programme in Karnataka", *Economic and Political Weekly* 19(26): A54-A58, June 30.

P38. 1984, Rao, V.M. "Rural development personnel: Location, status and development characteristics", in K. Singh, T.S. Papola and R.S. Mathur (eds.), *Economic Planning and Policies in India*. New Delhi: A Sterling Publications.

P39. 1984, Rao, V.M. "Income barrier in reaching food to the poor", in T.K. Lakshman and B.K. Narayan (eds.), *Rural Development in India - A Multi-dimensional analysis*. Bombay: Himalaya Publishing House.

P40. 1986, Rao, V.M. and R.S. Deshpande. "Agricultural production: Pace and pattern of growth", in M.L. Dantwala and others (eds.), *Indian Agricultural Development since Independence*. Bombay: Oxford and IBH Publishing Company.

P41. 1986, Thimmaiah, G. and V.M. Rao. "Problems and prospects of sericulture development in Karnataka: A field view", in H.G. Hanumappa (ed.), *Sericulture for Rural Development*. Bombay: Himalaya Publishing House.

P42. 1986, Rao, V.M. "Some reflections on institutional finance for rural development", in L.K. Naidu (ed.), *Bank Finance for Rural Development*. New Delhi: Ashish Publishing House.

P43. 1984, Rao, V.M. and R.S. Deshpande. "Agricultural growth in India: A review of experiences and prospects", *Economic and Political Weekly* 21(38-39): A101-A112, September 20-27.

P44. 1987, Rao, V.M. and R.S. Deshpande. "Agricultural growth in India: A review of experiences and prospects", in P.R. Brahmananda and V.R. Panchamukhi (eds.), *The Development Process of India*. Bombay: Himalaya Publishing House.

P45. 1987, Rao, V.M. "Changing village structure: Impact of rural development programmes", *Economic and Political Weekly* 22(13): A2-A5, March 28.

P46. 1987, Rao, V.M. and S. Erappa. "IRDP and rural diversification: A study in Karnataka", *Economic and Political Weekly* 22(52): A151-A160, December 26.

P47. 1987, Rao, V.M. "India in 2000 AD: A scenario for rural economy", An Invited Note sent to XII Indian Social Science Congress, Mysore, July.

P48. 1988, Rao, V.M. "Sustained development through people", *VIKALPA* 13(3), July-September.

P49. 1988, Rao, V.M. "Interventions for the poor: Critical dimensions, potentialities and limitations", *Economic and Political Weekly* 23(45-47): 2409-2420.

P50. 1989, Rao, V.M. "Impact of rural development programmes" in Irma Adelman and Sylvia Lane (eds.), *The Balance Between Industry and Agriculture in Economic Development*, Vol.4 - Social Effects, Proceedings of the Eighth World Congress of International Economic Association, Macmillan.

P51. 1989, Rao, V.M. "Relevance of Nehru's perspective for rural uplift", *Kurukshetra* XXXVIII(1), October.

P52. 1989, Rao, V.M. "Development strategy for the next phase: Perspectives and priorities", *Economic and Political Weekly* 24(1): 27-29, January 7.

P53. 1989, Rao, V.M. "Decentralised planning: Priority economic issues", *Economic and Political Weekly* 24(25): 1399-1405, June 24.

P54. 1989, Rao, V.M. "Fifty years of agricultural economics in India", *Economic and Political Weekly* 24(49): 2401-2402, December 9.

P55. 1989, Rao, V.M. "Prospects for food: Availability vs access", *Bulletin of Sciences* 5(2), Nov-Dec.

P56. 1989, Rao, V.M. "The economic environment for rural cooperatives", in Karnataka State Cooperative Agriculture and Rural Development Bank Ltd. (ed.) *Rural Development and Role of Cooperatives*. Bangalore: KSCARDB.

P57. 1990, Rao, V.M. "Village studies from the economic perspective: Some priority issues and themes", *The Administrator* XXXVI(3).

P58. 1990, Rao, V.M. "Interventions for the poor: Critical dimensions, potentialities and limitations", in K.S. Krishnaswamy (ed.), *Poverty and Income Distribution*. New Delhi: Oxford University Press.

P59. 1990, Dantwala, M.L., V.M. Dandekar, V.M. Rao, N. Rath, B. Tulpule, A.V. Desai and J.C. Sandesara. "Search for an employment-oriented strategy", *Economic and Political Weekly*, Symposium, 25(21): 1147-1162, May 26.

P60. 1990, Rao, V.M. and S. Erappa. "Development opportunities in dryland agriculture", in ISAE (ed.), *Agricultural Development Policy: Adjustments and Reorientation*, Golden Jubilee Volume of Indian Society of Agricultural Economics (ISAE), New Delhi: Oxford & IBH.

P61. 1990, Rao, V.M. "Land for the poor: A policy perspective for land reforms and use of common property resources", in *Study Group on Land Reforms and Common Property Resources*, National Commission on Rural Labour, New Delhi: Government of India.

P62. 1991, Rao, V.M. "Growth in the context of underdevelopment: The case of dryland agriculture", *Economic and Political Weekly* 26(13): A2-A14, March 30.

P63. 1991, Rao, V.M. "Technology for dryland agriculture: A note on experience in Karnataka", *Indian Association of Social Science Institutions Quarterly* 9(3), January-March.

P64. 1991, Rao, V.M. "Role of village studies in planning for integrated rural development", in B.N. Yugandhar and Neela Mukherjee (ed.), *Studies in Village India: Issues in Rural Development*. New Delhi: Concept Publications.

P65. 1992, Rao, V.M. "Change processes in dryland communities", *Indian Journal of Agricultural Economics* XLVII(1), January-March.

P66. 1992, Rao, V.M. "Fixing agricultural prices: Issues and experiences", *Economic and Political Weekly* 27(13): 639-645, March 28.

P67. 1992, Rao, V.M. "Inflation and cereals: Implications for policy", *The Economic Times*, 16th June.

P68. 1992, Rao, V.M. "Land reform experiences: A perspective for strategy and programmes", *Economic and Political Weekly* 27(26): A50-A64, June 27.

P69. 1992, Rao, V.M. "Land reforms: The next phase", in R. Bharadwaj and M.V. Nadkarni (ed.), *Planning for Social and Economic Development*. New Delhi: Sage Publications.

P70. 1992, Rao, V.M. "How secure is food security?", *Economic and Political Weekly* 27(48): 2598-2599, November 28.

P71. 1993, Rao, V.M. "The wheat story: Recent changes in price policy", *Economic and Political Weekly* 28(44): 2385-2386, October 30.

P72. 1993, Rao, V.M. "Decentralised planning: Priority economic issues", in *Critical Spectrum: Lectures on Current Issues*. Mangalagangotri: Mangalore University.

P73. 1993, Rao, V.M. "Government interventions in agriculture: A review of studies in developing countries", *Indian Journal of Agricultural Economics* 48(4), October-December.

P74. 1994, Rao, V.M. "Agriculture and liberalisation: Some implications for development policies", *Economic and Political Weekly* 29(16-17): 999-1003, April 16-23.

P75. 1994, Rao, V.M. "Farmers in market economy: Would farmers gain through liberalisation?", *Indian Journal of Agricultural Economics* 49(3), July-September.

P76. 1994, Rao, V.M. "Coping with liberalisation: The next phase in the anti-poverty strategy", *The Administrator* XL(1), January-March.

P77. 1995, Rao, V.M. "Beyond 'surpluses': Food security in changing context", *Economic and Political Weekly* 30(4): 215-219, Jan 28.

P78. 1995, Rao, V.M. "Looking ahead to the past", *Economic and Political Weekly* 30(20): 1165-1167, May 20.

P79. 1995, Rao, V.M. "Planning for liberalisation: ACRP in the changing context", *Economic and Political Weekly* 30(25): 1478-1479, June 24.

P80. 1995, Rao, V.M. "Coping with liberalisation: The next phase in the anti-poverty strategy", *Indian Journal of Social Science* 8(4), Oct-Dec.

P81. 1995, Rao, V.M. "Policies for rural labour: From relief to structural change", *Indian Journal of Labour Economics* 38(3), July-September.

P82. 1996, Rao, V.M. "Agriculture since independence", *Voices* IV(1).

P83. 1996, Rao, V.M. "Agricultural development with a human face: Experiences and prospects", *Economic and Political Weekly* 31(26): A50-A62, June 29.

P84. 1996, Rao, V.M. "Policy research for liberalised agriculture: Some illustrative research areas", *Indian Journal of Agricultural Economics* 5(1 & 2), Golden Jubilee Number, January-June.

P85. 1996, Rao, V.M. "Planning for liberalisation: ACRP in the changing context", in D.N. Basu and G.S. Guha (eds.), *Agro-Climatic Regional Planning in India: Concept and Applications* - Vol. 1. New Delhi: Concept Publishing Company.

P86. 1996, Rao, V.M. "Reconciling the two Indias", *Economic and Political Weekly* 31(19): 1135-1136, May 11.

P87. 1997, Rao, V.M. "Agricultural price policy: Issues for the next phase", in Bhupat M. Desai (ed.), *Agricultural Development Paradigm for the Ninth Plan Under New Economic Environment*. New Delhi: Oxford & IBH Publishing Company.

P88. 1997, Rao, V.M. "Adjusting to changing regimes: ACRP in the context of new policies", *Economic and Political Weekly* 32(48): 3047-3048, Nov. 29-Dec.05.

P89. 1997, Rao, V.M. "Role of industrialists: Private enterprise with a social perspective", in Abdul Aziz (ed.), *Industrialisation, Socio-Economic Externalities and State Policy*. New Delhi: Concept.

P90. 1998, Rao, V.M., V.J. Naidu and K.V. Raju. "Choosing among the equals: Beneficiary selection for anti-poverty programmes", *Indian Journal of Labour Economics* 41(2), April-June.

P91. 1998, Rao, V.M. "Development carnatic style", *Economic and Political Weekly* 33(13): 705-706, March 26- April 3.

P92. 1998, Rao, V.M. "Economic reforms and the poor: Emerging scenario", *Economic and Political Weekly* 33(29-30): 1949-1954, July 18-31.

P93. 1999, Rao, V.M. and H.G. Hanumappa. "Marginalization process in agriculture: Indicators, outlook and policy", *Economic and Political Weekly* 34(52): A133-A138, December 25.

P94. 1999, Rao, V.M. "Infrastructure for development: Towards a research agenda for the ninth plan", *ARPAN* 3(1), January-July, Ahmedabad: Agro-Climatic Regional Planning, Planning Commission.

P95. 1999, Rao, V.M. "Policy making for agricultural development: Why it misses the poor", *Indian Journal of Labour Economics* 42(1).

P96. 2000, Rao, V.M. "Mapping the periphery: The poor communities in the southern states", *Journal of Indian School of Political Economy*, April-June.

P97. 2000, Rao, V.M. "Where reforms do not reach: Rural poor in the vicinity of Bangalore", *Journal of Indian School of Political Economy* XII(1), January-March.

P98. 2000, Rao, V.M. "Towards human development: Glimpses from India and selected states", *The Indian Journal of Labour Economics* 43(2), April-June.

P99. 2001, Rao, V.M. "The making of agricultural price policy: A review of CACP reports", *Journal of Indian School of Political Economy* XIII(1), January-March.

P100. 2001, Rao, V.M. "Agricultural price policy and food security: The need for a new paradigm", in M.D. Asthana and Pedro Medrano, (eds.), *Towards Hunger Free India: Agenda and Imperatives*. New Delhi: Manohar Publications.

P101. 2001, Rao, V.M. "Don't Forget the Tortoise", *Economic and Political Weekly* 36(34): 3233-3235, August 25-31.

P102. 2002, Rao, V.M. "District governance: A foundation for grassroots development", in KWIRC and UNFDW (eds.), *In Search of Equitable and Just Development -Proceedings of a Round Table on Financing for District Level Development*. New Delhi: Karnataka Women's Information and Research Centre (KWIRC) and United Nations Development Fund for Women (UNFDW).

P103. 2002, Rao, V.M. and R.S. Deshpande. "Food security in drought prone area: A study in Karnataka", *Economic and Political Weekly* 37(35): 3677-3681, August 31.

P104. 2002, Rao, V.M. "Eradicating poverty: Some missing policy dimensions", in M. Govinda Rao (ed.), *Development, Poverty and Fiscal Policy*. New Delhi: Oxford University Press.

P105. 2002, Rao, V.M. "Growth, modernisation and poverty: The emerging institutional issues in Indian agriculture", in S.S. Acharya, Surjit Singh and Vidyasagar (ed.), *Sustainable Agriculture, Poverty and Food Security*. Jaipur: Rawat Publications.

P106. 2002, Rao, V.M. "Attacking poverty implications for the world bank's approach to poverty reduction", in World Development Report 2000-01, The World Bank, November.

P107. 2004, Rao, V.M. and D.V. Gopalappa "Agricultural growth and farmer distress: Tentative perspectives from Karnataka", *Economic and Political Weekly* 39(52): 5591-5597, December 25-31.

P108. 2004, Rao, V.M., R.Radhakrishna and Shovan Ray. "Beyond quantification of poverty: Emerging issues in poverty reduction", *Indian Journal of Labour Economics* 47(2), April-June.

P109. 2004, Rao, V.M. "Where reforms do not reach", in G.S. Aurora (ed.), *Poverty and Economic Reforms: The Social Concerns*. New Delhi: Academic Foundation in association with Institute for Social and Economic Change.

P110. 2004, Rao, V.M. "The poor communities in the southern states", in G.S. Aurora (ed.), *Poverty and Economic Reforms: The Social Concerns*. New Delhi: Academic Foundation in association with Institute for Social and Economic Change.

P111. 2005, Rao, V.M. "Development role of agricultural and rural diversification: Illustrative profiles from drought-prone villages", in Rohini Nayyar and Alakh N. Sharma (eds.), *Rural Transformation in India*. New Delhi: Institute for Human Development.

P112. 2005, Rao, V.M. "Towards effective poverty reduction: A global perspective", *Working Paper* No. 155, Institute for Social and Economic Change, Bangalore.

P113. 2005, Rao, V.M. "Is development economics user-friendly?", *Economic and Political Weekly* 40(44-45): 5754+5771-5772, Oct. 29- Nov. 04.

P114. 2006, Rao, V.M., D. Rajasekhar and J.Y. Suchitra. "Unorganised workers", *Economic and Political Weekly* 41(19): 1913-1919, May 13-19.

P115. 2006, Rao, V.M., D. Rajasekhar and J.Y. Suchitra. "Putting the cart before a non-existent horse", *Economic and Political Weekly* 41(32): 3488-3491, August 12-18.

P116. 2006, Rao, V.M. "Institutional reforms for poverty reduction: Current status and prospects", in R. Radhakrishna and Shovan Ray (eds.), *Handbook of Poverty in India: Perspectives, Policies and Programmes*. New Delhi: Oxford University Press.

P117. 2007, Rao, V.M. "Making safety nets effective for hardcore poor", *Economic and Political Weekly* 42(33): 3397-3403, August 18-24.

P118. 2008, Rao, V.M. "Through cloudy glasses: Viewing food insecurity from the top", *Economic and Political Weekly* 43(20): 35-37, May 17-23.

Keynote/Presidential Addresses and Memorial Lectures

K/P1. 1961, Rao, V.M. "Working of debt relief programme in the districts of Bombay deccan", presented in Golden Jubilee Souvenir of Social Service League, Bombay, March.

K/P2. 1980, Rao, V.M. "Rural diversification and the strategy for rural employment", presented in Round Table on Employment Policies, held in Poona under the joint auspices of International Economic Association and Indian Economic Association, March.

K/P3. 1984, Rao, V.M. "The place of village in planning for integrated rural development", The SDRSI Endowment Lecture delivered at Sri Venkateswara University, Tirupati on March 14.

K/P4. 1985, Rao, V.M. "From facts to interpretations: Some missing links", Keynote address delivered to the International Workshop on *Rural Economic Change* held jointly by the Social Science Research Council, New York and Indian Statistical Institute in Bangalore, August.

K/P5. 1988, Rao, V.M. "Decentralised planning: Priority economic issues", Keynote address delivered at 71st Annual Conference of the Indian Economic Association, Calcutta. (see also *Economic and Political Weekly* XXIV(25), June 24, 1989).

K/P6. 1990, Rao, V.M. "Horticulture and the rural economy: Some development issues", Keynote address delivered to the Workshop on *Horticulture Development: Opportunities and Challenges*, held by the National Horticulture Development Board, Bangalore, May.

K/P7. 1991, Rao, V.M. "Change processes in dryland communities", Presidential Address delivered at the 51st Annual Conference of the Indian Society of Agricultural Economics held at the Andhra Pradesh Agricultural University, Hyderabad, December 18 to 20. (see *Indian Journal of Agricultural Economics* XLVII(1), January-March, 1992.)

K/P8. 1994, Rao, V.M. "Beyond "surpluses": Food security in changing context", L.S. Venkataramanan Memorial Lecture delivered at Institute for Social and Economic Change, Bangalore, December. (see also *Economic and Political Weekly*, 28 January, 1995).

K/P9. 1994, Rao, V.M. "Farmers in market economy: Would farmers gain through liberalisation?", Keynote address delivered at Annual Conference of Indian Society of Agricultural Economics held in Kolhapur, November. (See also *Indian Journal of Agricultural Economics* 49(3), July-September, 1994).

K/P10. 1998, Rao, V.M. "Policy making for agricultural development: Why it misses the poor", V.B. Singh Memorial Lecture delivered during the 40th Conference of the Indian Society of Labour Economics, Hyderabad, December. (See also *Indian Journal of Labour Economics* 42(1), 1999).

K/P11. 2000, Rao, V.M. "Towards human development: Glimpses from India and selected states", Shri Mahadevappa Rampure Endowment Lecture delivered at Gulbarga University. (see also *The Indian Journal of Labour Economics* 43(2), April-June, 2000).

K/P12. 2001, Rao, V.M. "Sustainable agricultural development", Keynote Address delivered to International Research Symposium on Sustainable Agricultural Development, Bangalore, University of Agricultural Sciences, Bangalore, March 27.

K/P13. 2001, Rao, V.M. "Development of the scheduled castes: A systemic view", Keynote Address delivered at National Workshop on *Economic Development of the Scheduled Castes with special reference to Agricultural Landless Labourers*, organised by Gokhale Institute of

Politics and Economics and Development of Social Welfare, Government of Maharashtra, Pune, March 16.

K/P14. 2001, Rao, V.M. "Growth, modernisation and poverty: The emerging institutional issues in Indian agriculture", Keynote address delivered at Third Asian Conference of Agricultural Economists, Institute of Development Studies, Jaipur, October 18-20. (see S.S. Acharya, Surjit Singh and Vidyasagar (ed.), *Sustainable Agriculture, Poverty and Food Security*, Rawat Publications, Jaipur, 2002.)

K/P15. 2003, Rao, V.M. "The elusive goal of empowerment: A review of the emerging phase in poverty reduction", V.B. Singh Memorial Lecture on Political Economy of Development-2003, Giri Institute of Development Studies, Lucknow, April.

Section I

Aggregated Economic Development

3 Indian Economics in Disarray

Tragedy of a Forsaken Legacy

Dilip M. Nachane

3.1 The Pioneers of Indian Economic Thoughts

To be a pioneer across several disciplines is the natural destiny of a chosen few, and Raja Ram Mohan Roy was of this select band. Thus, students of Indian history would hardly be surprised to learn that he was possibly one of the earliest Indians to write on economic issues of British India. In the evidence given before the British House of Commons in 1831 on the question of the renewal of the East India Company Charter, he made a powerfully reasoned plea for lowering the rents of the *ryots* via a permanent settlement. Since then sporadic writings on issues of economic policy continued but a systematic critique of the Imperial government's economic policies really emerged only towards the closing decades of the 19th century under the intellectual triumvirate of Dadabhai Naoroji, Romesh Chander Dutt and Mahadev Govind Ranade. Together they may be regarded as the founding fathers of Indian economics. The sense in which this term is being employed will be clarified below, but first let us take stock of the major contributions of these three leading figures, albeit in a brief fashion.

Naoroji's contributions were basically two-fold. He is the first economist (Indian or British) to have compiled India's national income at £300 million (per capita income of 40 shillings or Rs. 20) using whatever data was possible in those days in a highly professional fashion. He published these in his celebrated paper "Wants and Means of India" (1870). From a modern perspective, two further features are noteworthy about these estimates *viz.*, that the estimates were broken down by the major provinces and further, a comparison between the per capita income and the money cost of "necessary consumption" defined as "what is necessary for the bare wants of a human being, to keep him in ordinary good health and decency." This latter feature anticipates the celebrated Dandekar-Rath thesis of "Poverty in India" by exactly a century.

Even more fundamental is Naoroji's challenge to Mill's free trade doctrine. He argued that the classical view about the benevolence of free trade was applicable (if at all) only to trade between free nations and emphatically, not to trade between an imperial power and its colonies. The Drain Theory which flowed naturally from this criticism related directly the growth in Britain to the "ungrowth" in India. Even so fine a scholar as Bhabatosh Datta failed to grasp the richness of Naoroji's criticism. Writing in 1962, Datta noted that "if only a full balance of payments account were available, Naoroji would probably have noticed that British capital was also being imported into India during this period." In truth, with the perspicacity of a truly great scholar, Naoroji was quite aware of this capital inflow—his regret being that mere influx of gold and silver into a country need not initiate prosperity. As a matter of fact in his deposition in the Report of the Revised Settlement of the Shahpur and Karnal Districts (1866, 1872), he attributed the inflation of food prices observed in the Punjab during 1861-1867 to "the large influx of silver from Europe now going on". Naoroji's work is thus very much a precursor of the strand of "anti-free trade" doctrine usually associated with Singer and Prebisch, Emmanuel, Wallerstein and more recently Krugman (and of course Marx and Lenin).

Romesh Chander Dutt is today remembered primarily as an economic historian but he was also deeply interested in contemporary issues. In his *Open Letters* to Lord Curzon (1901, 1902), he drew attention to the causes of rural poverty, focusing on the burden of land revenues, a theme touched upon by Raja Ram Mohan Roy 70 years earlier. From a contemporary point of view, however, his emphasis that investment be diverted from the expansion of the railway network to irrigation, may be seen as an articulation of the agriculture-industry debate which was to underpin the Soviet planning strategy two decades later (in the guise of the famous Neo-Narodniks *versus* Trotskyites debates involving Bukharin, Groman, Preobrazhensky and others) and in a less sharp perspective, the debates between the Mahalonobis proponents on the one hand and B.R. Shenoy, Vakil and Brahmananda on the other.

Of the triumvirate, however, Mahadev Govind Ranade was perhaps the most academically oriented, seeing economic issues not purely from the policy angle (as was the case with Naoroji who was first and foremost a "politician" in the noblest sense of the term), though a partisan and nationalist slant was never absent from his writings. Ranade was quite familiar with the writings of English classical economists such as Ricardo, Senior and Mill but also with the work of the German Historical School which had a deep impact on him. Thus, whereas his predecessors like Naoroji and K.T. Telang had attacked the classical doctrine of free trade, Ranade thrust deeper, at the very foundations of English classical economics itself. Among the classical postulates that he took exception to, were those of individual rationality, atomistic competition, free mobility of labour and capital, the Iron Law of Wages and most importantly the doctrine of *laissez-faire*. I reproduce below a rather lengthy quotation from a lecture delivered at Deccan College, Poona in 1892.

> These assumptions lie at the root of all dogmatical treatment of the subject. As these assumptions do not absolutely hold good of even the most advanced Societies, it is obvious that in Societies like ours they are chiefly conspicuous by their absence. With us an average individual man is, to a large extent, the very antipodes of the Economical Man. The Family and the Caste are more powerful than the individual in determining his position in life. Custom and State Regulation are far more powerful than Competition and Status more decisive in its influence than Contract. Neither Capital nor Labour is mobile... Wages and Profits are fixed, and not responsive to change of circumstances... In a Society so constituted, the tendencies assumed as axiomatic (by the classical theory) are not only inoperative, but are actually deflected from their proper directions... (see Chandra (1990)).

Ranade's views have a surprisingly modern flavour. Two affinities, in particular, are especially noteworthy. Firstly, the concept of X-efficiency introduced by Leibenstein (1983) has a ring similar to Ranade's views. X-efficiency, as is well-known, refers to a situation wherein a society falls short of its production potential owing to factors such as the following: (i) past customs and conventions dominating economic relations, (ii) inertia preventing agents from responding to economic incentives, (iii) non-enforceability of contracts, and (iv) lack of accountability.

Ranade in his writings underlined the importance of industrialisation for the removal of national poverty. He however felt that private initiative would not suffice to provide the needed stimulus and stressed the promotional role of the state in the mobilisation of savings and finance, in the development of banking and in promoting higher education. The importance attached to the role of the state by Ranade is echoed with a strong emphasis by modern institutionalists such as North (1981). The main emphasis of the neo-institutionalists is on institutional innovations and changes in property rights leading in turn to huge outward shifts in productivity. In this process, a crucial role is assigned to the state for removal of legal and other hurdles to institutional development. Government, as an agent of the state, can play a promotional role in internalising external economies and in modifying laws and procedures to enable the exploitation of existing commercial opportunities.

One of the important influences on Ranade's thinking was the German Historical School, which was shaped by the writings of Roscher (1843) and his disciples Hildebrand (1848) and Knies (1853). Strongly inflenced by Hegel (1807, 1813), this school was sceptical of the concept of theoretical systems in economics laying claims to universal applicability. They, thus inevitably were drawn into conflict with the Anglo-Saxon economies of Ricardo and Mill. Mill was a logician par excellence and even though he never claimed universality for economic laws either in his *System of Logic* (1843) or in his *Principles of Political Economy* (7th ed. 1871), his emphasis on the deductive method (or the *à priori* method) as the only valid method for economic inference could be easily construed as a plea for universality. Koopmans (1947) for example in his attack on Burns and Mitchell (1946) invokes Mills' logic to advocate the rather strange position that the structure of an econometric model should be based on *à priori* considerations with data supplying specific parametric values—an increasingly popular position with modern methodologists such as Leamer (1978) and Hendry (1980). Certainly, Mills' advocacy of the free trade principle had strong universal overtones. The German Historical School stressed the *à posteriori* principle and argued that economic laws were contingent upon their historical, social and institutional content. Inevitably, interdisciplinary perspectives have to be invoked in the derivation of economic laws. Thus, the study of the historical evolution in the interrelationship between the social and economic organisation of a nation should be the primary task of any economist. Ranade probably became acquainted with the German Historical School, through the writings of Cliff Leslie (1879), possibly the only English economist sympathetic to this School. The influence of the German School is very visible, when for example Ranade writes in 1892 that,

> The same Teachers and Statesmen, who warn us against certain tendencies in our Political aspirations, forget this salutary caution when the question at issue is one of Indian Economics. They seem to hold that the Truths of Economic Science, as they have been expounded in our most popular English textbooks, are absolutely and demonstrably true, and must be accepted as guides of conduct for all time and place whatever might be the stage of national advance. Ethnical, social, juristic, ethical or economic differences in the environments are not regarded as having any influence in modifying the practical application of these Truths. If Free Trade is good for England, it must be equally beneficial to all countries and prohibitive or protective duties are absolute evils, and no thought need to be given to the relative differences in civilisation, or the possession of natural advantages, or disadvantages.... (Chandra *op. cit.*: 323).

I looked for some reference to Ranade in Bhagwati's recent book *Free Trade Today* (2002) but was (predictably) disappointed. Ranade's relativist position led him to advocate the development of Indian economics as a distinct discipline in its own right.

3.2 Making of a Distinct Discipline of Indian Economics

It is my contention that the case for a distinct discipline of Indian economics remains as forceful today as it was when Ranade first made it in 1892. However, I restate his case in modern terminology so as to facilitate its communication to this learned audience. Economic laws in a society may be viewed as specifying interactions among agents optimising certain objectives subject to constraints. The culture, ethics and value systems of these agents will determine these objectives; the institutional framework will circumscribe the interactions among agents, while the stage of development will outline the constraints. Since values as well as institutions will vary across societies, economic laws in, say, India could be quite different from those in the US. To the extent that countries at similar stages of development could possibly share the same values and similarity of institutions, one could meaningfully talk of a separate economics for developing countries, though even this incorporates a certain level of generalisation. Thus, for a body of economic thought to qualify as Indian economics requires that it addresses the three issues of relevance, cultural conformity and institutional affinity. In other words, any theory which addresses issues of interest and relevance to India and pays due attention to the cultural and institutional contexts can rightfully qualify as a contribution to Indian economics. It is important to note that all the three criteria must, to some extent, be satisfied. Marxist reasoning often poses issues of strong relevance for less developed countries (LDCs) but is based on a value system totally alien to those prevailing in typical LDCs. Modern neo-classical economics reflects (implicitly) values like liberty and justice which are generally acceptable, but fails to pose questions of real relevance to LDCs. The anthropological strand in economics is once again sensitive to the cultural context and institutional features, but is silent on the major macroeconomic issues of LDCs.

In retrospect what is really remarkable is that a substantial and rich tradition of Indian economics flourished in the first seven decades of the twentieth century, gradually languishing from the 1970s till it has become virtually extinct in the last decade. It is not the purpose in this presentation, to take a detailed review of these developments—such a task is better left for a book-length publication. Nevertheless, it is necessary to outline the main contours of these developments, if the current crisis in Indian economic thinking is to be properly appreciated. The overview can hardly lay claim to completeness, and important omissions are inevitable.

Following Bhabatosh Datta (1962), it is now conventional for writers on the theme to distinguish three phases in the evolution of Indian economics:

(i) The Pioneering Phase (pre-1905).

(ii) The Nationalist Phase (1905-1939).

(iii) The Modern Phase (1939-1965).

To this, we may add a fourth phase which (for want of a better name and not from any considerations of intellectual fashion) may be termed as a post-modernist phase, spanning the last three decades.

As we saw earlier, Indian economics as a distinct discipline may be said to originate with Mahadev Govind Ranade. But important contributions were also made by his predecessors and contemporaries. Among his immediate predecessors, K.T. Telang deserves special mention for a paper entitled "Free Trade and Protection from an Indian Point of View" (1877), which presented a systematic case for protection of Indian industries and also advocated a concept of dependency, which is usually associated with the Latin American School of the 1950s. Another notable contributor in this area is a rather obscure writer called G.V. Joshi, who wrote on free trade issues around the 1880s, and whose work was brought to light through the sustained efforts of my teacher, the late Prof. Brahmananda. In this task, he received invaluable support from Dr. J.V. Naik, an eminent historian. Dr. J.V. Naik also contributed importantly to our understanding of this early period by discovering two important papers of Bal Gangadhar Tilak (see Naik, 1999).

As the name suggests, the dominant political mood underpinning the second phase was nationalism. The economic manifestation of this was the *Swadeshi* movement, which became a rallying point for the mass-based freedom movement after Gandhi assumed leadership of the same in 1921. *Swadeshi* was essentially an extension and accentuation of the earlier demand for protection via tariffs which was a common theme to writers like Ranade, Telang, Naoroji and others. Thus, protectionism continued to be a predominant theme among writers of economic issues during this period. But now the theme of protectionism was more closely aligned with the patriotic demand for indigenous industrialisation. Madan Mohan Malaviya made a strong plea for the development of manufacturing in his dissenting note to the Industrial Commission (1918). The twin calls for protectionism and industrialisation under the Swadeshi banner attracted domestic business interests. Vithaldas Thackersey, Dadiba Dalal and Purushottamdas Thakurdas were vocal advocates of *Swadeshi* (it is a serious error to attribute this enthusiasm of the trio for *Swadeshi* as purely motivated by self-interest—all of them were philanthrophists and nationalists of a high order).

But apart from *Swadeshi*, the first four decades of the twentieth century were witness to several other major economic issues. Three in particular need to be singled out—the steep inflation experienced over the decade 1905-1916, the problems of the external rupee parity and the issue of imperial preferences. In line with the tradition initiated by Ranade, Indian thinkers responded to these policy debates, keeping the Indian perspective uppermost in their minds.

The inflation issue saw a sharp drawing of lines with the official position represented by the Report of the L.K. Datta Committee and the Indian nationalist position being articulated by Gopal Krishna Gokhale. The nationalist position (systematised by Brij Narain in his book of 1926, reprinted in 1984) was Bullionist, attributing the inflation to currency over-issue and mismanagement, thus laying the blame squarely at the door of official policy. The Datta Committee tried to exonerate the official monetary and exchange management policies by citing natural factors such as the famines of 1899-1900 and 1907-08, the secular rise in population, and the decline in agricultural productivity as the critical factors (see Brij Narain (*op. cit.*) who even attempted to vindicate the nationalist position by developing an econometric model, which must be regarded as remarkably sophisticated by the standards then prevalent).

Possibly the richest debate on an Indian economic issue was the one generated over the external parity of the rupee. My colleague at Mumbai University, Dr. Avadhoot Nadkarni in a forthcoming paper has given an excellent and authoritative account of this debate. I recall here only the essential points of the debate, advising the interested reader to consult his paper for additional details. The drama had been building up a long time, as a matter of fact, ever since 1913, when a gold exchange standard was formally introduced with the rupee parity fixed at Re.1 = 2 sh. on the suggestion of J.M. Keynes. Overtaken by events, this parity proved unsustainable. The Hilton-Young Commission appointed to look into the problem recommended a new parity of Re.1 = 18 sh. (along with the recommendation to set up a Reserve Bank). This parity came up for sharp criticism from economists and domestic business interests such as G.D. Birla and Purshottam Thakurdas, who recommended a reversion to the pre-War parity of Re.1 = 16 sh. Gandhiji put his moral weight behind this group, which lent a nationalist flavour to what had been hitherto a purely technical controversy. The higher value of the rupee was favoured in the official line as it was felt that this would reduce the rupee equivalent of sterling expenditure within India (see B. Datta *op. cit.*), while the nationalist position (behind all the rhetoric) was essentially protectionist, especially with reference to the Indian cotton textile industry. It is against this background that Babasaheb Ambedkar's endorsement of the Hilton-Young higher parity (though not of the other recommendations of the Commission) has to be viewed. Displaying considerable moral courage, he opposed the nationalist position on grounds that it would be inequitous and would favour domestic business classes and hit the working classes and agricultural labourers, owing to the inflationary potential of the weaker rupee advocated by the nationalists (see Ambedkar, 1926). But Ambedkar must also be credited for a remarkably innovative insight *viz.*, the distributional consequences of devaluation. This issue remains as important today as it was in the 1920s and one may add, as unsettled now as then, largely owing to unavailability of data on income distribution by major classes in India, in spite of the heroic efforts of the noted scholar (and teacher to many of us at Mumbai University) Dr. (Ms.) Kanta Ranadive (1978).

The issue of imperial preferences was mainly political, with business interests opposing the special preferences (duty drawbacks etc.) given to goods imported from Great Britain into India, especially steel and cotton textiles. This opposition continued unabated till the Ottawa Agreement (1936) drew a curtain on the issue with the introduction of reciprocal preferences within the commonwealth.

An important but controversial contribution to Indian economics during this period was Gandhian economics. It holds a unique place in the history of economic thought, since it attacked the Western paradigm of development, not only on grounds of it being inappropriate to the institutional set-up in India (as had been done by Naoroji, Ranade and others) but also by rejecting the basic tenet that industrialisation was a pre-condition for removal of mass poverty. In this viewpoint, he was in fundamental contradiction not only with professional economic opinion in the West, but also with most contemporary economists in India. It must be emphasised, that the Gandhian thesis was radically different from the viewpoint of the pioneers from Raja Ram Mohan Roy onwards, all of whom were vocal advocates of industrialisation. As a matter of fact, these nationalists very often criticised the British government for being lackadaisical on this score.

By the late 1930s, a subtle change was evident in the methodology employed by Indian economists. The methodology was becoming increasingly more sophisticated, as more and more economists were being exposed to formal economic theories, via the various schools of postgraduate economics established throughout the country, since 1920s. But the economists of the entire period 1939-1965 (which we have adopted as the modern period) to their credit, focused exclusively on problems of interest to Indian policy, resisting the temptation to retreat into academic ivory towers. There was a serious attempt to appraise how appropriate or otherwise, were the predominant theories developed in the West, for analysing India's economic problems.

Dissatisfaction with Western models was specifically grounded in their inappropriate institutional specification (from the Indian perspective) and to some extent, on their focusing on questions having little bearing on issues of Indian interest. Except for J.K. Mehta (and of course, hardcore Gandhian economists such as J.C. Kumarappa), Indian economists in this phase kept clear of any involvement with ethical issues. In this sense, the modern Indian economists were much closer in spirit to Ranade and Naoroji than to Gandhi.

The initial years of what we have called as the "modern phase" of Indian economics were the heydays of Keynesian economics. It would have been an easy trap for Indian economists of that period to be deluded into confounding Keynes' cyclical unemployment with the structural unemployment characteristic of a pre-industrial society such as India's, and further, to suggest remedies for the latter along fiscalist lines. Parallely, demand management for controlling the inflation of the war years, would have been the obvious remedy of a naïve Keynesian. While it is true that several Indian economists of that period did fall tamely into such a trap, at least three notable exceptions saw clearly through the pitfalls of a purely Keynesian approach to India's macro-economic imbalances. Firstly, C.N. Vakil (1942), blamed the galloping inflation on the monetary pressures unleashed by the accumulated sterling balances. Secondly, V.K.R.V. Rao (1952) forcefully questioned the applicability of several Keynesian concepts, especially the income multiplier, in the Indian context and finally, A.K. Dasgupta gave a complete theoretical refutation of the applicability of the Keynesian theory to countries like India, suggesting in its place a notion of "shifting full employment" equilibria, as "With each expansion of capital equipment, the marginal productivity of labour rises and, the disutility curve of labour remaining constant, we have a higher level of full employment" (A.K. Dasgupta—originally published in 1954 and reprinted in the July 12, 2003 issue of *Economic & Political Weekly*).

The late 1940s and early 1950s were also witness to the evolution of the new discipline of development economics aimed at slaying "the dragon of backwardness" (to use Hirschman's (1981) colourful phrase) in the newly liberated nations of Asia and Africa, labouring under the dual handicaps of "rural underemployment" and "late industrialisation". The intellectual genesis of development economics lay in a profound dissatisfaction with the neo-classical models of economic growth coupled with the recognition that the "late industrialisation" handicap could only be overcome by an economically proactive state. From a policy angle, the crucial debates in developing societies then naturally revolved around the form that state intervention should take, as also the extent and degree of state control over the main levers of the economy. In India, two distinct schools of thought were evident—the heavy industries school with an extensive role envisaged for planning of the centralist type and the so-called "wage goods" school emphasising agriculture and light industries with a less centralised and more flexible role for state planning. The controversy came to a head around the time of the formulation of the Second Five Year Plan in the mid 1950s. The "heavy industry" school seemed to be strongly influenced by the teleological school of planning, represented by the Preobrazhensky faction in the Soviet planning debates of the 1920s and the Mahalonobis models of 1955, 1956 owed much to the mathematical encapsulations of the Preobrazhensky thesis embodied in the works of Soviet mathematical economists such as Khachaturov, Strumilin and Feldman. The "wage goods" thesis propounded by Brahmananda and Vakil (1956), owing allegiance to the genetic school of planning (Bukharin faction), and also drawing on some aspects of the Lewis-Nurkse thesis, was more elaborate but somewhat diffuse and lacked the mathematical cutting edge of its rival. Its Gandhian roots are stressed in a paper by Ajit Karnik (1997). It advocated concentration on agriculture and light consumer goods, with a strong exports orientation. The reasons as to why the wage goods school lost out to the heavy industry school are manifold. Vasudevan (2002) advances some basic theoretical flaws in the wage goods thesis itself, as the primary reason for its rejection, whereas in my obituary of Prof. Brahmananda (*Economic & Political Weekly*, 2003), I attributed the phenomenon to the contemporary Indian political ambitions of achieving a strong military-industry status for the nation. The controversy was revisited a few years later from a more sophisticated theoretical perspective by two scholars who were later to emerge as world class economic thinkers *viz.*, Amartya Sen (1962) and Sukhamoy Chakravarty (1969).

There is at least one more towering figure from that period, Prof. D.R. Gadgil who was Deputy Chairman of the Planning Commission over a brief period 1967-1969. Gadgil lamented the "great variety of prohibitions, directions and regulations" with which the planning process was riddled in the 1960s. He felt that there was "over-regulation" and felt the need to introduce a measure of competitiveness in Indian industry and some relaxation of the import-substitution philosophy, though he was not in favour of a full liberalisation (see Gadgil, 1972 and Tendulkar, 2000).

3.3 Indian Economics in Disarray

The above discussion is admittedly sketchy and does not do full justice to the richness permeating many of the debates. But, in spite of its brevity, I hope the discussion has served to indicate that by and large, a strong tradition of Indian economics flourished throughout the 70-year period, 1890-1960. Unfortunately, the tradition started to languish in the 1970s and is virtually extinct today. This is directly attributable to the ascendancy of what is called neo-classical economics; Hirschman (1981) termed it as "monoeconomics" and Sen (1983), only half-jokingly, likened it to a disease that "one could catch if not careful".

Following Lakatos (1970), a doctrine could be viewed as comprising:

(i) an immutable hard core and

(ii) a variable protective belt.

Eggertsson (1990) identifies the hard core of neo-classical economics as a set of three axioms *viz.*:

1. Stable preferences of economic agents
2. Rational choice, and
3. Equilibrium-based interactions among economic agents.

The protective belt of assumptions comprises three aspects:

1. Situational (including institutional) constraints
2. Assumptions about information available to agents
3. Type of interactions permissible among agents.

Modifications to the protective belt occur continuously but they do not constitute a paradigm shift. The latter is said to occur only when the hard core is touched. Thus, the important contributions to information theory, transaction costs and externalities by Arrow, Stigler, Stiglitz, Townsend, Coase, etc., do not represent a refutation of neo-classical economics, only its reaffirmation under more general boundary conditions.

Thus, essentially any challenge to neo-classical economics has to be based on a demonstrably convincing rejection of any of the three postulates listed above as comprising the hard core. The evident unrealism of these assumptions has been commented upon by numerous writers including such respected names as Frank Knight, Schumpeter and Keynes. The *General Theory* focused criticism on the rationality postulate, especially as it applied to expectations. Keynes in his typical style dubbed it as "a pretty polite technique" that tries "to deal with the present by distracting from the fact that we know very little about the future". Keynes also pointed to another fundamental methodological flaw, *viz.*, the neo-classical habit of deriving results for the economy as a whole by simply aggregating assumed relations at the micro level. This "fallacy of composition" (though Keynes himself does not use the term) is at the source of Keynes' famous statement that "savings is a private virtue but a public vice". A more recent perspective on this aspect may be had from Caballero (1992). The rational expectations revolution which has been hailed by the economics profession has virtually no foundations in psychology. Several studies of actual behaviour conducted by Tversky and Kahneman (1974) and several others have shown that real life expectations are not only irrational but very little learning or "convergence to rationality" is evident. At the most fundamental level, rational behaviour has been challenged by Herbert Simon (1957), who maintains that the model of the rational man optimising an objective function, subject to constraints hardly reflects the complex actuality of business decision-making, where survival, conventions, rules of thumb and other common business practices lead to what he calls as "bounded rationality" or "satisficing behaviour".

The ripostes of neo-classical economics to these criticisms are puzzling to say the least.

Firstly, as Hutchison (1984) has observed, neo-classicals sometimes adopt the defence that their assumptions are only designed as approximations to the real world and that attempts are continuously being made to relax the assumptions to fit real-world situations better. But if this is the defence, the neo-classicals have no right to make the kind of exaggerated claims for the real world applicability of some of the more extreme versions of their doctrines such as real business cycle theories and public choice theories.

A second line of defence pertains to what Hicks (1979) disapprovingly observes as a tendency to pursue economics "for no better reason than its intellectual attraction; it is a good game".

This "good game" approach lies behind the unforgivably ambivalent attitude of neo-classical economists to empirical verification. Alone among the empirical sciences, neo-classical economics prods along irrespective of how compelling the econometric refutation of its assumptions or predictions are. That economics is an "imperfect" science is hardly an excuse for this ostrich-like attitude. Other imperfect sciences, especially medicine, are simultaneously more modest in their claims and much more respectful and cautious towards the empirical verification of their theories.

A strand of neo-classical economists goes even further and rejects empirical verification altogether (Stewart, 1979; Machlup, 1978 and Caldwell, 1982). In this, they possibly drew inspiration from the philosopher Paul Feyerabend whose *Against Method* (1975) downgraded the importance of empirical arguments and in particular, Popper's falsification criterion by suggesting that aesthetic criteria and social factors play a more decisive role in the history of science than rationalist or empiricist methodology. But this kind of methodological anarchism (or "anything goes" attitude) has meant that neo-classical economics has not really countered its criticisms effectively but has rather flourished by ignoring its critics, ridiculing them or arraigning them as Marxists.

The real reasons why neo-classical economics reigns supreme and unchallenged in the world today have nothing to do with the soundness of its methodological position. Instead, they are to be located in three exogenous factors.

Firstly, it provides a seemingly infallible justification for the operation of free markets. (In the next section, I try to show that this is fallacious reasoning.)

Secondly, it cleverly confuses the issues of economic freedom and political liberty. A few days ago, *The Times of India* reproduced a quotation from Milton Fricdman to the effect that "Underlying most arguments against the free market is a lack of belief in freedom itself." Thus, everyone, from Keynes who justified public investment, to the advocates of the welfare state, to those who support public distribution schemes are all anti-libertarians!

Thirdly, it is one economic doctrine which lends itself easily to the use of a fair degree of sophisticated mathematics. This use of symbols often deludes neo-classicals into believing that they have rendered the subject of economics "scientific". By its very nature, economics is a soft discipline and as A.K. Sen once put it, it is better (in economics) "to be vaguely right, than precisely wrong."

Lastly, the collapse of the Soviet type economies, and the emergence of US hegemony has been heralded as a triumph of the market philosophy and neo-classical economics, though the US economy has always been, and continues to be, a heavily regulated economy.

It is noteworthy that neo-classical economics responds to criticism not by sacrificing its most valued tenets, but by trying to encompass additional phenomena. Thus, for example, neo-classical economics has long been criticised for neglecting institutional aspects. Recent years have witnessed the emergence of neo-institutional economics. The major thrust of this new discipline is to apply neo-classical principles such as rationality and competition to explain the evolution of social and political institutions. Thus, we have the concept of equilibrium institutions representing some kind of a Nash outcome of strategic interactions among individual agents (see in particular Coase, 1937; Alchian and Demsetz, 1972 and De Alessi, 1980). Historical experience is quite at variance with this view. To quote a familiar Indian example, the Hilton-Young Commission (1926) proposal to establish a Reserve Bank fell through on the political consideration that the Imperial government wanted the bank to be a shareholders' bank (so as to keep it out of the control of the legislature) while the Indian legislators and economists wanted it to be a state-owned bank (Datta, 1962).

A distinct but related strand of neo-classical thinking is even more ambitious. Thus, G. Becker and his colleagues at the Chicago school set out to explain the sociological phenomena on neo-classical principles. There appeared in the 1970s and 1980s, a string of articles in the *Journal of Political Economy* with such bizarre themes as Economics of Marriage, Economics of Divorce and even (believe me) Economics of Extramarital Affairs! The day is surely not far off when an enterprising neo-classical theologian is going to suggest an economic theory of the Almighty!

The sterile nature of much modern economic theorising and the perverted system of professional recognition is highlighted in this heavily ironic advice of a distinguished British economist to an aspiring economic theorist.

"The suggested Ph.D. thesis title 'n solutions to n-1 problems' is a very promising theme for an academic career devoted to High Theory. Nowadays, this is the super-highway to eminence and professional acclaim. And your status will rise in geometrical proportion to the irrelevance and obscurity of what you say and write. Abraham Lincoln was wrong here: you can fool all the people all the time without much effort either"—A.R. Prest (1983) "Letters to a Young Economist", *Journal of Economic Affairs.*

The intellectual pre-eminence that neo-classical economics has acquired in the last few years has had a corresponding impact on the way development issues have been viewed. The older politico-economy perspective has disappeared, as also the recognition that problems of LDCs are of a fundamentally different genre from the problems of growth in Western societies. The insistence that neo-classical economics is universal has meant that the subject of Indian economics now survives only as an exotic species. As a matter of fact, I could detect only three major macro studies in recent years which could qualify as contributions to Indian economics in the sense that we defined it earlier *viz.,* Dandekar and Rath, 1971; Rakshit; 1982 and Shetty, 1978.

The neo-classical paradigm of development economics links the existence of free markets to high growth rates in LDCs. But this causation cannot be supported unless each link in the following chain of arguments is validated.

1. Any move towards free markets is welfare improving.
2. A policy of free markets leads to an optimal static allocation of resources.
3. That this optimum is scientific in the sense of being value-free.
4. A series of static optima can be strung together to yield a dynamic optimum for the economy.
5. The resultant optimal path does not run up against resource constraints.

I will not go into a detailed refutation of each of these propositions. The refutation of the first principle forms the substance of the so-called "second-best theory" of Lipsey and Lancaster (1956) which to date holds its own. The invalidity of the second and third points follows from modern welfare economics (e.g. Little, 2002). As a matter of fact, this footnote from Little (*op.cit.*), (by no means a Marxist economist) makes interesting reading.

> The laissez-faire model, given enough assumptions, could bring about the "optimum" distribution of resources, as well as the socialist "blueprint". The socialist blueprint model is "superior" at the logical level in that it requires fewer postulates. It does not require the postulate of either a rising cost curve, or a perfectly elastic demand curve.

So far as point 4 is concerned, this is a rather technical point but its invalidity is well-known to optimal growth theorists. Finally, the invalidity of point 5 is intuitively obvious and has been emphasised in the "Limits to Growth" literature (which was banished from academic discourse mainly because it came into conflict with the neo-classical orthodoxy). Thus, while the refutation of any of the single links in the above schemata suffices to invalidate the presumed causal nexus between markets and growth, we have here performed an "overkill" by showing each of these links to be invalid.

My purpose has been simply to underscore a vital but neglected point *viz.*, that the presumed theoretical case for economic reforms simply does not exist. Whether freer markets will promote growth or otherwise is essentially an empirical issue or to pursue Hutchison's (1984) medical analogy "Keynes insisted on treating every patient as a separate problem rather than as one of a series of standard cases." The Chinese, with their Confucianism, have grasped this elementary truth, which somehow continues to elude our academics and policy makers alike.

If the fallacies of neo-classical economics had been confined to the textbooks and journals, much of the controversy surrounding it would have amounted to little more than a storm in an academic tea-cup. In the last two decades however, neo-classical economics has spilled over its academic boundaries and entered the arena of economic policy in a big way. Thus, the liberalisation wave of the 1980s has had neo-classical economics as its intellectual mainspring, and neo-classical reasoning has underlain many of the recommendations of the IMF and World Bank on structural adjustments.

Without going so far as to question the entire liberalisation philosophy, nor in any sense acting as an apologist for the "ancien regime", one could legitimately question the pace, direction and content of the liberalisation process. It is interesting to note that the questionable aspects of liberalisation are precisely those where the neo-classical influence is most in evidence. While several instances of this kind could be adduced, our case would derive additional strength if we challenge neo-classical economics on its favourite turf. The illustration below has been chosen with this consideration in mind. (I crave indulgence of my non-economist friends for retreating into technical jargon for a little while.)

In the aftermath of liberalisation, there has been an undue emphasis on capital market reforms and a special concern with stockmarkets, bordering on fetishism. A canard has been floated that economic growth (and even poverty removal) is conditioned upon the health of the sensex and nifty. The economic debate has shifted from issues of real and long-term concern to the purely transitory gyrations of the stock indices.

As I have just said, the stock market is the ideal turf of the neo-classicist. It meets most of the neo-classical assumptions for the "invisible hand" theorem: large numbers of buyers and sellers, free entry and exit, no externalities etc. Its role as an optimal allocator of capital is thus unquestionable to a neo-classical. The neo-classical view of stock market proceeds on two premises.

1. The value of a common share to an individual shareholder is simply the present discounted value of the future dividend stream from the share.
2. Managers maximise the present value of the firm by investing to the point where the marginal return on investment equals the firm's cost of capital.

From these two assumptions flows the famous Modigliani-Miller equation

$$i = (X/MV) + g$$

where i is the discounting factor, g the potential growth rate of a company, X its current profits and MV the firm's market value.

From this, it follows that firms with high growth potential undertake more investment relative to current earnings than do low growth potential firms. This movement of capital across companies should tend to equilibrate rates of return across firms if the invisible hand proposition is indeed correct.

The important findings of Shiller (1981) for US markets cast a great deal of doubt on the presumed neo-classical view of shareholder behaviour. His findings demonstrated that the variance in returns on the portfolio of all common shares far exceeded that which can be rationally justified by subsequent swings in dividend payments. Neo-classical economics has its own distinctive strategy of dealing with inconvenient empirical findings—*viz.*, to keep on adding auxiliary (untested) assumptions till these empirical findings are reconciled to the theory without jeopardising its fundamental normative implications. And thus, to explain away Shiller's findings as an aberration we have this entire body of the "rational expectations bubbles" literature. As a matter of fact, there is a far more obvious explanation of Shiller's observations, right there under our noses so to speak. It is that shareholders are playing on predicting market swings rather than a firm's future dividend profile. But because this "rent-seeking" behaviour is clearly out of line with the neo-classical view of the stock market as a device for allocating capital optimally, this explanation is never acknowledged.

Additional evidence of shareholder "irrationality" (in the neo-classical sense) proceeds from the persistent finding in the empirical literature of shareholders' preference for dividends over retained earnings. The neo-classical theory strongly posits that shareholders be indifferent between an extra unit of dividends and an extra unit of retained earnings, since a unit of retained earnings reinvested at a return equal to the cost of capital produces a unit of capital gains. As a matter of fact, given that dividend taxes are usually higher than capital gains taxes, one may even expect a preference for retentions over dividends. Thus, the empirical findings constitute a conclusive rejection of the neo-classical view of the stock market as an efficient allocator of capital.

The above detailed example should suffice to illustrate how neo-classical prescriptions, though offered with an appearance of moral authority, have often little theoretical or empirical basis. Similar illustrations pertain to other fields of economic policy such as foreign capital inflows, privatisation etc., and some of these have been touched upon by me in other studies.

3.4 Concluding Remark

It is a tragedy of our times that the great tradition of Indian economics, initiated by Mahadeo Govind Ranade in the nineteenth century and sustained throughout the major part of the twentieth century by a galaxy of Indian scholars, has now withered under the domineering onslaught of neo-classical economics.

Nothing illustrates the death of Indian economics more tellingly than an article published some time ago in a leading financial daily. To quote from the article

> "Dear Student...You would be better off studying "American Economics", "British Economics", "German Economics" or "Japanese Economics" than this balderdash (Indian economics).... Study other subjects... but don't study Indian Economics."

The crowning ivory of this piece of blasphemy is that it was published on 16 January 2001—Ranade's death centenary! Ranade, the father of Indian economics, (of whom Babasaheb Ambedkar had said "in worshipping him we have no feeling of kneeling before anything that is false"), had been most ironically forgotten in the land of his birth.

The great Russian playwright Anton Chekhov was once asked by the equally famous Russian director Stanislavski why his plays, which all had tragic themes, were called as comedies on the billboards. He gave a memorable reply, "When a person is aware of his impending tragic fate and resists it with a strong will, it is a tragedy, but when he is blissfully unaware of the impending fate and cheerfully acquiesces in it, it is a comedy." In that sense perhaps, the demise of Indian economics is not so much a conventional tragedy, as a Chekhovian comedy.

References

Alchian, A. and H. Demsetz (1972). "Production, information costs and economic organization", *American Economic Review* 62: 777-795.

Ambedkar, B.R. (1926). *Minutes of Evidence before the Royal Commission on Indian Currency and Finance.*

———. (1943). "Ranade, Gandhi and Jinnah", in *Dr. Babasaheb Ambedkar: Writings and Speeches* Vol. I, Govt. of Maharashtra, 1979.

Bhagwati, J. (2002). *Free Trade Today*. New Delhi: Oxford University Press.

Brahmananda, P.R. and C.N. Vakil (1956). *Planning for an Expanding Economy.* Bombay.

Burns, A.F. and W.C. Mitchell (1946). *Measuring Business Cycles.* New Jersey.

Caballero, R.J. (1992). "A fallacy of composition", *American Economic Review* 82(5): 1279-1292.

Caldwell, B. (1982). *Beyond Positivism: Economic Methodology in the Twentieth Century.* London: Allen & Unwin.

Chakravarty, S. (1969). *Capital and Development Planning*. Camb. Mass: MIT Press.

Chandra, Bipan (1990). *Ranade's Economic Writings*. New Delhi: Gian Publication.

Coase, R.H. (1937). "The nature of the firm", *Economica* 4: 386-405.

Dandekar, V.M. and N. Rath (1971). *Poverty in India*. Indian School of Political Economy.

Das, A. (1979). *Foundations of Gandhian Economics*. Bombay: Allied.

Dasgupta, A.K. (1954). "Keynesian economics and underdeveloped countries", *The Economic Weekly*, Annual Number.

Datta, K.L. (1914). *Report of the Enquiry into the Rise of Prices in India*. Calcutta.

Datta, B. (1962). *The Evolution of Economic Thinking in India*. Calcutta: Federation Hall Society.

De Alessi, L. (1980). "The economics of property rights: A review of the evidence", *Research in Law and Economics* 2: 1-47.

Eggertsson, T. (1990). *Economic Behaviour and Institutions.* Cambridge University Press.

Feyerabend, P. (1975). *Against Method*. London: Verso.

Gadgil, D.R. (1972). *Planning and Economic Policy in India*. Poona: Gokhale Institute of Politics & Economics.

Hegel, Georg (1807). *The Phenomenology of Mind.*

———. (1813). *The Objective Logic.*

Hendry, D.F. (1980). "Econometrics: Alchemy or science?", *Economica* 47: 387-406.

Hicks, J.R. (1979). *Causality in Economics*. Oxford: Basil Blackwell.

Hildebrand, B. (1848). *Economics of the Present and the Future.*

Hilton-Young Commission (1926). *Report of the Royal Commission on Indian Currency and Finance*. Vol. I-VI. London: His Majesty's Stationery Office.

Hirschman, A.O. (1981). *Essays in Trespassing Economics to Political and Beyond*. Cambridge University Press.

Hutchison, T. (1984). "Our methodological crisis", in P. Wiles and G. Routh (ed.), *Economics in Disarray*. Oxford: Basil Blackwell.

Karnik, A.V. (1997). "Development strategy initiated during the IInd Five Year Plan: A critical review", Univ. of Mumbai, Dept. of Economics, *Working Paper* No. 97/15.

Knies, K. (1853). *Political Economy from the Standpoint of the Historical Method.*

Koopmans, T.C. (1947). "Measurement without theory", *Review of Economics and Statistics.*

Kumarappa, J.C. (1958). *Economy of Permanence: A Quest for a Social Order based on Non-Violence*. Kashi: Akhil Bharat Sarva Seva Sangh Publication.

Lakatos, I. (1970). "Falsification and the methodology of scientific research programs", in Lakatos & Musgrave (ed.) *Criticism and the Growth of Knowledge*. Cambridge University Press.

Leamer, E. (1978). *Specification Searches : Ad Hoc Inferences with Nonexperimental Data*. New York: John Wiley & Sons.

Leibenstein, H. (1976). *Beyond Economic Man*. Harvard University Press.

Leslie, C. (1879). *Essays in Political and Moral Philosophy.*

Lipsey, R.G. and K. Lancaster (1956). "The general theory of second best", *Review of Economic Studies* 24.

Little, I.H.D. (2002). *A Critique of Welfare Economics*. Delhi: Oxford University Press.

Machlup, F. (1978). *Methodology of Economics and other Social Sciences*. New York: Academic Press.

Mahalonobis, P.C. (1953). "Some observations on the process of growth of national income", *Sankhya* 15: 307-312.

———. (1955). "The approach of operational research to planning in India", *Sankhya* 17: 3-62

Mehta, J.K. (1985). *Gandhian Thought*. South Asia Books.

Mill, J.S. (1843). *System of Logic.*

———. (1909). *Principles of Political Economy*. Longmans, Cream & Co.

Nadkarni, A. (forthcoming). "Political economy and economic rationale of nationalists thinking on Indian currency and exchange from Naoroji and Ranade to Ambedkar and Gandhi" (*mimeo*).

Naik, J.V. (1999). "Tilak on Karl Marx and class conflict (1881)", *Economic and Political Weekly* 18: 1023-25. 1-7 May.

Narain, Brij (1984). *Indian Economic Life Past and Present*. Delhi: Neeraj Publishers House. (originally published 1926).

North, D.C. (1981). *Structure and Change in Economic History*. New York: W.W. Norton.

Rakshit, M. (1982). *The Labour Surplus Economy*. Delhi: Macmillan.

Ranadive, K.R. (1978). *Income Distribution: The Unsolved Puzzle*. Bombay: Oxford University Press.

Rao, V.K.R.V. (1952). "Investment, income and the multiplier in an underdeveloped economy", *Indian Economic Review* I: 55-67 (February).

Roscher, W.G.F. (1843), *Outline of Lectures on Political Economy According to the Historical Method*.

Sen, A.K. (1962). *Choice of Techniques*. Oxford: Basil Blackwell.

———. (1983). "Development: Which way now?", *The Economic Journal* 93: 745-762.

Shetty, S.L. (1978). "Structural retrogression in the Indian economy since the mid-sixties", *Economic & Political Weekly*, Annual Number.

———. (2001). "Reviving the economy: Some explorations", *Economic & Political Weekly* 16(30): 2824-2830.

Shiller, R.J. (1981). "Do stock prices move too much to be justified by subsequent changes in dividends?", *American Economic Review* 71(3): 421-436.

Simon, H. (1957). *Models of Man*. NewYork: John Wiley & Sons.

Spulber, N. (1964) (ed). *Foundations of Soviet Strategy for Economic Growth*. Indiana: Bloomington. (Article by G. Feldman).

Stewart, I.M.T. (1979). *Reasoning and Method in Economics.* London: McGraw-Hill.

Tendulkar, S.D. (2000). "Planning and markets in Indian development process", *Artha Vijnana* XLII(3): 191-215.

Tversky, A. and D. Kahneman (1974). "Judgement under uncertainty: Heuristics and biases", *Science* 185: 1124-1131.

Vakil, C.N. (1942). *The Falling Rupee*. Bombay.

Vasudevan, A. (2002). Valedictory Speech "Comparative Perspectives on Indian Economic Thought", Seminar jointly held by the ICSSR and Department of Economics, University of Mumbai , 8 March.

4

Hindu Approach to Development

M.V. Nadkarni

Pari chin marto dravinam mamanyaad
Ritasya pathaa namasaa vivaaset/
Uta svena kritunaa samvadeta
Shreyaansam daksham manasaa jagribhyat//

—*Rigveda* 10.31.2

Let a man (or woman) ponder well on wealth and earn it by the path of Law (or Truth) and with humility. Let him (or her) take counsel with his (or her) own conscience and heartily gain justifiable (or upright) prosperity.

4.1 Introduction

Ever since the publication of Max Weber's *The Protestant Ethic and the Spirit of Capitalism* in 1930, interest in the influence of non-economic factors, particularly religion, on economic development has greatly increased. He regarded the impact of Protestantism as a positive and major factor in the rise of capitalism, and in contrast regarded the impact of religious ideas of Hinduism, especially of *karma* and *dharma* as negative, holding back economic development. While Protestantism was this-worldly, Indian religions were other-worldly, he felt. His work on Hinduism came in a later work—*The Religion of India* (published in English in 1958). Two more important western scholars also joined Weber in this critique of Indian religions in general and Hinduism in particular—Albert Schweitzer (1936) and W.J. Kapp (1963) among others. Max Weber felt that Indian religions were based on a worldview that took the world as false, which could not be a basis for any effort at economic (or capitalist) development. According to him, even Christianity also had stressed the primacy of the other world, the Kingdom of God, with a similar effect, until it was rescued by the new Protestant faith. The asceticism of this new faith was positive which helped accumulation and did not have to deny this-worldliness. Albert Schweitzer characterised Indian religions as world-and-life negating in contrast to Christianity, which by affirming the reality of the world and value of life, could give rise to ethical seriousness, enthusiasm for social welfare and hence, social service. Kapp analysed different value concepts such as *karma*, *dharma*, *aparigraha*, *maya* and *moksha* and tried to show how each of these is negatively associated with economic development.

Several Indian scholars took this western interpretation of Hindu values for granted without questioning it, though Dr. S. Radhakrishnan (1923 and 1939) had effectively countered it and showed that such an interpretation had no basis. It appears, however, that Radhakrishnan's rebuttal did not get as much publicity as the contention of the three western scholars cited above. India's low rate of economic growth up to 1980s at 3.5 per cent per annum was characterised by Raj Krishna as 'Hindu rate of growth'. Several scholars seriously believed that the Hindu 'other-worldliness' was a major factor in India's low economic performance, at least before the reforms of the nineties. Fortunately for Hinduism, nobody advocated eradication of Hinduism as the basis for the reforms. Instead, unnecessary controls and over-bureaucratisation of the economy were perceived as the major cause for the low performance of the past. The reforms were based on this perception and it worked!

Deepak Lal in his two-volume work on *The Hindu Equilibrium* did not attribute the low economic growth to Hindu philosophical thought and 'other-worldliness', but nevertheless took it for granted that it was associated with the Hindu society. He did not question the characterisation of Hindu society as having low motivation for growth and development, but only tried to find an explanation in factors other than scriptural values. According to him, low economic growth was due to the fact that the Hindu society showed a remarkable ability to adapt to adversities and maintain stability of the society even in the midst of severe political vicissitudes and hence, had little incentive to change. Lal clarifies: "The term Hindu is not to be taken in its religious sense." (Lal 1988: 5). Even the caste system, according to Lal was only an adaptation to scarcity of labour in an agricultural economy, which needed labour availability on a regular basis. In a situation of 'equilibrium' and adaptation to economic environment, 'the economy generates messages which do not cause agents change' (Hahn, 1973: 25, as quoted in Lal 1988: 6). The merit of Lal's approach is that low economic performance is not taken as intrinsic to Hindu worldview and its religion, but is on account of its 'equilibrium'! Once the economic environment changed which required agents also to change, there was nothing inherent and intrinsic in Hindu thought and religion to stop it from changing and promoting economic and social development. Otherwise, it would be difficult to explain how the same country which experienced a low 'Hindu rate of growth' till the early 1980s, experienced a spurt in growth thereafter, though the ethnic or religious composition of the country has hardly changed. If at all, Hindu-consciousness has grown, not declined.

This paper seeks to first dispel the misconception that Hinduism is world-and-life negating and that it was therefore indifferent to material progress, economic development and human welfare. Thereafter, it seeks to explain the Hindu worldview or development, human welfare and environment. The paper is not of just historical and academic interest. Its topical relevance consists in the fact that we have something to learn from the Hindu worldview on development in order to overcome dilemmas and crises being faced by humanity in the contemporary phase of economic development.

Though broadly, Hinduism can be said to include all religions and sects that originated in India, the reference here is mainly to what is known as *Sanatan Dharma* with three overlapping phases—the classical or Vedic phase of *vedas*, *upanishads*, the *Gita*, the great epics, *Puranas* and *Dharmashastras*; the phase of Bhakti movements during the medieval period; and the modern phase beginning with the 19th century. Since however, the main contention is about the scriptural values developed during the classical phase taken to be influencing people even now, and not about the Bhakti movements and the modern phase as such, our focus is mainly on the classical phase. This should not, therefore, be misinterpreted that the scope of Hinduism, according to the author, excludes the medieval and modern phase. The 'ism' in Hinduism here refers to its philosophy, which in spite of its diversity and dynamics had some remarkable unity, identity and continuity.

Buddhism and Jainism are not specially referred to in this paper, not because they are not relevant, but because of the author's lack of adequate knowledge of them. Since the main attack of western scholars is on Hindu concepts and value systems, and any way Hindus account for the bulk of the population following Indian religions, a focus on Hinduism in examining the impact on economic development is justifiable even otherwise. This in no way reduces the importance of other Indian religions like Buddhism and Jainism.

4.2 Misconceptions Dispelled

Though several ideas or values of Hinduism are attacked as negatively associated with economic and social development, the key concepts are *maya* (pronounced as *maayaa*), *tyaga* and the law of *karma*. If misconceptions about these are dispelled, it takes care of other concepts too.

It is to Shankaracharya (Shankara) of 8th century CE that the theory of the world being a *maya* is attributed. Though he has interpreted *upanishads* as supporting this theory, other *acharyas* have attacked this interpretation and have held that the world according to the *vedas*, *upanishads* and the *Gita* is a very real one. Shankara's *Advaita Siddhant* is one among several schools of thought in India, and none other than *Advaita* alone supports this theory. But even according to Shankara, *maya* does not mean absolute non-existence but only that compared to *brahman* which is fundamental, immutable and ultimate reality (*Paaramaarthika* truth), the mutable world is a lower level of reality (a *Vyaavahaarika* or *Aihika* truth). The world is unreal in the only sense that it is projection on *brahman*, rather than *brahman* itself. Thus, *maya* is appearance or projection, rather than illusion, and it is so only in a relative sense (see Radhakrishnan, 1999: 582-4 and Radhakrishnan, 1989: 27 for further explanation). Though several Hindu philosophers have used the word *maya*, it is only in the sense of creative power of the Supreme and not as an illusion. Even while conceding the mutable character of the world, Shankara himself took the world seriously. He did not neglect the worldly work of establishing a solid institutional framework for propagating his philosophy in the form of *mathas* or monasteries and starting monastic orders for the purpose. His concept of the world is better understood if the world is conceptualised as a drama. It is not real, compared to the real world. Yet, so long as actors act in it, they play their part quite seriously. To that extent, the drama is real, having a reality of its own. It is so real that the script is 'written' by the actors themselves and not predetermined and predestined (as we shall see below while discussing the law of *karma*).

If indeed Indian philosophy—particularly *Advaita*—had been so world negating as Schweitzer argued, it would have had a depressing impact on the initiative and enterprise of the communities, which adopted this philosophy as their own and shaped their life accordingly. Facts are otherwise. Communities that followed Shankara's *Advaita Siddhant* as their formal creed, come under the category of *Smaarta brahmins* among others. They comprise *Iyers*, *Havyakas*, *Chitpavans*, *Saraswats* (excluding Vaishnava Saraswats following Madhvaachaarya) and others. There is absolutely no evidence of any negative impact of *Advaita* philosophy on their initiative, enterprise and worldly success. Leading members of *Smaartas* can be found in business, science and technology, fine arts, media, bureaucracy, sports and even politics and have made big names.[1] It cannot be said that they ignored their philosophical roots. Most of them are quite religious and some have been good exponents of Hindu philosophy.

If this world is not real, even if only relatively real and not as real as *Brahman*, the ultimate and absolute reality, it is taken to mean that this world need not be taken seriously, and that the only happiness worth pursuing is the happiness of God realisation. It is thus that the values of renunciation (*tyaga*), controlling desires and monastic life are interpreted as more serious values than helping others and promoting social welfare. Liberation from illusion or ignorance, or *moksha* is thus the supreme goal. This attitude is interpreted as very negative and inimical to both social and economic development. Such a view again is a very misleading interpretation of Hindu spiritual values. Hindu scriptures have made it abundantly clear and in many places that even if this world is taken as a lower level of reality or mutable, as long as one

1. I am grateful to V.M. Rao for making this point and drawing my attention to the conspicuous—this worldly success of *Smaarta* communities, taking Chitrapur Saraswats as an illustration. There is a case study of Chitrapur Saraswats, who are followers of Shankara, by Frank Conlon (1977).

lives in this world, such a person has to take her/his role quite seriously and not neglect it, just as a good actor in a drama has to have all commitment to making the drama a success by acting her/his role with all earnestness and seriousness. Moreover, as already pointed out above, only one of the many schools of thought in India regards the world as relatively unreal, and others regard it as quite real. There is thus, no question of renouncing the world as long as one is in it. Even ascetics are not absolved from their role in the world; their role is to promote spiritual awareness, raise ethical standards and give guidance to people, though in this position, they have to be models of good (*saatvick*) behaviour, controlling their desires and possessiveness, be gentle and helpful to others.

Moksha is only one of the four goals of human existence, known as *purusharthas*. The other three are *dharma* (duty to society, conduct required for a moral social order which ensures human welfare), *artha* (acquiring means of material happiness) and *kama* (sensual pleasure, pronounced as *kaama*). All these three are rooted in this world. It is every one's right to seek them. No one is debarred. It is even suggested that *moksha* has to be sought after achieving all the three goals. *Dharma* is a social goal with an important role for individuals such that the social goal is achieved and everyone's happiness is ensured. This means that the individual goals—*artha*, *kama* and *moksha*, have to be tempered by *dharma*. Seeking *artha* and *kama* in ways not morally justifiable or as per *dharma* is not permitted. Even *moksha* cannot be sought by ignoring one's duty to society. The four *purusharthas* are thus interrelated and dominated by *dharma*. Moreover, *moksha* is not obtained only through renunciation or *sanyaasa*. Even householders who perform the role of *grihastha dharma* are entitled to spiritual liberation. *Tirukkural*, a Tamil classic by *Tiruvalluvar*, says: "If a man goes through the householder's life along the way of *dharma*, nothing is left for him to attain by becoming a recluse or going to the forest." (Rajagopalachari (ed. and tr.), 1999: 3). K.J. Shah (1982: 72) sums up the significance and interrelation of *purusharthas* thus: "*Artha* alone as a goal is greed, *kama* alone is lust, *dharma* alone is mechanical ritual, and *moksha* alone is escapism." The *purusharthas* are thus complementary and not conflicting with each other.

The value of limiting one's desires and needs in Hinduism was so interpreted by some economists that they believed that the normal supply curve which is upward sloping does not operate in India, particularly in agriculture. They thought that if the prices of farm produce are raised, farmers can satisfy their given needs with less money than before and would sell/produce less, making their supply curve backward sloping! It required the talents of economists like V.M. Dandekar and Raj Krishna to show that an Indian farmer is also governed by the same type of behavioural pattern and has shown evidence of responding to price stimuli in the same way as a western farmer. It looks that the Indian farmers knew their Hinduism better than economists who interpreted it in terms of its negative impact.

The law of *karma* is one of the most misunderstood concepts of Hinduism. It is not predestination or fate. It does not mean total helplessness of human beings with no freedom of will. *Karma* means action, and the law of *karma* applied to human situations is the law of action and reaction. The law very much belongs to the mundane world itself. *Karma* is determined by one's own action, may be past actions. What is more, it is possible to determine future destiny also by our own action in the present and move towards happiness. Belief in the law of *karma* is common to all Indian religions including Buddhism and Jainism. Because Hinduism (at least the mainstream of it) believes in God, the law of *karma* has two special features in Hinduism—the role of *kripa* or grace of God in alleviating the effect of the law of *karma* (or *karmaphala*) and the role assigned to *karma yoga* or *yoga* of pursuing altruistic action as a way of liberation from the law of *karma*. The law of *karma* has universal application according to Hinduism (and also Buddhism and Jainism) and not confined only to those who believe in it. Whether one believes in the law of gravitation and not, everyone is subject to it. The law of *karma* is believed to be as inexorable in the ethical/spiritual world as the law of cause and effect in the physical world. It does not mean that it curtails human freedom. As Arvind Sharma says, "The doctrine of *karma* no more prevents us from acting freely than the law of gravitation prevents us from moving around freely" (Sharma, 1996: 30). That the human beings have freedom of will is made clear in the *Bhagavad Gita* (the *Gita*, henceforth) itself, which says, "... reflecting critically over (whatever I said), you make your own decision" (18.63). Free will is evident also from another verse in the *Gita:* "A person should uplift oneself by own self (own effort), one should never destroy one's self, self is the (best) relative (or friend) of self, and self is also the (worst) enemy of self" (6.5).

In the eyes of the *Gita*, a human being thus is not a helpless puppet in the hands of a whimsical God, but has freedom and dignity that can be used for both material and spiritual success. The *Gita* also does not condemn desire (*kaama*), for it says *dharmaaviruddho kaamosmi*, endorsing *kaama* which is not against dharma or moral conduct. If this is so, what is the meaning of *karma yoga* where the path of work with detachment and without desiring fruit of work for personal gain is recommended for spiritual progress? The bulk of economic activity in the world is motivated by desire for personal gain or profit. Adam Smith showed that self-interest is not necessarily bad for the world. But Smith's view has not gone unchallenged. A natural order produced exclusively by narrow self-interest can be very unequal with a lot of exploitation of the weak by the strong and also environmentally unsustainable. What is needed is to rein selfishness, if not prevent it, so that it is within socially acceptable bounds. This can be done either by the government or through regulation and control, i.e., externally or, by voluntary self-restraint, or through both. What the *Gita* does is to emphasise voluntary self-restraint. This aspect of the *Gita* was later developed by Mahatma Gandhi who asked for treating property as a trust on behalf of the society and using it for the society, though there is bar on acquiring property by an individual. As per this approach, exploitation of humans by humans and exploitation of nature by humans is avoided—not through state control, not through communism, but through individuals' own voluntary self-control. The economy need not be run on the basis of altruism as such, but narrow self-interest is nevertheless transcended into enlightened self-interest in *loka-sangraha*—world construction ensuring peoples' welfare. If I act to promote world construction for people's welfare, I can also enjoy by sharing in it. One can earn a livelihood by socially acceptable and honest means, meeting not only basic needs, but also enough comforts to make a person efficient and productive in the long run. After all, according to the *Gita* itself, one should not destroy oneself (6.5). One can earn more according to each one's competence, but the surplus above one's legitimate needs (short term and long term) is to be used for the benefit of the society, for *loka-sangraha*. The way it is earned also is important. A teacher accepting a legitimate salary for work is not wrong; but if a person evaluates her students in an examination on the principle that one who pays more shall fair well but not others, it would be clearly unacceptable. Having once accepted the job of a doctor, a person cannot adopt the principle of 'whosoever pays more gets more attention'. Her work would be in the spirit of *karma yoga* if she pays equal attention to all patients as per their need, without extraneous or selfish discrimination, even if she makes a living out of her job. The *Gita* urges moderation, but not either narrow self-interest or self-destruction in the name of liberation. *Manusmriti* also makes the point clear by saying that no work, no action, is possible without a desire on the part of the doer (Ch.2.4), but what is important is that the action or work is in a morally right way (Ch.2.5). The morally right way, however, consists in going beyond being merely honest. According to the *Gita* at least, it is being proactive in contributing to the welfare of the world. Otherwise, it would amount to diluting the spirit of *karma yoga*.

In one of the most insightful books on the *Gita*, D.V. Gundappa observed wittily that *karma-phala-tyaga* (renouncing the fruit of action) does not mean cooking a tasty meal with all earnestness and skill and then throwing it in waste bin. Nor does it mean eating the meal, deliberately without enjoyment. It only means that we treat the meal as *prasaada* or grace of God (i.e., renouncing egoistic credit for it), to be shared with others whenever possible and thereby double the enjoyment of it. Having decided what is one's duty, detachment from its fruit means freedom from worry about its outcome and leaving it to God even while doing one's best (Gundappa, 2001: 333-5). It is clear, therefore, that neither the law of *karma* nor the recommendation of *karma yoga* can act as disincentive for economic action and for social and economic development of either the individual or the society.

Arvind Sharma points out that what Max Weber believed to be the major factors in Protestant ethic as behind the rise of capitalism, are present in Hindu scriptural values too, particularly in the *Gita*. Weber's emphasis was on the ascetic endeavour and not on profit seeking as the causal factor behind the emergence of capitalism. The main elements of the Protestant ethic which Weber identified as positively associated with economic development are present in the *Gita* as well (Sharma, 1980: 82-83). Thus, Luther believed that each individual was 'called' to do a particular job which was his 'calling' and that an individual by devoting himself wholeheartedly to his calling performed a spiritual duty. The *Gita*'s call to do one's *svadharma* is 'startlingly close' to Luther's concept of calling. *Svadharma* does not necessarily mean caste duty, but 'calling' as per one's aptitude, nature and ability (Nadkarni, 2003: 4786-87). The concept of asceticism in Weber's Protestant ethic is that the gains from the 'calling' are not to be dissipated in luxury, but saved and reinvested for the furtherance of the calling. The *Gita* does not recommend asceticism that involves renunciation of action. It recommends asceticism of a type where the action is undertaken but only the claim to the fruit of action is renounced particularly if it is beyond what is necessary to meet one's needs. Such asceticism comes close to what Weber had in mind, a positive asceticism which is favourable to economic development. Sharma identifies other elements also in Protestant ethic which are there in Hindu scriptures, especially the *Gita* (Sharma, 1980: 82-85). But those discussed here are the basic ones. We thus find that the criticism of western scholars about Hindu values being inimical to economic and social development are based on a complete misunderstanding; moreover, what they believed to be the positive factors in Christianity, particularly Protestantism, identified as being favourable to development, are very much there in Hinduism too.

4.3 Hindu View of Development

4.3.1 What We Look For

Development in the sense of continuous economic progress is new even in the West. It is post-Industrial Revolution thinking. Similarly, development in the sense of economic growth of GNP is also new even in the West. It would not be meaningful to look for a corresponding concept in Hinduism. What we can meaningfully and fruitfully look for is support to the idea of individual prosperity and welfare, as well as the community prosperity and welfare, and indications of how they have to be attained. Even more important, we shall see whether the ideas and values in Hinduism are suggestive of support to limitless economic growth, which is narrow in slope and also unsustainable in the long run in terms of particularly environmental costs, or support to a sustainable and holistic development consistent with human welfare in broad terms. In other words, is the idea of prosperity narrowly anthropocentric in Hinduism and purely materialistic or, is it eco-friendly and morally justifiable? What is the idea of human welfare in Hinduism? The answers to these questions cannot be directly and explicitly obtained in one source. We have to cast our net rather wide. However, we shall take in to account a few illustrative examples of what Hinduism stands for rather than make an exhaustive survey of scriptures and other works of Hinduism.

4.3.2 Economic Ideas in Ancient India

Arthashastra was recognised as a separate branch of knowledge in ancient India, worthy of specialised pursuit and subject of intense study by princes, scholars and administrators. *Arthashastra* did not mean economics or political economy in a narrow sense, and included even *Dandaneeti* (governance). Its economics part included a study of the economy—*varta* (pronounced as *vaartaa*), which in turn comprised of agriculture (*krishi*), animal husbandry (*pastupaalan or go-rakshaa*), commerce (*vaanijya*), money lending and banking (*kuseeda*), manufacturing, arts (*kalaa*) and crafts, sculpture and architecture. Agriculture, cattle rearing and commerce received the maximum attention, as they formed the main base of the economy of ancient India. Earning wealth was the result of pursuit of any of these businesses or professions (*vritti*). *Amarakosha*, a lexicon, mentions synonyms of wealth, which are suggestive. *Dhanam* or *vittam* used in singular meant wealth in general, while *dhanani* used in plural meant possessions, stressing the variety of forms in which it is held—land, cattle, gold coins and buildings. *Svaapateyam*, a synonym of *dhanam*, suggests its quality of being appropriated; *Artha* suggests its quality of being earned and accumulated; *Bhogyam* suggests it can be consumed or enjoyed; *Vibhavam* suggests that it is an indicator of one's prosperity; *Vyavaharyam* suggests that it is transferable or transacted, and can be a subject matter of disputes (Aiyangar, 1934: 20-21). *Dhanam* is also capable of *vriddhi* (growth, increment) when used judiciously and intelligently. *Vriddhi* is also used in the sense of interest on loans given. Mark the sophistication with which both the economy and wealth are treated as a subject matter with so many terms to reflect different nuances, which would not have been the case if the Hindus had indifference to it as claimed by western scholars like Weber *et al.*

The sources of economic ideas in ancient Hindu literature are several. Kautilya's *Arthashastra,* written during the reign of Chandragupta Maurya in 3rd Century BCE, is only one of the sources, though better known than others. Unfortunately, its text was almost lost for a long time though referred by several, until discovered by R. Shamasastry in 1904 at Mysore. He published the text in 1909 and its English translation in 1915. A critically edited text, with English translation and notes, was prepared by R.P. Kangle, published in three volumes between 1960 and 1965. A handy translation in English with detailed introduction and notes is now available (Rangarajan, 1992). Among other sources of economic ideas may be cited in *Shukra-Neetisaara* and also in *Dharmasootras* by Gautama, Apastambha, Vasistha, Baudhayana, Narada and Yajnavalkya. Aiyangar has made use of these sources to present and explain main aspects of ancient Indian economic thought (Aiyangar, 1934). P.V. Kane's five-volume *History of Dharmashastra*, published between 1930 and 1962, is also a useful source to trace economic, political, legal, management and governance ideas in ancient India, as contained in *Dharmashastras* (Kane, 1990).

Seeds of both labour theory of value and scarcity theory of value can be found in ancient Indian texts. *Shukra-Neetisaara*, for example, mentions clearly that price (*moolya*) depends on utility (capacity to satisfy desire—*kaama* or want), on the ease (*sulabha*) or difficulty (*a-sulabha*) with which the commodity can be obtained, and its scarcity—how rare (*apratima*) it is. It was also realised that these characteristics are not fixed or absolute, but vary according to *desha* (place) and *kaala* (time) (for concerned citations in support, see Aiyangar, 1934: 91-92).

Though the *Gita* advised voluntary restraint, *dharmashastra*s recommended state intervention to regulate the market, so that prices and interest rates charged are not unreasonable. The state also played an important role in resolving disputes in business transactions. This created the institutional framework necessary to create wealth, appropriate it and distribute it. There were also non-government institutions in the form of trade or craft guilds, which protected and promoted the interests of their members. There was an extensive trade both within India and outside and even across the seas. External marine trade was as old as the Harappan-Vedic era, since the *vedas* and other texts contain numerous references to such trade and also to ships.

Several foreign travellers have referred to the past opulence of India and its cities and its temples, suggesting that the Indian economy compared favourably well with other countries in the world before the British rule. David Washbrook, an eminent economic historian familiar with India's economic history, said in a lecture delivered at Bangalore (at the Institute for Social and Economic Change) in January 2003 (attended by the author), that based on a rough comparison of levels of living of respective classes, the per capita GDP of India on the eve of British rule appeared to be even better than that of Europe. The Indian economy would not have attained the diversity, complexity and the level of development it did, if the bulk of its inhabitants had a negative attitude to creating wealth and no interest in economic matters. Thinkers in India thought it necessary to coin different terms for different aspects of economy, developed rules for regulating economy and also the institutional framework required to monitor it and to take care of interests of trade as well as people. Milton Singer writes: "When I tell orthodox Hindus about Weber's theory, they are astonished. 'If that were true,' they would reply, 'how could we have lived and done so many things—built temples, ships, and empires, fought wars and organised agriculture, crafts and trade?'" (Singer, 1972: 275).

4.3.3 Qualifications to Earning Wealth

However, support to the earning of wealth was not unqualified. Take the *Rigvedic* verse cited in the beginning of this paper. It holds the key to the understanding of Hindu attitude to earning wealth. Wealth is not assumed to be coming unasked without effort. One has to consciously ponder (*pari chin*) over how it has to be earned by the path of moral law and truth (*ritam*) and not by dishonest means. It has to be earned with humility (*namasaa*) and not arrogance, since success depends on grace of God and one owes it to the society of which one is a member for making it possible. Consulting one's own conscience (*kritu*) also is important in deciding the ways in which it is earned. Once these qualifications are kept in mind, one can earn wealth heartily (*manasaa*) and gain justifiable or upright (*daksham*) prosperity (*shreyaansam*). Though *ritam* in *Rigveda* meant moral law, the later *dharmashastras* made it clear that wealth has to be earned according to the law of the land too, apart from being ethically correct. Eighth paper of *Shanti Parva* in *Mahabharata* suggests a circular influence between *dharma* and *artha*. *Artha* has to be earned according to *dharma* or moral law; but even *dharma* cannot be sustained in a situation of poverty since poverty breeds sin, but *dharma* flows out of wealth like a river from a mountain (*Dhanaaddhi dharmah sravati shailaadapi nadee tathaa*) (as cited in Aiyangar, 1934: 23). You hardly find poverty glorified. It is also made clear that wealth is not meant for hoarding or only for one's own selfish consumption. It should flow out to others like the waters gushing out from a rain-cloud or from a full lake. This is so particularly about the wealth of kings (*Mahabharata* XXII.8.33). A king was supposed to collect or accumulate wealth strictly for the benefit of others.

4.3.4 Holistic View

The Hindu view of development is holistic, not centred around personal acquisition, and not in terms of material wealth alone. This is evident from an ancient prayer known as *Swasti-mantra* chanted at all religious occasions in homes as well as temples, a part of which is cited here:

> *Sarvescha sukhinah santu*
> *Sarvessantu niraamayaah /*
> *Sarve bhadraani pashyantu*
> *Maa kaschit dukhamaapnuyaat //*
> *OM Shanti! Shanti! Shantihi!*
> (May all find happiness and
> Live without illness;
> May all find security, and
> May no one face sorrow!
> Oh Almighty! May peace prevail, may peace prevail,
> May peace prevail!)

This popular prayer is remarkable for several things. It is a prayer for the welfare of all humanity, not of one individual or family alone. What is sought here is not *moksha* or liberation from *sansaara* (world), but plain material happiness and freedom from sorrow. Welfare sought here is holistic, including good health and security for all and not material wealth as such. Peace, invoked here three times, also has its own significance. It is not just poetic emphasis alone. Peace is sought on three fronts: a) peace between human beings, between communities and between countries, b) peace with the natural world, including ecological balance and c) peace with one self, freedom from stress and tension and thus, realising oneness with the Almighty and all beings—sentient and non-sentient (Prime, 1994: 76). Peace on all the three fronts—social, ecological and spiritual—is very much a part of welfare, without which economic development and prosperity would have no meaning. What is cited above is not an exceptional prayer. Many Hindu prayers and *yajnas* seek this all round holistic welfare and peace, not just for the sponsor of the *pooja*s and *yajna*s but for all humanity, all the world.

This cosmopolitan spirit in religion as well as concept of welfare sought is evident from another well-known verse from *Hitopadesha*, a popular collection of stories:

Ayo nijah paro veti gananaa laghuchetasaam /
Udaara charitaanaam tu Vasudaiva kutumbakam //

It means: "This one is ours and that one is others—such a calculation befits only the narrow minded. For the broadminded, the whole world is one family." The source of this, *Hitopadesha*, is not regarded as a sacred scripture, but this verse is and has characterised the real spirit of Hinduism.

4.3.5 Knowledge as Development

Cosmopolitan outlook is only one of the several aspects of the holistic approach to development and welfare in Hinduism. While it did not shun acquisition of material wealth as part of it, as is evident from the above *Rigvedic* prayer and also from the several prayers in the *vedas* for material prosperity, the main thrust of development was towards acquisition of knowledge. With this heritage, it is no wonder if India is a leading country in an age of knowledge based development. The essence of *Gaayatri japa*, the most popular and regarded as the most sacred among *japas*, is praying for stimulus to the intellect (*dhiyo yonah prachodayaat*). Incidentally, this prayer is from *Rigveda* (3.62.10). That it is still a 'living' prayer, recited with devotion by millions, indicates the highest regard that Hinduism gave to intellect and knowledge. There could be no concept of human welfare without it. There are many prayers in the *vedas* to the same effect. Interestingly, the light of intellect and knowledge is sought for all, for people of all *varnas* or classes, including for the one who prays:

> *Rucham no dhehi braahmaneshu*
> *Rucham rajasu naskridhi/*
> *Rucham vishweshu shudreshu*
> *Mayi dhehi ruchaa rucham //*
>
> —*Taittiriya Samhita* V.7.6.3-4

It means: "Put light in our *brahmanas*, put it in our chiefs (kings), (put) light in *vaishyas* and *shudras*, put light in me by your light."[2]

4.3.6 Equity

Depriving women and *shudras* of the right to study *vedas*, which came later in Hindu society, was hardly consistent with this original spirit of Hinduism. A spirit of respecting equality and justice was very much a part of Hinduism. *Tirukkural*, an ancient text venerated by Tamils as Tamil Veda, authored by Tiruvalluvar, says: "Let him who thinks inequity be warned that ruin awaits him" (116th Aphorism). Again, "All men are born alike (equal), the differences are due only to differences in what they do" (972nd Aphorism).[3] *Vedanta* philosophy declares that there is divinity in every creature. Lord Krishna says in the *Gita* (Ch.6.30): "He who sees Me in all things and sees all things in Me, never becomes departed from Me, nor am I lost to him." The succeeding *verses* in the *Gita* also convey the same message. The Lord says again: "He who judges pleasure and pain in others by the same standard as he applies to

2. The original and the translation taken from P.V. Kane (1990) Vol.II Part I, p.34.
3. At least two translations of *Kural* are available in English—C. Rajagopalachari (1999; first edn. in 1965) and P.S. Sundaram (1990). While the former contains selected portions, the latter is a complete work.

himself, that Yogi is the highest" (Ch. 6.32). These principles can be basic to any just and equitable approach to development and welfare and go with cosmopolitanism referred above as crucial to the understanding of Hinduism and its approach.

4.3.7 Freedom

Amartya Sen's emphasis on 'development as freedom' is not new to the spirit of Hinduism. Max Weber, an otherwise trenchant critic of Hinduism observed: "The freedom of thought in ancient India was so considerable as to find no parallel in the west before the most recent age."[4] Hinduism encouraged pursuit of truth as a basic doctrine and encouraged openness and a scientific spirit both in spiritual and mundane matters. India had a lead in the development of mathematics, astronomy, medicine, surgery, metallurgy and chemistry in the ancient period right up to about 12th century. There were hot debates and disputations but no persons were burnt for repudiating what was earlier claimed to be true and for making scientific advance. Unfortunately, Hindus ignored defence and science and technology related to it and paid a heavy price for it. There was a reason for it. Hinduism was, and still is, a religion of peace, and even in warfare it wanted to follow *dharma.* Kings of course fought each other, but when peace returned, they patronised art, architecture and literature, but ignored updating war technology.

4.3.8 Health

A key ingredient in the Hindu concept of welfare is the emphasis on health. It is part of the *Swasti-mantra* cited above (*'Sarvessantu niraamayaah'*—may all be free from illness). With all its emphasis on *dharma* and spiritual progress, Hinduism still declared—*'Shareeramaadyam khalu dharma saadhanam'* (Human body is really the first instrument of *dharma*). To ignore human body and its illnesses was not considered proper, because it is primarily through our body and when we are alive that we can move along the path of *dharma* and realise the Divine. Hindus in ancient India developed the unique science

4. Quoted in p.364 of Srinivas and Shah (1968).

of *yoga,* integrating mental health with the physical, designed to tone up the whole body along with mind, and control several illnesses in addition to improve general health. Hindu physicians also developed a sophisticated system of medicine—*ayurveda*, based both on herbs (*vanoushadhi*) and chemicals (*rasoushadhi*). *Siddha* medicine was developed in South India, which is also equally popular in the South as *ayurveda*. Surgery was also developed on a scientific basis. *Shushruta Samhita* refers to as many as 120 surgical instruments. The ancient text gives also instructions in pre-operative, operative and post-operative care, including precautions against infections (Thakur, 2001).

4.3.9 State Responsibilities in Development

Health security had to be provided by the family rather than by the state. So also was the provision for education a responsibility of family. According to *Arthashastra*, however, the state had to undertake responsibility not only for law and order, but also for promoting economic and cultural activity including encouraging scholars, teachers, physicians, artists and craftsmen, and protection of weaker section of the society. If any one, particularly women, had no one to look after them, the state had to make provision for their support.[5] Consumer protection was also state responsibility. Forest conservation and maintaining cleanliness and access to water bodies were also state concerns. So also was construction and maintenance of infrastructure, particularly roads. Compared to the responsibilities that the present day state takes, the state in pre-modern India may look conservative, but it has to be compared with other contemporary states in the world and not with modern states. From this point of view, the state's role as seen from Kautilya's *Arthashastra* seems fairly proactive and progressive.

4.3.10 Gender Issues

An important criterion of the level of development of a civilisation is how it treats women. Judging Hindu civilisation of the past by this

5. Kautilya's *Arthashastra* (II.23) lays down that the state should provide facilities to destitute women to enable them to earn a living by spinning; it says that in the case of women who do not move out of house, raw material be supplied to them by state at home (Rangarajan, 1992: 332-3).

criterion is a very complex task, as one is struck by apparently ambivalent attitudes. On the one hand, Hinduism is the only religion to have conceptualised God in feminine form too, and followed it up by declaring *'yatra naaryastu poojyante ramante tatra devataah'* (where women are worshipped and highly honoured, it is a place where gods enjoy and become happy). Mothers enjoyed highest regard in traditional Hindu culture. Brides were looked upon as goddess Lakshmi incarnate. At religious functions and rituals, the wife has to be with the husband. He cannot perform any rites without the presence of his wife by his side. On the other hand, there were abominable practices like Sati and restrictions including severe dress codes for widows who did not opt to become *satis*. We can understand the situation better if the treatment of women and their right to education and property are seen in a historical perspective.

But first we should appreciate that it would be unfair to judge the pre-modern Hindu civilisation in this respect by present standards. The realisation that women deserve equal economic, political and cultural rights is a more recent development all the world over. Even Christianity is accused of misogyny. A Professor of religion, Malory Nye, observes: "Any reading of the Christian Bible cannot avoid the deep veins of misogyny, patriarchy, and in several places extreme violence by men against women that are found within the text. For feminist (and other) scholars of Christianity who are also Christians, the problem is one of how putative goodness of Christianity can be reconciled with a negative and abusive treatment of women" (Nye, 2003: 168). The Bible laid down that women "are not permitted to speak (in the church); but they are to be submissive. And if they want to learn something, let them ask their own husbands at home; for it is shameful for women to speak in the church" (The *New Testament* I Corinthians, 14, 34-35). Even in modern times, "down to 1850 AD in England a woman could not take a walk, much less a journey, alone; ...It was almost scandalous for a woman to address a public meeting. ...When the House of Commons was built in 1844, it was with great difficulty that a Ladies' Gallery was sanctioned. It was, however, decided to put a grille before it in order to screen the occupants from the public gaze. This grille was removed only in 1918." (Altekar, 1999: 178). Incidentally, 1918 was also the year when the

British Parliament granted franchise to British women and that too after some struggle in which women had to court imprisonment (Altekar, 1959: 192).

We may review Hindu attitudes to women in a historical perspective from three standpoints: (i) education, (ii) property rights and (iii) treatment of widows. Fortunately, we have a detailed study by A.S. Altekar (1959) on *The Position of Women in Hindu Civilization*, drawn from several primary sources. It is an objective, critical as well as a balanced study, which is used here. Altekar finds that during the ancient times right up to above 3rd century BCE, girls were given education, including access to *vedic* studies. Women authored several *vedic* verses. During the *upanishadic* period too, women took part in philosophical discussions. Even after 3rd century BCE, the situation was not very bad, since even as late as 8th century CE, the referee to the debate between Shankaracharya and Mandanamisrha was the latter's wife, who had a great reputation as a scholar in her own right. There were women physicians who specialised in women's diseases. The girls were given the right of *upanayana* (thread ceremony) along with boys, after which they were initiated into studies. Marriage of girls did not take place till they were at least 16-18 years of age and they had the right to choose their husbands. When political instability and insecurity started increasing, the age of marriage of girls started declining, and with it their access to education also declined. Higher education of girls became confined to royal or rich families, and to the class of dancing girls. There was this paradoxical phenomenon that girls from even respected families were kept illiterate, but dancing girls and courtesans went in for a good deal of education including fine arts and literature and they enjoyed a high status. Their houses even provided forum for intellectual discussions for the elite! They served as elite social clubs. For most of the women, however, there was no provision for education till almost the 20th century. The important point, however, is that Hinduism had nothing intrinsically against education of women. The adverse circumstances of history deprived women of chances of education for nearly one-and-half millennia.

According to Altekar, "The theory approved by the Hindu culture as early as the Vedic age was that the husband and the wife should be the joint owners of the household and its property. The husband was required to take a solemn vow at the marriage that he would never transgress the rights and interests of his wife in economic matters" (Altekar, 1959: 214). Altekar also says that in practice, all the logical corollaries of joint ownership were not respected. However, it helped the wife in securing a number of minor rights and privileges. For example, the wife had an absolute right of maintenance against the husband. "The husband could not proceed on a journey without making proper provision for her maintenance and the household expenditure. If he married a second time, the first wife had to be properly provided for" (Altekar, 1959: 215). The 12th century jurist, Vijnaneshwara, maintained that if a husband abandons a virtuous wife, willfully misappropriates her property and refuses to restore it, she could move a court of law to get her grievances redressed (Altekar, 1959: 215-6). Nevertheless, the wife had no proper guarantee of protection to her right in immovable property. This was also partly because the property rights particularly in land were not clearly defined even in general. To compensate for this, the concept of *streedhana* was evolved, which gave absolute right to moveable property to women. Interestingly, over time, the scope of *streedhana* was widened, and not shrunk. Apart from the bride price (a custom originally in vogue before it was replaced by dowry in the late medieval age) transferred by bride's father to daughter at the time of marriage, it included gifts by husband and other relatives given from time to time, and earnings by women such as through sale of milk from household cattle. *Streedhana* was normally held in the form of gold and gold ornaments, silver and also coins. Yajnavalkya mentions six forms of *streedhana,* which included property acquired by inheritance, purchase, partition, chance and adverse possession (Altekar, 1999: 219-222). Though this was the position in theory and law, in practice there were also occasional cases where women themselves were treated like chattel, but Altekar also says that this was the case in other societies too outside India. Probably, not all women could get property of their own, nor all women were used as chattel. It depended both on the class of women and also historical circumstances. Both in concept and practice, *streedhana* was common even among poorer classes at all times in India, though women did not have absolute right in landed property.

Though most of the anomalies of a patriarchal society were removed by the Hindu Law after Independence, there is still one at least. The head or the *karta* of a Hindu Undivided Family (HUF) is still a male as per law. But women owning immovable property came in to vogue much before, and so also woman-headed households managing immovable property. It was only in historical circumstances when, ownership in landed property could not be defended against encroachers by women and male help was needed for the purpose, that men came to dominate in property matters. But even here, women in Hindu societies had absolute right to *streedhana*.

It was unfortunately the widening of the scope of *streedhana* and strengthening of the absolute right of women over it, which could have influenced the heinous practice of Sati at least in some cases. According to Altekar, there was no practice of Sati in the *vedic-upanishadic* period. On the contrary, widows were encouraged to marry the younger brother or cousins of the departed husband. No Hindu scriptures have recommended or endorsed Sati. Sati came into vogue much later and that too strictly on a voluntary basis. There are references in texts when the near relatives dissuaded women from becoming a *sati*. During times when political instability increased and when the prospect of dishonour to women became inevitable at the hands of ruthless enemies after defeat and death of husbands in war, women became *satis* preferring death to dishonour. In the ancient period up to the end of the first millennium of CE, however, women were not normally dishonoured during or after wars. "Women were so sacred in India that even the common soldiery left them unmolested in the midst of slaughter and devastation" (Saksena, 1968: 35). Matters became worse during the medieval age when molestation of women became routine after wars. That is when the practice of Sati became more widespread. But even during the early British (in the late 18th and in the early 19th century) period, when Raja Ram Mohan Roy launched a campaign against Sati and got it outlawed, the practice was confined more to Bengal and was almost unknown in the south of India. The practice of Sati in course of time had degenerated so much that after the death of their husbands, women were subtly encouraged by husband's relatives to become *sati*, if not forced outright. This was mainly with the motive of cornering the *streedhana* of women. There was nothing intrinsic in Hinduism to support and encourage Sati.

In spite of the fact that India had a powerful woman Prime Minister and in late 2003 as many as five women Chief Ministers including in four supposedly backward northern states, women development is still a relevant and urgent issue of concern. Literacy among women is still lower, sex ratio is adverse, schooling and higher education among girls is lower, and there is still the practice of female foeticide. Dowry deaths still take place (which is not confined to Hindus). The representation of women in the Parliament, in Legislative Assemblies, and in educated employment is lower than what is warranted by the size of their share in population. This situation cannot be naively attributed to legacy of Hinduism. In a way, this is part of the problem of development and all the developing societies are facing this problem. It is encouraging, however, that women are breaking age-old barriers and coming to the front in every field, even in fields commonly the monopoly of men earlier. With progress in universalisation of primary and secondary education, with greater health care and with higher gender sensitivity among both men and women, matters are no doubt improving even if at lower pace than desired. Hinduism has not come as an obstacle in this great task.

4.4 Sustainable Development: Limits to Growth Revisited

Last but not the least, we come to the ecological dimension of development, to which Hinduism can make a valuable contribution. Lynn White Jr. in an article in 1967 which has since become famous suggested that anthropocentric biblical attitudes towards the earth tended to encourage over-consumption of natural resources and even a callous attitude towards the realm of the non-human.[6] Hindu philosophy in contrast cannot be considered as anthropocentric and has been emphatic on minimising our needs and consciously limiting our wants only to what is essential for leading a healthy and comfortable life, and on avoiding possessiveness and greed. The very first verse in

6. See White (1967), as referred in Chapple and Tucker (ed) (2001) p. xv.

Ishopanishad, which was Gandhiji's favourite, is pertinent here. It says: "Every thing in the Universe belongs to the Lord. Enjoy what is left for you as your share and do not covet what is not yours." It meant leading a simple life—simple living and high thinking. Eminent Hindu thinkers like Mahatma Gandhi drew inspiration from this precept and tried to set an example for others by leading a simple life. Such an attitude of non-acquisitiveness is very congenial for ecological balance and environmental conservation, because those who follow this ideal make minimum demands on the earth's natural resources.

Kenneth Boulding characterised the Earth as a spaceship with given resources. It meant that just as astronauts in a spaceship have to make things last as long as they are in the spaceship, the human beings too have to do so. Except for sunlight or solar energy that comes from outside, the Earth is constrained by its given resource endowments. Georgescu-Roegen (1971) drew attention to finiteness of the physical world, which sets limits on the economic process. This approach asks for conscious and planned limits on wants and artifacts, though not on development based on information and knowledge, cultural improvements and redistribution of income and wealth.

There were also several others who regarded these concerned scholars as pessimistic and felt that human ingenuity can take care of environmental problems of both pollution and depletion created by economic growth and implied that economic growth can be continued with the same relentlessness as in the past. There was also a protest from developing countries particularly to 'Limits to Growth' idea (Meadows *et al.*, 1972). The developing countries needed ccological space to grow to end poverty and deprivation. They felt that it is the developed countries, which brought about our ecological crisis through reckless growth, and now they have no moral right to ask developing countries to put limits on growth in the name of avoiding ecological crisis. Technological optimism was helpful to developed countries to project an idea that both developed and developing countries can grow, taking care of the environment through better technology in which of course the developed countries can provide technical know-how to developing countries at a cost. Business prospects of developed countries looked rosier than even before! There was no need, it appeared, to put limits on consumption and be afraid of depletion, because technology would always bring forth new substitutes for the resources that have depleted. The idea of sustainable development was advanced, with an implicit optimism that all that you have to do is to grow by taking care of environment and that it is still possible to eat the cake and have it too! The Brundtland Commission made it clear:

> Sustainable development seeks to meet the needs and aspirations of the present without compromising the ability to meet those of the future. Far from requiring the cessation of economic growth, it recognises that the problems of poverty and under—development cannot be solved unless we have a new era of growth in which developing countries play a large role and reap benefits. (WCED, 1987: 40).

If sustainable development is interpreted in such an optimistic way that everybody can continue to growth—the rich and the poor alike—and keep the Earth going as before, and that there would be technology available for any kind of crisis, it would be not only misleading but also disastrous. It is not appreciated that in a situation of finite resources, a continuously rising consumption of the rich—whether in developed countries and developing countries, can only be at the cost of the poor in both types of countries. It is unpleasant and politically difficult to accept that the Earth is a spaceship with limited resources on board. It is far more demanding to share given resources than to share growing resources. Nobody would like to solve the problem of poverty through redistribution of given income and wealth. It is so with environmental problems too. It is painful to share a given cake with growing appetites and growing numbers. It is far easier to believe that the cake can grow too than to curb appetites and control growing numbers. Unfortunately, we cannot eat the cake and have it too or keep it growing forever.

Though technological advance has helped us in the past to overcome the resource crunch, we also know that it has not been fast enough to cope with accumulating environmental problems. There are significant lags between emergence of environmental problems and development of technologies to alleviate them. There are further lags between development of technologies and their application on a wide scale in all problem areas. It is not enough for a technology to be environmentally benign; it has also to be economically efficient. But in the meanwhile, environmental degradation accumulates often in irreversible ways, so that it is difficult to undo the damage done. Even technology, therefore, has economic and social limits, apart from technological limits of entropy law. If the ecology of the Earth has already become so fragile, as it appears very likely, its degradation may become too fast and irreversible for any technology to tackle. Unfortunately, most of the ecological problems take place outside the price system, but application of technology has to operate within the price or market system. While the costs of preventing or controlling degradation are considered, the costs of degradation are hardly accounted for if they are to be borne by future generation. There is also one more aspect to the ecological costs. When the rich grow and create ecological costs, they have to be borne more by the poor. The ecological costs of growth were lower for developed countries in the past and they didn't even have to bear them. Now for the same quantum of growth, the ecological costs are higher for the developing countries and they have got to bear them. In other words, the more the rich grow, the more difficult it becomes for the poor to grow though they need to grow more than the rich.

Technology has another important limitation. It can give partial solutions and cannot address itself to overall and general scarcity of resources. Daly explains:

> As we attempt to recycle more and more of our produced foods, we will reach the point of diminishing returns; the energy expenditure alone will give rise to a ruinous amount of waste heat and thermal pollution. On the other hand, if we recycle too small a fraction of our produced goods, then non-thermal pollution and resource depletion become a severe problem (Daly, 1980: 181).

As Daly says further, wc can probably choose between the two depending on which of them is more efficient, reckoning environmental costs too. Yet, the hard reality is that such a choice does not enable us to have continuously increasing rates of material and energy consumption in the long term too.

If a collapse of the Earth's eco-system has not been reached so far in spite of the extremely high rates of consumption of the rich, it is not so much due to technological advance as due to the appalling sacrifice on the part of the poor in the world. They form the bulk of the world's population who are in no position to deplete and pollute, as they do not have the economic wherewithal to do so. But their deprivation cannot hold the balance of the world's eco-system any longer. Being impatient with inequity, they would strive to attain the same levels of consumption as the rich. Thus, inequity—even as it appears have prevented an ecological collapse so far—holds the promise of hastening it.

It is in this context that the Hindu worldview and attitude to development becomes relevant. According to Hinduism, God pervades the whole universe and transcends it too. To the extent that the universe with all its sentient beings and non-sentient things is a manifestation of God, Hinduism could be said to be pantheist. It is nothing to be ashamed of, even if some other religions have attacked pantheism. Hinduism does not authorise human beings to lord over the earth and exploit it in a whimsical, selfish and anthropocentric manner. It advises humans to enjoy the world and their life, but within reasonable limits that do not disrespect the earth itself. Humans can satisfy their wants but should also control greed. Gandhiji's famous saying that the earth has enough to satisfy our needs but not our greed, is very consistent with Hinduism. Hinduism considers earth as mother, *bhumata* (pronounced as *bhoomaataa*). The concept of *gaia* is not new to Hinduism. *Atharva veda* has a whole prayer in praise of earth (*prithivi sukta*). The Hindu concern for conserving biodiversity is reflected also in insistence on offering 21 varieties of leaves and 21 varieties of flowers to God in any formal ritual worship. The emotional attachment to cow protection and snake worship also have to be seen in this light. The *Gita* recommends commitment to the welfare of all beings—human and others (*sarvabhoota hiterataah*). Polluting air and water are a sacrilege according to Hinduism. The ecological concern of Hinduism is not, however, the same as deep ecology. For protecting wild life, for example, deep ecology may not mind ousting the inhabitants of a forest. But this is not consistent with the value of non-violence, which is also dear to Hinduism. Non-violence to nature has to be reconciled with non-violence to humans. Such as those who have to be shifted have to be compensated and resettled in such a way that they are better off.

There are ways in which human welfare can be advanced without involving violence to nature, without ecological costs. Development based on advancement of knowledge, culture, literature and arts is one such way. A part of human welfare also consists in ensuring that humans have enough leisure of their own in which they can advance their knowledge and enjoy art, literature and music and be more cultured. They should also have some time to reflect on the world and on one self—some time for meditation and reflection. Otherwise, creativity will die in a hectic over-busy world. It is senseless if human beings have to work all the while for earning livelihood by producing more and more of material goods. It is not enough if only a few specialise in producing culture goods, because if others have no time to enjoy these culture goods their production would go waste. Every human being should have some leisure, which she can enjoy. But this leisure should be voluntary, not forced. Bertrand Russell's *In Praise of Idleness* was published as early as in 1935. It has become more relevant today than ever before. More than cancer, stress and tension are taking a heavy toll in today's world, even among women. Productivity has increased enormously, thanks to labour-saving devices. This should have resulted in giving more leisure to employees, producing more with least wastage of both human and material resources. Russell, however, found the reality to be otherwise. There is forced idleness on the one hand, with a few employees working harder than they should have; there is also surplus production which is more than necessary to satisfy human needs (and even wants), with a lot of resources wasted on marketing the surplus production. Russell observes:

> In a world where no one is compelled to work more than four hours a day, every person possessed of scientific curiosity will be able to indulge it and every painter will be able to paint without starving... Above all, there will be happiness and joy of life, instead of frayed nerves, weariness, and dyspepsia. ...Modern methods of production have given us the possibility of ease and security for all; we have chosen, instead, to have over work for some and starvation for others. Hitherto we have continued to be as energetic as we were before there were machines; in this we have been foolish, but there is no reason to go on being foolish forever'. (Russell, 1960 edn: 20-21).

This has happened because we have viewed development mainly in terms of growth of GNP, not in terms of welfare. Knowledge, freedom, good health, opportunity for creativity and realising oneself as a cultured human being, and above all time to take delight in the joy of living in this beautiful world—they are all part of welfare and hence development. It is this holistic development, which is consistent with Hinduism, and not a relentless rat race.

Though this type of holistic development is projected above as Hindu view of development, it is not necessarily exclusive to Hinduism. It can be consistent with other religions too, and also with ethics in general freed from religious trappings. It would be humanistic development transcending commodities and promoting capabilities, using Amartya Sen's words.

References

Aiyangar, K.V. Rangaswami (1934). *Aspects of Ancient Indian Economic Thought* (Manindra Chandra Lectures at Benares Hindu University in 1927). Madras.

Altekar, A.S. (1999). *The Position of Women in Hindu Civilization: From Pre-historic Times to the Present Day*. Delhi: Motilal Banarasidass (1999 Reprint).

Boulding, Kenneth (1966). "The economics of the coming spaceship Earth", reprinted in Human Daly (ed.) (1980), *Environmental Quality in a Growing Economy*. John Hopkins Press. pp.253-263.

Chapple, Christopher Key and Mary Evalyn Tucker (eds.) (2001). *Hinduism and Ecology—The Intersection of Earth, Sky and Water*. New Delhi: Oxford University Press.

Conlon, Frank (1977). *A Caste in a Changing World: The Chitrapur Saraswath Brahmins, 1700-1935*. New Delhi: Thomson Press.

Daly, Human (1980). "The Steady-state economy: Toward a political economy of biopolitical equilibrium and moral growth" in Human Daly (ed.), *Economics, Ecology, Ethics: Essays Toward a Steady—State Economy*. New York : WH Freeman & Co.

Georgescu-Roegen, Nicholas (1971). *The Entropy Law and the Economic Process*. Cambridge Mass: Harward University Press.

Gundappa, D.V. (2001 Nov Edn.). *Shrimad—Bhagavadgita—Taatparya athavaa Jeevana-dharma: Yoga*, (Kannada). Mysore: Kavyalaya.

Hahn, F. (1973). *On the Notion of Equilibrium in Economics*. Cambridge.

Kane, P.V. (1990, first edn. 1930-62). *History of Dharmashastra*. Poona: Bhandarkar Oriental Research Institute (in five volumes).

Kapp, K.W. (1963). *Hindu Culture, Economic Development and Economic Planning*. New Delhi: Asia Publishing House.

Lal, Deepak (1988). *The Hindu Equilibrium, Vol. I Cultural Stability and Economic Stagnation: India* C.1500 BC – AD 1980. Oxford: Clarendon Press.

———. (1989). *The Hindu Equilibrium, Vol. II Aspects of Indian Labour*. Oxford: Clarendon Press.

Meadows, D.H., D.L. Meadows, J. Randers and W. Bervens (1972). *The Limits to Growth*. London: Pan Books.

Nadkarni, M.V. (2003). "Is caste system intrinsic to Hinduism? Demolishing a myth", in *Economic and Political Weekly* 38(45): 4783-93. 8 November.

Nye, Malory (2003). *Religion—The Basics*. London: Routledge.

Prime, Ranchor (1994). *Hinduism and Ecology: Seeds of Truth*. London: Cassell Publication.

Radhakrishnan, S. (1999: first publ. 1923). *Indian Philosophy*. New Delhi: Oxford India Paperback. Vol.2.

———. (1989: first publ. 1939). *Eastern Religions and Western Thought*. New Delhi: Oxford India Paperback, p.27.

Rajagopalachari, C. (1999–9th edn: first edn in 1965). *Kural: The Great Book of Tiruvalluvar*. Mumbai: Bharatiya Vidya Bhavan.

Rangarajan, L.N. (ed.) (1992). *Kautilya: Arthashastra*. New Delhi: Penguin India.

Russell, Bertrand (1960 edn; first in 1935). *In Praise of Idleness and Other Essays*. London: George Allen and Unwin.

Saksena, S.K. (1968) "The individual and social though and practice in India", in Charles A. Moore (ed.), *The Status of the Individual in East and West*. Honolulu: University of Hawaii Press. pp.347-359.

Schweitzer, Albert (1936). *Indian Thought and its Development*.

Shah, K.J. (1982). "Of artha and the arthasastra", in T.N. Madan (eds.), *Way of Life: King, Householder, Renouncer—Essays in Honour of Louis Dumont*. New Delhi: Vikas Publication. pp.55-73.

Sharma, Arvind (1996). *Hinduism for Our Times*. Delhi: Oxford University Press.

———. (1980). *The Hindu Scriptural Value System and the Economic Development of India*. New Delhi: Heritage.

Singer, Milton (1972). *When a Great Tradition Modernizes—An Anthropological Approach to Indian Civilization*. New York: Praeger.

Srinivas, M.N. and A.M. Shah (1968). "Hinduism", in David L. Sills (ed.), *International Encyclopedia of Social Sciences* 6: 358-366. The Macmillan Co. & the Free Press.

Sundaram, P.S. (1990). *Tiruvalluvar: The Kural, Translated from the Tamil with an Introduction*. New Delhi: Penguin.

Thakur, Vijay Kumar (2001). "Surgery in early India: A note on the development of medical science", in Deepak Kumar (ed.), *Disease and Medicine in India: A Historical Overview*. New Delhi: Tulika Books.

Weber, Max (2nd edn 1976; first in 1930). *The Protestant Ethic and the Spirit of Capitalism*. London: George Allen and Unwin.

White, Lynn Jr. (1967). "The historical roots of our ecological crisis", in *Science* 155: 1203-7.

World Commission on Environment and Development (1987). *Our Common Future* (Brundtland Commission Report). Oxford and New York: Oxford University Press.

5 Some Recent Developments on Measures of Quality of Life

Gopal K. Kadekodi

5.1 Introduction

To most statisticians of first day lesson, quality of life is synonymous to having good income. One need not disagree with that. But in the complexity of the world we live today, there is more to add to this definition. It can mean different things to different people. To some, it may mean good health status; to some others, it can be good food (not necessarily 'good' seen only as nutritional, but also as an assortment of different foods with different tastes). To many others, it may mean attaining basic needs such as fuel, drinking water and minimum shelter.

One can go on adding literacy, basic education, minimal sanitation and many more to this list of defining quality of life. Many of these attributes are 'individual characterisation' of quality of life. But there are several newer attributes that can also be considered. Can one not consider a thing of music, art, literature or other cultural dimensions forming part of quality of life? Are we not concerned about dignity of life, or security of life? Many of these may be broadly defined as social, civic societal and political. Examples of social indicators are gender equity, security from atrocities (e.g., gender, communal, child abuse), dignity of work status and so on. Civic societal and political indicators are dignity of life, democratic norms, rights and symmetric information and transparency, free from corruption and so on.

One always wondered how to measure these and get a feel of an aggregated measure of quality of life (Dreze and Sen, 1995; Sen, 1976; Dasgupta, 1993; Arrow, 1954). Three major issues are relevant here, to be distinguished to make the discussion more scientific. They are, quality of life at individual *versus* at societal levels, qualitative *versus* quantitative measures, and finally quality of life over time (even over generations). This paper is aimed at addressing some of these issues for discussion. As the notions are refined, estimates of quality of life and several allied indicators based on data from some selected villages from India are presented and analysed.

5.2 Quality of Life at Individual Levels

A distinction should be made, between individual *versus* societal quality of life. Not that they are totally independent, but they have different messages for understanding and for any follow-up action or policy imperatives. Indicators of quality of life measured at individual levels are very useful to take more and more precise and corrective policy measures to improve them. Given the fact that the society is more and more divided at the individual levels, measures of quality of life at individual levels are more easily understandable and appreciated.

However, for a country of about 1200 million people as in India, it may be too ambitious to construct individual indices of quality of life, though it would have been most desirable. Apart from this practical problem, there is a conceptual problem of aggregating a variety of attributes into one index to measure quality of life for each individual. One does not know how to add quality of dwelling (say *kuccha* house, *pucca* house, tiled house or/and RCC building) with say, amount of food consumption. Any monetary measure, even if worked out is devoid of aggregation problem.[1] Second, aggregation requires weighing different attributes. One does not know how to arrive at a unique set of weights to aggregate different attributes applicable to all individuals. The relative weights can differ from individual to individual. Third, even after arriving at some reasonable set of weights, there can be questions regarding interpretation of individual aggregated indices. Are they comparable between individuals? Can one say that one with an aggregated index of say, 1.5 is better than another individual with 1.3?

1. Suggestions such as adding annualised fixed assets with flows such as expenditures on food, clothing are mentioned and used by statisticians.

The answer depends upon how much weight the individual puts on different attributes of quality of life. Consider a case of an individual, who does not like to live in his own built house, but to stay only in a rented house, however shabby or inconvenient it may be. But he may like to have apples every day, be it winter or summer, be it at Rs. 30 a kg. or Rs. 100. Whose quality of life better? That is the kind of problems on which statisticians and social scientists in general have not been able resolve much.[2] Economic science took a safe course on this by saying that one does not indulge in 'inter-personal comparison'. But then, we still compare each other, for allocation and use of resources or policy statements. In general therefore, it is not practical to attempt constructing individual indices of quality of life.

5.3 Quality of Life at Geographical Scales or Societal Levels

An aggregated picture on quality of life, over geographical scales may have more useful messages. It may represent a measure of quality of life for a geographically confined population. But the question is how to construct an index, say for a state, or India as a whole? Or for that matter, at district, *panchayat* or village levels? This still requires some ways of aggregation over individuals and on geographical scales. This was the kind of problems that was faced in the middle of 19th century when the utilitarian school was emerging. Then, the issue was one of making sense from measuring welfare. Welfare may be measurable, but not its utility. A simple example will set this matter clear. Two persons A and B with incomes Rs. 100 and 200 respectively are comparable in their welfare sense, saying that B is better off twice as much as A. But the same can not be said about their utilities. Therefore, it was not easy to say that while the average welfare is Rs. 150 per capita, the same could not be said about average utilities. It was only in 1944 when von Neumann and Morgenstern came out with their postulate on the expected utility measures that one could estimate the average utility. Averaging is quite well known to statisticians. But the real question is one of getting the associated probability function (Savage, 1954).

2. McFadden (2001) refers to psychology of choice of consumer behaviour and makes an attempt at modelling discrete and continuous random choice models.

Dealing with societal and individual (i.e., personal) matters, one does not have a good theory of arriving at the probability laws in order to aggregate the preferences. Scholars such as Marschack, 1950; Arrow, 1954; Sen, 1977 dealt with this issue, and came to the conclusion that individual voting perhaps can be used, provided there are no interferences such as dictatorship. Much of the recent development on getting aggregated values on quality of life at societal level is based on such notions of equally weighted votings. In the process, we have forgotten the methodology suggested by von Neumann and Morgenstern.

Do we really need an aggregated measure of quality of life on a geographical scale? The answer is 'yes' for a specific policy purpose of measuring 'development with a human face'. This was the kind of issues raised when a concept of Human Development Index was first introduced (UNDP, 1990). There are severe limitations on the methods of computing such aggregative indices. There are further problems of interpreting them for purposes of policy making. Newer and newer dimensions are constantly being added to make the measure more and more representative of what sociologists would call 'qualitatively defined human development'.

Invariably, the aggregated measure is a linear additive function of various attributes as a transformation of the difference between the maximum and minimum of each attribute, and its actual. Since a large number of individuals are involved in between the maximum and minimum of the attribute, the probability distribution of that attribute is totally ignored. Consider the problem with an example from income distribution itself. While the range of income as maximum minus the minimum has some meaning, the income distribution itself is not taken into account in the aggregative measure based on such range measures. Similarly, in constructing an attribute of 'longevity of life', the difference between 85 years as the maximum and say 50 as the minimum of expectation of life at birth for the whole society (or country) are used as the measure. Clearly, the probability distribution of the population over the age groups is ignored. One can go on with several such examples.

5.4 Measuring Human Development: The Present Status

There have been considerable improvements recently on measuring human development, though the history of the world always debated on this. Starting with the first report of UNDP, *Human Development Report, 1990,* a large number of attempts have been made globally and nationally even in India, including the one by the Indian Planning Commission in 2001. Invariably, it is understood that given the complex mix of a large number of quality of life attributes involved, only some of them could be used to construct indices of human development. Three major attributes normally agreed are: longevity of life (measured as expectation of life at birth), knowledge (measured as literacy as access to knowledge), and command over resources needed for a decent living (measured by per capita income). It is further argued in the UNDP report of 1990 that these also reflect deprivation, and hence, it is a measure of quality of life. This is said to be attained from the measures of minimum and maximum of these attributes, and the distances from the maximum (as measures of deprivation) are to be estimated for a country.[3] Over time, different methods of aggregating these three attributes are evolved to improve its policy use. Among the many, mention can be made about gender development index, gender equity index, deprivation index etc. Attempts in India by the Planning Commission (2001), NCAER (1999), several state governments including Karnataka and Madhya Pradesh also followed roughly the same procedure. Planning Commission (2001) in its report improved the method by adjusting the attributes further in a number of ways. Inflation and inequality have been incorporated in the income or consumption measure; composite index of education is based on literacy and formal education; infant mortality has been added. Karnataka and several other states have estimated the HDIs at the district level.

Some of the major views, criticisms and challenges on these measures may be worth mentioning here. They are: measures reflecting attainment and deprivation or deficiency are not simply the two sides of

---

3. To the extent, the maximum and the minimum are contested limits, these measures can be questioned.

the coin. The indicators of attainment and that of deprivations can be different and there can be different degree of biases in their measurements. It is not as simple as saying 'disutility is the negative of utility'. Therefore, some kind of weighting diagram is necessary between them. Second, meanings of minimum and maximum values on these attributes (to be specified in advance) are very contextual. Third, absolute *versus* the probability distributional characteristics of the attributes make lot of difference in interpretations. Finally, fundamental distinction between 'point estimates' *versus* 'range estimates' based on variances or measures of dispersion always remains.

5.4.1 Quality in Qualitative Sense

There is a much more serious problem of measuring quality of life involving non-quantifiable attributes. When it comes to several civic society matters, the measures are likely to be more and more qualitative than quantitative. It is this aspect of the measures wherein the advancement in theory and application has been rather poor. Much of the social science approach on this is based on what is known as revealed preference of individuals. In doing so, only the individual preferences or orderings matter, which are not necessarily the societal matters. For instance, individually whether one prefers a clean road or not (an important indicator of quality of life, for sure) depends upon one's reveal on 'how much she or he is willing to pay' for it. One may not be willing to pay for it, given the choice of individual preferences. But as a societal matter, one may express that she or he is willing to pay for it. Likewise, there are counter examples to say that while people are willing to pay (an indicator of revealed preference) for water connection at the individual household levels, they may not like to pay for a public (i.e., societal level) water supply. Such basic difference comes from what is known as 'distinction between an individual and a citizen' (Blamey *et al.*, 1995). Hence is also the difference in the rankings towards quality of life. Since many social issues are non-tangible (i.e., non-measurable in physical or monetary terms), constructing a geographically definable index or measure of quality of life is still more difficult. The relative rankings could differ when people are asked to express their views as individuals, as citizens or collectively as a society. Devoid of a good theory, one does not interpret them as equivalent, or even integrate them. This may happen with matters such as importance of a forest, wildlife surrounding, clean air and water, good lighting, good roads, transparent information system and access to it, social amenities such as PHCs, schools, post office and so on.

The recently advanced theories of 'stated preference' are aiming at measures to bringing the societal preferences close to revealed individual preferences (McFadden, 2001; Adamowicz *et al.*, 1994; Hausman, 1993; Kahneman and Knetsch, 1992a). They can help in bridging the gap between market based individually revealed attainments or values and hypothetically revealed social attainments and values by the same individuals. Stated statistically, the gap between qualitative indicators and quantitative indicators, and their additivity are being resolved. The conceptual questions are still many, so also statistical methods of aggregation of these two.

5.4.2 A Case Study of Four Villages and Measures of Quality of Life[4]

A case study wherein some demonstration of the aggregation problems towards measures on quality of life involving both 'individual and societal matters' and both 'qualitative and quantitative measures' is present, is useful to look at. Such a case study can help in developing a more precise theory of aggregation of individual and societal based indicators and integration of quantitative and qualitative attributes of quality of life.

Ralegaon Siddhi is a village in Ahmednagar district of Maharashtra that has witnessed considerable transformation in quality of village life. Some of the neighbouring villages also followed the same trajectory, but many others did not. Secondly, it was Kishan Baburao Hazare (affectionately known as Anna Hazare) who returned to his village Ralegaon Siddhi in August 1975, initiated the process of transforming the village. Since then, three phases of village transformation can be highlighted: first, the phase of the village before Shri Hazare; second, the phase of his working on the village to improve the quality of life; and

4. Much of this section is drawn from Antia and Kadekodi (2002).

third as the period when he transferred the development tasks to the village communities in the village (for having moved to national level problems). As a contrast, three other villages may also be mentioned from the neighbourhood. Village Hirawe Bazar also had followed the paths of village development, but not under the guidance of Shri Hazare, but Shri Popatlal Pawar. This village has also has gone through several aspects of social and individual transformations, all adding to improved quality of life. On the other hand, an adjacent village to Ralegaon, namely Jategaon went through continued downturn in development, whereas the village Siri Koldara has been going through the 'usual' development, normally being observed universally (in the language of statisticians, one may coin this situation as a control village).

Let us take a look at Ralegaon village first. Can we measure the development of this village, in some what unconventional way, away from measures such as per capita income or investment or growth rate? The answer depends on how best one is able to measure the quality of life in the village. Table 5.1 shows the typically measurable attributes of village life, shown for the three phases of the village mentioned above. All the data are based on complete enumeration of the village households.

Table 5.1

Relative Position of Village Level Quality Life: In Three Phases of Time

Attributes	*Unit*	*Pre-Anna*	*Intensive Phase of Transformation*	*Mature Phase*	*Comments*
Family size	Average no.	3.33	2.87	1.48	Family size has gone down
Families having *pucca* houses	%	1.95	17.34	44.92	Better house conditions now
Families living in huts	%	32.47	16.76	5.88	Decline in poverty
Use of wood as cooking fuel	% of families	76.06	79.01	36.14	Decline in poverty
Use of LPG as cooking gas	% of families	0.00	2.47	20.18	Improvement in income status
Use of tap water	% of families	0.68	8.98	33.15	Improved quality of life
Use of community tap for water	% of families	2.03	7.78	18.48	Improved social amenities

Contd...

...contd...

Attributes	*Unit*	*Pre-Anna*	*Intensive Phase of Transformation*	*Mature Phase*	*Comments*
Use of water from open well	% of families	87.16	60.48	23.91	Decline in poverty
Distance travelled to fetch water	Average relative scale	2.72	2.03	1.28	Hardship reduced: Gender gain
Time spent in fetching water	Average minutes	43.30	35.10	25.67	Hardship reduced: Gender gain
Use of open field as toilet space	% of families	51.97	41.52	34.97	Improved hygiene
Use of community toilet	% of families	3.29	18.71	20.22	Improved social amenities
Family income	Average Rs.	9,000	17,040	20,000	Welfare
Crossbreed animals	% of families	1.45	12.71	33.83	Improved family asset position
Desi cows	% of families	49.28	44.92	15.04	Improved income avenues
Free grazing	% of families	32.80	10.75	6.45	Degradation of CPR reduced
Stall feeding	% of families	8.60	33.87	43.55	Social fencing
Milk yield (Litres)	Av. per family	1.58	3.49	4.96	Improved income
Milk consumed (Litres)	Av. per family	0.88	1.18	1.37	Improved nutrition
Own land as source for fuelwood	% of families	41.94	60.22	63.44	Self-sufficiency
Own land as source of fodder	% of families	34.75	50.27	52.69	Self-sufficiency
Dependency of forest for fuelwood	% of families	22.58	10.75	5.38	Forest conservation
Dependency on forests for fodder	% of families	12.30	4.28	4.84	Forest conservation
Distance travelled for fuelwood collection	Relative scale	2.70	2.30	2.03	Hardship reduced: Gender bias reduced
Distance travelled for fodder collection	Relative scale	2.55	2.22	2.07	Hardship reduced: Gender bias reduced
Time spent in fuelwood collection	Average minutes	106	94	88	Hardship reduced: Gender bias reduced
Time spent in fodder collection	Average minutes	101	86	84	Hardship reduced: Gender bias reduced
Size of land owned	Av. ha. per family	4.00	3.88	3.30	Growth of nuclear families in the village

Note: The three phases are: Before Anna Hazare's arrival, when Anna was working in the village, and after he handed over the village to village community. All the sample data were put to a test of statistical significance for the emergence of various attributes under the three phases. Out of 17 such tests, (basically c^2-square tests of independence), all of them showed significant difference during and subsequent developmental phase.

Source: Primary data.

Given the variety of attributes, can one say anything concretely about the three phases of village development or transition in quality of life? How does one gets a comprehensive picture of quality of life in the village? Multi-criterion analysis (MCA) is a recently developed method, which helps in the aggregation process over a variety of attributes or criteria (Arrow and Raynaud, 1986; Munda, 1995; 1993). When confronted with a variety of attributes with different units of measurements, to be aggregated into one index, the task becomes complicated if they are not easily additive. Secondly, aggregating qualitative and quantitative attributes is even more difficult. In the MCA, the individual values of all those attributes are organised as if they are coming from certain probability distribution and hence, they can be aggregated using the probability laws. Essentially, it is a variant of what von Neumann and Morgenstern propagated as a notion of expected utility in place of simple methods of linear aggregations of outcomes. Using the expected value method, the average aggregated ranks (scores) are computed for the quality of life in the three phases of Ralegaon village. For the purpose of analysis, the variables from the primary survey were grouped into four different categories according to: quality of life; hardship in living; personal status; and social status.

Table 5.2 shows the variables considered for each of these welfare and development groups.

The relative rankings of these indicators obtained as aggregated scores or ranks are tabulated in Table 5.3. Except for 'personal status', all other aspects of rural life have been ranked significantly high after the watershed and other developmental programmes were launched in the village. More significant is the revelation that, the villagers have been participating in a systematic way promoting the village welfare. Hardships in obtaining various basic needs (such as water, fuelwood, fodder etc.) have come down radically from a score of 0.92 to 0.37. The quality of life has improved from an index of 0.23 to 0.97. The social status has also improved considerably during the last 25 years. In the process, the personal status also has improved.

The ultimate objective of the rural development is improved quality of life together with increased income. This is assessed based on a PRA exercise. 'Wealth ranking' is a method of grouping households on the basis of income, wealth and other local measures of well-being. A social map of Ralegaon village was drawn by the villagers at the common place known as Yadav Baba Mandir. On the basis of the village map, the villagers identified three different wealth groups, namely rich, medium and poor. They marked the households, which were poor according to their perception. These included landless labourers having no regular source of income. The medium group included those having marginal land, and temporary jobs in factory in 3rd or 4th grade service or small business or as permanent factory workers. The rest were described as having better income from land, employment and business.

Table 5.2

Indicators of Village Level Attributes

Quality of Life	*Hardship in Living*	*Social Status*	*Personal Status*
• *Pucca* housing • Kerosene for cooking and lighting • LPG for cooking • Electricity for lighting • Tapped drinking water • Community tap • Tap water for bathing • Minimised distance, no. of trips, time spent for water collection • Private toilet • Milk consumption upto 3 litres per day	• Hutment housing • Use of wood for cooking • House lighting with fuels other than electricity and kerosene • Water from open well • Long distance, long time spent, and more trips made in fetching water • Use of open field as toilet space • No drainage • Long distance and time spent in fuelwood and fodder collection • Scarcity of fuelwood and fodder	* Community tap * Community toilet * Stall feeding	* Private clinic * Regular job * Self-employed * Annual income * Possession of livestock * Possession of crossbreeds * Milk yield above 6 litres * Fuel wood from owned land * Fodder from own land

Note: Social aspects of education and health are dealt under FGD.

Table 5.3

Aggregated Scores (Rankings) of Ralegaon Village in Different Phases over the Years

Particulars	*Phase 1*	*Phase 2*	*Phase 3*
	Pre-Anna Phase	*Intensive Phase of Transformation*	*Mature Phase*
Quality of life (15)	0.23	0.54	0.97
Hardship in living (27)	0.92	0.62	0.37
Personal status (9)	0.59	0.83	0.94
Social status (3)	0.34	0.79	0.97

Note: Numbers in brackets are number of variables considered.

A large number of qualitative indicators are developed, based on the FGD and PRA exercises and case studies carried out in the four villages including Ralegaon. Table 5.4 shows the relative picture of the four villages on a qualitative scale. Using this information, relative rankings of the four villages are arrived at. Once again, using the MCA numerical scales based on perceptions and qualitative rankings from as many as 29 attributes are derived.[5] An integrated score for each village is deduced using appropriate probability specifications. Table 5.5 shows the rankings under different groupings of the human development and quality of life attributes. At the aggregate level, Ralegaon village achieves the highest score of 0.77, as against, 0.50 for Hirawe Bazar, 0.33 for Siri Koldara and 0.23 for Jategaon village. Furthermore, the following specific findings can be noted:

- In terms of social amenities, Ralegaon ranks highest, followed by Hirawe Bazar and Siri Koldara. Jategaon has very low status on this score.
- Social assets, however, are low in Siri Koldara, and also limited in Hirawe Bazar.
- Government investments are very low in Siri Koldara.
- Community participation is fairly good in all villages except Jategaon.
- Private and personal developments are highest in Jategaon, followed by Ralegaon and Hirawe Bazar.
- On the whole, Jategaon lags far behind; Ralegaon tops the list, followed by Hirawe Bazar.

5.5 Conclusion

When it comes to measures of quality of life, there have been a large number of theoretical and empirical advancements on developing indicators and deducing policy directives. But the development and challenges in the emerging world on such measures have opened up a large number of additional issues. Firstly, beyond individual level measures such as income, consumption or employment status, the societal and civic amenities matters such as dignity of life, security, right to information, transparency, social amenities, governance, inter-

5. A statistical decision model package called DEFINITE is used to derive the integrated scores.

Table 5.4

Ratings of Village Infrastructure

Sr. No.	*Infrastructure*	*Ralegaon*	*Jategaon*	*Hirawe Bazar*	*Siri Koldara*
1.	Watershed (Irrigation)	+++++	Nil	++++	+++
2.	Drinking water facility	+++++	Nil	++++	++
3.	Primary school	+++++	++	+++++	+++
4.	Hostel facility	++++	Nil	Nil	Nil
5.	Higher secondary	+++++	Nil	Nil Till 8th std	Nil
6.	Primary health centre	+++	+++	Sub	Nil
7.	Hospital	Private Clinic	Nil	Nil	Nil
8.	Post office	+++	Nil	Nil	Nil
9.	Telephone facility	++++	+	++++	+++
10.	Bank	++++	Nil	Nil	Nil
11.	Milk co-operative	++++	+++++	++++	++++
12.	Credit society	++++	Nil	Nil	Nil
13.	Youth *mandal*	+++++	Nil	++++	+++
14.	Self help group	+++++	+++	+++	++++
15.	Veterinary hospital	++	Nil	+++	Nil
16.	Prohibition of liquor	+++++	++	+++	+++
17.	Transportation	+++++	++	++	++
18.	Adult education	—	+	—	+
19.	Temple as a centre of social activity	+++++	++	++	++
20.	Social forestation	+++++	—	+++++	++++
21.	Health awareness esp. about AIDS	+	—	—	—
22.	Fodder	++++	+	+++++	++
23.	Fuel LPG gas	++++	++++	+++	+
24.	Dependency on fuel wood	+	+++	++	+++
25.	Street lights	++	—	+++	Nil
26.	*Shramadaan* for public works	+++++	+	+++++	+++
27.	Organisation of social functions with local participation	+++++	+	+++++	+++
28.	Grain bank	+++++	—	—	—
29.	Flour mill	+++	+	++	+

Note: Excellent: +++++ Very Good: ++++ Good: +++
Average: ++ Low: + Poor: —

Table 5.5

Relative Dimensions of Rural Transformation

Development Indicator	*Ralegaon*	*Hirawe Bazar*	*Siri Koldara*	*Jategaon*
Social amenities	0.83	0.68	0.53	0.20
Social assets	0.81	0.37	0.16	0.20
Govt. investments	0.79	0.51	0.26	0.15
Community participation	0.89	0.67	0.53	0.29
Private	0.68	0.60	0.47	0.72
Over all dev.	0.77	0.50	0.33	0.23

generational bequeathing, and likewise, several ethical matters such as disease incidence and prevalence, fear of mind and social stigma etc., are equally important in measuring quality of life. Such attributes and measures open up more and more challenges for social scientists, statisticians and mathematicians to evolve scientific methods with minimal limitations.

Secondly, more than point estimates, the measures of their dispersal or range are far more informative to understand quality of life for better policy interventions. This is a matter of having good estimates of the associated probability distributions and their stochastic changes over time.

Thirdly, recent development in multi-criterion analysis has enabled to integrate quantitative and qualitative indicators (mainly order preserving types) and deduce some measures for policy purposes. Finally, challenges still remain as far as the 'individual *versus* societal' level values and preferences are concerned. Because of this, integration of societal and individual rankings is still prompted by normative considerations rather than on perceptions by people on their implications for quality of life.

References

Adamowicz, W., J. Louviere and M. Williams (1994). "Combining revealed and stated preference methods for valuing environmental amenities", *Journal of Environmental Economics and Management* 26: 271-292.

Antia, N.H. and Gopal K. Kadekodi (2002). *Dynamics of Rural Development: Lessons from Ralegan Siddhi*. The Foundation for Research in Community Health and Centre for Multi-Disciplinary Development Research, Pune.

Arrow, K.J. (1954). *Social Choice and Individual Values*. NY: Wiley.

Arrow, K.J. and H. Raynaud (1986). *Social Choice and Multi-criterion Decision Making*. Cambridge, MA: MIT Press.

Blamey, R., M. Common and J. Quiggin (1995). "Respondents to contingent valuation surveys: Consumers or citizens?", *Australian Journal of Agricultural Economics* 39(3): 262-288.

Dasgupta, Partha (1993). *An Inquiry into Well-being and Destitution*. Oxford: Clarendon Press.

Dreze, Jean and Amartya Sen (1989). *Hunger and Public Action*. New Delhi: Oxford University Press.

————. (1995). *India-Economic Development and Social Opportunity*. New Delhi: Oxford University Press.

Government of India, Planning Commission (2001). *National Human Development Report 2001*.

Government of Karnataka (1999). *Human Development in Karnataka*.

Hausman, J. (ed.) (1993). *Contingent Valuation: A Critical Assessment*. Amsterdam: North Holland Publication.

Kahneman, D. and J. Knetsch (1992b). "Contingent valuation and the value of public goods: Reply", *Journal of Environmental Economics and Management* 22(1): 90-94.

————. (1992a). "Valuing public goods: The purchase of moral satisfaction", *Journal of Environmental Economics and Management* 22(1): 57-70.

Marschak, J. (1950). *Rational Behavior, Uncertain Prospects, and Measurable Utility*. Cheltenham, U.K.: Elgar Publisher.

McFadden, D. (2001). "Economic choices", American *Economic Review* 91(3): 351-378.

Munda, G. (1993). "Multi-criteria decision aid: Some epistemological considerations", *Journal of Multi-Criteria Decision Analysis* 2: 41-55.

————. (1995). *Multicriteria Evaluation in a Fuzzy Environment: Theory and Applications in Ecological Economics*. Physica-Verlag-Heidelberg.

National Council of Applied Economic Research (1999). *India Human Development Report*.

Savage, L.J. (1954). *Foundations of Statistics*. New York: John Hopkins & Sons.

Sen, Amartya (1976). "Poverty-An ordinal approach to measurement", *Econometrica* 44(2), March.

————. (1977). "On weights and measures: Informational constraints in social welfare analysis", *Econometrica* 45, October.

United Nations Development Programme (1990). *Human Development Report*.

von Neumann, J. and Morgenstern, Oskar (1953). *Theory of Games and Economic Behaviour*. Princeton: Princeton University Press.

6 Kerala's Turnaround in Growth Role of Social Development, Remittances and Reform

K.P. Kannan

6.1 The Problem

While Kerala is well known for its remarkable achievements in social (and human) development, it is also referred to as a 'paradox of social development and economic backwardness'.[1] Despite a high level of social development, the disappointing performance of the economy led to a series of studies and debates. The generalised stagnation of the economy during the period 1975-76 to 1986-87 was the starting point for a number of studies on specific commodity producing and infrastructure sectors (see Kannan, 1990 and the papers in the special issues of the *Economic and Political Weekly* XXV(26&27), September 8 and 15, 1990). One of the scholars went to the extent of talking in terms of the 'limits to the Kerala model of development' based on the deteriorating public finance situation in Kerala (George, 1993). An International Congress on Kerala Studies held in 1994 debated the issue and witnessed a plethora of papers focused, among other things, on the economy of Kerala with a view to search for credible explanations and possible solutions (for a report on the Congress, see, Isaac and Tharakan, 1995). Popular print media was also actively involved in these debates and

1. This was the sub-title of a study on health status in Kerala by Panikar and Soman (1984) reflecting the mismatch between social development and economic growth.

provided a forum for the dissemination of various views.[2] Internationally, a debate was conducted in the *Bulletin of Concerned Asian Scholars* (30(1,3&4), 1998) that sought to raise issue of Kerala's 'development impasse' in the larger political economy context.[3] An earlier but short debate on Kerala's development experience drawing attention to its 'radical reform as development' appeared in the famed *Monthly Review* (see Frankie and Chasin, 1991; Amin, 1991 and Rammohan, 1991).

On balance, one finds that the western scholars have been net admirers (net of criticisms) of Kerala's development experience (often referred to as the 'Kerala Model') while scholars from Kerala, on an average, have been less enthusiastic about mere celebration of the human development achievements.

Economic analysis is very often conducted on an *ex post* basis. At the height of these debates, the Kerala economy was changing quietly leading to a different trajectory of growth that was no longer in consonance with the trend so far. However, it is my view that the issues raised in these debates—such as the fiscal crisis of the state in Kerala, the continuing high unemployment mostly of the educated, the slow but steady grip of a culture of rent-seeking, the contradictory

2. Issues in development continue to be an attractive topic for debate in the print media in Malayalam, the language of Kerala. The origin of this interest could perhaps be located in the issues of land reform and education that dominated the agenda of the first Communist Ministry in 1957. Later, especially in the mid-seventies, a number of people's organisations revived this debate with emerging issues and alternative perspectives. The people's science movement (known in Kerala as the Kerala Sastra Sahitya Parishad) was in the forefront of initiating such a debate with the publication of a volume titled *Keralathinte Sampath* (Kerala's Wealth) and its wide dissemination. Popular magazines in Malayalam often publish articles on developmental issues and initiates debates. A recent example is that by a weekly, *Malayalam Varika*, which debated the 'developmental impasse' week for a period of four months from 6 November 1998 to 5 March 1999, with contributions from a cross-section of political leaders, academicians and social activists. A recent volume containing selected papers on the development debate is edited by Sreekumar and Sajeev (2003).
3. The debate was initiated by Tharamangalam (1998) who reiterated and elaborated by the then well known observation that the 'Kerala Model' with its high social development has not been able to initiate a process of economic development necessary to make the social development sustainable. Some contributors agreed with this while others disputed it vigorously. See the contributions of Franke and Chasin, Omvedt, Heller, George, Govindan, Parameswaran and Tornquist (all 1998).

position of the organised working class in opposing technological change while successfully bargaining for higher wages and other benefits, and the inability of the state to attract adequate investment arising out of a negative image as an 'investor-unfriendly state'—remain pertinent and each of them deserve further detailed study and analysis. Despite these formidable constraints, the Kerala economy started responding to the national economic reforms initiated from the second half of the eighties. Such a response was made possible by two emerging undercurrents which in turn was the consequence of the high level of social development. These are: (i) the demographic transition, and (ii) the uninterrupted international labour migration started from the early seventies. The revival in growth has now covered a period of 15 years and the long-term average growth rate is close to six per cent per annum, which is also the national average for this period.

This paper is a modest attempt to place the debate on Kerala's 'lopsided development' in a balanced perspective by analysing the turnaround in growth that may well be the beginning of a virtuous cycle of growth based on human development. However, the sustenance and the realisation of the full potential of this virtuous cycle hinges, in my view, on the resolution of the main issues and constraints that were the subjects of the debates mentioned earlier.

6.2 From Stagnation to Growth

It was Ahluwalia's study (2000) that first highlighted the impressive growth performance of Kerala while examining the performance of the states in India. It benchmarked 1991 for examining the growth performance of the states since that year constituted the initiation of a new national economic policy by the Government of India in favour of increasing liberalisation both internally and externally. Subrahmanian and Azeez (2000) adopted the same logic while examining the performance of the manufacturing sector in Kerala *vis-à-vis* its neighbours and all India. As a prelude to our empirical exercise, a graphical analysis of the growth of the net state domestic product (NSDP) was carried out. It showed a kink in the trend in 1987-88 not only for the NSDP but also for the three broad sectors. Further, graphical analysis at the sub-sectoral level also showed a kink in 1987-88 or its neighbourhood. Therefore, this year has been taken as a break period for this study on the economic performance of Kerala covering more than three decades. The beginning of the period is taken as 1970-1971 since we wanted to start with the period before the international labour migration from Kerala (mainly to the countries in the Gulf). The revival in growth since 1987-88 however falls in the period when a limited form of economic reforms aimed at internal liberalisation was started in the country since 1985. Therefore, the beginning in the turnaround came immediately after the initiation of the first set of economic reforms; however the growth rate accelerated with the onset of the expanded economic reforms that included liberalisation of the external sector.[4]

By taking a long period of 30 years that starts prior to the labour migration to the Gulf countries, we are in a position to examine Kerala's growth performance in a long-term perspective. There is only one kink in the growth trend that falls on 1987-88. Therefore, the whole period is divided into two sub-periods; the first characterised by very low growth in state income (NSDP) and near stagnation in per capita growth and the second characterised by a turnaround and an acceleration in growth followed by a regime of stable growth. The overall growth performance along with that of the three main sectors for Kerala in comparison to all India is presented in Table 6.1.

The revival of the Kerala economy's growth in the second period is such that it has never before witnessed such an impressive performance since the formation of the state in 1956.[5] While Kerala's aggregate growth rate in the first period was considerably below that of all India,

---

4. The data on net domestic product (NDP) at the all India level were collected from various issues of National Accounts Statistics. The study uses the NSDP data published by the Central Statistical Organisation (CSO) in their publication, *Estimates of State Domestic Product in India*. The period of study is 1970-71 to 2002-03. The splicing method is used to make all the years data at 1980-81 prices. The growth rates of NSDP of Kerala shows that the growth rate is not uniform throughout the period. The rate is different before and after 1987-88. As a result we have to estimate growth rates separately for two sub-periods, 1970-71 to 1986-87 and 1987-88 to 2002-03. These were estimated using the kinked exponential model developed by Boyce (1986).
5. In an earlier paper, we had examined the growth rate during the sixties to the mid-seventies (1962-63 to 1974-75). During this period, the Kerala economy registered an aggregate growth rate of 3.21 per cent and a per capita growth rate of 1.11 per cent (see Kannan, 1990).

in the second period it has come close to the all India performance.[6] In per capita terms, the relative performance in the second period is much more impressive due to the 'demographic advantage' in the form of low population growth that Kerala has come to enjoy. As such, the per capita growth in income is 25 per cent higher than the all India rate. While the per capita growth during the first period was only half-a-per cent per annum, it was more than 5 per cent during the second period. Thus, Kerala appears to have gone past the syndrome of high social development and low economic growth that has been the central theme of much of the debate mentioned earlier.

Table 6.1

Sectoral Growth Rate of Net State Domestic Product (1993-94 Prices)

Sector	*Kerala*		*All India*	
	Period I	*Period II*	*Period I*	*Period II*
Primary sector	-0.14	2.90	2.69	3.47
Secondary sector	2.38	6.13	5.02	6.53
Tertiary sector	3.28	7.55	5.19	7.48
Aggregate	1.89	5.79	4.08	5.98
Per capita NSDP/GDP	0.52	5.03	1.87	4.01

Note: Period I = 1970-71 to 1986-87 and Period II = 1987-88 to 2002-03.
Source: The Table is based on 1) *National Account Statistics* (Various issues) and 2) *Estimates of State Domestic Product* in India, published by Central Statistical Organisation, Ministry of Statistics and Programme Implementation, Government of India. Please refer to footnote no. 4 for complete details.

The sectoral growth performance also brings out a few important changes. First of all, the turnaround in growth is contributed by all three sectors of the economy. While the tertiary sector remains the lead sector in both the periods, the performance of the secondary sector (industry and construction) is quite impressive. Though a similar pattern is discernible at all India level too, the relatively slow growth of the primary sector (more so in Kerala than all India) is to be noted. From this picture of sectoral growth, it would appear that the growth performance in the Kerala economy has kept pace with the all India trend. In order to examine whether this is really the case at a more disaggregated level, we examined the growth performance for the 14 sub-sectors of the economy. The results are given in Table 6.2.

6. In fact, the growth performance of Kerala between 1987-88 and 1998-99 was marginally higher than all India. During the last few years, the growth rate seems to have declined leading to the long-term average being less than, even if marginally, all India.

Table 6.2

Sub-sectoral Annual Growth Rates of Net State Domestic Product

Sl No.	Industry	Kerala		All India	
		Period I	Period II	Period I	Period II
1.1	Agriculture	0.17	3.0	2.76	3.31
1.2	Forestry & logging	-2.49	40.3	-1.44	1.02
1.3	Fishing	-2.61	23.13	4.37	6.81
1.4	Mining & quarrying	6.10	7.80	6.45	5.45
	Primary Sector	-0.14	2.90	2.69	3.47
2	Manufacturing	3.10	5.18	5.36	6.75
2.1	Registered	4.13	5.47	5.81	7.24
2.2	Unregistered	1.89	4.96	4.64	5.89
3	Construction	4.06	5.72	3.34	5.53
4	Electricity, gas and water supply	-0.05	16.01	7.78	7.04
	Secondary Sector	2.38	6.13	5.02	6.53
5	Transport, storage and communication	6.55	12.71	5.45	7.37
6	Trade, hotels and restaurants	0.88	6.29	4.79	7.12
7	Banking & insurance	9.19	12.21	8.63	11.51
8	Real estate, ownership of dwellings and business services	-0.71	-20.15	5.63	7.18
9	Public administration	8.77	6.40	5.72	5.82
10	Other services	3.27	6.14	3.70	7.05
	Tertiary Sector	3.28	7.55	5.19	7.48
	NSDP/GDP	1.89	5.79	4.08	5.98

Note: Period I = 1970-71 to 1986-87 and Period II = 1987-88 to 2002-03.

Source: Same as Table 6.1.

In the primary sector, Kerala's lead is only in mining and quarrying (related to the demand for sand and granites for construction) while in the secondary sector it is in construction and electricity, gas and water supply. Three sub-sectors in the tertiary sector have registered a lead over all India namely, transport, storage and communication, banking and insurance, and public administration. On the whole, Kerala seems to be marching along with the all India situation and its better performance should be seen as a catching-up process because of its considerably lagged behaviour in the first period. As we shall see later, the remittance factor seems to have helped in the catching-up process leading to a situation where the Kerala per capita income is now well above the all India level.

A few more remarks are called for while interpreting the growth performance for the whole period. The growth performance is in terms of the domestic product. For Kerala, this imposes a serious limitation because of the significant size of remittances it receives from its people abroad. This only means that the stagnation during the first period must have been somewhat offset by the accrual of income from abroad. As we shall see later, this will be shown as a higher per capita income than the official figures. Secondly, since the remittances are not counted in the state income, the growth in income for both the periods must have been somewhat higher than the ones based on domestic product. That would place the performance in the second period in a more favourable light than has been revealed here.

Figure 6.1

Trend in State Income (NSDP) of Kerala

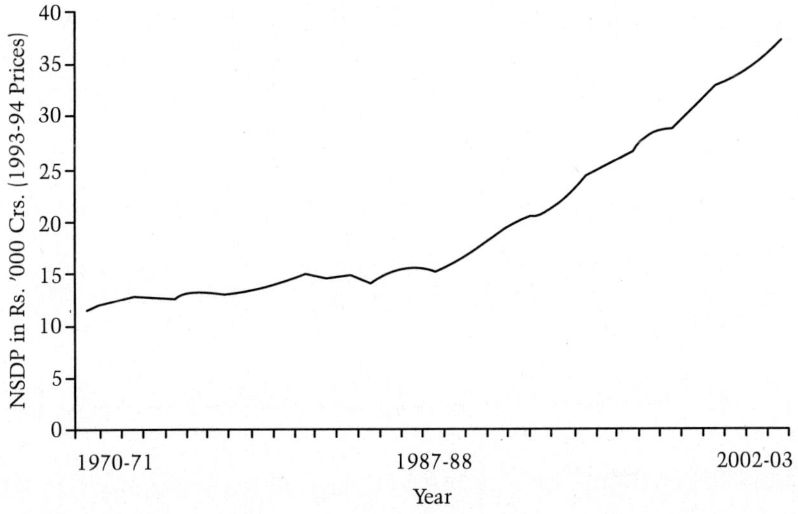

6.3 Linking Remittances and Reform to High Growth

The debate on India's economic performance during the nineties has linked the economic reform as a proximate cause for the high growth regime. However, it is also well known that the growth performance during the eighties has been equally impressive. This is also seen to be an outcome of the limited but significant reforms initiated during the early eighties but picked up faster since the mid-eighties under the Prime Ministership of Rajiv Gandhi.

In the case of Kerala, the turnaround in growth is immediately after the economic reforms started during the mid-eighties. We hypothesise that the proximate reason for the turnaround in Kerala's economic growth is the economic reforms initiated during the mid-eighties. The acceleration and intensification of these reforms from the beginning of the nineties seems to have provided further impetus to the growth process. However, for such a low income economy as Kerala with a weak industrial sector, the economic reforms *per se* could not have triggered such a high growth regime spanning over a period of more than 15 years now. We, therefore, further hypothesise that the underlying factor in generating such a high growth regime was the income received from abroad and its persistence in the form of flow of remittances to the Kerala economy. An important outcome of economic reforms i.e., the discontinuation of fixed-exchange rate system in favour of a market-determined one, seems to have contributed to the strengthening of the role of remittances. It meant a higher rate of growth in remittance income as a result of the depreciation of the rupee. From a long-term point of view, it is important to locate the increasing role of remittances in the Kerala economy. This means that the international labour migration was an unintended but positive consequence of the slow but steady process of social development attained in Kerala. A generalised process of enhancement of basic capabilities of the people (e.g. increasing educational attainments, better health and heightened awareness of opportunities beyond one's locale) made it possible, especially for the younger generation, to seize job opportunities abroad. Here it is pertinent to note that nearly two-thirds of migrants from Kerala to the Gulf countries have only school level of education with skills in such manual work as construction, building maintenance, driving and related occupations.[7] It is this linkage of social development with remittances that could respond positively to economic reforms to break out of the low growth/stagnation trap that Kerala found itself in for more than a decade prior to 1987. This warrants an explanation as to why

7. This was the situation during the late 1990s. A recent CDS survey (2003) suggest that this ratio has declined to 50 per cent indicating an increasing share of better educated among the emigrants. For example, between 1999 and 2004 the share of graduates and above increased from 10 to 20 per cent (see Zachariah *et al.*, 2004).

remittances did not act as a catalyst in the first period and how it worked itself out in the second period. A tentative explanation is attempted here.

Although Kerala was a net in-migrating state till the 1930s, it quickly turned itself into a net out-migrating state with the onset of the economic depression of the thirties (see Zachariah *et al.*, 2003: Ch.2). A high rate of growth of population (largely due to faster decline in mortality) without commensurate economic growth meant the continuation of the net out-migration phenomenon. However, a significant part of this migration was to other parts of India. As a result of the oil boom in the Gulf countries, Kerala's labour started responding almost immediately to the boom in demand for labour in those countries. Starting on a modest scale in early seventies it continued to grow. Based on a primary survey of ten thousand households conducted by the CDS, it was estimated that there were 1.36 million people who maintain a household link in Kerala working abroad.[8] Of this, around 95 per cent were in the Gulf countries[9] (see Zachariah *et al.*, 2003: 129).

Since the remittances are not counted in the computation of state domestic product, they are not reflected in the calculation of per capita income for the state. Remittance income data are available only for the country as a whole and not for its constituent provinces and hence difficult to find out the exact magnitudes. A number of attempts have been made to estimate remittances for Kerala, for example, by attributing a certain share according to the Kerala's share of Indian workers abroad (e.g. Gulati and Mody, 1983) or by indirectly estimating by taking a proxy variable like per capita bank deposits (Krishnan, 1994). With somewhat better informational base we have estimated the flow of remittances by using the first method for a period of nearly three decades beginning from the early seventies (Kannan and Hari, 2002). These estimates show that remittance income as a proportion of NSDP

---

8. The figure based on the primary survey led by K.C. Zachariah was 1.36 million. However, he stated that the "estimate of the number of emigrants at the state level (1.36 million) has a tolerance limit (95 per cent standard error) or 0.19 million (plus or minus). Thus, we concluded that in the second half of 1998, the number of emigrants from Kerala was somewhere between 1.55 million and 1.17 million (see Zachariah *et al.*, 2003: 17).

9. The 2003 survey revealed a decline in the share of Gulf countries to around 90 per cent indicating a slow diversification of destinations.

is around 23 per cent during the second half of the nineties.[10] Using these estimates of remittances, a series of modified state income (NSDP plus remittances) was constructed. Table 6.3 shows the trend in per capita state income as measured by the NSDP as well as MSI as a percentage of the per capita NDP for all India.[11] It is quite clear that remittance factor has been an important factor in contributing to a higher per capita income in Kerala than the all India one since the early nineties. Kerala's per capita income crossed the all India level in 1993-94 reaching 60 per cent above the latter in 2002-03 when remittances are included and 34 per cent when remittances are excluded.

Table 6.3

Per Capita Income Excluding Remittance (PNSDP) and Including Remittance (PMSI) for Kerala and PNDP for India

(Rs. in Current Prices)

Year	*PNSDP Kerala*	*As % of (6)*	*PMSI Kerala*	*As % of (6)*	*PNDP All India*
1	2	3	4	5	6
1991-92	5140	84	6004	98	6129
1992-93	5768	84	6818	99	6866
1993-94	7938	101	9278	118	7834
1994-95	9539	106	11646	129	9021
1995-96	11469	111	13882	135	10306
1996-97	13050	111	16257	138	11740
1997-98	14231	110	17814	138	12909
1998-99	16029	107	19571	131	14927
1999-2000	17709	109	22114	136	16203
2000-01	19951	118	23987	142	16878
2001-02	22668	125	26767	148	18100
2002-03	25764	134	30609	160	19185

Source: Government of India (2003).

10. Our study estimated the flow of remittances from 1972-73 to 1999-2000. In this paper we have updated the figures up to 2002-03. These figures show that the remittances continue to increase but as a share of state domestic income they are around 19 per cent during 2001-2003.

11. Since net state domestic product (NSDP) representing state income is net of depreciation, the appropriate comparison with the national income is that of net domestic product (NDP) which is net of depreciation as opposed to gross domestic product (GDP) which includes depreciation.

An indirect method to find out the growth in per capita income that would reflect the influence of remittances is the growth in per capita consumer expenditure. This shows that there has been a higher rate of growth in consumption in Kerala compared to all India (see Table 6.4). In fact, Kerala's per capita consumer expenditure was lower than all India till 1976-77 but steadily exceeded all India since and was 41 per cent higher than the latter in 1999-2000 (for details see Kannan and Hari, 2002). This could not have been possible but for the accrual of extra income in the form of remittances.[12]

Table 6.4

Growth Rate of Monthly Per Capita Consumption Expenditure

Kerala		*All India*	
Period I	*Period II*	*Period I*	*Period II*
10.71	10.73	8.96	9.59

Note: Period I = 1970-71 to 1986-87 and Period II = 1987-88 to 2002-03.
Source: Kannan and Hari (2002).

The question however is: why did remittances not induce economic growth during the first period? Growth during the first period was mostly accounted for by the growth in the tertiary sector, which was a reflection of the increasing consumer expenditure. Even with an initial lag remittances did not contribute to growth. Earlier studies have partly answered this question. These include that migrant workers, most of whom belonged to low-income if not poor households had to pay back the loans incurred for migration, pay back the outstanding debts of the family and incur expenses for marriage of young women in their families. These are the first charges on the savings from remittance income. Next comes investment in land (real estate) and construction of better houses. While these are not productive investments, these are long-term investments in social status and the gains arising out of them cannot be easily quantified in the Indian social milieu with a high premium on upward social mobility. In fact, there

12. This shows that the per capita income, including remittances, may well have exceeded the all India level by mid-seventies. This might well have been the case since our estimate of remittance income was based on legal flow of remittances as opposed to the illegal flow which was quite substantial during the 1970s and 80s due to the fixed exchange rate system.

was a boom in construction during the first period as well. Given the limited avenues for financial investment then, a good part of the savings might have ended up in the form of gold and bank deposits.

As noted by Saith (1992), majority of the migrant labour of the kind we are discussing are not 'investing-savers' and hence their investment behaviour (in land construction, gold and bank deposits) can be seen as rational behaviour. However, the economic system in Kerala could not utilise these funds, especially in the banks, for purposes of investment in productive sectors. This is related to Kerala's record in labour relations and the absence of compensating factors such as a well-functioning infrastructure. Elsewhere we have tried to understand this analytically (see Kannan, 1990). The message is that wage effect induced by remittances via pressure on an inter-related labour market reinforced the institutional power of labour (early and high level of unionisation) and drove away much of Kerala's early labour-intensive industries such as coir processing/manufacturing, cashew processing and tile manufacturing. A transition to a technologically advanced high productivity industrial sector was thwarted by the power of organised labour. Technological change, especially using machines, was also opposed in agriculture where the problem was compounded by the failure of public investment in such productivity-enhancing critical infrastructure as land and water management. With productive sectors unable to attract investment, the tertiary sector attracted investment in quick-profit ventures to take advantage of the growing consumer demand. In such a scenario, the state that had retained much initiative in investment decisions (through controls, regulations, licensing and public investment) could not provide the necessary leadership in initiating a process of renewed growth.

The onset of economic reforms changed the situation mainly in two ways. One, it led to a release of the pent-up demand in a number of consumer goods and services that were not previously available. This meant that effective demand was building up in the Kerala economy but were facing supply constraints for certain specified commodities. The acceleration and intensification of economic reforms contributed further to removing the remaining supply constraints. The role of remittances here should be seen as removing the effective demand constraint in a developing economy and the role of reforms as removing the supply constraints. The continuing flow of remittance income sustained this situation. The second factor was in removing a number of minor and major constraints to investment, import of technology and raw materials. Along with market-determined exchange rate, this set of reforms provided a far more favourable climate for investment. However, Kerala does not seem to have been in a position to take advantage of the situation in the large industrial sector. This is related to the continuing image problem of Kerala as an 'investor unfriendly state' arising, largely if not only, out of the record in managing labour relations. To this should be added the inability of the state to manage its public sector, which continues to be on a declining path in terms of profitability and efficient management.

Given a steady flow of income to the households, part of it was translated into effective demand. Commodities (traded items) in which Kerala did not have a comparative advantage (either due to higher labour costs without a commensurate increase in labour productivity) were procured from outside the state whereas those goods and services that are of a non-tradeable nature experienced an increase in their supply. These were mainly in construction, trade and commerce, banking and insurance, travel and tourism, education, and health care. From an analytical point of view, increases in effective demand in a regional economy like Kerala led to an increase in investment in non-tradeable goods and services while it also expanded the market for traded goods and services emanating from outside the region. As such, the benefits arising from remittances to Kerala benefited both the regional and national economies.

6.4 What has Happened to Employment and Unemployment?

While Kerala's growth performance since the first round of economic reforms is quite impressive especially against its background of a long period of stagnation, it cannot be perceived as a meaningful one unless it is related to its impact on employment. This of course holds good for a developing economy but much more so for a state like Kerala with a historically high incidence of unemployment. The availability of data on employment in the organised sector as well as the information from various NSS rounds on employment and unemployment, especially the last one for 1999-2000 has been of immense help in relating growth to employment.

The analysis brings out certain important and far-reaching outcomes which, we think, will be quite crucial in the future trajectory of development of Kerala. First, for the first time in its history, Kerala has registered a structural transformation in employment away from agriculture and related activity (see Table 6.5). Along with an earlier structural transformation in income generation, this employment transformation means that Kerala is no more an agrarian economy. Although it is yet to fit into the description of a modern economy, a high proportion of income as well as employment are generated outside of agriculture and related primary sector activities.

Second, the employment transition is not accompanied by a significant increase in organised sector employment but by an increase in the so-called unorganised sector. The organised sector employment in 2001 is around 1.2 million or 10 per cent of total workforce. This means the quality of employment for a majority of workers continued to be of a low order.

Third, there is a marked reduction in unemployment since 1987-88 but this occurred between 1987-88 and 1993-94 (see Table 6.6). Since then the unemployment rate for men and women either remained the same (for men) or experienced an increase (for women). These rates remain considerably higher than the all India average. In terms of chronic unemployment (measured by Usual Principal Status), male unemployment at 7.4 per cent is more than two-and-half times the all India rate. In the case of women, it is nine times that of all India.

This is despite the large-scale international migration of people from Kerala. If this workforce of around 1.2 million (out of a total migrants of 1.36 million) is included, then the 1999-2000 estimate of workforce (as per NSS) at 39 per cent of the population will go up to 43 per cent. Note that the Kerala workforce abroad (in 1998) was equal to the organised sector workforce within Kerala.

Table 6.5

Structural Transformation of the Kerala (and All India) Economy as seen through Sectoral Shares of Income and Employment

Year	Primary	Secondary	Tertiary
1983			
Income	35 (41)	25 (22)	40 (37)
Employment	50 (69)	22 (13)	28 (18)
1987-88			
Income	35 (35)	22 (24)	43 (41)
Employment	52 (66)	20 (15)	28 (19)
1993-94			
Income	32 (33)	20 (24)	48 (43)
Employment	49 (65)	21 (14)	30 (21)
1999-2000			
Income	26 (28)	19 (24)	55 (48)
Employment	32 (60)	28 (16)	40 (24)

Note: Figures in parenthesis gives the all India figures.

Source: For income: Government of India (2003).

For employment: *For Kerala:* NSSO, Report No.341/3, Report on the Third Quinquennial Survey on Employment and Unemployment, February 1988, *Sarvekshana*, Special Issue, State Series, Kerala, January 1992, NSSO Report No.409, Report on the Fifth Quinquennial Survey on Employment and Unemployment in India, March 1997 and NSSO Report No.458, Report on Sixth Quinquennial Survey on Employment and Unemployment in India.

For All India 1983: *Sarvekshana* Issue No.35, Vol.XI, No.4, April 1988. For 1987-88: *Sarvekshana*, Special Number, September 1990. For 1993-94 and 1999-2000: Same as Kerala.

Table 6.6

Incidence of Unemployment: Unemployed as a Percentage of Labour Force (UPS)

Year	Rural			Urban			Total		
	Male	Female	Persons	Male	Female	Persons	Male	Female	Persons
1977-78	13.6	29.2	19.2	16.2	39.5	23.5	14.0	30.6	19.8
	(2.2)	(5.5)	(3.8)	(6.5)	(17.8)	(11.9)	(3.1)	(8.0)	(5.5)
1983	10.6	17.0	12.6	11.9	25.6	15.6	10.8	18.4	13.1
	(2.1)	(1.4)	(1.8)	(5.9)	(6.9)	(6.4)	(3.0)	(2.7)	(2.9)
1987-88	12.5	25.0	16.6	14.2	34.0	19.6	12.8	26.3	17.1
	(2.8)	(3.5)	(3.1)	(6.1)	(8.5)	(7.2)	(3.6)	(4.7)	(4.2)
1993-94	7.2	15.8	9.4	7.6	24.4	12.0	7.3	18.2	10.1
	(2.0)	(1.4)	(1.8)	(4.5)	(8.2)	(5.2)	(2.6)	(2.5)	(2.6)
1999-2000	7.6	19.7	10.9	6.9	26.4	12.5	7.4	21.5	11.4
	(2.1)	(1.5)	(1.9)	(4.8)	(7.1)	(5.2)	(2.8)	(2.4)	(2.7)

Note: Figures in parenthesis gives the all India figures.

Source: Same as Table 6.5.

The structural transformation that Kerala has undergone during the last decade of the twentieth century is significant. Historically, Kerala had a higher share in non-agricultural activities because of its specialisation in low-labour absorbing cash crops, high labour-absorbing agro-processing industries and the consequent employment in trade and related activities. This showed up the structure of income generation. By the beginning of 1980s, a major share of income was generated outside of the primary sector. But the employment structure remained largely agrarian in the context of a slow growth of the secondary sector. What seems to have contributed to this structural transformation are two contradictory processes. One is the acceleration in the decline in agricultural employment as a result of faster pace of substitution of rice with low-labour absorbing perennial and more profitable crops (see, e.g. Kannan, 1999). So much so that agriculture showed a negative rate of employment since 1987-88 affecting women more adversely than men. The other is the fast rate of growth in employment in the construction sector followed by transport and other services, which registered impressive growth in employment that was more favourable to men than to women. Migration, especially international migration, also helped ease the unemployment problem. But this has also worked more in favour of men than women since more than 80 per cent of the migrants are men.

That the organised sector hardly contributed to the growth in employment is a striking feature of this changing employment scenario. Within the public sector it is related to the declining share of public investment as well as the declining performance of public enterprises in the state. In the organised private sector the growth is equally slow. In our opinion, this is related to the reluctance of the private sector in Kerala to invest in relatively bigger enterprises in a significant way despite the increased availability of loanable funds in the banking system. Although this situation is changing somewhat slowly especially in the emerging sectors of tourism, health, higher education and information technology it is still to attract other avenues. Hence, much of employment generated is in what may be called small and medium enterprises in the industrial and service sectors.

6.5 Emerging Challenges

The fundamental changes that are taking place in the Kerala economy present considerable opportunities for accelerating the process of economic development. However, such opportunities are embedded in formidable challenges. The ultimate challenge is to enhance labour productivity and to create conditions for secure and decent work (for which there is immense social pressure) on the one hand and generate higher growth of such employment on the other. For realising such a goal there exists significant favourable factors unavailable to many other states in India. Equally important to note is the presence of strong unfavourable factors that call for imaginative and bold public policy as well as efficient provisioning of infrastructure facilities such as power.

The favourable factors are largely the outcome of an uninterrupted process of human development for the last three decades. These are:

(1) A demographic transition leading to a very low rate of population growth and near stable population within the next 10 years. This has already resulted in an increase in the share of working age population (15 to 59 years) to more than 60 per cent of the total population and a corresponding decline in dependent population.

(2) An educated labour force, especially in the younger age group of 15-35, majority of which have at least 10 years of schooling. This is accompanied by the demand for higher education for specialised knowledge and skills cutting across social and economic status groups.

(3) A structural transformation of the economy by the nineties in which two-thirds of employment and around 70 per cent of income are generated outside agriculture.

(4) An uninterrupted period of international labour migration for the last three decades exposing more than two million adults (migrants and return migrants) to international work experience, exposure to working with people from different cultures as well as familiarisation with new and modern forms of organisation and management of work and business.

In addition, one should also count the new national economic environment offering more favourable conditions for investment, and adoption of technology in a regime of high growth and consequential expansion in effective demand.

What are the strong unfavourable factors?

(1) First of all, human development *per se* is not going to lead to a process of broad-based growth and development unless critical and complementary factors are present. In Kerala's case, the failure in providing such critical infrastructural goods as electric power and water control (mainly irrigation) is as spectacular as the achievements in human development indicators. The continuing inefficiency and inadequacy in supplying quality power by the Kerala State Electricity Board should be counted as a strong unfavourable factor.

(2) Given the high wage rates in the unorganised sectors of the economy and the relatively higher educational qualifications of the labour force, Kerala should be charting on a path of technological change in all sectors of the economy. However, the political society has no consensus on the need for technological change. It is actively opposed in agriculture and agro-processing industries. The role of trade unions in this respect has been shortsighted and self-defeating in that much of the investments that would have taken place in Kerala has moved to the neighbouring states. However, there is no resistance to the introduction of high technology-intensive industries/services in new ventures.

(3) There is a serious problem of quality of education at all levels that may not be unique to Kerala. But Kerala has an urgent necessity to focus on this issue since most of its unemployment problem is that of the educated especially those without any skill or specialised knowledge. This is partly responsible for the low level of knowledge-intensive industries and services. Quantitative expansion of higher education has started in recent years but there is hardly any meaningful initiative in improving the quality of education.

(4) Kerala's image as an 'investor-unfriendly state' has got stuck for some time. Although political parties and trade unions are taking steps to change this image, it takes time to change the perception of people, especially prospective investors. A sustained campaign highlighting Kerala's favourable factors and backed by the provision of high quality infrastructure facilities might help remove this negative image.

To these should be added the fiscal crisis being faced by the state leading to a declining share of capital expenditure in total public expenditure. This has exacerbated the state's capacity to enhance the quality and quantity of public and collective goods especially those that are infrastructural in nature.

In sum, Kerala has left behind the phase of high human development and low economic growth but it faces many a hurdle in translating its high human development and relatively high growth into meaningful development outcomes especially in meeting the challenge of high unemployment of its educated people. It is this theme that is engaging the attention of a number of researchers at the Centre for Development Studies, Trivandrum.

References

Ahluwalia, M.S. (2000). "Economic performance of the states in the post reform period", *Economic and Political Weekly* 35(17).

Amin, Samir (1991). "Four comments on Kerala", *Monthly Review* 42(8), January.

Boyce, J.K. (1986). "Kinked exponential models for growth rate estimation", *Oxford Bulletin of Economics and Statistics* 48(4).

Centre for Development Studies (1975). *Poverty, Unemployment and Development Policy: A Cast Study of Selected Issues with reference to Kerala*. New York: United Nations.

Frankie, Richard, W. and Barbara H. Chasin (1991). "Kerala state, India: Radical reform as development" in *Monthly Review*, January.

———. (1998). "Kerala: A valid alternative to the new world order" in *Bulletin of Concerned Asian Scholars* 30(3)

George, K.K. (1993). *Limits to Kerala Model of Development: An Analysis of Fiscal Crisis and its Implications*. Trivandrum: Centre for Development Studies.

———. (1998). "Historical roots of Kerala model and its present crisis", in *Bulletin of Concerned Asian Scholars* 30(4).

Government of India (2003). *National Accounts Statistics*. New Delhi: Central Statistical Organisation.

———. (2003). *Estimates of State Domestic Product in India*. New Delhi: Central Statistical Organisation.

Govindan, Parayil (1998). "The perils of trying to be objective without being reflective: The Kerala model revisited", *Bulletin of Concerned Asian Scholars* 30(3).

Gulati, I.S. and Asoka Mody (1983). "Remittances of Indian migrants to the Middle East: An assessment with special reference to migrants from Kerala", *Working Paper* No.182, Centre for Development Studies, Thiruvananthapuram.

Heller, Patrick (1998). "Problematizing the Kerala model", *Bulletin of Concerned Asian Scholars* 30(3).

Isaac, Thomas, T.M. and P.K. Michael Tharakan (1995). "Towards a new agenda", *Economic and Political Weekly*, August 5-12.

Kannan, K.P. (1990). "Kerala economy at the crossroads?", *Economic and Political Weekly*, September 1-8.

———. (1998). "Political economy of labour and development in Kerala", *Economic and Political Weekly*, December 26.

———. (1999). "Rural labour relations and development dilemmas in Kerala: Reflections on the dilemmas of a socially transforming labour force in a slowly growing economy", *Journal of Peasant Studies*, Jan-March 1999. Also in Byres, T.J., Karin Kapadia and Jens Lerche (eds.) (1999), *Rural Labour Relations in India*. London: Basil Blackwell.

Kannan, K.P. and K.S. Hari (2002). "Kerala's Gulf connection: Remittances and their macroeconomic impact", in Zachariah, K.C., K.P. Kannan and S. Irudaya Rajan (eds.), *Kerala's Gulf Connection: CDS Studies on International Labour Migration from Kerala State in India*. Centre for Development Studies, Thiruvananthapuram.

Krishnan, T.N. (1994). "Foreign remittances, consumption and income" (*mimeo*), Paper presented at the *International Congress on Kerala Studies* organised by the AKG Centre for Research and Studies, Thiruvananthapuram.

Omvedt, Gail (1998). "Disturbing aspects of Kerala society", *Bulletin of Concerned Asian Scholars* 30(3).

Parameswaran, M.P. (1998). "Kerala 'Model': What does it signify?", *Bulletin of Concerned Asian Scholars* 30(4).

Rammohan, K.T. (1991). "Understanding Keralam: The tragedy of radical scholarship", *Monthly Review* 43(7), December.

Saith, Ashwani (1992). "Absorbing external shocks: The Gulf crisis, international migration linkages and the Indian economy, 1990 (with special reference to the impact on Kerala)", *Development and Change* 23(1), January.

Sreekumar, T.T. and Sajeev S. (ed) (2003). *Katha Ithu Vare: Kerala Vikasana Samvadangal* (The Story Thus Far: Debates on Kerala's Development). Kottayam: D.C. Books.

Subrahmanian, K.K. and Abdul Aziz (2000). "Industrial growth in Kerala: Trends and explanations", *Working Paper* No. 310. Thiruvananthapuram: Centre for Development Studies.

Panikkar, P.G.K. and C.R. Soman (1984). *Health Status of Kerala: Paradox of Economic Backwardness and Health Development*. Trivandrum: Centre for Development Studies.

Tharamangalam, Joseph (1998). "The perils of social development without economic growth: The development debacle of Kerala", *Bulletin of Concerned Asian Scholars* 30(1) and 'A Rejoinder' in 30(4).

Tornquist, Olle (1998). "Beyond romanticism: Remarkable popular reorganizing", *Bulletin of Concerned Asian Scholars* 30(4).

Zachariah, K.C., E.T. Mathew and S. Irudaya Rajan (2003). *Dynamics of Migration in Kerala: Dimensions, Determinants and Consequences*. Hyderabad: Orient Longman.

7 Environment and Economic Development

K.V. Raju

7.1 Introduction

Rapid population growth coupled with development has spurred on unplanned urbanisation and extensive industrialisation, which has placed increasing strains on the environment. In the process, the world has landed in the middle of an ecological crisis. It has experienced with the loss of forests, poisoning of waters, erosion of lands and rendering the millions of people as homeless and resource less. According to UN estimates, the world's urban population reached 3 billion in 2003 and is expected to increase to 5 billion by 2030. It is projected to exceed 50 per cent of the global population by 2007. This means that for the first time in history the world will have more urban residents than rural residents. With more than half of the world's population is expected to be concentrated in urban areas by 2007, agencies like the World Wide Fund for Nature (WWF) and the United Nations Environmental Programme (UNEP) have expressed concern at the unregulated growth of cities.

As reported by the World Conservation Union and the United Nations Environment Programme, the 'roof of the world', as well as other mountains in Asia, are being slowly degraded by unchecked human activity that will affect the water supply of millions of people and the region's rich biodiversity. The mountains of Asia, including the Himalayas, are facing accelerating threats from a rapid increase in the number of roads, settlements, overgrazing and deforestation. The report voices concern that the region's water supply, fed by glaciers and the monsoons and vital for around half the world's population, may be harmed alongside the area's abundant and rich wildlife. According to Surendra Shrestha, Director of the UNEP's regional office for Asia and the Pacific, "Most serious is the situation in parts of Pakistan, northern India, Bangladesh, Myanmar and South-East Asia." Here, human population pressures and piecemeal development for logging and other purposes can have a great impact on biodiversity and watersheds, he added. Many of the rivers in the region have been affected by deforestation and increased use of water for irrigation. Climate change as a result of the burning of oil, coal and other fossil fuels is likely to aggravate water problems. Studies carried out by the UNEP and other environmental agencies have pinpointed some 50 lakes that have formed in Nepal and Bhutan in recent years as a result of melting glaciers. These lakes, held back by soil and stones, could burst their banks sending torrential floods down valleys threatening villages and homes.

China is also facing the problem of melting glacier. Estimates show that the country's glaciers are shrinking by an amount equivalent to all the water in the Yellow river each year. The Chinese Academy of Science says 7 per cent of the country's glaciers are vanishing annually and that, by 2050, as many as 64 per cent of China's glaciers will be disappeared. Up to half of Asia's mountain region is affected by infrastructure development; by 2030 this could rise to over 70 per cent if trends continue unchecked. The biggest impacts will be on river catchments and wildlife along the Karakoram highway, Pakistan, the Indian and southern side of the Himalayas and in southeastern Tibet and the Yunnan and Sichuan provinces of southwestern China.

Overgrazing along road corridors in dry regions of Pakistan and China, resulting in erosion, landslides and dust storms, is also a huge problem. All countries in the region are likely to see a decline in the abundance of wildlife over the next three decades, on current trends. Lowland areas may see a decline of up to 80 per cent in their historic abundance of wildlife, the decline depending on measures taken to steer development into more environment-friendly ways.

The nation's ongoing population explosion has placed great strain on the country's environment. This rapidly growing population, along with a move toward urbanisation and industrialisation, has placed significant pressure on India's infrastructure and its natural resources. Deforestation, soil erosion, water pollution and land degradation continue to worsen and are hindering economic development in rural

India, while the rapid industrialisation and urbanisation in India's booming metropolises are straining the limits of municipal services and causing serious air pollution problems. India has made substantial progress in most spheres of development over the last 50 years, particularly the last two decades. During the last two decades, the Indian economy has been growing at about 6 per cent per annum, making it one of best performing economies in the world.

Currently, India is the largest contributor (21 per cent) to world population growth, adding about 17 million people every year to an already huge population of over one billion. Although more than two–thirds of India's population still lives in the rural areas, it has experienced rapid urbanisation over the last two decades. However, the benefits of this impressive growth have been substantially offset by environmental degradation. Even though India has a rich tradition of environment conservation, large–scale environment degradation has resulted from population pressures, industrialisation and the indiscriminate use of forest areas for fuel, power generation and irrigation purposes. The spread of input–intensive green technology has given India a certain measure of food security, but it has been at the cost of falling water tables, degrading soils, poor management of irrigation systems and the harmful side–effects of increasing pesticide and fertiliser use. Industrial growth and uncontrolled urbanisation pollute water, air and land. Similarly, rapid economic growth-led changing lifestyle such as increasing use of automobiles and plastics are also putting an immense stress on resources (energy) and the environment.

The national impact of environmental degradation is now becoming increasingly clear. Loss of topsoil, salinity, pollution, shortage of water and biomass has caused serious declines in agricultural productivity in many areas, making the food security situation bleak. A World Bank study reported that the cost of environmental damage due to pollution is 4.5 per cent of the GDP. Polluted air poses serious threats to human life, the short-term effects of which can be seen as health hazards and diseases. India is spending about Rs. 4,600 crore every year to make up for health damages due to ambient air quality. The Centre for Science and Environment's Fifth Citizen's Report (1999) states that in the 33 Indian cities for which air quality is available, deaths, particularly due to air pollution went from 40,000 to 52,000, an increase of 30 per cent in just 3 to 4 years. Noise levels are so high that certain areas record over 90 decibels for the better part of the day.

Loss of biodiversity has increasingly marginalised and impoverished many tribals and other forest-dependent communities which directly depend on various components of biodiversity for food, drink, medicine, culture, spirituality, etc. The indirect impact of degradation—such as severe drought or deforestation-induced floods—also hits the poor hardest. Poverty in these cases is a direct outcome of environmental destruction. Millions of hectares of land are utilised for dams or mining or urban growth and other 'development' projects. This is because those who benefit from these projects, mostly urban consumers, industrialists, contractors, politicians and big farmers, have greater control over land than small farmers, pastoralists and others whose land is taken over and who are displaced by these projects, often with minimal or no compensation.

Inappropriate technologies and the mismanagement of resources are certainly responsible for environmental degradation. But they are not the root of the crisis. At the root is the socio-political structure of the country. Over-population in third world countries is often cited as the root cause of environmental degradation.

7.2 Land and Soil Degradation

Land is the most threatened resource in India. In 1980, the union ministry of agriculture admitted that 175 million hectares of the total landmass, i.e., 53 per cent of the total area, is degraded to some extent. In 1994, Sehgal and Abrol placed this figure higher at 187.2 million hectares, of which 162.4 million hectares are degraded by water and wind erosion and 21.7 million hectares by salinity and waterlogging. The remaining 4 million hectares are affected by the depletion of nutrients.

According to the National Remote Sensing Agency and Forest Survey of India, 80 million hectares of the 142 million hectares under cultivation are substantially degraded and about 40 million hectares of the 75 million hectares controlled by the forest department have canopy cover of less than 40 per cent (Gadgil, 1993). Nearly 12 million hectares of pasture lands are also substantially degraded. Thus, a total of 132 million hectares representing 40 per cent of the country's total landmass have productivity well below their potential (UNEP, 2001).

7.2.1 Causes of Land Degradation

The main causes of land degradation are:

- Deforestation.
- Ignorance of soil conservation practices.
- Extension of cultivation to marginal lands.
- Improper crop rotation.
- Imbalanced fertiliser use.
- Surface irrigation ironically designed to increase land productivity.
- Rapid growth in population, paucity of land.
- Economic pressures and poverty.

7.2.2 Vanishing Forests

India lost 26,245 sq km of dense forest cover between 2001 and 2003, with mining projects and industrial development considered to be the chief culprits, according to the latest countrywide forest report conducted by the Forest Survey of India. However, its overall forest cover increased marginally by 2,795 sq km, or 0.41 per cent, mainly due to afforestation. India's forest cover currently stands at 678,333 sq km, or 20.64 per cent of the country's geographical area, as against 675,538 sq km, or 20.55 per cent, in 2001. The forests cover 23.68 per cent or 778,229 sq km of India's land area—up a marginal 0.65 per cent from 2001. This includes trees in non-forested areas. Dense forest cover, or forest cover with a canopy density of 40 per cent covers a total of 390,564 sq km of land in India. Open forests cover 287,769 sq km, an increase of 29,040 sq km from the 2001. Of the country's total forest cover, dense forests constitute 51,285 sq km (1.56 per cent), moderately dense forests 339,279 sq km (10.32 per cent) and open forests 287,769 sq km (8.76 per cent) of total land area. Of 593 districts, 199 have less than 5 per cent forest cover; this includes 59 districts with less than 1 per cent forest cover (State of Forests Report, 2003).

Till 1980, India's forest cover was being lost at the rate of 144,000 hectares per year. This slowed to 23,533 hectares between 1981 to 1995. Between 1975 and 1982, India lost a total of 1.4 million hectares of forest cover. According to a Food and Agriculture Organization (FAO) report (1994), the annual rate of deforestation in India is 0.6 per cent (0.34 million hectares). In 1990, the total forest area was 70.6 million hectares, of which 27 per cent was under commercial plantation, especially of eucalyptus, teak and pine. The area allotted for forestry plantation is increasing by 15.5 per cent a year since 1981. As a result of this, the total area under forests is increasing even as the extent of natural forests is decreasing.

7.2.3 Causes of Degradation of Forest Resources

- Over-exploitation by communities residing in the vicinity of forests for subsistence or economic use such as collection of fuel wood, fodder, non-timber forest produce, etc.
- Overgrazing by livestock.
- Commercial extraction of timber and non-timber forest produces by state agencies.
- Unregulated urbanisation and increased consumption needs of urban populations.
- Rapid industrialisation.
- Diversion of forestland to non-forest use such as mining industry, timber-based industry, paper and pulp industry.
- Submergence of forest land in river valley projects.
- Conversion of forest land for agricultural purposes, including encroachments.

7.2.4 Water Resources

The per capita water use in the country has decreased from around 5,277 cubic metres in 1955 to 2,464 cubic metres in 1990. Per capita availability of water, which was 6,008 cubic metres in 1947, has fallen to 2,266 cubic metres in 1997. This gives a broad indication of the growing water scarcity in the country since Independence and consequently, the serious drought situation year after year in various parts of the country

(Engelman and Roy, 1993). According to the Eighth Five Year Plan document (1992-1997), the total irrigation potential of the country was 71.8 million hectares. However, according to land use statistics, the net area irrigated is less than one-third of the net area sown.

7.2.5 Impact on Surface Water

Indian rivers are a classic example of rapid, unplanned development at the cost of an important natural resource. For example, from the time the river Yamuna enters Delhi, about 1,700 million litres of untreated sewage are discharged in it per day. This was, till recently, in addition to the industrial waste from about 93,100 small- and large-scale industries (CSE, 1999). The situation is similar in almost all large urban centres. Twenty-five large towns on the banks of the Ganga generate 1,340 million litres of sewage every day, which was directly discharged into the river till the Ganga Action Plan was started in 1985 to clean it up (CSE, 1999). Therefore, river systems passing through major cities and towns serve as open sewers to carry untreated effluents (domestic and industrial). Over 70 per cent of India's surface water is seriously polluted. The Economic Survey of 1995 stated that 95 per cent of the water in India's 241 class II towns was polluted. Recent surveys show that more than 50 per cent of industries may be discharging effluents above the prescribed standards.

A report by the Central Pollution Control Board (CPCB) reveals startling facts about pollution levels in Gujarat's rivers. The percentage rise in pollutants found in rivers since the last count in 2001 is the highest in the Sabarmati. The area now ranks among the highest pollution zones, the fourth in the country. Until 2001, the Sabarmati figured nowhere near the top 10 most polluted rivers. Officials blame this on the failure of the local administration to regulate the flow of untreated sewage into the river, and also the activities of polluting industries in the city. These are the two most important factors contributing to the pollution. The river currently resembles a nullah, with 32 canals dumping chemical effluents and sewage into the river, and slums lining its banks. Wastewater from a sewage treatment plant, which also processes industrial waste from the Pirana/Narol industrial estates, flows into the Sabarmati river. Plastic bags containing hazardous chemicals float in the puddles of water that are left; washermen scrub clothes in the water, which is pink, interspersed with black sewage flowing from the sewage treatment plant. The water's Bio-chemical Oxygen Demand (BOD) level has risen by 28 milligrams per litre, from 72.9 mg in 2001 to 100.3 mg in 2004. BOD is a measure of how much dissolved oxygen is being consumed as microbes break down organic matter. Higher BOD levels are a clear indicator of pollutants in the water as they show the presence of a higher quantity of organic waste. The standard BOD level required to sustain aquatic life is 10 mm per litre. By this estimate, the existing BOD levels in most Indian rivers are alarmingly high.

7.2.6 Causes of Degradation and Pollution of Water Resources

- *Poor technology:* Many industries in India have obsolete pollution control technology. They still follow the 'dilute and disperse' principle for treating effluents. Very few industries in India have in-built techniques for pollution prevention and waste minimisation.
- *Over-extraction:* Serious degradation of water resources is caused by excessive water withdrawal for various reasons such as irrigation, industry, domestic consumption, etc. The effect of this is compounded by the fact that the catchments of these water resources are now seriously degraded, hampering groundwater recharging.
- The natural drainage and water flow of many important rivers has been altered due to the withdrawal of water and construction of big dams. In the absence of optimum water flow, river systems lose their capacity of self-cleansing.

7.2.7 Impact on Groundwater

Pharma factories poison groundwater in Punjab village: In Toansa village of Punjab, the department of water supply and sanitation has marked local handpumps with red crosses to stop people from drawing and using the water, which has been contaminated by effluents from pharmaceutical companies and a paper mill. Ranbaxy Laboratories, Montari Industries (now closed), Max India, DSM India and a paper mill in the area have poisoned the area's groundwater with their toxic waste, to such an extent that the department of water supply and sanitation in Nawanshahr has stamped its 200-odd hand pumps with red crosses. These symbols warn that the water pouring out of the pumps is unsafe for consumption. The department, through a notice on November 2005, sent to the village *panchayat* (local governing council), wants villagers warned through the public address system that water from the handpumps contain hazardous chemicals. People in Toansa suffer skin diseases; many children have asthma, men and women complain of nausea and headaches.

Pollution of groundwater in urban fringe villages: The Hootagalli village in the outskirts of Mysore city in Karnataka is affected by groundwater contamination caused due to the discharge of effluents from chemical industries manufacturing potassium nitrate. At Hootagalli, the surrounding industries adopt various methods to discharge the waste generated—dumping it into dried borewells, by digging pits (40-50 feet depth) and dumping into Bommannahalli tank situated at a distance of about half a kilometre (Manasi and Deepa, 2004). The contaminated water tastes bitter and has a strong pungent odour.

People started to realise the negative effects at different situations. However, it took some time for them to link the reasons with water. Youth in the village noticed that a small tank where they reared fish started dying suddenly. Frogs in the same pond were dying too. People experienced varied health problems at different parts of the village—skin rash, stomach upsets and hair loss became more common. Clothes washed did not look clean and any amount of soap did not give lather. Death of two cows triggered the issue linking the situation largely to water.

Excessive contamination of groundwater in Meerut: High levels of chemicals in drinking water, soil and sludge in Daurala, near Meerut in Uttar Pradesh, high enough to put the region among the top 50 most polluted habitations in the country. High toxic untreated effluents are released by industry in the area and used as irrigation water by local villagers, are spelling a slow death for the 18,000-odd residents of the village-cum-industrial estate of Daurala. Local residents battle chronic bronchial asthma, gastrointestinal diseases and throat cancer. Out of 192 people who have died in the region over the past 5 years, 54 died from thyroid cancer, 33 of heart disease and 42 due to various gastrointestinal disorders. "The reason for these ailments is supposed to be the presence of alarming levels of heavy metals like arsenic, lead, aluminium and lethal compounds like cyanide in the drinking water, wastewater, agricultural soil and sludge samples tested at the Indian Institute of Technology, Roorkee" (Janhit Foundation). Tests conducted in nearby villages in Meerut district also show that the groundwater is heavily contaminated with chromium, nickel, zinc and aluminium. Local and municipal water pumps in the district reveal levels of magnesium and chlorine that are above the permissible limit.

7.2.8 Air Pollution

Industrialisation and urbanisation have resulted in a profound deterioration of India's air quality. India has more than 20 cities with populations of at least 1 million, and some of them—including New Delhi, Mumbai, Chennai and Kolkata—are among the world's most polluted. Urban air quality ranks among the world's worst. Of the 3 million premature deaths in the world that occur each year due to outdoor and indoor air pollution, the highest number are assessed to occur in India. Sources of air pollution, India's most severe environmental problem, come in several forms, including vehicular emissions and untreated industrial smoke. Continued urbanisation has exacerbated the problem of rapid industrialisation, as more and more people are adversely affected and cities are unable to implement adequate pollution control mechanisms.

To add to these hazards are the mushrooming chemical industries and nuclear power plants, both of which have shown terrible safety records in India. The Bhopal disaster of 1983, in which several thousand people died inhaling toxic gas, was only the most visible sign of the dangers posed. Smaller accidents of that kind happen frequently in the country. Though no major accident has so far taken place in nuclear facilities in India, the possibility is certainly not remote. Most Indian nuclear power plants have been plagued by small reactor accidents. The

Rajasthan Atomic Power Plant has perhaps the most radioactively contaminated interiors in the world.

Pesticides are another category of environmental contaminators. Many pesticides are known to have a biomagnifying character, i.e., having a cumulative effect after many years of accumulation in the body or magnifying in concentration while entering from prey to predator in the foodchain. The use of seriously poisonous pesticides has resulted in the decline of many bird species and caused serious ailments among humans.

One of the most affected cities is New Delhi, where airborne particulate matter (PM) has been registered at levels more than 10 times India's legal limit. Vehicles are the major source of this pollution, with more than three million cars, trucks, buses, taxis and *rickshaws* already on the roads. With vehicle ownership rising along with population and income, India's efforts to improve urban air quality have focused in this area. In New Delhi, emissions limits for gasoline- and diesel-powered vehicles came into effect in 1991 and 1992, respectively, and the city has prohibited the use of vehicles more than 15 years old. Emissions standards for passenger cars and commercial vehicles were tightened in 2000 at levels equivalent to the Euro-1 standards of the European Union, while the even-more-stringent Euro-2 standards have been in place for the metropolitan areas of Delhi, Mumbai, Chennai and Kolkata since 2001. Furthermore, the sulphur content of motor fuels sold in the four cities has been restricted to 500 parts per million (PPM) since 2001 in order to be compatible with tighter vehicle emissions standards. Motor fuel sulphur content in all other regions of India has been limited to 2,500 PPM since January 2000.

India's high concentration of pollution is not due to the absence of a sound environmental legal regime, however, but to a lack of environmental enforcement at the local level. Regulatory reforms aimed at improving the air pollution problem in cities such as New Delhi have been difficult to implement. In 1998, India's Supreme Court issued a ruling requiring all the city's buses to be run on compressed natural gas (CNG) by March 31, 2001. Compliance was to be achieved either by converting existing diesel engines or by replacing the buses themselves.

However, only 200 (out of a total fleet of 12,000) CNG-fueled buses were available by the initial deadline and public protests, riots and widespread "commuter chaos" ensued as some appearance of some 15,000 taxis and 10,000 buses in the city were banned from use. To ease the transition, the local government changed course and allowed for a gradual phase-out of the existing diesel bus fleet.

In addition, India's reliance on coal-fired power plants for its electricity generation has undermined some of the vehicular-oriented air quality improvement initiatives. Despite the fact that India is a large coal consumer, its Central Pollution Control Board has been slow to set sulphur dioxide (SO_2) emissions limits for coal-fired power plants, mainly because most of the coal mined in India is low in sulphur content. Coal-fired power plants do not face any nitrogen oxide (NO_x) emissions limits either, although thermal plants fueled by other fossil fuels are subject to particulate matter emission standards. Again, however, the government's support for air quality standards has been undermined by the lack of enforcement of these standards.

7.2.9 Causes of Air Pollution

- Various regulatory legal provisions exist for emission levels from industry and vehicles. However, malpractice and a lack of political will render their implementation ineffective.
- Lack of a sense of responsibility and awareness of the direct impact of pollution among the people.
- Use of bad fuel quality for short-term gains.
- Use of obsolete technology for energy production in vehicles and industry.

7.2.10 Energy Consumption

India's energy consumption is increasing rapidly, from 4.16 quadrillion Bt (quads) in 1980 to 12.8 quads in 2001. This 208 per cent increase is largely the result of India's increasing population and the rapid urbanisation of the country. Higher energy consumption in the industrial, transportation and residential sectors continues to drive India's energy usage upwards at a faster rate even than China, which experienced a 130 per cent increase in energy consumption from 1980 to 2001.

Despite the rapid growth between 1980 and 2001, India's energy consumption is still below that of Germany (14.35 quads), Japan (21.92 quads), China (39.67 quads) and the United States (97.05 quads). In addition, India's per capita energy consumption, which stood at 12.6 million Btu in 2001, is well below most of the rest of Asia and is one of the lowest in the world (although this may be more the result of India's large population rather than a low level of energy consumption). The 103 per cent rise in India's per capita consumption between 1980, when per capita energy usage was just 6.2 million Btu and 2001, is more problematic in the long-term, however.

Figure 7.1

India's Fuel Share of Energy Consumption, 2001 (Btu)

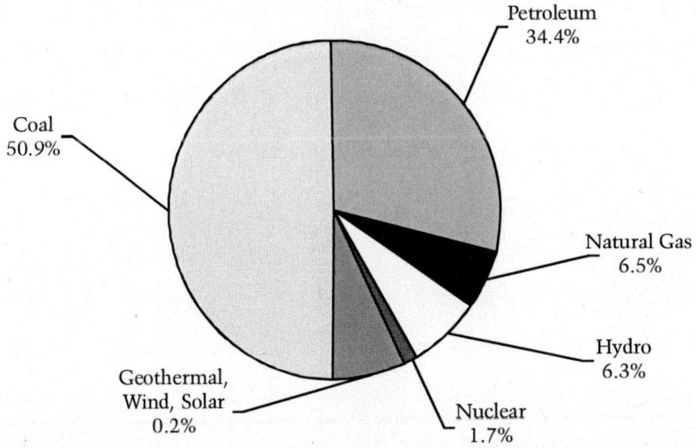

Source: EIA.

Coal accounts for just over 50 per cent (6.5 quads) of India's energy consumption. The power generation sector uses the majority of this coal, with heavy industry a distant second. Petroleum (4.4 quads) makes up 34.4 per cent of India's energy consumption, while natural gas (6.5 per cent) and hydroelectricity (6.3 per cent) account for much of the remainder. Natural gas is growing in importance, as its share of India's energy consumption has risen from just 1.4 per cent in 1980, while hydroelectricity—which made up 11.5 per cent of the country's energy usage in 1980—has declined in relative importance. Nuclear (1.7 per cent) and geothermal, wind, solar and biomass (0.2 per cent) made up a very small share of the country's energy consumption in 2001.

Case studies for Andhra Pradesh and Bihar states facing different energy challenges with varying resources show that the financial performance of the power sectors in both states will impose an unsupportable financial burden on their respective state governments. The rate of return on capital in Andhra Pradesh will become increasingly negative, reaching 18 per cent by 2015; in Bihar it will average 14 per cent from 1996 through 2015. The financial resources needed to maintain and operate the power plants at the level needed to meet the projected demand are unlikely to be forthcoming. Under current policies, emissions of environmentally damaging combustion products may be expected to increase rapidly, doubling in Bihar and quadrupling in Andhra Pradesh by the year 2015. Extrapolating the results to India as a whole reveals serious conditions.

7.2.11 Causes

Small particles from combustion eventually reach the ground, threatening human health and property.

- Disposing of the ash that is produced as a byproduct of combustion requires large amounts of land; leaching ash can contaminate groundwater.
- Carbon dioxide released from fuel by combustion contributes to global warming and climate change.
- Power stations may require large, frequently environmentally valuable, land areas. Large hydro and coal projects require resettlement and rehabilitation and affect people.
- Acid gases that are produced when fossil fuels are burned are eventually precipitated as acid rain.

7.3 The Biodiversity Crisis

The Indian subcontinent has been identified as one of the top 12 hotspots of biodiversity in the world. India harbours 8 per cent of the total number of species in the world, estimated to be 1.6 million, with possibly twice or thrice that number still to be discovered. However, conservative estimates suggest that at least 10 per cent of India's recorded wild flora and 20 per cent of its mammals are on the threatened list. Many of these would now be categorised as 'critical', i.e., on the verge of extinction. In fact, no one can say how many species have already been lost. According to one estimate, 23 species of different animals and plants are extinct, including the cheetah, one-horned rhino, pink-headed duck, mountain quail, forest spotted owlet, and plants like the hubbardia heptaneuron. The latter disappeared when a hydroelectric dam was built upstream of its riverine habitat. Many species have gone extinct either because they were not 'glamorous' enough to attract attention like the larger mammals or because their existence was simply not known to us.

India's domesticated biodiversity suffers the same plight. The Indian subcontinent is recognised as one of the world's major centres of crop and livestock origin and diversity. For example, till not so long ago, Indian farmers grew about 50,000 to 60,000 varieties of rice. The use of a diverse range of crop species and varieties ensured that several human needs (food, fodder, thatching, medicines, ritual uses, etc.) are fulfilled, and that there are back-up crops if some are affected by disease, pests or natural calamities. Hundreds of varieties of cattle, chickens, camels, goats and sheep are still bred and used by communities all over the country.

7.3.1 Threats to Biodiversity

- Ever-increasing market pressures, poaching and smuggling of timber.
- Over-exploitation of natural resources.
- Widespread pollution in combination with habitat destruction.
- Large-scale introduction of exotics have endangered a large portion of biological diversity.

References

CSE (1999). *State of India's Environment The Citizen's: Fifth Report*. New Delhi: Centre for Science and Environment.

Engelman, R. and P. Le Roy (1993). *Sustaining Water: Population and Future of Renewable Water Supplies*. Washington D.C., USA: Pollution and Environment Program, Population Action International.

Environment News Service, August 5, 2005.

Gadgil, M. (1993). "Biodiversity and India's degraded lands", *Ambio* 22: 167-172.

Manasi, S. and N. Deepa (2004). "Pollution of groundwater due to effluent seepage: Conflict between people and industrialists at Hootgalli village, Mysore", A Case Study. ISEC, Bangalore.

Meeting India's Future Power Needs—Planning for Sustainable Development. Environmental Issues in the Power Sector.

Reuters, November 17, 2005.

State of Forests Report 2003.

The Hindu, July 23, 2005.

UNEP (2001). *India: State of the Environment 2001*. Pathumthani: United Nations Environment Programmes (UNEP), Thailand.

www.gujaratiworld.co.uk, November 21, 2005.

www.indianexpress.com, December 18, 2005.

www.pollutedplaces.org, August 2, 2005.

www.cpcb.nic.in/adsorbs20.htm

www.oneworld.net, December 6, 2005.

www.oneworld.net, August 6, 2005.

www.lnweb18.worldbank.org

www.eia.doe.gov

www.un.org, June 5, 2005.

www.oneworld.net, June 5, 2005.

www.unep.org, August 4, 2005.

www.peopleandplanet.net, September 8, 2005.

www.ias.unu.edu

Section II

Agricultural Development

8 Redrafting the Agenda for Agricultural Development

N.A. Mujumdar

8.1 False Start

It is now admitted that the process of liberalisation of the Indian economy, introduced through economic reforms initiated in 1991, has largely by-passed the agricultural sector. "Agricultural development must be viewed as a core element of the Plan, since growth in this sector is likely to lead to the widest spread of benefits especially to the rural poor. The first generation of reforms concentrated on the industrial economy and reforms in the agricultural sector were neglected. This must change in the Tenth Plan."[1] What is worse, such reforms as have been actually introduced or contemplated by contemporary policy makers are mainly inspired by market theology, and are not grounded in the India-specific socio-economic milieu. Hence these reforms have given, as it were, a false start to agricultural development. These reforms constitute a bundle of contradictions. Food subsidy is not consistent with market theology and abolishing it will raise the issue prices of food grains distributed through the public distribution system (PDS). The minimum support price (MSP) system has resulted in the emergence of large surpluses of rice and wheat and hence, MSP should be done away with. The cropping pattern should be diversified with a perceptible shift in acreage away from rice and wheat to, say horticultural crops. Huge stocks of food grains, mainly rice and wheat, accumulated with the Food Corporation of India (FCI) reaching some 62 million tonnes at one point of time: this was highly embarrassing to policy makers who, alas, did not know what to do with them. They found the easiest way out, by exporting them. Exports of rice and wheat reached an unprecedented

1. *Tenth Five Year Plan, 2002-2007*, Vol. I, p.9.

level of 11 or 12 million tonnes on 2003-04. Shri Sharad Yadav, Minister for Consumer Affairs, Food and Public Distribution, exults in this achievement: "Today, India has emerged as the world's second largest exporter of rice and the seventh largest exporter of wheat. The country has earned foreign exchange of $ 4 billion through these exports. Though maintaining domestic food security will continue to be top priority, the country's newly-acquired position as a major exporter of food grains will be protected."[2]

8.2 The Under-Fed and the Under-Nourished

It is this agenda for agricultural development drawn up by contemporary policy makers inspired by market theology which needs to be urgently redrafted. Is there a real surplus of food grains in today's India? India continues to remain the abode of the largest number of under-fed and under-nourished persons in the world, despite the high level of production of food grains. FAO defines food security as: "The physical and economic access for all people at all times for enough food for an active, healthy life, with non-risk of losing such access and as such is directly connected with livelihood in developing countries." The so-called "surplus", the basic premise on which contemporary policy makers seem to build their strategy for agricultural development, is only "effective demand surplus" and not a genuine surplus. If domestic food security is to be ensured, where is the "surplus" for exports? In fact, as a consequence of raising the issue prices of food grains in the PDS, the off-take of food grains declined significantly clearly indicating that food grains became increasingly inaccessible to the poorer sections of the population. Even otherwise the per capita availability of cereals actually declined from 450 grammes per day in 1991 to 395 grammes in 2001. Against this background, exports of food grains on a massive scale as in 2003-04 are a travesty of development. Strangely enough, the Tenth Plan which otherwise provides a scholarly analysis of agricultural and food policies, does not make even a casual reference to the mountain of food grains co-existing with a mass of under-fed population, nor to the targets of reaching food security in a meaningful sense, described above.

---

2. For excerpts from the interview with the Minister, see *Swagat Magazine*, December 2003.

Even the list of 11 "Moniterable Targets" of the Tenth Plan does not include the food security target. On the other hand, the Tenth Plan grandiloquently promises: "All villages to have sustained access to potable drinking water within the Plan period."[3] Is it because the Planning Commission experts assume that food security has already been achieved? Would it not have made better sense to ensure food security with food grain supplies already available, than to promise potable water which is yet to be made available?

Experts of the Reserve Bank of India (RBI) also seem to believe that we have already attained food security and it is high time we move away from producing rice and wheat to production of high value-added agricultural products such as milk, fruits and vegetables, poultry and fisheries. They hold MSP as the villain of the distorted cropping pattern. "The minimum support price (MSP) policy has distorted the relative prices between rice and wheat, on the one hand and other food and non-food crops, on the other, giving rise to a distorted cropping pattern. It has contributed to a steep rise in the ratio of procurement to production over the years. The higher increase MSPs of rice and wheat relative to prices of other agricultural commodities has contributed to an incentive structure that favours production of rice and wheat at the cost of other crops. The policy has contributed to a burgeoning stock—far in excess of food security requirements, adding to the carrying costs and locked-in bank credit, which could have been otherwise deployed for funding productive activities. In view of the associated costs, there is a need for re-examining the price support mechanism to eliminate the distortion of agricultural product composition. In line with diversification of the consumption basket of a representative Indian household, there has been some acceleration in the growth of high value added agricultural products such as milk, fruits and vegetables, poultry, meat and fisheries during the 1990s. It is essential that this trend is reinforced in the coming years from the viewpoint of enhancing producer incomes and nutrition of consumers. Higher agricultural growth will come from crop diversification to non-traditional activities that are in line with the changing agricultural demand pattern."[4]

3. *Tenth Plan*, Volume I, see Box 1.1 on p.6.

4. *Report on Currency and Finance, 2001-02*, Reserve Bank of India, March 2003 (page VIII–2).

While RBI experts' concern for improving the nutrition of consumers is indeed touching, the danger underlying the philosophy of both Government of India and RBI needs to be exposed. Both are trying to push below the carpet the stark reality of a sizeable population continuing to remain in what may be called a state of semi-starvation. According to FAO, more than 225 million Indians remain chronically under-nourished and the UNDP estimates that over one-half of all Indian pre-schoolers suffer from malnutrition. Eliminating hunger should therefore be the first priority on the redrafted agenda of agricultural development. This can be achieved immediately because fortunately we have been able to successfully generate adequate supplies of food grains, mainly rice and wheat. Enriching the consumer basket of the relatively better off thus becomes a priority of the second order. We must first look at those consumers whose baskets are practically or nearly empty.

Conventional wisdom stipulates that the problem of poverty can be tackled through higher GDP growth, expansion of employment and generation of supplementary income through secondary occupations and soon. But the process is a long haul and may take at least two decades, as the recent experience of China has demonstrated. The Tenth Plan which has analysed the trends in poverty reinforces this conclusion clearly that the mandated reduction in poverty rate of 5 percentage points during the Tenth Plan and another 10 percentage points during the Eleventh Plan will still leave more than 11 per cent of the population or about 130 million people below the poverty line in 2012. It is as if the policy makers are throwing up their hands declaring that the situation is hopeless. Do the contemporary policy makers expect the "semi-starving India", to remain with us always?

In the redrafted agenda, therefore the approach should be: In the India-specific unique situation, plan to eliminate hunger first and poverty later. The co-existence of embarrassingly large stocks of food grains with FCI and sizeable unsatisfied demand for food grains is an anachronism. Policy makers should grow out of their market theology and address the issue head-long. In any other country, such a situation would have exploded into a revolution. Ours is an ancient civilisation known for its quiescence. Exporting of a small quantity of high-value branded commodity like *basmati* rice is certainly welcome, but massive exports of 10 to 12 million tonnes of ordinary quality rice and wheat is totally unwarranted. What is worse, our exports of food grains are highly subsidised. For instance, during the four years 2000-01 to 2003-04, the price realised on rice exports has been generally lower than the issue price of rice provided to families below the poverty line (BPL). This is taking the "export optimism" to its absurd heights. In other words, the same market theologists who are advocating the abolition of domestic food subsidy are encouraging subsidising foreign consumers of Indian food grains! Food policy has thus become a bundle of contradictions. To reiterate, we need all the cereals we produce for domestic consumption and in fact the rate of production of cereals needs to be accelerated. Even modest projections of demand for cereals in 2020 place the estimate at 260 million tonnes, as compared to the production level of 187 million tonnes in 2001. The enormous gap between demand and supply is thus obvious. Logically, therefore the incentive machanism to promote production of rice and wheat—the MSP, procurement of food grains by FCI and the public distribution system must also be reinforced. This does mean that there is no scope for modification or rationalisation of this mechanism. The point is that market theologists should be warned of the grave dangers to food security, if this incentive mechanism is dismantled on the specious ground of "surpluses" of food grains. Our policy makers should disabuse their mind of the illusion of "surpluses". RBI experts, quoted earlier, have an important point. We do need to produce more fruits and vegetables, milk, poultry and fisheries products etc. But this is not an "either or" proposition. We do not have to cut down our acreage under rice and wheat to be able to produce other products. There is enough scope to raise the production of these products without impinging on the production of cereals. For instance, some states like Maharashtra have made, in more recent years, remarkable progress in horticulture without encroaching upon the production of cereals. The substitution of rice/wheat by horticultural crops could, at best, be marginal. In fact, the thrust for growth of agriculture and allied activities must emanate in the coming years, from agriculture in its extended sense, particularly the livestock sub-sector, which holds out great promise for growth. The extended arms of the agricultural sector should therefore receive greater prominence in the redrafted agenda.

8.2.1 Reaching Food to the Poor

The tragedy of Indian planning is that, over the years, we have developed the technology and the institutional framework to produce adequate quantities of food grains or cereals at any rate: but we simply do not know how to reach the food grains so produced to the needy. The muddle-headedness of food management policy discussed earlier reflects this tragedy. In fact, the issue is so important that the Tenth Plan should have devoted a whole paper to find an appropriate solution to the problems of food delivery mechanism which ensures food security. Food security in a meaningful sense is ensured not merely by producing adequate quantum of food grains but also by reaching the food to the needy. The latter task is inextricably interwoven with the livelihood or employment, because a majority of the poor is not only assetless but also without any assured or a continuous employment. This brings to the employment situation.

The current backlog of unemployment is around 9 per cent or equivalent to 35 million persons and thus, is far too high. This is on top of the large underemployment or disguised unemployment. On the basis of the Prime Minister's vision of creating 100 million employment opportunities over the next 10 years, the Tenth Plan has set a target of creation of 50 million jobs during the next 5 years. If this target is achieved, unemployment is likely to decline to some 5 per cent by the end of the Tenth Plan. To be able to realise the target, the focus will have to be on a wide range of sectors such as agriculture and allied sectors, construction, tourism, transport, small scale industries (SSI), retailing, etc. To facilitate growth in these sectors, supportive policies need to be put in place. Here is the rub.

Unfortunately, as I have demonstrated elsewhere, the financial sector reforms introduced in the 1990s have, in effect, succeeded in alienating the financial system from the business of development.[5]

5. For detailed discussion see: Mujumdar, N.A. (2002). *Financial Sector Reforms and Indian's Economic Development*, New Delhi: Academic Foundation.

Admitting this conclusion, the Tenth Plan states: "It is becoming evident however, that the organised financial sector in India is either unable or unwilling to finance a range of activities that are of crucial importance both for growth and development. Agriculture, unorganised manufacturing, and services and various types of infrastructure are instances of such sectors. The recent financial sector reforms have naturally focussed primarily in improving viability and stability of financial institutions, without adequately addressing this issue. It is therefore necessary to consider methods of encouraging the financial sector to finance such activities without impinging on its viability or compromising on prudential concerns."[6] Public sector banks have failed even today to meet the credit target of 18 per cent of net bank credit to agriculture, the actual level being some 15 per cent in 2002-03. PSBs should enhance their presence in the rural sector with a view to facilitating not only faster agricultural growth, but also a wide range of activities in the non-farm sector, self-employment, retail trade, services and generally decentralised development. One has to foster decentralised growth of a multitude of micro-enterprises in the rural and semi-urban sector, the Chinese experience is illuminating in this context. To facilitate such broad-based growth we have to organise and build self-help groups (SHGs), micro-credit institutions and increasingly seek to involve NGOs in the process. It is encouraging to note that RBI has begun to take recently some initiatives in this direction. While on this subject, it is refreshing to note that the Exim Bank has recently identified the agriculture and processed food sector as a thrust sector in its business strategy. It has identified certain products as having maximum export potential[7] and has started financing export-oriented contract farming and organic farming and related activities. One hopes PSBs and NABARD would emulate this example in their respective areas.

Employment expansion is an ideal way by which the poor would be empowered to have access to food grains. This method needs to be supplemented by other modalities to achieve the objective in the

6. *Tenth Plan*, Vol. I, p.13, para 1.52.
7. The identified products include frozen shrimp, prawns, coffee (green and not decaf) fresh grapes, melon, papayas, avocado, guava, mangoes, malt extract, oil cakes of soyabean, raw cane sugar, dried and shelled chickpeas, whole cloves, garlic, bovine meat, sheep meat and black tea.

immediate run: linking of rural development works like micro watershed development programmes to utilisation of food grains, instituting "Grain Loans Facility" for all institutions involved in financing rural development programmes like rural co-operatives, RRBs, even NGOs. I have spelt out these possibilities elsewhere.[8] There is also the need to activate the mid-day meals schemes to provide children in government and government assisted primary schools with prepared meals. This scheme confers multiple benefits to the economy. In fact, universal and nutritious mid-day meals would be a great leap forward toward the realisation of right to food. The main point to drive home is that productive utilisation of all the food grain domestically—and not through exports—should be the dominant objective of development policy subsuming all other objectives.

The founding fathers of the Indian Society of Agricultural Economics had in their wisdom inscribed in the Society's logo the following motto: "*Dhan Dhanyam Vipulam Bhavatu*", or "Let there be surpluses of wealth and food grains". We have achieved this objective because our foreign exchange reserves have soared to the unprecedented level of beyond $ 100 billion and we have been living with the so-called food grains surpluses, for the past 3 or 4 years, the food stocks with FCI, at one point, exceeding 60 million tonnes. Little did these forefathers realise that contemporary policy makers in the 1990s and early 2000s, soaked in the market theology would frustrate the cherished objective of ensuring adequate food to all in the country, by exporting large quantities of food grains. The redrafting of the agenda for agricultural development has therefore become imperative. We have now to pursue food security in the holistic sense. It is not enough to produce adequate quantities of food grains: it is also necessary to ensure that food grains produced reach all the needy. If this extended concept of food security is to be achieved, agricultural development itself assumes different connotations. Employment must be expanded not only in agriculture but also in allied sectors like livestock. Investment in agriculture does not end with investment in large and medium irrigation projects, but it would also involve pursuit of micro watershed

8. "Rural Development: New Perceptions", *Economic and Political Weekly*, September 28, 2002.

development projects on a massive scale and rainwater harvesting. Empowering the rural poor through employment expansion, both wage-paid and self-employment, so as to enable them to access food grains should constitute an integral part of agriculture development strategy. Of course, these programmes need to be supplemented with special programmes aimed at benefiting specific target groups like school-going children.

8.3 Concluding Comments

The agenda for agricultural development needs to be redrafted immediately because the contemporary policy makers soaked in the market philosophy of IMF and World Bank have produced a food management policy which is muddle-headed. This policy is founded on the premise that India has large surpluses of rice and wheat. This is reflected in the massive exports of rice and wheat of more than 10 million tonnes in 2003-04. What is worse, these exports are highly subsidised. The same market theologists who cry hoarse against the domestic food subsidies are encouraging subsidisation of foreign consumers of Indian rice and wheat. What a travesty of development! India is the abode of the largest number of under-fed and under nourished persons in the world. The premordial objective of development in this context should therefore be to eliminate hunger; all other objectives should be subsumed in this primordial objective. The starting point of the redrafted agenda would therefore be that there are no "exportable surpluses" of food grains; what we observe today as surplus stocks are effective demand surpluses. For ensuring meaningful food security, it is not enough to produce adequate quantities of food grains; it is also necessary to ensue that these food grains reach the needy and the poor. The Tenth Plan which does not make even a reference to the co-existence of huge stocks of food grains with large unsatisfied demand for food grains, should have devoted a whole paper to this question of reaching available food grains to the poor or needy. Several modalities of reaching food to the poor have been discussed including "food for work" programmes, employment expansion programmes, linking of micro watershed development programmes to utilisation of food grains, institution of a "Grain Loans Facility" and so on. There are schemes like mid-day meals aimed at benefiting specific target groups. In this sense, agricultural development should have the twin objectives of producing adequate quantum of food grains and also facilitating access of the poor to these food grains. This holistic concept of food security assumes greater significance because removal of poverty is a long haul. Even if the targeted reduction in poverty is achieved, as stipulated in the Tenth and Eleventh Plans, about 130 million persons would continue to remain poor by 2012. In terms of "immediacy" therefore, providing minimum food gains in terms of caloric requirements becomes a viable alternative as a "second best" solution. Indian cannot afford, at this stage, to institute a comprehensive social security scheme on the lines of those prevalent in, say, the UK or the USA. Through the various modalities discussed earlier and with appropriate supportive policies in place, India can atleast seek to guarantee the right to food to all its citizens.

9 Diversification in Indian Agriculture during Nineties

S.S. Acharya and R.L. Jogi

9.1 Introduction

Diversification essentially means moving away from a single enterprise or activity to a number of enterprises or activities. Diversification helps the individual farmer in: (a) fuller and better utilisation of land, labour, water and other resources; (b) realising regular and quicker returns; and (c) reducing risks arising out of crop failures, yield losses and market failures. Diversification of agriculture has also been realised as an effective strategy for achieving the objective of food and nutrition security, employment generation, poverty alleviation, income growth and sustainable development.

The diversification in Indian agriculture can be analysed by looking at: (a) diversification from crop enterprises to non-crop enterprises like livestock and fishing; (b) diversification in employment; and (c) crop area diversification. In this paper, we have concentrated on crop area diversification only. As regards the crop area diversification, it needs to be mentioned that ever since the launch of the First Five Year Plan, till late seventies or early eighties, the major thrust of the agricultural development strategy was to increase the production of food grains. The new strategy of agricultural development launched in the country in mid-sixties also aimed at accelerating the growth of food grains production. It was only in early eighties when the balance between demand and supply of cereals was in sight, the thrust of the agricultural policy was changed from 'maximising production of food grains' to 'evolving a production pattern in line with the demand pattern' (Government of India, 1986). The crop diversification in Indian agriculture is, therefore, expected only during eighties and nineties.

The objective of this paper is to analyse the trends in diversification in Indian agriculture during nineties. The changes in the share of agricultural sector in GDP and employment are presented in Section two. Land use changes at macro level in India are analysed in the third section. In the fourth section, we have analysed crop area diversification at the all-India level. Product diversification in terms of value of crop output is discussed in the fifth section. State level analysis of crop area diversification is presented in the sixth section. Estimates of diversification index for different states and at all-India level are shown in the seventh section. Some concluding observations are given in the last section.

9.2 Share of Agriculture in GDP and Employment

The declining trend in the share of agriculture in the country's economy continued during the eighties and nineties. The combined share of crops and livestock sector in GDP, which decreased from 48.7 per cent in 1950-51 to 34.7 per cent in 1980-81, declined further to 28.7 per cent in 1990-91 and 22.2 per cent in 2000-01 (Table 9.1). The share of forestry and fishing also followed the same trend. In 2000-01, the combined share of agriculture and allied sectors in GDP was only 24.2 per cent.

Table 9.1

Indian Agriculture—Shares in GDP and Employment

Particulars	*1950-51*	*1980-81*	*1990-91*	*2000-01*
Share of GDP				
• Agriculture	48.7	34.7	28.7	22.2
• Forestry & fishing	6.7	3.4	2.2	2.0
Total	55.4	38.1	30.9	24.2
Rural population				
• Million persons	298.6	523.9	628.7	741.7
• % of total population	82.7	76.7	74.3	72.2
Working population				
• Million persons	140.0	244.6	314.1	402.5
• % of total population	38.8	35.8	37.1	39.2
Cultivators				
• Million persons	69.9	92.5	110.7	127.6
• % of total workers	49.9	37.8	35.2	31.7
Agricultural labourers				
• Million persons	27.3	55.5	74.6	107.5
• % of total workers	19.5	22.7	23.8	26.7
Total workers in agriculture				
• Million persons	97.2	148.0	185.3	235.1
• % of total workers	69.4	60.5	59.0	58.4

Source: EPW (1995); Government of India (2002a).

Rural population in India has continued to increase but the share of rural population in the total population has continued to slowly decline. Even then, preponderance of rural life continues unabated. The share of rural population in total population of India, which came down from 82.7 per cent in 1950-51 to 76.7 per cent in 1980-81 declined marginally to 74.3 per cent in 1990-91 and further to 72.2 per cent in 2000-01. In 2001, rural population in India was estimated as 741.7 million.

As regards the ratio of working population to total population, there appears to be a reversal of trend during the eighties and nineties. Working population as a proportion of total population, which had declined from 38.8 per cent in 1950-51 to 35.8 per cent in 1980-81, recovered to 37.1 per cent in 1990-91 and increased to 39.2 per cent in 2000-01.

A noticeable change in agricultural sector during the nineties has been the acceleration in the rate of increase in the proportion of agricultural labourers in the total workforce. While the proportion of workers in agriculture remained at around the same level of 59 per cent between 1990-91 and 2000-01, the proportion of agricultural labourers went up from 23.8 per cent in 1990-91 to 26.7 per cent in 2000-01. It may be mentioned here that: (a) the cultivators as a proportion of total workers has been continuously decreasing in the country; (b) the proportion of agricultural labourers in total workforce has been continuously increasing; and (c) total workers in agriculture as a proportion of entire workforce which declined between 1950-51 and 1980-81, declined only marginally during the eighties and did not change much during the nineties. Continued dependence of around 59 per cent of the population for livelihood on agriculture and increasing proportion of agricultural labourers in the workforce should be a matter of concern for food security and alleviation of rural poverty.

9.3 Trends in Land Use in India

As far as land under major use categories is concerned, there does not appear to be any significant change during the eighties and nineties except some marginal decline in culturable wastelands and corresponding increase in non-agricultural uses (Table 9.2). The cultivated area (net sown area plus current fallow lands) which increased sharply from 129.5 million hectares (mha) in 1950-51 to 154.8 mha in 1980-81 increased only marginally to 156.7 mha in 1990-91 and declined slightly to 156.1 mha in 2000-01. The area under forests, pastures and trees has stayed at around 83 mha between 1980-81 and 2000-01. Substantial potential culturable area (old fallows and culturable wastes) continues to remain without productive use. Such areas were estimated as 26.6 mha in 1980-1981, 24.7 mha in 1990-91 and 23.9 mha in 2000-01. As these areas require considerable investment for bringing them under productive use, several states have launched special schemes to encourage private sector, entrepreneurs and farmers groups to come forward in this endeavour.

9.4 Crop Area Diversification in India

Crop area diversification was analysed from several angles. First, we looked at changes in area under food grains and non-food grains as groups. As already mentioned, crop area diversification away from food grains at aggregate level was not expected before 1980-81. In fact, this is reflected from the area allocation figures also. Between triennium ending (TE) 1952-53 and TE 1980-81, while the gross cropped area (GCA) went up from 134.3 mha to 172.4 mha, the proportion of GCA allocated to food grains had remained nearly the same at 73.6 per cent (Acharya, 2003). It was only during the last two decades that a shift in area away from food grains is noticed.

Area under food grains as proportion of GCA declined from 73.6 per cent during TE 1980-81 to 69.5 per cent during TE 1990-91 and further to 64.3 per cent during TE 2000-01. Correspondingly, the area under non-food grain crops went up from 26.4 per cent to 30.5 per cent and further to 35.7 per cent during this period (Table 9.3). It may be mentioned that there was no absolute decline in area under food grains during the eighties. It was only during nineties that the area under food grains came down from 127.4 mha during TE 1990-91 to 122.7 mha during TE 2000-01. However, the increase in area under non-food grain crops was considerably more than the decline in food grains area. The area under non-food grain crops, which had gone up from 45.4 mha during TE 1980-81 to 56.0 mha during TE 1990-91, further increased to

68 mha during TE 2000-01. The increase in area under non-food grain crops during nineties occurred owing to both expansion and substitution effect. About 61 per cent of the incremental area under non-food grain crops (12 mha) was contributed by extension in GCA and 39 per cent by the replacement of food grains during the nineties.

Table 9.2

Trends in Land Use in India

Land Use Classes	1950-51		1980-81		1990-91		1998-99	
	Mha	%	Mha	%	Mha	%	Mha	%
I. Cultivated								
Net sown	118.8	36.1	140.0	42.6	143.0	43.5	142.6	43.4
Current fallow	10.7	3.3	14.8	4.5	13.7	4.2	13.5	4.1
Sub-total(I)	129.5	39.4	154.8	47.1	156.7	47.7	156.1	47.5
II. Other agricultural related uses								
Forests	40.5	12.3	67.5	20.5	67.8	20.6	69.0	21.0
PP & GL	6.7	2.0	12.0	3.6	11.4	3.5	11.1	3.4
MTC & G	19.8	6.0	3.6	1.0	3.8	1.2	3.6	1.1
Sub-total (II)	67.0	20.3	83.1	25.2	83.0	25.3	83.7	25.5
III. Potential for use								
Old fallows	17.4	5.3	9.9	3.0	9.7	3.0	9.9	3.0
Wastes	22.9	7.0	16.7	5.1	15.0	4.6	14.0	4.3
Sub-total (III)	40.3	12.3	26.6	8.1	24.7	7.6	23.9	7.3
IV. Non-agriculture								
In use	9.43	2.9	19.7	6.0	21.1	6.4	22.8	6.9
Barren & uncultivable	8.24	11.6	20.0	6.1	19.4	5.9	19.6	6.0
Sub-total (IV)	7.6	14.5	39.7	12.1	40.5	12.3	42.4	12.9
V. Not reported	44.3	13.5	24.5	7.5	23.8	7.1	22.6	6.8
Total geographical area (I to V)	328.7	100.0	328.7	100.0	328.7	100.0	328.7	100.0

Note: PP & GL = Permanent Pastures and Grazing Lands, MTC & G – Miscellaneous Tree Crops and Growers and Mha = Million Hectares.

Source: Government of India (2002a).

Table 9.3

Area under Food Grains and Non-Food Grain Crops in India

Period	Food Grains			Non-Food Grains			Gross Cropped Area		
	Mha	%	Incremental Mha	Mha	%	Incremental Mha	Mha	%	Incremental Mha
TE 1980-81	127.0	73.6	-	45.4	26.4	-	172.4	100.0	-
TE 1990-91	127.4	69.5	0.4	56.0	30.5	10.6	183.4	100.0	11.0
TE 2000-01	122.7	64.3	(-)4.7	68.0	35.7	12.0	190.7	100.0	7.3

Source: Government of India (2003).

Second, we looked at season-wise changes in area under food grains during eighties and nineties (Table 9.4). The decline in absolute area under food grains, observed during nineties, was entirely among *kharif* food grains. Not only this, the decline in area under *kharif* food grains during the nineties was considerably higher than the decline observed in area under all food grains owing to the increase in area under *rabi* food grains. While the area under *kharif* food grains declined from 81.4 mha during TE 1990-91 to 74.1 mha during TE 2000-01, the area under *rabi* food grains went up from 46 mha to 48.6 mha during this period.

Table 9.4

Area under Kharif and Rabi Food Grains in India

Period	*Kharif*		*Rabi*		*Total*	
	Mha	*%*	*Mha*	*%*	*Mha*	*%*
TE 1980-81	82.3	64.8	44.7	35.2	127.0	100.0
TE 1990-91	81.4	63.9	46.0	36.1	127.4	100.0
TE 2000-01	74.1	60.4	48.6	39.6	122.7	100.0

Source: Government of India (2003).

Third, we analysed the changes in area under cereals and pulses during the nineties. It was observed that the decline in area has occurred under both cereals and pulses during this period (Table 9.5). The area under cereals declined from 103.7 mha to 101.1 mha and that under pulses declined from 23.7 mha to 21.6 mha between TE 1990-91 and TE 2000-01.

Table 9.5

Area under Cereals and Pulses in India

Period	*Cereals*			*Pulses*			*Total*		
	Mha	*%* *	*Incremental Area (Mha)*	*Mha*	*%* *	*Incremental Area (Mha)*	*Mha*	*%* *	*Incremental Area (Mha)*
TE 1980-81	104.2	60.4	-	22.8	13.2	-	127.0	73.6	-
TE 1990-91	103.7	56.5	(-) 0.5	23.7	13.0	0.9	127.4	69.5	0.4
TE 2000-01	101.1	53.0	(-) 2.6	21.6	11.3	(-)2.1	122.7	64.3	(-)4.7

Note: * % of gross cropped area.

Source: Government of India (2002a).

Fourth, we looked at the changes in area under individual cereals during the nineties (Table 9.6). It was observed that the decline in cereal area occurred only under coarse cereals, other than maize during this period. The combined area under *bajra*, *jowar*, *ragi*, small millets and barley declined from 31.7 mha during TE 1990-91 to 23.3 mha during TE 2000-01. The decline in area under these cereals, which commenced in eighties, was reinforced during the nineties. Contrarily, the trend of increase in area under rice, wheat and maize continued during the nineties. The incremental area under these three staple cereals aggregated to 5.8 mha during the nineties.

Table 9.6

Area under Major Cereals in India

(Million Hectares)

Period	*Rice*	*Wheat*	*Maize*	*Other Coarse Cereals*	*Total*
TE 1980-81	40.0	22.4	5.8	36.0	104.2
TE 1990-91	42.2	23.9	5.9	31.7	103.7
TE 2000-01	44.7	26.7	6.4	23.3	101.1

Source: Government of India (2002a).

Fifth, we analysed the changes in area under individual non-food grain crops. Under oilseeds, the increasing trend of area continued during the nineties but the rate of increase appears to have slowed down. The area under oilseeds, which went up from 17.42 mha during TE 1980-81 to 22.95 mha during TE 1990-91, increased to 24.59 mha during 2000-01. The area under all other major non-food grain crops and crop groups also recorded increase between TE 1990-91 and TE 2000-01 (Table 9.7).

Table 9.7

Area under Non-Food Grain Crops

(Million Hectares)

Crops	*TE 1980-81*	*TE 1990-91*	*TE 2000-01*
Oilseeds	17.42	22.95	24.59
Cotton	8.02	7.49	8.88
Jute+mesta	1.26	0.95	1.03
Sugarcane	2.79	3.49	4.19
Potato	0.74	0.94	1.29
Onion	0.23	0.31	0.47
Tobacco	0.43	0.40	0.41
Coconut	1.07	1.46	1.79
Cashewnut	0.47	0.53	0.70
Others*	12.97	17.48	24.65
Total	45.40	56.00	68.00

Note: * Include fruits, other vegetables, spices, plantation crops, guar seed and fodder crops.
Source: Government of India (2002a).

The direction of crop diversification in Indian agriculture observed above is also substantiated by the estimates of compound growth rates of area under different crops and crop groups (Table 9.8) generated by the Directorate of Economics and Statistics, Ministry of Agriculture (Government of India, 2002a). While the growth of area under rice and wheat accelerated during the nineties as compared to that during the eighties, the area under coarse cereals continued to decline both during the eighties and nineties. In the case of pulses, the rate of decline in area accelerated during the nineties. The area under oilseeds and all other non-food grain crops or crop groups, for which the estimates are presented in Table 9.8, recorded positive and/or accelerated growth rates during the nineties.

Table 9.8

All-India Compound Growth Rates of Area

Crops/Crop Groups	*1980-81 to 1989-90*	*1990-91 to 1999-2000*
Rice	0.41	0.62
Wheat	0.46	1.67
Coarse cereals	-1.34	-0.54
All cereals	-0.26	-.0.08
All pulses	-0.09	-0.61
Food grains	-0.23	-0.17
All oilseeds	1.51	1.14
Cotton	-1.25	2.36
Jute+mesta	-2.90	0.95
All fibres	-1.50	2.16
Tobacco	-2.79	1.28
Sugarcane	1.44	1.81
Non-food grains	1.12	1.37
All principal crops	0.10	0.25

Source: Government of India (2002a).

9.5 Product Diversification in Indian Agriculture

One other way of looking at the diversification in Indian agriculture is to analyse the changes in product composition within agriculture. This can be done by comparing the changes in value of agricultural products. In value terms, the agricultural basket is tending to tilt towards nutritionally rich livestock products. The share of livestock products in total value of agricultural products (crop plus livestock) has continued to increase during the nineties. It went up from 20.5 per cent in 1980-81 to 23.4 per cent in 1990-91 and further to 25.2 per cent in 1999-2000.

The value of entire basket of crop products (at constant 1993-94 prices) went up from Rs. 1876 billion during TE 1990-91 to Rs. 2421 billion during TE 2000-01 (Table 9.9), registering a point to point compound growth rate of 2.58 per cent per annum. The growth rate during the nineties was considerably lower than that during the eighties (3.51 per cent per annum). Several aspects of product value diversification of Indian crops sector can be observed from Table 9.9. First, food grains as a group account for less than 44 per cent of the total value of crop output in the country. The share of food grains in the total value of crop output, which was 43.2 per cent during TE 1990-91, declined to 39.5 per cent during TE 2000-01. The decline is observed in the share of both cereals and pulses separately as groups. Second, across individual cereal crops, the share of only wheat recorded an increase from 10.6 per cent to 11.3 per cent during this period. The share of rice and coarse cereals in total value of crop output declined during the nineties.

Third, rice continues to be the single largest crop in terms of value of crop output, despite its share declining from 20.5 per cent during TE 1990-91 to 19.1 per cent during TE 2000-01. The share of coarse cereals declined from 5.5 per cent to 4.1 per cent and of pulses from 6.6 per cent to 5.0 per cent of the total value of crop output during this period.

Fourth, among non-food grain crops, the share of fruits and vegetables as a group recorded a considerable increase during the nineties. The share of fruits and vegetables in total value of crop output went up from 17.6 per cent during TE 1990-91 to 23.0 per cent during TE 2000-01. The share of other oilseeds (mainly soyabean and sunflower seeds), sugar crops and spices/condiments also went up during the nineties. Fifth, as a reversal of the past trend, the share of oilseeds as a group has tended to decline during the nineties mainly due to decline in the share of two major oilseeds *viz.*, groundnut and rapeseed/mustard. Between TE 1990-91 and TE 2000-01, the share of groundnut declined from 4.4 per cent to 2.8 per cent and that of rapeseed/mustard declined from 2.5 per cent to 2.1 per cent. The decline in the share of oilseeds is a reflection of structure of import duty on edible oils which was kept at considerably lower levels during the most part of nineties.

Table 9.9

Changes in Crop Value Composition of Indian Agriculture (At 1993-94 Prices)

Crop/Crop Group	TE 1980-81		TE 1990-91		TE 2000-01	
	Value in Crore Rs.	%	Value in Crore Rs.	%	Value in Crore Rs.	%
Rice	26528	20.0	38481	20.5	46334	19.1
Wheat	13120	9.9	19986	10.6	27421	11.3
Maize	1977	1.5	2815	1.5	3547	1.5
Other coarse cereals	7138	5.3	7475	4.0	6185	2.6
All cereals	48763	36.7	68757	36.6	83487	34.5
All pulses	9627	7.24	12429	6.6	12203	5.0
All food grains	58390	3.9	81186	43.2	95690	39.5
Groundnut	5302	4.0	8227	4.4	6830	2.8
Rapeseed/mustard	2067	1.6	4669	2.5	5173	2.1
Other oilseeds	3587	2.6	7554	4.0	12882	5.4
All oilseeds	10956	8.2	20450	10.9	24885	10.3
Sugar crops	9653	7.3	14122	7.5	18701	7.7
Fibres	6282	4.7	8255	4.4	9742	4.0
Spices & condiments	3689	2.8	5567	3.0	9004	3.7
Fruits & vegetables	24996	18.8	32924	17.6	55633	23.0
Tobacco	850	0.6	1022	0.5	1255	0.5
Tea & coffee	1742	1.3	2232	1.2	1304	1.3
Byproducts	9745	7.3	14695	7.8	15999	6.6
Miscellaneous	6640	5.1	7187	3.9	8079	3.4
All non-food grains	74553	56.1	106454	56.8	146402	60.5
Total value	132943	100.0	187640	100.0	242092	100.0

Source: Government of India (2001, 2002).

Sixth, the trend in area diversification appears to be generally consistent with the need for shift towards high value crops without jeopardising the objective of food security. The average value productivity of coarse cereals (other than maize) is the lowest among all crops/crop groups. Value productivity of rice, wheat, oilseeds and other non-food grain crops is considerably higher than coarse cereals and even pulses (Table 9.10). Thus, shift of area away from coarse cereals towards rice, wheat, oilseeds, fruits, vegetables and spices has helped in not only improving the supply of these much needed basket of commodities but also in improving the farm value productivity and nutritional status without sacrificing the national food security.

Table 9.10

Value of Crop Output Per Hectares in India (At 1993-94 Prices)

(Rs. Per Hectare)

Crops/Crop Groups	*TE 1990-91*	*TE 2000-01*	*Compound Growth Rate (% Per Annum)*
Rice	9119	10366	1.29
Wheat	8362	10270	2.08
Maize	4771	5542	1.51
Other coarse cereals	2358	2655	1.19
All cereals	6630	8258	2.22
All pulses	5244	5650	0.75
All food grains	6373	7790	2.03
Oilseeds	8891	10116	1.30
Other non-food grains	26062	27999	0.72
All non-food grains	19010	21530	1.25
All crops	10231	12695	2.18

Source: Computed from Tables 9.5, 9.6 and 9.9.

9.6 Crop Diversification at the State Level

We have analysed the extent and direction of diversification at the state level also. However, the limitations of analysing crop diversification at the state level should be kept in view. Around 110 million farm families in thc country take the decisions relating to the area planted under different crops. Further, the agro-climatic conditions of the region influence the decisions of the farmers in this regard. Therefore, the most appropriate unit for assessing the degree of diversification is the individual farm. As one aggregates the farms for analysing the extent and direction of diversification, considerable information is lost. For illustration, assume that there are five agro-climatic zones, each covering 20 per cent of gross cropped area. Further, assume that the farmers in each zone specialise in a single crop (different across zones). In this case, while each farm is a specialised farm, the aggregate analysis would reveal that the country or region has well diversified agriculture i.e., five crops occupying 20 per cent area each. Higher and higher levels of aggregation obviously obscure the assessment of diversification.

Percentage area under important crops/crop groups at two points of time i.e., 1990-91 and 1999-2000 are shown in Table 9.11. Several aspects of crop area diversification at the state level can be discerned from this table. First, except Kerala and Gujarat, in all the states, food grains account for more than 53 per cent of the GCA of respective states. In Kerala, food grains accounted for only 19.5 per cent of GCA in 1990-91, which declined further to 12.7 per cent in 1999-2000. In the case of Gujarat, food grains occupied 45.7 per cent of GCA in 1990-91, which declined to 33.7 per cent in 1999-2000. Second, there was considerable difference among states in terms of diversification from food grains to non-food grain crops. In Gujarat, Orissa, Rajasthan and MP, the percentage point shift in area from food grains to non-food grain crops during the nineties was between 7.7 and 12.0. In Kerala, Andhra Pradesh and Maharashtra, the shift in area was 5.4 to 6.8 percentage points. In West Bengal, UP and Assam, there has been an increase in area under non-food grains (and corresponding decrease under food grains) which ranged from 2.6 to 3.0 percentage points of GCA during this period. In Punjab and Bihar, there was negligible change in distribution of GCA between food grains and non-food grain crops during the nineties. In Haryana, Tamil Nadu and Karnataka, there had been a reversal leading to some increase in area under food grains by 2.2 to 4.2 per cent of GCA during this period.

Third, rice alone accounts for more than half of GCA in eastern states of Assam, Bihar and West Bengal. In Orissa also, rice occupies considerable part of GCA, 45.9 per cent in 1990-91 and 54.0 per cent in 1999-2000. During the nineties, while in some states, the share of rice in GCA went up, in others it declined. The area under rice as a proportion of GCA increased in Haryana (11.2 per cent to 18.0 per cent), Orissa (45.9 per cent to 54.0 per cent), Punjab (26.9 per cent to 31.6 per cent) and Tamil Nadu (28.0 per cent to 33.8 per cent). Fourth, in the case of wheat, while the percentage area increased in Haryana (31.3 per cent to 38.4 per cent), Rajasthan (9.4 per cent to 13.7 per cent), Bihar (18.7 per cent to 21.2 per cent), MP (16.0 per cent to 17.7 per cent) and

UP (33.6 per cent to 35.3 per cent), it declined in Punjab (43.6 per cent to 41.1 per cent). Fifth, the percentage area under coarse cereals declined in all the states (except Bihar) during the nineties. Sixth, the share of pulses in GCA declined in all the states except Karnataka and Maharashtra, where some marginal increase in percentage area under pulses is observed during the nineties. Seventh, in the case of oilseeds, while there was increase in their share in GCA in Gujarat, MP and Rajasthan, it declined in AP, Karnataka and Orissa. And eighth, the area under other non-food grain crops (other than oilseeds) as a proportion of GCA increased in almost all the states except some decline in Haryana and Tamil Nadu.

We also examined the status of first five crops in each state in terms of their ranks and dominance in GCA. Both in 1990-91 and 1999-2000, out of 15 states for which the analysis is presented in Table 9.12, rice continues to be the most important crop in seven states. The dominant crop was wheat in three states (Haryana, Punjab and UP); *jowar* in two states (Karnataka and Maharashtra) and groundnut (Gujarat), *bajra* (Rajasthan) and coconut (Kerala) in one state each. There was no change in the rank of these crops between 1990-91 and 1999-2000. However, there was considerable difference in the percentage of GCA occupied by the first crop across states. The general tendency is that wherever rice is the first crop, the relative area occupied by the first crop is considerably higher than where the first crop is other than rice. Closely followed by rice is wheat. Where wheat is the first crop, the percentage of GCA occupied by the first crop is higher than where *jowar, bajra*, groundnut or coconuts emerge as the first crop. There was considerable difference across states in terms of second and other crops among first five crops.

In 11 states, there was no change in the ranking of second crop during the last 10 years. In Gujarat, cotton replaced *bajra* as second crop, in Karnataka rice replaced groundnut as second crop, in Kerala rubber replaced rice as second crop and in Rajasthan, wheat replaced other pulses as second crop. Between 1990-91 and 1999-2000, the percentage of GCA occupied by the first two crops declined in seven states and increased in eight states. As regards the first five crops, the percentage of GCA occupied by these crops, declined in as many as nine states and increased in only six states.

Table 9.11

State-wise Percentage of Gross Cropped Area under Major Crops

Year/State	*Rice*	*Wheat*	*Coarse Cereals*	*Total Cereals*	*Pulses*	*Food Grains*	*Oilseed*	*Other Non-Food Grains*	*Gross Cropped Area*
1990-91									
Andhra Pradesh	30.6	0.1	15.8	46.5	12.4	58.8	23.7	17.5	100.0
Assam	65.6	2.2	1.1	68.8	3.2	71.8	8.4	19.8	100.0
Bihar	51.4	18.7	8.6	78.7	11.2	89.9	2.3	7.8	100.0
Gujarat	5.1	6.9	24.0	36.0	9.6	45.7	26.2	28.1	100.0
Haryana	11.2	31.3	14.0	56.4	12.5	68.9	8.2	22.9	100.0
Karnataka	10.0	1.7	34.4	46.1	13.8	59.9	21.7	18.4	100.0
Kerala	18.5	0.0	0.3	18.8	0.8	19.5	0.8	79.7	100.0
M.P.	21.3	16.0	16.7	53.9	21.0	75.3	16.7	8.1	100.0
Maharashtra	7.2	4.0	40.0	51.2	14.9	66.1	13.0	20.9	100.0
Orissa	45.9	0.4	5.4	51.7	22.2	73.9	11.9	14.2	100.0
Punjab	26.9	43.6	3.2	73.7	1.9	75.6	1.5	22.8	100.0
Rajasthan	0.6	9.4	36.3	46.3	16.4	65.3	15.9	18.8	100.0
Tamil Nadu	28.0	0.0	17.8	45.8	13.2	58.6	17.3	24.1	100.0
U.P.	22.0	33.6	12.6	68.2	12.4	80.4	6.6	13.0	100.0
W. Bengal	67.1	3.1	1.2	71.4	3.7	75.0	5.9	19.1	100.0
1999-2000									
Andhra Pradesh	30.0	0.1	11.2	41.3	11.9	53.2	19.7	27.2	100.0
Assam	63.8	1.9	0.8	66.4	2.8	69.2	7.9	22.9	100.0
Bihar	50.4	21.2	9.6	81.2	8.9	90.1	2.4	7.5	100.0
Gujarat	6.5	4.8	15.5	26.7	6.9	33.7	27.6	38.8	100.0
Haryana	18.0	38.4	12.5	68.9	2.2	71.1	8.0	20.9	100.0
Karnataka	12.0	2.2	33.2	47.4	15.5	62.9	16.2	20.9	100.0
Kerala	11.7	0.0	0.2	11.9	0.8	12.7	0.3	87.0	100.0
M.P.	20.4	17.7	9.9	48.1	19.5	67.6	22.6	9.8	100.0
Maharashtra	6.8	4.7	33.1	44.6	16.1	60.7	12.2	27.1	100.0
Orissa	54.0	0.1	2.2	56.3	8.1	64.3	4.1	31.6	100.0
Punjab	31.6	41.1	2.4	75.1	0.8	75.9	1.4	22.7	100.0
Rajasthan	1.0	13.7	29.1	43.9	12.9	56.8	18.8	24.4	100.0
Tamil Nadu	33.8	0.0	15.9	49.7	13.1	62.8	16.4	20.8	100.0
U.P.	22.3	35.3	10.1	67.6	10.1	77.7	5.6	16.7	100.0
W. Bengal	64.7	3.8	0.6	69.1	2.9	72.0	5.2	22.8	100.0

Source: Government of India (1992, 2000); Government of India (2002b).

Table 9.12

State-wise Percentage Area under First Five Crops

Year/State	*First*	*First Two*	*First Five*	*Crops in Order**
1990-91				
Andhra Pradesh	30.6	48.7	71.8	Rice, Groundnut, Pulses, *Jowar*, Cotton
Assam	65.6	73.3	84.8	Rice, Mustard, Tea, Pulses, Jute
Bihar	51.4	70.2	87.1	Rice, Wheat, Pulses, Maize, Gram
Gujarat	16.4	27.5	52.1	Groundnut, *Bajra*, Cotton, *Jowar*, Oilseeds
Haryana	31.3	42.4	72.0	Wheat, Rice, Gram, *Bajra*, Cotton
Karnataka	18.3	28.6	56.4	*Jowar*, Groundnut, Rice, *Ragi*, Oilseeds
Kerala	28.8	47.3	68.0	Coconut, Rice, Rubber, Black Pepper, Cashewnut
M.P.	21.3	37.3	66.5	Rice, Wheat, Gram, Oilseeds, Pulses
Maharashtra	29.0	41.4	64.7	*Jowar*, Cotton, *Bajra*, Rice, Pulses
Orissa	45.9	65.9	76.2	Rice, Pulses, Groundnut, Sesamum, *Ragi*
Punjab	43.6	70.5	83.7	Wheat, Rice, Cotton, Maize, Sugarcane
Rajasthan	25.1	35.3	60.5	*Bajra*, Pulses, Mustard, Wheat, Gram
Tamil Nadu	28.0	42.5	65.7	Rice, Groundnut, Pulses, *Jowar*, *Bajra*
U.P.	33.6	55.7	73.4	Wheat, Rice, Sugarcane, Pulses, Gram
West Bengal	67.1	72.9	83.6	Rice, Jute, Mustard, Pulses, Wheat
1999-2000				
Andhra Pradesh	30.0	43.7	65.1	Rice, Groundnut, Cotton, Pulses, *Jowar*
Assam	63.8	70.8	80.9	Rice, Mustard, Tea, Pulses, Wheat
Bihar	50.4	71.6	88.4	Rice, Wheat, Maize, Pulses, Jute
Gujarat	18.0	33.1	53.6	Groundnut, Cotton, *Bajra*, Rice, Wheat
Haryana	38.4	56.4	82.6	Wheat, Rice, *Bajra*, Cotton, Mustard
Karnataka	16.7	28.7	54.0	*Jowar*, Rice, Groundnut, Pulses, *Ragi*
Kerala	29.9	45.7	67.6	Coconut, Rubber, Rice, Black Pepper, Cashewnut
M.P.	20.4	38.1	73.0	Rice, Wheat, Oilseeds, Gram, Pulses
Maharashtra	23.0	37.6	61.4	*Jowar*, Cotton, Oilseeds, *Bajra*, Pulses
Orissa	54.0	60.1	64.6	Rice, Pulses, Oilseeds, *Tur*, Chilies
Punjab	41.1	72.7	81.8	Wheat, Rice, Cotton, Maize, Sugarcane
Rajasthan	20.4	34.1	60.2	Bajra, Wheat, Mustard, Pulses, Gram
Tamil Nadu	33.8	46.6	70.8	Rice, Groundnut, Pulses, *Jowar*, Sugarcane
U.P.	35.3	57.6	74.5	Wheat, Rice, Sugarcane, Pulses, Mustard
West Bengal	64.7	71.1	81.9	Rice, Jute, Wheat, Mustard, Potato

Note: * Pulses in this table mean other than gram and *tur*; and oilseeds mean soyabean, sunflower seed, nigerseed and/or safflower.

Source: Government of India (1992, 2000); CMIE (2002); *http/agricoop.nic.in/statistics/st.3.htm*; Government of India (2002b).

9.7 Diversification Index

For assessing the extent of crop diversification and changes therein during the nineties, an index of diversification was worked out at the national as well as state level at two points of time i.e., 1990-91 and 1999-2000. The diversification index (DI) was computed following the formula of Simpson Index as given by Odum (1975) for measuring bio-diversity. Specifically, DI was computed as follows:

$$DI = (1 - \Sigma pi^2 fi)\ 100$$

Where pi = percentage of GCA under ith crop divided by 100

fi = frequency (number of crops) of pi

i = 1 to n (number of crops)

The DI varies between zero and 100. It takes a value zero when a single crop occupies entire GCA and it approaches 100 as n tends to infinity. The advantage of using Simpson Index over the one used by Acharya (2003) for working out index of diversification (ID) is obvious. A comparison of DI and ID will make the difference clear. If there are only four crops, each occupying 25 per cent of GCA in a region or a farm, while ID will come out to be 100, DI will be 75. Take the other case where there are 10 crops, each occupying 10 per cent of GCA, while the ID will come out to be 100, DI will be 90. In another case, where there are 100 crops, each occupying one per cent of GCA, while ID will again come out to be 100, DI will be 99. Thus, ID approaches 100 only when n (number of crops) increases, which is not the case for DI. Therefore, if the objective function is diversification towards a defined number of crops, ID is superior to DI. But, if the number of crops is not assumed to be limited, DI is superior to ID.

The estimates of DI for 1990-91 and 1999-2000 for each of the 15 important states and for country as a whole are shown in Table 9.13. At the national level, there is already a very high degree of crop area diversification, the index being 91.1 for 1990-91 and 90.7 for 1999-2000. The DI estimated from the crop values was however lower than that from the crop areas and appears to have marginally declined during the nineties. However, there is a considerable difference among the states in terms of extent and change in the status of diversification.

The estimates of DI at the state level vary from 55.7 to 93.4 for 1990-91 and 58.3 to 95.0 for 1999-2000. During 1990-91, the DI was relatively low for West Bengal (54.1) and Assam (55.7) and relatively high for Kerala (93.4), Gujarat (92.9) and Karnataka (91.4). During nineties, the crop diversification considerably increased in West Bengal and Assam, which are low diversified states. Maharashtra, Andhra Pradesh, Kerala and Rajasthan also recorded increase in diversification during the nineties. On the contrary, there was considerable decrease in crop diversification in Haryana, Orissa and Tamil Nadu. Out of 15 states for which DI has been estimated, 8 states recorded increase and 7 recorded a decrease in crop area diversification during the nineties.

Table 9.13

Crop Diversification Index

Item/State	***Number of Crops/ Crop Groups*	*1990-91*	*1999-2000*	*% Change*
Andhra Pradesh	25+15	85.1	87.0	2.23
Assam	20+20	55.7	58.3	4.67
Bihar	25+15	68.7	68.8	0.15
Gujarat	24+16	92.9	92.0	-0.97
Haryana	18+22	85.2	79.5	-6.69
Karnataka	26+14	91.4	92.2	0.88
Kerala	21+19	93.4	95.0	1.71
M.P.	25+15	89.0	87.7	-1.46
Maharashtra	25+15	87.2	89.4	2.52
Orissa	25+15	74.3	69.8	-6.06
Punjab	17+23	72.7	72.6	-0.14
Rajasthan	21+19	89.6	90.6	1.12
Tamil Nadu	22+18	87.4	84.3	-3.55
U.P.	24+16	82.3	81.1	-1.46
W. Bengal	21+19	54.1	57.2	5.73
All India (Area)	39+20	91.1	90.7	-0.44
All India Value				
(Current Prices)	71	71.9	67.5*	-6.12
(Constant Prices)	71	71.5	70.7*	-1.12

Note: * For TE 2000-01.

** The number after + sign indicates the number of crops considered as tail i.e., 'others' group whose area was assumed to be equally distributed among these crops.

9.8 Concluding Observations

The process of diversification in Indian agriculture had commenced in early eighties after the objective of agricultural development strategy shifted from 'maximising the production of food grains' to 'evolving a production pattern in line with the demand pattern'. The declining trend in the share of agriculture and allied sectors in GDP, which had set in since Independence, has continued during the nineties. Similarly, the share of rural population in total population has continued to decline, though at a much slower pace than the decline in agriculture's share in GDP. Another disturbing trend, which continued during the nineties, has been increasing proportion of agricultural labourers, which nullified the decrease in the proportion of cultivators in total workforce. During the nineties, there has been no substantial change in land use (broad categories) except some marginal decline in culturable wastelands and corresponding increase in land under non-agricultural uses. However, substantial potential culturable area continues to remain without productive use for the want of capital investment, despite special schemes launched to encourage entrepreneurs and farmers groups by several state governments.

The agricultural basket is tending to tilt towards nutritionally rich livestock products, with the share of livestock products in total agricultural products going up during the nineties. As regards crop area diversification, there was considerable shift away from food grains to non-food grain crops. Unlike during the eighties, there was also an absolute decline in area under cereals as well as pulses during the nineties. Correspondingly, there was considerable increase in area under non-food grain crops, with the share in GCA going up from 30.5 per cent in TE 1990-91 to 35.7 per cent in TE 2000-01. However, there was no decline in area under staple cereals like rice, wheat and maize. The decline in area occurred only under coarse cereals like *bajra, jowar, ragi* and small millets. In the case of wheat, even its share in value terms improved during the nineties. However, rice continues to be the single largest crop in terms of share in the total value of crop output in the country.

Among non-food grain crops, the share of fruits and vegetables in total value of crop output recorded a substantial increase from 17.6 per cent in early nineties to 23.0 per cent 10 years later. The share of other oilseeds (soyabean and sunflower), sugarcane and spices in the total value of crop output also increased during the nineties. However, as a reversal of past trend, the share of oilseeds as a group has tended to decline mainly due to decline in the share of two major oilseeds *viz.*, groundnut and rapeseed/mustard during the nineties. Analysis of shift in crop areas and average value productivity reveals that these shifts have helped in not only improving the supply of nutritionally rich farm products but also in increasing the farm value productivity, without sacrificing the national food security.

The state level analysis provides some additional insights into crop diversification of Indian agriculture. In most states, food grains occupy more than 53 per cent of GCA, with the exception of Kerala and Gujarat. In all the states except Tamil Nadu, Haryana and Karnataka, the share of food grains in GCA declined during the nineties. In three eastern states of Assam, West Bengal and Bihar, rice alone accounts for more than half of GCA. In Haryana, Orissa, Punjab and Tamil Nadu, proportionate area under rice increased and in Assam, Kerala, West Bengal and Madhya Pradesh, relative area under rice decreased during the nineties. In the case of wheat, the proportionate area increased in major states except Punjab. In oilseed dominant states, proportionate area under oilseeds further increased. The crops, which dominate the cropping pattern, are different in different states. The ranking of first five dominant crops in different states has undergone conspicuous changes during the last 10 years.

Overall, the degree of crop diversification is relatively low in West Bengal and Assam and relatively high in Kerala, Karnataka and Gujarat. During the last 10 years, there has been considerable increase in crop diversification in West Bengal and Assam. There was also a marginal increase in crop diversification in Karnataka, Gujarat, Rajasthan and Andhra Pradesh. In other states, there was a decrease in the degree of crop diversification during the nineties. By and large, at the all-India level, the crop diversification index was estimated to be quite high at around 91.

The analysis of crop diversification at the national and state levels reveals that aggregates conceal lot of information. However, by and large, the degree of diversification is quite high. The emerging changes in demand pattern and trade environment coupled with the increased responsiveness of farmers to these changes suggest that Indian agricultural sector is poised to take a great leap forward with crop diversification taking place at micro level.

A pre-condition for sustaining the process of crop diversification is the availability of adequate marketing infrastructure and enabling environment for emergence of marketing support services. Infrastructure needed for sustaining crop diversification include rural roads, storage structures, transportation facilities, cold storages, reefer vans, packaging services, processing facilities, branding systems and quality testing facilities. The legal regulatory framework also needs to be simplified to enable the private sector to invest in creating these market support services for agricultural products. These apart, training of farmers in maintenance of quality of products and producing in accordance with the demand pattern and creation of some minimum post-harvest handling facilities like cleaning, sorting/grading and packaging of the produce at the farm gate or village level will be quite important in sustaining and accelerating the process of crop diversification in Indian agriculture. In this context, recent initiatives of the government in encouraging private sector for investment in agricultural marketing services is a step in the right direction.

References

Acharya, S.S. (2003). "Crop Diversification in Indian Agriculture", Invited Paper sent to *Agricultural Situation in India,* Independence Day Special Issue.

Centre for Monitoring Indian Economy (CMIE) (2002). *Agriculture*. Mumbai, December.

Economic and Political Weekly (EPW) (1995). "National Accounts Statistics of India – 1: Macro Aggregates", *EPW Research Foundation (EPW)* XXX(46): 2955-64. November 18.

Government of India (1986). *Agricultural Price Policy—A Long Term Perspective*. New Delhi: Ministry of Agriculture.

———. (1992, 2000). "Statistical Abstracts of India", CSO, Ministry of Statistics and Programme Implementation, New Delhi.

———. (2001, 2002). *National Accounts Statistics*. New Delhi: Central Statistical Organization, Ministry of Statistics and Programme Implementation.

———. (2002a). *Agricultural Statistics at a Glance*. New Delhi: Ministry of Agriculture.

———. (2002b). *Report of the Commission for Agricultural Costs and Prices for the Crops Sown during 2001-02 Season*. New Delhi: Ministry of Agriculture.

———. (2003). *Reports of the Commission for Agricultural Costs and Prices for the Crops Sown during 2002-03 Season*. New Delhi: Ministry of Agriculture.

Odum, Eugene P. (1975). *Ecology—The Link Between the Natural and Social Sciences*. New Delhi: Oxford and IBH Publishing Co Private Ltd. pp. 232-33.

10 Agricultural Development

Policy and Planning

R.S. Deshpande and K.V. Raju

10.1 Introduction

In the context of changing global scenario towards open market economy, the agricultural policy of most of the nations is under severe stress of domestic reforms. The stress is mainly due to the insistence on weeding out the trade distorting agents, freer competition, and increase in efficiency in the production with best allocation of natural resources. Therefore, the present normative and theoretical concerns about policy studies are precisely directed at trying to improve the ability of a society and its governance to replace the earlier issues with the new and fundamental issues. It involves changing the pattern of past policies towards the present one and analyse the impacts of these likely changes. In the process of trade led growth, where international trade serves as the main engine of growth, the trade related decisions are likely to be taken by the central power (Union Government), but the welfare implications of these decisions essentially involve the sub-national governments. In this context, the nations with federal constitution will be placed in a tricky situation. Therefore, in such situation, a clear design of the policy is an essential pre-requisite.

Policy making in agriculture inevitably passes through difficult contours. One can enlist at least five bold reasons qualifying such difficulties. First, agriculture is an unorganised sector and therefore policy responses could not be predicted *a priori* with objective probabilities. Second, the information flow to agricultural sector is not as quick as it takes place in other sectors. The information asymmetry in the absence of objective probabilities about outcomes virtually authenticates to formulate disjointed policies in isolation, without detailed homework or arbitrarily. Third, the sector in most of the agro-climatic regions has a strong proverbial weather dependence and thus a quick fire-fighting job is usually the core of the policy. Fourth, significant factor is the income and asset distribution in the sector that has always been a point in question. This is further complicated by the income and price variations, a peculiarity mark of the sector. The policies framed needs to keep these variations in view. Last, the sector has a strong link with consumers and other industries. The growth of the aggregate economy of any country is sensitive to the fluctuations in the sector. Therefore, agricultural policies in India as well as in many countries have a strong state dependence.

Indian agriculture has made rapid strides over the last 50 years. It has contributed significantly to achieve self-sufficiency in food production and avoiding food shortages. Food grain production has reached 206 million tonnes (1999) from a mere 51 million tonnes in the early fifties. Still, the agriculture sector confronts the very same constraints, in its growth pattern which were on scene at the time of Independence albeit with reduced intensity such as: a) uneven development across regions, crops, and across different sections of farming community; b) it is characterised by low levels of productivity; c) degradation of natural resources in some areas. Economic viability of the agricultural sector is affected by: a) capital inadequacy; b) lack of infrastructural support; c) demand side constraints such as controls on movement, storage and sale of agricultural products, etc. These constraints pull down the rate of growth of agriculture. Agriculture has also become a relatively unrewarding profession due to generally unfavourable price regime imposed by the government and low value addition. Depeasantisation and increasing migration to urban areas are two prominent features. But these too do not result into net welfare gain for the sector. Yet, over two-third of the billion population of India still work in agriculture and allied activities for their survival.

Our experience of policy formulation in India is largely from two sources, namely the five year plans and various schemes initiated by the concerned development departments. There is a general lack of awareness about the theory of policy making and therefore, to a significant extent the policy is understood often as the problem solving steps taken in the context of severity of the issue and/or a common denominator of various programmes. Actually, "a policy aims at specific-often quantifiable-objectives, deploys an array of instruments to achieve them and operates according to a pre-planned time frame for implementation. It lends itself to standardised monitoring and evaluation procedures to assess the outcome and to identify those responsible for the success/failure of the policy." (Rao, 1998: 1). In this study, we have tried to analyse the policy making in India, initially through a theoretical perspective on policy making, followed by the experience of agricultural policy during the last five decades at the country level. This is followed by an empirical study of policy making across the states in the country.

10.2 Towards an Agricultural Policy

The emergence of agricultural policy in the Indian context can be traced back to the official documents beginning from Food grains Policy Committee of 1943 (Gregory, 1943). Gregory's policy was framed in the context of the food situation forced due to the Second World War and cessation of rice supplies from Burma. The Committee therefore focused on food availability, control prices, supplies and distribution. It did not address to any long term issue facing the sector, as food was the main issue. At the time of Independence, availability of food continued to be the haunting challenge for the new government. The Food grains Policy Committee (1947) under Thakurdas was appointed to look into the food distribution aspects and the Committee recommended a revolutionary step to progressively decontrol food. The salient features of the policy included gradual withdrawal of control and removal of restrictions on movements of food grains. This policy of decontrol could not be pursued due to persistent shortage and large imports. This was followed by three committees under Maitra (1950), Mehta (1957) and Venkatappaiah (1966) which were appointed to enquire into the food problem of India and the means to solve them. These were the important documents flagging the milestone in making of agricultural policy *nay* food policy during the first two decades. Food production was treated as equivalent to the agricultural development as it was the main problem. Draft on any long term policy for agricultural sector was far away even in the thinking process during those days.

There was no significant and holistic agricultural policy resolution so far though Industrial Policy Resolution was adopted as early as 1948. Agricultural policy was not considered save, drafting and issuing of it in the melee of schemes. Most of the measures taken in past were either focused on crises management, or for political gain, otherwise backwardness of Indian agriculture cannot be explained (GoI, 1990). Among the available papers, referred to in this study, only the High Power Committee Report (1990) touches the umbilical cord of the Indian rural mass. It lays greater emphasis on improving the human resource base to uplift the agriculture. The report (1990: 74) rightly suggests, "Indian agriculture need not remain backward and the rural masses amongst the poorest in the world. Both can be uplifted by improving the human resources base increasing the farmers' efficiency through greater user of science and technology, suited to their conditions and placing them at par with others in prices, incomes, facilities and opportunities" (High Power Committee, 1990: 74).

Rarely, any paper focuses on the vision for Indian agriculture. This had led to a scattered thinking and not weaving a central theme for the policy and prevented crafting the focused objectives and thrust areas. It then led to incoherent statements along the path; they remain mutually contradicting too. An unclear institutional mechanism complicated any further sailing of the whole policy. (We have given a comparative statement in the Annexure Table A-10.1.) The study commissioned by traders lobby (ASSOCHAM, 1998), owing to the authors' business first approach, they were able to chalk out a vision for Indian agriculture by 2020 that included: a) become the driving force of the Indian economy through increased contribution to export earnings, b) generate additional income, savings and investment in the economy, c) through rapid growth of output, reduce and effectively remove poverty and starvation, d) generate exportable surplus of food grains and non-food grains after meeting the domestic demand at the world prices, e) increase labour productivity to offset any increase in the cost of inputs including wages, f) provide good quality raw materials for industrial at competitive rates, generating demand for industrial goods and services. What is more interesting is the assumptions made by the study to realise the vision.[1]

Nothing prevented successive governments during the last five decades to arrive at a meaningful policy document on agricultural sector. Several drafts of agriculture policies were put forth but every time a new government was sworn in, they promised to do something robust and different than the earlier efforts. The same thing cannot be said about the other sectors. For example, Industrial Policy Resolutions were introduced since mid-fifties for promoting industrial growth. Similar examples are there even for sub-sectors having negligible share in the GDP. All these speak volumes on the nature and extent of lack of state initiative towards a comprehensive policy for agriculture.

During late eighties, a Committee was appointed to look into the problem of agriculture. This Report of the High Power Committee (1990), chaired by Shri Bhanu Pratap Singh made recommendations covering all major sectors of agricultural economy. Following this, various policy statements were issued till the Agricultural Policy Document of 2000. Most of the agricultural policy documents came during the decade of nineties, not so much due to lack of policy, but mostly due to the incessant problems faced by the sector during the decade. The first draft agricultural policy resolution came into being under the Prime Ministership of Shri V.P. Singh, and Shri Sharad Joshi was largely responsible in putting the draft together. The High Power Committee, under the chairmanship of Shri Bhanu Pratap Singh was constituted during 1990 and the committee provided a full view of agricultural policy. This is one of the comprehensive documents, dealing with agricultural policy in the most of the needed form.

From here, a clue was taken by the state of Karnataka and the policy document was prepared during 1995 for the state as such. To the

1. The assumptions are: average annual compound rate of population growth will be 1.6 per cent during 1997 to 2000; labour supply will grow at the rate of 1.85 per cent per annum over this period; growth of work/trade in agriculture products will be substantially higher during the next two decades on account of major changes in international trade environment; seed, feed and wastage constitute 12.5 per cent of the gross output; income elasticity of demand for food grains other than coarse cereals is 0.4 and it is 0.12 for coarse grains in India.

best of our knowledge, this was the only existing policy document at state level for agricultural sector as a whole. Even at that time, there was no accepted policy document at the Centre, not so much because agriculture is a state subject, but possibly due to the apathy towards the sector. The government under the Prime Ministership of Shri Deve Gowda, prepared a document on agriculture policy during 1999. However, due to the instability of the government the document could never make it to the floor of the house. There was no serious attempt after that, to formulate a policy till the New Agriculture Policy came into being. However, none of these could culminate into a full-fledged policy document for agriculture sector. Therefore, the only first authenticated and hurriedly prepared policy document for agriculture sector is the Agricultural Policy 2000. During the future plan periods, it is necessary to keep in view the lessons learnt through this experience. Briefly during the last five decades we have witnessed broadly four important policy directions namely: (i) food security, (ii) institutions for agricultural administration, introduction and dissemination of technology, (iii) under-developed regions, classes, farmers and crops, and (iv) input and technology distribution.

Efforts towards framing the National Agricultural Policy (NAP) were quite intensive during the nineties both due to the pressure from farm lobby and the lately descended realisation that for the last decades after Independence we never had one. Finally, it was introduced in the monsoon session of the Lok Sabha in July 2000. Different ministers, bureaucrats and advisers have contributed to shape the present version of the policy document. Needless to add, several researchers and policy makers might have also shared their might behind the screen. In this long sojourn, each driver and his passengers had their own intentions and steered the policy document accordingly. Result is a collation of ideas and ideals of different vintages without a theme or link. This time it was an enviable opportunity to gain from the collective wisdom of professionals, formal and informal organisations working on agriculture and related aspects and put together a cohesive document. Rao aptly summarises it as, "The difficulty here is that, 'policy maker' refers not to a few identifiable individuals and government bodies but a confusing collage of elites, pressures groups and lobbies each operating with its own agenda not necessarily conforming to the national goals and priorities. The result is chronic inability of the policy makers to read the signs of crisis sufficiently in advance and to deal with them in a systematic manner; the crises he faces are challenging but certainly not beyond our capabilities to handle" (Rao, 1998: 7).

10.3 National Agricultural Policy

As discussed earlier, India never had a formal and comprehensive policy on agriculture in the five decades since Independence. Not that there were no pronouncements of policy on agriculture. In fact, there were quite a few: some on land redistribution, some on this or that specific input, infrastructure, on technology. Statements on food situation were plenty; but the policies, or absence thereof, they contain concern supplies for the public distribution systems, and only incidentally, production and productivity. A policy statement defines the role of agriculture in the overall economy and its development is conspicuously absent (GoI, 1990).

The NAP (2000) seeks to realise by 2020: a) vast untapped growth potential of Indian agriculture; b) strengthen rural infrastructure to support faster agricultural development; c) promote value addition; d) accelerate the growth of agro-business; e) create employment in rural areas; f) secure a fair standard of living for the farmers and agricultural workers and their families; g) discourage migration to urban areas and face the challenges arising out of economic liberalisation and globalisation. The policy aims stated in the document to achieve these are: a) a growth rate of 4 per cent per annum; b) efficient use of natural resources and bio-diversity; c) growth with equity; d) protect from economic liberalisation and globalisation by demand driven growth and catering to domestic markets and maximise agricultural exports; e) environmentally, technologically and economically sustainable growth.

The NAP concentrates on:

- "A growth rate of excess of 4 per cent per annum in agricultural sector;

- "Growth that is based on efficient use of resources and conserves our soil, water, and bio-diversity;
- "Growth with equity i.e., growth which is widespread across regions and farmers;
- "Growth that is demand-driven and caters to domestic markets and maximises benefits from exports of agricultural projects in the face of the challenges arising from economic liberalisation and globalisation;
- "Growth that is sustainable technologically, environmentally and economically"

(GoI, NAP, 2000: 2).

The rest of the policy document covers nine broad areas *viz.*, sustainable agriculture, food and nutritional security, generation and transfer of technology, inputs management, incentives for agriculture, investments in agriculture, institutional structure, risk management and management reforms. In the next section, we have attempted to describe the main features of these focus areas along with the promised potential inadequacies. The method of this review process is indirect and we try to locate the assumptions and actuals in each of the focus areas.

It could have helped to showcase the vision of the second largest populated country of the world. All this seems to be conspicuously absent and the policy document fails to evoke any interest of academics, polity or administration. It provides little vision for the window of future developments. Hence, this paper attempts to analytically review a few major features of the NAP, its inadequacies, and discuss these in the light of earlier efforts made for formulating a policy frame. Lessons could have been drawn from worthwhile efforts made earlier at national level and by some states for formulating a more useful policy for agricultural development.

Commenting on the National Agricultural Policy, the Standing Advisory Committee under the chairmanship of the farmer leader Sharad Joshi suggested (compared to broad objectives of the Policy) more specific and robust objectives: a) production of articles of nourishment—both direct and derived, b) creation of exportable surplus, c) generation of further surplus for creation of capital for improved technology and infrastructure, so as to improve productivity, d) generation of further surplus for capital formation in backward and forward linkage activities and other secondary and tertiary sectors, e) regulation of the deployment of surplus so that the aggregate capital-output ratio corresponds to the proportion between the surplus produced and the labour force required to be taken away from agriculture, f) reduction of unemployment and underemployment so that not more than 10 per cent of the rural labour force is wasted at the end of the next two decades, g) planned shifting of population from agriculture to 50 per cent by the year 2010 and the absolute number reduced, h) raising the per capita income in the agrarian sector by 2010, i) vesting in the hands of rural women who perform about 2/3 of agricultural work, at least 1/2 of agricultural income and 15 per cent of agricultural land by the year 2010, j) restoration of pasture and forest lands encroached in the heat of the 'grow more' food campaign in the 1950s and 1960s, k) establishment of a parity between the facilities available for education and medical care in the countryside and those in towns, and l) initiating of a 'real green revolution' that would be less dependent on the rapidly depleting petroleum resources.

10.3.1 Focus Areas

Ten years of drafting and redrafting of the policy document has led to the current shape of the NAP. Apparently we need to look at its focus areas and the way they are dealt and projected for the next 20 years. In Table 10.1, we have provided focus on area-wise salient features, extracted from NAP.

The NAP has taken note of some of the expected changes in the country. In the spirit of market-driven forces of growth, NAP mentions corporatisation of agriculture in a significant manner but does not comment on the role of public sector. It also suggests commercialisation of all the services, including agricultural extension (p.19). The NAP indications may be summarised here. Primarily, the whole policy is drafted (surely, not crafted) from the view point of Central government despite the fact that under India's Constitution, agriculture is a state subject. Even though 'decentralisation' and 'participation' are the buzz

Table 10.1

Towards Sustainable Agriculture

Thrust Areas	*Policy Options*
1. Promote technically sound, economically viable, environmentally non-degrading, & socially acceptable use of country's natural resources—land, water & genetic environment.	1. Contain biotic pressures on land & control indiscriminate diversion of agricultural lands for non-agricultural purposes. 2. Use unutilised wastelands for agriculture & afforestation.
2. Improve the quality of land resources.	3. Increase cropping intensity, through multiple-cropping & inter-cropping
3. Promote rational utilisation & conservation of water resources.	4. Reclamation of degraded & fallow lands & problem soils.
4. Conservation of bio-resources through their *ex situ* preservation and *in situ* conservation in their natural habitats.	5. Integrated and holistic development of rainfed areas. Management of grazing and long-term perspective plan for sustainable rainfed agriculture.
5. Sensitisation of farming community with the environmental concerns.	6. Conjunctive use of surface and groundwater.
6. Promote agro-forestry & social forestry for maintenance of ecological balance & augmentation of biomass production in the agricultural systems.	7. Recharge and control groundwater table. 8. Efficient use of water and use of *in-situ* moisture management techniques, and promote pressured irrigation systems.
7. Pool, distil and evaluate traditional practices, knowledge & wisdom for sustainable agricultural growth.	9. Promote water harvesting structures and suitable conveyance systems in hilly and high rainfall areas.
	10. Encourage community irrigation management.

Note: Based on GoI (2000).

words of this decade the policy document failed to note the need for state specific approach. There is no clarity on role of the state in agriculture; particularly demarcation of the role of Central government and the state governments. Consultation process, if any, was confined to meetings with the state level agricultural secretaries and ministers in 1995 and 1997. The NAP clearly states that, "The effective implementation of policy initiatives will call for comprehensive reforms in the management of agriculture by the Central government and the state governments. The Central government will supplement/complement the state governments' efforts through regionally differentiated Work Plans, comprising crop/area/target group specific interventions formulated in *inter-active* (emphasis added) mode and implemented in a spirit of partnership with the state" (p.15). On one side, the policy argues for decentralisation and on the other it provides greater leverage to the Central government. With the NAP, total flow of funds to states from the Central government may reduce over time and direct transfer of funds to districts may begin. Otherwise also, the central support is only for three items: a) minimum support price, b) inputs subsidies, and c) centrally sponsored schemes. The policy is not clear on what kind of incentive structure is needed to increase productivity; mere dismantling of minimum support price structure would certainly not help. The replacement has to be competent enough to deal with the price issue.

Main worry is the thrust on corporatisation of agriculture. It is biased in favour of the traders and farmers are largely taken for granted as mute participants. In corporate agriculture, investment figures do not indicate employment generated (e.g. in coastal Karnataka, Rs. 3000 crore investment will employ only 350 persons). The supporters of corporatisation of agriculture argue that we need to come out of the myths surrounding Indian agriculture: a) subsistence agriculture; lot of farmers' produce to sell, rather than for own consumption. What they need is good marketing and commercialisation of agriculture; b) food security; in the era of globalisation, we need to know what are our comparative advantages in growing some crops. Why should these crops be grown at high cost, and then demand high support price; c) subsidies in agriculture sector; it is well known fact that, most of the subsidies have failed to reach the target group. That points out towards need to revamp the structure. This skips the attention in the policy document.

10.3.2 Missing Threads

A policy is a statement of government's agenda for the sector. However, the elaborated agenda as given in the NAP, should have taken care of current and future challenges of the agricultural sector and its allied activities. It falls short in reflecting the sector's endogenous and exogenous strengths and constraints, which control and steer the sector for the next two decades. The NAP has some incompatibility of its instruments to achieve the goals. For example, the NAP seeks to create better infrastructure for agricultural growth, while one of the aims indicates protection from liberalisation and globalisation. This may keep farmers away from the mainstream. Mechanisms are not properly designed for implementing the NAP. These mechanisms should have been spelt out, based on the objectives of the NAP.

It is clear. The NAP has not followed some simple steps in evolving a national level policy frame. So, it is design default. The process may include, setting up a core group, review of earlier experience crafting a draft, discussions in regional workshops and in national workshops, inviting comments, putting the draft on websites (like population policy), revising the draft, sending it for a peer review, getting a group of experts to deliberate on various dimensions of the policy (financial, infrastructure, capacity building and others for the next 20 years), then finalising it and having a discussion in the Lok Sabha. Many of these steps are not followed at all in evolving the NAP. One of the best, among the available documents, is the High Power Committee report (Chairman, Bhanu Prathap Singh) in 1990. A comparative analysis of these available documents, dealing with the agricultural policies is given here. Annexure Table A-10.1 provides main thrust areas suggested by various documents during the last 10 years.

10.4 Federalism and Agricultural Policy

Globally, intervention in agriculture by different levels of government is well documented, so also in India. This is despite the fact that agriculture is a private activity in its content. But there has been a lack of coordination between the Centre and the states to achieve a well-defined set of policy objectives. There have been mutually inconsistent policies amongst economy—wide macro policies like foreign trade policies, industrial policies on the one hand and agricultural macro policies on the other. These have large and offsetting impacts on agriculture (Srinivasan, 1998).

While determining the role of Central governments in formulating agriculture policy, the views of the leaders at the time of Independence were of great importance. In a memorandum to the Cabinet during 1947, it was stated that agricultural production policy, price control of agriculture products, the establishment of the Central higher technical institutions, food distribution and then setting up of a twisted emission refer agriculture and industrial development as vital problems and the Central government should take steps to correct these. It was inherently accepted that Central government should have an authority of its own to coordinate agricultural production in the country as a whole and play an increasingly active role in the development of both industry and agriculture (Austin, 1966). The objective of the framers of the Constitution was to make states, primarily and directly responsible of all matters concerning the development of agriculture and rural poor, and at the same time, the Central government owning the responsibility to oversee such arrangements. The powers over agriculture, and the responsibility for its development, where thus ambiguously divided between the Centre and the state. This exercise was quite fragile as the federal inaction in its own spear can render the policy ineffective, either by the state or by the Centre. No wonder, neither the states nor the Centre could formulate an agriculture policy of longstanding.

The functions directly undertaken by the Central government and the functions that it coordinates may be listed as below:

- Providing financial assistance to the states for their agricultural plans through grants and loans.
- Overall planning and coordination of agricultural development in the country; coordinating state agricultural plans; assuring the efficient implementation of development plans; and their evaluation.
- Providing technical assistance to the states in planning and executing agricultural programmes.
- Assisting the states in securing the requirements of agricultural inputs such as pure seeds, imprudent amends, fertilisers and pesticides in adequate quantity and timely supply.
- Providing credit; assisting the states in organising marketing storage and transport facilities.
- Price stabilisation; enforcing incorporation with the states on minimum and maximum prices for agriculture produce; regulating interstate trade and movements of the commodities.
- Laying down import and export policies in respect of agricultural requisites and products.

- Providing cooperation to the states for betterment of extension services to the farmers.
- Coordinating programmes of land use and development; soil conservation and utilisation of water sources.
- Fundamental and applied research on agriculture, better sciences, agricultural economics, fisheries, home science and nutritional problems.
- Maintaining the standards of higher education in all agricultural sciences.
- The administration of external assistance in the agricultural sector.

Agricultural plans of the states are not built from below, but it is often claimed as that. There is hardly any consultation either with the Panchayati Raj bodies, or farming interests and farmers bodies. Mostly it is the department officials who prepare the plans and these are usually the step-up plans with little innovative approach. Even within the Agriculture Department there is hardly any machinery that can monitor the policy goals and exercise online corrections. Usually the plans are made at the headquarters, broken into district segments and later split into local plans. The idea of farm plans, built in the villages culminating into block level, district level and finally, state level plans, has never been practiced, and possibly may not be practiced even after introduction of Article 243 of the Constitution of India. The states are hardly expected to plan realistically keeping in view their constraints and opportunities, and consultation down with the district or other tiers of governance is clearly a distant dream.

10.5 Macro Agricultural Policy

In Indian economy, agricultural policy at macro level (country level) is needed essentially from two viewpoints. First, is to monitor the allocation of resources and sustain the relative growth rates and second, to manage the employment in the sector. Public spending on agriculture as a proportion of GDP in India has been much higher than in many other Asian countries, while Indian agriculture growth has been slower. A question about the efficiency in use of investment crops up here and that has to be answered by placing investible resources in the sub-sectors with better returns. World Bank studies show two broad reasons for this (as quoted on Srinivasan, 1998): a) composition of public spending across categories/regions/states is not geared towards a more rapid broad-based and poverty alleviating agriculture growth, b) On one hand, public expenditure has been very much skewed towards subsidies, and against growth-enhancing capital spending and operation and maintenance; on the other hand, such skew contributes to the poor quality and poor reliability of delivery of inputs such as power and water. In the absence of any policy document, most of the allocation of resources was taking place through the National Planning Commission. The policy directive was thus coming largely from the Plan documents. We have tried to put together the policy pointers emerging from the policy documents right from the First Five Year Plan.

10.5.1 Agricultural Policy: An Experience of Five Decades

The plan documents over the last five decades made it quite clear that policy for agricultural sector is of prime importance to the plan and the steps taken could be seen from Table 10.2. One expects a significant shift in the strategy during the Tenth Plan. Keeping with this expectation the Approach Paper to the Tenth Plan makes it clear that, "First, agricultural development must be viewed as a core element of the Plan since growth in this sector is likely to lead to the widest spread of benefits, especially to the rural poor including agricultural labour. Also, since the majority of women workers are engaged in agriculture, investments in this sector have enormous implications for gender equality and must be designed to have maximal impact on this dimension. The first generation of reforms concentrated on reforms in the industrial economy and reforms in the agricultural sector were neglected. This must change in the Tenth Plan" (Approach Paper to the Tenth Five Year Plan, GoI, 2001).

From the First Plan onwards, the plan documents are replete with ideas and objectives towards agricultural sector. In the process of planned development we have achieved significant strides in the sector but the experience of the earlier plans rarely becomes a background for the policy. During the last three plans the planning process has been revitalised incorporating specific working groups, drawing on the experience of the experts and circulation of the drafts for discussions. It is interesting that the First Five Year Plan emphasised organisation of agriculture through a continuous extension process and the community development programme was the instrument. The development philosophy underlying this was to involve participation from below starting at the grassroot. Opening paragraph of the approach to Ninth Plan reiterates our commitment accepting little achievement in the direction. Plan documents and successive appraisal reports stand in the testimony of our riverine policy (flowing like a river directed by mountainous constraints and flows of successes in terms of streams). It is during the Seventh Plan that a medium term development perspective was evolved (GoI, 1985: 8). The aim was to create, by the year 2000, the conditions for self-sustaining growth in terms of both the capacity to finance internally and the development of technology. The perspective plan for agriculture documented in Seventh Plan emphasised on self-sufficiency, employment, technology, extension and by-passed regions (rainfed agriculture) (GoI, 1985: 15). The emphasis was continued through Eighth Plan. But in response to the NEP and liberalisation, the Ninth Plan had set the market participation and trade sector as the main diversions.

Over the last five decades we have learnt a good number of lessons in our planning exercise and appraisals of the plan programmes. Objectives have more or less stayed the same and revolved around poverty reduction, empowering poor sections, self-sufficiency, and assimilating by-passed regions and groups. But the instruments to achieve these have significantly changed. These together give varied choice and rich experience in framing policies.

Table 10.2

Agricultural Policy Formulation through Five Year Plans

Plan Period	*Major Issues and Policy Thrust*
First Plan 1951-1956	Severe food availability constraints. Maximisation of agricultural production. Making food available to masses. Food distribution network. Nationwide community development (CD) programme institutions for village development. National extension and community projects skewed land distribution, inefficiency in production and thus land reforms—abolition of intermediaries. Bringing the fallow lands under cultivation and increase in land use efficiency. Tenants to be given the rights to cultivate land.
Second Plan 1956-1961	Concern about low land productivity and thrust on irrigated agriculture. Irrigation development for the rainfed areas. Land reforms enactment of laws. Tenancy reforms & ceiling on holdings. Soil conservation as an important programme. Co-operative development institutions, national extension service blocks created. Training and extension work for the technology through community development network.
Third Plan 1961-1966	Food security concerns continued to dominate. Technological change and adoption of improved technology to increase land productivity. Cultivable wasteland to be brought under cultivation. Brining the lagging regions under mainstream growth. Area development as an approach for development. Intensive area development programme adopted for selected districts. Extension of non-agricultural activities in rural areas. An integrated land policy approach. Soil surveys were taken up.
Fourth Plan 1969-1974	Emphasis on food security continued as minimum dietary requirements to be met. Deep concern about poverty. Regional inequality and correction of regional imbalances. Incentives created for diversion of land towards food crops and enhancing the capacity of such land. Increased emphasis on irrigation and soil conservation in dryland regions and technological change introduced. Higher cropping intensity was the concern. Emergence of agricultural price policy. Concern about domination of large holding sizes and low allocative and technical efficiency. Second phase of land reforms with land ceiling acts and consolidation of holding. Encouragement to cooperatives. Institutional changes in credit, agri extension and training.
Fifth Plan 1974-1979	Twenty point economic programme. Concern to eradicate poverty intensified. Area development strategy continued. Drought-prone areas attracted attention. Allocation on drought-prone area development programme, desert area development programmes, and soil conservation was enhanced. New impetus to dry farming Problems of land degradation land management in irrigated command areas surfaced. Modernisation of irrigation in selected irrigation command areas.
Sixth Plan 1980-1985	Minimum needs programme. Providing clean drinking water, elementary education and basic health facilities. Larger attention to unemployment and under-employment. Target group specific programmes for poverty alleviation. IRDP, NREP and RLEGP programmes were undertaken for employment and income

Contd...

...*contd*...

Plan Period	*Major Issues and Policy Thrust*
	generation. Under-utilisation of land resources. Drought-prone areas continued to attract attention. Further attention for lagging areas on the backdrop of green revolution. Land and water management programme under drought-prone area programme in selected districts.
Seventh Plan 1985-1990	Direct attack on poverty, unemployment and regional imbalances continued. Soil erosion and land degradation surfaced as major issues. Larger share of land was going out of cultivation. Soil and water conservation was needed for averting land degradation. National watershed development programme, oilseed and pulses development programmes, wasteland development programmes, and long term view of land management was initiated.
Eighth Plan 1992-1997	Priority for employment generation, strengthening of infrastructure, liberalisation and globalisation in agricultural sector. Trade sector priorities by generating surplus of agricultural commodities for exports. Emphasis on oilseed sector increased. Agro-climatic regional planning approach was incorporated. Productivity enhancement schemes. Horticulture sector to be encouraged. Degradation of land in irrigated command areas attracted attention. Peoples' participation surfaced as major issue in land management at village level. Emphasis on watershed development approach. Soil conservation merged with watershed programmes.
Ninth Plan 1997-2002	Priority to agricultural sector. Generating adequate productive employment through employment assurance. Renewed assault on poverty. Accelerating growth with stable prices. Food and nutritional security for vulnerable sections. Providing basic needs for environmental sustainability. Growth with social justice and equity. Foreign trade to be tailored for accelerating growth. Boost to agricultural research. Development of infrastructure and increasing investment in infrastructure. Export-oriented growth and emphasis on horticultural crops for exports. Land degradation increased significantly. Integrating watershed development programme across various components. Rethinking on land reforms. Gap between potentials and actual crop yields need to be bridged. Need for a long term policy document. Bringing the under-utilised land under cultivation. Management of wastelands. Maintenance of village commons. Decentralised land management system. Panchayat Raj institutions to manage the village lands. Rethinking on land legislation.
Tenth Plan 2002-2007	Creation of employment. Improving pace of growth in agriculture. Sustaining demand for labour. Employment generation programme to concentrate in diversification of agriculture and agro processing. Land use policy. Process oriented programmes focusing on poor. Universalisation of joint forest management or macro management approach. Precision farming. Organic farming. Wastelands to be brought under economic use. Strengthening R&D for slow growth crops.

Source: From various plan documents. These are however not exhaustive statements but only indicative of the thrust.

10.5.2. Three Dimensions of Liberalisation[2]

The changes in the macroeconomic thinking during nineties have placed the agricultural policy at crossroads. Macroeconomic crisis of early nineties was the beginning of the process of calibrating trade globalisation in the economy and agriculture was no exception. The problems confronted include: Forex reserves touching rock bottom, unfavourable trade balance, decelerating earnings in foreign exchange, mounting and uncontrolled fiscal deficits, and strong protectionist policy in trade sector. Even though the basic current emerged actually during mid eighties, it could acquire a visible proportion only by early nineties (Sen, 2000; Rao, 2001). As is well known, the crisis began when the foreign exchange reserves touched a critical bottom level, adverse balance of payment condition was evident and a near debt trap situation became imminent (Joshi and Little, 1996). An alternate view is about the very necessity of getting into the policy change itself (Ghosh, 1997). One must not forget the fact that Forex reserves did not evaporate overnight and the process began under the very administration that endeavoured to sort it out later. If one looks carefully at the data on National Accounts Statistics, it is quite visible that the trigger of the situation leading to the crisis was located in the expansion of non-agricultural sectors during mid-eighties beginning with the historical budget presented by the then Finance Minister Shri V.P. Singh. The performance of the agricultural sector during that period was certainly impressive and contributed significantly to the national growth. It is also a fact that the situation of the balance of payments did not emerge without prior signals. Even though agricultural exports were increasing during this period, it was felt that the situation was beyond the capacity of the economy to rescue, and following this, the structural adjustment programme was undertaken and globalisation was given as an unavoidable policy alternative. Incidentally, it was the time when the entire world was considering this policy alternative from various angles. These changes are naturally expected to have impact on the agricultural policy.

2. These viewpoints are gathered through the deliberations at various academic meets and represent broad common denominator, but may exclude a few specific views. This part is based on Deshpande (2002).

In the academia, we have three distinct viewpoints pertaining to the current transition phase. The proponents of these viewpoints can be grouped as 'committed liberalisers', 'advocates of no-change' and 'cautious liberalisers'. The first view is marked by the faith in the paradigm of growth leading to a fair distribution. It is believed that the agricultural sector is more controlled and thus, it is not allowed to achieve its natural growth potential. The intervention of the state has been continuously present in the sector right from Independence and intensified during seventies and eighties. Initially, it was a necessity but the gradual withdrawal was expected. This 'statisation' of the sector has to be reduced firmly to improve production and allocative efficiency of the sector. The interventions in the agricultural sector both in the product market as well as factor markets have been responsible for depressing the initiatives coming from the producers. Thus, while liberalisation is an essential process, it must be accompanied with firm withdrawal of the state thereby releasing the growth potential. International trade sector was hitherto, based on the residual exportable surplus. Now it is necessary to capture the new avenues in international trade. India must negotiate towards greater advantage of the country by making use of the provisions in the legal text of WTO. Well preparedness for the negotiations is an essential component and if we fail on that, probably we will miss the bus.

The second viewpoint advanced by the 'advocates of status quo' favouring the earlier policy regime of protected agriculture sector, emphatically record that the present pace of liberalisation may leave out the weaker sections and fragile regions. It is felt that India's food grain sector is being mishandled and we must continue to hold a wedge between border and domestic prices. The productivity trends during nineties have not been very encouraging. Based on this a strong view is expressed that after eight years from the beginning of economic liberalisation, instead of experiencing any unprecedented boom in the growth pattern, the agricultural sector is showing signs of decelerated growth. It has been estimated that agricultural output recorded an annual compound rate of growth of 3.46 per cent between 1980-1990 as against 2.38 per cent during 1990 to 1999. Though the decline in the rates of growth cannot be directly connected to the process of globalisation, it is pointed out that the technological advances in agriculture have slowed down and due to this, the pace of capital formation has also been declining. It is also argued that the transfer of labour from developing sector to the developed sector (Lewis process) has failed in the country. That has caused dampening effect on the growth in incremental rural income. Given the distribution of land across various classes it is stated that phenomenally, large portion of Indian farmers have holdings below two hectares and this leaves the marketable surplus management and the market participation only to the remaining minority farm groups. The process of growth thus leaves out the most vulnerable section among the farmers from partaking the benefits. Therefore, the process of marketisation will lead to incremental income for a small minority that may lead to increased inequality.

The third viewpoint (largely similar to the first group but more cautious in their approach and therefore termed as 'cautious liberalisers') emerging in the process of liberalisation, is expressed by those who believe that the process of liberalisation would usher in new trends in growth of Indian agriculture. Similarly, they expect that the quality of growth will also undergo significant changes in addition to increased efficiency. They believe that competitive forces will spur growth but this viewpoint is marked by its distinct and careful approach to the process of liberalisation. While it is argued that we must take greater advantage of trade generated growth by properly negotiating under WTO regime but at the same time, the domestic reforms in order to avoid the probable welfare loss must get due priority. This viewpoint emphasises earnest requirement of domestic market reforms and infrastructural facilities to precede the process of liberalisation. It is argued that this has to be supported by intensive domestic market reforms relaxing the present control regime on factor as well as product markets. More than that, the immediate task is to reduce the current market inefficiencies embarking upon the deep domestic reform process. On one hand, it is important to utilise the opportunity of investing for creating better infrastructure and boosting–up the investment trends, whereas, on the other hand, the domestic price policy should be carefully monitored in order to pass on legitimate advantages to the producers. Distortions in fertiliser prices and the subsidy regimes in fertilisers, electricity, credit and water have caused uneconomic use of resources and inefficiency in the production process. Serious and bold interventions are required to undo the uneconomic uses of subsidies. Here again, a finer difference has to be marked between the two groups arguing for the process of the withdrawal of the state from the sector. The 'cautious liberalisers' do not necessarily feel that the state should withdraw its controls at once from the agricultural sector, but believe that this can be done extremely gradually over years and can be graded positively.

Keeping these three currents featuring in academic discussions in view, it will be necessary to take a pragmatic path of policy. For the past several years, we have not gone through a proper drill of policy making as expounded by the theorists of policy. But even the accumulative policies have demonstrated clear intentions of the policy bodies. These outline the policy thrust though in a fashion of formation of a river through different currents.

10.6 Major Features of States Selected

This study begins with the premise that any attempt to frame agricultural policy must begin at the state level and there too constructed from below. Essentially such exercise requires basic understanding at the state level and discussions with the stakeholders that include: policy makers, administrators, farmer leaders, farmers, traders and researchers in the field. As indicated above, the discussions were format free and were directed more towards finding out the strengths, weaknesses, opportunities and threats. These were to be located from the standpoint of the concerned state and not in the centralised perspective. Thirteen state reports could be collected over a period of three years to put this consolidated report together. These include: Punjab; Himachal Pradesh; Andhra Pradesh; Karnataka; Maharashtra; Madhya Pradesh; Gujarat; Rajasthan; Assam; Bihar and Uttar Pradesh. Despite repeated reminders, Haryana and West Bengal could not submit their reports. These are certainly notable exceptions.

Analytical understanding required putting the states into policy groups based on the inherent current indicated in the documents. The first group of states includes the forerunners in the context of new economic structure with marketisation as the leading growth initiative. Punjab as a state had always been on the forefront of development even during the British rule (Blyn, 1966). Recent trends in Punjab agriculture have clearly indicated preference of the farmers towards diversification towards commercial crops (Bhalla and Singh, 2001; Bhalla, 2004). The farmers of Punjab have adopted paddy (*basmati* and other export-friendly varieties) as one of the major crops deviating from the traditional cropping pattern. Similar is the case of Haryana, where farmers prefer cash crop-oriented cropping pattern. The third state falling in this category is Himachal Pradesh, not so much by the shift in the decision making process of the farmer but largely due to the agro-climatic conditions and the traditional cropping pattern. Fruit crop growers of Himachal Pradesh have taken up the challenge to confront the fruits entering in India from other countries.

The second group of states includes those, which did not enjoy the prime position in leading agricultural development of the country prior to Green Revolution (1966-67), but have come up after successfully negotiating with the major agro-climatic constraints and placed themselves in leading the agricultural growth scenario of the country. This group includes Andhra Pradesh, Karnataka, Gujarat and Rajasthan. Among these four states, Andhra Pradesh and Karnataka have already made a place in the international trade scene by diversifying into trade-oriented crops, whereas, Gujarat and Rajasthan have been successful in encashing the opportunity by relying upon the traditional rainfed crops.

Assam has a unique position as an eastern state and that fits well with West Bengal. It is finding the most needed growth initiative by diversifying into market-oriented crops. Bihar and Uttar Pradesh are the proverbial low productivity states and have to strive hard to come out of the low productivity trap. These states have extremely good potential for development and thus, the objective in these states should be to overcome these constraints forcing its agricultural sector to low productivity.

The basic features pertaining to agricultural sectors of the states are given in Tables 10.4 and 10.5. One can easily observe four emerging groups from this table based on a cross-classification of natural resource position and state-led agricultural development efforts (See Table 10.3).

Table 10.3

Cross-classification of the Selected States

	Naturally Well Endowed Regions	*Regions Not So Well Endowed in Natural Resources*
Significant state-led development efforts	Punjab, Haryana, Western Uttar Pradesh, Tamil Nadu, Kerala, Himachal Pradesh	Gujarat, Northern Rajasthan, Andhra; Western Maharashtra, South Karnataka
Lacking in development efforts	Assam, West Bengal, Orissa, North Bihar, North-Eastern States	Southern Rajasthan, Northern Karnataka, Central Maharashtra, Rayalseema (AP), South Bihar

The first group of states are those, which are naturally well endowed, as well as the state initiated development efforts have put them well ahead in the growth. These states are depicting strong emergence of diversification towards commercial cropping pattern. These states also show better irrigation facilities and higher rates of growth. These have recorded higher cropping intensity and a clear shift away from traditional crop pattern to the crop combination suitable for the new technology. Therefore, in all ways these are the leaders in the growth process till now. This group includes Punjab, Haryana, Kerala, Himachal Pradesh, Uttar Pradesh and Tamil Nadu. The second group of states is the well-placed region in terms of natural resource endowments but could not take advantage of this vantage position due to failure of well-directed development efforts. Hence, these states/regions could not record on the count of growth performance. This group includes Bihar, Orissa, Assam, West Bengal and Madhya Pradesh. The third group includes the states with significant natural resource constraints but still performing better under the shadow of such threat. These regions or states could record respectable growth rates and therefore need to be encouraged to step up further. These include Gujarat, Andhra Pradesh, Karnataka and parts of Madhya Pradesh, along with parts of Andhra Pradesh (Coastal Andhra), Maharashtra (Western Maharashtra) and Rajasthan (Northern Rajasthan). The fourth group of states includes the regions not so well endowed with natural resources, as well as lacking in state led developmental efforts. These include Southern Rajasthan, Northern Karnataka, Central Maharashtra, Rayalseema (AP), South Bihar. One of the important characteristics of this group is the natural constraints that it faces. Some of the regions have been successful in overcoming such constraints. But a good amount of investment is required in order to circumvent these constraints and provide opportunities across sectors for the purpose of development. It's only a deliberate and well-planned agriculture policy, which can get this implemented.

Table 10.4

Basic Performance of Agriculture in the States Selected

States	*Overall Performance in Agriculture*
Andhra Pradesh	The agricultural growth rate was witnessing sharp acceleration throughout the 60s and 70s except for a slight deceleration during 80s. Along with the net sown area, the area under food grains, especially that of coarse cereals, continuously declined. On the other hand, area under commercial crops like groundnut and sunflower were on the rise. The state has high levels of area under irrigation and the fertiliser use has been increasing tremendously.
Assam	Both the growth in agriculture and that of the cropped area were reasonably high until the 80s after which a thorough deceleration is experienced. But, the productivity levels had been at moderate levels and the use of modern inputs had also been on the increase at moderate levels.
Bihar	Until the 80s, agri and productivity growth rates had been stagnating with a slight acceleration effect during 80s. The net sown area had been declining after the 70s and infact, negative throughout with slight decreases in cropping intensity. The use of modern inputs in particular, the fertiliser consumption increased tremendously.
Gujarat	Agriculture witnessed a positive but low growth rate on the whole with moderately high growth rate of productivity. The extension of wheat and rice technology increased growth and productivity substantially during 70s but for a stagnation during 80s owing to the persistent droughts. The net sown area declined continuously in the 80s with a moderate increase in cropping intensity. Coarse cereals like rice and wheat, which dominated the cropping pattern during 70s, gave way to oilseeds during the 80s recording a decline in the area under coarse cereals. The fertiliser use increased considerably.
Haryana	The agricultural economy recorded very high rates of growth in general owing to the confinement of the new wheat technology only to the irrigated areas. The growth rate in net sown area went negative during the 80s while increases in cropping intensity were seen. The state has high percentage of irrigated area. The area under food grains declined sharply and the oilseeds were gaining importance in the region with a significant increase in their area. The rate of mechanisation is also high in the state.
Himachal Pradesh	Agriculture growth in the state has been stagnating during the 70s after which there was a spurt in growth during the 80s while maintaining moderately high growth rates in the productivity levels. The cropped area had been declining continuously after the 70s to witness a negative growth in the 80s leaving the NSA more or less the same. The area under food grains remained almost the same with a shift in the cropping pattern to rice, wheat, cotton and sugarcane. The use of modern inputs had been minimal except for an increase in the use of fertilisers.

Contd...

...contd...

States	*Overall Performance in Agriculture*
Karnataka	A medium to high growth rate was attained in the agri-sector all through the period also recording very high growth rate in yield, in general. The growth in cropped area has been increasing right from the 70s, primarily because of changes in rainfall and remained reasonably high even during the 80s. The area under food grains, especially coarse cereals, declined with a shift towards oilseeds and sunflower. There has been a tremendous increase in the use of pumpsets and fertiliser consumption.
Madhya Pradesh	Growth in agriculture sector gained momentum after the 80s and hence a positive but low growth rate was recorded both in the overall and productivity growth rates all through the period. The growth in the cropped area in the state remained reasonably high even during the 80s. The area under coarse cereals declined greatly while the area under oilseeds, especially soyabean, increased. The use of modern inputs was very high in the state with special reference to the fertiliser use.
Maharashtra	Wide fluctuations were experienced in the growth of the agri-sector leaping from a negative growth in the 60s to a very high growth in the 70s and further a deceleration during the 80s owing to persistent droughts in the late 80s. Primarily, a higher growth rate occurred in the cropped area and later the 80s witnessed a decline. A decline in area under coarse cereals took place with a shift to oilseeds especially sunflower. The use of all modern inputs was on the rise.
Rajasthan	The state has been experiencing stagnation in agriculture during the 70s. Otherwise, very high growth rates in agriculture and its yield were recorded. Primarily, because of changes in rainfall, the cropped area grew at a moderately high rate with a moderate increase in cropping intensity too. The area under irrigation was more than doubled. There has been a considerable decline in the area under coarse cereals and a shift to oilseeds—rapeseed and mustard was seen. The use of fertilisers shot up tremendously along with the increase in the usage of tractors and pumpsets.
Uttar Pradesh	High growth rates were experienced right from the 60s with moderately high growth rates in yield, as the state had been a beneficiary of the new technology right from the start. The cropped area declined severely to become negative during the 80s with the cropping intensity increasing throughout. There has been a considerable increase in the area under irrigation along with tremendous increases in the use of modern inputs. With a very sharp increase in area under rice the area under food grains has been increasing continuously while area under oilseeds registering a decline.
West Bengal	Owing to the benefits of the wheat revolution, higher growth rates were recorded in agriculture in the initial period but for a severe decline in the 70s. The performance was creditable in the 80s with a spurt in output to unprecedented levels. Area under crops grew at a moderate rate, with the introduction of HYV wheat facilitating an increase in intensity of cultivation, and later remained at reasonably higher growth rates. But, the NSA showed a negative rate during the 80s. Higher use of modern inputs and higher levels of area under irrigation were recorded. Wheat dominated the cropping pattern during the initial stages at the cost of pulses. After 80s, the area under oilseeds also saw a rise.

Source: Bhalla and Singh (2001).

Table 10.5

Features of States Selected

States	*Predominant Crops (based on CCR)*	*Irrigated Area (%) and the Irrigation Intensity (II)*		*Cropping Intensity*		*Growth Rate in Food Grains Output*		*Growth Rate of Output of Major Crops*	
		1987-1990	*1997-2000*	*1987-1990*	*1997-2000*	*1970-71 to 1989-90*	*1990-91 to 1999-2000*	*1970-71 to 1989-90*	*1990-91 to 1999-2000*
Andhra Pradesh	Castor, groundnut, sunflower, cotton, sesamum, pulses, *arhar*, rice, *jowar*, *ragi*	39.87 (1.28)	43.82 (1.32)	1 19	1.23	2.50	1.47	Rice – 3.61 *Jowar* – -1.34 Groundnut – 5.15	Rice – 1.61 *Jowar* – -5.63 Groundnut – -5.83
Assam	Tea, rice, rapeseed & mustard, food grains, sesamum		11.38 (1)	1.39	1.47	1.83	1.07	Rice – 1.70 Mustard – 5.85	Rice – 1.06 Mustard – -1.79
Bihar	Maize, rice, wheat, food grains, pulses, *ragi*, small millets	39.74 (1.26)	47.06 (1.31)	1.37	1.35	1.54	3.60	Rice – 1.35 Wheat – 3.05 Maize – 2.90 Gram – -0.26	Rice – 4.91 Wheat – 3.13 Maize – 3.85 Gram – -3.83
Gujarat	Castor, groundnut, cotton, sesamum, *bajra*, *arhar*, maize, rapeseed & mustard	24.33 (1.18)	34.86 (1.24)	1.12	1.11	0.22	1.74	*Bajra* – -1.38 Groundnut – -0.73 Cotton – -1.16	*Bajra* – 1.45 Groundnut – 8.13 Cotton – 10.36
Haryana	Rapeseed & mustard, wheat, cotton, *bajra*, gram, rice	NA	81.08 (1.76)		1.71	4.22	3.44	*Bajra* – -2.20 Wheat – 6.27 Gram – -4.92	*Bajra* – 3.96 Wheat – 3.78 Gram – -9.52
Himachal Pradesh	Maize, wheat, small millets, food grains sesamum, pulses, *ragi*	17.63 (1.74)	18.7 (1.76)	1.68	1.74	1.0	-0.01	Maize – 1.63 Wheat – 2.27	Maize – 0.53 Wheat – -0.28
Karnataka	*Ragi*, sunflower, safflower, *jowar*, groundnut, *arhar*, pulses, maize, cotton, sesamum	20.68 (1.24)	25.46 (1.24)	1.13	1.16	0.74	1.60	*Jowar* – -0.03 *Ragi* – 2.68 Cotton – 1.51	*Jowar* – 1.06 *Ragi* – 2.02 Cotton – 1.60

Contd...

...contd...

States	*Predominant Crops (based on CCR)*	*Irrigated Area (%) and the Irrigation Intensity (II)*		*Cropping Intensity*		*Growth Rate in Food Grains Output*		*Growth Rate of Output of Major Crops*	
		1987-1990	*1997-2000*	*1987-1990*	*1997-2000*	*1970-71 to 1989-90*	*1990-91 to 1999-2000*	*1970-71 to 1989-90*	*1990-91 to 1999-2000*
Madhya Pradesh	Small millets, gram, pulses, wheat, maize, food grains, rice, *arhar*, rapeseed and mustard	16.15 (1.03)	19.62 (1.04)	1.17	1.75	2.20	1.91	Rice – 1.98 Wheat – 3.68 Gram – 2.56	Rice – -0.11 Wheat – 5.39 Gram – 4.26
Maharashtra	Safflower, *jowar*, cotton, *arhar*, sunflower, *bajra*, pulses, food grains, gram, sesamum	14.20 (1.26)	16.47 (1.23)	1.14	1.24	3.97	0.98	*Jowar* – 5.27 Groundnut – 2.99 Cotton – 3.41	*Jowar* – -13.41 Groundnut – -3.53 Cotton – 6.72
Punjab	Wheat, cotton, sunflower, rice, food grains, barley, potato, sugarcane, maize		95.08 (1.91)		1.90	5.56	2.26	Rice – 12.52 Wheat – 4.97 Cotton – 3.32	Rice – 2.52 Wheat – 2.26 Cotton – -11.22
Rajasthan	*Bajra*, rapeseed & mustard, gram, sesamum, pulses, maize, food grains, wheat	25.62 (1.23)	32.40 (1.24)	1.16	1.26	1.17	3.57	*Bajra* – 0.09 Wheat – 4.09 Gram – -1.13	*Bajra* – -0.82 Wheat – 6.47 Gram – 5.93
Uttar Pradesh	Wheat, maize, rapeseed & mustard, food grains, rice, gram, pulses, sesamum, *bajra*	56.53 (1.39)	49.84 (1.42)	1.45	2.02	4.33	2.52	Rice – 5.44 Wheat – 6.11 Sugarcane –	Rice – 3.05 Wheat – 3.17 Sugarcane –
West Bengal	Tea, rice, sesamum, food grains, rapeseed & mustard, *ragi*		30.32 (1.48)	1.56	1.71	2.05	2.61	Rice – 2.65 Rape & Mus. – 13.88 Jute –	Rice – 2.57 Rape & Mus. – -3.03 Jute –

Note: CCR: Crop Concentration Ratio.

10.7 Focus of this Study

Policy can be considered as a response of the government indicating its position on an area of significant concern to a political and administrative system. Such sectors are of course connected with the other segments of the economy and more than that with the polity, bureaucracy and the outside pressure groups. Inter-relatedness of policies and their outcomes therefore cannot be fully explored a *priori* but their probable direction of impact can be visualised. Hence, the study of policy making will require understanding of the institutional dynamics and case studies in order to analyse the emergence of the situation and the resolution of possible conflicts in goals. One of the important points of discord and subsequent resolutions is the understanding between the Central and the state governments, even keeping aside the other important players for a moment. According to the Indian Constitution, agriculture is in the state list but many facets of the sector are either in the central list or under the concurrent list. Even being on the state list, the policies pertaining to agriculture are mostly initiated at the Centre, sometime after consultation with the state. The only way of handling such a tricky issue is to understand the policy matrix through revealed juxtaposition.

Therefore, an attempt was made to formulate policy for agricultural sector with active participation of the players at the state level (Deshpande, 2006). Among the important interest groups we included the polity, administrators, bankers, farm leaders, academicians, processors and traders, agricultural labour unions, NGOs engaged in agriculture and rural development activities, and other stakeholders. It was felt necessary that the policy statement emerge out of the felt needs and resource availability at these locales. Such policy statement will emerge, as a matrix having the states on one axis and the felt needs on the other. The cells will speak about the type of initiatives needed for handling the underlying issues. We have also attempted a SWOT analysis in the context of the states.

10.8 Objectives

Keeping in view the above-stated background and considerations, the present study focuses on the following specific themes across states in terms of objectives:

i. To review the available material (including policy documents at selected country levels, five year plans at the Centre and at state level, policy statements made at the state level, etc.) at the state level dealing with policy interventions after the formation of the state.

ii. To identify important constraints and review the efforts made by the state in the past to meet major challenges pertaining to agriculture and allied activities.

iii. To record the state's response to the already formulated National Agricultural Policy, that is, to find out precisely how and where the state would like to suitably supplement, modify and re-articulate the National Policy in the local context.

iv. To discuss with the important stakeholders (as identified above) the requirements for formulation of a policy document at the state level, in response to the country's growing concerns at home and abroad (i.e., in response to challenges arising from WTO or otherwise).

v. To elaborate on the initiatives taken to meet the challenge of diversification, technology, resource management and price policy at the state level.

vi. To assemble these views in the form of a meaningful policy requirement matrix, relating problems/issues to action points suggested/recommended and also trying to spell out the agencies, which should undertake such actions.

Given the objectives as spelt out above, the study would have three broad components—first, description of agricultural policy scenario at the state level in general and identification of state level concerns and priorities in the pre-WTO era (objectives i to iii); second, enlisting of the state's reactions and responses to the country's obligations to meet the WTO requirements and the emerging constraints in the current global scenario (objectives iv & v). These are being dealt in this study whereas, the state's desired response to the emerging challenges (due to WTO or otherwise) in the form of policies will be attempted in a separate study by CMA Indian Institute of Management, Ahemedabad. The pre-WTO component of this document (i.e., objectives i to vi) will be coordinated by ADRT of ISEC, Bangalore, while the post-WTO part (i.e., the rest of the objectives) will be coordinated by CMA of IIM, Ahmedabad. Thus, the overall study is expected to bring out and document in historical perspective (i.e., during pre-WTO and post-WTO era) the state's perceptions of various challenges confronting its agricultural economy and effectiveness of the initiatives undertaken so far in response to those challenges. Although many of the underlying issues will come for discussion in almost all stages, in order to have clarity in understanding of the problems and subsequent presentation of the document, an attempt may nevertheless be made to undertake as far as possible the above-stated three components of the study in three successive stages, beginning with the first.

This study is aimed at achieving the twin goals of sensitising all important stakeholders of state agriculture on the emerging challenges at home and abroad, on the one hand, and on the need for making a continuous and concerted move for appropriate policy changes in today's circumstances, on the other. Naturally, the AER centres conducting this study are expected to continue to play a pivotal role in achieving these twin goals even after completion of this study.

10.9 Study Methodology

The methodology for the study involves a thematic review of the existing material at both international level (to see through review of mainly website literature by the two coordinating centres how at least some of the important and major players from Indian viewpoint like the EU, the USA, Canada, Australia, Brazil/Argentina, China, Japan, Israel, Thailand/Malaysia are repositioning themselves) and state level (to be reviewed by the AER centres) and interview with the stakeholders (also to be conducted by the AER centres) on crucial issues. The state level exercise should take into consideration the documents prepared by the agro-climatic regional planning groups across various states as well as strategy papers prepared by some of the state governments in response to WTO or otherwise. Plan documents both at Centre and state level should be reviewed. However, the intention here is to go beyond that in terms of preparing a policy document, as prevailing at the current moment, irrespective of the fact whether such policies are explicitly stated or not. The expected output from the first two stages of this exercise will be a systematic policy document for the concerned state. Although interaction with important stakeholders of state agriculture would be useful to get access to prevailing and pre-existing documents and thus to bring out the current policy status during the first two stages of the study, such interaction would be of crucial importance during the third and last stage of this exercise. Obviously, the spirit of this interaction would be positivist (i.e., to bring out the prevailing factual position without any ideological or normative preoccupation) during the first two stages, while it has to be essentially normative in nature (i.e., to bring out the desirable features as per the wishes and aspirations of various stakeholders) during the last stage. Naturally, the AER centres conducting this exercise would be applying logical introspection and analytical skills to present the findings in a systematic, consistent and coherent structure. Conflicts in desired policy changes across stakeholder groups would be an essential feature, which the study should bring out together with feasible prescriptive measures to resolve those conflicts.

Looking into the experience of agricultural development across the states, one can broadly group the states into six groups. We follow these broad groups for the purpose of our analysis.

Table 10.6

Agricultural Development Experience across the States

Groups	*Names of States*
Towards high commercialisation	Punjab, Haryana and Himachal Pradesh
Diversifying for trade	Andhra Pradesh, Karnataka and Tamil Nadu
Infrastructure for take-off in trade	Maharashtra and Madhya Pradesh
Encashing on rainfed crops	Gujarat and Rajasthan
Need for diversification	Assam and West Bengal
Evading low productivity trap	Bihar and Uttar Pradesh

These groups indicate the force of development in the context of the forces of liberalisation prevailing in these states. The states of Punjab, Haryana and Himachal Pradesh have a better promise of growth and it is essential that these states carefully transform themselves into pockets of commercial agriculture through policy initiatives, in order to participate positively and effectively in international trade. Punjab and Haryana have a significant natural advantage in growing food commodities and pulses as well as oilseeds, whereas Himachal Pradesh is known for its horticultural produce. Our analysis focuses on the strong points of these three states. The states of Andhra Pradesh, Karnataka and Tamil Nadu are traditionally food grain growing states. It would be prudent now that some diversification takes place towards trade-oriented crops in some selected pockets in these states. Our attempt is to locate such pockets and indicate the crops and crop groups for the purpose of development. In Central India, Maharashtra and Madhya Pradesh are still to come out of the constraints of the inadequate and low level infrastructure and public investment. The domination of food commodities in the cropping pattern of these two states is quite visible. It would be necessary to set a take-off stage in these states through better infrastructure and focusing on comparative advantages. As we have seen historically, Rajasthan and Gujarat are the major rainfed regions of India and these also have large portions under desert conditions. These would require a totally different strategy to deal with and that should be focused on negotiating the capabilities of rainfed crops as well as other allied agricultural activities. Livestock development is one of these activities and could be considered as an alternative here. Far eastern states of Assam and West Bengal remained out of the mainstream growth for a long time. It is only after the implementation of the S.R. Sen Committee Report, that these two states have shown signs of resurgence. With the abundance of natural resources, it will be essential to inject a proper incentive structure to provoke diversification towards high value crops and increase the productivity on the base of technology. The sixth group of states consists of Bihar and Uttar Pradesh, which are trapped in the low value-low productivity trap and that needs to be sorted out through proper policy change. Given this broad framework, we intend to analyse the state level reports keeping this frame of analysis in mind.

References

Agriculture Canada (1989). *Growing Together: A Vision for Canada's Agri-Food Industry*. Ottawa: Government of Canada.

ASSOCHAM (1998). *Strategic Plan for Indian Agricultural Sector*. New Delhi, July.

Ash, Robert F. (1988). "The Evolution of Agricultural Policy". *The China Quarterly* No. 116: 529-555, December.

Austin, Granville (1966). *The Indian Constitution: Cornerstone of a Nation*. Bombay: Oxford University Press.

Bhalla G.S. (2004). *Globalisation of Indian Agriculture—State of the Indian Farmer: A Millennium Study*. New Delhi: Academic Foundation.

Bhalla G.S. and Gurmail Singh (2001). *Indian Agriculture: Four Decades of Development*. New Delhi: Sage Publication.

Blyn, George (1966). *Agricultural Trends in India1891-1947: Output, Availability and Productivity*. Philadelphia: University of Pennsylvania Press.

Bordoloi, Jotin (2004). *Agricultural Policy in India: A Policy Matrix in a Federal System—A Study in Assam, AERC Report*. Jorhat: Assam Agricultural University.

Coleman, William D., Skogstad Grace and M. Atkinson Michael (1997). "Paradigm Shifts and Policy Networks: Cumulative Change in Agriculture", *Journal of Public Policy* 16(3): 273-301.

DeBrauw, A., J. Huang and S. Rozelle (2001). "Sequencing and the Success of Gradualism: Empirical Evidence from China's Agricultural Reform", *Working Paper*, Davis: Department of Agricultural and Resource Economics, University of California.

Deshpande, R.S. (2002). "Suicides by Farmers in Karnataka: Agrarian Distress and Possibly Alleviatory Steps", *Economic and Political Weekly* 37(26): 2601-2610, (June 29-July 5).

Deshpande, R.S. and J. Prachitha (2006). *Agricultural Policy in India: A Policy Matrix in a Federal System*. Bangalore: Agricultural Development and Rural Transformation Unit, Institute for Social and Economic Change.

Epstein, Paul J. (1997). "Beyond Policy Community: French Agriculture and GATT", *Journal of European Public Policy* 4(3): 355-72.

Ethiraj, K. (2004). *Agricultural Policy in Tamil Nadu: A Policy Matrix in a Federal System*. AERC Report. Chennai: University of Madras.

Finagold, Kenneth (1981). "From Agrarianism to Adjustment: The Political Origin of New Real Agreement Policy", *Politics and Society* 2(1): 1-27.

GoI (1980). *Report of the Special Expert Committee on Cost of Production Estimates* (Chairman: S R Sen). New Delhi: Ministry of Agriculture, Department of Agriculture and Cooperation.

———. (1985). *Seventh Five-Year Plan*. New Delhi: Planning Commission.

———. (1990). *Agricultural Policies and Programmes: Report of the High Power Committee* (Chairman: Shri. Bhanu Pratap Singh), July, New Delhi.

———. (1999). *Imperatives for Agricultural and Rural Development in India*. A Memorandum submitted to Prime Minister of India by H.D. Deve Gowda, Former Prime Minister of India on 17 February.

———. (2000). *National Agricultural Policy*. New Delhi: Department of Agriculture and Cooperative, Ministry of Agriculture, July.

———. (2001). *Approach Paper to the Tenth Five-Year Plan*. New Delhi: Planning Commission.

———. (various years). *Five year Plan Documents: First Five-Year Plan to Tenth Five-Year Plan*. New Delhi: Planning Commission.

Ghosh, Jayati (1997). "India's Structural Adjustment: An Assessment in Comparative Asian Context", *Economic and Political Weekly* 32(20-21): 1113-1131, (May 17-30).

Gregory, Sir Theodore (1943). *Report of the Food Grains Policy Committee*. New Delhi: Government of India.

Gupta, S.K. (2004). *Agricultural Policy in Madhya Pradesh: A Policy Matrix in a Federal System*. AERC Report for Madhya Pradesh and CHattisgarh. Jabalpur: JNKVV.

Hall, Peter A. (1993). "Policy Paradigms, Social Learning and the State: The Case of Economic Policy Making in Britain". *Comparative Politics* 25: 275-297.

Hill, Brian E. (1984). *The Common Agricultural Policy: Past, Present and Future*. London: Methuen.

Huang, J. and S. Rozelle (2001). "The Nature and Extent of Current Distortions to Agricultural Incentives in China", Paper presented at the second project meeting on WTO Accession, Policy Reform and Poverty Reduction in China. Beijing: World Bank Resident Mission. October 26-27.

Jha, Ugra Mohan and Rajiv Kumar Sinha (2003). *Agricultural Policy in Bihar: A Policy Matrix in a Federal System*. AERC Report for Bihar and Jharkhand. Bhagalpur: T.M. Bhagalpur University.

Jordan Grant, William A. Maloney and Andrew M. McLaughlin (1994). "Characterizing Agricultural Policy Making", *Public Administration* 72: 505-526 (winter).

Joshi, Vijay and I.M. Little (1996). *India's Economic Growth: 1991-2001*. New Delhi: Oxford University Press.

Kueh, Y.Y. (1985). "The Economics of Second Land Reforms in China". *The China Quarterly*, Vol. 101, March.

Kumar, Sanjay and S.D. Grover (2004). *Agricultural Policy in Punjab: A Policy Matrix in a Federal System*. AERC Report. Ludhiana: Punjab Agricultural University.

Lardy, N. (2001). *Integrating China in the Global Economy*. Washington D.C.: Brookings Institution.

Lasswell, Harold (1956). *The Decision Process*. Maryland: University of Maryland.

Maitra, Laxmi Kanta (1950). *Report of the Food Grains Investigation Committee*. New Delhi: Government of India.

Malik, R.P.S. (2004). *Agricultural Policy in India: A Policy Matrix in a Federal System—A Case Study of Haryana, AERC Report*. New Delhi: University of Delhi.

Mehta, Ashok (1957). *Report of the food Grains Enquiry Committee*. New Delhi: Ministry of Food and Agriculture, Government of India.

Mishra, J.N. (2004). *Agricultural Policy in Uttar Pradesh and Uttaranchal: A Policy Matrix in a Federal System*. AERC Report. Allahabad: University of Allahabad.

Narayanamoorthy, A. and S.S. Kalamakar (2004). *Agricultural Policy in Maharashtra: A Policy Matrix in a Federal System*. AERC Report, Pune: Gokhale Institute of Politics and Economics.

Nyberg, A. and S. Rozelle (1999). *Accelerating China's Rural Transformation*. Washington D.C.: The World Bank.

Paarlberg, Robert (1997). "Agricultural Policy Reform and the Uruguay Round: Synergistic Linkage in a Two Game?", *International Organisastion* 53(3): 413-44.

Paarlberg, Robert and David Orden (1996). "Explaining US Farm Policy in 1996 and Beyond: Changes in Party Control and Changing Market Conditions". *American Journal of Agricultural Economics* 78: 1305-1313, (December).

Patel, Arun, S. (2004). *Review of State Agriculture Policy in Gujarat and Rajasthan. AERC Report*. Vallabh Vidyanagar, Gujarat: Sardar Patel University.

Rahim, Kazi M.B. and Debashis Sarkar (2004). *Agricultural Policy in West Bengal: A Policy Matrix in a Federal System*. AERC Report. Visva Bharti: Santiniketan.

Rao, C.H. Hanumantha (2001). "WTO and Viability of Indian Agriculture", *Economic and Political Weekly* 36(36): 3453-3457, (Sept. 8-14).

Rao, V.M. (1998). "Policy Making for Agricultural Development: Why it Misses the Poor", V.B. Memorial Lecture delivered during the 40th Conference of Indian Society of Labour Economics, Hyderabad (Later published in *The Indian Journal of Labour Economics*, Vol. 42(1), 1999).

Ratnam, C. (2003). *Agricultural Policy in Andhra Pradesh: A Policy Matrix in a Federal System*. AERC Report. Vishakhapatnam: Andhra University.

Sen, Sunanda (2000). *Trade and Dependence: Essays on Indian Economy*. New Delhi: Sage Publications.

Singh, Ranveer, S.P. Saraswat and Partap Singh (2004). *Agricultural Policy in Himachal Pradesh: A Policy Matrix in a Federal System*. AERC Report. Shimla: University of Summer Hill.

Srinivasan. T.N. (1998). *Eight Lectures on India's Economic Reforms*. New Delhi: Oxford University.

Swinbank, Alan (1989). "The Common Agricultural Policy and the Politics of European Decision Making", *Journal of Common Market Studies* 24(4): 303-322.

Venkatappaiah, B. (1966). *Report of the food Grains Policy Committee*. New Delhi: Department of Food, Ministry of Food and Agriculture, Government of India.

Walkar, K.R. (1984). "Chinese Agriculture during the Period of Readjustment". *The China Quarterly* Vol. 100 (December).

William, James Adams (1999). "The Political Economy of Agriculture in France's Fifth Republic", *Explorations in Economic History* 36(1): 1-29.

Annexure Table A-10.1

A Comparative Analysis of the Agricultural Policy Documents

Parameters	*Memorandum by H.D. Deve Gowda,[1] 1999*	*Draft Agricultural Policy Resolution,[2] 1990 (for India)*	*Strategic Plan for Indian Agricultural Sector,[3] 1998*	*Agriculture Policy Resolution by Karnataka,[4] 1995*	*National Agricultural Policy,[5] 2000*	*High Power Committee Report,[6] 1990*
1	*2*	*3*	*4*	*5*	*6*	*7*
1. Resources-land, water, labour, technology, risk and natural hazards	Better utilisation of natural resources, stress on dryland farming, promote cost-effective minor irrigation works and pressure irrigation (drip and sprinkler).	Efficient management of land and water resources and conservation of natural resources. Dryland farming, creation of jobs, better utilisation of irrigation resources.	Increase the area under irrigation, transfer irrigation management to corporate sector, HYV seeds for dryland farming, increase yield rates.	Necessary amendments for land act to facilitate expansion of sunrise industries, fisheries and others. Increase irrigation water fees.	Promote technically sound, economically viable, environmentally non-degrading, and socially acceptable use of country's natural resources. Development of rainfed and irrigated lands, evolve national livestock breeding strategy, & genetic upgradation of indigenous/native cattle, efforts towards food security, National Agriculture Insurance Scheme to protect from natural calamities and price fluctuations.	Natural resources should be guarded against abuse and misuse, and ensure their upgradation. New techniques of production should be financially viable. More stress on dryland farming. Increase support for minor irrigation works (groundwater and tanks) and micro-irrigation, and increase their efficiency, and emphasis on backward regions.

Contd...

...*contd*...

1	2	3	4	5	6	7
2. Linkages, infrastructure, supportive mechanism, safety net, attending to specific problems, regional imbalance	Efficient use of extension and training methods, schemes & programmes for small and marginal farmers, support allied activities (livestock, fisheries), improve quality of rural life, encourage direct producer-consumer links, PDS to mainly support poor.	Provide for agriculture and allied activities, profitable technology, extension service, input support, incentive process & processing facilities. Incentive price policies and efficient price support mechanisms. Agro-processing facilities in rural areas, farming systems approach.	Encourage regional specialisation, develop appropriate HYV seeds, adoption of new technology by farmers, making new technology more viable to farmers.	Establishment of new rural financial institutions, on the line on NABARD to supplement the credit operations of the existing institutions. Restructure extension system. Adopt ACRP approach to reduce regional imbalances.	Promote allied activities to generate rural employment, stress on sunrise sectors, generate and disseminate appropriate technology for agriculture and allied activities of livestock and fisheries, evolve location-specific and economically viable options in various sectors, regionalisation of agricultural research. Inputs management, priority for rural electrification, stress on market insfrastructure and forward linkages, promote micro-credit and self help group-banking linkage system, popularise and support renewable sources of energy.	Safeguard the purchasing power of farmers, and not merely reimbursement of their cost of production. Encourage and enable to create direct producer-consumer links. Public distribution of food grains restructured to provide freedom to farmers to participate from process-transport-sales anywhere in the country. PDS should help genuinely poor. In desingning schemes and programmes, stress on marginal and small farmers. Reorient research and extension to cater to small farmers. More stress on allied activities.
3. Institutions, governance, agricultural administration, preparedness for new trends, & challenges, capacity building, Role clarity	Enforce land ceiling laws, consolidation of land holdings, promote participatory irrigation management, krushi vignana kendras at district level, set up National Academy of	Development of appropriate institutional infrastructure to enable production for domestic consumption and export. Strengthen institutional infrastructure for a creative partnership between Central and	Long-term political commitment to the vision, mission and goals, shared vision and cooperation from all state governments, efficient bureaucracy, corporate sector	Encourage ACRP approach for planning agriculture development with emphasis on planning from below. Activate district planning boards.	Application of frontier sciences, strengthen research and extension linkages, encourage KVKs, NGOs, and user organisations, corporate sector, commodity-wise strategies and arrangements for protecting the grower	Improve human resource base by providing necessary knowledge, skills and attitudes, improve quality of life in rural areas. Enforce land ceiling laws & consolidate holdings. Review share-croppers role. Involve users in irrigation

Contd...

...contd...

1	2	3	4	5	6	7
(Central and state govt, users, corporate)	Agricultural Administration, focus on capacity building	state, and between state & local bodies & farmers. Land reforms, & consolidation of land holdings. Increase exports of both traditional & non-traditional commodities, programme for the landless, research in frontier sciences, reorientation of extension system. State and Central govts. to be partners, involvement of NGOs, role of panchayat raj institutions, research to be small holder oriented.	participation, effective coordination among various levels of implementing agencies.		from liberalisation and globalisation, consolidation of land holdings, redistribution of surplus lands and waste lands among landless, tenancy reforms, development of lease markets for increasing holding size and for agri-business, recognition of women's rights in land, promote private sector participation and contract farming and land leasing arrangements, progressive institutionalisation of rural and farm credit, revamp cooperatives, policy initiatives for reforms in agriculture management by the Central and state govts, centre to move towards macro-management and role do advocacy and facilitation.	management and developmental projects. Focus on small and marginal farmers for all demonstration effects. Stress on farmers training and revive farmers training centres. Establish districtwise krushi vignana kendras and rejuvenate them. Set up National Academy of Agricultural Administration to upgrade knowledge and skills of personnel of agriculture and allied fields.
4. Performance monitoring, data base, information system, efficiency, policy feed back process				Launch separate TV channel for dissemination of information on agricultural activities —include market/ price information.	Upgradation and dissemination of market intelligence, strengthen database and ensure greater reliability of estimates and forecasting, harness	

Contd...

...contd...

1	2	3	4	5	6	7
					remote sensing and information technology, develop agriculture on-line capacity.	
5. Finance, investments, capital formation		6% growth in output and 40% of the plan outlays needed.		Incentives on the lines of those given to industries for promoting investment. Establish rural credit institution on the lines of NABARD to promote investment activities in rural areas.	Favourable economic environment for increasing capital formation and farmer's own investments, increase public investment to reduce regional imbalances, review resource allocation regime, energise small farmers agro business consortium and promote public and private investments in agri-business, financial viability of extension services.	Double the outlay on agricultural research and extension. Mount technology missions for new and thrust areas.
6. Aim/goal	Improve quality of rural life, realise full potential of agriculture.	Build a vibrant agricultural economy for securing a better life for the farm community and an efficient institutional structure to fulfil the goals of economic effciency, employment, export, equity and ecological conservation.		To incorporate competition in the agriculture sector, particularly for commercial crops and high value low volume crops. Simultaneously provide safety net to the poor.	Growth rate of 4%, efficient use of resources, growth with equity, demand driven, and sustainable.	Realise full potential of agriculture to help resolve, self-sufficiency in food grains, poverty, unemployment and deficit trade balance.

Contd...

...contd...

1	*2*	*3*	*4*	*5*	*6*	*7*
7. Vision				To promote agricultural exports in the area of flowers, fruits and vegetables; to adopt ACRP approach; to declare agriculture as industry.		

Note: 1. Imperatives for Agricultural and Rural Development in India. A memorandum submitted to Prime Minister of India by H.D.Deve Gowda, Former Prime Minister of India on 17 February 1999.
2. Draft Agricultural Policy Resolution, 1990. Prepared by the Ministry of Agriculture, Government of India.
3. Strategic Plan for Indian Agricultural Sector, ASSOCHAM, New Delhi. July 1998.
4. Karnataka Agriculture Policy Resolution, 1995. Government of Karnataka.
5. National Agricultural Policy, 2000. Ministry of Agriculture, Government of India, July 2000.
6. Report of the High Powered Committee on Review of Agricultural Policies and Programmes. 1990. Ministry of Agriculture, Government of India.

Section III

Irrigation

11 On Researching Irrigation Institutions*

A. Vaidyanathan

11.1 Introduction

My interest in institutions was kindled by my efforts to understand the factors that influence the impact of irrigation on agricultural productivity and the distribution of increased production due to irrigation among various groups and regions.

Irrigation works differ in terms of source, scale and the institutional arrangements for managing them. The two main sources are surface water and groundwater. The former range from small storages and diversion of local stream flows serving a single village or a small group of contiguous villages, through networks of local storages drawing water from barrages across rivers with a wider catchments severing a large number of villages, to canal systems fed by large storage reservoirs serving extensive areas (sometimes hundreds of thousands of hectares). Groundwater has become an increasingly important source of water supply for all uses.

The contribution of irrigation systems to increasing the quantum and reliability of water supply and its impact on agricultural productivity is conditioned in considerable degree by agro-climatic conditions and the nature of the water source. Thus, small storages depending on local catchments are likely to contribute much less in these respects compared to larger storages drawing their supply from wider catchments. And perennial rivers are likely to contribute more than seasonal rivers. The distribution of surface water involves considerable losses and

* Draft note for discussion at the Conversations with Economists and Anthropologists II being held in Goa, August 1-4, 2003.

regulating its delivery to match crop water needs is far more difficult both technically and managerially compared to groundwater.

Given the nature of the water source, irrigation impact in terms of raising agricultural productivity, ensuring equitable distribution of the increased production and safeguarding the interests of long term sustainability depends partly on a combination of factors: the engineering design of the system, the state of agricultural technology, and the water management institutions. These are inter-related. Given system design and agricultural technology, the functioning of irrigation institutions has a crucial bearing on the end results.

11.2 Evolution of Irrigation Institutions

Water by nature is a fluid, common pool resource serving diverse uses and numerous users. The conditions necessary for an effective market mechanism to mediate allocations (and in particular clearly defined and enforceable private property rights) is near impossible to fulfil. Entitlement to access (geographical and by use) to a given source (which could be a tank, a reservoir, a river basin or an aquifer) as well as the sharing the available supplies from that source among claimants entitled to access the source is therefore everywhere subject to social.

Historically, irrigation and water control works were mostly small and localised. Questions regarding entitlement and allocation were decided and enforced locally by the concerned community and in the case of multi-community systems—of which there are a sizeable number—through mutual negotiation without any significant involvement of higher levels of authority and power. There were of course significant exceptions: the mammoth flood control works of ancient China, extensive canal deltaic irrigation systems in the Nile and the Cauvery being some notable examples. These were exceptions and were associated with the emergence of centralised authority holding sway over wide areas.

Over time, the local systems went through a process of expansion and integration covering several contiguous communities. This process, of which there are well-documented accounts in the case of China, Japan, India and Indonesia, seems to be result of a combination of local level interest in exploiting potential for increased production through expansion of irrigation as well as encouragement and support from regional chieftains interested in expanding their domain and revenues. The latter seem to have played basically a facilitating role.

The physical works in extended multi-village systems was largely constructed at the initiative of the beneficiary communities with support and encouragement from supra-local chieftains and kings. The institutional arrangements for managing multi-community systems were more complex calling for more elaborate rules concerning the rights of different communities, scheduling of water and sharing it in time times of scarcity, as well as mechanisms for monitoring, enforcement and conflict resolution. These mechanisms again were set up and managed largely by the concerned communities. However, it seems likely that the scope and need for involvement of extra-local centres of authority also increased.

All these elements are liable to change. Major changes in land tenure, increased contacts with the outside world (through for example migration, integration with wider markets and spread of education), and incursion of extra-local institutions and centres of power (such as state government and its bureaucracy, political parties and the judicial system) into the community can significantly change the configurations of local power and the working of local institutions. Changes in the agricultural technology through the introduction of new crops, new varieties and non-traditional inputs can change the level and pattern of water demand by raising returns to irrigated agriculture generally and shifting the relative returns to different crops. The introduction of energised pumps and electrification of rural areas has given a strong impetus to private irrigation using groundwater. Insofar as access to well irrigation reduces dependence on tank irrigation, the institutions for managing the latter are weakened. Nevertheless, it is significant that community management of maintenance and water allocation in times of scarcity continues wherever tanks are the only source of irrigation.

In recent times, the state has become more and more involved in improving existing local surface systems, building new works and in regulating their management. This tendency has become more pronounced as advances in civil and hydraulic engineering technology has made it possible to construct large storages and canal systems. The growing pressure of demand for water for increasing food and fibre production has been a strong impetus for their growing importance. The resources and organisation needed to implement them are far beyond the capacity of local communities. So is the task of balancing of competing claims between different regions, uses and users. All this has led to the state playing an increasing role in setting up and managing such works.

Handling these tasks also calls for huge, complex, multi-tiered organisations managed by a professional bureaucracy based on formal rules and procedures. The nature and extent of state involvement varies: in some cases, it is limited to legislating the framework of general principles leaving each system to be managed by more or less autonomous organisations. More typically, the state specifies regulations concerning the structure, composition and role of these organisations and procedures and mechanisms for dispute settlement. In the extreme—and India is a typical case in point—the Government takes over all the tasks from conception through design, engineering and financing of construction, continuing maintenance and management and settling conflicts.

By contrast groundwater, though a common pool resource in a given aquifer, can be easily tapped from wells and tubewells and lifting devices that are within the capacity of individuals and can be adjusted, within limits, to their water needs. Exploitation of groundwater is therefore mostly in the private sector but usually subject to government regulations. The extent of groundwater irrigation was relatively limited until the advent of energised pumping greatly reduced costs by making it possible to tap deeper aquifers and lift much larger volumes per unit of time. Improvements in agricultural technology (notably the introduction of high yielding varieties) and the spread of electricity to rural areas gave a strong fillip to expansion of groundwater use in recent decades.

The agro-climatic conditions, sub-surface geology and other features of the physical environment as well as the state of agricultural and engineering technology thus have a significant influence in shaping the organisation and management of irrigation. So do the socio-political context in which they function. At the same time, given physical environment and technology, the impact of irrigation in terms of increased productivity and its distribution, as well as the externalities generated by it, depend crucially on the way water is managed.

11.3 Framework for Study of Institutions

The literature on irrigation institutions highlights the diversity of their forms, structure and functioning, and to some degree their historical evolution. It is rich in description but rather less so in throwing light on the reasons underlying variations in these respects and in their effectiveness. Collective action theories help in exploring the working of community level institutions to some extent. But they are inadequate when local institutions are part of a wider network of institutions and more so for studying organisations managing large irrigation systems.

Much of the discussion of these aspects tends to view them from a management perspective and focus on particular aspects such as technical design of systems, ability to ensure proper maintenance of facilities, pricing policies, monitoring and enforcement of rules, and corruption. Much is also written about the relative merits of centralised *versus* decentralised management, bureaucratic *versus* self-managed systems and markets *versus* public regulation. These provide useful partial perspectives but are inadequate to comprehend differences in structure and functioning of networks of inter-related institutions and large organisations.

Organisation theories and the new institutional economics offer a promising framework for analysing different types of institutions. Institutions, in the more general sense, comprise a set of rules and conventions to regulate behaviour of individuals and groups in pursuit of their goals and of procedures to ensure their compliance. They also seek to specify what goals are permissible and which are not; rules governing relations between individuals and groups; and procedures for conflict resolution. Organisations are the media through which these functions are implemented.

Irrigation institutions share 411 these features. However, unlike individuals and private enterprise they are 'public systems'. Water institutions are required to balance multiple social objectives (efficiency, equity and sustainability of water use) and open to state intervention and political forces to a much greater degree than private enterprise. Whether and how the theory of institutions needs to be modified for application to public systems is a moot point. The following discussion merely explores how the basic concepts and insights of institutional analysis can be used to better understand the way water institutions are structured, function and change, and for the differences in these respects.

It is also necessary to take note of the fact that these different dimensions are inter-related in complex ways. Most analysts recognise this but is rarely incorporated adequately in empirical studies of water institutions. This led me to think about a common framework in which the structure and functioning of water institutions can be better comprehended. What follows is a preliminary and sketchy outline of my reflections on this issue. They are frankly and explicitly eclectic. They do not, and cannot, claim to be an integrated 'theory'. Nevertheless, I feel that the concepts of rules, authority and power provide the elements of a common framework for analysing water institutions, and indeed institutions generally.

11.4 The Relevance of the Institutional Economics Perspective

Let me start with a relatively simple case of an irrigation tank in Tamil Nadu. Typically it serves a section of farmland within the village. It is considered to be the common property of the village community. Access to and use of the water is supposed to be governed by customary rules and conventions. Originally—often several centuries back—these were constructed under the leadership of local temples, prominent landowners or local chieftains with contributions of material and labour by members of the community.

The purpose of the rules is to make proper use available water and ensure that it is distributed in a fair manner among the users. Typically they also spell out the contribution expected of members of the irrigation community to the maintenance and upkeep of the tanks and its distribution network and remunerating the functionaries appointed by it. The rules allow for flexible adaptation to different contingencies of scarcity. Note that 'proper use of available water' is relative to a particular understanding of water-productivity relations and seldom quantified. The notion of equity is also fuzzy sometimes focusing on head to tail allocations; sometimes to fair sharing of available supplies in times of scarcity; but rarely of equal access to different classes of farmers. In all these respects actual practice, if not the rules, changes over time.

The authority to make and change rules, as well as to enforce sanctions for non-compliance, is supposed to be vested with community. In fact, however, the exercise of this authority is in effect delegated to leaders. The leaders have usually been drawn from the relatively well-to-do landowners belonging to the dominant caste in the community. That the proper observance of the rules is in their personal economic interest (namely obtaining good yields) and that a substantial, if not the bulk, of the benefits accrue to them gives them a strong incentive to make sure that rules are observed. There are designated functionaries to attend to monitoring and enforcement. Within a small community, getting reliable and timely information on rule compliance is relatively easy and inexpensive.

The economic and social position of the dominant users gives them the power to enforce compliance if need be through coercive, and even violent, means. Their personal interest is not always harmonised with that of other, less well-endowed members or of the community as a whole. In that event, the dominant group is in a position to use their authority and power to manipulate the rules and their application in their favour. That, by virtue of their position and experience they may be better informed about the intricacies of functioning of the system also makes it possible for them to manipulate the use of such information to their advantage.

This does not mean that everyone will be satisfied with the way the system is managed or with all decisions of those in authority. Nor does it mean that there are no conflicts over water among users. Nevertheless, the disaffected may be content to acquiesce in the situation so long as the attitudes and responses of the latter to different contingencies are predictable. Conflicts are not pushed to the brink of breakdown because there are also costs to defying the authority and because members of the irrigation community are inter-related at several levels and in diverse ways and have to maintain long-term relationships with each other. So long as the local power relations are stable, the interpretation and enforcement of 'rules' under different contingencies is predictable. Most participants acquiesce in the arrangement and let it work more or less smoothly.

The picture gets more complicated in the case of local systems serving several communities like the system tanks and tank cascades in south India, and the 'melons on vine' of China. Often they are evolved by expanding and integrating pre-existing local systems through a process of trial and error and mutual negotiations among the concerned communities with the support and active encouragement of supra-local authority (chieftains, kings). The institutions to manage them are more complex than that of works serving single communities. They are known to have evolved elaborate conventions concerning the rights of different communities, scheduling of water and sharing it in times of scarcity, as well as mechanisms for monitoring, enforcement and conflict resolution.

Authority and power do play an important role in formulating and implementing the rules but are more diffused than in a single community. Built-in containment mechanisms are much weaker than within individual villages. Consequently, constituent communities put in more effort to monitor each other's activities in relation to the system and rely more on mutual accommodation through negotiation. The relative power of leadership of constituent communities has an important role in the process but cannot always handle conflicts amicably without external intervention. Institutions of governance at higher levels have to intervene by laying down a framework in which local institutions are to function and be involved in the settlement of disputes is therefore greater. The extent of this involvement and intervention has vastly increased in recent times. Changes in the external environment—technological, economic, social and political—have also affected the working of these institutions.

Intervention by regional and national level governments in all aspects, and at all levels, of water resource development has greatly increased in recent times. This role covers: (1) rights of individuals and organisations other than government to construct and manage water control projects; (2) the basis on which guiding allocation of water between different uses and users is to be decided; (3) regulations relating to financing and management of water control works and pricing policies; (4) conflict resolution mechanisms.

The nature and extent of government role varies. At one extreme is a situation in which the government chooses to confine itself to setting the broad legal framework for water resource development, and creating regulatory and dispute settlement mechanisms without direct involvement in the construction and management of projects. At the other extreme is a situation—as in India—where the government not only legislates general principles but also takes over direct responsibility for all these functions. Most countries fall between these extremes.

Even when the government chooses the first course, and its direct involvement in setting up and managing individual systems is limited, it has to devise credible and effective mechanisms to strike a balance between efficient use of available water from a common source (basin, ~b-basin, aquifer); its equitable distribution between competing uses and users of that source; minimise adverse effects by way of displacement of people and loss of productive land and forests; and ensure long term sustainability. Since these objectives are not all mutually consistent, this balancing is inherently difficult. So is the task of deciding how the costs and benefits are to be shared between various groups involved.

In principle, these issues can and should be decided on the basis of careful, transparent and public consideration by independent experts of alternative feasible patterns of exploitation and use, their implications in terms of costs and the impact on different claimants, and trade-offs among them. However, expert bodies, no matter how independent and knowledgeable they are, cannot strike a balance between different claims wholly on objective considerations. They have to take into account societal preferences about the relative importance to be attached to efficiency of use as against equity in distribution, and to outcomes over different time horizons.

Societal preferences are decided through the political process through which diverse interests and different perceptions of good and bad, desirable and undesirable are mediated. Politicians have a well-known propensity to skirt around or sweep contentious issues under the carpet. They are also bothered more about the consequences of their choice to their immediate political future than about long-term impacts. Moreover, all the concerned interest groups and regions are not equally placed—in terms of knowledge and resources—to articulate their interests effectively before such bodies or through the media and other public forums. Those better equipped to do so are therefore in a better position to influence the ultimate decisions in their favour. More so given the possibility of 'regulatory capture', a tactic widely and successfully adopted by powerful vested interests. That the political process is notoriously biased and seldom leads to a clear and unambiguous resolution is all too obvious.

Collective preferences of the polity reflected in constitutional directives, policy statements and legislations are not necessarily shared by those charged with implementing them. Even when they do, there can be a serious 'principal-agent' problem when they are perceived by those responsible for implementing them (namely the politicial executives and the bureaucracy) to be against their interests. Politicians are naturally concerned with retaining power, or wresting it from opponents, both at a personal level and for the party/group to which they belong. This concern becomes stronger when politics is in a fluid state, and tenures are short and uncertain. Under these conditions, the short term interests of the political class, whether they are in or out of office, acquires salience over long term societal concerns in the making and implementation of public policy. It gets reflected in many spheres of governance, including decisions on the scale of investment and the specific projects to be taken up by the government and its agencies.

Public expenditure on projects offers opportunities for mobilising funds for the ruling party, patronage to cadres and supporters and to woo electoral support of particular constituencies. There is therefore, a strong incentive for them to: (a) favour large public spending on 'development' projects, and sanction more and more projects funds; (b) approve projects without proper scrutiny and techno-economic evaluation of designs; (c) violate contracting procedures meant to ensure that projects are implemented at minimum cost; (d) make operational rules fuzzy and give themselves considerable discretion to change them as they deem fit; and (e) avoid independent audit of projects and their performance of completed projects.

There are of course formal mechanisms to keep these propensities in check. They include independent expert scrutiny and techno-economic evaluation of projects before being cleared for implementation; procedures for award of contracts based on *operis*, competitive bids; statutory public audit reporting to parliaments; anti-corruption laws; and regulatory bodies to review and approve pricing decisions. Not all of them are in place. In any case, their effectiveness depends on the autonomy and integrity of these mechanisms, the cooperation of the executive in providing full and correct information, and the seriousness with which findings of oversight agencies are used to initiate corrective action. Of particular importance is the existence of a vigilant civil society willing and able to generate strong public protests against wrongful decisions, abuse of power and hampering the functioning of check and balance mechanisms.

The extent to which these conditions are met varies. It is strongest, though far from ideal, in democratic societies which have a tradition of maintaining separation of powers between legislatures, executive and judiciary; independent regulatory bodies and vibrant and vigilant institutions in civil society. Even in such societies, the executive is known to adopt stratagems to evade check and balance mechanisms. Their authority to appoint regulators and judges gives them the opportunity to bias if not pack the regulatory bodies and courts. The political executives of government can exercise considerable influence on legislators belonging to their party to support them. They are also well positioned to hamper the oversight agencies, as well as the public at large, by withholding or delaying information and even giving false and misleading information. Failure to provide full and free public access to information on executive decisions and their underlying rationale, severely limits the capacity of interest groups to exert pressure for corrective action.

Specifically in respect of irrigation institutions, when users and private enterprises contribute a substantial part of the investment costs, participate actively in management of maintenance and water allocation, and the operation is required to be financially self-reliant, they are likely to have strong interest in ensuring that projects are designed carefully, and implemented at minimum cost. Large systems will need a professional bureaucracy to manage the system but they will be accountable to the management. There will be greater pressures on them to ensure that rules are clearly defined and strictly implemented; and that users pay charges to cover costs of water supplied to them.

Incentives to ensure these in practice will be weakened when the government finances the bulk of the investment and users have no role in management. The political and bureaucratic executives will have greater scope to use their authority to manipulate rules and their implementation to serve particular interests selectively. Fuzzy operational rules leave much scope for discretionary changes in their application to serve the interests of particular groups or regions selectively. This may be used collusively by political interests and the managerial for mutual benefit. The difficulties and the high cost of monitoring ground level operations in a large system give ample opportunities for discretionary use of authority by lower level functionaries for their personal benefit. Principal-agent problems are thus greatly aggravated in such situations.

Incentives for transparent, fair and accountable management are weakest when the government funds the entire investment in water supply projects and supplies water at highly subsidised rates. If anything, such a dispensation leads to such a perversion of the incentive structure that the political executive does not only fail to enforce rules for fear of losing support, but often permits and even encourages violations.

As for users, those with the means or political influence can bend or flout the rules to their advantage. Not having much of a financial stake in good management, users as a class are least concerned about the enormous drain on the exchequer. Instead, they can be readily mobilised to protest against any increase in water rates and even to demand a further reduction in the rates! The rest of the community that is denied of investments for much needed public goods and infrastructure (including extension of irrigation to new areas) is too diffuse to counter this trend. In this 'worst case' scenario, the executive is able to use its authority and power to emasculate the oversight and review institutions and do pretty much what it pleases to serve the short-term interests of the individuals and the party who run the government.

11.5 The Indian Experience

The current Indian situation is pretty close to the 'worst case' scenario. However, it was not always so. Nearly two centuries back, the colonial government assumed the responsibility for maintenance of much of the traditional local systems and for construction of new surface irrigation works. The so-called 'major' works were managed entirely by the government bureaucracy with practically no user participation. Neither efficiency (in terms of output impact) nor equity in distribution was the central consideration. There were of course complaints on both scores that were left to be dealt with by the bureaucracy. Political considerations and pressures did play a role but not in the degree and manner observed currently. The policy was to undertake fresh investment in irrigation (except in protective works) only when there was an assurance that it will earn a net return in terms of government revenue. There are instances of the government taking up less viable projects on condition that the beneficiaries contributed a substantial part of the investment.

After Independence, the organisational structure for irrigation and water management remained much the same but there were major changes in strategy and policy. These include: (1) a vigorous policy of expansion of irrigation facilities under the auspices of the government; (2) an enormous expansion in funds allocated for irrigation development; (3) abandonment of financial return as the criterion for investment decisions; and (4) procedures and criteria for technical scrutiny and social cost benefit analysis of project proposals as a precondition for approving their implementation.

With the government undertaking to finance the entire cost, the demand for starting irrigation projects soared. Their potential as means of cultivating and expanding electoral support made elected governments eager to accede to these demands. This led to promises to launch far more projects than could be accommodated within available funds. Many were based on inadequate investigations and poorly designed.

Pressures for relaxing and diluting the appraisal processes grew. Many projects were taken up without prior approval. The fund raising potential of construction contracts further distorted the programme and eroded procedures for technical and financial audits to the point of nullity. There were no countervailing forces to check these trends. On the contrary, pressures for going soft on cost recovery increased.

The policy that irrigation projects should bring a reasonable net return on investment had been given up soon after Independence. It was considered sufficient to ensure that current operation and maintenance costs were recovered from users. As current costs increased rapidly, rates had to be raised to meet this requirement. But faced with strong and increasingly organised resistance from users, governments, irrespective of party affiliation, found it politically expedient to give up attempts to raise water rates. Problems of under assessment and low recoveries seem to have worsened. Losses on account of irrigation even in relation to current O&M costs increased apace. Including capital costs, which were also soaring partly because of inflation, defective designs, growing dependence on borrowings and steep rise in interest rates, the losses to the public exchequer mounted to staggering proportions.

Countervailing political pressures to check these trends have been weak. Given the fluidity of politics, and the attendant insecurity and shortness of tenure of governments, expediency and populism continue to inhibit any major reforms and serious efforts to implement them. Nevertheless, Governments have had to confront persistent and growing criticisms, both internally and from external funding agencies, regarding high cost, inordinate delays, inefficient and inequitable use of water, and poor cost recovery. The acute fiscal crunch facing practically all levels of government is forcing them to address these problems. This has triggered some changes reflected in greater emphasis on rehabilitation and modernisation of existing systems, measures to improve efficiency of water use, restructuring of water resource management with greater user participation and reviews of cost recovery policies. While these have not gathered much momentum, the very fact that they are happening is a sign of the system trying to respond, however disjointedly and hesitantly, to objective compulsions. Whether and how soon they will lead to major reforms is a question impossible to answer.

11.6 By Way of Summing Up

This paper has turned out to be more discursive than I had intended. My intention was to highlight: (a) the need to view water institutions in the context of the larger physical, socio-political and technological environment in which they operate; (b) the usefulness of concepts and insights from organisation theory and institutional economics to analyse the structure and functioning of water institutions; and (c) the fact that the evolution of institutions is shaped not merely by their internal dynamics but equally, perhaps more importantly, by changes in different elements of the overall context.

In exploring the dynamics of institutions, it is important to remember that even to begin with, the physical context in which a system is planned, its engineering design, the patterns of use and the objectives they are meant to achieve and the rules and procedures to implement them seldom are coherent and internally consistent. This happens for several reasons: inadequate or wrong information on water availability, water requirements of different crops, cropping patterns suited to the specific agro-climatic context, losses in conveyance and application, design deficiencies due to inadequate investigations and compromises to accommodate competing claims of efficiency and equity under political pressures. These inadequacies and resulting inconsistencies surface once the systems become operational. They are invariably compounded because the patterns of cropping that users find profitable differ from what the planners considered desirable and managers find it difficult to enforce the original rules. The functioning of the system in several related dimensions goes through a process of readjustment until some sort of stable and workable state is reached.

That state, though invariably very different from the original intentions, can and does continue till it is disturbed by changes in one or more of its elements: it could be the physical context (for instance reduced water supplies due to increased extraction upstream, deterioration of water quality due to pollution), the advent of a new technology (such as conjunctive use of different sources, introduction of new crops or crop varieties), changes in demand emergence of new markets affecting economic returns, socio-political changes (shifts in land distribution and regional balance of power) and changes in the way the management is organised and functions. The system then goes through another phase of change and adjustment to the new context till a different but reasonably stable configuration is reached. This process is of course never ending. Nor can one confidently project its trajectory.

Clearly the study of institutions and their dynamics has to be informed by an inter-disciplinary and historical perspective. This does not mean a search for an integrated inter-disciplinary theory. That would be futile. What it calls for is an internalisation of inter-disciplinary perspective in the research. Researchers need to have a basic knowledge (not expertise) of key elements other than institutions that determine the scope, extent and modes of hamessing water and their impact on outcomes (productivity, distribution, sustainability). Analysis must take explicit account of the interactions among these elements *inter se* and with institutions. The methodology will have to be eclectic and comparative. After all, techniques of gathering relevant information, analysing various aspects and interpreting them are necessarily different. We need to get out of the mindset which presumes that the methodology of different disciplines are uniquely and inseparably tied to the substantive issues that motivate their inquiries.

12 Economics of Reviving Natural Resource Systems in Fragile Environments

V. Ratna Reddy

12.1 Background

The age-old water harvesting and storage systems such as tanks and ponds are becoming things of the past due to the absence of any maintenance by the state or civil society. Traditionally, local people through institutional arrangements managed these systems. These traditional systems of resource management have degenerated over time due to the state interventions and due to the socio, political and economic dynamics at the village level. As a result, irrigation under these water bodies too experienced a growing gap between capacities, often created much before Independence, and the net area irrigated. In fact, by 1999-2000, the net area irrigated by tanks was just 6.52 lakh hectares, almost half of the 13.71 lakh hectares in 1950-51. Loss of capacity of the tanks is not only the loss of tank irrigation but also loss of groundwater recharge in the tank dominant regions, which are relatively dry and drought-prone and dependent on wells as much (Reddy, 1998). The decline in groundwater tables in some of the regions has become alarming in the recent years resulting in the widespread phenomenon of desertification. Well irrigation recorded a phenomenal rise since 1950-51 i.e., moved from third position to first position in terms of area irrigated by a single source. This has, in turn, created enormous ecological and social problems.

Tanks replenish groundwater table and help maintain the ecological balance. The declining tank irrigation coupled with the expansion of groundwater development is a recipe for disaster, especially in the fragile resource regions like Rayalaseema in Andhra Pradesh. The literature on tank irrigation identifies numerous reasons such as socio-economic, institutional and physical for the decline of tank irrigation (von Oppen and Subba Rao, 1980a; Reddy, 1990; Shankari, 1991; Reddy *et al.*, 1993; Janakarajan, 1993; Reddy, 1995; Gireesh *et al.*, 1997). Historically, the decline in tank irrigation is linked with increasing population density (von Oppen and Subba Rao, 1980b). The relation between tank irrigation and population density is portrayed as an inverted 'U' shaped curve indicating that tank irrigation would increase along with population density till a certain point and then declines with any further increase in population density. This may be due to the reason that as the benefits from tanks decline due to increased population pressure (declining carrying capacity), communities lose interest in maintaining them and let them decay. Decline in tank irrigation is also linked to the development of well irrigation though it is difficult to determine the cause and effect. For, as the benefits from community based technology/ source (tank) decline, people shift toward individual based technology/ source (well). This, however, connotes a wrong notion of substitutability between tank and well irrigation while tanks complement groundwater development in reality. The decline therefore is a cumulative effect of policy and institutional neglect.

Traditionally tank systems were providing protective irrigation on a limited scale. They were maintained by village communities, which were nurtured by the benevolent local rulers. Institutional arrangements such as *Dasabandam* and *Kudimaramat* were in place to protect these systems from decay.[1] Under *Dasabandam*, tank lands were created and given to a person in the village (*poligars*) for the purpose of maintaining the tank. Under *Kudimaramat,* community voluntarily participates in maintaining the tank. However, the policy shift towards major and medium irrigation during the British period coupled with the change in the policy perception about irrigation development i.e., treating it as a productive (revenue generating source) rather than a protective source has resulted in the degeneration of these institutions. Besides, overall

1. There are numerous examples of institutional arrangements for managing traditional water harvesting systems across the country. For details, see Agarwal and Narain (1997).

environmental degradation resulting from population pressure, especially in the drought-prone regions, led to silting of tanks and shrinking of their capacities. This, in turn, has led to the shift towards the individual based well irrigation. The declining tank irrigation and expansion of well irrigation has stabilised towards the end of British period and continued till 1980s.

The second phase of this trend was triggered by the advent of energisation of groundwater lifting mechanisms. The new technologies in pumping systems during 1980s coupled with the benefits of green revolution have resulted in an unprecedented expansion of groundwater development. Further, the capital-intensive nature of these technologies, especially during the initial stages, has made the groundwater resources privy to large and medium size farmers. For, number of open wells has started drying up in the drought-prone regions. In fact, well failure (including bore wells) has become a common phenomenon in the recent years indicating an impending ecological disaster. All the while, unfortunately, the state has been a silent spectator and party to this ecological mismanagement. While there is every reason to protect and strengthen the traditional systems like tanks, there is need for examining their viability and sustainability in the long-run. Economic viability of the tanks, given their scale, is crucial for the communities to realise their importance in improving their livelihoods. Tanks being common pool resources (CPRs), collective action is a pre-requisite to manage them in a sustainable manner. This becomes important in the changing socio-economic and political scenario. This study is an attempt to explore the economic as well as ecological rationale in strengthening and promoting tank systems in drought-prone regions and their sustainability in the long run.

12.2 Objectives and Setting

This paper is an attempt to examine the impact of tank restoration on rural livelihoods in the context of fragile resource regions. Some of the important aspects in this regard include: viability of tank irrigation practices in the context of their size, distribution of water resources across farm size classes and the role of communities in the process. The specific objectives of the study include:

- to examine the impact of the tank restoration programme on rural livelihoods in terms of changes in crop pattern, crop intensity, yield rates, employment, equity, etc., and,
- to critically evaluate the viability, replicability and sustainability of the programme and suggest further interventions for sustainable water resource management in these regions.

Society for Promotion of Wasteland Development (SPWD) has been carrying out the tank restoration programme with the help of local non-governmental organisations (NGOs) in the Rayalaseema districts of Andhra Pradesh. So far 38 tanks have been restored and some of them are converted in to percolation tanks. Rayalaseema region has fairly good elevation, slope from south to north. About three fourths of the soils are red and the rest are black cotton soils. The climate is dry with a normal rainfall ranging between 520 mm to 720 mm, the lowest in the state. This region, due to its topography, has limited scope for canal irrigation. Proportion of area irrigated in this region is about 20 per cent of the net sown area. Canals contribute 30 per cent of the area under irrigation while tanks and wells contribute the rest. Crop failure and drought is a common phenomenon, especially in Anantapur district. Non-farm sector is also relatively backward and hence, seasonal migration is widespread in most parts of the region. Tanks occupy a prominent place in the region's agriculture. Tanks are life saving mechanisms in most parts of these perennially drought-prone regions.

Table 12.1

Tank Irrigation in the Rayalaseema Districts

District	*1955-56**		*1999-2000#*	
	Number	*Area (ha)*	*Number*	*Area (ha)*
1. Anantapur	2237	37254	2182	20997
2. Chittoor	6626	72024	8270	63187
3. Cuddapah	1187	29806	1582	13270
4. Kurnool	518	24472	426	4752
5. Prakasam	—	—	701	9765

Note: * net area irrigated by tanks; # command area of tanks. Presently, Prakasam district is not part of Rayalaseema, but parts of the present Praksam district originally from Rayalaseema.

Source: Reddy *et al.* (1993) for 1985-86 and GoAP (2000) for 1999-2000.

Tanks are the traditional rainwater harvesting and storage systems consisting of a major embankment across and (along) the line of the drainage with two side embankments running backwards up to the line of the drainage gradually losing their height. It resembles a rectangular (or semi-circle) catchment basin with only three embankments and the fourth side left open for runoff and drainage water to enter (Rao, 1999). Tanks provide direct as well as indirect irrigation benefits through recharge of groundwater and hence, safeguard the economic and ecological sustainability of these districts. However, the importance of tanks is on the decline, especially in terms of area irrigated (Table 12.1). More than 75 per cent of these tanks are small in size (less than 100 ha of area irrigated). In Chittoor, the proportion of small tanks is above 90 per cent (Reddy *et al.*, 1993). Though the importance of wells as a source of irrigation has gone up substantially, one should not undermine the importance of tanks due to the complementarity between these two in the fragile regions.

Given the importance of tanks in these districts and based on their past experience, the SPWD has initiated a network for 'promotion of people's management of small irrigation schemes in Rayalaseema' with 18 NGOs. The network envisages that people should be involved at all stages of the processes from identification of the problem, planning of the rehabilitation package and execution of the work. The involvement of the people is ensured through a mandatory contribution of 25 per cent of the total costs by all the beneficiaries, either in cash or labour. Tank management committees (TMCs) will be set up to facilitate people's participation. The salient features of the TMCs include:

a) TMC is representative of all sections of the village community though contributions are collected only from the farmers in the tank command area (TCA). Size of TMC will vary from 5 to 20 members depending on the size of the village.

b) A third of the members are women. To the extent possible, women will be recruited (by NGOs) as organisers for collecting information and interacting with village people about the tanks.

c) Elections are conducted every year and any person can be a member for a maximum of two terms.

d) Official minimum wages will be paid on the basis of volumetric rates. Contributions are also valued at these rates.

e) NGOs will open bank accounts jointly with TMCs and operate them jointly.

12.3 Approach

For the purpose of evaluating the impact of tank restoration on livelihoods we have selected three restored tanks in three districts of Anantapur, Chittoor and Prakasam. SPWD has initiated the tank restoration programme in the early 1990s itself. We have grouped the restored tanks into the ones restored prior to 1996-97 and post 1996-97. The reason for this bifurcation is to examine the sustainability of the restoration programme and its impact. For the purpose of our study, we have selected one tank from the tanks restored prior to 1996-97 and two tanks from post 1996-97. Besides, a matching sample of one village each for the restored tank village where there is no restoration programme, is selected to compare with and without situations. That is, a sample of three control villages are selected from the respective districts. Details of the sample villages are presented in Table 12.2.

Both qualitative and quantitative information were elicited. Group discussions, transect walks, discussions with local NGOs and SPWD were conducted to get an overview of the situation. This process has also helped us in selecting the sample tanks and finalising the structured questionnaire. Before and after as well as with and without approaches are used to evaluate the impact of the tank restoration. Both these methods are used as complementary, as either of these methods is fraught with problems such as memory lapse in the case of before and after and estimation problems in the case of with and without approach (see for an interesting analysis in this regard Ravallion, 2001). This is known as the 'double difference' method. Here, the problem of memory lapse in getting 'before' information is not serious as the time lag is seven years in the case of Anantapur and less than three years in the case of Chittoor and Prakasam districts.

Table 12.2

Details of the Sample Tanks

Tank/Village Name	*Mandal*	*District*	*Year of Restoration*	*Total No. of HH*	*No. of Command Area Farmers*	*Command Area (acres)*	*Tank Size (acres)*
I. Restored tanks							
1. Adepalli/Adepalli	Chilamathur	Anantapur		73			
(a) Adepalli cheruvu			1993-94		a) 35	a) 23.96	19
(b) Nallarathi kunta			1993-94		b) 14	b) 12.40	08
(c) Jammala Kunta			1993-94		c) 12	c) 09.18	07
2. Venglavaripalli	Emanapalli	Chittoor		54			
(a) Yerrappagari kunta			1997		a) 03	a) 0.52	—*
(b) Nagannagari kunta			1997		b) 07	b) 2.42	—
(c) Tatappagari kunta			1997		c) 13	c) 4.50	—
3. Akkapalli	Kammarolu	Prakasam		118			
(a) Kannela kunta			1997-98		a) 65	a) 62	a) 23
(b) Rekula Kunta			1997-98		b) 80	b) 146	b) 60
II. Unrestored tanks (control)							
1. Korla kunta	Chilamattur	Anantapur	—	195	68	70	65
2. Valasapalli	Madanapalle	Chittoor		150			
(a) Nagula cheruvu			—		a) 25	a) 80	a) 60
(b) Akkulavani kunta			—		b) 20	b) 15	b) 09
3. Pottipalli	Komarole	Prakasam	—	125	40	60	60

Note: *These are very small ponds (*kuntas*).

Source: Village schedule and also based on the discussions with the community.

Three structured questionnaires were prepared in order to elicit information at the NGO (implementing agency), village and household levels. A sample of 25 households was selected from the beneficiaries of each restored tank. These sample farmers were selected using the probability proportionate sample (PPS) to size of the land holding. Another sample of 25 households was selected from a nearby village, which matches with the restored tank village in terms of various socio-economic attributes, except for the restored tank, using the same method of sampling. This would facilitate with and without scenario analysis. At the same time, we have collected before and after information from the same households in order to cross-check the scenarios. An attempt is also made to get the scenario when the tank was functional in the control village, though the reliability of the information depends on the time lag since the tank became defunct. On the whole, we have collected detailed information from 150 households i.e., 75 from the 3 beneficiary villages and 75 from the 3 controlled villages. Field visits and data collection were organised during the months of March, April and May 2001. The sampling details are presented in Table 12.3. Our sample coverage ranges between 21 and 46 per cent of the total households in the programme villages and ranges between 13 and 20 per cent in the control villages. In terms of beneficiary farmers (programme villages), sample coverage is much higher. There are no landless households in the sample villages though majority of the households belong to small and marginal category in most of the villages.

Table 12.3

Details of the Sample Selection

Tank/Village Name	*Marginal*		*Small*		*Medium*		*Large*		*Total*	
	Act.	*Samp.*	*Act.*	*Samp.*	*Act.*	*Samp.*	*Act.*	*Samp.*	*Act.*	*Samp.*
Restored tanks										
1. Adepalli	28	09(38)	30	10(41)	13	04(18)	02	02(03)	73	25(34)
2. Venglavaripalli	25	12(46)	17	07(31)	08	04(15)	04	02(07)	54	25(46)
3. Akkapalli	21	05(18)	30	06(25)	67	14(57)	00	00(00)	118	25(21
Unrestored tanks (control)										
1. Korla kunta	28	06(40)	25	03(13)	72	08(37)	19	02(07)	195	25(13)
2. Valasapalli	79	12(19)	62	10(41)	50	08(33)	10	01(10)	150	25(17)
3. Pottipalli	23	05(18)	63	12(50)	24	05(19)	15	03(12)	125	25 (20)

Note: Act.= Actual number of households in the village; Samp.= Sample households selected.

Figures in brackets are respective percentage to the total households. There are no landless households in any of the villages.

12.4 Profile of the Sample Villages

As indicated earlier, we have two sets of sample villages. Three villages belong to the group where tanks have been restored during the recent years (programme villages) and in the other three villages no tank restoration work was taken up, though they have tanks (control villages). Important socio-economic features of these villages are presented in Table 12.4. There are wide variations between these villages regarding their socio-economic features. Village size in terms of number of households and average family size differ. In all the cases, control villages are bigger compared to programme villages. Average farm size of the household also differ between and within the groups of villages. The average farm size ranges from 3.25 acres to 4.48 acres. In two of the districts, average farm size is more in the case of control villages. On other hand, programme villages have larger SC/ST population. Control villages are better off economically in two districts indicating that households are better off even without tank restoration. Average household income is higher in the control villages in the case of two districts.

Table 12.4

Socio-economic Characteristics of the Sample Villages

Village	*No. of HH*	*% of Sample*	*Avg. Size of HH*	*Avg. Size of Land-holding (acres)*	*% of Households Belonging to (farm size)*				*% of HH belonging to SC/ST*	*Avg. Income (Rs.)*
					Large	*Medium*	*Small*	*Marginal*		
Programme villages										
1. Adepalle	73	34	5.26	3.79	3	18	41	38	56	8820
2. V.V. Palli	54	46	5.35	3.44	7	5	31	47	15	5495
3. Akkapalli	118	21	5.33	3.25	0	57	25	18	17	6837
Control villages										
1. Korla kunta	195	13	4.72	4.48	10	37	13	40	26	6650
2. Valasapalli	150	17	5.64	3.30	7	33	41	19	0	6039
3. Pottipalli	125	20	4.12	3.96	12	19	50	19	3	12926

Note: HH= Households.

Agriculture is the major source of income in all the villages. But, income from agriculture is much higher in the villages where tank restoration programme was taken up. Agriculture accounts for above 70 per cent of the household income in all the villages, programme as well as control. Dependence on agriculture is slightly higher in the programme villages. Livestock rearing is the second largest livelihood activity followed by labour activity in the sample villages. There seems to be substitutability between these two activities. That is, households having livestock are less dependent on labour. Large proportion of labour income is from farm labour within the village in the case of programme villages while some migration takes place in the case of control villages. Dependency on common pool resources (CPRs) and other sources is substantial in two villages, one each from programme and control villages. Presently, these two sets of villages do not differ much as far as their livelihood activities are concerned.

12.4.1 Status of Irrigation

All the sample villages have irrigation tanks of different sizes, more than one tank in some villages (Table 12.5). In the programme villages all the existing tanks are restored with repairs to bund, feeder channels, distributory channels, etc. Two tanks in Adepalli are converted in to percolation tanks. In Adepalli, the tanks were restored during the year 1993-94, while in the other two villages they were restored after 1996-1997. Tanks are the major source of irrigation in all the sample villages. The extent of area irrigated ranges from 24 to 33 per cent in the programme villages and 15 to 36 per cent in the control villages. These figures are based on the command area of the tanks and not necessarily the effective area under irrigation. Effective area under irrigation would be determined by the quality of tank and the local rainfall during a particular year. Size of the tanks in the programme villages is much smaller compared to the tanks in the control villages. This is mainly due to the reason that small tanks are given priority in the restoration programme. It appears that small tanks are characterised with substantial representation of SC/ST population. The first indicator of impact of tank restoration is reflected in the quality of tanks. The command area served by each acre of tank bed is higher in the programme villages compared to the control villages despite the fact that control villages have larger size tanks (Table 12.5). These ratios, however, reflect the extent of damage to the tank and the local rainfall, though rainfall is controlled to some extent by the selection of neighbouring villages. Further, size of the tank seems to influence the command area per acre of tank bed.

Well irrigation complements tank irrigation in most of the sample villages. Both open and bore wells exist in these villages (Table 12.6). However, all the open wells have dried up in all the villages in the recent years. This is a common feature in the entire region indicating the ecological stress. As a result, dependence on bore wells is on the rise. Functioning of the bore wells is critically linked with groundwater recharge in the region. Groundwater, like any other renewable resource, can be exploited indefinitely as long as extraction rate does not exceed replenishment rate. The mismatch between these two is clearly reflected in the sample villages, where even bore wells are drying up especially in the control villages. This is despite the fact that most of these wells are located in the tank command area. The situation is much better in the programme villages. For instance, in Pottipalli (control village) where 52 bore wells have come up in recent years, they serve only 10 acres of land since most of the wells have dried up and the extraction rates are quite low. The high density of wells coupled with the poor management of tank has further depleted the water tables in this village. On the other hand, the situation is not bad in Adepalli (programme village) where bore well density is quite high. For, in Adepalli three tanks are restored, two of them are converted in to percolation tanks. This clearly establishes the complementarity between tank and well irrigation and emphasises the rationale for tank restoration in this region. Apart from the ecological consequences, well failure imposes severe economic burden on the households.

Table 12.5

Details of Tanks in the Sample Village

Village Name	*No.*	*Tank Size (acres)*	*Command Area (acres)*	*No. of Tanks Restored*	*Command Area/Tank Size*	*NGO Responsible*
Programme villages						
1. Adepalli	3	34	45.54	3.00	1.34	Chaitanya
2. V.V. Palli	3	6.44	07.44	3.00	1.15	Krushi Samstha
3. Akkapalli	2	83	208	2.00	2.51	CAFORD
Control villages						
1. Korla kunta	1	83	70	0.0	0.84	—
2. Valasapalli	2	69	95	0.0	1.38	—
3. Pottipalli	1	60	60	0.0	1.0	—

Note: CAFORD= Collective Action For Rural Development.

12.4.2 Institutional Set-up in the Sample Villages

It seems that there was no historical background of institutional arrangements as such in the villages. That is, prior to tank restoration programmes there were no institutional arrangements in the villages, formal or informal, to manage CPRs. In the wake of tank restoration programmes, the implementing agencies (NGOs) have evolved the institutional arrangements for managing the tanks. Depending on the vision, commitment to the development and proper understanding of the dynamics of the village problems, different NGOs have adopted different approaches in the villages, as far as the management of tanks are concerned. Enabling the beneficiaries to manage the tank on their own after the NGOs have withdrawn or in the long run is totally absent. The attitude of dependency or looking for external help to carry out works on the tanks is still prevalent among the communities.

Table 12.6

Details of Wells in the Sample Villages

Village	*No. of Wells Present*		*Density of Wells (No./Cropped Area)*		*Density of Wells (No./Command Area)*		*Area Irrigated by Wells (Acres)*	
	Open	*Bore*	*Open*	*Bore*	*Open*	*Bore*	*Open*	*Bore**
Programme villages								
1. Adepalli	06	27	0.02	0.10	0.16	0.72	Dried	38
2. V.V. Palli	02	02	0.01	0.01	0.27	0.27	Dried	13
3. Akkapalli	08	13	0.02	0.03	0.04	0.06	Dried	70
Control villages								
1. Korla kunta	12	12	0.01	0.01	0.17	0.17	Dried	Dried
2. Valasapalli	05	15	0.01	0.03	0.05	0.16	Dried	45
3. Pottipalli	08	52	0.02	0.11	0.13	0.87	Dried	10

Note: * Bore wells are located in the command area in all the villages except V.V. Palli. Hence, they serve the command area with assured water supply rather than irrigating extra area.

However, some attempts have been made in Adepalli and V.V Palli in this direction. Tank management committees (TMC) have been formed by the farmers in both the villages with specific objectives (collecting money, organising the community, monitoring works, etc.), where NGOs play the role of facilitators. In Adepalli, Conflict Resolution Federation (CRF) is formed at the *mandal* level, represented by experienced members from different TMCs. The role of CRF is to resolve the conflicts that come up in the process of tank management. This establishes the relationship among the TMCs and their activities in particular and all the villages in general. One of the important role that TMCs in Adepalli play is that of restrictions, which they imposed on farmers, especially on cropping pattern in the command area to manage the water effectively. V.V Palli is a small village with quite less number of beneficiaries. Theoretically, the emergence of collective action is expected to be much easier in such cases (Olson, 1965). But, the TMC in V.V. Palli is not as effective as expected. For, the TMC mainly confined to maintenance of bank accounts and monitoring the works. Lack of efforts towards capacity building of the community is hindering effectiveness of the TMC. This reflects the commitment on the part of the PIA (NGO).

The situation in Akkapalli is different, as no attempt has been made from the NGO side to form any committee to involve farmers in the process of tank restoration, though the beneficiaries are quite enthusiastic about the tank management. The size of the two tanks is large. These tanks are poorly maintained, as one can observe the tanks with weeds and siltation. Some people are coming forward voluntarily to contribute towards desiltation and removing weeds from the tank bed. This is an interesting case where after restoration of one tank, farmers realised the benefits from the restored tank and slowly mobilised themselves to request the NGO to restore another tank. This is where the collective action (institution) evolved spontaneously, though serious efforts are needed from the implementing agency to make it effective and sustainable.

12.4.3 Process of Tank Restoration

The process of tank restoration initiated through consultations with the farmers by the NGOs. According to the implementing agencies (NGOs), initially farmers did not show interest at all. Later on when they came to realise the benefits of restored tanks, farmers themselves initiated the works enthusiastically and came out with new proposals to carry out similar works in other tanks or in the same tank. In Adepalli, the impact of the percolated tank spread even to other nearby villages, i.e., demonstration affect. According to the NGO (Chaitanya), by seeing the impact of the percolation tank, neighbouring villagers forcibly closed sluices of their tanks to make it a percolation tank.

The process of tank restoration started in Adepalli village in 1993-94 whereas it started in 1997 in V.V Palli and Akkapalli. In the case of Adepalli tanks, which were restored in 1993, the long run sustainability of the restored tanks can be examined. The TMC, which formed at the time of restoration, is working fairly well with the help of NGOs. Out of three tanks, two are percolation tanks and the other is irrigation tank. The nature of work carried out in Adepalli include closing down of sluices for percolation tank, desiltation, treatment of catchment area, feeding channels and strengthening of bunds, etc. The entire work took three months to complete. The total expenditure incurred on restoration is Rs. 1,84,000 of which Rs. 95,000 is contributed by SPWD and the remaining amount is contributed by the farmers in the command area (Table 12.7). The share of beneficiary contribution is quite high (48 per cent) by any standard. Beneficiaries have contributed in terms of labour and materials (cement, etc.) voluntarily. Besides, desiltation was carried out by the farmers at their own cost i.e., those interested in using the silt. The donor's contribution is used only towards tractor hiring charges at the rate of Rs. 500 per day for a total of 190 tractor days. Tractors are provided to transport the silt to the farmer's fields.

The TMC was formed with nine members, of which three are women. The TMC is headed by a chairperson and supported by a secretary/treasurer. These members were selected/elected unanimously. So far no elections were conducted to elect the members and the chairperson. They do not even follow the rotation system to change the members or the office bearers. The PIA has left the process of establishing the TMC entirely to the community. In order to manage the limited water in the tank in an equitable manner among all the farmers in the command area, the implementing agency (NGO) with the help of TMC imposed restrictions on water intensive cropping pattern and other agricultural practices. Farmer's response to such restrictions is rather encouraging. At the beginning of the year, the TMC organises a meeting of the command area farmers where the cropping pattern is determined based on the availability of water in the tank. In the event of water shortage, the TMC requests the farmers to reduce the area under paddy. Farmers growing paddy continuously are asked to rotate their cropping pattern. This arrangement seems to be working satisfactorily so far.

Table 12.7

Details of Costs of Tank Restoration

Village	*District*	*NGOs*	*Amount Spent by the NGO (Rs.)*	*Contribution from the Farmers (Rs.)*	*Total Costs (Rs.)*
Adepalli	Anantapur	Chaitanya	95000	89000(48)	184000
V.V. Palli	Chittoor	Krushi Samstha	47978	0	47978
Akkapalli	Prakasam	CAFORD	200000	34000(17)	234000

In V.V. Palli, the restoration work started in the year 1997 and took two months to complete the work. The work was carried out on three small ponds at the cost of Rs. 47,978. Almost all the expenditure is borne by SPWD and PIA (Krushi). Here farmer's contribution is in a different form i.e., working at a low wage rate. Those farmers having land in the command area were paid Rs. 20 per day and those who do not have land in the command area were paid Rs. 25 per day towards wage. The difference in wage rate (Rs. 5) is the contribution of the farmers. Besides, beneficiary farmers used to put extra hours (1-2) of work every day. Moreover, all the households, beneficiary and non-beneficiary, worked at less than market wage rate indicating the community support for the activity. The main works carried out are desilting (78 per cent of the expenditure), stone revetment (10 per cent), slice (10 per cent) and green cover (2 per cent). Here also, TMC was formed with eight members and two of the members were women. The chairperson of the TMC is a woman.

In Akkapalli, the restoration work started in 1997 on two tanks and it took nearly seven months to complete. These tanks are fairly big compared to the ones in Adepalli and V.V. Palli. The nature of work includes strengthening bunds, sluice repairing, etc., on two tanks. Here, the beneficiaries have contributed money (a minimum of Rs. 80 per acre) towards the restoration work. The villagers also took the responsibility to clear the weeds in the tank. But due to unexpected rains at the time of restoration, they could not complete the work. However, the cleaning of tank bed is still pending due to various reasons. The tanks are quite big in size and degraded due to long negligence. As a result, it required more investment and time to bring them back to the functional form. It was also found that before the restoration the tanks were almost defunct. In fact, some of the households had shifted their occupation to non-agricultural activities due to the total failure of cultivation. Farmers are visibly happy about the condition of the tanks. They are very enthusiastic about protecting the tank, as the tank brought back their normal life. By the time of our field visits (March-April 2001), no TMC was formed though farmers were keen to form one. The farmers themselves with contributions are carrying out maintenance work. This village seems to be a highly potential location for collective action.

The cost of tank restoration depends on the size of tank and the nature of works carried out. Most of the restoration works are common to all. The major difference is in terms of contributions from the beneficiaries. Beneficiary contribution is not uniform, as it ranges from a negligible amount in V.V. Palli (in monetary terms) to 48 per cent in Adepalli. While V.V. Palli may be an exception due to its smallness (and also nature of people's involvement), the difference between Adepalli and Akkapalli reflects the involvement of the people as well as the role and commitment of the implementing agency.

12.5 Impact of Tank Restoration: Economic and Ecological

Impact is measured in terms of changes in various indicators due to the tank restoration programme. The measurement of impact is based on the information collected from 25 sample households from each village. Impact is measured across different size classes of holding in order to examine the distributional aspects of the impact. Impact indicators are grouped under economic, social and ecological categories. Economic impact is measured in terms of changes in area under irrigation, productivity (yield) of land, value of land, livestock holding and employment. Social impact is measured in terms of changes in migration, health, education and differences in gender equity. Ecological impact is measured in terms of changes in CPRs, drinking water, fodder and fuel wood. In what follows is the assessment of the impact of tank restoration on these factors separately.

Changes in area under irrigation are the prime indicator of any impact on rural livelihoods, especially where the major livelihood activity is farming. It is observed that proportion of area under irrigation has increased, though marginally, among all the households in the programme villages after the restoration of the tanks (Table 12.8). The changes range from 5 to 10 per cent in the three programme villages.[2] The increase is more in the case of small and marginal farmers in two of the villages while medium farmers gained more in Adepalli. However, area under irrigation in absolute terms is the lowest for marginal farmers in all the villages though in proportionate terms it is in favour of small and marginal farmers. Distribution of area under irrigation is more favourable to small and marginal farmers but this is not due to the programme. On the other hand, area under irrigation is stagnant in the control villages. Apart from the quantitative changes in the area, qualitative changes in the availability of irrigation in terms of throughout the season regular and assured supplies are equally, if not more, important in improving the economic conditions of the farmers. This aspect is reflected in the changes in land productivity, which is measured in quintals of food grains per acre. Food grains include mainly paddy, maize, *ragi*, *jowar*, etc.

In all the programme villages, land productivity has gone up while it remained same in the control villages. Productivity gains range from 26 per cent in V.V. Palli to 44 per cent in Adepalli, which is the first village of tank restoration. Productivity gains are more in the case of small and marginal farmers, which may be explained with the help of production conditions in agriculture. That is, small and marginal farmers are more efficient in terms of land productivity due to the availability of family labour. Along with land productivity, land value also has gone up in all the programme villages as well as in two of the control villages. The increase in land value is much higher in the programme villages compared to the control villages. While land values have gone up by 28 to 37 per cent in the programme villages, they have gone up by 3 to 12 per cent in the control villages (Table 12.8). Interestingly, the increase in land prices across size classes does not commensurate with the increase in land productivity. This indicates that small and marginal farmers are at a disadvantageous position in the land market perhaps due to the small size of their holdings.

2. The changes are in terms of effective irrigation, as the command area remains same before and after the restoration.

Table 12.8

Impact of Tank Restoration on Area and Productivity in the Sample Households

Village/ Size-class	*% Area Irrigated*	*Percentage Change in*		
		Area Irrigated (per household)	*Yield/Acre (quintals)*	*Value Per Acre (Rs.)*
Programme villages				
1. Adepalli	10.55	05.26	44.39	37.30
Large	03.94	02.50	36.28	22.95
Medium	06.83	38.10	44.67	25.00
Small	16.93	03.78	41.49	78.57
Marginal	12.02	05.56	61.00	23.15
2. V.V. Palli	10.75	08.82	26.57	33.33
Large	04.76	00.00	25.00	33.33
Medium	00.74	00.00	28.33	33.33
Small	19.60	00.00	26.75	33.33
Marginal	14.73	216.67	22.93	33.33
3. Akkapalli	29.53	10.34	36.25	28.67
Large	00	00	00	00
Medium	39.06	01.13	27.99	29.35
Small	31.54	11.40	33.30	28.97
Marginal	28.87	21.43	48.98	27.84
Control villages				
1. Korla kunta	26.33	00	00	00
Large	11.11	00	00	00
Medium	26.51	-16.67	00	00
Small	12.15	00	00	00
Marginal	16.57	00	00	00
2. Valasapalli	45.15	00	00	11.50
Large	45.45	00	00	00
Medium	53.24	00	00	12.00
Small	19.10	00	00	20.59
Marginal	25.00	00	00	15.79
3. Pottipalli	35.35	00	00	02.77
Large	29.04	00	00	16.66
Medium	22.81	00	00	00
Small	28.89	00	00	-8.33
Marginal	36.71	00	00	00

Income and Consumption: Assessing the impact in terms of annual income and consumption is a tricky business, as they are expected to be plagued with strategic bias of the respondents. It is often observed that respondents strategically under report their income and over report their expenditure. In the case of consumption, figures are often not accurate due to measurement problems as food items are bought in small quantities in regular intervals. However, the present analysis is relative rather than absolute and hence, the biases may not be a serious problem. Both income and consumption levels have gone up in all the sample villages and even across all, except one, size classes (Table 12.9). Between the programme and control villages, two important deviations can be noted. Firstly, the increases in income and consumption are higher in the programme villages. Secondly, income increases are higher than the increases in consumption expenditure in the programme villages while the reverse is true in the case of control villages. This indicates that net gains are positive in the programme villages.

Average household income per year has gone up by more than 35 per cent in the programme villages while the increase is just 1 per cent in two of the control villages and 14 per cent in one village. Except in Prakasam district the average income is higher in the programme villages. Similarly, average consumption per household is also higher in the control villages. In the programme villages, the household consumption has increased between 26 and 39 per cent in the programme villages while the increase ranged between 21 and 23 per cent in the control villages (Table 12.9). In most of the cases, small and marginal farmers have recorded higher growth in household income in both control and programme villages. On the other hand, in the case of consumption the changes are either neutral or biased in favour of large farmers. Therefore, income gains are not converted into consumption benefits for small and marginal farmers, which may be due to low profitability of farming among these sections (Reddy, 1993).

Table 12.9

Change of Average Annual Income and Consumption of Sample Households

Village Name/Size-class	*Average Income (Rs./year/household)*			*Average Consumption (Rs./year/hh)*		
	Before	*After*	*% Change*	*Before*	*After*	*% Change*
Programme villages						
1. Adepalli	18230	26872	47	3839	5339	39
Large	35833	55167	54	4768	7224	52
Medium	13750	18250	33	4694	6265	33
Small	8586	14571	70	2952	4015	36
Marginal	8750	8250	-06	2943	3850	31
2. V.V. Palli	11895	16329	37	3928	5261	34
Large	14000	19000	36	6104	7967	31
Medium	10100	13332	32	3915	5623	44
Small	8480	11232	32	3331	4369	31
Marginal	6086	9021	48	2363	3085	31
3. Akkapalli	9452	13999	48	3507	4420	26
Large	0	0	00	0	0	00
Medium	14657	21946	50	4388	5488	25
Small	7000	10000	43	2902	3711	28
Marginal	6700	10050	50	1804	2349	30
Control villages						
1. Korla kunta	17465	17810	02	4227	5111	21
Large	23000	23000	00	5176	6366	23
Medium	17625	17850	01	4221	4874	15
Small	18400	18650	01	4566	5558	22
Marginal	10833	11741	08	2945	3645	24
2. Valasapalli	14597	16609	14	4378	5374	23
Large	17000	17000	00	4676	5712	22
Medium	16714	19786	18	3369	4257	26
Small	12241	14942	22	5575	6784	22
Marginal	10643	12250	15	3891	4743	22
3. Pottipalli	19454	19704	01	3121	3785	21
Large	26667	26667	00	4362	5354	26
Medium	17050	18050	06	3446	4064	18
Small	21950	21950	00	2951	3436	16
Marginal	12150	12150	00	1825	2286	25

12.5.1 Ecological Impact

Economic impact is critically linked with ecological impact in the agrarian economies. Productivity of land and livestock are dependent on the quality of natural resources such as land, water, common grazing lands, etc. Here we examine the linkages between the tank restoration and natural resources. Our focus is mainly on the availability of fodder, fuel, drinking water and groundwater.

Fodder and Fuel Wood: Fodder availability is seen in terms of dependence of cattle on different sources of feed. The main sources of feed are stall-feeding, common grazing lands (CPRs) and own fields (feeding on crop residue and in fodder fields). Dependence on market for fodder (purchase) is also there but on a very limited scale. Stall-feeding is the single most important source followed by grazing in own lands and CPRs. Availability and quality of CPRs determine the relative shares of CPRs and own lands in the respective villages. Over a period of 3 to 7 years, the importance of stall-feeding has declined though it continues to be the most important source in all the villages (Table 12.10). However, the decline is more prominent in the programme villages. In fact, in one of the control villages (Pottipalli) the incidence of stall-feeding has gone up. In most of the villages, the decline in stall-feeding is compensated by both grazing on own fields and CPRs. Across the size classes, the dependence on CPRs is more in the case of small and marginal farmers. On the whole, the impact of tank restoration on the availability of fodder is only indicative at the best.

Household's fuel wood needs are met by collections from CPRs and their own sources. Fuel is also purchased in the market in a limited scale. Here also the impact on fuel wood is seen in terms of household's dependence on different sources. Since purchase of fuel wood by the households is minimal, we focus on own and CPR sources. Time spent by the households in collecting the fuel wood reflects the improvement in the fuel wood availability, especially in the CPRs near the village. Own sources like crop residues and wood from own trees is the single most important source of fuel wood in all the villages. In terms of quantity of fuel wood used, small and marginal farmers use more when compared to large farmers because large farmers have alternative sources

Table 12.10

Changes in the Availability of Fodder

Size-class/ Village	Before (Cattle using Various Sources in % of Days)			After (Cattle using Various Sources in % of Days)			Percentage Change		
	Stall fed	CPR	Own field	Stall fed	CPR	Own field	Stall fed	CPR	Own field
Programme villages									
1. Adepalli	77.6	11.9	10.4	46.9	28.9	24.2	-39.5	141.5	132.1
Large	75.3	11.6	13.0	69.8	14.0	16.3	-7.4	20.0	25.0
Medium	67.3	16.7	16.0	42.3	30.8	26.9	-37.1	84.6	68.0
Small	84.1	10.2	5.7	41.9	35.5	22.7	-50.2	248.0	295.5
Marginal	76.1	10.6	13.3	0.0	14.9	58.1	-100.0	294.9	337.4
2. V.V. Palli	76.2	9.1	14.6	66.9	11.5	21.6	-12.3	26.0	47.7
Large	81.0	9.5	9.5	65.1	14.0	20.9	-19.6	46.5	119.8
Medium	100.0	0.0	0.0	89.3	0.0	10.7	-10.7	0.0	0.0
Small	68.8	18.8	12.5	68.3	19.0	12.7	-0.7	1.6	1.6
Marginal	75.0	0.0	25.0	73.0	0.0	27.0	-2.6	0.0	7.9
3. Akkapalli	68.4	13.4	18.1	61.7	16.1	22.2	-9.8	19.7	22.5
Large	0.0	0.00	0.0	0.0	0.0	0.0	0.0	0.0	0.0
Medium	75.0	9.8	15.2	64.6	16.3	19.1	-13.9	66.3	25.6
Small	48.2	23.9	27.9	47.6	24.9	27.4	-1.2	4.3	-1.6
Marginal	50.0	25.0	25.0	45.9	24.6	29.5	-8.2	-1.6	18.0
Control villages									
1. Korla kunta	78.1	9.3	12.6	46.9	23.0	30.1	-40.0	146.9	138.9
Large	75.3	12.4	12.4	75.3	12.4	12.4	0.0	0.0	0.0
Medium	64.7	15.9	15.9	62.6	16.5	20.9	-3.2	3.8	7.6
Small	90.6	4.0	4.0	74.4	11.1	14.4	-17.8	180.4	164.3
Marginal	50.0	17.6	17.6	48.3	20.7	31.0	-3.4	17.2	-4.1
2. Valasapalli	53.6	23.2	23.2	50.8	24.4	24.8	-5.3	5.4	6.8
Large	0.0	0.0	0.0	0.0	0.0	0.0	0.0	0.0	0.0
Medium	77.5	11.2	11.2	77.0	11.2	11.9	-0.7	-0.7	5.9
Small	37.9	31.0	31.0	29.4	35.3	35.3	-22.5	13.7	13.7
Marginal	33.3	33.3	33.3	33.3	33.3	33.3	0.0	0.0	0.0
3. Pottipalli	62.3	12.3	25.3	70.4	11.2	18.4	12.9	-9.2	-27.2
Large	63.8	8.1	28.2	58.5	9.2	32.3	-8.3	14.5	14.5
Medium	53.8	15.4	30.8	53.8	15.4	30.8	0.0	0.0	0.0
Small	90.5	4.0	5.5	74.4	11.1	14.6	-17.8	178.1	162.2
Marginal	68.4	10.5	21.1	68.4	10.5	21.1	0.0	0.0	0.0

of fuel such as coal, dung cakes, kerosene, gas, etc. The major source of fuel wood is CPRs in all the villages (Table 12.11). The dependency on CPRs is more in the case of small and marginal farmers. Similarly, small and marginal farmers spend substantially higher time in fetching fuel wood when compared to large farmers. Over the period, there is a marginal decline in the dependence on CPRs in all the villages irrespective of the status of the tank. However, the impact of tank restoration can be seen in terms of time spent in fetching fuel wood. Time spent in fetching fuel wood has declined in two of the programme villages while it has increased in all the controlled villages. This indicates the improvement in the availability in the vicinity as well as in good quantity and quality. This could be termed as ecological impact because the increased fuel wood demand is met either by CPRs or own lands, which reduces drudgery in the programme villages while it is met by an increase in the drudgery in the control villages. For, purchase of fuel wood is on a very limited scale in the before and after situations in the programme as well as control villages.

Groundwater: Impact on groundwater is the major positive externality of tank restoration. Tank restoration is expected to have a positive impact on groundwater availability. The impact would be more conspicuous in the case of percolation tanks. Here we examined the impact in terms of number of wells, open as well as bore, depth of the wells. Besides, improvement in groundwater situation will ease the drinking water problems. Hand pumps are the main source of drinking water in all the villages. Since none of the sample villages face any shortage of drinking water, it is difficult to assess the impact even if there is improvement in groundwater availability in the programme villages. On the other hand, other indicators reveal a clear change in groundwater situation in the sample villages.

Table 12.11

Changes in the Availability of Fuel Wood

Size-class/ Village	Before (% Quantity from)			After (% of Quantity from)			Percentage Change		
	CPR	Own	Time Spent for Collection (days per year)	CPR	Own	Time Spent for Collection (days per year)	CPR	Own	Time Spent for Collection
Programme villages									
1. Adepalli	81.25	18.75	21	76.47	23.53	20	-5-88	25.490.0	-4.76
Large	0	100	4	0	100	4	0.0	0	0
Medium	75	25	14	75	25	12	0.0	0.00	-14.29
Small	80.95	9.52	35	80.95	9.52	35	0.0	0.00	0
Marginal	84.21	15.79	33	84.21	15.79	30	0.0	0.00	-9.09
2. V.V. Palli	84.62	15.38	13	86.67	13.33	13	2.42	-13.33	0
Large	100	0	4	100	0	4	0.00	0.00	0
Medium	50	25	8	77.78	22.22	8	55.6	-11.11	0
Small	93.33	6.67	16	93.75	6.25	15	0.5	-6.25	-6.25
Marginal	91.67	8.33	26	92.59	7.41	25	1.01	-11.11	-3.85
3. Akkapalli	45.67	54.55	18	38.46	61.54	19	-15.4	12.82	5.56
Large	0	0	0	0	0	0	0.00	0.00	0
Medium	33.33	58.33	30	33.33	59.26	32	0.00	1.59	6.67
Small	50	50	15	40	60	17	-20.0	20.00	13.33
Marginal	66.67	33.33	8	66.67	33.33	8	0.00	0.00	0
Control villages									
1. Korla kunta	64.71	35.29	18	61.11	38.89	22	-5.56	10.19	22.22
Large	0	100	8	0	100	8	0.0	0.00	0
Medium	40	60	24	36.36	63.64	30	-9.09	6.06	25
Small	33.33	50	10	28.57	87.14	14	-14.3	14.29	40
Marginal	92.31	7.69	30	88.89	11.11	35	-3.7	44.44	16.67
2. Valasapalli	57.14	42.96	27	56.52	43.48	30	-1.09	1.45	11.11
Large	0	100	6	0	100	8	0.00	0.00	33.33
Medium	40	60	30	42.86	57.14	35	7.14	-4.76	16.67
Small	44	56	32	42.31	57.69	35	-3.85	3.02	9.38
Marginal	83.33	11.11	40	78.95	15.79	44	-5.26	42.11	10
3. Pottipalli	65	35	37	61.92	38.10	39	-4.76	8.84	5.41
Large	0	83.33	20	0	85.79	24	0.00	2.86	20
Medium	47.62	28.57	35	45.45	31.82	38	-4.55	11.36	8.57
Small	46.14	38.46	45	44.44	37.01	46	-3.70	-3.70	2.22
Marginal	78.95	10.53	48	83.33	16.67	48	5.56	58.33	0

Table 12.12

Changes in the Status of Wells in the Sample Households

Size-class/Village	No. of Wells		Depth of Wells (ft)		% Change	
	Before	After	Before	After	Number	Depth
Restored villages						
1. Adepalli	08	19	240	178	138	-25.80
Large	02	03	220	170	50	-22.72
Medium	02	03	240	165	50	-31.25
Small	01	05	260	185	400	-28.85
Marginal	03	08	250	190	167	-24.00
2. V.V. Palli	0	01	0	0	@	0
Large	0	0	0	0	0	0
Medium	0	0	0	0	0	0
Small	0	01 (dug)	0	30	@	0
Marginal	0	01	0	0	0	0
3. Akkapalli	02	0	260	165	400	-36.54
Large	0	0	0	0	0	0
Medium	02	08	260	165	300	-36.54
Small	0	02	0	170	@	0
Marginal	0	0	0	0	0	0
Control villages						
1. Korla kunta	05	07	210(40)	253	40	20.48
Large	02	04	210	270	100	28.57
Medium	02 (dug)	01+00 (dried up)	40	260	-50	0
Small	0	01	0	250	@	0
Marginal	01 (dug)	01+00 (dried up)	35	230	0	0
2. Valasapalli	09	10	220(42)	255	11	15.91
Large	3 (dug)	00 (dried up)	40	0	@	0
Medium	02	08	220	260	300	18.18
Small	02 (dug)	02+0 (dried up)	40	250	0	0
Marginal	02 (dug)	00 (dried up)	45	0	@	0
3. Pottipalli	0	11	0	249	@	0
Large	0	03	0	265	@	0
Medium	0	02	0	220	@	0
Small	0	05	0	260	@	0
Marginal	0	01	0	250	@	0

Note: Number of wells includes bore wells and dug (open) wells. Dug wells are indicated in the brackets. Changes are calculated on the basis of functioning wells.

@ indicates changes from zero to positive and vice-versa.

Number of irrigation wells has gone up in all the sample villages. Number of bore wells is increasing over time as the dug wells are getting dried up. All the dug wells of the sample households in the control villages have dried up. This is true at village level also. Despite the drying of dug wells, number of wells have increased in all the villages though the increase is much higher in the programme villages (Table 12.12). More importantly, groundwater depth[3] has declined substantially (above 20 per cent) in the programme villages while it has increased in the control villages. Groundwater levels are high in the control villages prior to the restoration of the tank in the programme villages. After the restoration, groundwater levels have risen in the programme villages. Also, after the restoration, the difference in the groundwater depth has become substantial between programme and control villages. It may be noted that the improvement in groundwater situation is prominent in Adepalli (Anantapur district) village. This could be due to two reasons, one is that in Adepalli tank restoration was carried out during 1993-94 itself and hence, there was sufficient time for recharge and second is that two of the tanks in Adepalli are converted in to percolation tanks, which is more effective in terms of groundwater recharge. In fact, improved groundwater availability in Adepalli had a demonstration affect on the neighbouring villages where villagers came forward to restore their tanks. Another important observation is that there is a structural change in the ownership of wells in the recent years. It may be noted that wells, especially bore wells, are no longer privy to large farmers, as more and more small and marginal farmers seem to be investing in bore wells (Table 12.12). This may be due to the decline in the cost of bore wells during the recent years. Perpetuation of this trend results in equitable distribution of water resources in these fragile regions. However, this is critically linked with the sustainability of groundwater recharge and the quality of technology that is available at cheap prices. For, there are reports (news papers) that frequent well failure in these regions is attributed to poor quality of the equipment. Average capital cost of a bore well range from Rs. 33000 to Rs. 83000 across the villages and these costs tend to be lower in the case of small and marginal farmers.

3. Depth of the bore wells was assessed based on the information provided by the sample household on the depth at which groundwater is available before and after the restoration of the tank.

Thus, the positive impact of the programme is reflected in all the economic indicators such as area irrigated, land values, land productivity, employment and livestock economy. The improvement in all these indicators in the case of before and after the programme scenarios and with and without the programme scenarios unequivocally supports the rationale for tank restoration in the drought-prone regions. And the impact is more in the case of small and marginal farmers when compared to large farmers. Economic impact is closely linked with ecological impact, which is evident from the improved groundwater situation in the programme villages. In fact, availability of groundwater has made growing of *rabi* crops possible and enhanced the yield rates. Further, the ecological impact is reflected in the livestock economy of the programme villages. Economic and ecological impact of the programme is emphatic in the case of the tanks restored prior to 1995-1996. This reflects the long run nature of the ecological benefits and sustainability of the programme. Economic as well as ecological indicators support the viability of the programme, as the short run viability of the programme is often determined by the economic returns from the programme to the community. This in no way belittles the economic value of the ecological benefits, which are expected to be much higher than the economic benefits. Though measuring the ecological benefits is beyond the scope of the study, ecological impact in value terms, partially and indirectly, is covered in the economic impact on crop production and livestock sector. The economic impact is an indicator of the success of the programme but it does not say much about the economic viability of the programme. Comparing the actual costs and benefits would establish the economic viability of the programme. Therefore, the economic analysis is taken up in the next section.

12.6 Economics of Tank Restoration

In this section we examine the economic viability of the tank restoration programme in the drought-prone regions. For this purpose, economic returns due to restoration of tank are compared with the actual costs of restoration. The purpose is to have an idea regarding economic returns, which are immediate and conspicuous. For, farmer's interest and commitment to tank restoration and management will directly depend on these returns. In the absence of tangible and immediate economic benefits, farmer's involvement in the programme will be temporary because of the financial support from outside. Their contribution, cash or kind, to the programme may depend on the expected benefits from the programme and on the motivation from the local NGOs. This may not sustain in the long run without any real economic gains to the households.

Measurement of benefits from any programme or project is a complex issue, especially when environmental and social benefits are involved. It is difficult to value some of the benefits such as social benefits and ecological benefits. Therefore, we have restrained ourselves to pure economic benefits to the households, which are measured in terms of increased area under irrigated crops and productivity of land. Moreover, farmers are more concerned about these benefits rather than ecological and social benefits. However, economic benefits also reflect some of the ecological benefits such as groundwater improvement. Besides, households have also benefited from increased labour demand. Employment benefit may not be entirely a net benefit, as some of the households were getting employment outside the village prior to the restoration. Hence, increased labour demand from within the village partially reflects the net benefit and partially reflects the social impact due to reduced migration. Here we restrict our analysis to the command area farmers only though groundwater recharge and employment benefits could spread beyond the command area. And, only the incremental benefits from crop production are considered for the economic analysis of tank restoration. These benefits will include the benefits from increased area under irrigation and cropping intensity. For, as the area under irrigation increases per acre, incremental returns from crop production will also increase.

12.6.1 Measurement of Costs and Returns

The costs of tank restoration are one time costs. These costs are mainly incurred on desilting, clearing the tank bed weeds, strengthening the tank bunds, repairs to sluices, repairs to feeder and distributory channels and treatment of catchment area. These costs include contribution from the donors (SPWD) as well as contribution from the farmers. Actual costs of tank restoration are obtained from the respective implementing agencies (NGOs). It is assumed that the works carried out through this one time investment would last for 10 years (scenario-I). Alternatively, an assumption of 15 years of life (scenario-II) is also used for the purpose of simulation of costs and returns. Based on these two assumptions, the investment on tank restoration is amortised to arrive at the annualised fixed cost by using the formula (Gireesh *et al.*, 1997):

$$AC = I\,[1 + i)^t \times i] \,/\, [(1 + i)^t - 1]$$

Where,

AC = amortised cost of tank restoration per year;

I = one time investment or expenditure on tank restoration;

i = interest rate at 10 per cent;

t = life of the works (10 or 15 years).

The incremental benefits accruing to the command area farmers/ households are assessed in terms of increased agricultural productivity and area under irrigated crops. These aspects were discussed in detail in the previous chapter. The incremental returns from agriculture are estimated on the basis of before and after scenarios. Here also the returns are assumed to continue as long as the life of the assets i.e., 10 or 15 years. Further, these returns and costs are assumed to be constant over the period of 10 or 15 years. Costs and returns, before and after the restoration, data are obtained directly from the sample households. The estimated annual amortised costs for the three tanks are presented in Table 12.13. These costs include contribution from the farmers also.

Table 12.13

Amortised Costs of Tank Restoration Per Year

Village/ Tank	*NGOs*	*Total Costs (Rs.)*	*Amortised Cost Per Year (Rs.) (Life = 10 years)*	*Amortised Cost Per Year (Rs.) (Life= 15 years)*
Adepalli	Chaitanya	184000	29945	24186
V.V. Palli	Krushi Samstha	47978	7808	6306
Akkapalli	CAFORD	234000	38082	30758

The main crops grown in the command area of tanks are paddy and irrigated dry crops like *ragi*, *jowar* and maize. Groundnut crop is grown in Adepalli of Anantapur district. Costs, returns and the incremental income from these crops are presented in Table 12.14. In Adepalli, the cropping pattern has shifted in favour of groundnut over the period of five years after the restoration of tank, whereas it remained same in the other two villages. More importantly, *rabi* crops are being grown in Adepalli and V.V. Palli after the restoration of the tanks. As a result, the incremental returns from crops are quite high in these two villages. Though desilting was done in most of the tanks silt was not sold to farmers. Farmers themselves at their own cost carried out desilting. On the other hand, in Adepalli tractors were provided by the PIA to transport the silt to the farmer's fields. These costs are included in the total cost. But, the labour charges incurred by the farmer are not included in the costs. These costs could be equated with the value of silt. The incremental income from crop production is positive for all the tanks and it is proportional to the tank command area.

Similarly, expenditure on tank restoration is proportional to the tank size. But the per unit expenditure is inversely proportional to tank size and command area (Table 12.15). We have also included the operation and maintenance costs though there is no system of collecting water charges for operation and maintenance (O&M) in any of these tanks. Maintenance of the tank is carried out on ad hoc basis. In some cases whenever there is need for repairs, all the command area farmers contribute towards the work, cash or kind. In other words, individual farmers who benefit more from the tank (number of bore wells, area irrigated, etc.) contribute towards repairs (Adepalli). Nevertheless, since maintenance costs are involved we have assumed that the requirement for O&M would be Rs. 50 per acre of command area per year.

Net returns turned out to be positive in all the three tanks for both the scenarios (Table 12.15). Interestingly, net returns are not proportional to size of the tank. This indicates that the high per unit costs in the case of small tanks is more than upset by the higher incremental returns from crops, which is facilitated by double cropping. This also reflects the quality of service provided in the case of better-managed tanks. On per acre basis the net returns are higher in Adepalli, which may be due to the high value-cropping pattern (groundnut). At the same time, the high returns in Adepalli even after five years of tank restoration reflect the sustainability of the programme. This can be interpreted in two ways: i) programme is sustainable due to the high returns to agriculture, and ii) sustainability is due to the involvement of the community and the PIA even after the completion of the works, which has ensured high returns. But these two aspects are very much inter-linked. For, in the absence of sustained benefits it is difficult to ensure community involvement. This is supported by the fact that there was no further expenditure on the works by the PIA. In fact, PIA is interested in further strengthening the tanks and looking for support from SPWD.

Table 12.14

Returns and Costs of Crops in the Tank Command Area

Particulars	*Before (only kharif)*			*After (kharif + rabi)*			*Incremental*
	Paddy	*Irri/Dry*	*G. Nut*	*Paddy*	*Irri/Dry*	*G. Nut*	*Income (Rs.)*
1. Adepalli							
Area (acres)	23.0	19.0	04.0	20	19	40.0	—
Production (qtls)	230	152	16	280	228	280	—
Rate (Rs./qtl)	500	500	1200	500	500	1200	—
Gross income (Rs.)	115000	76000	19200	140000	114000	33600	379800
Cost of production (Rs.)	58650	24320	7200	72000	36000	0	89830
Net income (Rs.)	56350	51680	12000	68000	78000	72000	289970
2. V.V. Palli						264000	
Area (acres)	7.47	—	—	14.94	—	0	—
Production (qtls)	60	—	—	180	—	—	—
Rate (Rs./qtl)	500	—	—	500	—	—	—
Gross income (Rs.)	30000	—	—	90000	—	—	60000
Cost of production (Rs.)	14044	—	—	41832	—	—	27788
Net income (Rs.)	15956	—	—	48168	—	—	32212
3. Akkapalli							
Area (acres)	139	69	—	139	69	—	—
Production (qtls)	1390	552	—	2085	828	—	—
Rate (Rs./qtl)	500	500	—	500	500	—	—
Gross income (Rs.)	695000	276000	—	1042500	414000	—	485500
Cost of production (Rs.)	326650	88320	—	486500	131100	—	202630
Net income (Rs.)	368350	187680	—	556000	282900	—	282870

Table 12.15

Costs and Benefits of Tank Restoration

Particulars	*Adepalli*		*V.V. Palli*		*Akkapalli*	
	S-I	*S-II*	*S-I*	*S-II*	*S-I*	*S-II*
1. Total expenditure on tank restoration (Rs.)	184000	184000	47987	47987	234000	234000
2. Investment per acre of command area (Rs.)	4000	4000	6424	6424	1125	1125
3. Investment per acre of tank size (Rs.)	5412	5412	7451	7451	2819	2819
4. Life of restoration (years)	10	15	10	15	10	15
5. Amortised cost per year (Rs.)	29945	24186	7808	6306	38082	30758
6. Annual O&M costs @ Rs. 50 per acre	2300	2300	374	374	10400	10400
7. Incremental net return from crops (Rs./year)	289970	289970	32212	32212	282870	282870
8. Total costs (4+5)	32245	26486	8182	6680	48482	41158
9. Net return/tank (Rs./year)	257725	263484	24030	25532	234388	241712
10. Net return per acre of command area (Rs./year)	5603	5728	3004	3192	1127	1162

Note: S–I = Scenario I where expected life of restoration is 10 years; S-II= Scenario II where expected life of restoration is 15 years.

The economic viability of tank restoration is also reflected in the cash flow measures, which are often used to take investment decisions (Table 12.16). Benefit-cost ratios are quite high in both the scenarios for all the three tanks. Net present value of the benefits is positive for all the three tanks. And internal rate of return is quite high for all the tanks. Usually investment decisions would be made favourably when benefit-cost ratios are above one or net present value of the benefits is positive or internal rate of return is above the standard rate (say 10 to 12 per cent). Of these three methods, net present value is preferred as it gives the total cash flows from the investments made. On the basis of net present value, all the three tanks merit positive investment decisions. Large size tanks seem to perform better with regard to all these measures.

On the whole, the economic analysis of tank restoration brings out clearly that tank restoration in drought-prone regions is a viable proposition. One of the reasons for the viability of the tank restoration programme is that only cost effective measures such as strengthening the bunds are given more emphasis under the restoration programme. Unlike in the case of state promoted *neeru-meeru* (water-you) programme, desilting of the tanks is not given priority. Desilting is costly unless silt is valued and sold. In fact, one of the studies in Karnataka has observed that tank restoration is economically viable even under the conditions of heavy desilting, as the silt has generated substantial income through auctioning (Gireesh *et al.*, 1997). Otherwise, desilting may adversely affect the economic viability of the tank restoration programme. Economic viability in the context of desilting depends on the market for silt in location. In the case of *neeru-meeru* programme, entire cost of desilting is borne by the state without generating any income from the silt. Moreover, desilting may be suitable in the case of percolation tanks rather than irrigation tanks. Wherever, appropriate farmers may be encouraged to desilt the tanks on their own rather than spending money directly and this should be carried out on a regular basis. TMCs can facilitate this activity and generate income as well.

Table 12.16

Different Cash Flow Measures

Particulars	*Adepalli*		*V.V. Palli*		*Akkapalli*	
	S-I	*S-II*	*S-I*	*S-II*	*S-I*	*S-II*
1. Benefit-cost ratio	7.99	9.95	2.94	3.82	4.83	5.87
2. Net present value (Rs. in lakhs)	14.52	18.38	1.36	1.79	13.67	17.43
3. Internal rate of return (%)	140	143	49	53	100	103

It may be noted that the above analysis is purely based on the economic viability based on returns to crop production and hence, not a comprehensive benefit-cost analysis. As mentioned earlier, substantial ecological and social benefits accrue to the households. As we are not in a position to estimate the benefit flows from the ecological impact here, we list out some of these benefits (scooping) that could be converted in to economic benefits. The most important benefit is that of groundwater recharge. Impact of groundwater recharge is medium term (2-3 years) when compared to short run (one year) impact of the tank. Thus, regions with groundwater aquifers can withstand drought for longer periods. This, in turn, could check desertification in the presence of extensive and effective tank network. Availability of water in sufficient quantities and quality would improve health and sanitation conditions in the region. Firstly, availability of potable water in nearby locations would reduce the household drudgery (especially of women and children) of carrying water from long distances. Time saved from this activity can be used in more productive economic activities. This would also facilitate livestock rearing. In the presence of tanks, soil moisture and greenery will increase in the vicinity of the tank. These benefits, especially ecological, become tangible as the groundwater availability improves in the areas beyond the command area in the long run. These benefits continue to increase along with the life of the tank. In fact, these benefits would be growing over the period, as our experience showed in the case of Adepalli. In the long run, this would lead to stability in crop production.

12.7 Sustaining Traditional Water Harvesting Systems: Some Insights

The rationale for tank restoration is valid not only from the equity and stability points but also from the economic angle. For, per unit costs of restoration are marginal compared to creating new irrigation systems, canal or tank. Tank restoration has another important benefit in terms of groundwater replenishment. There are two ways of restoring these traditional systems. One is restoring them to the old type for providing direct irrigation and another is to convert them in to percolation tanks. Though both of them have advantages and disadvantages, percolation tanks seem to perform better in terms of productivity. On the other hand, irrigation tanks are more equitous. More investments and follow up measures are required to safeguard equity in percolation tanks. Our analysis of costs and benefits of irrigation tanks made it clear that benefits outweigh costs in all situations irrespective of tank size though benefits are proportional to the size of the tanks. Apart from crop production, tank restoration has other economic benefits such as employment, livestock, etc., ecological benefits such as groundwater recharge, improvement in CPRs, etc., and social benefits such as checking out-migration, equity, etc.

Therefore, restoring these systems will go a long way in addressing the issues of food security, regional imbalances, ecological balance, etc.

While there is urgent need for policy intervention in this regard, the need for managing these resources in a sustainable manner is equally important. For, the role of policy in managing these systems is rather limited[4], as these systems fall under common pool resources (CPRs). Collective action is a pre-requisite for CPR management. Understanding and promoting collective action is central to common management. While the role of institutions in promoting collective action in CPR management is well recognised, the process of institutional innovation and change is less understood. An attempt is made here, based on our case studies, to gain some insights regarding how to sustain these systems in the long run.

12.7.1 Lessons for Future

The policy initiative of SPWD to restore tank irrigation is rational as far as achieving the objective of improving the rural livelihoods in the drought-prone regions. While the immediate benefits of tank restoration are conspicuous, sustaining these benefits in the long run is the crux of the problem. This aspect is well recognised and the model adopted by SPWD is practical and effective. However, there are certain aspects, which need attention in order to sustain the systems in the long run. These aspects are:

- There is no second opinion about the benefits accruing to beneficiary households due to tank restoration. However, communities in these villages need to have stronger commitment towards protecting these systems in sustainable manner. The economic benefits can further be enhanced through supporting the community beyond the restoration works in terms of providing irrigation benefits to larger area. That is, providing more irrigation facilities through community bore wells, etc. In this context, converting the small tanks into percolation tanks would provide access to water to more households. While large tanks can provide both direct irrigation and percolation benefits, small tanks could be more productive as percolation tanks. In this regard conflict resolution and equity aspects need attention.

4. This is not to say that policy does not have any role in this regard. Policy can provide conducive environment for institutional innovation and hence, plays a role of catalyst.

- The most important aspect our study brings out as far as sustaining the traditional water harvesting systems are concerned is the selection of the PIA (local NGO) for implementing the programme. Selection of PIA appears to be critical in the whole process. For, success of the programme depends on the commitment and sincerity of the PIA. In fact, sustenance of the programme is conspicuous in the villages where good NGOs like Chaitanya in Anantapur, are working.
- The concept of user charges is not properly followed in the programme. Maintenance works are carried out on ad hoc basis. This is not done in the case of small systems where economic returns are small. Farmers expect that PIAs have the responsibility to carry out these repairs. Similarly user contribution, labour or cash, of 25 per cent of the costs is not followed. Imbibing these concepts in the programme ensures not only the financial sustainability of the systems but also increases the stakes (responsibility) of the farmers towards maintaining the system.
- Another important aspect is the follow-up action on the part of the funding agency. This is mainly to ensure equity in water distribution, especially in the case of percolation tanks, through supporting measures to increase the access to water to greater number of households.
- On the whole, the demand driven approach needs more emphasis in the whole process. Though this is in-built at the SPWD level, this approach is not taken forward by the local PIAs. In most of the cases, farmers are enthused and request for the works to be carried out. This is due to the demonstration effect. Efforts on the part of PIA to conduct some orientation programmes and educational tours to the community before selecting the villages and taking up the programme would be useful. This again will depend on the commitment and sincerity of the PIA.
- While the non-beneficiaries or non-command area farmers are provided place in TMC, they do not have any right to water. Therefore, they evince little interest in the activities relating to tank. Though this is a complex issue and needs lot of efforts towards conflict resolution, this is possible through delinking

water and land rights. This is effectively done by *pani panchayats* in Maharashtra. That is, rights on water are given to the households including landless. All the households in the village contribute equally to the development of the lift irrigation schemes and get equal rights to water irrespective of whether the household owns land or not. Every household gets water rights for irrigating 0.5 acres per each household member (adult) and not more. Landless households can exchange or sell these water rights in terms of share cropping, etc. When a household sells its land, water rights are not transferred and hence, there will not be any concentration of irrigated lands in the hands of few. Private exploitation of groundwater is strictly prohibited (for details, see Deshpande and Reddy, 1991). However, this is not to suggest that it is feasible in the given framework of the implementing agency. This requires proper and stronger institutional arrangements and its replicability is rather difficult in the absence of policy support.

For, this kind of approach needs more intensive work towards institutional arrangements apart from the requirement of macro policy and legal support. In the absence of such support at the policy level, it is rather difficult to ensure equity in resource distribution. Its feasibility gets further complicated in the context of restoring the old systems where customary rights are already established. The approach of SPWD in expanding the tank restoration programme through demonstration effect rather than directly pumping money would set the stage for demand driven approach though it is too early to see the impact on a large scale.

Demonstration will be effective when the economic benefits are substantial. Economic benefits tend to increase with the increase in access to water, qualitatively and quantitatively. In scarcity conditions and drought-prone regions, this could be possible either increasing the availability of water through rainwater harvesting, conjunctive use of water or reducing the pressure on agriculture. As far as institutional feasibility is concerned, reducing the pressure on land and water would be more effective. It is envisaged in the Vision 2020 document of Andhra Pradesh that people depending on agriculture would be halved by the year 2020. The state should work towards providing appropriate policy and legal environment in order to make effective use of the resources in a sustainable manner.

References

Agarwal, A (2000). "Drought? Try capturing the rain", *Briefing Paper for Members of Parliament and State Legislatures*, July (*www.cseindia.org*).

Agarwal, A. and S. Narain (1997). *Dying Wisdom: Rise, Fall and Potential of India's Traditional Water Harvesting Systems.* New Delhi: CSE.

Bardhan, Pranab (ed) (1989). *The Economic Theory of Agrarian Institutions*. Oxford: Clarendon Press.

Chopra, K., G.K. Kadekodi and M.N. Murty (1990). *Participatory Development: People and Common Property Resources.* New Delhi: Sage Publications.

Deshpande, R.S. and V. Ratna Reddy (1991). "Differential impact of watershed based technology: Some analytical issues", *Indian Journal of Agricultural Economics* XLVI(2), April-June.

Easter, K.W. and K. Palanisami (1984). "Irrigation tanks of South India: Management strategies and investment alternatives", *Indian Journal of Agricultural Economics* 39(2).

Gireesh, M,N. Nagraj and M.G. Chandrakantha (1997). "Rehabilitation of irrigation tanks in eastern zone of Karnataka—An economic analysis", *Indian Journal of Agricultural Economics* 52(2): 231-43.

GoAP (2000). *Water Conservation Mission, The Information and Guidelines*. Hyderabad: Government of Andhra Pradesh.

Janakrajan, S. (1993). "In search of tanks: Some hidden facts", *Economic and Political Weekly* 28(26), June.

Jodha, N.S. (1986). "Common property resources and the rural poor", *Economic and Political Weekly* 21.

———. (1990). "Rural common property resources: Contributions and crisis", *Economic and Political Weekly* XXV(26), 30 June.

Leach, Melissa and Robin Mearns (1991). "Poverty and environment in developing countries: An overview study", Report, Institute of Development Studies, Sussex, Brighton, U.K.

Olson, Jr. Mancur (1965). *The Logic of Collective Action: Public Goods and the Theory of Groups.* Cambridge: Harvard University Press.

Pagare, Ganesh and Vasudha Pagare (1994). "A village like Ralegan", (The World Report on the Environment), *Economic Times*, June.6

Rama, Govindasamy and K. Palanisami (1990). "Optimum modernisation for tank irrigation system using a sustainable model", *Indian Journal of Agricultural Economics* XLU(2), April-June.

Raju, K.V. (2000). "Participatory irrigation management in Andhra Pradesh: Promise, practice and a way forward", *Working Paper* No. 65, ISEC, Bangalore.

Rao, G. Bhaskara (1997). "Irrigation tanks in Anantapur district: Andhra Pradesh", Paper Presented at the *Workshop on Traditional Water Management Solutions*, National Museum of Man, Bhopal, 16-18 September.

———. (1999). "In search of the owners for the abandoned treasure: SPWD's tank restoration programme in Rayalseema", Paper presented at *Workshop on Tank Irrigation*, ANSSIRD, Mysore, 13-14 July.

Rao, V.M and M.G. Chandrakantha (1984). "Resource at the margin: Tank irrigation programmes in Karnataka", *Economic and Political Weekly* 19(26), June.

Ravallion, Martin (2001). "The mystery of the vanishing benefits: An introduction to impact evaluation", *The World Bank Economic Review* 15(1).

Reddy, M. Atchi (1995). "Irrigation tanks in Rayalaseema", in B.C. Barah (ed.), *Development of Water Resources and its Ecological Implications (The Role of Minor Irrigation)*. New Delhi: Delta Publishing House.

Reddy, V. Ratna (1990). "Irrigation in colonial India: A study of Madras Presidency during 1860-1900," *Economic and Political Weekly* XXV(18 and 19), May 5-12.

———. (1993). "New technology in agriculture and changing size productivity relationships: A study of Andhra Pradesh", *Indian Journal of Agricultural Economics* 48(4), October–December.

———. (1995). "Environment and sustainable agricultural development: Conflicts and contradictions", *Economic and Political Weekly* XXX(12), 25 March (Review of Agriculture).

———. (1998). "Environmental movement in India: Some reflection," *Journal of Indian School of Political Economy* 10(4), Oct.-Dec.

———. (2000). "Sustainable watershed management: Institutional approach", *Economic and Political Weekly* 35(38).

———. (2001a). "User valuation of renewable resources: A study of arid zone", in V. *Ratna Reddy (ed.), User Valuation of Renewable Natural Resources: The User Perspective*. New York: Nova Science Publications.

———. (2001b)."Political economy of irrigation development in Andhra Pradesh", *Centre for Economic and Social Studies*, Hyderabad.

Reddy, D.N., B.C. Barah and T. Sudhakar (1993). "Tradditional water harvesting system: *Tank in the drought prone areas of Andhra Pradesh", Indian Journal of Agricultural Economics* XLVIII(1): 76-87. Jan.-March.

Sengupta, N. (1991). *Managing Common Property*. Delhi: Sage Publication.

Shankari, Uma (1991). "Tanks: Major problems in minor irrigation", *Economic and Political Weekly* 26(39).

Sing, K. (1994). *Managing Common Pool Resources-Principle and Case Studies*. Delhi: Oxford University Press.

Thilo, Hatzius (1994). "Reconsidering agrarian reform and agricultural production co-operatives in northern coastal Peru—A neo-institutional perspective", *Quarterly Journal of International Agriculture* 33(1).

von Oppen, M. and K.V. Subba Rao (1980a). "Tank irrigation in semi-arid tropical India: Part I: Historical development and spatial distribution", *Progress Report* 5, Economics Programme, ICRISAT, Hyderabad, February.

———. (1980b). "Tank irrigation in semi-arid tropical India", *Progress Report* 9, Economics Programme, ICRISAT, Hyderabad, May.

Vyas, V.S. (1991). "Agrarian structure, environmental concerns and rural poverty", *Elmhirst Memorial Lecture*, XXI International Conference of Agricultural Economists, Tokyo, Japan, 22 August.

13 Decentralisation Trajectories with Multiple Institutions

The Case of PIM Programme in India

R. Parthasarathy

13.1 Introduction

One of the offshoots of the planned economic development model in India has been the increasing emphasis on effective local governance. While some scholars lay emphasis on financial decentralisation, others view decentralisation as a political process involving strong local self-governments that plan and execute local developmental needs. The political parties and the people alike have also argued time and again for greater 'administrative freedom' at local levels. Strong Panchayat Raj (local government) institutions are viewed as a step in this direction. During the first few decades in independent India, the state governments adopted legislative and administrative measures with a view to expanding and developing local self-government. Policy makers were influenced by the Gandhian view, democratic constitution of the country and the five year plans, which emphasised the promotion of peoples' participation in management especially for rural development through tiered representative institutions.

In the past few decades, however, with newer models of implementing programmes, incremental steps in governance and institution building have assumed importance. These models of development are an outcome of both the recognition of local level governance and the importance of users' involvement in programme conceptualisation and implementation. Examples of this type are: the user groups formed for joint forest management (JFM), watershed programme, water users associations (WUA) under the participatory irrigation management (PIM) programmes and so on. One predictable outcome of this approach has been the multiplicity of user groups in a small geographical area like village.[1] The membership to these groups sometimes comes from a single village *panchayat*, while in others membership is spread over different villages or *panchayats*. This process of decentralisation, theoretically at least, has brought into fore different trajectories and dynamics in the space assumed to be for *panchayats*.

The new user groups could be viewed as logical extensions of the decentralisation process, thus hypothesised as complementing the *panchayat* committees. It is also possible that a plethora of institutions at the village level may work at cross-purposes; worse they may appear competitive as most groups are vested with managerial functions and with special funds. The fear is that these might lead to a further fragmentation of the society by providing fertile political grounds. In a flourishing democracy, however, it could be argued that politics is an integral part of the set-up, yet, insofar as the influential members of these new user groups belong to a caste or class group, the political powers unleashed by such groups may have an adverse impact on various parameters.

On the contrary, it would be simplistic to view decentralisation process having a last, identifiable, administrative layer. It would be easy to argue, as some do, that the *panchayats* should be recognised as the last level in the hierarchy of decentralised political institutions. Therefore, both in terms of finance as well as on managerial aspects, *panchayats* should be supreme and all other (emerging) user groups should function under the *panchayat* umbrella. There is also a school, which argues that all programmes in a *panchayat* area should be implemented at the behest of the *panchayat*. In the course of reforms and decentralisation of power and functions, this aspect of institutional dynamics is often ignored. The present paper sets out to explore this class of issues by considering the case of participatory irrigation management (PIM) programme. Largely, the cases are drawn from the

1. In Andhra Pradesh for instance, there are user groups formed to manage irrigation canals and water distribution; WUAs, watershed committees, development programme implementation committees under *Janmabhoomi*, school management committees, etc.

field studies carried out in Andhra Pradesh and Gujarat. The paper is organised as follows: Section 2 shares the understanding of the problem. Section 3 presents an overview of the PIM programme. Section 4 discusses the various aspects of financial and managerial functions of the new institutions set up under the PIM programme. In both these sections, the interrelationships between the newly set up organisations and the *panchayats* are discussed. The last section summarises the findings.

13.2 *Panchayats* and User Groups: Competing Spaces?

Functions of a *panchayat* include local administration, water resources development and management, sanitation and health, public works, school and adult education, community development, agriculture and animal husbandry, forest and village industries and so on. Over time, the government has also transferred various other functions and development schemes to be administered by them. A part of the finances for the *panchayat* now come directly from different government departments, besides, they also collect local taxes, rents, levies, rates, fees, etc., as authorised by the acts (For a comprehensive review of Pachayati Raj in India, see, RGF, 2000).

During the British rule and after Independence, there have been assessments and reviews on the performance of the self-government *panchayat* institutions by the government and academics like, the Ashok Mehta Committee (GoI, 1978); Shivaiah, 1986; GoK, 1996; RGF, 2000, etc. The striking feature of all these reviews and studies is their recommendation on ways and means of further strengthening the *panchayat* system. Thus, the village *panchayat* as a unit of decentralised administration has come to be accepted and importantly reviewed periodically. Indeed, this is an important signal for local level institutions that they are not only recognised but attempts are also on to strengthen them periodically.

Inter alia, the Government of India and the various state governments have also started recently emphasising direct involvement of participants at local level in their various programmes. These new efforts are partly due to attempts at downsizing of the government roles but largely based on the experiences of NGOs and donor insistence. By and large, the user-involved programmes are based in rural areas[2] and often revolve around managing resources like land, water or forests. As mentioned, the *panchayats'* portfolio of work also includes tasks that are now managed by separate user groups. In fact, in some tribal areas like the Central India regions and in other scheduled areas, there is an apparent conflict between the *panchayats* and the local bodies of tribal *panchayats* and hill councils. The power and jurisdiction of these bodies are matters of dispute and affect the development. So far no resolution is in sight probably because the tribal councils also enjoy similar powers in matters of administration like the *panchayats* and would be reluctant to give up. However, it is clear that the users group roles and responsibilities (discussed in subsequent sections) are indeed different. Yet, can these new institutions be viewed as the ones competing for the same space of work, authority and power? This paper uses one such user group, namely water users associations (WUA) set up under the participatory irrigation management (PIM) programme to analyse the institutional dynamics at the local level.

13.3 PIM: A Brief Overview

During the British times and after Independence during the successive five year plan period, there has been an expansion of the irrigated area and some efforts to improve the maintenance of the irrigation systems. The significant qualitative attempts are directed toward increases in irrigation efficiency, introducing better methods of water control under the recently introduced participatory process in irrigation management (in some states).[3] The importance of institutions in all these aspects is obvious; yet there are relatively fewer attempts to relate the structure of these new institutions and their working to the larger context of decentralisation initiatives.

2. There are some urban area based programme as well, like SJRY, Development of Women and Children in Urban Areas (DWCUA), Infrastructure Support and so on.
3. However, the persistent underutilisation of irrigation potential and the continued slow growth of yields suggest that the effectiveness of irrigation management is lower than its potential.

In line with the National Water Policy 1987, several states have enacted or are in the process of enacting irrigation policies/laws with an emphasis on users managed irrigation system. In Gujarat and Andhra Pradesh, the governments have taken initiatives in sponsoring irrigation management transfer (IMT) but the approach and process have been different (for a synoptic view, see Table 13.1 and for details, see Parthasarathy, 2000). In the case of Gujarat, a Government Resolution in 1994 authorised the creation of 13 pilot projects in some major and minor irrigation schemes.[4] In the case of Andhra Pradesh, the state government enacted a law, The Andhra Pradesh Farmers Management of Irrigation Systems Act (1997) and created 10,262 water users associations (WUAs) in the command areas of major, medium and minor irrigation projects.

The Gujarat approach emphasised on the consultations with farmers and the main feature has been a gradual approach rather than a forceful push by the government like in Andhra Pradesh.[5] While the PIM programme in Gujarat envisages a complete turnover of operation and maintenance (O&M) to the WUAs, the Andhra Act empowers farmers to manage the irrigation systems themselves. In both the cases, canals remain government property and major repairs continue to be the responsibility of the irrigation department, however, the day-to-day functioning of the system passes on to the users associations.

In Andhra Pradesh, active membership starts with the electoral process of the WUA executive committee. However, in both the states voting rights are vested in the landowners in the command area irrespective of the farm size. Tenants have no voting rights in either state, although the APFMIS Act acknowledges their membership in the WUAs. Repair and rehabilitation of the infrastructure has been the most important component in both IMT programmes (Table 13.2). But, the major functions of WUAs are water distribution management and day-

4. The implementing agency in six projects was an NGO; in the remainder, government officials undertook the transfer programme. These agencies besides motivating the farmers also aimed to build their capacity to manage the WUAs. The notable feature of the PIM scheme is its emphasis on the social engineering aspect (for details, see, Parthasarathy, 2000).

5. It should however, be mentioned that Gujarat too is considering the legislative route to PIM programme and is in the process of drafting an act.

Table 13.1

Some Features of the Irrigation Management Transfer Programme: Gujarat and Andhra Pradesh

Details	*Gujarat*	*Andhra Pradesh*
Name of the Programme	*Participatory Irrigation Management (PIM)*	*Farmers Management of Irrigation Systems*
Year of commencement	1995	1997
Status of the programme	Pilot phase (13 pilot schemes were chosen to serve as learning laboratories)Plans are to cover 50 per cent of irrigated area (of 15 million hectares) in the state by year 2003.	State wide coverage (excluding tribal areas)
No. of WUAs formed	13 in the pilot phase (There are however, WUAs formed prior to the PIM, like Mohini, Chopadvav, etc. Claims on the exact number of such WUAs vary; even the most optimistic estimate does not exceed 45).	10,292 WUAs have been formed in all the 22 districts of Andhra Pradesh covering major, medium and minor irrigation projects in the state.
State's role in water distribution	To provide water at the outlet (off-take) stage.	Commitment to ensure adequate water supply at the outlet level.
Membership criteria in WUA	Landowners in the WUA area.	Landowners and tenants in the WUA area. Other water users to be co-opted in to the WUA.
Status of women representation in WUA	Rules of the WUA state that one-third of the managing committee members will be women.	No explicit provision.
Members' voting rights	Landowners in the WUA area.	Landowners in the WUA.
Procedure for electing WUA management committee	Varies between WUA.	District collector in charge of the election. Managing committee will hold office for three years. Provision to recall the President or a Chairman or a member of the WUA.
Federating WUAs	Not so far attempted.	Three-tier management structure. At the primary level is the WUA, at the secondary level, a distributory committee (DC), and at the apex level, there is a Project Committee (PC), which has DC presidents as members.
Involvement of NGOs in the programme	NGOs play a larger role in policy making and programme implementation.	Under the new act no clear role for the NGOs.

Source: Parthasarathy and Joshi (2001).

to-day operation and maintenance of the canal and field channels under their jurisdiction.[6] Due to the differences in the prevailing system of water distribution and water charge collection,[7] intra-scheme water distribution to the farmers fundamentally changes under the PIM programme in Gujarat but remains almost the same under APFMIS in Andhra Pradesh.

Table 13.2

A Summary of Repair and Rehabilitation Programme: Gujarat and Andhra Pradesh

Components	*Gujarat*	*Andhra Pradesh*
Rehabilitation and repair support	State expenditure vary and are established on the basis of a joint survey of irrigation department and farmers.	State expenditure of fixed amount of Rs. 100 per acre. The irrigation department continues to assess the needs for R&R, certify and authorise works. Funds are channelled via the irrigation department.
Tiered rehabilitation and repair responsibilities	Not applicable.	The PC is responsible to attend to the problems relating to repairs and rehabilitation (R&R) and operation of the main delivery systems. The DC is responsible for the O&M of the distributory level structures and at the WUA, the farmers are responsible to manage the field level distribution.

Source: Parthasarathy and Joshi (2001).

There have been efforts to make the WUAs financially viable. Though charging economic rates for water had been a very difficult task in all the states, the WUAs in Gujarat at least had begun fixing and

6. While the WUAs in Gujarat are responsible for the collection of the demand forms and water charges, in Andhra Pradesh the collection of water charges is the responsibility of the revenue department. In Andhra Pradesh, the water charge is part of land tax collected by the officials of the revenue department and the amount depends upon the classification of land like, wet or dry and the farm size. It is expected that the WUA will eventually take over the responsibility of water fee collection, which will then be disconnected from land taxes (Table 13.3).

7. In Gujarat *sejhpali* system is in vogue, which is based on the farmers' demand for water allocation and water payment is based on crop area to be paid to the irrigation department. The new WUAs take over the collection of water demand and employ operators for the canal gates and inspection of water distribution. The operators being paid by WUAs replace the local-level functionaries of the irrigation department officials (*chowkidar*).

collecting water charges from member farmers. There are also attempts to strengthen the finances of the WUAs by the government. In Gujarat for instance, there are two types of grants for the WUA. The first is related to the performance, where the WUA retains 30 per cent of the water charges collected toward O&M expenditure and another 20 per cent of the total water charges collected for administrative expenditure. The second grant consists of a contribution of Rs. 250 per hectare from the state government, Rs. 200 from the Central government and Rs. 50 from the members of the WUA. Insofar as the first type of grant is based on a proportion of the total water charges collected, there is an incentive for the WUAs to raise the water charges (see for details, Parthasarathy, 2000). In Andhra Pradesh too, funds for repairs have been disbursed to all the WUAs and federating bodies *albeit* through the irrigation department. In 1997-98, the actual amount to be spent on maintenance works was fixed at Rs. 100 per acre and a total of Rs. 10.6 million was allocated for repairs and rehabilitation. The lump sum grant was shared in the following way: 50 per cent to the WUA, 20 per cent to DC, and 20 per cent for the PC. Importantly, the remaining 10 per cent was earmarked for the village *panchayat* to undertake development programmes.

Table 13.3

Highlights of Water Distribution: Gujarat and Andhra Pradesh

Components	*Gujarat*	*Andhra Pradesh*
State's role in water distribution	Irrigation department continues consultation with farmers (now the WUA) on timings of water allocation. WUA either employs own operator, or local-level ID official distributes (*sejhpali*-based on water demand forms).	Irrigation department (through its local level *luskars*) continues to distribute water (*warabandhi* no water demand forms).
State's role in water supply	Commitment in the Act to ensure adequate water supply at the outlet level.	Commitment in the Act to ensure adequate water supply at the outlet level.
Water charges: Rates and collection	WUA collects water demands forms. It sets the water rate, but often had raised it compared to the period before PIM. WUA collects water charges and the recovery rate has improved, perhaps due to the provision of rebate for payment of water charges on time.	Water rate was tripled in 1997. Department continues to collect the water charges as part of the land tax. No legal provision has been made as yet to delink water charges from land cess. To transfer the water charges to the WUA.

Source: Parthasarathy and Joshi (2001).

Thus, there has been some attempt in Andhra Pradesh to bring about a link between the new water management institution, WUA and the *panchayat*.[8] The fact that Andhra Pradesh Act is touted as the model of irrigation sector reform, it is possible that other states, which use the Andhra Act as basis, would also try and forge similar links with the *panchayats*. There exist other linkages, weak though. Of the members of the WUA, around one-fifth in Gujarat and one-fourth in Andhra Pradesh hold some office in the village *panchayat* (Table 13.4) but there are variations in pattern among the WUAs. The (slightly) higher proportion of the members of the WUA involved in *panchayat* activities in Andhra Pradesh than Gujarat also reflects the political process used for the constitution of the WUAs. Conversely, in Gujarat the fact that more than 21 per cent of the WUA members also hold active office in the village *panchayat* indicates that consciously

Table 13.4

Distribution of Members having Association with Other Organisations: Gujarat and Andhra Pradesh

Name of the WUAs		Number of Members in				
		WUAs	Panchayat	Cooperative	Political Party	Total Members
	Gujarat					
1	Tranol	98	24	4	2	30
2	Thalota	113	22	5	0	27
3	Laxmipura	91	17	2	1	20
4	Digas	39	11	4	1	16
	Total	341 (100)	74 (21.7)	15 (4.4)	4 (1.2)	93 (27.27)
	Andhra Pradesh					
1	Ellabotharam	121	30	4	—	34
2	Peddapalakaluru	118	27	—	—	27
3	Jantaluru	120	30	—	—	30
	Total	359 (100)	87 (24.2)	4 (1.1)	—	91 (25.3)

Note: Figures in parentheses indicates percentage to total members.
Source: Parthasarathy and Joshi (2001).

8. In the subsequent year, though the government had planned to maintain this level of grant for maintenance works, a new dimension of farmers sharing/contributing 15 per cent has been added. Like in Gujarat, in Andhra Pradesh too, no fixed commitment of grants for the PIM programme has been made (except the first two years in Andhra Pradesh).

insulating WUAs from either *panchayats* or the political process is nearly impossible. It is recognised that taking part in the *panchayat* activities is not the same as involvement in party politics, yet, there is a fair play of party politics at the *panchayat* level that should be kept in view. This sort of linkages if sustained proves that decentralisation is not an exclusive or static process or that the newer institutions' "encroachment" into *panchayats'* "space" is necessarily a competitive phenomenon. Few institutions in a developing democracy can be viewed as sacrosanct to the extent that parallel or competing institutions should be forbidden. It is plausible that *panchayats* may view the newer institutions in its area as beneficial additions since they not only bring in additional resources but take away some of the management responsibilities as well in to small 'homogenous' groups. The challenge, therefore, is to find a proper balance of institutional arrangements at the local level that promotes development effectively. This balance is not easily determined as they shift in tandem with the performance and changes in the new institutions.[9]

13.4 An Assessment of WUAs' Performance

For assessing the performance of the newly formed WUAs a sample was drawn that would represent different regions and irrigation schemes in each state. In Gujarat for instance, Thalota in the Dharoi irrigation scheme and Laxmipura in the Dantiwada scheme represent the North Gujarat region; Tranol in the MahiKadana project and Digas in the UkaiKakrapar irrigation project were chosen from the Central and Southern regions.[10] In Andhra Pradesh, one WUA was selected from

9. According to the 9th Plan document, to ensure that the *panchayat* act in the most effective manner, the involvement of people and facilitators in planning, prioritisation and implementation of programmes and in monitoring of their activities is essential. To circumvent the problem of disparity in the allocation of available financial resources between the main village and the hamlets, there is, perhaps, a need for developing appropriate principles of allocation of resources at the micro level. The second constraint can be removed through training and retraining of the *panchayat* members. Public administrators, managers of co-operatives and social activists/leaders could design training courses and manage training centres. The states should evolve appropriate mechanisms to ensure harmonious working of different tiers of the *panchayats*, perhaps, legislative actions would also be required.

10. In Thalota and Laxmipura, the PIM programme was implemented by an NGO. In Tranol and Digas, the irrigation department implemented the programme.

each of the following irrigation schemes and regions: Sriramsagar in Telangana, Nagarjunasagar in Coastal Andhra Pradesh and Cuddapah-Karnool and Thungabhadra in Rayalaseema region. In all, seven WUAs, four in Gujarat and three in Andhra Pradesh were studied. Including Gujarat (341) and Andhra Pradesh (359), 700 households representing different socio-economic statuses were surveyed. Tables 13.5 and 13.6 provide details about sample households.

Table 13.5

Distribution of Sample Households: Gujarat

Categories	*Tranol*	*Thalota*	*Laxmipura*	*Digas*	*Total*
Up to 0.5 ha. males	15 (15.3)	15 (13.3)	15 (16.5)	1 (2.6)	46 (13.5)
Up to 0.50 ha. female heads	2 (2.0)	3 (2.7)	2 (2.2)		7 (2.1)
Up to 0.50 ha. female respondents	13 (13.3)	12 (10.6)	11 (12.1)	1 (2.6)	37 (10.9)
0.51-1.0 ha. males	15 (15.3)	15 (13.3)	15 (16.5)	6 (15.4)	51 (15.0)
0.51-1.0 ha. female heads	2 (2.0)	2 (1.8)	2 (2.2)		6 (1.8)
0.51-1.0 ha. female respondents	13 (13.3)	13 (11.5)	13 (14.3)	1 (2.6)	40 (11.7)
1.01-2.50 ha.	15 (15.3)	15 (13.3)	15 (16.5)	15 (38.5)	60 (17.6)
2.51+ ha.	15 (15.3)	15 (13.3)	15 (16.5)	15 (38.5)	60 (17.6)
Tenant male	5 (5.1)	8 (7.1)	2 (2.2)		15 (4.4)
Tenant female headed		1 (0.9)	1 (1.1)		2 (0.6)
Tenant female respondent	3 (3.1)	14 (12.4)			17 (5.0)
Total no. of households	98 (100.0)	113 (100.0)	91 (100.0)	39 (100.0)	341 (100.0)

Note: Figures in parentheses indicate percentage to total.
Source: Parthasarathy and Joshi (2001).

13.4.1 Water Distribution and Management

As mentioned, the important difference between Gujarat and Andhra Pradesh is that they adopt different systems of water distribution—*sejhpali* in Gujarat and *warabandhi* in Andhra Pradesh. In *warabandhi,* each farmer is entitled to a fraction of the total flow available to the

Table 13.6

Distribution of Sample Households: Andhra Pradesh

Categories	*Ellabotharam*	*Peddapalakaluru*	*Jantaluru*	*Total*
Up to 0.5 ha. males	15 (12.4)	14 (11.9)	15 (12.5)	44 (12.5)
Up to 0.50 ha female heads headed	1 (0.8)	7 (5.9)	7 (5.8)	15 (4.2)
Up to 0.50 ha. female respondents	14 (11.6)	7 (5.9)	9 (7.5)	30 (8.4)
0.51-1.0 ha. males	15 (12.4)	16 (13.6)	14 (11.7)	45 (12.5)
0.51-1.0 ha. female heads	5 (4.1)	2 (1.7)	4 (3.3)	11 (3.1)
0.51-1.0 ha. female respondents	10 (8.3)	13 (11.0)	11 (9.2)	34 (9.5)
1.01-2.50 ha.	15 (12.4)	15 (12.7)	15 (12.5)	45 (12.5)
2.51+ ha.	16 (13.2)	14 (11.9)	15 (12.5)	45 (12.5)
Tenant male	14 (11.6)	15 (12.7)	15 (12.5)	44 (12.3)
Tenant female headed	2 (1.7)	1 (0.8)	4 (3.3)	7 (1.9)
Tenant female respondent	14 (11.6)	14 (11.9)	11 (9.2)	39 (10.9)
Total no. of households	121	118	120	359

Note: Figures in parentheses indicate percentage to total.
Source: Parthasarathy and Joshi (2001).

system proportional to his land area in the canal command. Water is supposed to be delivered to farmers below each outlet by means of a strict rotation schedule. During his turn each farmer gets the full flow from the outlet. Under *sejhpali* system, every farmer is required to apply for irrigation each season indicating the crop and the area. Under the decentralised set-up, after receiving necessary guidance from the irrigation department, WUAs in Gujarat began to perform various water distribution and management related tasks. Some of the WUAs had framed rules however, as expected their effectiveness varied from one WUA to another. In some measure, the process of PIM has been able to introduce important changes through the local institution; such as an increase in accessibility of water to tail portions, expansion of area under irrigation and prevention of wastage of water by carrying out repair and rehabilitation work.

It is evident that the WUAs have addressed (though with varied level of success) some of their specific problems that had prevailed before their formation. For instance in the two states, appropriation of water by farmers in the head reaches of the canal and improper field channels were reported as two major reasons responsible for inadequate supply of water before (the formation of WUA). After the PIM, it was R and R work and management by WUAs, which led to a better supply of water than before. Two important reasons for the reported inadequacy of water even after the PIM are the location of plots and insufficiency of water in the reservoirs.[11] Evidently, both these problems are beyond the scope of WUAs influence and functions and hence, the PIM programme's impact on water distribution and management through its new institutions namely, the WUA appears to be modest so far.

Regardless of its modest success, why does the government planners, donor institutions and the observers of the development process continue to promote and support the new local-level institutions? This could partly be due to the recognition that, "while in principle the *panchayats* could be effective bodies for local planning and implementation, they may not be so in practice because of a number of constraints. First, all *panchayat* members do not necessarily seek to achieve social goals and hence may not be sensitive to the needs of the people. Diversion and misuse of resources have been reported even where the PRIs are involved in the implementation of programmes. It has also been found that the *gram pradhans* who are mostly elected from the main village (71 to 92 per cent in different districts of a state) ignore the development of hamlets. Second, most of the members do not have the necessary background in planning and implementation of development programmes. Third, unless there is a functional link between the various tiers of the *panchayats* in terms of administrative and financial control, the required coordination in planning and implementation may not come through. Fourth, the *panchayats* need

11. In Gujarat, insufficient supply of water, plots located in the tail-end and poor R and R work seemed to be major limitations for the adequate supply of water before the formation of WUA (for details, see van Koppen *et al.*, 2002).

flexibilities in operational rules, authority and financial resources if they are to participate actively in planning and implementation of development programmes" (IX Plan document, Vol. I, Planning Commission). Although the President of *gram* (village) p*anchayat* is the head, s/he does not exercise the status of the executive as done by the *taluk* and district *panchayats*. "In practice, the Secretary exercises more powers than the President. All correspondence and communication between the village *panchayat* and other *panchayats* and departments are done through the Secretary. Since he is the only recognised official at the *panchayat* level the members depend very much on the Secretary (than the President) for carrying their works and panchayat activities" (RGF, 2000: 67).

Even in the case of WUAs, the proposed solution of simple transfer of the responsibilities of the existing government department like say irrigation, that was handling these functions without bringing about necessary changes in their (department's) role, attitude and without fostering linkages to the already existing (local level) institutions is like setting up newer priority to the older methods. As a result, these steps fail to have the force of a corrective measure aimed at improving efficiency. Similarly, creating newer institutions (or even accompanying them with awareness creation and training modules) will not *per se* bring about changes since the efficiency and effectiveness of these new institutions depend on the performance of the new actors. Yet, to expect existing institutions like the *panchayat* to learn the intricacies of specific functions like water distribution and management and liasoning with the irrigation department tasked with this role also appears difficult. Some states have already created institutions for the training of *panchayat* members but the effective functioning of the *panchayat* depends on facilitative functional relationship in terms of coordination, cooperation between the elected and official functionaries. Further, "it is a prerequisite of a democracy that administrative wing should function under deliberative wing, that is, bureaucracy should be answerable and accountable to the elected political leadership. In most states the bureaucracy was found to be in a prime position over elected leadership (RGF, 2000: 11)." One of the reasons for this outcome is the fact that local leaders, be it *panchayat* or the WUA are seen by the bureaucracy merely as communicators and beneficiaries (now, termed *(sic)* participants) in the programme and not as channels to planners and implementers. To a large extent, then, participation of users in the programme would only be treated as adjuncts and only marginally influence the implementation or reform process. "Commenting on the relationship between non-officials and the officials (in a *panchayat*), the P.R. Nayak Committee states that the role of Government officials within the Panchayati Raj institutions should be facilitative and executive rather than authoritative" (RGF, 2000: 68).

In some programmes implemented by a *panchayat,* it is found that they enter into a contract with *taluka panchayat* as 'contractors;' similar to the NGOs under PIM. Under the circumstance, the *panchayats* do appear as an agency meant as fast a channel mechanism. In fact, *panchayats* seldom initiate a planning process for its income and expenditure and priorities. Nor are the *panchayats* always consulted while initiating programmes like building tanks or check dams within the village area. It is reported that on many occasions, the government or other agencies do not even care to obtain the mandatory no objection certificate (NOC) from *panchayats*. Worse still, the *panchayats,* in some cases are not even aware of programmes or processes that NGOs or other governmental agencies set up in the village. Similar is the case of investments in a village under the Member of Parliament or Member of Legislative Assembly discretionary funds. In the present set-up, the *Talati* or Secretary (lowest level revenue officials) is more powerful than the collective of a *panchayat* to the extent that the *Talati* dictates on how funds are to be disbursed and the quantum of grants/funds that the *panchayat* should demand every year. A close look at the devolution of powers and functions to *panchayats* reveals that, "the State Government has retained many regulatory, controlling, supervising powers and some important functions like public distribution system. More importantly, the personnel of the *panchayats* are very much controlled by the State Government, both in terms of requirements and transfers." (RGF, 2000: 70).

Against this background, it is difficult to assume that a *sarpanch* of a village *panchayat* would be willing and able to take on roles in diverse specialisations from distributing water and fixing up water charges to planning and executing watershed works including construction of check dams and so on besides the regular work of the *panchayats*. The other major drawback in the *panchayat* administration is that once a work is planned and tasks cut out, *panchayats* do not have the right to refuse even when they find the process or programme difficult. Thus, there is a real danger that even in the event of some of these programmes not working, some ways would 'officially' be found to make them appear working.

13.4.2 Farmers Participation in PIM Programme

In most of these new programmes including PIM, the key to successful operation is the kind and degree of participation by water users. The evidence suggests that participation varies according to local socio cultural, economic and political factors. The policy approaches are also found to create different contexts for participation and the initial arrangements heavily influence the establishment of norms of participation as well as impacts. For example, in Gujarat, the joint (users-department-NGO if present) surveys undertaken to decide the extent of R and R work needed and in estimating the costs prior to handing over of the canal management to the WUAs, reveal that only 12 per cent of the households had participated. Incidentally, a majority of them have their lands either in the head or in the middle portions of the canal. In Andhra Pradesh, participation in joint surveys only meant involvement of the department and the WUA President. In some WUAs, territorial committee (TC) members have also taken part yet, most of the ordinary members are not even aware of these surveys. As far as different WUA activities are concerned, both in Gujarat and in Andhra Pradesh the involvement of farmer-members was found to be minimal and there was no discernable difference between the two states (Table 13.7). Members had shown relatively higher level of involvement in motivation of fellow farmers to join the WUA and R and R work as compared to their involvement in other activities.

Level of attendance in meetings is often considered to be an important indicator for assessing participation. Participation in annual general meetings (AGM) was higher in Gujarat (22 per cent) than in Andhra Pradesh (13 per cent). Awareness about the programme is a pre requisite for members to participate. It is striking to note that in

Andhra Pradesh, more than 50 per cent of the households were not even aware of the WUA. In Gujarat also, 22 per cent of the member-households were not aware of the WUA. This significant variation between the two states could partly be due to the impact of the differences in the approaches adopted.[12]

Table 13.7

Distribution of Households Involved in WUA Activities

Details	*Gujarat*	*Andhra Pradesh*
No. of households	341	359
Participation in following activities:		
Motivation	15 (4.4)	9 (2.5)
Contribution collection	7 (2.1)	3 (0.8)
Registration of WUA	4 (1.2)	NA
Election of WUA members	NA	25 (7.0)
R and R work	21 (6.2)	21 (5.8)
Water distribution	4 (1.2)	4 (1.1)
Demand forms/water charges	2 (0.6)	1 (0.3)

Note: Figures in parentheses indicate percentage to total participants.
Source: Parthasarathy and Joshi (2001).

Another important yardstick in the PIM process are the meetings of WUA. Usually, the Executive Committee of the WUA is supposed to meet every month in Gujarat and once in a fortnight in Andhra Pradesh. In practice however, in both the states the meetings are held 'as per the requirement' of the individual WUAs. Level of participation in committee meetings was found to be significantly higher in Andhra Pradesh (72 per cent) than in Gujarat (48 per cent). And in Gujarat,

12. There are, however, other aspects to the level of involvement in the IMT. Unawareness about the WUA was prominent among the farmers having smaller land holdings and belonging to socially and economically backward communities. As expected, the importance of the political process in the formation of Andhra Pradesh WUA is evident from the fact that 7 per cent of the members had reportedly taken part in the electoral process of the WUA president or TC members.

involvement of committee members in meetings was significantly higher in NGO-led WUAs compared to others.

The argument that user-specific groups, say a WUA, would have a greater advantage over a congregation of all village members (in a *panchayat*) is obviously based the premise that these specific groups will not only have higher stakes because of the 'homogeneity' but will also have a deeper understanding of the issues. Given the differences between member-farmers with respect to land holding size, location of plots, class and caste, it is difficult to expect the WUA to be a homogenous entity. As far as the effectiveness of the committee members' involvement either during the planning stage or in executive capacity is concerned, this would vitally hinge on their understanding of the area and on their relationship with other members of the WUA. Further, these committee members as leaders are also supposed to execute the decisions taken during the meetings. One of such activities is their ability to motivate other members to join the WUA and act as a collective. In Gujarat, the role of the committee members is evident during the motivation work, at the time of R and R work, negotiations with the irrigation department and NGO, collection of water charges and dissemination of information. And, in Andhra Pradesh, the committee members were found to be involved in R and R work and water distribution and management. Though in Andhra Pradesh the irrigation department manages water distribution, committee members reporting their involvement in this activity were mainly engaged in supervision. Their involvement in other activities like dissemination of information and motivational activities was found to be modest. These modest successes are however, only at the beginning stage of the programmes and hence with greater authority and resources to perform their new roles, it is possible that the user-specific groups like the WUA will bring in the skills and understanding of irrigated agriculture of their members to manage the functions effectively. In the early stages, it is indeed possible that they act as an extensions of centrally established organisational controls. This could partly be due to the fact that establishing political and administrative linkages involve some gestation time and that recognition of authority hinges on the political clout, at least in a democracy.

13.4.3 Politics and WUAs

For reasons not clear through a provision in the byelaw of the WUAs in Gujarat, politics was consciously kept out of the purview, whereas the post of the president of the WUA in Andhra Pradesh has been a coveted one from the beginning. It is possible that such posts enhance their visibility and help further their political ambition, while it also suggests that only the influential sections of the society could afford to become leaders of the WUAs—as is the case with other institutions including the *panchayat*. Interestingly, in many Andhra Pradesh WUAs, farmers reported that party politics did not play any role. Plausibly, use of money in the elections might be due to the attraction of the financial stakes involved in managing the WUAs. The funds handled by a WUA annually were substantial (at least in the initial years) and hence, a vested interest could have developed in acquiring control over them. However, in the subsequent years the quantum of money handled by a WUA in Andhra Pradesh has declined and it remains to be seen in the subsequent rounds of elections to the WUAs, whether the WUA posts continue to be viewed as stepping stones to the political ambitions of the people or are they perceived to be important as seats of authority by themselves, parallel to *panchayats*!

13.5 Conclusion

It should be recognised that taking part in user group activities is not the same as involvement in (party) politics, yet, there is a fair play of party politics even at the village level. This sort of linkages if sustained proves that decentralisation is not an exclusive or static process. Few institutions in a developing democracy are held sacrosanct to function without competition. For a *panchayat*, newer institutions in its area could also be viewed as beneficial additions, as they not only bring in additional resources but also manage specific functions in small 'homogenous' groups. The challenge, therefore, is to find a proper balance of institutional arrangements at the local level that promote development effectively. This balance is not easily determined as they shift as the performance of the new institutions change.

The performance of a WUA is based on three specific functions. First is the technical function of maintaining the canals and distributing water. Evidently, a group of irrigators is better suited to perform this role rather than a set of elected people whose stakes in the functions or performance of irrigation systems are limited. As indicated, for a *panchayat* to learn the intricacies of specialised functions of irrigation in one case, watershed in another is difficult if not impossible. The other important difference in these functions is that, unlike the general administrative and facilitative roles involved in routine or in implementing programmes with a set of defined rules and targets, irrigation or watershed management would involve varying degrees of work in each agricultural season and year and considerable process component. Secondly, the WUA also has a set of managerial functions to discharge that are specific to the functions it performs. For instance, accounting the area actually irrigated for levying and collecting water charges. This function would certainly call for some degree of indifference to the legal status of the plots irrigated. It is implicit in the argument that the WUAs unlike the *panchayats* have to perform its functions in a market mode rather than on purely as a routine task. Third is the set of coordinating functions. Besides coordinating with the irrigation department, one of the major coordination roles is in organising and motivating member-farmers and resolving conflicts that may arise out of water distribution. It is thus, apparent that the WUAs or similar user groups are by design different from the *panchayat* institutions. In the course of discharging these specific functions, there is elfin element of overlap between the user groups' institutions and the *panchayats*. Insofar as there is no overlap or competing interests, there is no reason to presuppose that *panchayat*, as a village level institution should be the last layer in decentralised administrative process. As mentioned, many of these new user groups together could possibly complement the existing local level institution.

One must take cognisance of the reasons behind the modest performance of the new institutions. Partly the fact that they are in the formative stages could explain the level of performance. It could also be partly due to the structure, yet the difficulties in evaluating the impact of new decentralised institutions on new programmes and on the existing local institutions are obvious. Essentially, most of these institutions are formed through political process, though a number of non-political institutions could be involved as channels like the line departments, apolitical local institutions or NGOs. As discussed, one advantage of the *panchayat* institutions is that there have been periodic commitments to strengthen and review them. In the case of the user group institutions being created, there is a real danger that these could be viewed variously as the ones to offload functions the government does not want to do anymore. Few institutions in a developing democracy can be viewed as sacrosanct to the extent that parallel or competing institutions should be forbidden. It is plausible that *panchayats* may view the newer institutions in its area as beneficial additions since they not only bring in additional resources but take away some of the management responsibilities also. The challenge, therefore, is to find a proper balance of institutional arrangements at the local level that promote development effectively. This balance is not easily determined as they shift in tandem with the performance and changes in the new institutions. There is thus a need to be cautious and careful while crafting and tasking the new institutions.

References

Andhra Pradesh Farmers Management of Irrigation Systems Act (1997). *Act and Rules, (Act 11 of 1997).* Department of Irrigation and Command Area Development, Government of Andhra Pradesh.

Government of India (1978). *Report of the Committee on Panchayati Raj Institutions* (Chairman Ashok Mehta). Ministry of Agriculture and Irrigation, New Delhi.

Government of Karnataka (1996). *Report on the Expert Committee on Karnataka Panchayati Raj Act, 1993.* (Chairman: P.R. Nayak).

Parthasarathy, R. (2000). "Participatory irrigation management programme in Gujarat: Institutional and financial issues", *Economic and Political Weekly* 35(35&36): 3147-3154.

Parthasarathy, R. and Harish Joshi (2001). "Access to water and equity dimensions of irrigation management transfer: A comparison of Gujarat and Andhra Pradesh, India", A Report Submitted to the International Water Management Institute, Colombo, Sri Lanka.

Rajiv Gandhi Foundation (2000). *Panchayati Raj in India: Status Report 1999.* Task Force on Panchayati Raj, New Delhi.

Shiviah, M. (1986). *Panchayati Raj: A Policy Perspective.* National Institute of Rural Development, Hyderabad.

van Koppen, Barbara, R. Parthasarathy and Constantina Safiliou (2002). "Poverty dimensions of irrigation management transfer in large-scale canal irrigation in Andhra Pradesh and Gujarat, India", *Research Report 61.* International Water Management Institute, Colombo, Sri Lanka.

14 Hyperbolic Discounting in Analysing Investment in Groundwater Irrigation in India*

M.G. Chandrakanth, N. Rashmi, H. Chandrashekhar, P.S. Srikantha Murthy, N. Nagaraj and Lalith Achoth

14.1 Preamble

Financial institutions have been charging simple interest rate on agricultural borrowings. However, when borrowers default, they are charged at the compound (exponential) interest. Due to recurrent droughts in agriculture, default by farmer borrowers has been a rule than an exception. Thus, such farmers are put to financial stress in addition to drought. The 'exponential' discounting overestimates the interest payable by borrowers due to the exponential growth. This 'interest rate' is subsumed to incorporate: (i) opportunity cost of capital, (ii) uncertainty in investment, and (iii) intensity of time preference. The 'hyperbolic' discounting separately incorporates the intensity of time preference.

This paper has three purposes: (a) to analyse the differences in loan repayment using exponential and hyperbolic discounting for groundwater irrigation to financial institutions; (b) to compute the real rate of change in investment per irrigation well in hard rock areas, and (c) draw implications on the choice of discount rate and discounting method while analysing natural resource economics and ecological economic issues.

* The senior author thanks the Ford Foundation, New Delhi for the grant no. 995-1103 which made this study possible.

14.2 Hyperbolic Discounting

The process of discounting at a higher rate to get a payoff sooner and at a lower rate to get a payoff over long time horizon is 'hyperbolic' discounting. When a person has a choice that s/he can receive Rs. 10 today *versus* Rs. 11 tomorrow, s/he prefers immediate payment, even at high discount rate; but, when s/he has a choice of Rs. 11 in 101 days compared with Rs. 10 in 100 days, s/he prefers Rs. 11 in 101 days, even though the gap between both the payments is still one day. Thus, individuals discount the future hyperbolically, with a much greater discount rate in the short run than in the long run. Hyperbolic discounting was first used by psychologists (Jonathan, 2000; Chung and Herrnestein, 1967) to characterise animal behaviour and later applied to humans. Others used hyperbolic discounting to inter-generational utility flows and for intra-personal utility flows (Laibson, 1996). Researchers are increasingly finding that discounting is closer to 'hyperbolic' than an 'exponential' function (Dasguptha and Maskin, 2004). This difference between exponential and hyperbolic discount rate is due to 'dynamic inconsistency' as demonstrated in the example above.

Thus, 'hyperbolic' discount function is characterised by high discount rate over short time horizon and a relatively low discount rate over long horizons. From today's perspective, the discount rate between two far off periods 't' and 't+1', is a long-term low discount rate. From the perspective of time t, the discount rate between 't' and 't+1' is a short-term high discount rate. Thus, if borrowers are 'hyperbolic': (i) they prefer low levels of liquid wealth, (ii) indulge in frequent credit card borrowing, (iii) consumption and income co-move, (iv) consumption drops at retirement and so on (Laibson, 1996).

Hyperbolic discounting is a declining function, where the degree of discounting is inversely proportional to time 't', qualified by degree of time preference 'α', as given in:

$$\text{Present value}_t = \text{Future value}/[1 + \alpha t]^{(r/a)}$$

Where t = time, r = interest rate and α = intensity of time preference, varying between 0 and 1, with 0 representing low or no time preference and 1 representing high time preference. Obviously if there is no time preference, present value = future value. If time preference or α = 1 or 100 per cent, and if r is a fraction (say 5 per cent), then, present value in hyperbolic discounting is lower than that in exponential discounting, because 't' is non-exponential in 'hyperbolic', while 't' is exponential in exponential rule. Hence, degree of discounting/ compounding in 'hyperbolic' is lower than in 'exponential' method.

Thus, the higher the value of α, lower is the difference between the discounted values obtained in the near and distant future. The lower the value of α, wider is the difference between discounted values obtained in the near and distant future. Due to hyperbolic discounting, the present values fall less drastically compared to exponential discounting as the interest rate is weighted by alpha, the parameter, indicating degree of time preference. Hyperbolic discounting provides smoothened cash flows (Table 14.1 and Figure 14.1). The exponential discounting is as usual given by Present value$_t$ = Future value / $[1 + r]^t$.

Table 14.1

Hyperbolic Discount Functions under Varying Values of Intensity of Time Preference 'α' (at r = 5 per cent and 10 per cent)

Time 't' in Years	Hyperbolic Discount Value of Rupee 1 at r = 0.1 and		Hyperbolic Discount Value of Rupee 1 at r = 0.1 and		Hyperbolic Discount Value of Rupee 1 at r = 0.1 and	
	α=0.05	α=0.1	α=0.3	α=0.5	α=0.7	α=0.9
0	1.0000	1.0000	1.0000	1.0000	1.0000	1.0000
1	0.9070	0.9091	0.9163	0.9221	0.9270	0.9312
2	0.8264	0.8333	0.8550	0.8706	0.8824	0.8919
3	0.7561	0.7692	0.8074	0.8326	0.8508	0.8647
4	0.6944	0.7143	0.7689	0.8027	0.8264	0.8440
5	0.6400	0.6667	0.7368	0.7784	0.8066	0.8274
6	0.5917	0.6250	0.7095	0.7579	0.7902	0.8136
7	0.5487	0.5882	0.6858	0.7402	0.7760	0.8018
8	0.5102	0.5556	0.6650	0.7248	0.7637	0.7915
9	0.4756	0.5263	0.6465	0.7111	0.7528	0.7824
10	0.4444	0.5000	0.6300	0.6988	0.7430	0.7743
11	0.4162	0.4762	0.6150	0.6877	0.7341	0.7669
12	0.3906	0.4545	0.6013	0.6776	0.7261	0.7602
13	0.3673	0.4348	0.5888	0.6683	0.7187	0.7540
14	0.3460	0.4167	0.5772	0.6598	0.7118	0.7483
15	0.3265	0.4000	0.5665	0.6518	0.7055	0.7429
16	0.3086	0.3846	0.5566	0.6444	0.6995	0.7380
17	0.2922	0.3704	0.5473	0.6375	0.6940	0.7334
18	0.2770	0.3571	0.5386	0.6310	0.6888	0.7290
19	0.2630	0.3448	0.5304	0.6248	0.6838	0.7249

Figure 14.1

Hyperbolic Discount Function with Varying Levels of Intensity of Time Preference 'α' at Rate of Interest = 10 Per cent

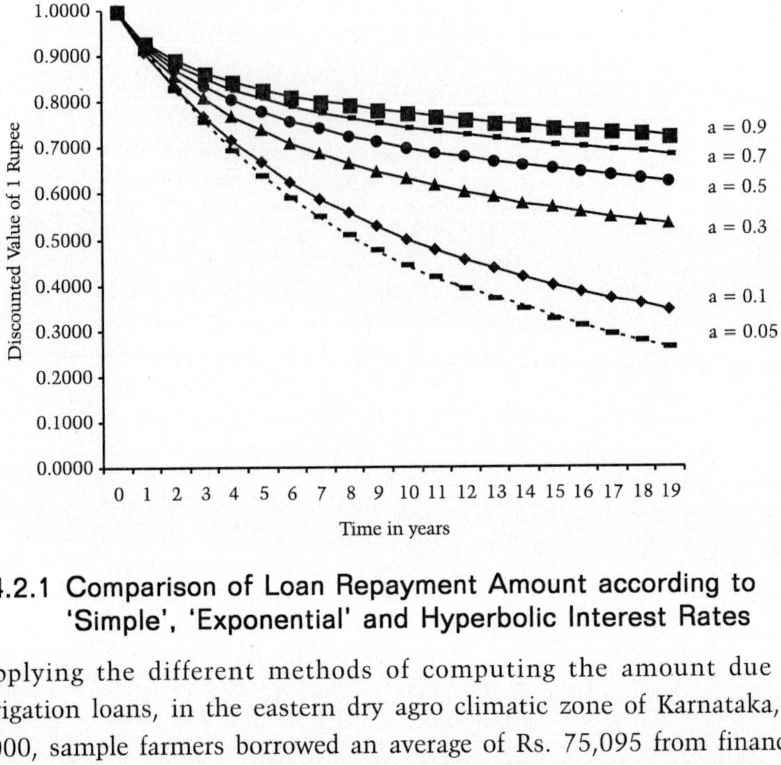

14.2.1 Comparison of Loan Repayment Amount according to 'Simple', 'Exponential' and Hyperbolic Interest Rates

Applying the different methods of computing the amount due on irrigation loans, in the eastern dry agro climatic zone of Karnataka, in 2000, sample farmers borrowed an average of Rs. 75,095 from financial institution to drill an irrigation bore well (430 feet deep) and installed a 12 HP/12 stage submersible pump set. The average gross irrigated area is around 3.8 acres. The financial institution charged an interest rate of 9 per cent for a repayment period of 10 years. As this is an agricultural loan, the terms of repayment on simple interest rate basis amounted to Rs. 1,42,680 (Table 14.2).

However, as farmers were unable to repay the loan in time due to groundwater overdraft and associated scarcity factors in hard rock areas in addition to recurrent drought, the repayment will no longer be on simple interest basis due to default. Thus, the repayment is converted to 'exponential' or 'compound' interest basis with which the total repayment works to Rs. 1,77,777. This substantially increases the burden on farmer due to compounding process in the exponential compound growth function.

Table 14.2

Total Repayment Due on Irrigation Well Loan, from Financial Institution on the Basis of Simple Interest, Compound Interest and Hyperbolic Interest for T = 10 Years, R = 9 Per cent

Sl.No.	Dry Agro-Climatic Zone of Karnataka	Initial Investment on Irrigation Well (Rs.)	Total Repayment due on Simple Interest Basis	Total Repayment due on 'Exponential' or Compound Interest Basis	Total Amount Due on 'Hyperbolic' Interest Basis at		
					$\alpha = 0.1$	$\alpha = 0.5$	$\alpha = 0.9$
1	Northern	53,478	101608	126602	99793	73831	67324
2	Central	45,000	85500	106531	83973	62126	56652
3	Eastern	75,095	142680	177777	140132	103676	94539

However, using the hyperbolic basis, for 10 years, at 9 per cent, for $\alpha = 0.9$, the total repayment amounts to Rs. 94,539, while it amounts to Rs.1,40,132, for $\alpha = 0.1$. Thus, weighting the interest rate by intensity of time preference in computing repayment amount will benefit farmers on 'hyperbolic' basis. In addition, irrespective of the value of α, the intensity of time preference, the 'hyperbolic' basis repayment will be lower than even the 'simple interest' basis, *ceteris paribus* the discount rate and the period t of repayment.

The purpose of 'hyperbolic' basis of discounting is to reflect the reality of the future/present valuation of long term lending to irrigation, where in by accommodating the intensity of time preference, the future value is allowed to oscillate in a narrow plausible range, unlike exponential discounting, where future values not only range widely but are also unrealistic. Thus, by adopting 'hyperbolic' basis, financial institutions lending at least for agriculture purposes will have adopted a procedure, which is equitable for farmers to invest in agriculture.

14.3 Choice of Discount Rate in Resource Economics Analysis

Researchers are often confronted with the choice of discount rate as well as the method of discounting for estimating the amortised cost of long-term investment in agriculture including groundwater irrigation. The obvious choice is to use the opportunity cost of capital, which is the prevailing rate of around 9 per cent (compounded in exponential basis), charged on long-term agriculture loans. However, using the 'exponential' basis does not provide a realistic amortised cost of irrigation as it over estimates the value of investment due to 'exponential' basis as demonstrated above. In order to obtain an empirical estimate of this rate of interest, using field data from farmers in three dry agro-climatic zones of Karnataka (Shamsundar, 1996; Sripadmini, 2001; Chaitra, 2002; Rajendra, 2003), nominal investment per irrigation well is considered (Table 14.3). The nominal investments are then deflated using the index number of wholesale prices (with 1993-94 as base year).

Table 14.3

Nominal and Real Investment Per Irrigation Well in Different Agro-Climatic Zones of Karnataka

Zones##	Investment per Irrigation Well				Nominal Interest Rate* (%)	Real Interest Rate ** (%)	Estimated Cost of Irrig Well in 2005 @ Nominal Int Rate# (Rs.)
	Initial Year and Wholesale Price Index Number in Parentheses	Nominal (Actual) Investment in Initial Year (Rs.)	Terminal Year and Wholesale Price Index Number in Parentheses	Nominal (Actual) Investment in Terminal Year (Rs.)			
(NDZ) Dug well	1982 (38.71)	25833	2002 (161.2)	53478	3.7	-0.17	59578
(CDZ) Bore well	1984 (43.63)	18480	2000 (150.9)	45000	5.7	-2.17	59193
(EDZ) Bore well	1985 (44.99)	32857	2000 (150.9)	75095	5.6	-2.5	97702

Note: * Nominal interest rate refers to the estimated exponential interest rate using nominal investment per well between initial and terminal years.

** Real interest rate refers to the estimated exponential interest rate using deflated nominal investment per well between initial and terminal years using index numbers of wholesale prices with 1993-94 base.

estimated cost of well in 2005 is the nominal investment per well in the initial year compounded in 2005 (using exponential interest rate).

(NDZ)-Northern Dry Zone; (CDZ)- Central Dry Zone; (EDZ)- Eastern Dry Zone.

Considering nominal and real change in investment per irrigation well between the 1980s and 2000s in the three agro-climatic zones of Karnataka, with 'exponential' discounting, the nominal investment per well is found to be increasing between 3.7 and 5.7 per cent. This shows that the amortisation of groundwater investment hovers in the range of

3 to 6 per cent. The real (exponential rate of) interest is computed for deflated initial year investment and terminal year investment per irrigation well deflated using the 1993-94 base all India wholesale price index numbers. It is found that in real terms, the investment per well is falling between –2.5 per cent and –0.17 per cent (Table 14.3). This fall in real investment is due to increased competition by rig owners in offering an almost uniform rate of drilling (in relation to inflation) over the years in several aquifers of Karnataka. For instance, the price of drilling has been between Rs. 35 and Rs. 50 per feet between 1985 and 2005 for shallow bore wells. The phenomenon may not be very different in other states of hard rock regions in the country.

A comparison of nominal investment in terminal year and the estimated cost of well in 2005 indicates that in the northern dry zone, the nominal change in investment per well is 3.7 per cent while the real change in investment per well is –0.17 per cent. Thus, the investment per well in 2002 (terminal year) being Rs. 53,478 and in 2005 (current year) being Rs. 59578 is comparable. But in the central dry zone, while the nominal investment per well in 2000 is Rs. 45,000, the estimated investment in 2005 is Rs. 59,193, which is an unrealistically high exponential growth obtained by compounding the initial investment of Rs. 18,480 from 1984 to 2005. Similarly, in eastern dry zone while the actual investment per well in 2000 is Rs. 75,095, the estimated investment per well in 2005 works to Rs. 97,702, which is an overestimated growth. The real rate of change in investment per irrigation well being negative in different agro-climatic zones is one of the reasons for mushrooming of irrigation wells in Karnataka, since this makes investment affordable across different classes of farmers.

Apparently, the above analysis has two messages: (i) the nominal rate of interest used for amortising investment on irrigation well to cost the groundwater, can be around 3 to 6 per cent and (ii) the real investment per well is falling.

14.4 Implications

Considering the associated risks and uncertainties in agriculture in general and in groundwater irrigation in particular, financial institutions can choose to adopt 'hyperbolic' discounting method to compute the dues in long term groundwater irrigation loans including agriculture loans. This will reduce the loan burden on farmer borrowers and serve the purpose of equity. While amortising investment on irrigation wells, resource economists need to consider a realistic nominal growth rate of around 3 to 6 per cent. However the real rate of interest is negative ranging from –0.17 per cent to –2.50 per cent. Natural resource economists/ecological economists valuing contribution of groundwater irrigation on farms irrigated by wells can use a social rate of around 2 per cent hyperbolic, considering the inter-generational equity, sustainability in groundwater use and the societal concerns.

References

Chaitra, B.S. (2002). *Valuation of Synergistic Role of Canals and Tanks in Groundwater Recharge in the Framework of Optimal Control Theory*. M.Sc. thesis (unpublished). Submitted to UAS. Bangalore.

Chung, S.H. and R.J. Herrnestein (1967). "Choice and delay of reinforcement", *Journal of Experimental Analysis of Behaviour* 10: 67-74.

Dasguptha, Partha and Eric Maskin (2004). *Uncertainty and Hyperbolic Discounting*. Faculty of Economics, University of Cambridge and Institute for Advanced Study, Princeton, University of Princeton, pp. 1-21.

Jonathan, B. (2000). "Can we use human judgements to determine the discount rate?", *Working paper*, Department of Psychology, University of Pennsylvania, p. 16.

Laibson, D. (1996). "Hyperbolic discount functions under saving and savings policy", *NBER working paper*, 5635, Cambridge, Manchester.

Department of Economics, Princeton University.

Rajendra, A. (2003). *Optimal Extraction of Groundwater Resource in Canal, Tank and Well Irrigation Commands in Karnataka-An Application of Control Theory*. M.Sc. thesis (unpublished), Department of Agricultural Economics, University of Agricultural Sciences, Bangalore.

Shyamasundar, M.S. (1996). *Interplay of Markets, Externalities and Equity in Groundwater Development-An Economic Study in the Hard Rock Areas of Karnataka*. M.Sc. thesis (unpublished), Department of Agricultural Economics, University of Agricultural Sciences, Bangalore.

Sripadmini, R. (2001). *Relative Economic Performance of Watershed Development Project under Different Management Protocols in Karnataka*. M.Sc. thesis (unpublished), Department of Agricultural Economics, University of Agricultural Sciences, Bangalore.

Section IV

Poverty

15 Seven Lessons of Poverty Alleviation Programmes

V.S. Vyas

15.1 Introduction

I value this opportunity to join friends and admirers of Dr. V.M. Rao in felicitating him. Our association goes back to the years when we both were research students in what was then, Bombay School of Economics and Sociology, working under one of the most sagacious and erudite teachers, Prof. M.L. Dantwala. During those days, and ever since then, Dr. Rao has impressed everyone who came in contact with him by his scholarship and rigour. To those of us who have the added advantage of his warm friendship, his human qualities are equally impressive. This rather rare combination of scholarship, transparent sincerity and empathy for the downtrodden finds best expression in his writings on poverty, deprivation and inequality. I thought, therefore, appropriate that I should share on this occasion my own views on a subject close to Dr. Rao's heart, namely, lessons we have learnt on poverty alleviation in our country.

Right from Independence, in fact even in the pre-Independence era, India's leaders have accepted poverty alleviation as a major objective of economic policy. During all these years, there has been a national consensus on achieving this goal. Such consensus could emerge due to the participatory character of India's struggle for freedom, in which the poor masses played an active role, while a majority of upper classes sided with the colonial power. Former, naturally, expected a better deal after Independence. In the competitive, multi-party, democratic political system in our country it became necessary to woo them to obtain their electoral support. The emphasis on poverty alleviation in India's development strategy continued also due to the lingering influence of Gandhi with his plea to reach the benefit of freedom "unto the last".

It was not only an articulation of national consensus by leaders of all important political parties and social organisations on various fora. The goal of poverty alleviation was translated in huge public investment for a variety of poverty alleviation programmes (PAP) in each successive five year plan. One or the other type of PAP was initiated right from the inception of the planning era. The focus of these programmes shifted from time to time: from a community development programme to land reforms legislation to the targeted programmes for disadvantaged sections and marginal areas. Effort to reach the poor was made through different types of institutional arrangements: state bureaucracies, Panchayati Raj institution, cooperatives, specialised institutions, NGOs etc.

The programmes in the past as well as those perused currently have encompassed all the different forms of poverty alleviation measures. There are policies of income transfers as reflected in PDS; there are employment generation programmes as well as the programmes for self-employment in the household enterprises; various schemes for rejuvenating natural resources, especially in the dry and marginal areas, have been launched. Safety nets for the old and handicapped are provided. Special dispensations are made to provide the basic facilities of health, education and housing for the poor. It is fair to say that there is hardly any form of public intervention for poverty alleviation, which is not tried out in India.

The results on the other hand, are not commensurate either to the proclaimed objective of poverty alleviation or to a sizeable investment in a variety of programmes and projects designed to meet this objective. At best, the poverty reduction since the early 1970s, when we started collecting more reliable data through carefully conducted national sample surveys, to the end of the nineties has averaged approximately 1 per cent per annum. The pace might have slightly quickened in the last quinquennium of the nineties. The proportion of the poor households to the total households, which was around 52 per cent in the early 70s, is now hovering around 26 per cent. There are indications that the pace of poverty reduction has probably accelerated a little during the mid nineties. However, some reputed scholars have challenged this conclusion. A number of the developing countries, who did not proclaim poverty alleviation as a national goal, have fared much better than India in this respect.

The moot question, therefore, is why we have not been able to achieve the objective of poverty reduction to a substantial extent.

15.2 Seven Lessons of Poverty Allevation Programmes

After a review of the experiences of poverty alleviation in the country as a whole, and with more detailed examination of poverty alleviation programmes in different states of the Union, I would advance following important conclusions from the experience of decades of poverty alleviation programmes in this country.

15.2.1 Economic Growth Matters, but the Pattern of Economic Growth is More Important

The overall economic growth in India till very recently was not substantial, the per capita income rose between 2 to 3 per cent per year during the last three decades. Therefore, the relationship between rapid economic growth and poverty alleviation cannot be established firmly at the national level. However, there is ample evidence to suggest that the states which had a poor record of economic growth, had also a miserable record of poverty alleviation. The reverse, however, is not always true. There are states where relatively speaking, better growth in GDP was recorded without a proportionate decline in poverty. A close examination of the impact of economic growth on poverty alleviation suggests that the growth, which was accompanied with the development of the infrastructure and/or triggered by agricultural development, made salutary impact on the poor. In other words, the 'trickle down' effect of economic growth is strong only when the growth is accompanied with infrastructure development which permits speedy percolation of the benefits and is lead by a labour absorbing sector, such as agriculture.

15.2.2 Macro Policies Matters, More So Their Impact at the Micro Level

Micro initiatives can be supported or frustrated by pricing, trade, monetary and fiscal policies at the macro level. It is becoming clear that the macro policies addressed to generating employment and keeping down the "real" price of food are helpful to the poor. The role of macro policies has become particularly important in the present context when significant changes are expected in the thrust of major economic policies with the emphasis on competition at domestic as well as global levels. If the two important objectives, *viz.*, employment generation and stable food prices, were not woven into the policy framework, incidence of economic adjustment would unjustly fall on the poor.

15.2.3 Decentralisation of Decision-making is Important for an Effective Programme

Poor is not a homogeneous mass. In terms of the nature and extent of deprivations, asset ownership and geographical location, the poor households differ from one another. Centralised decision-making and resource allocation cannot be discriminatory to the extent warranted by the specific characteristics of different groups of disadvantaged households. The approach to have uniform programmes for all poor households has not succeeded. The earlier efforts to address, distinctly and separately, a particular disadvantaged section (e.g. through small and marginal farmers development agencies or landless labourers development agencies) was substituted by a more general approach in the recent years. This has proved to be a retrograde step. It is clear that the poverty alleviation programmes have to be location-specific and section-specific. If that is agreed, then by very definition they can be managed effectively only in a decentralised way. Strengthening of the Panchayati Raj institutions may help in the better implementation of the programmes, provided the *panchayats* are made truly participatory and are given adequate resources. In this respect, after the initial spurt, one can now discuss a 'fatigue'; with PRI losing support in the decision-making quarters.

15.2.4 Access to Assets, Reproducible or Non-reproducible is Important

Even in a dynamic market economy, certain sections can remain at the periphery and continue to be marginalised. The poor can respond to the market stimuli only if they have resources to respond to market signals. Such resources could be land, other productive assets, marketable skills or even physical stamina.

It is proving to be increasingly more difficult to redistribute a non-reproducible resource such as land. This, however, is not a critical handicap for poverty alleviation as the non-land assets, which are by and large reproducible, are gaining in importance. For example, in the rural areas non-farm enterprises supported by research, extension, marketing and credit can contribute more to poverty alleviation than the distribution of land in tiny plots, though the latter may have justification on social and political grounds. Along with productive assets, access to health, education and skills formation also improve endowment of the individuals, and can make significant contribution in bringing the poor households in the mainstream of development.

15.2.5 Improving Market Value of the Activities of the Poor is Important

Investment in providing assets to the poor by itself has not succeeded in achieving the objective of poverty alleviation. We have the Integrated Rural Development Programme (IRDP) type of poverty alleviation initiatives, which have proved extremely costly and at best, only partially successful in achieving the stated objective. The value-added by resources owned by the poor, be it land or animal or other productive assets, is extremely low. It is only when the activities of the poor result in adding value to their produce that they are able to cross over the poverty line. This underlines the importance of "value addition" to the produce of the enterprises owned by the poor. In this context, appropriate technology of production and effective marketing arrangements play critical roles. A neglected area in this respect is the mitigation of enhanced risks which the changeover to high value activity, generally, entail.

15.2.6 The Congruence between the Delivery System and the Recipients is Important

India has extensive network of institutions catering to various needs. However, these institutions take as their clients the middle and upper middle strata of the society; in case of rural areas, the medium and the large farmers. They find it difficult to cater to the needs of the poor, mainly because of the high transaction cost of dealing with the groups who demand/offer goods and services intermittently and in low quantities. Special institutions have to be designed which can cope with the characteristics of the poor both as the consumers and as the producers. It is possible to design such delivery mechanisms even in a competitive market situation, as proved by the self-help groups organised for the dispension of credit, or the Amul pattern of milk cooperatives to market milk produced in the poor households. Delivery systems which are attuned to the characteristics of the poor have made significant and positive impact in terms of the "value addition" in the poor households and enterprises owned by the poor. Lack of institutional support makes the task of the poor, as producers as well as consumers, all the more difficult.

15.2.7 Uni-dimensional Approach to Poverty Alleviation has Failed

The poverty is measured, mostly, in economic terms, i.e., in reference to a benchmark income. The poverty, in fact, is a reflection of the deprivations which are not only economic but also social, political and even cultural. The lasting measures of poverty alleviation would also imply, for example, providing dignity to the poor, providing respect and regards for the women folk and, respect for and pride in their culture and way of life. There are several instances in our country, as in other countries, which show that removal of income poverty by public interventions does not result in alleviating deprivations in the social and cultural spheres. It only leads to a "dependency syndrome", or moral perversion, or both. This suggests the importance of emphasis on social and political awakening along with the economic upliftment, and also underlines the role of social movements, social reforms and social institutions.

These lessons have important implications for designing and implementing poverty alleviation programmes to meet one of the important Millennium goals, i.e., reducing poverty to significant extent within quarter of a century.

16 Improving Food Security for the Poor*

R. Radhakrishna

16.1 Introduction

Achievement of food security, particularly, for the poorest segments of the population, has been a major goal of development policy in India since the beginning of planning. This can be accomplished through increased food production, though arguably a necessary, but not a sufficient condition. The improvement in food production contributes to meeting the needs of the poor if it takes place in an environment of pro poor growth. Since growth has not been inclusive, the government has been implementing specific policies for achieving the food security of the poor and relying on numerous policy instruments such as targeted food rationing, price subsidies, employment programmes and feeding schemes. Stability of food grain prices, besides being a direct measure of food security, is considered important for both employment generation and poverty alleviation.

During the mid sixties when the food situation was critical, India opted for a production strategy of spreading the high yielding variety (HYV) seed-fertiliser technology in a few high potential regions through a policy package consisting of output price support and input price subsidies. The policy choice was based on the presumption that positive agricultural price incentives would accelerate food grain output through the spread of new technology, particularly in high potential areas in both small and large holdings. There was an explicit recognition that the new strategy might aggravate inter-regional and inter-class inequalities, but such adverse consequences were sought to be neutralised through a

---

* This paper draws on Radhakrishna *et al.* (2004) and Radhakrishna (2005).

public distribution policy[1] (Dantwala, 1976). Since then, food management in India has come to include a food procurement programme (with support prices as major policy instrument), a public distribution system (which moves grains from the surplus to the deficit states) and a buffer stock policy for stabilising food grain prices. The intervention system has remained more or less the same even in the post-reform period.[2]

During the past four decades, government intervention in the food grain market has expanded in scale. Procurement as a proportion of gross output has risen from 1.76 per cent in 1961-1965 to 17.5 per cent in 1998-2001 (these proportions would double if marketed surplus is considered instead of gross output); government supplies (allocations) as a proportion of total domestic supply (net availability) increased from 8.3 to 19.7 per cent and government's food grain stocks increased from a negligible level in the early sixties to 48.2 million tonnes in January 1993 which formed about one quarter of gross output and exceeded the buffer stock norm by a factor of three. In 2003-04, the intervention package, in the form of food subsidy, costed the government Rs. 25160 crore.

In the early years, the efforts have produced beneficial effects. Producer incentives have resulted in a steady increase in the production of rice and wheat and, in the second half of the 1970s, the food economy witnessed the beginning of its transition from food grain scarcity to food grain surplus. In the most recent period, India has exported food grains.[3] The current level of food grain production is adequate to meet

---

1. Since assured water is a prerequisite for the adoption of HYV, the new technology could spread only in the areas with irrigation facilities as well as with high rainfall. The problem of equity has also arisen because the principle of cost recovery has not been followed for water, electricity etc.

2. The instruments of intervention include: (a) minimum support price for 24 agricultural commodities, (b) buffer stocking of rice and wheat, (c) levy on rice and sugar mills, (d) subsidy on fertilisers, (e) lower user charges for canal water and electricity for irrigation, and (f) regulation of domestic trade practices such as restrictions on private stocks (see for details, Acharya and Chaudhuri, 2001).

3. Liberalisation of exports undertaken during the 1990s has facilitated India to emerge as a major exporter of rice, accounting for about one-fifth of global rice trade. However, the price received for Indian exports was substantially lower than that in the international market for a comparable grade (Chand and Jha, 2001).

the basic food requirement of each and every person. India was also able to protect its domestic food prices from the volatility of prices in the international market. Notably, domestic rice and wheat prices showed less variability as compared to international prices.

The food management system has come under severe criticism on several grounds, particularly after the implementation of the recent economic reforms (Radhakrishna *et al.*, 1997; GoI, 2002). The reasons include: the system consumed substantial budgetary resources; fertiliser and food subsidies absorbed nearly 8.4 per cent of Central government expenditure and 1.4 per cent of GDP in 2001-02. The input subsidies benefited only the big producers and traders. Moreover, this type of subsidies results in inefficient use of resources.

Another major criticism is that the price support measures are highly selective, benefitting only the producers of rice and wheat from the surplus states of Punjab, Haryana and Uttar Pradesh and parts of Andhra Pradesh (Government of India, 2002). Consequently, the growth of food grain output is biased in favour of rice and wheat which helps these four states. The regulatory framework, it is argued, has become producer-driven and the formulation and implementation of price policy is being constrained by pressures from the farm lobbies. Thus, the price support system has contributed to the widening regional inequality in agricultural growth.

It is also being argued that the government supplies through PDS are not very effective in raising the food security levels of the poor particularly in states like Bihar and Orissa which have high incidence of poverty as well as food insecurity (Radhakrishna *et al.*, 1997). Food grain offtake by states for distribution among beneficiaries has been progressively falling short of the Central allocations in some of the poorest states because of fiscal crunch. What is worse is that the retail delivery system does not exist in some states and even if it exists, it is non-functional and is used only for the distribution of kerosene.

It is being argued that the food management system which was mainly evolved in response to the food crisis in the mid-sixties has remained morbid, although the macro food grain scenario has experienced transition from scarcity to surplus situation. It is suggested that the food policy should be reoriented taking into consideration the ongoing changes in the domestic and international economic scene which places greater reliance on market forces and give a greater role to NGOs, private sector etc., in the implementation of the food policy. However, the fact that there are vulnerable groups mainly in the adverse agro-climatic regions, slums, etc., exposed to the risk of chronic food insecurity should not be lost sight of. In case of increasing reliance on the market, measures to counter abnormal situations such as floods and droughts occurring once in a while, should be firmly put in place.

The reforms undertaken in the 1990s in agricultural sector were slower than in other sectors. The major reforms include: abolition of restrictions on inter-zonal trade, increasing the role of private agencies in the distribution of inputs, provision of services and in extension, etc. Nevertheless, the role of Food Corporation of India (FCI) in interregional trade remained more or less intact and in fact, FCI has crowded out private agencies in interregional trade (GoI, 2002).

The agricultural terms of trade have improved during the reform period, though the improvement can be attributed mainly to the reforms undertaken in the industrial sector and in trade and exchange rate. The membership of WTO may force India to undertake further reforms in agricultural institutions as well as in its supportive institutions (GoI, 2002). Whether India becomes a food secure nation by 2020 depends on the efficacy of domestic reforms that ensures pro poor growth.

It is widely believed that the macroeconomic reforms introduced in the 1990s have had an adverse impact on the key determinants of food security of the poor. The flow of resources to the agricultural sector especially to the traditional one has been slowed down in the post reform period, as evidenced by the decline in the public investment in agriculture as well as in the flow of institutional credit. The reforms were also not successful in accelerating the employment growth. In fact, the annual growth rate of employment declined from 2.0 per cent during 1983 to 1993-94 to less than 1.0 per cent during 1993-94 to 1999-2000. These trends need to be reversed for improving food security of the poor. The allocations of public expenditure to wage employment programmes and public distribution of subsidised food have been increased but these are only short term and partial solutions. To achieve labour-intensive growth as well as price stability in the medium term, it is desirable to have a conducive macroeconomic policy environment.

In the post-reform period, especially after India's entry into the WTO, there has been perceptible shift in policy emphasis towards promotion of diversification and commercialisation of agriculture; a value addition through growth of agro-processing industry as well as vertical integration between farmers, processors and retailers; and improvement in the share of agricultural exports in the world market. The impact can be seen in the increased share of fruits and vegetables in agricultural GDP from 18 per cent in 1990-91 to about 32 per cent in 2002-03 and in the emergence of food processing as a major sector. A substantial portion of bank term (investment) credit that was given to the private sector was invested in high tech, storage, marketing, godowns, etc. During 1998-2003, nearly half of the term credit was disbursed for the above sub-sectors. Since the term credit constitutes two-thirds of private investment in agriculture, it can be inferred that a major portion of private investment has been utilised in the modern agriculture.[4] To what extent these developments will improve the food security of the poor depends on their impact on the incomes of small and marginal farmers who constitute nearly 80 per cent of the farmers while their share is only one-third of the total cultivated area.

Recent policy initiatives have benefitted the modern agricultural sector significantly. The deep-seated structural obstacles faced by the traditional agriculture that fall in the domain of agrarian relations were not touched. The other obstacles that include declining soil fertility, declining water table, vulnerability to external shocks etc., were not addressed adequately. What is worse, the role of the state in the development of agriculture is shrinking as evidenced by declining public investment, breaking down of extension machinery and so on. It is widely believed that private sector may not have incentives to perform some of the roles being performed by the government, at least in the medium term, because of the externalities and risks involved. Whether

4. Potential for private investment is high in reforming the food chain systems. It appears that it can absorb Rs.1,40,000 crore.

the modern sector can complement the traditional security in providing food security needs to be examined. The ongoing policy initiatives are likely to drive a wedge between the traditional and modern sectors and these may lead to social disarticulation. Hence, significant attention should be paid to the development of the traditional sector and integration between the traditional and modern sectors is essential. Useful lessons can be drawn from the Asian experience.[5]

Following the brief discussion of changes in the food policy and food management, it is important to make an assessment of the current food security situation and examine the major challenges to realise a food secure world for the poor. Inclusion of malnutrition and identifying the key actions required to overcome malnutrition broadens the concept of food security. This paper utilises the two approaches that are generally used in the assessment of malnutrition, *viz.*: (i) food energy intake and (ii) nutritional status based on anthropometric measures. It also examines whether the food based safety nets have improved food consumption of the poor or not.

16.2 Food Supply

India has made significant progress over time in food production (Table 16.1). The annual growth rate of food production (cereal + non-cereal food) accelerated from 1.87 per cent in the 1960s to 3.0 per cent in the subsequent decade and further to 3.38 per cent in the 1980s. Food production barely kept pace with the population growth in the 1960s, slightly exceeded the population growth in the 1970s, but in the 1980s per capita food production increased at a satisfactory rate of 1.3 per cent per annum. The turnaround in the food supply can be attributed to the significant strides made in cereal production whose annual growth rate increased from 2.48 per cent in the 1960s, to 2.76 in the 1970s and

5. Rao (1996) observes that the impact of post-liberalisation growth on poverty reduction in Asian countries is the greatest in situations where land reforms have been implemented and a high priority has been accorded to physical infrastructure and human resource development. Yield improvements and growth of rural non-farm sector have contributed to the diversification of employment opportunities. This has been the process of transition from an agrarian economy towards an industrial one in many East and South-East Asian countries which experienced sharp reductions in poverty levels (Barker and Dave, 2001).

further to 3.10 per cent in the eighties. The growth patterns are similar between agricultural and food production. The per capita calorie supply growth rates are close to those of per capita food supply. There seems to have been some diversification in food production in the 1980s on account of the impressive growth of output of oilseeds and livestock products (Bhalla and Singh, 2001). The diversification of food production more or less conformed to the growth pattern of domestic demand.

Table 16.1

Food Production Growth Rates

(Per cent per annum)

Year	*Food Production*		*Cereal Production*		*Agricultural Production*		*Calorie Supply*
	Aggregate	*Per Capita*	*Aggregate*	*Per Capita*	*Aggregate*	*Per Capita*	*Per Capita*
1961-1963 – 1971-1973	1.87	-0.42	2.48	0.17	1.86	-0.42	-0.13
1971-1973 – 1981-1983	3.00	0.84	2.76	0.60	2.92	0.76	0.51
1981-1983 – 1991-1993	3.38	1.29	3.10	1.03	3.34	1.26	0.99
1991-1993 – 2001-2003	2.34	0.56	1.29	0.33	2.27	0.49	0.31

Source: FAO STAT.

After an impressive performance in the eighties, the food economy exhibited sluggish growth in the nineties (see Table 16.1). The growth of food production slipped to 2.34 per cent per annum and cereal production to 1.29 per cent. What is disquieting is that the annual growth rate of cereal production has been lower than the historical growth rate of 2.4 per cent during 1960-2003 and has been less than the population growth rate. Ironically, even at the slow growth rate of cereal production, the cereal supply has outstripped the effective market demand and the public food grain stocks have increased to unsustainable levels. Food grain stocks constitute more than one-third of the annual consumption of food grains and are close to three times the norms fixed by the government.

The real cereal price, which showed a decline in the seventies and eighties, registered a rise in the nineties. An increase in cereal price significantly reduces the calorie intake of the poor as is brought out by the available food price elasticity estimates. For the very poor, the food (calorie) elasticity with respect to cereal price is estimated to be –0.51 (–0.74) for rural areas and –0.37 (–0.57) for urban areas (Ravi, 2000). The upward trend in the real price of cereals in the nineties had coincided with a slowdown in the decline of rural poverty during the initial years of reform.

Despite favourable terms of trade for agriculture and the normal behaviour of the South-West monsoon, the growth of food production has been less impressive in the nineties and the crop diversification, from coarse cereals towards oilseed crops, has come to a halt in the poorer rainfed areas. The sluggish growth could be attributed to:

- The decline in public investment in agriculture especially for irrigation sector witnessed since the early 1980s (the annual growth rate being 4.0 per cent in 1980s, slipped to 1.9 per cent in the 1990s), slowed the expansion in irrigation. The public investment in agriculture (at 1993-94 prices) declined from Rs. 6,443 crore per annum in the 1980s to Rs. 4,837 in the 1990s while that of private investment increased from Rs.7,840 per annum to Rs. 12,299 per annum.[6]
- Low public investment on R&D (0.5 per cent of agricultural GDP as against the one per cent recommended by the ICAR) has affected the technological progress.
- The share of agricultural in total bank credit declined from 16 per cent in March 1990 to 10 per cent in March 2003. The share is way below the stipulated norm of 18 per cent.
- Decline in the annual growth rate of fertiliser use from 7.8 per cent in the 1980s to 4.3 per cent in the 1990s.
- Deceleration in the annual growth rate of area under HYV from 4.9 per cent in the 1980s to 2.8 per cent in the 1990s.

6. The bulk of the private investment seems to have been utilised for hi tech, storage, marketing infrastructure, etc., and only a small share for minor irrigation and land improvement. For instance, during 1998-2003, in the bank term credit advanced to the agricultural sector which accounts for two-thirds of the private agricultural investment, only 10 per cent was utilised for minor irrigation, about 5 per cent for land improvement while 49 per cent had been advanced towards hi tech, storage, marketing and so on (NABARD, *Annual Report 2002-03*).

- The intensive cultivation and rice-wheat rotation year after year has tended to impoverish soil nutrients in the north-western region.

The substantial increase in the minimum support prices for rice and wheat coupled with almost free supply of electricity, although shielded farm incomes from the deceleration in agricultural growth, has resulted in the excessive allocation of land to high cost, water-intensive rice and wheat (GoI, 2002). There has been a shift of cultivation from coarse grains to wheat and rice although yields of coarse cereal have improved. The fixation of minimum support prices and pricing of inputs such as water and electricity are resulting in inefficient resource use and over-exploitation of groundwater.

India has to address the current concerns of decline in public investment, low public investment on R&D and policy distortions and also meet the challenge of limits to growth imposed by land and water resources. Of late, though private investment has registered an up-trend, public investment has stagnated. It should be realised that public and private investments are complimentary and private investment is not a perfect substitute for public investment and normally, the positive externalities cannot be internalised.

16.3 Food Consumption

16.3.1 Cereal Consumption

The NSS data reveal that the per capita cereal consumption has been declining since the early seventies despite a significant increase in per capita cereal production (Radhakrishna and Ravi, 1992; Rao, 2000). The cereal consumption in rural areas fell from 15.35 kg./per capita/month in 1970-71 to 12.7 kg. in 1999-2000 and in urban areas from 11.4 to 10.4 kg. The declining trend is discernible in most of the states particularly in Punjab and Haryana where the decline is as much as 6 kgs per capita per month. What is most conspicuous is the low per capita intake of cereals in a prosperous state like Punjab (10.58 kg. in rural and 9.21 kg. in urban areas in 1999-2000) and higher intake in a backward state like Orissa (15.09 kg. in rural and 14.51 kg. in urban areas). The sharp decline in cereal consumption can be attributed to changes in consumer tastes and preference from food to non-food items, and within the food group from cereals to non-cereal food items and from 'coarse' to 'fine' cereals (Radhakrishna and Ravi, 1992). More recently, Rao (ibid) has shown that the decline in cereal consumption has been greater in rural areas, where the improvement in infrastructure increased the availability of other food and non-food. It has been argued that the reduction in hard manual work in agriculture due to farm mechanisation might have put downward pressure on the nutritional requirements. Rao further observes that a reduction in the intake of cereals on this account should not be taken as deterioration in human welfare.

16.3.2 Food Consumption and Calorie Intake

The per capita cereal expenditure, at constant prices, declined in rural and urban areas during 1970-1998 but the decline was greater in rural areas than in urban areas (Table 16.2). The fall in cereal consumption was more than compensated by the increased consumption of non-cereal food items during the 1970s and 1980s and as a result, per capita calorie intake increased at a moderate rate in both rural and urban areas. However, this did not continue in the 1990s when the per capita calorie intake tended to stagnate (Table 16.3). The leveling of non-cereal food intake in the later part of the 1990s should be a matter of concern. This is due to the changing preferences towards non-food items in the later part of nineties.

In the case of the bottom 30 per cent of the population, there has not been much improvement in the cereal and calorie intake in the rural and urban areas despite a significant improvement in their real per capita expenditure. There has been a substantial diversification of the consumption basket in favour of non-cereal food items and non-food items. These tendencies would not be a major cause of concern if the intake levels were nutritionally adequate. Food diversification is justifiable from a nutritional perspective only if it enhances the nutritional status by increasing the intake of micronutrients, even though it may not add much calories to the diet. Given the state of knowledge, it is extremely difficult to infer about the impact of dietary diversification on the nutritional status. However, what is worrisome is the low per capita calorie intake (1600-1700 k.cal/day) of the bottom 30 per cent which falls short of the required norm. What is still worse, intra-family distribution of food is inequitable in the poor households and the pre-school children get much less than their physiological needs as compared to the adult males and females (NNMB, 2000).

Table 16.2

Annual Growth Rates of Per Capita Total Expenditure, Per Capita Food Expenditure and Per Capita Cereal Expenditure at 1990-91 Prices

(Per cent per annum)

	Bottom 30%	*Middle 40%*	*Top 30%*	*All Classes*
Rural				
Per capita cereal expenditure				
1970-1989	0.09	-0.58	-1.28	-0.69
1990-1998	-1.38	-2.34	-2.43	-2.14
1990-2000*	-1.38	-2.27	-2.30	-2.06
Per capita food expenditure				
1970-1989	1.34	0.87	0.74	0.89
1990-1998	-0.48	-0.78	-1.12	-0.88
1990-2000*	-0.17	-0.40	-0.34	-0.33
Per capita total expenditure				
1970-1989	1.71	1.40	1.45	1.54
1990-1998	1.19	1.11	1.23	1.18
1990-2000*	1.49	1.32	1.41	1.40
Urban				
Per capital cereal expenditure				
1970-1989	0.07	-0.33	-0.18	-0.18
1990-1998	-0.67	-0.55	0.30	-0.28
1990-2000*	-1.36	1.30	-0.73	-1.12
Per capita food expenditure				
1970-1989	1.29	1.19	0.69	0.97
1990-1998	0.08	0.03	-0.23	-0.08
1990-2000*	-0.39	-1.30	-0.73	-1.12
Per capita total expenditure				
1970-1989	1.44	1.50	1.40	1.45
1990-1998	1.70	2.27	3.31	2.77
1990-2000*	1.49	2.11	2.55	2.27

Note: * Includes NSS 55th round.

Source: Updated figures of Ravi (2000).

Micronutrient deficiency is common among the people. Diets of about 80 per cent of rural population contain less than half of normal requirement of Vitamin A (ibid). This deficiency leads to preventable blindness which is common in the rural children. Iron deficiency is widely prevalent among the pregnant women. As per the National Family Health Survey (NFHS-2), about half of the pregnant women suffer from iron deficiency and consequent anaemia. This results in a high incidence of low birth weight children, which in turn contributes to malnutrition.

The most important problem to be attended to is to increase the energy intake of the bottom 30 per cent of the population and at the same time, facilitate diet diversification to meet the micronutrient deficiency. The food gap which works out to about 10 million tonnes per annum can be met from the existing food grain stocks in the medium term and by increasing the purchasing power of this segment of population in the long run. The micronutrient deficiency can be rectified through supplementary nutrition and supply of fortified food.

Table 16.3

Average Per Capita Calorie Intake and its Growth Rates in India

	K. Cal./Day				
Expenditure Classes	*1972-73*	*1977-78*	*1993-94*	*1999-2000*	*1972-2000 Percentage Annual Growth Rate*
Rural					
Bottom 30%	1504	1630	1678	1696	0.6
Middle 40%	2170	2296	2119	2116	-0.1
Top 30%	3161	3190	2672	2646	-0.8
All groups	2268	2364	2152	2149	-0.3
Urban					
Bottom 30%	1579	1701	1701	1715	0.4
Middle 40%	2154	2154	2438	2136	-0.0
Top 30%	2572	2979	2405	2622	0.1
All groups	2107	2379	2071	2156	0.1

Source: Radhakrishna *et al.*, 2004.

16.4 Nutritional Status

16.4.1 Child Malnutrition

The National Nutrition Monitoring Bureau (NNMB) reports provide estimates of child malnutrition based on Gomez classification and chronic energy deficiency of adults based on body mass index. The NNMB estimates show that in rural areas, the incidence of child malnutrition, even though slowly declining, was alarmingly high at 47.7 per cent in 2000-01, which was higher than the income poverty level (Table 16.4). The nutritional status of the tribal children is worse. In 1998-99, over 60 per cent of the tribal children suffered from malnutrition (Table 16.5). NFHS estimates of malnutrition based on standard deviation classification show that in rural areas in 1998-99, 20.3 per cent of children were severely malnourished, another 30.2 per cent were moderately malnourished and 50.5 per cent were malnourished (severe + moderate); in urban areas, 12 per cent were severely malnourished, 27 per cent were moderately malnourished and 39 per cent were malnourished (Table 16.6). Hence, half of the children of India might not have reached their physical or mental potential and about one-fifth might be functionally impaired.[7] Such a high level of wasting away of human resources should be a cause of concern.

While poverty explains the high level of child malnutrition in India, additional factors are responsible. Radhakrishna *et al.* (2004) shows that the risk of child malnutrition decreases with mother's nutritional status, mother's education, consumption of leafy vegetables and increases with household size and birth order.

The decline in malnutrition during 1975-2001 is uneven across states. Kerala and Tamil Nadu states with progressive social and food security have comparatively better nutritional achievements. Orissa showed no improvement. There are also substantial inter-state variations in the decline in malnutrition among the tribal children. Surprisingly,

7. Children of the poor communities suffering from malnutrition not only do not achieve full genetic growth potential and end up as adults with small body size but are also exposed to a greater risk of child mortality. Pelletier *et al.* (1995) identify malnutrition as a major cause of child death in developing countries. Their results reveal that malnutrition, by virtue of its synergistic relationship with infectious disease has a powerful impact on child mortality in India.

there was no improvement during 1985-1999 in the nutritional status of tribal children in Tamil Nadu, a state which witnessed substantial decline in the incidence of child malnutrition in its rural areas. The incidence of malnutrition among the tribal children of Maharashtra was very high and there was no progress in its reduction.

Table 16.4

Per cent Distribution of Children (Aged 1-5 Years) by Nutritional Status (Weight for Age—Gomez) in Rural Areas of Selected States

		Nutritional Grades			
State	*Period*	*Normal*	*Mild*	*Moderate*	*Severe*
Kerala	1975-1979	7.5	35.7	46.5	10.3
(KER)	1991-92	17.6	46.7	29.6	6.0
	2000-01	20.8	50.4	26.9	1.9
Tamil Nadu	1975-1979	6.2	34.2	47.0	12.6
(TN)	1991-92	8.0	39.7	41.7	5.7
	2000-01	10.5	50.6	35.3	3.7
Karnataka	1975-1979	4.6	31.1	50.0	14.3
(KAR)	1991-92	3.6	33.6	54.5	8.3
	2000-01	7.2	45.2	45.2	2.4
Andhra Pradesh	1975-1979	6.1	32.4	46.1	15.4
(AP)	1991-92	9.9	39.2	41.9	8.9
	2000-01	11.5	48.6	35.8	4.1
Maharashtra	1975-1979	3.2	25.4	49.5	21.9
(MAH)	1991-92	4.5	33.3	44.9	17.3
	2000-01	8.2	39.6	48.0	7.2
Gujarat	1975-1979	3.8	28.1	54.3	13.8
(GU)	1991-92	2.4	34.9	50.8	11.8
	2000-01	7.4	43.7	40.0	8.9
Madhya Pradesh	1975-1979	8.4	30.3	45.1	16.2
(MP)	2000-01	5.8	30.4	49.2	14.7
Orissa	1975-1979	7.5	35.9	41.7	14.9
(OR)	1991-92	6.0	38.2	42.5	13.3
	2000-01	6.7	38.9	47.2	7.2
West Bengal	1991-92	9.3	30.1	42.7	17.9
(WB)	2000-01	7.4	43.0	42.9	6.7
All states*	1975-1979	5.9	31.6	47.5	15.0
	1991-92	7.2	36.3	45.1	11.1
	2000-01	9.0	43.3	41.3	6.4

Note: Based on National Centre for Health Statistics (NCHS), standards.

* Pooled estimates for Kerala, Tamil Nadu, Karnataka, Andhra Pradesh, Maharashtra, Gujarat, Madhya Pradesh and Orissa.

n.a.: not available.

Source: National Nutrition Monitoring Bureau (1999). "Diet Nutrition Status of Rural Population Second Repeat Survey", *Technical Report* No.18. National Nutrition Monitoring Bureau (2002). Diet Nutrition Status of Rural Population, *Technical Report* No.21.

Table 16.5

Undernutrition among Tribal Children

Period	*KER*	*TN*	*KAR*	*AP*	*MR*	*GJ*	*OR*	*WB*	*Pooled*
1985-1987	71.8	60.7	82.6	72.3	74.2	73.7	68.1	68.2	71.8
1998-99	55.2	62.6	45.5	56.9	73.6	61.1	62.6	53.8	60.2

Source: National Nutrition Monitoring Bureau (2000). *Diet and Nutritional Status of Tribal Population*. Report of the first Repeat Survey, National Institute of Nutrition, Hyderabad.

NFHS data also reveal substantial inter-state variations in the malnutrition levels in both rural and urban areas (Table 16.6). The percentage of moderately and severely malnourished children among major states in rural areas varied between 29 in Kerala and 59 in Madhya Pradesh and in urban areas from 21 in Jammu and Kashmir to 45.5 in Orissa. In terms of nutritional status of children, middle-income states such as Kerala, Tamil Nadu and Andhra Pradesh performed better than higher-income states like Gujarat, Maharashtra and West Bengal. Not surprisingly, poorer states such as Madhya Pradesh, Bihar and Orissa showed the worst performance.

Inter-state variations reveal weak correlation between nutritional status and per capita SDP as well as between nutritional status and per capita calorie consumption. The state-level mismatch between food intake and nutritional status could be attributed to the differences in women's status, education, health, availability of safe drinking water, environmental sanitation and personal hygiene which intervene between the food intake and nutritional status.[8] A better environment would reduce food wastage caused by infections and diseases.

8. Kerala and Tamil Nadu have better health care and educational facilities and coverage of the PDS. The per child public expenditure on nutrition as well as per capita public expenditure on social sector has been high in these two states for the past few decades.

Table 16.6

NFHS-2 Estimates of State-wise Incidence of Undernutrition (Weight-for-Age) among Children under Age Three

(Percentage)

	Severe Undernutrition			*Moderate Undernutrition*			*Undernutrition (Severe+Moderate)*		
	Rural	*Urban*	*All*	*Rural*	*Urban*	*All*	*Rural*	*Urban*	*All*
Andhra Pradesh	11.6	7.2	10.5	30.4	21.5	28.2	42.0	28.7	38.7
Assam	14.1	7.5	13.7	23.1	19.8	22.9	37.2	27.3	36.6
Bihar	27.4	13.3	26.1	28.4	34.4	28.9	55.8	47.7	55.0
Goa	3.6	6.5	4.7	26.8	21.0	24.6	30.4	27.15	29.3
Gujarat	20.8	10.7	17.0	29.3	28.7	29.1	50.1	39.4	46.0
Haryana	10.7	7.6	10.0	25.8	23.7	25.3	36.5	31.3	35.3
Himachal Pradesh	12.6	6.3	12.1	33.6	24.1	32.9	46.2	30.4	45.0
Jammu & Kashmir	9.2	6.7	8.8	28.5	14.6	26.2	37.7	21.3	35.0
Karnataka	20.1	10.5	17.0	27.2	28.5	27.6	47.2	39.0	44.6
Kerala	5.1	2.9	4.7	23.5	19.5	22.8	28.6	22.4	27.4
Madhya Pradesh	26.2	19.9	24.8	32.8	24.9	30.9	59.0	44.8	55.7
Maharashtra	22.5	11.4	18.1	32.1	33.5	32.6	54.6	44.9	50.7
Manipur	5.4	6.1	5.6	23.1	21.2	22.6	28.6	27.3	28.2
Meghalaya	11.9	15.5	12.3	27.0	22.1	26.4	38.9	37.6	38.7
Mizoram	7.7'	2.3	5.1	25.0	19.6	22.4	32.7	21.9	27.5
Nagaland	8.2	3.2	7.4	17.4	14.9	17.0	25.6	18.1	24.3
Orissa	21.8	16.8	21.2	34.6	28.7	34.0	56.4	45.5	55.2
Punjab	10.0	6.1	9.1	22.8	13.0	20.5	32.8	19.1	29.6
Rajasthan	22.7	15.2	21.1	29.8	31.4	30.1	52.5	46.6	51.2
Sikkim	4.2	5.9	4.4	16.3	17.6	16.5	20.6	23.5	20.9
Tamil Nadu	11.5	10.1	11.0	27.9	24.5	26.7	39.4	34.6	37.2
West Bengal	18.5	9.3	16.8	35.0	23.7	32.9	53.5	33.0	49.7
Uttar Pradesh	23.4	16.7	22.2	31.1	26.6	30.3	54.5	43.3	42.6
New Delhi	27.6	8.8	10.6	25.0	24.0	24.1	52.6	32.8	34.7
Arunachal Pradesh	8.3	4.9	7.8	18.5	14.6	17.9	26.8	19.5	24.7
All India	20.3	12.0	18.4	30.2	27.0	29.4	50.5	39.0	47.8

Note: Children below 2 SD from the international reference population median are treated as suffering from undernutrition.

Source: Estimated from the unit level data of the NFHS-2.

16.4.2 Chronic Energy Deficiency Among Adults

Table 16.7 shows that in rural areas in 2000-01, 37.4 per cent of adult males and 39.4 per cent of adult females suffered from chronic energy deficiency (CED). The inter-state variations in CED are similar to those of child malnutrition. CED was found to be lower in Kerala (22.4 per cent for males and 18.7 per cent for females) and Tamil Nadu (26.7 per cent for males and 38.7 per cent for females) and higher in Gujarat, Maharashtra and Madhya Pradesh (above 40 per cent). Gender differences seem to exist in some states, particularly in Tamil Nadu and was also comparatively higher in West Bengal. As expected tribals suffered more from chronic energy deficiency.

Table 16.7

NNMB Estimates of Chronic Energy Deficiency (CED) among Adults in Rural Areas of Selected States

	Percentage of Adults with BMI less than 18.5			
	Rural Population in 2000-01		*Tribal Population in 1998-99*	
	Males	*Females*	*Males*	*Females*
Kerala	22.4	18.7	39.3	50.4
Tamil Nadu	35.5	38.2	58.1	59.3
Karnataka	36.2	41.7	47.2	53.4
Andhra Pradesh	37.4	42.0	52.4	62.5
Maharashtra	41.3	45.1	57.7	62.3
Gujarat	37.1	33.3	53.9	50.5
Madhya Pradesh	42.8	41.9	47.2	50.0
Orissa	38.6	46.0	43.7	51.6
West Bengal	40.5	45.9	50.6	64.6
Pooled	37.4	39.4	49.3	55.4

	*Pooled BMI for Rural Population**	
	Males	*Females*
1975-1979	55.6	51.8
1988-1990	49.0	49.3
1996-97	45.5	47.7

Note: * Pooled BMI estimate is based on the BMI estimates of 7 states—Kerala, Tamil Nadu, Karnataka, Andhra Pradesh, Maharashtra, Gujarat and Orissa.

Source: Same as Tables 16.4 and 16.5.

16.5 Food Based Safety Nets

India has had a niche for food based safety nets. The emergence of food grain surplus soon after the advent of green revolution has led to food based interventions at household and individual levels. The major food based interventions include the public distribution systems (PDS), integrated child development services (ICDS) and midday meals programme (MDM). Currently, PDS absorbs about 1 per cent of GDP. Public spending on ICDS, MDM, micronutrient programmes and other nutrition programmes amounted to 0.19 per cent of GNP in 1997-98 (Measham and Chatterjee, 1999).

16.5.1 The Public Distribution System

The present public distribution system—a producer price-support-cum-consumer subsidy programme—has evolved from the food grain shortages of 1960s. In the beginning, it was mainly confined to urban and food deficit areas with an emphasis primarily on price stabilisation which continued till the late seventies. Its welfare (distribution of subsidised food especially to the poor) component received attention in the early eighties and the PDS coverage was extended to rural areas. In the wake of economic reforms, the PDS is perceived to be the main safety net to protect the poor from potential short-run price-induced adverse effects. Central food subsidy at Rs. 25,160 crore in 2003-04 accounted for 1.0 per cent of the GDP.

The recent abnormally large increases in procurement prices and the consequent upward revisions in the central issue prices have had an adverse impact on the efficacy of the PDS (see Government of India, 2002). It has resulted in large and unjudicious food stocks with the open ended procurement system, benefiting largely surplus farmers in selected regions. While costs have mounted, the average consumer has not benefited much.

It is important to find out whether the PDS is effective in distributing food to the poor. Many recent evaluation studies have highlighted the severe biases in the inter-regional distributions of the PDS supplies—states with high incidence of poverty like Bihar, Orissa and Madhya Pradesh received a lower share, much lower than their share in poverty. The per capita monthly purchases of cereals from PDS in rural areas in 1999-2000 was lower than half a kg in poorer states in Bihar, Madhya Pradesh, Rajasthan and Uttar Pradesh—while it was 4.6 kg in Kerala, 3.3 kg in Tamil Nadu and 2.3 kg in Andhra Pradesh—states with low incidence of poverty (Table 16.8). The picture is similar in urban areas as well (Table 16.8). Despite its many shortcomings, it should be mentioned that PDS is very effective in protecting the poor by smoothening their consumption from shocks caused by droughts, cyclone etc. Shortcomings in PDS functioning in normal periods should not cloud our assessment of its role in food security. However, reforms are necessary for strengthening its role in the fulfilment of its multiple goals.

Table 16.8

Per Capita Purchase from PDS in 1999-2000

Kg/person/month

Sl.No.	*Rural*			*Urban*		
	Poor	*Non-poor*	*All*	*Poor*	*Non-poor*	*All*
1. Andhra Pradesh	2.56	2.30	2.33	2.32	1.42	1.77
2. Assam	0.98	0.58	0.74	1.02	1.12	1.12
3. Bihar	0.20	0.32	0.26	0.11	0.22	0.19
4. Gujarat	1.11	0.92	0.95	1.47	0.59	0.84
5. Haryana	0.07	0.04	0.04	0.08	0.09	0.09
6. Himachal Pradesh	3.53	2.93	2.97	2.85	2.39	2.43
7. Karnataka	1.50	1.50	1.50	1.35	1.74	1.58
8. Kerala	5.49	4.53	4.62	4.91	4.34	4.47
9. Madhya Pradesh	0.44	0.32	0.36	0.53	0.34	0.43
10. Maharashtra	1.14	1.13	1.13	0.91	0.86	0.87
11. Orissa	1.71	1.46	1.58	0.33	0.85	0.64
12. Punjab	0.00	0.00	0.00	0.01	0.03	0.03
13. Rajasthan	0.22	0.19	0.20	1.07	0.71	0.82
14. Tamil Nadu	3.49	3.30	3.34	2.08	1.99	2.03
15. Uttar Pradesh	0.27	0.20	0.25	0.23	0.21	0.21
16. West Bengal	0.45	0.27	0.32	1.34	1.89	1.76
17. Other states & UTs	3.08	2.32	2.39	3.38	3.15	3.19
All India	0.83	1.08	1.02	1.23	1.21	1.22

Source: B. Sambi Reddy and K. Hanumantha Rao (2003). "Assessment of Targeted Public Distribution System in India", National Institute of Rural Development, Hyderabad.

16.5.2 Integrated Child Development Services

The ICDS launched in 1975 is a centrally sponsored, state-administered nation-wide direct nutrition intervention programme, which integrates supplementary nutrition with primary health care and informal education. It provides six services to under six year old children and mothers: i) supplementary feeding,[9] ii) immunisation, iii) health check ups, iv) referral services, v) health and nutrition education to adult women, and vi) non-formal pre-school education to 3-6 years old. The programme is organised through a chain of projects each of which is located at a community block covering around 1,00,000 population in rural and urban areas and 35,000 population in tribal areas.[10] The *anganwadi* (child care centre) is the focal point in the delivery of services at the village level covering 1000 population. Currently, 34 million children consisting of 23 per cent of the children in the relevant age group and 4.8 million mothers are being provided with supplementary nutrition.

Evaluation studies reveal that most of the beneficiaries belong to the vulnerable groups highlighting the self-targeting nature of the programme design. Moreover, utilisation of Vitamin A, folic acid and immunisation service is better in the ICDS areas. However, the overall impact of ICDS on malnutrition is very limited which could be due to meagre allocation of budgetary resources and faulty project design. Field studies reveal poor quality of services and identify the shortcomings such as: i) irregular supply of food by the state government, ii) lack of community participation either in the running or monitoring the functioning of the ICDS, and iii) housing of *anganwadi* in a dilapidated building located in unhygienic environment. It is suggested that until the quality of services is improved, the coverage of ICDS should not be expanded (Measham and Chatterjee, 1999). It should, however, be stressed that the potential impact of ICDS on malnutrition is high and it is within reach, provided some changes in the programme design are made (ibid).

---

9. The ICDS provides to a child food ration for 300 days, containing 300 k.cal and 12.5 gms protein and to pregnant and lactating women food ration containing 500 k.cal and 12-15 gms protein.

10. The ICDS project located at a community block targets to provide food supplement to 40 per cent of 17,000 children aged under six years and 40 per cent of the pregnant and lactating women.

16.5.3 Midday Meal Programme

The National Programme of Nutritional Support to Primary Education (NPNSE) commonly known as midday meal programme launched in 1995 is another nation-wide central scheme intended to improve enrolment, regular attendance and reduce dropouts as well as improve the nutritional status of primary school children. It provides to a child aged 6-14 years, cooked food comprising 100 gms of food grains (rice or wheat) per school day or 3 kg food grains per month. The scheme is being implemented by *panchayats* and *nagarpalikas*. The scheme covered 108 million primary school children in 2003-04.[11]

The central allocations of food grains have fallen short of the entitlement (Saxena, 2004). Moreover, many state governments do not even meet the norm of Re.1.0 per child fixed by the Centre for their expenditure. According to Saxena (2004), the impact of the programme can be improved by: (a) providing clean space separately for storing and cooking the midday meal with hygienic food items and clean water, (b) utilising the employment programmes for constructing kitchen sheds, (c) giving the task of food preparation to women self-help groups, and (d) supplementing the meal with micronutrients like iron, Vitamin A and iodine. Some of these suggestions are equally applicable to the ICDS.

16.6 Concluding Observations

India has achieved self-sufficiency in cereal availability and emerged in the recent past as a net exporter of cereals. Yet, its high incidence of food insecurity at the household level remains a key concern. This high incidence of food insecurity is due to diets deficient in food energy as well as micronutrients. It is notable that even before food energy needs are met, the consumption basket of the poor is getting diversified; shifting away from food to non-food items; from cereals to non-cereals within the food group; and from coarse to fine cereals within the cereals. This phenomenon seems to be exacerbated in rural areas with

11. For running the scheme, the Central government provides free food grains, meets the salary of the cook and helper and provides transport subsidy of Re.0.50 per quintal for transporting food grains from FCI depo to the school. The state government meets the cost of other food items and other costs involved in running the programme. The Central government spent Rs.1375 crore during 2003-04. The states spent between Re.0.47 and Rs.2 per child (Saxena, 2004).

adequate infrastructure facilitating easier access to outside world. Given these ongoing trends, substantial expansion of the incomes of the poor as well as reduction in gender (intra-household) inequality is required for tackling the chronic food insecurity problem. While food based interventions play a supplementary role, pro poor growth alone can eliminate chronic food insecurity in the long run.

The performance of food based interventions needs to be improved by making them more demand driven. Merely scaling up the coverage of the programmes without improving their quality may not be the best way to reduce malnutrition. For example, PDS provides less than 1 kg. per month to a person under poverty in rural areas despite absorbing 1 per cent of GDP. It is essential to reform the PDS to serve the poor better and simultaneously release some resources needed by the ICDS and MDM. Essentially, all the current food based interventions play a complementary role in mitigating malnutrition over the life cycle of an individual.

References

Acharya, S.S. and D.P. Chaudhuri (2001). "Domestic agricultural marketing practices, incentives, and integration", in S.S. Acharya and D.P. Chaudhuri (ed.), *Indian Agricultural Policy at the Crossroads*. Jaipur: Rawat Publications.

Barker and David Dowe (2001). "The Asian rice economy in transition: Challenges ahead", *Keynote Address*, International Workshop on Medium and Long-Term Prospects of Rice Supply and Demand in the 21st century, International Rice Research Institute, Los Banos, Philippines, 3-5 December.

Bhalla, G.S. and Gurmail Singh (2001). *Indian Agriculture: Four Decades of Development*. New Delhi: Sage Publications.

Chand, R. and D. Jha (2001). "Trade liberalisation, agricultural prices and social welfare", in S.S. Acharya and D.P. Chaudhuri (ed.), *Indian Agricultural Policy at the Crossroads*. Jaipur: Rawat Publications.

Dantwala, M.L. (1976). "Agricultural price policy since Independence", *Indian Journal of Agricultural Economics* 22(2): 1-25.

Government of India (2002). *Long Term Grain Policy*, Department of Food and Public Distribution.

National Nutrition Monitoring Bureau (1999). *Diet and Nutrition Status of Rural Population*. Second Repeat Survey, Technical Report No.18, National Institute of Nutrition, Hyderabad.

———. (2000). *Diet and Nutrition Status of Tribal Population*. Report on First Repeat Survey, National Institute of Nutrition, Hyderabad.

———. (2002). *Diet and Nutrition Status of Rural Population.* Technical Report No.21, National Institute of Nutrition, Hyderabad.

Measham, Anthony R. and Meera Chatterjee (1999). *Wasting Away: The Crisis of Malnutrition in India*. Washington D.C.: World Bank.

Pelletier, D.L., E.A. Frongillo Jr., D.G. Schraeder and J.P. Habicht (1995). "The effects of malnutrition on child mortality in developing countries", *Bulletin of the World Health Organization* 73(4): 443-48.

Radhakrishna, R. (2005). "Food and nutrition security of the poor: Emerging perspectives and policy issues", *Economic and Political Weekly* 30.

Radhakrishna, R. and C. Ravi (1992). "Effects of growth, relative price and preferences on food and nutrition", *Indian Economic Review* 27: 303-323.

Radhakrishna, R., K. Hanumantha Rao, C. Ravi and B. Sambi Reddy (2004). "Chronic poverty and malnutrition", *Working Paper* No.11, Chronic Poverty Research Centre, IIPA.

Radhakrishna, R., K. Subba Rao, S.Indrakant and C. Ravi (1997). "India's public_distribution system: A national and international perspective", World Bank *Discussion Paper* No. 380.

Ravi, C. (2000). *Complete Demand Systems, Welfare and Nutrition: An Analysis of Indian Consumption Data*. Centre for Economic and Social Studies, Hyderabad.

Rao, C.H.H. (2000). "Declining demand for food grains in rural India: Causes and implications", *Economic and Political Weekly*, January 22.

Rao, V.M. (1996). "Agricultural development with a human face: Experiences and prospects", *Economic and Political Weekly* 31(26): A50-A62 (June 29).

Sambi Reddy, B. and K. Hanumantha Rao (2003). "Assessement of targeted public distribution system", (*mimeo*) National Institute of Rural Development, Hyderabad.

Saxena, N.C. (2004). "Food based programmes as safety nets in India", National Workshop on *Protecting the Vulnerable Poor in India: The Role of Social Safety Nets*, World Food Forum, New Delhi, October 6-8.

17

Linkages between Population, Poverty and Environment

*An Exploratory Study from Gujarat State**

Sudarshan Iyengar** and
Jyothis Sathyapalan

17.1 Introduction

Gujarat is one of the most economically developed states in India, ranking fourth in terms of per capita state domestic product (GoG, 1998; Iyengar, 1998). The performance of the State has been better in terms of reduction in poverty level and this is quite evident from a significant decline in poverty level from 41 per cent to 21 per cent during 1972-73 to 1993-94 (Annexure Table A-17.3). However, though overall poverty shows declining trend, urban poverty reveals a sharp increase during the period of 1987-88 to 1993-94, whereas rural poverty remained more or less stagnant. This is very critical issue for development strategy of the state and need careful analysis of problem.

Gujarat's overall decline in poverty can be attributed to mainstream growth strategies and centrally-funded anti-poverty programmes. The focus of these strategies on direct public investment in infrastructure and other services has worked well for regions that have had good potential for the development of the agriculture, industry and service

---

* We are thankful indeed to Dr. Derek Johnson for his painstaking effort in reading and editing the draft paper and providing thoughtful comments. We alone are responsible for the views expressed.

** It was sometime in 1978 when I registered for my Ph.D. and started reading on irrigation economics that I came across Prof. V.M. Rao's writings. His clarity and scholarship impressed and since then it has always been a pleasure and a learning experience reading his work. Much later in 1998, I had an opportunity to contribute an article "Gujarat" in a volume that Prof. V.M. Rao edited on the issue of poverty in India. I am happy that I am now contributing a paper in the volume in his honour along with one of my colleagues on the same poverty theme with some new dimensions that we have been able to bring in.

sectors. The benefits from mainstream approaches have not been evenly spread, however. NSS data demonstrates that poverty continues to persist in some areas and among some groups. Our analysis shows that the areas where poverty persists are also those where environmental degradation is severe and where populations remain highly dependent on the diminished resource base. On first glance, the coexistence of these phenomena would seem to confirm the argument, common in development studies, that poverty is the root cause of environmental degradation. The situation in poverty-prone regions of Gujarat does indeed support the idea of a vicious cycle of poverty and resource degradation. Careful analysis of the circumstances leading to this cycle, and reinforcing it, however, demonstrates that it is a product of larger forces related to the development process itself. The policy implications of our analysis are two-fold. First, further reduction of poverty in Gujarat requires a shift to poverty reduction strategies that better identify and target the poor. Second, these strategies have to engage with the broader social, economic and political factors that lead to the perpetuation or indeed, deepening of poverty. This means that we cannot blame ecological degradation primarily on the poor, though their activities do exacerbate such degradation. We also have to consider the direct and indirect ecological impacts of advantaged groups, including industrialists, wealthy farmers and state departments.

The vicious circle relationship between population, poverty and environment in developing countries has been the focus of extensive analysis (cf. Dasgupta, 1998). As the poor in developing countries depend foremost on their local natural resource base, when these resources are depleted, more hands are needed to gather fuel and water for daily use. This stimulates a high birth rate which, over time, increases pressure on the local resource base and provides further incentive for increased fertility. This is the vicious circle, where poverty, fertility and environmental degradation reinforce one another in escalating manner (Mäler, 1997). The basic reasoning is that desperation impels resource over extraction (Jodha, 1998). In this context, the poor are particularly vulnerable to natural calamities, environmental degradation and ecological disasters (Nadkarni, 2000). The implication of this argument is that the poor are the cause of population growth and the numerous environmental problems of developing countries. It distracts attention from other matters that demand urgent action, such as the need for land reform, poverty alleviation, waste reduction and cleaner and more appropriate technologies. While the vicious circle of poverty and resource degradation is indeed pernicious, the nexus between population, poverty and environment has to be placed in the context of broader forces and agents of development.

17.2 Data and Methodology

It must be stated at the outset that the existing database on natural resources, ecological parameters and environmental indicators is very poor not only in Gujarat but also at the national level. The attempt to collect and create an environmental database is relatively recent. The Central Statistical Organisation (CSO) brought out the first Compendium of Environment Statistics in 1997 following the recommendations of an inter-disciplinary committee struck by the Indian Department of Statistics. CSO has since published the second updated version of the Compendium in 2003. Since it is a new effort, the data for all important parameters and variables are not available at the state level and elements of the database have limitations. Iyengar (2003), for example, has pointed out specific problems with respect to land use database in Gujarat. It may be a long time before such data is compiled and published and an analysis of the kind that we are suggesting can be undertaken on a comprehensive basis. Therefore, this paper should be regarded as a preliminary attempt to examine the linkages between environment and poverty using the data presently available from various sources such as the National Sample Survey Organisation (NSSO), Census records and selected publications of the Gujarat Ecological Commission.

Ideally, we would have liked to examine the population, poverty and environmental data for different ecological and environmental regions within Gujarat. However, systematic and well-accepted regionalisation of Gujarat on the ecological basis has been undertaken only since the mid 1990s. We have, therefore, chosen to base our analysis on the regionalisation undertaken by the NSS. There is some logic to this as their secondary data on population, fertility and poverty by different NSS regions does reflect some distinct environmental characteristics. One of the limitations of this exercise is that we have taken districts as a unit and not as a block (*taluka*). The NSS regions have included all or some blocks in a district in its scheme of regionalisation but for our paper, we have classified the entire district in one particular region avoiding any overlap of districts in more than one NSS region. In order to make data comparable, information provided in Murthi *et al.* (1999) has been used to categorise Census districts in accordance with NSS regions of Gujarat state. The classification of Census districts in conjunction with NSS regions is presented in Table 17.1.

Table 17.1

Classification of Census Districts in Conjunction with NSS Regions of Gujarat State

NSS Regions of Gujarat State	*Census Districts*	*Key Characteristic of the Region*
Gujarat eastern	Surat, Dang, Valsad, Navsari	Tribal area with degraded forest resource base. Tribal *talukas* covered under Tribal Sub-Plan.
Gujarat plain southern	Bharuch, Panchmahal, Dahod, Narmada, Vadodara	Tribal area with degraded forest resource base. Tribal *talukas* covered under Tribal Sub-Plan.
Gujarat plain northern	Sabarkantha, Mehsana Gandhinagar, Ahmedabad Kheda, Anand,	Except Sabarkantha, other districts are non-tribal districts.
Dry region	Kachchh, Banaskantha, Patan, Surendranagar	Arid and semi-arid region covered under drought-prone areas programme and desert development programme.
Saurashtra region	Rajkot, Jamnagar, Junagadh Bhavnagar, Amreli Porbandar	Semi-arid region. Covered under drought-prone areas programme and desert development programme.

Source: Murthi *et al.* (1999).

Among the five NSS regions, Gujarat eastern and Gujarat plain southern are areas with substantial tribal populations with relatively degraded natural resource bases. The eastern and southern plains are also characterised by high level of industrialisation. Industrial development has been highly uneven across the regions, with Kachchh and Saurashtra getting a very small share of the investment in the years following liberalisation (Kundu, 2000). Among the district of northern Gujarat plain, Sabarkantha district is also a tribal area. The dry region that consists of Kachchh, Banaskantha and Patan is poor in terms of the natural resource base that would be suitable for irrigated agriculture. The Saurashtra region mostly consists of semi-arid districts. The data pertaining to poverty, population and natural resource base are analysed across different NSS regions as well as districts.

17.3 Population, Poverty and Natural Resource Base

17.3.1 Population and Poverty

Until 1997, Gujarat state had 19 districts. Some of the districts were bifurcated into two in 1997. A detailed estimation of population for the Census years prior to 2001 has yet to be undertaken and hence, in this paper we present the population growth data for 19 districts distributed within the NSS regions. Annexure Table A-17.1 contains the data on population growth between 1901 and 1991 by NSS regions and districts. Gujarat experienced high population growth between 1941 and 1981. The decadal increase was between 18.69 and 27.67 per cent. The eastern tribal districts experienced higher population growth between 1961 and 1991. The growth during 1981-1991 was higher than that of the state average even when one considers Valsad and Dang districts only, which do not attract labour immigrants from other states in the country, as is the case with Surat district. Districts with major cities such as Ahmedabad, Vadodara, Surat, Rajkot and Gandhinagar in general experienced faster growth in population between 1961 and 1991 due to the high rate of urbanisation. In other NSS regions, districts with tribal population and the dry and arid district of Banaskantha experienced higher population growth between the 1961 and 1991 Census years. Thus, apart from the major cities in Gujarat, population pressure has increased most in dry and arid districts and in some of the districts already having substantial population.

The provisional totals for Gujarat state in 2001, shows that the state ranked 10th among Indian states with respect to population. It is a thinly populated state (258 persons per sq km in 2001) as compared to the national average density of population about 324 persons per sq km in 2001. The state ranks 21st in India in terms of population density. The change in the density of population in 2001 as compared to 1991 was around 22.27 per cent. This is very much nearer to the decadal growth rate of population during the same period. The decadal growth rate of population for the decade 1991-2001 has increased in comparison to 1981-1991 from 21.19 to 22.45. The sex ratio and female literacy were also low in the 2001 Census as compared to many other Indian states. The fertility rate in many parts of Gujarat state is closer to the national average. Gujarat in 2001, thus displays peculiar demographic characteristics. It would be of interest to examine the picture at the NSS regional and district levels.

Detailed information on the selected demographic indicators in different NSS regions and districts has been presented in Annexure Table A-17.2. The regional figures are presented for change in population, fertility, female literacy and poverty. It is remarkable that the Gujarat eastern region with its substantial tribal population experienced significantly higher growth in the population between 1991 and 2001 compared to other regions. While Gujarat state recorded decadal growth of 21.44 per cent, the Gujarat eastern region recorded growth of nearly 30 per cent. Again discounting for Surat and therefore, Surat city, population growth in Valsad and Dang was also substantially higher with figures of 29.66 and 29.58 per cent respectively. The dry region also experienced growth rate equal to the state average. In the remaining three NSS regions, the growth in population was on average lower than the state average. Interestingly, the economically well-developed Gujarat northern plain region comprising of Sabarkantha, Mehsana, Gandhinagar, Ahmedabad, Kheda and Anand districts and semi-arid Saurashtra districts experienced low growth in population with about 18 per cent increase between 1991 and 2001.

The sex ratio is lowest in the northern plain region. The northern plains, which have relatively better economic status, have an adverse sex ratio. Sex selective abortions in rural and urban areas have resulted in a serious imbalance in the sex ratio. The 0-6 population age group sex ratios present a further serious picture with respect to adverse sex ratio. Tribal *talukas* on the whole do not appear to be affected deeply by this menace. The rate of female literacy at around 60 per cent is relatively homogeneous for all areas of Gujarat except for the dry and tribal regions. The state has significant SC and ST populations, which as social groups carry known disadvantages. The tribal population is concentrated in the south and south-east districts and to some extent in two dry districts (Iyengar, 2001).

As per the 2001 Census, the dry and eastern region registered a fertility rate of 3.47 and 2.70 respectively. The literacy rate of the dry region is 43.21 per cent while it 50.19 in the plain southern region. The district-wise analysis provided in Annexure Table A-17.1 also shows that the fertility rate of Banaskantha district in the dry region is around 3.9 and female literacy is about 34.54. A similar case has been reported in a tribal district of Dahod which belongs to the southern plain region and has a fertility rate of 4.30 and female illiteracy of about 31.7 per cent. These are the pockets having high incidence of poverty in Gujarat state.

Table 17.2

Region-wise Variations in Poverty, Population and Fertility

NSS Regions of Gujarat	*Poverty-Headcount Ratio 43rd 50th and 55th Rounds of NSS*			*Population*			
	Rural Poverty 1987-88	*Rural Poverty 1993-94*	*Rural Poverty 1999-2000*	*Decadal Growth of Population (1991-2001)*	*Total Fertility Rate (TDR) (2001)**	*Sex Ratio 2001**	*Female Literacy 2001**
Dry area	40.47	20.72	8.35	22.04	3.47	926	43.21
Eastern region	25.79	19.78	18.34	29.88	2.70	924	61.09
Plain southern	18.08	19.19	9.75	20.45	3.10	942	50.19
Plain northern	20.27	19.76	5.56	17.85	2.52	918	62.18
Saurashtra	14.55	8.97	2.49	18.09	2.48	949	58.75
Gujarat	23.83	17.68	8.89	21.44	2.85	919	55.08

Note: Own estimates; similar district-wise table has been provided in Annexure Table A-17.1; Headcount ratio are based on official poverty line (OPL); Estimate are based on poverty line Rs. 49 in 1973-74 prices.

* Unweighted average for the districts falling in the respective regions.

Source: Jha and Sharma (2003), Guilmoto and Rajan (2002), Census of India (2001).

Table 17.2 shows that the incidence of poverty is also high in the dry and eastern regions as compared to other NSS regions, although it registered a decline in 1999-2000. The southern plain and dry regions where the headcount ratio was 9.75 and 8.35 during the 55th round of NSS survey follow the eastern region. These regions are homes for the tribal population of Gujarat state. Hirway (2000), using the estimates based on the expert group official poverty line (EOPL), has also shown that even in 1993-94, the Gujarat eastern NSS region ranked first in both rural and urban poverty. This gives an indication that the incidence of poverty is considerably higher in dry and tribal regions of Gujarat where we see high fertility and low female literacy levels. The southern plains region also has a substantial tribal population and one finds that both poverty and TFR are high. It may be seen thus that in the dry areas and the eastern tribal region, poverty is high along with relatively high TFR and higher poverty levels.

Most areas of developing countries are biomass based subsistence economies, where households generally do not have access to reliable sources of energy and water. Therefore, in addition to agriculture related activities, people in these economies have to spend considerable time fetching water, fodder and fuel wood. Labour productivity in these economies is also low not only because capital is scarce, but also because the environmental resource base is scanty (Dasgupta, 1998). Child labour is a common phenomena in most of these areas. Children are engaged in the workforce either to supplement household income or to support household enterprises (Visaria and Jacob, 1995). It is recorded that children between 10 to 15 years of age work one and a half times the number of hours adult males do (Centre for Science and Environment, 1990).

The links between poverty and fertility is very clear in many parts of the state. It has been argued that one prominent motive for having more children arises from their being an end in themselves. Other motives include children as productive assets (Becker, 1981 cited in Dasgupta, 1998). A study conducted in one of the districts of the dry region of Gujarat state reported that children who worked according to the 'usual status' concept[1] (including subsidiary activity) formed 26 per cent of the girls and 21 per cent of the boys in rural areas. Among these children, 58 to 63 per cent are engaged in work at the 'behest of parents'. The study also found that 83 to 87 per cent of the working children supplement household income or help household enterprises. Further, the study noted that the most important determinant of child labour seemed to be poverty and illiteracy. The proportion of households judged as poor on the basis of 'insufficiency of food availability' or 'inadequacy of clothing for female members' was higher among households with any child labour than among other households (Visaria and Jacob, 1995).

An econometric analysis of the factors determining fertility in rural Lesotho, Bakane-Tuoane (1997) showed that households demand

1. By usual status here is meant a child that usually works for salary/wage.

children to provide old age support and general social security, to serve as full-time productive agents, and to generate income to supplement household earning (cited in Mäler, 1997). Therefore, it is argued that high fertility and low educational attainment is also a self-sustaining mode of behaviour in developing societies. Such societies may get stuck in such modes of behaviour even when in principle, this same society could have sustained a mode of behaviour characterised by low fertility and high educational attainment (Dasgupta, 1998).

In developing economies, the higher participation of the population in the workforce in the initial stages reflects low-income earning capacity of the workers. More people in a family have to work to earn enough to survive. Table 17.3 shows share of population, share of workers and share of agricultural labourers by different NSS regions.

Table 17.3

Shares in Population, Agricultural Workers and Area under Cultivation in 2001

Regions	*Percentage Share in Population*	*Percentage of Workers to Total Population*	*Percentage Share of Workers in Agricultural Sector*
Dry area	13.29	43.81	65.08
Eastern region	15.46	45.97	57.18
Plain southern	18.15	46.37	69.63
Plain northern	29.54	42.22	47.48
Saurashtra	23.56	39.98	52.55
Gujarat	100	43.67	58.38

Source: Census 2001.

It can be seen that dry and tribal regions (eastern and plain southern) together constitute 46.9 per cent of the state's population. In these regions, work participation and involvement in the agriculture sector is found to be quite high as compared to other regions. For example, the percentage share of workers in the agriculture sector in dry, eastern and plain southern region are 65.08, 57.18 and 69.63 respectively. Of all the agricultural labourers in the state, 41.75 per cent were in tribal districts. Both regions have higher populations in rural areas that do not own land, the basic production asset (Iyengar, 2001). Therefore, the important issue is whether the present resource base or poverty alleviating intervention helps these societies to attain a self sustaining mode of behaviour with high income, low fertility and high educational level. What type of social effort will help to shift such a society from the pernicious hold of high fertility rates and poverty? In this context, it would be worthwhile to review the status of environmental resource base of these regions.

17.3.2 Poverty and Natural Resource Base

Although there is considerable theoretical reasoning behind the links between poverty and local environmental degradation, it is difficult to substantiate this with data in Gujarat since such specific data are hardly available. However, some indications are available from data related to deforestation, groundwater depletion, and reduction in the area of grass lands, mangroves etc. Table 17.4 provides environmental indicators compiled from various publications of Gujarat Ecological Commission.

Table 17.4

Region-wise Variations in Environmental Indicators

NSS Regions of Gujarat	*Percentage Change in the Dense Forest Cover between 1960 and 1997*	*Groundwater Table Drop in Levels between 1980 and 1997 (%)*	*Grass Land Reduction in Percentage between 1990 and 1996*	*Loss of Mangroves*
Dry region	No estimate available	162	20	72.5 per cent during 1960 to 1993 in the Gulf of Kachchh area
Eastern region	-40.78	Not available	Not available	Not applicable
Plain southern region	-68.88	Not available	50	96 per cent during 1960 to 1993 in the Gulf of Khambhat area
Plain northern region	-64.49	104	Not available	Not available
Saurashtra region	-34.98	132	Not available	Not available
Gujarat	-52.68	132.66	13	84

Note: Own estimates based on data provided by the Gujarat Ecological Commission (undated); Similar district-wise table has been provided in Annexure Table A-17.2.

Source: Gujarat Ecological Commission (undated).

Based on the forest survey of India data, Gujarat Ecological Commission has estimated district-wise change in the dense forest area which shows that the area under dense forest cover has been reduced by about 0.58 million ha in the last 35 years. We observed that the worst affected districts belong to the eastern and southern plains regions where a substantial percentage of the tribal population lives. Panchmahal district (including the present Dahod district) registered a nearly 70 per cent decline in dense forest area. Bharuch and Surat also show very high losses of dense forest area, around 67.17 and 54.78 respectively. Across different NSS regions, the Saurashtra region registered comparatively low level of deforestation.

The decline of groundwater levels is also very pronounced in the dry region as compared to other areas. Table 17.4 also shows drops in the levels of groundwater in different regions in Gujarat. In the dry region, the water table went down by 162 per cent between 1980 and 1997. The quality of drinking water has also declined in many parts of the state due to high salinity ingress. The worst affected are coastal districts of the dry region. A study conducted on drinking water quality of two blocks of Surat district, which is not a dry or semi-arid region, found high salinity ingress and chemical contamination in the groundwater source (Joshi and Jyothis, 2004). The situation in semi-arid Saurashtra coast is worse. The Royal Netherlands Embassy supported a special drinking water programme in Ghogha coastal area in Bhavnagar district in 1999.

The loss of grasslands and mangroves in the dry and semi-arid regions are also high. Permanent pasture and revenue grasslands have also reduced in many districts namely Panchmahal 58 per cent, Vadodara 34 per cent, Bharuch 31 per cent, Valsad 23 per cent, Sabarkantha 22 per cent, Kachchh 18 per cent and Mehsana 17 per cent. The reason for the sharp decline in the grassland can be attributed to the increasing number of livestock population in these areas. A nearly 30 per cent increase in livestock population has been observed from 1972 to 1992 with another 5 per cent increase from 1990 to 1995 mostly in the districts of Mehsana, Panchmahal and Sabarkantha (Gujarat Ecological Commission). As we see in the case of population and poverty indicators, the environmental degradation indicators also distributed unevenly across the state. Therefore, it is very important to consider the spatial variations in these indicators while policies relating to poverty, population and environmental problems are planned.

17.3.3 Poverty and Population Sections

We have observed in the foregoing analysis that in Gujarat, the NSS regions also broadly overlap with particular environmental features. Gujarat eastern, for example has a larger, although degraded, forest base. We now proceed to show that there are particular population groups that are poor and that they are concentrated in particular NSS regions. Visaria (1995) tabulated the NSS data for Gujarat for 1982-83 and 1987-1988 rounds for households by scheduled tribes and caste and by occupation. Annexure Table A-17.4 contains the details of his tabulations. He established that in both years, scheduled tribe and scheduled caste households were the poorest in the total population. Similarly, he also established that landless and other casual labourers were poorer than other occupation holders including the land holding population. If we now superimpose the population group specific data on the NSS regions, we realise that poverty in NSS regions with substantial tribal population is higher because the tribal people are poorer compared to non-tribal people. The second NSS region where poverty has persisted to a greater degree than other regions is the dry area. The dry region, which has the second highest poor population, includes Kachchh, Banaskantha, Patan and Surendranagar districts. As per the 1991 Census, the percentages of scheduled caste population in the total population in Surendranagar, Kachchh and Sabarkantha (undivided districts in 1991) were 11.29, 11.90 and 10.63 respectively. These were well above the state average of 7.41 per cent. In all other districts in Gujarat, percentages were below 9.50. A brief description of the tribal and scheduled caste populations is attempted below.

17.3.4 Tribal Population

This discussion is based on the analysis of tribal situation in Gujarat by Iyengar (2002). Tribals in Gujarat live in the north-east and eastern belt, which is hilly and where terrain is undulating. Tribal populations in Gujarat are poor and socially distinct. Efforts to alleviate their condition started with educational programmes by Gandhi's followers prior to Independence. The Government of India set up Dhebar Commission in 1960, which is the most comprehensive effort to document the status of tribal people and suggest remedies. In the late 1970s, the Government of Gujarat introduced the Tribal Sub-Plan for tribal development.

Most tribal areas were ruled by princely states. The administration then did not interfere much with tribal way of life. Except for forced labour *veth,* tribal people were not bothered. Forest cover was good and it provided a sustainable livelihood for a small and stable tribal population. People were not rich, but it appears that there was no destitution and hunger among them. With the declaration of Independence, the native princely states were to merge with the Indian Union. During the process, most native states that had good forest cover ordered the clear felling of all their forests. They did this in order to convert forest wealth into cash before handing over power to the Indian Union. Contractors also reaped maximum benefit. Tribals were used as labourers. There was a temporary gain for them too. But good stocks of forest were lost in most places and the flow of goods for survival thinned. One factor for tribal poverty started taking effect.

With the merger of states into the Indian Union, control of the forest department over the forests increased. The department's relationship with the tribal inhabitants was not sympathetic. The department officials considered the tribals as threat for conservation and regeneration of forests. Except for some customary rights relating to the collection and gathering of non-timber forest produce, fuel wood and grass, the department did not allow and plan for tribals and their development along with forest development. Over time, tribals also came to distrust forest officials. Policing by the department intensified and thus, the department ended up becoming oppressive in the forest areas of Gujarat. Forests, therefore, could no longer be considered as a source of livelihood for tribals. Tribals in the process became more vulnerable. The District Gazetteers have recorded the process in great details (1981).

Some tribals in the forests had legal land ownership due to historical reasons. The forest department also invited a few tribal families to settle in the middle of the forest to fight fires and other contingencies. The department offered eight acres of land to each family in such cases. Tribals did not follow the mainstream culture of property transfer after death of the legal landowners. The property was *de facto* divided among the legal heirs, but on paper and revenue records the name transfers did not take place. *Talatis* (*Patwaris*) hardly visited these villages. As tribals were neither literate nor educated, they did not understand the importance of this aspect. This lapse hit the tribals very badly when the development processes unfolded in the rural areas. First, without their name in the land records, they could not avail the loan subsidy facilities available to tribal farmers under special schemes. The second disadvantage unfolded in a big way during the implementation of development projects that affected land, house and hearths of tribal families. The total impact on the tribals of the development projects was quite devastating but the immediate effect was on their entitlements for compensation. Persons who cultivated land all by themselves, but did not have names in the records were not entitled for compensation. They were treated as landless labourers. They were simply displaced.

The overall impact on the tribals of the development projects meant for the benefits of the downstream population was negative. In most cases, the tribals lost their livelihood. Compensations offered were limited to cash compensation for land at government regulated land prices, alternative habitation, and inferior and inadequate physical and social infrastructure. This happened not only in Gujarat but also all over the country and it has been well documented. The end result has been that the development of the mainstream society seems to have taken place at the cost of immiserisation of the tribal population.

The coping mechanisms shown by the tribals have not been good either for them or for the society. One major way in which they have tried to cope is by cultivating the ecologically fragile degraded forestland that has fallen vacant because of clear felling. Such cultivation is not legal because the land is under the control of the forest department. Encroachments in the forest area are significant in size and are a serious problem in Gujarat. Two voluntary organisations working in tribal areas, ARCH-Vahini, Rajpipla and DISHA, Sabarkantha of Gujarat have raised the issue forcefully. Both organisations have pointed out that the tribal population is growing in number but is experiencing a severe shortage of cultivable land. Tribal families have no option but to take up cultivation of degraded forestland. Both voluntary agencies organised tribals around the issue of unauthorised cultivation of degraded forestland and started a statewide agitation. The Government of India's Ministry of Environment and Forest agreed to release 60,000 hectares of forestland for cultivation. The land to be released had already been brought under cultivation before 1980. Between 1980 and 2004, still more area would have been encroached. There are not any published statistics on this issue, although the forest department may have the data in its files. The point is that the problem has not been solved by such one-time release. It is a very ad hoc and temporary solution. Without any effective income earning opportunity, tribals will continue to encroach upon new lands and yet, as we have seen from the statistics, tribals continue to be poor.

The second and most commonly undertaken coping mechanism is seasonal migration. Tribals in Gujarat are known to migrate from rural to rural and rural to urban areas. Some of it may be "pull" migration, but most of it is "push" migration. Interestingly, the state transport bus services have connected a large number of origin and destinations connecting tribal area villages and towns from where the tribals migrate with the villages and towns that are destinations for the tribal migrants. If one looks at the state transport bus routes that have been started from the late 1980s, the increased magnitude and distances migrated may be gauged. "Push" migration is obviously for survival. The process by which the large tribal population was pushed into poverty is described here to make the point that more poverty leads to the degradation of environmental resources; it is the degradation and depletion of natural resource base, including forests that induced poverty among tribal people.

17.3.5 Scheduled Caste (SC) Population

An important social factor that needs attention particularly in the rural areas of Saurashtra, Kachchh and Banaskantha is untouchability. Despite sincere efforts by Gandhi, the problem of untouchability has yet to vanish and strong caste biases are still prevalent. Atrocities, including violent attacks on men and molestation and sexual assaults on women, continue to occur despite significant constitutional provisions for their safeguarding and development. With the rising scarcity of natural resources, caste biases appear to be further strengthened. The rising resource crunch in dry and semi-arid rural regions seem to be generating more caste based tensions. There seems to have been considerable erosion of traditional economic entitlements among the SCs. Common property resources are one such example.

The Government of Gujarat acquired a total of 100,000 hectares of land under the Land Ceiling Act in 1960 and 1976. Out of this, 56,000 ha could be taken into possession. 22,277 holdings with an average size of 2.5 ha were distributed to the landless. A large majority of them were from scheduled castes. One study noted that a large majority of the landholders found land productivity to be low and the allottees did not have necessary wherewithal to improve and cultivate it productively. Instances of illegal sale of land to big landowners in the villages by the SC beneficiaries have also been noted. Creating an asset base with the poor has thus not been particularly successful in Gujarat. This is true even in case of the Integrated Rural Development Programme (IRDP), Government of India's anti-poverty programme for the families living below poverty line, through which productive asset base was to be created for poor that would guarantee a steady flow of income to elevate them above the poverty line. Traditional occupations, social ostracisation and lack of productive asset base make the poor SCs one of the most vulnerable communities.

17.3.6 Agarias (Saltpan Workers) in Surendranagar Dry Region

Gujarat for centuries has been a traditional salt producer in India. Gujarat produces both marine and inland salt. Marine salt production is concentrated mainly in Gulf of Kachchh from Jakhau to Kandla in Kachchh district. The inland salt production area falls in the four districts of Kachchh, Banaskantha, Surendranagar and Rajkot. The major area of inland salt production is known as Little Rann of Kachchh and falls under the three districts of Banaskantha, Surendranagar and Kachchh—all forming part of the NSS dry region. The production process is largely manual and hence, salt production is akin to farming. The primary producers of salt i.e., those who work the saltpans, are locally known as Agaria. Most of them belong to the Koli community, which is a socio-economically backward and/or schedule caste. The inland salt producers are the poorest.

Inland salt production is largely undertaken as self-employment. It requires working capital that is supplied by traders in most cases. This sets in a process of borrowing, partial repayment and further borrowing. The workers are not able to extricate themselves from this vicious circle. Since production takes place in the interiors of the Rann area, the family moves to the production pans and children are pushed out of school. The next generation also is thus deprived of human capital formation. There have been some efforts to improve the economic status of Agarias but private traders are very powerful and rule the market. Salt production and its market need to be analysed before designing any interventions.

17.3.7 Maldharis—Communities involved in Animal Husbandry

Maldharis known variously as Rabaris, Bharwads and Charans broadly belong to Maldhari group. The meaning of *maldhari* is owner of *mal*, which means stock. Maldharis originally lived and operated in semi-arid Saurashtra and arid districts of Kachchh and Banaskantha. A large number of them were migratory. Between November and June, the groups migrated from their main habitats in arid and semi-arid Gujarat to places in south Gujarat and Maharashtra. With the onset of monsoon they returned. With changing conditions even at the destinations such as intensification of irrigated agriculture, privatisation of common grazing lands and changes in cropping pattern, Maldharis are finding this pattern difficult to sustain. Some of them have permanently settled in parts of Gujarat, which were hitherto migration destinations.

Kachchh and Banaskantha, the dry region as per the NSS regionalisation, and parts of the Saurashtra region were originally pastoral areas. Agriculture was practised in a way in which pastoral occupations were supported and strengthened. The rulers then recognised the need for common property land and granted access and use rights exclusively to the Maldharis. Even in villages, where cultivation was the main occupation for survival, the village *panchayat* administered land in a way which could accommodate the requirements of Maldharis. The dominant species herded by the Maldharis was cows.

Maldharis are excellent breeders of some cattle breeds such as Kankrej in Banaskantha and Kachchh and Gir in Saurashtra. The survival of Maldharis almost entirely depended on the common land that was made available to them as groups. In the north and north-east parts of north Gujarat comprising of Banaskantha and Sabarkantha, good forest cover before 1947 also acted as a rich land base for supporting animals owned by Maldharis. It is known that Maldharis had a route and routine, which they followed by season. Loss of common lands has been the major cause leading to poverty among most Maldharis.

In the post-Independence era, pressure on land increased because of faster increase in population and because of privatisation of land. We have seen in Annexure Table A-17.1 that between 1951 and 1991, population growth in Gujarat was high. The absolute number of families, which depended on given areas of common and private land has increased significantly over time. This increase has created pressure on private as well as common lands. Secondly, increased priority on food production in the first two decades after Independence led to the privatisation of land and the extension in the area under crop cultivation. Subsequently, irrigation facilities were enhanced leading to intensive agriculture. In most of the dry and semi-arid regions in Gujarat, land was cultivated mainly in the *kharif* or monsoon season. After the harvest in October-November of every year, privately owned and cultivated lands were open for grazing. Thus, private lands turned into seasonal commons. With the intensification of agriculture, the extent of the seasonal commons reduced. The reduction was generally larger than the areas under irrigation or second crop because farmers also closed the adjacent uncultivated areas. They were afraid of intrusion of animals onto the cultivated land if they gave them access to the fallow areas. Therefore, the effective seasonal commons declined considerably over time even in the arid and semi-arid Gujarat and the options of the Maldharis narrowed.

The responses have been varied. Coping mechanisms have been adopted, but all have had more detrimental effects on the Maldharis' own welfare and on the quality of the resource base. One response has been to change the composition of livestock. Cattle have been replaced by sheep and goats and, in some areas, with buffaloes. The former shift to small ruminants has the potential to lead to further degradation, as these animals are browsers who eat the roots also. The composition shift has been accompanied by encroachment on private agricultural land and on public wasteland. Lopping, which was a coping mechanism during extreme drought and stress years has become a regular practice. Since the tree population is either very thin or non-existent on the common land, the lopping is more on trees standing on private farms. Obviously, this has led to verbal and physical conflicts between farmers and Maldharis. It is unfortunate that the state and its administrative wings have ignored the frequency, magnitude and seriousness of these conflicts. In yet another significant move, the Government of Gujarat has offered *gauchar* and revenue wasteland to persons desirous of setting up industries in rural areas at a price. In places where traditional stakeholders do not have any other alternatives have lost their stake overnight without any compensation. Common property has been privatised. This has already led to further conflicts and if not addressed appropriately, it may lead into violence in villages.

The analysis of these selected population groups, which the NSS identifies as prone to poverty, brings out an important aspect of the poverty-environment debate. The cases of tribals and Maldharis show that the degradation of forest and other natural resources and the loss of access to common lands has induced poverty among both groups. These livelihood impacts also appear to be true for SCs, who are largely asset less and depended on CPRs for non-farm livelihood support. It appears that degradation and loss of access to environmental resource base to the poorer sections leads to further poverty and that in turn creates additional pressure on the resource base. The people and resource are then on a downward spiral.

17.4 Conclusion

This paper has focused on the linkages between poverty, population and environmental degradation in Gujarat state. A comparative presentation of national sample survey and census data revealed that certain pockets of Gujarat, especially dry and tribal regions, are trapped in a vicious circle of poverty, high fertility and low educational attainment. Therefore, it is argued that Gujarat needs a concerted, region-specific social effort to break the cycle and move to another equilibrium mode of behaviour with low fertility, high educational levels and a better natural resource base. The foregoing secondary data analysis suggests that the natural and economic bases of dry and tribal regions are weak. Obviously, this is not a new finding, but it has been established that these areas are stuck with a particular mode of behaviour as far as poverty and the natural resource base are concerned. Importantly, it is also to be noted that while general poverty levels have come down substantially in Gujarat, they continue to persist in resource poor and degraded tribal and dry regions. We have also shown and argued that population pressure and poverty have not created the initial pressure on the natural resource base in these two regions, but external interventions by the government policies and programmes and private initiatives in clear and/or unsustainable felling of forests and intensive irrigated agriculture in water scarce dry region districts have put pressure on the asset less and entitlement less people who had no other alternative but to over use the degraded natural resource base for their survival.

The development policies promoted and supported by the state despite its welfare and distributive focus augmented the economic growth strategies that ignored sustainable development. As is believed that 'development is the best contraception' so is perhaps the belief in the working of the environment Kuznet Curve, which roughly means that there would be a rise in the economic prosperity and environmental pollution in the first few years and as the economic prosperity will reach a threshold, concern for clean environment will start taking effect and ultimately there will be high economic status and clean environment. This thesis deters any inquiry on the lifestyle and uncontrolled consumption by the humanity. Despite imposition of social and environmental costs, developing nations such as India are yet to question the conventional development model. The 'Golden Corridor' in Gujarat that covers Mehasana-Ahmedabad-Vadodara-Surat-Vapi broad gauge railway strip from North to South, is emitting carbon and other obnoxious gases and effluents that pollute air, water and land. The natural resource base in the downstream of these discharge channels is being speedily destroyed. People depending on these resources for livelihood are fast losing economic and utility value of these polluting resources. The good forest and water resources are already overexploited to supply the ever-increasing urban demand due to rise in income from industrialisation in a limited area. If the environmental pollution is not abated effectively and if the natural resources quality is not restored quickly, there may be a rise in poverty due to loss of livelihood and income among those who depended on these polluted land and water resources.

For further reduction in poverty in rural Gujarat and also in urban Gujarat particularly in the dry and tribal regions, restoration of ecological balance is a priority. The Government of India has rightly initiated the watershed development programme as its mainstay under the rural development ministry. In the case of Gujarat, specific population groups like the ones identified above should be identified and anti-poverty programmes should specifically focus on them for further reducing poverty. Serious efforts will also have to be made to clean pollution and restore the production potential of the polluted resources.

For improving the economic status of tribals, their direct stake in the forest resources will have to be created. Since most of the undulating hilly terrain in the forest area may not be suitable for agriculture, forestry will have to be developed. The forest department cannot do it by policing alone or by hiring tribals as casual labour on plantations and for protection. Substantial stake of the tribals will have to be created in the potential forest wealth. Joint forest management, which is a participatory forest management programme, is just a beginning step in the right direction. It will have to be more substantial and tailor-made for the tribal population in different parts in Gujarat.

Human capital formation is one of the most important contributors to reducing poverty. The presence of teachers, doctors and other functionaries in the service sectors will have to be improved significantly. The government may have to devise incentive schemes for performance of the paid functionaries. A related and perhaps more relevant and important component of the service delivery in human capacity building among poor is the course content of the curriculum. Scheduled caste and tribal children should be trained well in english, mathematics and computers. Gaps in the opportunities, standards and quality of education between rural and urban and tribal and non-tribal SC and other caste people are enormous. These gaps will have to be overcome. Improvement in human capacities will help in developing non-farm occupations in rural areas, which will provide employment and income to a large population.

The decline in poverty in Gujarat may be attributed to the rise in per capita income with improved employment opportunities. In the 1990s, poverty has come down sharply in Gujarat. Economic growth, expressed by the growth in SDP, suggests that growth appears to have contributed more than distributive programmes. Market friendly policies did indeed lessen structural poverty. The poverty that now remains, although structural in nature, will require state and community level interventions including creation and enforcement of entitlements and perhaps some income transfers in some cases as suggested above. The next round of poverty reduction in Gujarat will have to be specifically focused on well-identified areas and population groups. Simultaneous improvement in and restoration of the quality of the natural resource base and in income accrual opportunities have more promise for sustainable development and poverty removal in rural Gujarat.

References

Bakane-Tuoane, Manane (1997). "The economic and fertility interactions in agricultural production in Lesotho", *Beijer Institute Discussion Paper Series* 98. Stockholm.

Becker, G. (1981). *A Treatise on the Family*. Cambridge M.A.: Harvard University Press.

Centre for Science and Environment. (1990). *Human Nature Interaction in a Central Himalayan Village: A Case Study of Village Bemru*. New Delhi: Centre for Science and Environment.

Dasgupta, P. (1998). "Economics of poverty in poor countries", *Beijer Reprint Series No 101*. Stockholm: Beiger International Institute of Ecological Economics, The Royal Swedish Academy of Sciences.

Government of Gujarat (1981). *Gazetteer of Banaskantha District*. Director of Gazetteers, Gandhinagar.

———. (1998). *Socioeconomic Review*. Directorate of Economics and Statistics, Gandhinagar.

Gujarat Ecological Commission (undated)

Gulimoto, C.Z. and S. Irudaya Rajan (2002). "District-level estimates of fertility from India's 2001 Census", *Economic and Political Weekly* 37(7): 665-672 (Feb.16-22).

Hirway, Indira (2000). "Dynamics of development in Gujarat: Some issues", *Economic and Political Weekly* 35(35-36): 3106-3120 (Aug. 26-Sept. 28).

Iyengar, S. (1998). "Gujarat", in V.M. Rao (ed.). *The Poor in a Hostile Society: Glimpses of Changing Poverty Scenario in India.* New Delhi: Vikas Publishing House Pvt. Ltd. pp. 108-145.

———. (2001). "Locating and describing poverty in Gujarat: An exploration", in *Gujarat 2010 Challenges and Opportunities* (seminar volume). Ahmedabad: Sardar Patel Institute of Economic and Social Research.

———. (2002). "Gujaratna adivasiona prashno", in S. Iyengar and D. Oza (eds.) *Gujarat: Ek Sarvayyu* (in Gujarati). Mumbai: Navbharat Sahitya Mandir.

———. (2003). "Environmental damage to land resources: Need to improve land use database", *Economic and Political Weekly* 38(44): 3596-3604 (August 23-29).

Jha, R. and Anurag Sharma (2003). "Spatial distribution of poverty: Last three quinquennial round of NSS", *Economic and Political Weekly* 38(47): 4985-4993 (Nov. 22-28).

Jodha, N.S. (1998). "Poverty and environmental resource degradation: An alternative explanation and possible solutions", *Economic and Political Weekly* 33(36-37): 2421-2428 (Sept. 5-8).

Joshi, V. and S. Jyothis (2004). "Socio economic baseline study, Suvali Hazira area", Surat: Centre for Social Studies (*Mimeo*).

Kundu, A. (2000) "Globalising Gujarat urbanisation employment and poverty", *Economic and Political Weekly* 35(35-36): 3172-3182 (Aug. 26-Sept. 8).

Mäler, K-G. (1997). "Environment, poverty and economic growth", *Beijer Reprint Series No 100.* Stockholm: Beiger International Institute of Ecological Economics, The Royal Swedish Academy of Sciences.

Murthi, M., P. V. Srinivasan, S. V. Subramanian (1999). *Linking the Indian Census with the National Sample Survey*. Bombay: Indira Gandhi Institute of Development Research.

Nadkarni, M.V. (2000). "Poverty, environment, development: A many patterned nexus", *Economic and Political Weekly* 35(14): 1184-1190 (April 01-07).

Visaria, Pravin (1995). "Levels of living in India: Correlates and determinates", (*Mimeo*) Gujarat Institute of Development Research, Ahmedabad.

Visaria, P. and P. Jacob (1995). *Child Labour in India, Results of a Methodological Survey in Surendranagar and Surat Districts of Gujarat State.* Ahmedabad: Gujarat Institute of Development Research.

Annexure Table A-17.1

District-wise Decadal Variation in Population (1901-1991)

(Percentage)

State/NSS Region/District	Percentage Decadal Variation in Population								
	1901-1911	1911-1921	1921-1931	1931-1941	1941-1951	1951-1961	1961-1971	1971-1981	1981-1991
Gujarat	7.79	3.79	12.92	19.25	18.69	26.88	29.39	27.67	21.19
Eastern									
Surat	6.94	0.38	9.94	20.64	18.66	25.72	36.01	39.53	36.29
Valsad	6.94	0.38	9.94	20.64	18.66	21.38	25.57	24.17	22.52
Dang	57.78	-16.54	38.74	20.13	17.51	51.36	31.60	20.68	26.77
Southern Plain									
Vadodara	18.05	8.32	16.38	19.02	15.92	26.02	29.64	29.19	20.78
Bharuch	14.60	1.53	13.33	19.41	10.40	24.31	24.40	16.84	19.26
Panchmahal	29.29	16.35	19.01	15.06	19.55	29.85	25.86	25.58	27.34
Northern Plain									
Mehsana	-0.37	8.22	10.64	13.38	19.08	21.63	28.14	21.81	15.26
Sabarkantha	13.32	10.23	18.69	17.15	19.39	34.29	29.29	26.49	17.23
Gandhinagar	2.38	7.50	10.81	26.16	24.39	14.51	46.39	44.08	41.48
Ahmedabad	5.20	6.80	10.98	38.70	28.66	32.55	36.62	33.17	23.89
Kheda	-2.00	1.57	8.79	18.97	20.66	22.64	23.96	22.99	14.12
Dry Region									
Banaskantha	-4.26	5.36	8.27	14.96	26.90	28.72	27.03	31.81	29.66
Surendranagar	12.39	2.12	9.92	12.32	17.99	30.97	27.51	22.32	16.89
Kachchh	5.21	-5.63	7.42	-2.42	11.76	22.70	22.02	23.58	20.22
Saurashtra									
Amreli	7.57	-0.47	14.40	20.57	14.78	24.01	27.09	27.14	16.08
Bhavnagar	7.83	-1.85	14.13	21.68	15.88	26.40	25.54	33.73	21.96
Jamnagar	2.12	0.01	18.31	21.71	19.13	34.29	34.15	25.35	12.24
Junagadh	10.68	7.90	18.13	26.24	13.66	26.13	33.00	26.80	14.00
Rajkot	17.92	-0.65	15.73	17.83	16.27	29.94	34.39	28.88	20.12

Source: Statistical Abstract of Gujarat State 2000, Directorate of Economics and Statistics, Government of Gujarat, Gandhinagar.

Annexure Table A-17.2

District-wise Variation in Poverty, Population and Fertility

Regions	Districts	Decadal Growth 1991-2001	Sex Ratio 2001	Female Literacy 2001	Total Fertility Rate	Percentage of Population in Primary Occupation	Rural Head Count Ratio 43rd Round 1987-88	Rural Head Count Ratio 50th Round 1993-94	Rural Head Count Ratio 55th Round 1999-2000
Gujarat	Gujarat	21.44	919	58.60					
Dry Area									
	Surendranagar	22.40	923	48.72	3.40	64.8			
	Banaskantha	26.31	931	34.54	3.90	66.48			
	Patan	14.08	933	46.36	3.10	63.97			
	Kachchh	25.37	918	NA	NA	58.6			
	All	22.04	926	43.21	3.47	65.08	40.47	20.72	8.35
Gujarat	**Saurashtra**								
	Rajkot	28.95	930	67.64	1.90	43.8			
	Jamnagar	22.40	941	56.9	2.40	49.67			
	Junagadh	17.08	955	56.92	2.60	64			
	Bhavnagar	19.29	936	54.46	3.00	44.79			
	Amreli	6.45	986	57.77	2.50	63.71			
	Porbandar	14.35	946	58.83	2.50	49.34			
	All	18.09	949	58.75	2.48	52.55	25.79	19.78	18.34
Gujarat	**Eastern**								
	Surat	47.04	835	66.71	2.50	33.88			
	Dang	29.58	986	48.99	3.80	86.04			
	Valsad	29.66	919	59.92	2.50	52.14			
	Navsari	13.22	955	68.74	2.00	56.64			
	All	29.88	924	61.09	2.70	57.18	18.08	19.19	9.75
Gujarat	**Plain Northern**								
	Sabarkantha	18.30	948	52.85	2.90	62.99			
	Mehsana	12.04	926	63.96	2.50	47.97			
	Gandhinagar	23.88	911	64.85	2.40	40.18			
	Ahmedabad	26.61	892	71.12	2.30	18.23			
	Kheda	13.24	922	57.77	2.60	58.87			
	Anand	13.04	910	62.53	2.40	56.61			
	All	17.85	918	62.18	2.52	47.48	20.27	19.76	5.56
Gujarat	**Plain Southern**								
	Bharuch	19.32	920	65.42	2.50	55.13			
	Panchmahal	20.36	939	45.43	3.50	77.82			
	Dahod	28.35	985	31.7	4.30	82.73			
	Narmada	14.40	948	47.16	2.80	79.24			
	Vadodara	19.80	919	61.24	2.40	53.21			
	All	20.45	942	50.19	3.10	69.63	14.55	8.97	2.49

Note: 1. The regional averages given in the 'all' rows are unweighted.

2. Headcount ratio are based on official poverty line (OPL); estimates are based on Rs. 49 per month per capita at 1973-74 prices.

Source: Jha and Sharma (2003), Guilmoto and Rajan (2002), Census of India 2001.

Annexure Table A-17.3

Poverty in India and in Gujarat 1972-73 to 1993-94

Year	Region	India		Gujarat	
		Persons (Lakh)	Percentage	Persons (lakh)	Percentage
1972-73	Rural	2442	54	87	44
	Urban	473	41	27	34
	Combined	2915	52	114	41
1977-78	Rural	2531	51	95	43
	Urban	537	38	28	30
	Combined	3068	48	123	39
1983-84	Rural	2215	40	68	28
	Urban	495	28	20	17
	Combined	2710	37	88	24
1987-88	Rural	1960	33	56	21
	Urban	417	20	17	13
	Combined	2376	30	73	18
1993-94	Rural	2440	37	62	22
	Urban	763	32	43	28
	Combined	3203	36	105	24

Source: Department of Rural Development, Government of Gujarat.

Annexure Table A-17.4

Percentage of Poor (Households and Population) in Gujarat by Region, Caste/Tribe and by Household Occupation (in per cent)

Characteristics of the HHs	*Rural*				*Urban*			
	1983		*1987-88*		*1983*		*1987-88*	
	HHs	*Pop.*	*HHs*	*Pop.*	*HHs*	*Pop.*	*HHs*	*Pop.*
1. Region								
Eastern (tribal)	56.0	61.4	41.5	49.9	28.3	39.3	38.3	39.0
Northern plains	30.2	35.7	33.2	38.2	24.9	31.3	28.5	33.2
Eastern plains	31.7	36.6	27.5	32.6	37.6	41.7	25.9	32.5
Dry areas	41.1	46.8	54.3	59.8	40.2	51.1	48.1	53.1
Saurashtra	19.7	23.5	27.4	31.6	38.5	41.5	45.2	54.8
Total	34.8	39.0	36.0	41.4	32.5	39.0	33.7	40.7
2. Caste/tribe								
Scheduled tribe	59.8	65.4	50.6	60.3	62.4	64.2	53.5	60.0
Scheduled caste	41.5	48.8	42.3	50.2	56.3	63.3	51.7	60.4
Others	25.8	29.8	30.0	34.4	29.6	37.0	26.0	33.0
Total	34.8	39.0	36.0	41.4	32.5	39.0	33.7	40.7
3. Household Occupation								
Self-employed in agriculture	29.6	32.7	23.7	27.2	-	-	-	-
Self-employed in non-agriculture	23.0	27.5	21.6	27.0	36.7		34.9	39.7
Agricultural labour	49.1	55.1	51.9	60.3	-	-	24.8	31.0
Other labour	52.3	60.8	47.4	55.4	-	-	61.6	71.0
Other households	14.7	17.4	14.1	17.4	30.8	37.8	25.6	32.8
Total	34.8	39.0	36.0	41.4	32.5	39.0	33.7	40.7

Source: Visaria Pravin (1995). "Levels of Living in India: Correlates and Determinates". (*Mimeo*) Gujarat Institute of Development Research.

18 An Empirical Study of the Contractual Mix between Cash and Kind Wages*

Samar K. Datta, Rahul Nilakantan and Saurabh C. Datta

18.1 Background and Objectives

Although there is ample and compelling evidence in favour of the presence of a kind component in agrarian wages in general and especially in developing agrarian economies in particular, a unifying economic framework based on strong microeconomic foundations and capable of explaining variations in the composition of cash and kind in wages in diverse socio-economic settings, seems to be missing from the economic literature. A number of economic arguments are generally advanced to explain the presence of a kind component in agrarian wages. There are three broad strands of thought in this context. First, in-kind wage payment (e.g., meals, shelter, credit, insurance, water and other services) arises essentially in situations where markets for such services are either incomplete or imperfect, and self-production is costly and infeasible from the worker's viewpoint, often leading to the worker's dependency on his employer. Second, economies of scale in the production of kind goods and services may prompt the employer to go for a kind component in wages, which will be most welcome by the worker especially if a part of the benefits of economies of scale flow to the latter in the form of higher wages. Such economies of scale may also arise due to reduction of risks (e.g., in conversion of cash into kind goods) and/or transaction costs (e.g., provision of midday meal on the

* This paper is based on a study sponsored by the Research and Publications Committee of the Indian Institute of Management, Ahmedabad.

job, which can prevent loss of worker's time and energy to visit his home for food) through use of greater kind component in wages. Third, use of a larger in-kind component in wages (e.g., through supply of on-the-job meal or a staple good like rice or wheat to carry back home) would allow the employer, even if it costs him a bit more at the beginning, often ensures that the worker gets sufficient nutrition (and doesn't waste his cash wages, for example, on liquor) to maintain and even increase his productivity.

The above-stated lines of reasoning have however, three main drawbacks. First, these arguments seem to be flowing in bits and parts, thus failing to put together all necessary ingredients and assumptions, to produce the desired explanation. Second, the above-stated arguments, though they have some explanatory power in the context of cross-village variations in wage mix, are apparently incapable of explaining the frequently observed variation in the relative importance of cash and kind mix of wages within villages. Third, most of the above-stated arguments run in terms of unequal market power on the part of the employer, thus raising a suspicion that the standard neo-classical economics as often couched in terms of competitive market structures is incapable of explaining as simple a matter as existence of a mix of cash and kind in wages within its rigorous format.

Fortunately, the above-stated deficiency of standard neoclassical economics is overcome in a paper by Datta, Nugent and Tishler (to be referred to as DNT hereafter)[1] wherein the observed inter-village and intra-village variation in the composition of wages is explained in a standard competitive general equilibrium model involving a representative worker and a representative employer. Apart from production risk, which is solely borne by the landlord-employer, there is inter-temporal price risk (in converting output into cash), which both the parties want to share, given their usual averseness to risk. Although the fixed-wage worker cannot provide any hedge to his employer from

1. Datta, Samar K., Indian Institute of Management, Ahmedabad; Nugent, Jeffrey B., University of Southern California; and Tishler, Asher, Tel Aviv University, "Determination of Contractual Mix between Cash and Kind Wages of Casual Workers in an Agrarian Economy", Revised, August 15, 2003, forthcoming in *Review of Development Economics*.

production risk, he is often in a position to offer a partial hedge against price risk even though the worker is usually more risk averse than his employer-landlord, as long as the former has stronger and more rigid consumption preferences in favour of the kind good (assuming that the output is a staple good) *vis-à-vis* cash. The model provided by DNT also allows for negative correlation between price and output, where one kind of risk can offset the other, besides demonstrating the possibility of a corner solution (i.e., cent per cent cash or kind wages), and even side payments (i.e., overpayment in cash or kind, thus implying inter-linkage between wage and credit contracts). The various comparative static exercises performed by DNT thus provide a fertile ground to test against empirical evidence their singular explanation in terms of differences in consumption preferences and attitudes towards risk between the two contractual parties. The purpose of this paper is to do precisely the same.

The paper is organised as follows. The next section attempts to provide a diagrammatic and intuitive reformulation of the essential ingredients of the DNT model. Section 3 enlists the comparative static hypotheses arising out of the DNT model. Section 4 attempts to explain the observed features and trends in agrarian wages, as described in separate case lets on three selected West Bengal villages. Section 5 performs a rigorous statistical test of the DNT model against a small but carefully collected set of micro-data[2] from six selected villages of West Bengal. The last section concludes this paper.

18.2 A Diagrammatic Exposition of the DNT Model

The essential message of the DNT model that a cash-kind combination of wages can often be seen as an equilibrating device by two risk-averse agents (namely, employer and employee) confronting price risk and a choice between cash and kind wages or a combination thereof, can be shown in a simple consumer-cum-labourer choice framework, as

2. For details, see, Datta *et al.* (1997): "Role of Markets, Government and Cooperatives in Shaping Contractual Relations for Rural Development—An Empirical Study of Selected Villages from West Bengal, Gujarat and Maharashtra", Study sponsored by Indian Council of Agricultural Research, New Delhi and IIM, Ahmedabad, February.

demonstrated in Figures 18.1(a) to 18.1(c), duly supported by Figures 18.2 and 18.3. In all the first three figures, AB is worker budget line where he can get either OA amount in kind income or OB amount in cash income given a constant and certain price for the kind good. When price of the kind good is uncertain, the budget line swings to AB° where BB° is the premium, the risk-averse worker is willing to pay to totally avoid price risk. In other words, AB° is the actual budget line being confronted by the worker, when he is averse to price risk. The size of the risk premium to hedge against price is constant, increasing or decreasing in Figures 18.1(a), 18.1(b) and 18.1(c), respectively (thus making the worker budget line look like either a straight line as before, but with a smaller intercept on the vertical axis, or concave to the horizontal kind axis, or convex to the horizontal axis, respectively), the larger the quantum of kind wages is placed for conversion from kind into cash by the worker.[3] Given usual convex to the origin consumer indifference curves of the worker, an interior equilibrium signifying choice of a mix of cash and kind goods in the consumption basket is likely to occur. The introduction of uncertainty in the price of kind and risk-averse behaviour on the part of the consumer signals as if the price of cash has increased at a constant, increasing or decreasing rate in these three diagrams. Naturally, the demand for cash would fall for a normal consumer as a result of the above-stated 'price effect'.[4] However, Figures 18.1(a) to 18.1(c) capture merely the choice of the worker as consumer between cash and kind income in the presence of price risk. We need to move to Figures 18.2 and 18.3 to understand how the worker decides to alter his supply of labour for cash and kind wages.

Following DNT, we assume that the representative worker has only one unit of labour. He sells a part (m) for cash wage, W and the rest for kind wage in terms of the staple good (say, rice) produced by the

3. As long as the landlord-employer gets his entire output in kind, given his risk-averseness to price risk, he should always be prepared to provide as much kind wages as possible, thus minimising his own dependence on the market for conversion of kind into cash to satisfy his as well as his worker's demand for cash consumption.

4. The same result would hold even if the price risk (i.e., variance of the price of kind) increases. However, under normal circumstances, demand for the kind good may not increase if the implied 'price effect' involves a very strong income reduction effect.

landlord-employer. It is assumed that the price of the kind good, P is subject to uncertainty such that E (P) =1. Given the fact that both sides are risk-averse, it would immediately follow that trade in cash wages can take place if and only if W<E (P) = 1, but W can't be less than the lowest possible value of P. Following DNT, it is further assumed that the worker has a constant elasticity of substitution (CES) utility function with á and 1-á as the parameters capturing preference for kind and cash goods, ó as the elasticity of substitution (assumed to be positive) between the two goods and μ (less than unity) as the risk-averseness parameter.[5]

Figure 18.1(a)

Change in Worker's Consumption Behaviour with Constant Risk Premium

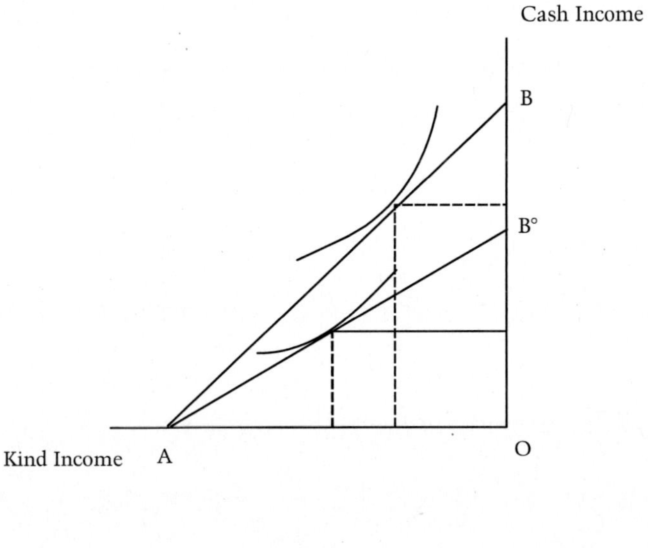

5. A similar assumption has been made by DNT regarding landlord-employer's utility function with á * (and 1- á *), ó * and μ*, respectively, as the corresponding taste preference, elasticity of substitution and risk-averseness parameters. It is important to mention in this context that DNT have further assumed that á > á *, ó > ó * and μ< μ* - a natural set of assumptions, for deriving suitable comparative static results from their model (to be reported in the next section and tested in later part of this paper).

Figure 18.1(b)

Change in Worker's Consumption Behaviour with Increasing Risk Premium

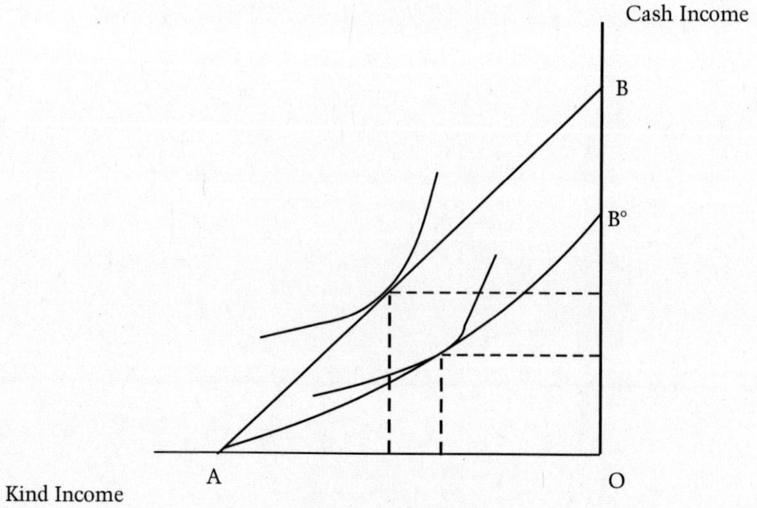

Figure 18.1(c)

Change in Worker's Consumption Behaviour with Decreasing Risk Premium

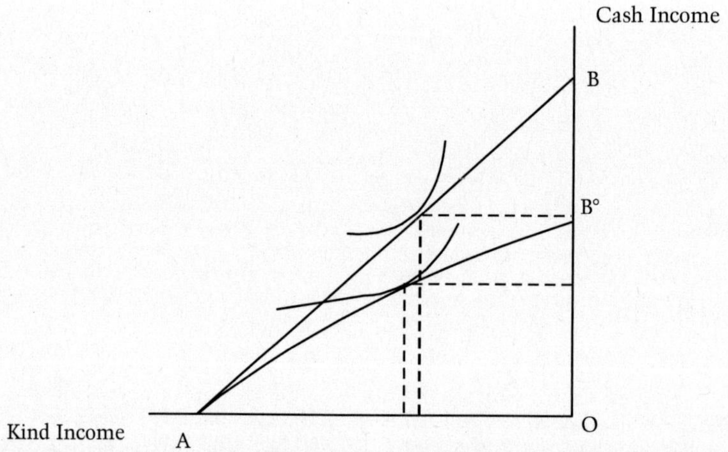

Figure 18.2

Change in Cash-Kind Composition of Wages and Consumption Mix with Price Risk

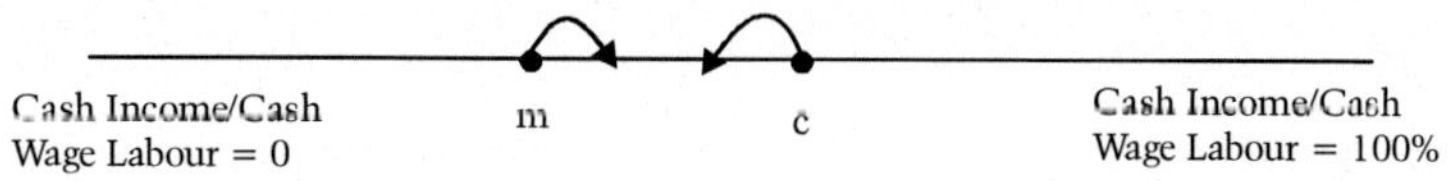

Figure 18.3

Determination of Cash-Kind Composition of Wage

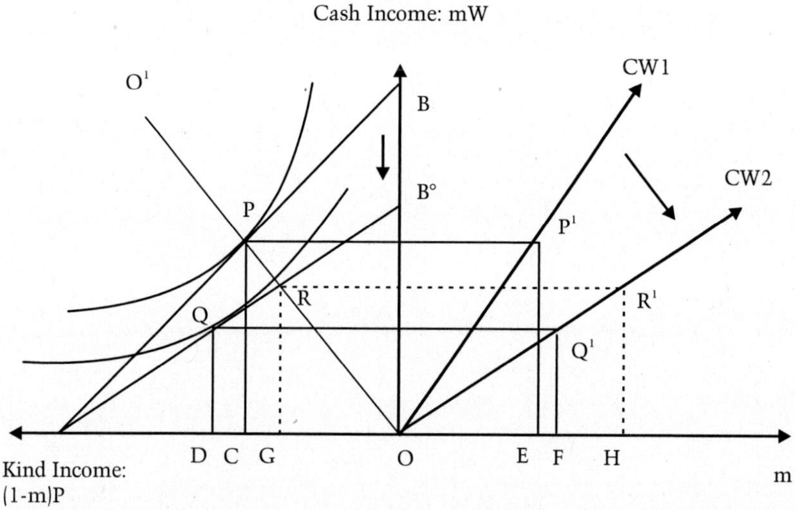

As mentioned earlier, in the given circumstances, the worker must always be converting kind into cash in equilibrium, as shown in Figure 18.2. The implication of uncertainty in kind price and risk-averseness on the part of the worker-consumer (as discussed above in Figures 18.1(a) to 18.1(c)) is to shift his choice of the consumption bundle point from c to c* (i.e., in favour of less cash consumption) in Figure 18.2. The relevant question at this juncture is: will his choice of the composition of cash and kind wages, m, remain unchanged in this situation?

Figure 18.3 combines the worker's consumption choice (on the left-hand quadrant) with his work choice for cash or kind wages (on the right-hand quadrant). His cash income is mW. In the presence of price uncertainty (or, increased risk-aversion of the landlord-employer), the landlord will be prepared to provide risk-hedging to the worker by offering some cash wages if and only if the worker is willing to accept a lower W (thus, paying a risk-premium to his employer). This is shown in the right-hand panel of Figure 18.3 by a downward shift of the cash wage ray from CW1 to CW2, indicating a lower wage rate. With the worker-consumer choosing a smaller cash income and larger kind income as consumption bundle in the left-hand panel of the same figure, an increase in m, the composition of cash wage contract, follows as a result. Thus, in the presence of increased price uncertainty (or, increased risk-aversion of the worker), increased supply of cash wage labour, implying a smaller gap between desired consumption bundle and acquired consumption basket (through labour supply against cash or kind wages) to overcome through conversion of kind into cash in the market, as pictured in Figure 18.2, follows as a natural consequence. A reduction in ó, i.e., elasticity of substitution between cash and kind in the consumer's preferences, which amounts to having a greater exchange risk for the worker due to price uncertainty, will have a similar upward adjustment in m, the composition of cash wages, as can be easily gauged by assuming the perfectly L-shaped consumption indifference curves, necessitating a relatively smaller decline in cash wage income and a relatively larger rise in m (for equivalent decline in W), as shown in Figure 18.3.

As claimed earlier, this diagrammatic reformulation of DNT is also capable of demonstrating the potency of this unifying framework to explain various alternative hypotheses (spelt out in the first section of this paper) on cash-kind composition in wages prevalent in the literature. For example, the first hypotheses on existence of a kind component in wages due to market failure or market imperfection problem in kind goods supply can be interpreted as arising from greater uncertainty with cash wages (i.e., greater exchange risk in converting cash into kind), leading to increased demand for kind wages by risk-averse worker. Similarly, economies of scale in production of kind goods or economies in transaction costs due to increased use of kind wages, which the landlord is willing to share with the worker, can be interpreted as lesser risk associated with kind wages not only for the landlord-employer, but also for the worker (meaning an expansion of the worker's budget line along the kind axis, as displayed in Figure 18.4), thus leading to a change in the cash-kind composition in consumption and labour supply. Efficiency wage hypothesis, on the other hand, has dynamic implications over time. In terms of the DNT model, it can be interpreted as future economies of scale in production of kind good, which the landlord-employer can expect to reap, if the worker is paid a higher wage rate in kind (i.e., an increase in the kind component of wages), which will have a 'feedback effect' on production of kind goods through increase in labour productivity.[6]

Figure 18.4

Economies of Scale in Provision of Kind

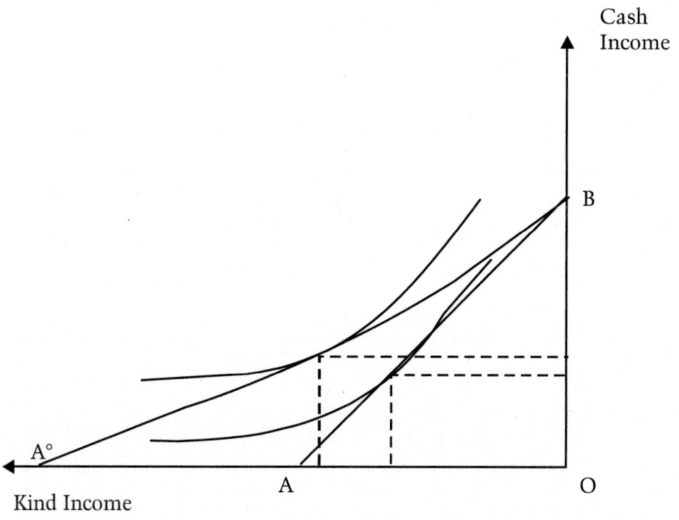

6. Comparative static hypotheses producing change in the composition of cash and kind wages in opposite directions (e.g., due to increased risk-averseness of both parties) can't produce unambiguous results, unless the relative sizes of the two parties and the interaction between the two sides are explicitly modeled, as done by DNT. In order to keep things simple, the reformulated DNT model attempts to explain changes only for one party at a time in a partial equilibrium framework.

18.3 Comparative Static Hypotheses and Methodology for Testing

The major comparative static hypotheses, arising out of the DNT model, which we shall attempt to test in this paper, are summarised in Table 18.1.

Table 18.1

Comparative Static Hypotheses Arising Out of DNT Model

Nature of Parametric Change	*Partial Effect on the Worker*	*Partial Effect on the Landlord*	*Full General Equilibrium Effect on the System*
(a) $\alpha \downarrow$ [i.e, $(1-\alpha) \uparrow$]	m $\downarrow$	-	m $\downarrow$[7]
(b) $\alpha^* \downarrow$ [i.e, $(1-\alpha^*) \uparrow$]	-	m $\uparrow$	m $\uparrow$
(c) $\mu \downarrow$	m $\uparrow$	-	m $\uparrow$
(d) $\mu^* \downarrow$	-	m $\downarrow$	m $\downarrow$[8]
(e) V (P)$\uparrow$	m $\uparrow$	m $\downarrow$	m $\downarrow$
(f) $\sigma \downarrow$	m $\uparrow$	-	m $\uparrow$
(g) $\sigma^* \downarrow$	-	m $\downarrow$	m $\downarrow$
(h) F $\uparrow$	-	m $\uparrow$	m $\uparrow$
(i) |Cov (F, P)| $\uparrow$	-	m $\uparrow$	m $\uparrow$[9]

Note: The parameters from the landowner side are designated with asterisk (*). F stands for any production augmenting parameter—whether technological or institutional.

It may be pointed out in this context that some of the above-stated results can be further utilised to assess the impact of a change in worker side parameter *vis-à-vis* the same from the landlord side. For example, a relative decline (i.e., relative to the landowner) in the worker's preference for cash consumption, or a relative decline in the worker's risk-aversion parameter, or a relative fall in the worker's elasticity of

7. With more exchange risk following from a stronger need to convert kind into cash, the worker arranges for income compensation for him by switching more toward kind and less towards cash wages, given the fact that W<1. The landlord, on the other hand, responds to a similar situation by offering more employment at cash wages, given the fact that W<1.

8. However, the representative landlord being several terms larger than the representative worker, the induced decline m due to landlord side effect is likely to be much stronger as compared to the oppositely working effect from the worker side, thus resulting a fall in m under conditions of general equilibrium.

9. A rise in absolute value of the covariance term between F and P (assuming that the productivity augmenting parameter has random consequences, which are negatively correlated to the uncertain price variable) can be interpreted as, as if, F is increased, or V (P) has fallen, or μ^* has increased for the landlord, due to the fact that price uncertainty is now hedging to some extent the impact of production uncertainty.

substitution between cash and kind goods will have a similar and rising effect on the cash-composition of wages.

The present paper proposes to test the above-stated hypotheses as far as possible against: (1) small case studies of three carefully selected villages of West Bengal (in terms of variation in the incidence of price and production risks across them, as displayed in Table 18.2) capturing the stylised features and recent trends in agricultural wages therein, and (2) a micro data of 64 such contracts available to the first author out of one earlier research project sponsored by the Indian Council of Agricultural Research during 1993-1995. While intuitive reasoning based on the DNT model hypotheses is used to explain the observed stylised facts and trends in agricultural wages in the selected villages, linear single-equation regression analysis is performed on the available micro data of 64 observations to explain, once again in terms of the comparative static hypotheses of the DNT model, the observed mix of cash and kind wages of the pairs of worker and landlord households and their respective villages.

18.4 Trends in Agricultural Wage Contracts in Selected Villages

An attempt is made in this section to briefly describe the stylised facts, features and recent trends in agricultural wages in three carefully selected West Bengal villages, and to try to explain the same in terms of the hypotheses emanating from the DNT model. A semi-structured questionnaire was used to seek information from these villages during April-June 2002 through group interviews of a representative small cross-section of both employer and employee households. Naturally, help and support of local level organisations and personnel were sought to conduct these group interviews in the presence of the first author. In course of these interviews, attempts were made to observe and relate variations in cash and kind components of wage rate to the observed variation in village characteristics (especially, cropping pattern, proximity to towns/cities, and imperfections in existing village infrastructure to cope with production and price risks and to minimise costs of conducting transactions by the villagers). In order to ensure some variation in both price and production risks across the villages, they were selected so as to conform to the following design.

Table 18.2

Characterisation of Selected West Bengal Villages in terms of Price and Produce Risk

		Production Risk	
		High	*Low*
Marketing/Price Risk	High	Village 1 = Dharrasole	Village 2 = Sridharpur
	Low	Village 3 = Sirol	-

It may be noted in this context that terms like 'high' or 'low' used in the sample design for selection of villages are only relative ones. For sake of convenience, the fourth cell is deliberately left out.

18.4.1 Dharrasole

Dharrasole is an interior village of West Bengal, located about 22 kilometres to the west of the nearest town and the district headquarters of Midnapur. The district town of Midnapur is the nearest railway station as well as the nearest police station for this village. Although the village is connected by a bus route, there is no metal road connecting this village. There is no commercial bank operating in this small village of only 64 households, the nearest one being a branch of the United Commercial Bank operating in the nearest village of Chandra (about 5 kilometres from Dharrasole). There is neither any cold storage nor any shop in the village, wherefrom the villagers can purchase their agricultural inputs and implements. As many as 56 of the village households are owner-cultivators (i.e., cultivating their own land mostly with family labour and only partly with hired labour, wherever necessary); only 4 are pure labourer households (in view of their landlessness) and another 4 households are engaged in mainly non-agricultural occupations. Irrigation facilities are not well-developed at Dharrasole, so that the cropping intensity is a low 102 per cent figure and the extent of dependence on *kharif* paddy is as high as 81 per cent, as it can be seen from Table 18.3 below, displaying the broad cropping pattern[10] across the three selected villages:

10. The cropping pattern has undergone very little changes over the years, except that the incidence of summer paddy has increased to some extent at Dharrasole and Sirol, thanks to moderate use of shallow tube wells by several households in these villages.

Table 18.3

Cropping Pattern and Cropping Intensity in Selected Villages

Villages	*Dharrasole*	*Sridharpur*	*Sirol*
A. Crops			
Kharif paddy	81	44	63
Summer paddy	1	17	0
Wheat	2	3	0
Patato	2	31	0
Mustard	7	4	0
Sesame	4	0	0
Betel leaf	0	0	25
Rid	0	0	10
Horticulture	0	1	3
B. Cropping intensity	102	206	122

Note: Cropping pattern indicates percentage share of a crop to gross cropped area; and cropping intensity gross cropped area as percentage to net cropped area.

Source: Datta *et al.* (1997). "Role of Markets, Government and Cooperatives in Shaping Contractual Relations for Rural Development—An Empirical Study of Selected Villages from West Bengal, Gujarat and Maharashtra", Study Sponsored by ICAR and IIM, Ahmedabad.

Although Dharrasole is a relatively poor and backward village, as compared to the other two, landholdings are fairly evenly distributed in this village (as compared to the other two), as it can be seen from the fact that the percentages of households in the categories of landless, marginal (0-1 ha.), small (1-2 ha.) and medium (2-4 ha.) size groups are 4.7 per cent, 67.2 per cent, 21.9 per cent and 6.3 per cent, respectively. In the absence of widespread landlessness, the extent of dependence of this village for outside supply of food is relatively less. However, at the same time, this village has very little marketable surplus to dispose off in the market. Given its poor infrastructure, especially in terms of irrigation facilities and supply of critical agricultural inputs, Dharrasole is exposed to a fairly large order of production risk. Because of interior location of this village, price of rice[11] (of low-moderate quality, as used by villagers) is also found to vary quite a lot within the year from Rs.6.8 to Rs.9 per kilogram. The village also confronts occasional deficiency in supply of labour, especially in busy seasons like sowing and harvesting, when demand for labour suddenly rises to very high levels, especially for several land-rich households which cannot be met from within those households or even from within the village. Casual agricultural labour is

11. Paddy-rice conversion ratio is roughly 1.5:1.

usually paid a cash wage component equal to Rs.30 plus a breakfast (valued at about Rs.5-10), i.e., a total daily wage of about Rs.35-40. The regular working hours are from 8 a.m. to 3.30 p.m. The incidence of attached seasonal labour is negligible, but not nil. Attached seasonal labourers usually work from 7.30 a.m. to 5.30 p.m., and they get Rs.30 plus one meal (valued at Rs.10) plus breakfast (valued at Rs.5-10), i.e., a total daily wage rate of Rs.45-50 in equivalent terms. Although price and output seem to have been always negatively correlated in the past in this interior village, the villagers allege that price of rice hardly goes up significantly in recent post-WTO years, even though there is a significant shortfall in production. After noting the stylised facts and features of wage contract in this village, the authors were wondering: (1) why a two-tier labour contract system (i.e., casual daily labour contract along side attached seasonal labour contract) with differential wage rate and composition of cash and kind had evolved in this village, and (2) why the incidence of cash component in daily wage was relatively higher in this village as compared to the village of Sridharpur (being discussed below), even though the former is more distant from urban area and less exposed to urban influences as compared to the latter. Could the DNT theory be suitably applied to explain these phenomena?

18.4.2 Sridharpur

The village of Sridharpur is located at a distance of about 11 kilometres from the nearest town and block headquarters of Memari, which is believed to be the most prosperous block of the most prosperous district of West Bengal in terms of agricultural development. Sridharpur is an affluent and large village of 600 households with a well-functioning multipurpose primary agricultural credit cooperative society (PACS) working since 1917. Memari is the nearest railway station on Howrah-Burdwan mainline track. Sridharpur is well-connected by bus, even though it is about 3 kilometres away from the metal road bus route. It has a post office, one commercial bank, one daily market and as many as five potato cold storages in its vicinity, besides having private shops to sell groceries and agricultural inputs and implements. The multipurpose PACS called Sridharpur Bank is a versatile organisation, which provides all kind of services (including credit, input supply, irrigation, tractor, storage and marketing services) to its members. While the activities of Sridharpur Bank seems to have significantly cut down on agricultural input risk and thus production risk, it has been only partially successful in handling price risk, though it has invested quite a lot in godowns and cold storages. The distribution of land in Sridharpur, however, is fairly unequal, with as much as 67 per cent of households as landless, 29 per cent as marginal landholders, and only 3 per cent and 1 per cent as small and medium landholders, respectively. This land distribution pattern coupled with high importance of agriculture with a cropping intensity of 206 per cent has led to the following occupational distribution: only 15 per cent of the households are owner-cultivators, while another 12 per cent are tenant-cultivators, 45 per cent are primarily labour households, and 27 per cent are mainly engaged in other occupations. As it can be seen from Table 18.2, Sridharpur's cropping pattern is highly concentrated in production of staple crops like *kharif*/summer paddy and wheat. Even mustard is grown mainly for home consumption, whereas potato is produced mainly for the market.

Because of marketing intervention of Sridharpur Bank, the farmers in this village have always experienced a slightly higher rice price than an average West Bengal village. Nevertheless, variation in rice price is still considerable—price generally varies between Rs.8 and Rs.12. In recent times, however, the price distribution seems to have shifted somewhat to the left—varying between Rs.6 and Rs.10 with a hump towards the left-hand side, which the farmers allege to have happened as an effect of the WTO-induced opening of markets, which has considerably reduced illegal poaching of rice from West Bengal into the neighbouring country of Bangladesh just across the border, resulting in gains of other countries like Thailand on this score. Two types of casual labour wage payment systems are found in Sridharpur: full cash payment at the rate of Rs.50, or two kilograms of rice plus Rs.32, though mix wage payment systems are more common than the other. However, in recent times, the incidence of full cash wage payment is rising. Even though share payment system is fraught with legal complications due to possible recording of non-transferable rights of the tenant to the land, whereas leasing out of land against fixed rent is totally banned, incidence of seasonal leasing out of land against share or even rent contract in place of wage contracts seems to be on the rise. Given the results of the DNT model, therefore, one needs to explain for this village: (a) in co-existence of exclusive cash wages along side mix wages to casual labourers, (b) the gradual preference over exclusive cash wage contracts fixed at Rs.50 per day, and (c) the movement away from wage towards share and even rent contracts.

18.4.3 Sirol

Sirol is a small village of only 127 households in the district of Howrah in West Bengal. It is located at a distance of about 11 kilometres from the nearest town and block headquarters of Bagnan, which is also an important railway station (only about 20-25 kilometres from Howrah) on the Howrah-Kharagpur railway track of the South Eastern Railways. Sirol is very conveniently located at a distance of only one kilometre from the metal road and direct bus route to Kolkata. Besides its close proximity to Kolkata, Sirol has apparently very good infrastructure in the form of post office, commercial bank, PACS (though not well-functioning), daily market and shops for purchase of agricultural inputs, groceries and implements. However, it has a serious infrastructural lacuna due to vagaries of the river Damodar, which not only disconnects the village during flood (a regular annual feature due to high silting) in the absence of an all-weather bridge, but also keeps large tracts of land of this village under flood during the crucial rainy season, besides regularly affecting the soils with salinity during high tides. As a result, only 30 per cent of available land area of this village is fit for cultivation of regular crops during the *kharif* season and irrigation continues to be a problem even in the *rabi* and summer seasons. In these circumstances, there is no wonder that this village has a very high incidence of labour households (as many as 117), only 2 owner-cultivator households and another 8 households engaged mainly in non-agricultural occupations. About 69 per cent of the households are landless and the rest of them are either marginal or small farmers. Most of the land in this village is owned by absentee landlords with this primary source of income arising from trade and services.

Naturally, Sirol is a food-deficit area, but it being a part of the greater Kolkata rationing zone, there is no serious food problem, nor any serious marketing problem for food crops. As a result, there is hardly any inverse correlation between agricultural production and price, a phenomenon more prominently observed in the other two villages. On the other hand, variation in the price of rice across the year is rather low; it varies within a narrow range of Rs.7.5 to Rs.8.5 during the year. Given the vagaries of nature, this village is mostly engaged in production of cash crops like *betel* leaf and *rid* (see Table 18.3). Cropping intensity is as low as 102 per cent and only a small fraction of the available land area is devoted to production of *kharif* or summer paddy, though the incidence of the latter is increasing in recent times. Production of summer paddy however continues to be problematic not only because of intrusion of saline water, but also because of pest attack and heavy dependency of this crop on labour, which is very much prone to unrest and indiscipline.

Detailed discussion with the farmers of this area revealed that assuming an average production of 24 quintals of paddy per acre, paddy cultivation gives a gross return of Rs.14,000 against a cost is Rs.8,000 (exclusive of labour cost). Labour cost in summer paddy is generally 66 man-days at Rs.50, i.e., Rs.3960. So, a paddy cultivator enjoys on average a net income of Rs.2040. Under seasonal share-cropping, however, a farmer gets about Rs.3000 income per acre, whereas under fixed renting the owner of land gets Rs.2500 to Rs.3000 per acre.

In this village, there is hardly any incidence of kind wage payments. Workers are usually paid fully in cash. However, the *kharif* wage rate is usually Rs.50 per day, whereas the same for *rabi* and under *rabi* paddy is Rs.60-100, i.e., much above the *kharif* rate. Kind wage rate is hardly provided except under special occasions—for example, during festivals or when excess work is required from labour. However, there is a strong recent tendency to move away from wage contract towards renting contract on the part of the landlords. Questions, which therefore arise in the context of Sirol, are: (a) how to explain frequent use of exclusive cash wages and use of cash-kind mix only sparingly; (b) how to account for application of cash wages and in fact, higher cash wages in summer paddy cultivation; and (c) how to explain the consistent movement towards renting contact in summer, using the insights from the DNT model?

An attempt is being made in the following paragraphs to explain the observed stylised features of labour contract in the selected study villages as far as possible in terms of the comparative static hypotheses of the DNT model:

Village: Dharrasole

(a) Why do we observe a two-tier labour contract system (i.e., casual daily labour contract along side attached seasonal labour contract) with differential wage rate and composition of cash and kind in this village?

Most people in this village are engaged in self-cultivation, but there are several large land-holding households, who have high excess demand for labour during critical and short-lived periods of sowing and harvesting operations. Employment of seasonal labour at a higher overall wage rate may be looked upon as a mechanism used by these landlords to overcome uncertainty in labour supply to them. So, the higher overall wage paid to seasonal attached labour may be interpreted as an efficiency wage. This ensures that the labourers do not leave the landlord, as the opportunity cost of doing so becomes large. Employment of attached labour to overcome uncertainty in availability of labour may be interpreted as if the landlord has become more risk-averse. Therefore, he offers a higher kind component in attached labour wage, thereby offering an insurance premium (since kind wage is higher than cash wage in expected terms) to his attached labourers.

(b) Why is the incidence of cash component in daily wage relatively higher in this village as compared to the village of Sridharpur (being discussed below), even though the former is more distant from urban area and less exposed to urban influences as compared to the latter?

The incidence of cash component in daily wage in Dharrasole (Rs.30 out of an expected Rs.37.5, i.e., 80 per cent for casual labour) is relatively higher than in Sridharpur (Rs.32 out of an expected Rs.52, i.e., 62 per cent), even though Dharrasole is more distant from urban areas and less exposed to urban influences as compared to Sridharpur. The possible reason for this is that the landlords in Dharrasole are relatively less (exchange) risk averse than the landlords in Sridharpur, and can therefore offer a higher cash component in the mix. Being more distant from urban areas, the rice market in Dharrasole is more fragmented than that in Sridharpur. Even though the negative correlation between output and price has been declining off late, it may still be higher in absolute terms than that in Sridharpur. As a result, production risk offsets price risk, and the total risk is thus reduced in Dharrasole to a greater extent than in Sridharpur. As a result, landlords in Dharrasole may be relatively less risk averse than landlords in Sridharpur, and offer a higher cash component in the mix. Further, being an interior village less exposed to urban influences than Sridharpur, it is likely that the elasticity of substitution in consumption of cash and kind goods by the labourers is less in Dharrasole. This mean, the Dharrasole labourers would demand a relatively larger cash component in the mix than do the labourers in Sridharpur.

Village: Sridharpur

(a) How can we explain the co-existence of exclusive cash wages along side mix wages to casual labourers?

The exclusive cash wage contract at Rs.50 per day and the cash-kind mixed contract (with 2 kg of rice and Rs.32 per day) are equivalent if the realised price of rice is Rs.9 per kg. Rice prices in the village usually range from Rs.8 to Rs.12 a kg. The expected price of rice, assuming a symmetric distribution, is Rs.10 per kg of rice. The worker's expected wage at Rs.10 per kg of rice is therefore

Rs.52. The relatively less risk-averse workers will opt for the risky (larger kind component, therefore greater exchange risk in conversion of kind into cash) mix contract with the higher expected wage. Relatively more risk-averse landlords will be willing to accept the less risky (lower cash component, thus lower exchange risk of converting kind into cash to pay to the worker) mix contract and pay a higher expected wage. The more risk-tolerant worker may thus actually be insuring the risk-averse landlord by accepting greater exchange risk and thus reducing the landlord's exchange risk. In return, the landlord pays the worker an insurance premium of Rs.1 per kg of rice. The worker could thus insure the landlord because of their differences in risk-aversion behaviour.The relatively more risk averse workers will opt for the less risky (no kind component, therefore no exchange risk in conversion of kind into cash) cash contract with a lower expected wage. Relatively less risk-averse landlords will opt for the risky (full cash wage, so greater exchange risk for the landlord who has to convert kind into cash to pay to the worker) cash contract and pay a lower wage. In this case, the landlord is thus insuring the worker by accepting more exchange risk and reducing the worker's exchange risk. In return, the worker pays to the landlord an insurance premium through accepting a lower expected wage.The co-existence of both cash and mixed contracts is thus explained by differences in risk-bearing abilities of the worker and the landlord within the village.

b) How can we explain the gradual preference for exclusive cash wage contracts fixed at Rs.50 per day?

Over time, the price distribution has shifted towards the left, with rice prices ranging from Rs.6 per kg to Rs.10 per kg. Further, it has become peaked towards the left, meaning that low prices occur more often than high prices. The expected price of rice will therefore be slightly less than the mid-point of the price range, i.e., slightly less than Rs.8, say Rs.7.5 per kg. As a result, the worker's expected wage under the mix contract will be only Rs.47. (See Annexure A-18.1 and Figure 18.5). Risk-neutral (and even risk-averse) workers will opt for the cash contract as they expect to get more than 2 kg of rice at Rs.7.5 per kg plus Rs.32 out of an exclusive cash wage rate of Rs.50 per day. Only the risk loving workers will be willing to bear the exchange risk (in converting kind into cash, for example, at the rate of Rs.10 per kg) and opt for the mix contract, in the hope that rice price would exceed Rs.9 per kg. On the other hand, risk-averse landlords will opt for the mix contract. Only risk-loving landlords will be willing to bear the exchange risk and pay a cash wage that is higher than the expected value Rs.47 of the mix wage, on the belief that the realised rice price would be greater than Rs.9 (and thus the mix would cost him more than Rs.50). The gradual preference for exclusive cash wage contracts means that more and more landlords are becoming risk-lovers (which is extremely unlikely), or that the workers are continuing to remain or becoming more and more risk-averse (more likely). Since the village consists primarily of labour households, it appears that increasing competition for employment among the workers would confirm the latter rather than the former hypothesis.

c) How can we explain the movement away from wage towards share and even rent contracts?

All risk-averse landlords are badly affected by the shift in rice price distribution as they have to bear more exchange risk, and pay a cash wage (Rs.50) that is higher than the expected value of the mix wage (Rs.47). The landlord would then prefer mix wages, while the worker would prefer exclusive cash wages. Thus, the model would fail to arrive at an equilibrium wage through equating the marginal risk-premium, the two parties will be willing to pay to hedge against price risk. Earlier a total wage of Rs.50 meant a cash component of Rs.32 plus 2 kg of rice evaluated at a price of Rs.9 (less than the expected price of Rs.10 per kg of rice), thus providing to the landlord an expected risk premium of one rupee for choosing cash wages. But after the shift in the price distribution, a total wage of Rs.50 would mean Rs.32 in cash plus more than 2 kg of rice. Now, for the landlord to continue to bear exchange risk through supply of a cash component would require the cash wage rate and the cash component of Rs.32 to go down. Unfortunately, that is not happening in this village. When the cash-kind framework fails to offer an acceptable result to both parties, it is expected that they would go for an alternative contractual framework such as share or even rent contracts, which is what is observed in this particular village.

Figure 18.5

Recent Shift in Price Distribution in Sridharpur

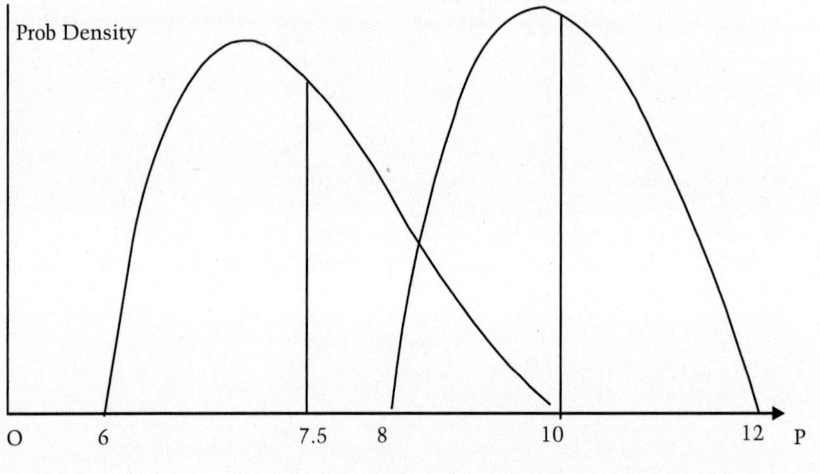

Village: Sirol

(a) How can frequent use of exclusive cash wages and sparing use of cash-kind mix be explained?

The frequent use of exclusive cash wages can be explained by the fact that the village is engaged mainly in the production of cash crops. From the landlord's point of view, the payment of a kind component in the wage will involve a double exchange risk—first, in converting cash crop into cash, and then, cash into kind in order to pay the worker a kind wage. When the landlord is risk-averse, he may be willing to offer the labourer an insurance premium in the form of a higher cash wage in order for the labourer to accept the cash contract than to offer any kind wage, which would augment his exchange risk. The worker gets an insurance premium because he now bears an increased exchange risk in conversion of cash into kind. Note that given a normal performance for a mix in consumption, a risk-averse labourer is always in favour of some cash contract. Here the premium in the form of higher cash wage will induce the worker to go for an exclusive cash wage contract, even though it may involve conversion of some cash into kind on his part. This tendency to move towards cash wage contract would be there, as long as the village is engaged in production of cash crops. If price is relatively steady, i.e., V(P) is small, as in fact is the case in this village, the worker would not mind converting some cash into kind. Even though the absentee landlords in this village are engaged in production of summer paddy, a staple crop, it amounts to production of virtually a cash crop mostly for market sale by such rich landlords. The production of a staple crop combined with the fact the landlord has now stronger incentives to ensure steady availability of labour during the critical sowing and harvesting seasons, is expected to lead to occasional use of a cash-kind combination of wages by absentee landlords in this village.

(b) How can we account for application of higher cash wages in summer paddy cultivation?

Higher cash wages are paid for summer paddy cultivation as the problem of labour scarcity and even labour unrest (this village being close to the industrial estates near Kolkata) is quite severe. The higher wage is like an insurance premium the production-risk averse landlord pays to the labourer in return for the labourer's cooperation in smooth harvesting operations.

(c) How can we explain the consistent movement towards renting contract in summer paddy production?

A renting contract for summer production offers unambiguously higher returns to the landlord than cultivation through employment of wage labour. Moreover, it is less risky for the landlord, as the entire production and price risk is borne by the tenant. The labourers will prefer renting the land to offering wage labour to the landlord as there is tremendous competition among the labourers for wage employment, there being 117 labour households in this village. Labourers are therefore expected to take this opportunity to increase their income through use of non-standard labour, which they cannot offer for sale under a standard wage contract. A sharecropping arrangement may yield the landlord a higher return than a rent contract, but it is more risky, as the landlord bears a part of the production risk. Moreover, as most of the landlords in Sirol are absentee landlords, the monitoring costs are extremely high. The landlord will opt for a sharecropping contract only if the returns (share of output) from doing so compensate for the high monitoring costs and the production risk. In the case of Sirol, summer production of paddy is rendered difficult because of pest attacks and salinity of the soil. Thus, it is unlikely that the output of paddy will be high enough for the landlord to consider bearing a part of the production risk and the monitoring costs under a sharing system. The sharecropping contract being an intermediate form of contract between a wage contract and a rent agreement in terms of risk-sharing is only however a step along the way in the consistent movement towards a rent contract in summer paddy production.

18.5 Testing of DNT Model against Micro Data

This section proposes to test the hypotheses of the DNT model against a small set of micro data of 64 observations generated out of one 1993-1996 ICAR research project of the first author. The data was collected from a random sample of 64 pairs of landlords and their casual labourers across six West Bengal villages over successive seasons of two consecutive years: 1994-95 and 1995-96. Information collected pertained to various terms and conditions of casual labour contract, besides the attributes of the villages and the corresponding landlord and worker households. Annexure A-18.1 enlists the descriptive statistics on selected variables of this data set, which are interpreted as proxy for some of the parameters of the DNT model. PCASH, percentage of cash component in the total value of agricultural wages, is found to vary between 41 to 100 per cent across these villages. DIFCASTE stands for difference in the caste dummies of the worker and the landlord, a value of -1 arising when worker has a higher caste[12] than his employer-landlord and a value of 1 if the worker's caste is not higher than the landlord's. DIFCASTE can be interpreted as capturing difference in relative taste preference for cash between the two sides—precisely, [(1-á*) – (1- á)]. RELLAND is a quantitative variable representing the ratio between the operational landholding of the worker *vis-à-vis* the same for the landlord, which is found to vary from 0 to 28.57. DIFLAND, on the other hand, is a qualitative dummy assuming a value of 0, if the worker is landless, and a value of 1, if the worker possesses a positive amount of land. Both RELLAND and DIFLAND can be interpreted as capturing difference in flexibility in consumption preferences of the two sides—a lower value standing for a relatively larger elasticity of consumption substitution of the worker and a larger value meaning relatively less elasticity—typical of more affluent families—of the worker. DIFEXT, DIFINVST, DIFM and DIFHIRE stand for differences in household extension, agricultural investment, out-migration and agricultural labour hiring status, respectively, between worker and landlord households. Each of these four variables assume three possible values, -1, 0 and 1, depending on whether the status of the worker household is

12. Higher caste is represented by 1, whereas lower caste is represented by 2, for both the sides.

lower, same or higher, respectively, *vis-à-vis* the same for the landlord family. Thus, a value of -1 for DIFEXT means the worker has got a nuclear family, whereas the landowner has an extended family. A zero value of DIFEXT means either both families are nuclear type, or both are extended type. Similarly, a unitary value of DIFEXT means the worker has an extended family, whereas the landlord has a nuclear family. Thus, a higher value of DIFEXT means lesser relative risk-averseness of the worker family.[13] Similarly, a higher value of DIFINVST signifies relatively larger incidence of worker investment in machinery than that of the landlord, signifying a relatively lesser risk-averseness of the worker *vis-à-vis* the landlord, thus inducing a lower value of m in equilibrium. Similarly, a larger value of DIFM signifies a larger incidence of out-migration from the worker family *vis-à-vis* the landlord family, meaning relatively larger income flow through remittance into the worker household and therefore lesser relative risk-averseness of the worker family. A larger value of DIFHIRE, implying a larger incidence of labour hiring by the worker family than in the landlord family, because of fixed contractual commitments to pay hired labour, leads to a drop in the elasticity between cash and kind for the worker than for the landlord. Hence, as per the comparative static hypotheses of the DNT model, it is expected to raise m. A larger value of SUP, supervision dummy (equal to unity as compared to cases where no supervision is provided and as such SUP=0) means lesser realisation of market value from an equal amount of efforts on the part of the landowner, thus raising the value of V(P) to the landlord. CROPDUM, a dummy for the cropping pattern, has two values—0 and 1, depending on whether the village under consideration is mostly concentrating on staple crops (which can be directly consumed) or cash crops (crops which have to be invariably sold in the market for cash).

Table 18.4 has tabulated the values of cash-kind composition of wages (PCASH) for possible values of the above-stated parameters. Although tabular analysis displays variation in only one parameter and has no way of ensuring the constancy of other parameters (i.e., no way of fulfilling *ceteris paribus* conditions), this simple tabular analysis is

13. Horizontally, extended households are presumed to offer more opportunities of risk-hedging inside the family as compared to nuclear ones.

performed below to provide a first-hand feel for the empirical test being performed in this paper. An increase in the value of DIFCASTE, signifying a stronger relative preference for cash on the part of the landlord, has led to a larger value of m from 70.21 to 71.69 in this table, consistent with the comparative static hypotheses of the DNT model in Table 18.1. Unfortunately, DIFCASTE couldn't be used in Table 18.5, which performs a more rigorous regression analysis, due to multi-collinearity of this variable with other explanatory variables.

Table 18.4

Variation in Cash-Kind Composition of Wages Within and Across Villages

Variables	*Minimum Value*	*Maximum Value*	*Mean*	*Std. Dev*
DIFCASTE = -1 (18)	41.32	100	70.21	22.23
DIFCASTE = 1 (46)	40.58	100	71.69	21.62
DIFLAND = 0 (23)	47.46	100	70.15	20.49
DIFLAND = 1 (41)	40.58	100	71.90	22.45
CROPDUM = 0 (43)	40.58	100	59.29	12.89
CROPDUM = 1 (21)	47.46	100	95.81	13.51
SUP = 0 (6)	56.25	100	82.20	20.71
SUP = 1 (58)	40.58	100	70.14	21.57
DIFHIRE = -1 (21)	47.46	100	73.66	22.04
DIFHIRE = 0 (39)	40.58	100	70.51	21.71
DIFHIRE = 1 (4)	49.23	100	66.1	23.02
DIFM = -1 (2)	47.63	100	73.82	37.03
DIFM = 0 (61)	40.58	100	71.37	21.58
DIFM = 1 (1)	60.00	60.00	60.00	-
DIFINVST = -1 (8)	55.17	76.92	74.69	6.91
DIFINVST = 0 (43)	41.32	100	66.54	22.18
DIFINVST = 1 (13)	40.58	100	70.6	23.72
DIFEXT = -1 (12)	49.25	100	74.86	21.9
DIFEXT = 0 (43)	40.58	100	55	22.4
DIFEXT = 1 (9)	47.63	62.07	54.85	4.48

A higher value of DIFLAND, signifying lesser relative elasticity of substitution of the worker (i.e., a lower value of ó-ó*) seems to have led to an increase in cash-kind composition from 70.15 per cent to 71.90 per cent, once again confirming the comparative static hypotheses. In regression analysis, we have however used a quantitative explanatory variable, RELLAND, i.e., relative landholding of the worker, as a substitute for DIFLAND, and it too is found to have a positive impact on m, which is statistically significant at 5 per cent level for two-tailed test.

An increase in the value of CROPDUM, the crop dummy from 0 to 1, i.e., with a movement towards villages with greater concentration on production of cash crops, the landlord is being exposed to two-fold price risk—first, while converting cash crop into kind and then, while converting cash into the requisite mix between cash and kind, as a result of which he would like to minimise his burden of the exchange risk by offering more cash and less kind wages. In the latter situation with double exchange risk, a risk-averse landlord is simply unwilling to offer greater kind wages to his worker. So, the average value of PCASH rises from 59.29 per cent to 95.81 per cent. CROPDUM is also found to be highly significant (at 1 per cent level for two-tailed test) in regression analysis in Table 18.5.

Table 18.5

Regression Analysis to Explain PCASH

(Percentage of Cash in Wages)

Independent Variables	*Coefficients*	*t-values*	*Prob > |t|*
Intercept	70.64	13.09	0.0001
Operated land area of worker as ratio of the same for the landlord, RELLAND	0.86	1.99	0.0559
Difference between household extension dummies of the worker (0 or 1) and the landlord (0 and 1) DIFEXT	-4.57	-1.80	0.0765
Difference between agricultural investment dummies of the worker (0 or 1) and the landlord (0 and 1) DIFINVST	-7.74	-295	0.0047
Difference between out-migration dummies of the worker (0 or 1) and the landlord (0 and 1) DIFM	-18.53	-2.74	0.0083
Difference between labour-hiring features of the worker (0 or 1) and the landlord (0 and 1) DIFHIRE	7.05	2.57	0.0128
Supervision of the worker dummy (0 or 1), SUP	-12.43	-2.33	0.0237
Crop dummy, CROPDUM (0 if a staple crop; 1 otherwise)	40.54	13.07	0.0001

Note: F-value = 27.25; Adjusted R-square = 0.74.

A rise in DIFEXT from -1 to 0 and from 0 to 1 means an increase in relative size of the worker household, which can be presumed to provide a greater risk-hedging opportunity to the worker, thus making him relatively less risk-averse (i.e., leading to a rise in $\mu - \mu^*$), which should lead to a decline in cash-kind composition of wages, m. In Table 18.4, the result is not clear, as m rises from 70.60 per cent to 74.86 per cent as DIFEXT rises from -1 to 0, but it falls from 74.86 per cent to

55.00 per cent when DIFEXT rises further from 0 to 1. DIFEXT is found to have a negative effect on m in Table 18.5, but the relevant regression coefficient is statistically significant only at 10 per cent level for a two-tailed test. An increase in DIFINVST means relatively more investment in machinery by the worker, meaning some decline in relative risk-averseness of the worker, that is, a rise in $\mu - \mu^*$, leading to a drop in m, as warranted by the comparative static hypotheses. This is confirmed by regression results in Table 18.5, displaying negative and statistically significant (at 1% level for two-tailed test) coefficient for this variable. However, in simple tabular analysis (Table 18.4), PCASH increases initially from 60.57 per cent to 74.69 per cent as DIFINVST rises from -1 to 0, but then it falls to 66.54 per cent when DIFINVST rises further to reach a value of 1.

An increase in the value of DIFM means a rise in the relative incidence of out-migration in the worker family, implying a spurt in the flow of remittances into the worker family, which is expected to increase the worker's relative risk-bearing capability, i.e., a rise in $\mu - \mu^*$, leading to a decline in the demand for the cash component in wages, m. This comparative static hypothesis is confirmed by regression analysis in Table 18.5 (by a negative and highly significant, at 1 per cent level, of the coefficient of DIFM) as well as by simple tabular analysis in Table 18.4 (where m falls from 73.82 per cent to 71.37 per cent and further down to 60.00 per cent, when DIFM falls from -1 to 0 and again down to 1).

A rise in the relative incidence of hiring of labourers by the worker family as a result of an increase in the value of DIFHIRE is expected to result in a drop in the value of ó - ó *, which should raise the value of m, as confirmed by the positive and statistically significant (at 1 per cent critical level for two-tailed test) value of the estimated coefficient of DIFHIRE in Table 18.5. However, the tabulated values of m for possible values of DIFHIRE in Table 18.4 do not confirm positive impact, which is quite possible as the values of other parameters are not controlled in tabular analysis. As argued earlier, a rise in the value of the supervisory dummy, SUP, from 0 to 1 amounts to a rise in V(P) from the landlord side, inducing a drop in the value of m. This is confirmed by negative and statistically significant (at 5 per cent level for two-tailed test) value of the regression coefficient of SUP in Table 18.5. Tabular analysis in

Table 18.4 also confirms a drop in m from 82.20 per cent to 70.14 per cent, as SUP rises from 0 to 1. Although the formal DNT model talks of a situation where agricultural production involves growing of a staple crop and thus results in conversion of kind into cash by both the parties in equilibrium, the insight from this model can still be used to interpret results in a situation where a cash crop is grown, thus resulting in two-fold exchange risk for the landlord—first, while converting cash crop into cash, and then cash into kind good for himself as well as for his worker. In this situation, a mix of cash and kind wages as an equilibrating mechanism to ensure adequate exchange risk-sharing between two risk-averse agents, the worker and the landlord, may fail and the landlord may end up paying the entire wages in cash (thus avoiding the second exchange risk while converting cash into kind) and may thus simply refuse to pay any kind (thereby hedging the worker from exchange risk in converting cash into kind) to his worker. This is precisely what is happening when the selected villages in the data set do vary in terms of incidence of cash crops in their cropping pattern. This is confirmed by a positive and statistically highly significant (at less than 1 per cent critical level for two-tailed test) and positive value of the regression coefficient of CROPDUM in Table 18.5. Table 18.4 also shows rise in the average value of m from 59.21 per cent to 95.81 per cent as the value of CROPDUM rises from 0 to 1.

18.6 Concluding Observations

While the DNT model attempts to provide an unifying general equilibrium framework to explain observed variation in the mix of wages, it does not minimise the utility of alternative hypotheses like efficiency wages, which allows for dynamic interaction between the worker and the employer to justify wages (and those in kind) higher than the market rates. In fact, the existence of efficiency wage hypothesis seems to have strengthened the explanatory power of the DNT model by extending this framework to capture a variety of situations. Although the DNT model is couched in terms of a situation, wherein only kind crops are grown and market exchange by both parties involve conversion of only kind into cash, as this paper has shown, the insights from this model can be applied to explain situations involving production of cash crops and market exchange in the opposite direction.

Although this paper has fairly reasonably explained the observed empirical data, it must nevertheless be conceded that it suffers from absence of a comprehensive and large-sample data, which can sharply distinguish between measures of different parameters (e.g., elasticity of substitution, risk aversion and preference) used in the DNT model. Thus, this paper calls for creation of a more comprehensive data set which can provide a more satisfactory testing ground to examine validity of multiple hypotheses arising from general equilibrium models of the DNT type. One possible solution would be the latest NSS farmer level data, which is now been processed, if it is made available in a form such that the researcher can relate the households from one module to those in other modules of this large data set (e.g., through use of a common numerical code, without revealing the true identity of households). A more comprehensive data will also allow for simultaneous determination of a number of variables and estimation of simultaneous equations (e.g., of the cash-kind mix as well as the cash wage rate).[14]

One interesting area where the DNT model has ample scope for testing is the organised business sector enterprises, where the incidence of kind wages in various forms seems to be on the rise, unlike in agriculture, where the incidence of cash wages seems to be rising apparently due to gradual spread of commercial forces within traditional agriculture.

14. This could not be performed in this paper due to data limitations-precisely, in the case of enough variables to explain variations in the wage rate.

Annexure Table A-18.1

Descriptive Statistics on Selected Variables

Variables	*Minimum Value*	*Maximum Value*	*Mean*	*Std. Dev*
PCASH	40.58	100.00	71.27	21.62
PRDRISK	1.00	2.00	1.67	0.47
DIFCASTE	-1.00	1.00	0.44	0.91
RELLAND	0.00	28.57	0.66	3.58
DIFLAND	0.00	1.00	0.64	0.48
DIFEXT	-1.00	1.00	-0.05	0.58
DIFINVST	-1.00	1.00	0.08	0.57
DIFM	-1.00	1.00	-0.22	0.22
DIFHIRE	-1.00	1.00	-0.27	0.57
SUP	0.00	1.00	0.91	0.29
CROPDUM	0.00	1.00	0.33	0.47

19 Reforms, Children and India's Human Face

What Have Been the Impacts of Macroeconomic and Policy Changes on the Welfare of Children in India?

Jos Mooij

19.1 Introduction[1]

The impact of the reforms on children has received considerable attention in the late 1980s and early 1990s, especially after the publication of UNICEF's *Adjustment with a Human Face* (Cornia *et al.*, 1987). Based on experiences in 10 countries, mainly in Latin America, Africa and East Asia, this study showed that adjustment often had very negative effects on the welfare of children. In many countries, there had been deteriorations in most indicators of child development during the adjustment period. This was especially so because social investments in health, nutrition and education had been reduced, but also because unemployment and loss of family income meant that families had less money to spend on their children.

The UNICEF report has played a significant role in subsequent reform discussions and practices, and since the early 1990s, donors, international financial agencies as well as country governments introducing reforms have become much more 'human face' conscious, in any case in their rhetoric. India was no exception in this regard. When the reforms took off in 1991, the Indian finance minister made it immediately clear that the government "was committed to adjustment

1. This paper is based on work done for the 'Young Lives' project in India, which is implemented by Save the Children and funded by DfID.

with a human face".[2] This reassurance, however, was not sufficient to remove the concerns of large numbers of people about the social impact of the reforms. From the start onwards, there have been many apprehensions that the reforms would lead to a decline in social welfare in general, and child welfare in particular. So far, however, very few comprehensive studies have been done to assess the impact of the reforms specifically on children[3] and the present paper can be seen as an attempt to address this gap and to stimulate more research and debate on this important topic.

This paper is about reforms, welfare of children and the relationship between the two. The term reforms are used loosely. It refers to macroeconomic changes regarding fiscal, monetary and financial policies, but it also refers to sectoral policies changes (in agriculture, industry or social sectors) as well as to changes in the system of administration or mode of governance. Instead of 'reform', the paper, hence, also uses the term 'macroeconomic and policy changes'.[4]

Welfare of children can be understood in terms of capabilities and/or rights. The most basic capabilities for children are:

- Material well-being.
- Survival and health.
- Education and development.

A fourth fundamental human capability that is necessary to live a meaningful life (Sen, 1992) is 'social inclusion', the possibility and freedom to participate in a meaningful way in social and political affairs. This capability is important for teenagers, but less for younger children, and receives therefore less attention in this paper. The three capabilities correspond with the main elements of the UNDP Human Development Index and with the main rights adopted during the 1989 Convention of the Rights of the Child.

---

2. Budget Speech of Finance Minister Manmohan Singh, 1991–92, point 8. See also point 45 of this budget speech.
3. An early study is Saleth (1993). This paper develops a model of linkages and mechanisms through which structural adjustment and child welfare are related, in order to say something about likely strategies of the government and of pro-child professionals.
4. See White and Masters (n.d.).

The relationship between reforms and welfare of children is not easy to establish. Often policies do not all work in the same direction. In fact, even a relatively coherent cluster of policies that can be grouped together as 'economic reform' can have contradictory effects on children. The effects of policies can also be mitigated or reinforced by other developments. Moreover, children themselves do not form a homogeneous group, they are differentiated along lines of gender, class, caste, religion, age, etc., and policies may have a different impact on different categories of children. So, rather than trying to draw a uniform picture, the main objective of the paper is to distinguish and discuss the mechanisms through which (some elements of the) reforms could have an impact on rights and capabilities of (particular groups of) children in India. This discussion will be based on data and secondary literature, pertaining mostly, but not exclusively, to India. Various kinds of mechanisms, more direct and more indirect ones, will be distinguished and discussed.

The paper begins in the second section with a short review of the various reforms that have been introduced in India. Section 3 discusses changes in children's welfare since 1991, focusing particularly on: a) material well-being, b) survival and health, and c) education and development. The fourth section discusses various mechanisms through which reforms (could) influence rights and capabilities of children. It will be impossible to draw firm conclusions, but this discussion leads to a number of questions and issues that could be taken up in further research. These are summarised in the concluding section of this paper.

19.2 Macroeconomic and Policy Changes since 1991

The year 1991 is often referred to as the start of the economic reform process in India. There had been earlier episodes of economic liberalisation: first, during the post-Emergency rule of Indira Gandhi (1980–1984) and later during Rajiv Gandhi's regime (1984–1989), but the extent to which liberalisation policies were pursued in the 1990s is incomparable to that in the 1980s. In 1991, a new government, headed by P.V. Narasimha Rao and with Manmohan Singh as Finance Minister, announced its first reform measures almost immediately after it assumed office in June 1991. The immediate trigger was an acute balance of payment crisis: foreign exchange reserves barely sufficed to cover two weeks of imports. The rupee was devaluated, and various international loans helped to resolve the most pressing problems. The government continued to introduce new reform measures in various key economic sectors during its term. The reforms continued after 1996 when the Congress (I) government was replaced by a coalition headed by the Janata Dal and later when various coalitions led by the Hindu-fundamentalist Bharatiya Janata Party (BJP) ruled the country.

Table 19.1 summarises the main reform policies that have been introduced since 1991. The greatest changes have taken place in trade and industrial policy. The import tariffs were brought down considerably from a weighted average rate of 87 per cent in 1990–91 to 29 per cent in 2001–02. Although these tariffs are still much higher than those of many other developing countries, they are much less than what they used to be (Williamson and Zagha, 2002: Tables 19.3 and 19.7). The import licensing system was abolished in 1991 (with the exception of most consumer items). Industrial licensing was also abolished for all but 18 industries, and the number of industries reserved for the public sector has been reduced from 17 in 1991–92 to 3 in 2000–01 (Srinivasan, 2003: 13). The controls on foreign capital inflows have been relaxed, and foreign investment up to 51 per cent equity holdings is now automatically approved for 34 high priority industries. In other sectors, however, the reforms have been much less radical (e.g., agriculture, disinvestments and privatisation of public sector units, and labour).

Children have never received much explicit attention in India's economic policies. They are hardly mentioned in the annual budget speeches, or in other crucial policy documents. This may be related to the fact that India is a federation with a Central government taking responsibility for certain subjects and state governments assuming responsibility for other subjects. Most subjects that affect children most directly come under the state list (e.g., public health and education) or the concurrent list (e.g., education—but primary education is taken up primarily by the state governments). Most issues that have to do with household livelihoods (agriculture, land, fisheries, water) are state government responsibilities; social security, (un)employment and workers' welfare come under the concurrent list.

Table 19.1

Reforms in India after 1991

Reforms	*Main Reform Policies*	*Further Comments*
Fiscal, monetary and financial policy	1991—18% devaluation of the rupee. After 1991—Gradual introduction full convertibility for current account transactions. Liberalisation of foreign exchange dealings. Attempt to reduce fiscal deficit. Limited tax reforms. 1991—Liberalisation of banking. Gradual freeing interest rates. 1999—Reform of insurance sector.	Fiscal deficit was initially reduced but started to increase again from 1993–94 onwards. Recommendations on tax reforms of Kelkar committee (2002) not implemented; VAT not (yet) implemented. But there have been changes in tax rates and a shift towards direct tax collection.
Trade policy	1991—Virtual abolition of import licensing controls. From 1991—gradual reduction of custom duties and tariffs. 1991—Elimination import quantity. restrictions on intermediate and capital goods. 1998–2001—Elimination of quantity restrictions on consumer goods.	
Industrial policy and foreign capital	1991—Virtual abolition of industrial licensing; further abolition in 1998–99. Sharp reduction of industries reserved for public sector (opening up of electricity and telecommunications). 1991 and 1997—Substantive relaxation of foreign investment up to 51% equity. Gradual liberalisation of foreign direct and portfolio investment.	Reservation of products for small scale industry still largely in place. Power: unbundling took place; 10% of generation is in private hands; distribution still by and large done by PSUs; tariff increases meet with resistance. Telecommunications: reforms widely regarded as success.
Agricultural policy	Abolition of restrictions on movements of commodities and liberalisation of agricultural trade. Liberalisation of exports.	Continuation of subsidy on fertiliser, food and power. Basic staple prices controlled by minimum support prices.
Social sector	After 1993—Gradual shift away from wage employment anti-poverty schemes to human development programmes. 1997—Introduction of targeting in public food distribution system. 2001—Enactment of 93rd Amendment to the Constitution, making education a fundamental right. 2002—New Health Policy moving away from the idea of comprehensive primary health care (which was never implemented anyway before) towards more modest goals. Various new schemes for children generally and girl children.	
Labour policies	2001—Proposals were made to reduce 'labour market rigidities'.	Proposals still not formally accepted, but in actual reality gradual changes have taken place.

Contd...

...contd...

Privatisation and disinvestments	1991—Disinvestments policy started officially. Greater autonomy/accountability for public enterprises.	Large-scale disinvestments and privatisation still to take place, but from 2001 onwards the policy started to gain momentum (VSNL, Maruti).
Governance and administration	1992—Enactment of 73rd and 74th Amendments of the Constitution about decentralisation to local elected bodies. 1997—Implementation salary revisions as recommended by Fifth Pay Commission Report.	No significant reduction in the size of government, despite various recommendations.

Source: Acharya (2002); GoI Budget Speeches; Jenkins (1999); Mooij and Dev (2002); RoyChowdhury (forthcoming); Srinivasan (2003); Williamson and Zagha (2002).

Nevertheless, several all-India developments and trends that could affect children directly are noteworthy. The 93rd Amendment has made elementary education a fundamental right.[5] In 1992, India ratified the UN Convention on the Rights of the Child, and it formulated a National Plan of Action for Children and the Girl Child. A number of programmes were initiated, including the Child Survival and Safe Motherhood Programme to provide integrated antenatal, intranatal and postnatal care to women as well as children; a special package for girl children belonging to families below the poverty line, consisting of an incentive for the mother at the time of delivery and annual scholarships for school-going girls; and the programme of Nutritional Support to Primary Education, known as mid-day meal scheme to provide all children attending government (assisted) primary schools with a hot meal during at least 200 days in a year. More generally, there has been a partial shift away from 'traditional' ways of poverty alleviation (mainly through rural wage employment schemes) to human development/basic needs schemes (Mooij and Dev, 2002). The emphasis in poverty programmes and rhetoric is no longer primarily on income and work,

5. Whether this Amendment will help in universalising good quality education is, however, a contested issue. Some people have welcomed the Amendment, but critics have pointed out that the Amendment legitimises (and will reinforce) the already existing trend towards a parallel stream of education where poor children receive education by poorly trained and poorly paid para-teachers for just three years. Education, according to such critics, is increasingly reduced to literacy only. Moreover, by placing a duty on the parents, not just to send their children to school, but also to 'provide opportunities for education', the door has been opened to gradually transfer the state's obligation to provide education to the parents. See, for instance, Sadgopal (2001) and (2002).

but more on education, health, housing and rural roads/connectivity. There has been an attempt to reduce and target the food subsidy[6] and cost-recovery measures have been introduced in health provisioning. The question is how these and other policy changes have affected child welfare.

19.3 Changes in Welfare of Children: An Aggregated Picture

The question addressed in this section is how capabilities and rights of children have changed in the period after 1991. The focus will be only on: a) material well-being, b) survival and health, and c) education and development. This section only describes aggregate trends.

19.3.1 Material Well-being

Material well-being can be operationalised in terms of income or poverty levels. Poverty figures do not exist for different age groups, but are based on household data. What is available, however, are data about child nutritional status.

There has been a lot of debate about whether poverty has been decreased or increased in the 1990s, but the consensus now seems to be that poverty has decreased, but that: a) inequality has increased, and b) the "rate of poverty reduction in the 1990s is slightly lower than the 1980s, and lower than one would have expected given the growth in the 1990s" (Datt *et al.*, 2003: 355).

Table 19.2 provides data of poverty trends. The official data are estimates made by the Planning Commission based on National Sample Survey (NSS) data.[7] One of the problems with these estimates is, however, that the 1999–2000 NSS data are not completely comparable to

6. The policy reform has been a failure: the food subsidy did not come down, and the poor were not better served. In fact, the reform led to severe crisis in the public distribution system, with food stocks mounting and the delivery system unable to reach the desperate and hungry people.

7. In this paper, I make use of several statistical databases, in particular the National Sample Surveys. I am aware of the fact that some scholars have questioned the reliability of these data sources (Vaidyanathan, 2001; Hirway, 2002 in relation to labour force data), although it remains surprising how little critical analysis there is of the validity and reliability of NSS data.

the data collected in earlier rounds due to changes in the questionnaire. Deaton and Dreze (2002) developed an alternative methodology adjusting for this (as well as some other) problem(s).

Table 19.2

Poverty Head Count (Per cent)

	Rural			*Urban*		
	1987–88	*1993–99*	*1999–2000*	*1987–88*	*1993–94*	*1999–2000*
Official methodology	39.4	37.1	26.8	39.1	32.9	24.1
Adjusted estimates	39.0	33.0	26.3	22.5	17.8	12.0

Source: Deaton and Dreze (2002).

The two methodologies lead to different estimates, especially in the case of urban poverty, which is much lower according to the adjusted figures. The overall trends in poverty following from these two methodologies are, however, the same. Both methodologies show a rather sharp decline in poverty incidence between 1993–94 and 1999–2000. The inter-state variation is large, as can be seen from Table 19.3. The decline of poverty in the 1990s was large in Haryana, Kerala, Tamil Nadu and Karnataka, but the percentage of poor people did not come down much in Assam, Madhya Pradesh and Orissa.

Table 19.3

Incidence of Poverty across States

	1973–74	*1993–94*	*1999–2000*
Andhra Pradesh	49	22	16
Assam	51	41	36
Bihar	62	55	43
Gujarat	48	24	14
Haryana	35	25	9
Karnataka	54	33	20
Kerala	60	25	13
Madhya Pradesh	62	43	37
Maharashtra	53	37	25
Orissa	66	49	47
Punjab	28	12	6
Rajasthan	46	27	15
Tamil Nadu	55	35	21
Uttar Pradesh	57	41	31
West Bengal	63	36	27
India	55	36	26

Source: Dev (2003: Table 8), based on NSS data.

While poverty (head count) has decreased on the whole, inequality has increased. This, according to Deaton and Dreze (2002: 3739-40) has three dimensions. First, there has been an increasing divergence between per capita consumption across states. Second, rural-urban inequalities in per capita expenditure have increased. Third, economic inequalities have increased within states, particularly within the urban sector.

Table 19.4 provides data regarding the nutritional status of children, based on weight for age ratios. Severe and moderate malnutrition has come down. If these two categories are taken together, the incidence has come down from 56.2 per cent in the whole of India in 1991–92 to 47.7 per cent in 2000–01. The trend is in the right direction, but still almost half of the children is moderately or severely malnourished and the nutritional status of only 9 per cent of the children can be considered as normal. This percentage is 20 per cent in Kerala, while it is only 6 per cent in Madhya Pradesh (Dev, 2003: Table 19.5).

Table 19.4

*Nutritional Status of Children (Aged 1–5 Years)**

		Malnutrition		
	Normal	*Mild*	*Moderate*	*Severe*
1991–92	7.2	36.3	45.1	11.1
2000–01	9.0	43.3	41.3	6.4

Note: * The figures relate to rural India, and are based on data from 8 sample states.
Source: Dev (2003: Table 19.5), based on National Centre for Health Statistics.

19.3.2 Survival and Health

The main indicators for survival and health are infant and child mortality rates. As can be seen from Table 19.5, infant and child mortality rates continued to decline in the 1990s, although not dramatically and less than in the 1980s. While the IMR declined by 2.9 per cent per year in the 1980s, it declined by only 1.5 per cent in the 1990s—a reduction of almost 50 per cent. Progress is highly uneven (Table 19.6), with Haryana, West Bengal and the southern states (except Andhra Pradesh) doing well, while in some other states (Madhya Pradesh, Punjab, Rajasthan) infant mortality rates have even gone up between 1988–1992 and 1994–1998.

Table 19.5

Infant and Child Mortality Rates

	1981	*1988–1992*	*1994–1998*
Infant mortality rates	115	78.5	67.6
Under five mortality rates	152	109.3	94.9

Source: 1981 data from GoI (2002a), based on census reports; other data from National Family Health Surveys 1 (1992–93) and 2 (1998–99), available from *www.nfhsindia.org*

Table 19.6

Infant Mortality Rates across States

	1988–1992	*1994–1998*
Andhra Pradesh	70.4	65.8
Assam	88.7	69.5
Bihar	89.2	72.9
Gujarat	68.7	62.6
Haryana	73.3	56.8
Karnataka	65.4	51.5
Kerala	23.8	16.3
Madhya Pradesh	85.2	86.1
Maharashtra	50.5	43.7
Orissa	112.1	81.0
Punjab	53.7	57.1
Rajasthan	72.6	80.4
Tamil Nadu	67.7	48.2
Uttar Pradesh	99.9	86.7
West Bengal	75.3	48.7
India	78.5	67.6

Source: National Family Health Surveys 1 (1992–93) and 2 (1998–99), available from *www.nfhsindia.org*

Moreover, there is a stark difference between the survival chances of boys and of girls (See Table 19.7). The juvenile sex ratio (i.e., number of girls per 1000 boys) continues to decrease, and reached an all-time low in 2001, suggesting female foeticide and/or neglect of girl children. So, while the overall health and survival chances of children improved in the 1990s, the relative survival chances of girls as compared to boys declined. The juvenile sex ratio in 2001 is lowest in the relatively well developed states: Punjab (793), Haryana (820), Gujarat (878) and Delhi (865). The north-eastern states have relatively high juvenile sex ratios (i.e., around 960–970) (Premi, 2001: Table 19.2).

Table 19.7

Juvenile Sex Ratios for India, 1961–2001

	Sex Ratio
1961	976*
1971	964*
1981	962*
1991	945**
2001	927**

Note: * 0–4 years, ** 0–6 years.
Source: Chunkath and Athreya (1997); Athreya (2001); based on Census.

19.3.3 Education and Development

There are two main indicators for education and development, namely literacy rates (an outcome indicator) and school attendance rates (a process indicator). Literacy has increased considerably in the 1990s and faster than in the 1980s: the annual rate of decline of illiteracy (+7) was 2.8 in the 1990s, while it was 1.5 in the 1980s. The increase in female literacy has been more than the increase in male literacy, which means that the gender gap decreases, albeit slowly. Still, in 2001, just over 50 per cent of the women are literate while about three-fourth of the male population is literate.

Table 19.8

Literacy Rates

	1981	*1991*	*2001*
Rural	36.01	44.69	59.21
Urban			80.06
Female	29.76	39.29	54.03
Male	56.38	64.13	75.64
All India	43.57	52.21	65.20

Source: GoI (2002a), based on Census.

Increases in overall literacy have to do with access of children to school, but also with adult literacy campaigns. Table 19.9 is about child literacy. Unfortunately, age-specific data are not yet available from the 2001 census, but based on 1998–99 data from the National Family Health Survey it is nevertheless possible to observe that literacy rates among children have increased significantly in the 1990s. Table 19.10 gives information on school attendance, which has increased in the 1990s. Again, girls are catching up with boys. There is almost universal education among girls in Kerala and Tamil Nadu, but there are still many states in which a substantial proportion of the girls do not go to school (Table 19.11).

Table 19.9

Literacy Rate by Age Group

		1981	*1991*	*1998–99*
7–14	Male	60.8	70.3	
	Female	41.3	55.8	
	Total	51.3	63.3	
10–14	Male	66.1	76.9	
	Female	44.7	59.5	
	Total	55.9	68.6	81.8

Source: NIEPA (2002: Table 23.1) based on Census; 1998–99 data from Srivastava (2002) based on National Family Health Survey 2.

Table 19.10

Proportion of Children Aged 6–14 Attending School (%)

	1992–93	*1998–99*
Male	76	83
Female	59	74

Source: Dreze and Sen (2002: Table A3), based on publications of the International Institute of Population Sciences.

Table 19.11

Proportion of Girl Children (6–15 years) Attending School across States

	1992–93	*1998–99*
Andhra Pradesh	55	71
Assam	66	75
Bihar	38	54
Gujarat	68	73
Haryana	75	86
Karnataka	64	78
Kerala	95	97
Madhya Pradesh	55	71
Maharashtra	77	87
Orissa	62	75
Punjab	78	90
Rajasthan	41	63
Tamil Nadu	79	89
Uttar Pradesh	48	69
West Bengal	63	77
India	59	74

Source: National Family Health Surveys 1 (1992–93) and 2 (1998–99), available from *www.nfhsindia.org*

To conclude this short overview of changes in children's welfare, there are a few points worth mentioning.

1. On the whole, the situation of children has improved in the 1990s. The proportion of malnourished and illiterate children has come down. More children survive and go to school. The overall situation, however, is still far from satisfactory. Almost half of the children in India is moderately or severely malnourished. Almost 10 per cent of the children that are born alive will not reach the age of five, and about 20 per cent of the children does not attend school. The situation is worse for girls than for boys.
2. Although there is an overall improvement, there does not seem to be a positive trend break after 1991. In the 1980s, too, there was a gradual improvement in the overall situation of children. The only area in which the 1990s showed an acceleration as compared to the 1980s is literacy. While literacy rates increased annually by 1.5 per cent in the 1980s, the increase was 2.8 per cent in the 1990s. The annual rate of improvement in infant mortality rate, however, was much lower in the 1990s than in the 1980s.
3. In the area of literacy, women are catching up with men. The relative survival chances of girl as compared to boys, however, have further deteriorated in the 1990s.
4. There are huge inter-state differences, both in trends as well as in outcomes. Some states do well in some respects while they do poorly in other respects.

19.4 Reforms and the Welfare of Children

Section 2 of this paper showed that the 1990s witnessed some major changes in the macroeconomic and policy environment in India. Section 3 discussed aggregate trends in some important indicators of capabilities and rights of children. The question is: is there a relationship between the macroeconomic and policy changes on the one hand, and child welfare on the other? If so, what is this relationship?

On the basis of the above discussed trends, it is impossible to deduce a clear, let alone, causal relationship. First, there is too much variation within India. Correlations that seem to exist in one state do not seem to exist elsewhere. Andhra Pradesh and Gujarat are both states at the forefront of the reform process, but while literacy rates increased by 20 per cent in AP between 1991 and 2001, they increased by only 5 per cent in Gujarat in the same decade. Uttar Pradesh is hardly reforming, but the literacy rate increased by 17 per cent from 37 per cent in 1991 to 54 in 2001 (GoI, 2002a). Second, even if there seems to be a correlation, it is difficult to assess to what extent is this caused by reform policies. We do not know, for instance, how literacy rates would have changed in the absence of the reform. Third, the category of children is very diverse. The above discussion illustrated already that while, on the whole, infant mortality rates have improved, the relative survival chances of girls have deteriorated. Overall poverty may come down, while simultaneously the poverty of specific groups may have intensified. An aggregated picture is likely to hide important variations within the category of children.

Despite these difficulties to observe or deduce clear or causal relationships at the aggregated level, it may nevertheless be possible to say something about the relationship between macroeconomic and policy changes and children's welfare. In principle, it is possible to distinguish different kinds of hypothetical mechanisms through which reform policies could influence children's rights and capabilities. These mechanisms can be studied in more detail, and by doing so, it may be possible to establish a relation between reforms and children's welfare. Four different mechanisms can be distinguished.

1. Direct Effects on Public Provisions. Some sectoral policies may have a direct effect on children's rights and capabilities. The introduction of targeting in the public food distribution system or the introduction of user fees in the government health system are examples of policy changes that may have a direct impact (positive or negative) on the welfare of children.

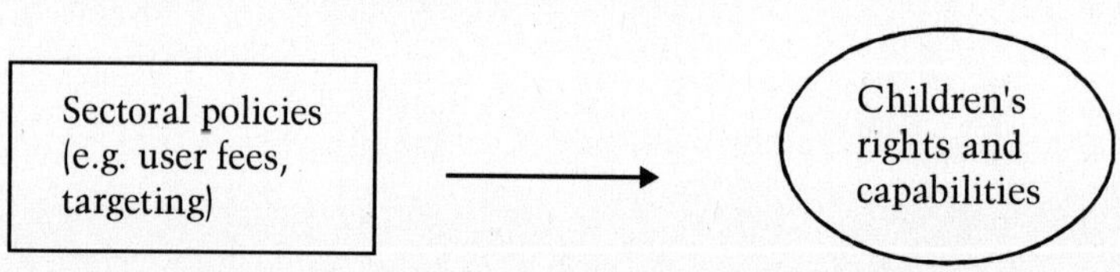

2. Livelihood Effects. Some general economic policy changes may have an effect on livelihoods of some households, which will have an effect on the rights and capabilities of children in these households. Negative effects may occur because employment opportunities decrease, wages decrease or price increase, for instance, as a result of subsidy cuts.

3. General Policy Effects. Some policies, such as administrative reforms or economic policies may have effects on more general administrative and economic conditions. They may affect budget allocations; they may lead to growth or stagnation; they may improve or deteriorate the quality of governance. In turn, these effects may have consequences for social sector service provisioning and the rights and capabilities of children.

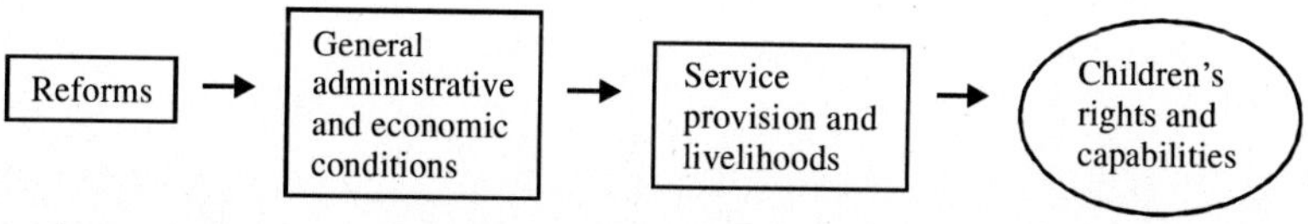

4. Indirect Fallout. The macroeconomic and policy changes may have an effect on the more general social and cultural climate, lifestyles and aspirations of people. These broader changes can impact on rights and capabilities of children.

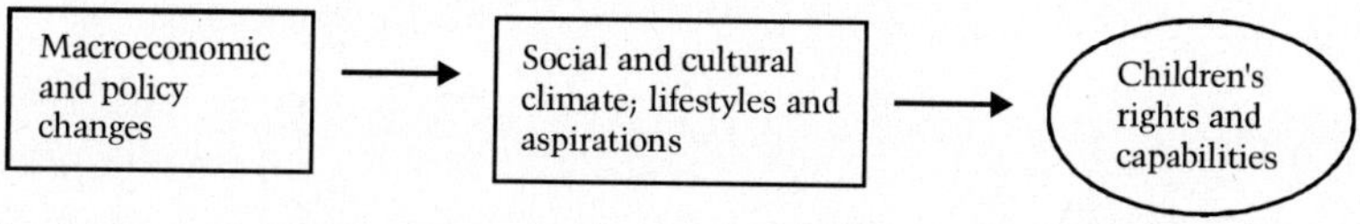

These four mechanisms are generic descriptions of possible ways in which reforms are linked to outcomes in terms of children's rights and capabilities. They are generic in the sense that they do not yet refer to specific causal relationships linking specific policy changes to specific effects. They only refer to possible relationships, because whether or not these relationships exist and how they work in actual practice is still to be investigated in empirical research. In the following, I will elaborate each of these mechanisms and will discuss some more specific possible causal relationships that may (or may not) exist. In other words, I will formulate some hypotheses linking reforms with welfare of children and discuss existing literature and preliminary findings for some of these hypotheses as far as these exist. The hypotheses and discussion is far from exhaustive, although some of the most important issues are covered.

19.4.1 Direct Effects on Public Provisions

Some sectoral policies are about the organisation of social services and could therefore have a direct impact on rights and capabilities of children. Two examples spring immediately to mind: the introduction of targeting in the Public Distribution System (PDS) and the introduction of user fees in the provision of government health services.

19.4.1.1 Targeting of the Public Distribution System[8]

In 1997, the Government of India decided to introduce targeting in the so-far largely universal public food distribution system. The rationale was two-fold. Targeting was supposed to reduce government expenditure and it was supposed to increase the programme's effectivity. The PDS was (and still is) one of the major subsidies given by the Central government. A reduction of this subsidy fitted into the government's overall aim to reduce its fiscal deficit, and was also suggested by the international financial agencies. By focusing the subsidy especially on those who are most in need, targeting seemed to cut both ways.

The targeted PDS (TPDS) involved a subdivision of the whole population in two sections: BPL families and APL families, where BPL means below poverty line and APL means above poverty line. The policy is that BPL families receive a certain quantity of rice and wheat (initially 10 kilos per month; later increased to 25 kilos) at subsidised prices, while APL families would gradually be phased out from the system. The allocation of subsidised food grains to the various states would take place on the basis of a (head count) estimation of poverty in these states.

Targeting of food subsidies, one can hypothesise, increases food intake of poor children. After all, it is poor households which would

8. See also Mooij (1999).

benefit from a redirection of the subsidies away from the rich to the poor. The extent to which children in these households benefit depends on intra-household distribution of food and substitution effects, but the effect can be expected to be positive.[9]

In actual reality, however, it is doubtful whether targeting has benefited the poor, or poor children. First of all, the introduction of targeting caused a major crisis in the whole delivery system. APL households lost their interest to buy food grains from the ration shops through which the PDS commodities are sold. As a result, the overall income of the ration shop dealers (based on a fixed commission) came down. It became more difficult to run PDS shops and the quality of the delivery system suffered.[10]

Second, targeting was done poorly. As we know from the theoretical literature on targeting, there are two types of targeting mistakes: wrong inclusion of the rich, and wrong exclusion of the poor. Both mistakes are probably common, as Table 19.12 suggests, but they are of different nature. While wrong inclusion of the rich results in fiscal or financial costs, wrong exclusion of the poor leads to welfare costs (Swaminathan, 2000: 102). Table 19.12 shows that the per capita allocation to the poor is higher that that to the non-poor, but that the non-poor nevertheless benefit disproportionately. An average poor person in India receives only 0.85 kilo of food grains per month, while a non-poor person receives 1.09 kilos. The allocation ratio of poor/non-poor is 1.33, while the actual PDS-consumption ratio is only 0.78. This aggregate picture of poor targeting is confirmed by various micro studies. A recent study

9. Bhalotra (2002) estimated the benefits for children from the PDS before targeting was introduced. Based on data collected in 1994 by the National Council of Applied Economic Research (NCAER), she concludes that: a) in every state, PDS use by households leads to a positive increase in the total food that is purchased in these households (Bhalotra, 2002: 19), and b) the PDS has a significantly positive effect on childhood nutritional status, although the size of this effect is small (*ibid*: 24). The effect is slightly larger for boys than for girls, but the difference is not significant.

10. Procurement operations, however, remained uninterrupted. The result was an expansion of the foodstock held by the Government of India. This exceeded 60 million tonnes in the middle of 2002. As a result, the food subsidy has not come down—which was one of the initial objectives of the targeted PDS. While the food subsidy was 51.7 billion rupees in 1996–97 (2.46 per cent of government expenditure), it was 176.1 billion rupees in 2001–02 (4.84 per cent of government expenditure) (Virmani and Rajeev, 2002).

undertaken by the Centre for Economic and Social Studies in six villages in Andhra Pradesh found that 25–30 per cent of the beneficiaries were not poor, and therefore wrongly included. About half of the poor were wrongly excluded (Dev and Ravi, forthcoming). Swaminathan and Mishra showed on the basis of a village study in rural Maharashtra that the shift from universal to targeted coverage led to a reduction of wrong inclusion, but a sharp increase in wrong exclusion from about 5 to about 50 per cent of the poor.

Table 19.12

Effectiveness of Targeting, 1999–2000

	Poor	*Non-Poor*	*Ratio (poor/ non-poor)*
Per capita allocation of food grain (kgs/month)	2.4	1.8	1.33
Per capita average consumption from PDS (kgs/month)	0.85	1.09	0.78

Note: This table is only about quantities of food grain, and not about subsidies. The poor are assumed to pay less for a kilo than the non-poor, and would therefore receive more subsidies per kilo than the rich.

Source: PDS consumption data from handout prepared by Jean Dreze and Reetika Khera for a workshop on 'Reform of the PDS' held at the Centre for Development Economics (Delhi School of Economics), 9 January 2003, based on NSS 55th round (1999–2000; per capita allocation of food grain calculated on the basis of allocation figures from Abjihit Sen Committee (2002: 203–4) and poverty figures (GoI, 2002a: Table 2.21).

All this does, however, not mean that the poor do not benefit from the PDS. Based on data from the 1986–87 and 1999–2000 National Sample Surveys, Dev and Ravi (forthcoming) calculated the income gains from PDS (See Table 19.13). The income gain for the rural poor is almost 2 per cent in 1999–2000, a percentage point more than what it was in 1986–87. There was a marginal reduction, however, in income gain for the urban poor. There is considerable inter-state variation. In Andhra Pradesh, Kerala, Tamil Nadu and Orissa, the income gains for the poor are the largest. In Uttar Pradesh, Rajasthan, Madhya Pradesh and Bihar, they hardly exist.

Table 19.13

Income Gain from PDS Food Grain Distribution, as % of Consumer Expenditure

	Rural		*Urban*	
1986–87	0.97	0.51	1.31	0.49
1999–2000	1.98	0.53	1.29	0.45

Source: Dev and Ravi (forthcoming: Chapter 4, Tables 19.5 and 19.6).

To conclude, it is hard to say whether and to what extent poor people (and poor children) have benefited from the introduction of targeting. The high percentages of wrong exclusion suggest that targeting has led to access problems for the most vulnerable among the poor (seasonal migrants, split families, etc.) On the other hand, the income gains for the rural poor from the PDS are higher in 1999–2000 than in 1986–87, which could be related to the introduction of targeting. It is, however, important to differentiate between states—in several states, there are virtually no income gains at all. A much more detailed study is necessary to get a better idea of who exactly is excluded from the PDS and why, and what the benefits are for various categories of poor people in different states and regions.

19.4.1.2 Introduction of User Charges in Government Health Services

Health is a state subject and changes in health policy are, hence, primarily made at the level of the state.[11] Several states, such as Punjab, West Bengal, Karnataka and Andhra Pradesh have introduced health care reforms. In these states, the reforms were supported by the World Bank, and fitted in with the World Bank approach to health as laid down in the 1993 World Development Report. Cost recovery through the introduction of user charges became important, as well as promotion of market forces through contracting out services in public hospitals to the private sector and by encouraging the expansion of private sector health care facilities (Baru, 2001).

User charges have been introduced in the secondary hospitals, but usually not in the primary health care centres. The poor are often exempted from user charges. According to the advocates of user charges, user charges may help to: a) discourage unnecessary use of health facilities, b) create greater accountability, by making health consumers more conscious of quality issues and more demanding in case of quality lapses, and c) create funds which may be invested in order to improve the availability and quality of services. Seen from this perspective, one

11. The Central government is important particularly in the area of disease campaigns and epidemics. There are a number of vertical programmes related to malaria, leprosy, AIDS, tuberculosis etc., which are initiated by the Centre and implemented more or less in the same fashion all over India.

could hypothesise that the introduction of user charges improves the welfare of (poor) children. There is, however, also an alternative position, which emphasises the fact that the introduction of user charges creates additional barriers in public health care and will lead to a restriction of access for poor people.

Purohit (n.d.) discusses experiences in other countries. On the whole, these show a reduction in health care utilisation as a result of user charges. "For example, in Zaïre it was observed that a price increase in health services overall led to a fall in utilisation rate from 37 per cent to 31 percent (...). Generally it is the poor who tend to respond negatively to price increases thereby affecting equity" (Purohit, n.d.: 5–6). There are, however, exceptions to this general rule. As far as I know, so far no studies have been published that assess the impact of user charges on utilisation of government health care by the poor in India, but it would be likely that, if anything, it has restricted access, rather than improved quality of care.[12] First, the user charges come on top of other costs already incurred, related to transport to the hospital, food to be bought from outside for the patient and caretakers, medicines, bribes to hospital staff and workers, etc. For a poor person, going to the hospital is always a costly affair (Krishnan, 1999). Second, although BPL ration cardholders are exempted from user charges, many poor people do not have a BPL card, as was discussed above. Third, altogether, the fees that are collected is small as compared to the costs of running a hospital and are unlikely to result in major quality improvements. Most people who make use of government hospitals are desperately poor—otherwise they would have gone to a private hospital. Large-scale collection of user charges from this group of people is impossible, and one should, hence, have only modest expectations as regards to what can be done with the collected user fees (Baru, 2001).

12. Ravi Duggal (Centre for Enquiry into Health and Allied Themes – CEHAT, Mumbai) mentioned that there has been an (unpublished) study on the introduction of user charges in Maharashtra, which showed that user charges initially reduced access of the poor, but that this effect lasted only for two years (personal communication).

19.4.2 Livelihood Effects

There is no doubt that the macroeconomic and policy changes of the past 12 years have had important negative effects on the livelihoods of particular sections of the population, even though this is not visible in overall trends in poverty. This livelihood deterioration is likely to have a negative impact on the welfare of children in these households. Several mechanisms may be important in eroding livelihoods. The following discussion focuses primarily on employment, and less on changes in purchasing power as a result of price increases or subsidy cuts (such as, for instance, the price hike in kerosene).

Trade liberalisation may have adverse effects on particular categories of producers. The list of people/households who may be affected is almost endless: handloom weavers, tailors, labourers in spinning mills that have been closed, producers of groundnuts who have been negatively affected by imports of soya and palm oil; silk spinners and twisters who lost their jobs because of imports of 'China–Korea' silk yarn; workers in local small-scale automobile spare parts or light bulb industries that could not compete with imports, etc. For many day-to-day consumer items that were previously produced in local markets, there is now a ready-made alternative, sometimes imported and sometimes produced in India in a joint venture. Many people have lost their livelihood. This could be compensated, of course, by the creation of new employment opportunities, for instance, as a result of increased export possibilities.

An important question is, hence: what happened to the general employment scenario? Was there jobless growth, as some of the opponents of the reforms argue (Kothari, 1997), or did employment opportunities increase? Table 19.14 summarises the overall employment growth between 1983 and 2000. It shows that employment growth did not decline up to 1993–94, but that it did significantly between 1993–94 and 1999–2000, both in rural and urban areas. Further disaggregation shows that, as far as there was employment creation in the rural sector, it was in the non-farm economy rather than in agriculture (Dev, 2002).

Table 19.14

Employment Growth (% per year)

Period	*Rural*	*Urban*
1983 to 1987–88	1.36	2.77
1987–88 to 1993–94	2.03	3.39
1993–94 to 1999–2000	0.67	1.34

Source: Dev (2002: Table 3), based on NSS data.

One should, however, not give too much weight to these overall employment figures. After all, as Ghose (1999: 2595) argues, in a poor country like India, where self-employment and casual wage employment predominate, 'supply of labour creates its own demand to a significant extent'. This means, for instance, that when substantial percentages of the labour force would withdraw because of increased participation in schooling (something that is happening, according to Chelliah and Sudarshan, 2001: 36), the statistics would show that employment growth would come down. Ghose, therefore, suggests to use different indicators to assess improvements in general employment conditions (namely, speed of inter-sectoral labour transfers and tendency of convergence of sectoral labour productivities) and then concludes that "general employment conditions in India actually appear to have been deteriorating even though employment growth apparently kept pace with labour force growth" [which was the case only up to 1993–94 and no longer afterwards—see Table 19.14] (Ghose, 1999: 2596).

Another impact of the reforms is that they have led to further casualisation or informalisation of labour relations. The existence of informal labour arrangements is nothing new in India (Breman, 1996). As Harriss–White (2003: 240) writes, "[the vast majority of the Indian workforce has no formal contracts with employers (...). [Their] livelihoods (...) come from (casual) wage labour and self-employment—dispersed and fragmented petty production and trade. Only about 3 per cent of the workforce are unionised (...)." But what the reforms have done is informalise some of the rare labour that was formal, and give a justification and legitimacy to this feature of the Indian economy.

Ghose (1999) constructed an employment quality index in order to get a better idea of this casualisation[13] (See Table 19.15). The maximum value of 1.00 means that 100 per cent of employment is regular wage employment in the organised sector. The lowest possible value is 0.50, which means that 100 per cent of employment is casual wage employment. The table shows that quality of employment deteriorates over time in the aggregated economy as well as in each of the three main sectors. The quality is highest in the service sector and lowest in agriculture. The rate of deterioration is highest in industry and lowest in services.

Table 19.15

Trends in Employment Quality Index

	1977–78	*1983*	*1987–88*	*1993–94*
Aggregate economy	0.723	0.717	0.715	0.706
Agriculture	0.694	0.688	0.687	0.675
Industry	na	0.749	na	0.715
Services	na	0.791	na	0.782
Male	0.737	0.731	0.725	0.717
Female	0.687	0.680	0.686	0.675

Source: Ghose (1999: Tables 9 and 15).

Casualisation or informalisation is an explicit component of the reform agenda, except that it is often called 'privatisation' or 'contracting out to the private sector'. It is not only the government, but also the private sector that is informalising. RoyChowdhury (forthcoming) shows how, despite the fact that the Industrial Disputes Act, 1947 and the Contract Labour (Abolition and Regulation) Act, 1970 remained essentially unchanged throughout the nineties, the actual practices have changed considerably. With the help of three case studies of multinational companies in Bangalore, she is able to argue that contract labour is on the increase and trade unions lack the power to reverse this trend. Moreover, this development is endorsed by the state. While in an

13. The EQI $= w_1.e_1 + w_2.e_2 + w_3.e_3 + w_4.e_4$, where w_1 refers to regular wage-employment in the organised sector, and gets a weight of 1.00; w_2 refers to self-employment which gets a weight of 0.80; w_3 refers to regular wage-employment in the unorganised sector, which gets a weight of 0.65, and w_4 refers to self-employment, which gets a weight of 0.50, while e_{1-4} represents the share of this particular form of employment in total employment.

earlier era, the state mediated between capital and labour, the "process of globalisation has largely diluted the state–labour pact. (...) [I]n each of the case studies (...), the state appeared to side with the management when conflicts arose." The result has been detrimental for the workers. "Labour's bargaining power in the unorganised sector is minimal and is declining even in the so-called organised sector (...) Thus while the state's patronage has declined, the market has not emerged as an alternative source of support for the workforce."

When livelihoods are threatened, the welfare of children within these households is also affected. How exactly this happens, is a matter of empirical investigation, and depends on a lot of variables, including the existence of alternative livelihood (strategies) and the position of child(ren) within the household. A question that is of particular relevance is whether, and in what way, child labour becomes part of the livelihood strategy. One could hypothesise that, when 'traditional' livelihoods break down, child labour will increase.

There are, indeed, a few scholars who have argued that child labour is on the increase, or more cautiously, that it is plausible that child labour is increasing (Gayathri and Chaudhri, 2002; Gulrajani, 1994; Raman, 1997; Vidyasagar, 1999; Wazir, 2002). Raman, for instance, argues that reforms lead to casualisation and more pauperisation, particularly among the scheduled castes, scheduled tribes, other backward classes and Muslim communities. The bulk of the child workers come from these communities. In order to survive, she argues, these communities are forced to sell their labour power far below subsistence levels, and also put their children to work. This is the 'push–factor' argument. There is also a pull–factor argument, as formulated, for instance by Gulrajani (1994: 192–3): "Recent developments in the world capitalist system have increased the economic motivation for the use of the cheapest sources of labour in Third World countries. Arrangements like GATT provide for free trade of goods and capital without allowing for free movement of labour. They push Third World countries to export commodities in which comparative cost advantage rests solely on extremely low labour cost." In a similar vein, Gayathri and Chaudhri (2002) argue that, in the post-liberalisation period, Indian children have been drawn into the production process as a source of cheap, least demanding and pliable labour.

The empirical evidence for these arguments is, however, weak. Raman (1997) and Gayathri and Chaudhri (2002) claim that 'studies' have shown that liberalisation policies increase child labour, but it is not clear to which studies they refer. Gulrajani (1994) describes a case study (the carpet industry in north India), but, although she argues extensively that the survival of this industry depends on cheap labour, she does not show that child labour is actually increasing. In fact, she says that the number of children might have come down marginally as a result of mounting national and international pressure (ibid: 202)—which is an aspect not so much of reforms, but certainly of globalisation (White, 1996).

Table 19.16 shows work participation rates of children as reported by the NSSO. These aggregate figures do not suggest that there is a wholesale increase of child labour.

Table 19.16

Work Participation Rates and Estimates of Child Labour by Sex

Year	*Boys*	*Girls*	*Total*
Work participation rate (per cent)			
1983	11.9	10.6	11.2
1987–88	8.8	7.9	8.3
1993–94	6.4	6.0	6.2
1999–2000	4.0	3.6	3.8
Workers (in millions)			
1983	12.0	9.49	21.45
1987–88	69.5	7.43	16.94
1993–94	17.24	5.94	13.18
1999–2000	5.18	3.98	9.16
Per cent change per annum			
1983—1987–88	–5.9	–6.1	–5.9
1987–88–1993–94	–4.5	–3.7	–4.2
1993–94–1999–2000	–5.6	–6.7	–6.1

Source: Deshpande (2002: Table 2), based on NSS data.

It is, however, possible that these figures underestimate the extent of child work in India. Vidyasagar (1999) and Deshpande (2002) express their doubts about the reliability of both Census and NSS data, among other things because "girls, employed as helpers and in unpaid family work are likely to be missed from the count of workers" (Deshpande, 2002: 53).[14] Moreover, it could also be that expansion of child labour in certain sectors does occur but is masked by a decline elsewhere. This is suggested by some rare case studies which show an increase of child labour in particular localities, such as Swaminathan's study about child labour in urban Gujarat (the city of Bhavnagar, in particular) between the early 1980s and the mid–1990s (Swaminathan, 1998).[15] Perhaps it is possible to find this variation confirmed in Table 19.17, which gives a sector-wise break-up of child labour. Unfortunately, I have not been able to find the 1999–2000 figures, but a comparison between 1983 and 1993–94 suggests that the decline in child labour is mainly in agriculture and services, while the share of industrial child labour increases. If this trend had continued after 1993–94, it would lend support to the 'pull–factor' argument mentioned above.

Table 19.17

Child Labour Distribution by Sector

Sector	*1983*	*1987–88*	*1993–94*	*1999–2000*
Agriculture	80.1	75.4	75.2	
Industry	8.4		15.8	
Services	11.5		9.0	
Total	100	100	100	100

Source: Ghose (1999: Table 19), based on NSS data.

Finally, there does not seem to be a clear relationship between economic growth and per capita income on the one hand, and a decline in child labour on the other. Swaminathan's (1998) case study shows that even in the context of rapid economic growth, child labour may

14. Dev (forthcoming) compares the figures from the National Family Health Survey (1998–99), the NSS (1993–94), the Census (1991) and the National Council for Applied Agricultural Research (1994). The NSS gives the highest percentage of child labour (7.2 per cent in the whole of India); the Census says 6.4 per cent; NCAER says 4.3 per cent, and the NFHS concludes that 4.08 per cent of the children in rural areas and 1.65 per cent of the children in urban areas are working. All are about children between 5 and 14 years old.

15. R. Vidyasagar (National Institute for Rural Development, Hyderabad), too, states that child labour has increased in the powerloom sector, the export processing zones as well as the so-called traditional craft productions which have expanded as a result of increasing integration in the global market (like silk, gems, carpets) (personal communication).

increase (as in Bhavnagar in Gujarat). Dev (2001) compares state per capita income levels with incidence of child labour, and also concludes that there is no linear relationship. This means that, even when the reforms become very successful in the sense of economic growth achievements, there is no reason to assume that this will automatically lead to the elimination of child labour.

19.4.3 General Policy Effects

Macroeconomic and policy changes are likely to have an impact on some general administrative and economic conditions. They may change the overall administrative and economic environment in which policies are implemented and services are provided, and thereby also the benefits that children may derive from these policies and services. I will focus on two such general policy effects, related to decentralisation and government budgets.

19.4.3.1 Decentralisation

One of the new legislations introduced in the 1990s is the 73rd and 74th Amendment to the Constitution, devolving powers from the state government to rural and urban elected bodies. The 73rd Amendment lists 29 subjects for devolution. These include some key social services, such as sanitation, health and primary education, which are of immediately relevance to the welfare of children.

Decentralisation has been advocated for several reasons. First, it is thought that decentralisation could improve governance. Reducing the distance between those who plan and those who are supposed to benefit would help in raising accountability. Second, decentralisation would enhance political participation and therefore deepen democracy. Third, decentralisation would help to improve the quality and suitability of services, as programmes could become more needs-based when designed by (people close to) the target group, rather than by a state-level bureaucracy. Given these arguments in favour of decentralisation, one could hypothesise that poor children would benefit from decentralisation.

In an all-India study covering both health and education, Mahal *et al.* (2000) have tried to test whether decentralisation has led to improved outcomes in rural India. Their conclusion is that "indicators of democratisation and public participation, such as frequency of elections, presence of non-governmental organisations, parent–teacher associations, and indicator variables for decentralised states generally have the expected positive effects, although these are not always statistically indistinguishable from zero" (ibid: 73). The database used in this study was the 1994 survey by the National Council of Applied Economic Research, so the study captured inter-state variation in decentralisation, and not so much the impact of the 1992 Amendment to the Constitution.

In general, most scholars of decentralisation in India emphasise that there are potential benefits for the poor, but that decentralisation can also provide the rural rich with an additional arena in which they can assert their power (Mathew and Nayak, 1996). In his review of the literature, Johnson (2003) states that "[s]tudies of decentralisation have consistently highlighted the fact that the 73rd Amendment and earlier attempts at decentralisation have failed to prevent a local (and primarily landed) elite from controlling local *panchayats.* Micro-level studies have shown that *gram sabha* often fail to fulfil their role as deliberative bodies or as mechanism for accountability. (...) Even when there are reservations to ensure that marginal groups have a place in the *panchayat* system, there is evidence to suggest that these formal institutions have been usurped by more informal patterns of domination and power. Reservations for women, for instance, are notoriously prone to corruption by male relatives (...). Similar patterns have been observed among [Scheduled Castes and Scheduled Tribes], whose economic well being is dependent on the patronage of local elites" (Johnson, 2003: 29). Moreover, experiences elsewhere have shown that good quality service delivery at the local level sometimes requires primarily an effective Central government that stimulates and fosters a culture of accountability between local officials and the poor (Moore and Putzel, 2000; Tendler, 1997).

An additional issue that is to be taken into account is that the term 'decentralisation' can refer to different processes. Different states in India have implemented the 73rd and 74th Amendments to different degrees and have also experimented with different modes of decentralisation. In Andhra Pradesh there is, for instance, hardly any devolution of powers to the elected *panchayats*, but there is a wide-scale attempt to establish stakeholder committees in relation to virtually all development subjects (for example, village education committees, patent–teacher associations, village health committees etc.). More generally, in actual practice, decentralisation has sometimes taken place only with regard to the functions the state governments were no longer willing to perform. Decentralisation can become a means of shedding government responsibilities, rather than of increasing meaningful participation. Altogether, this means that the question whether decentralisation has contributed to the welfare of poor children is too crude. The issue to explore is, rather, which modes of decentralisation, under which conditions, have led to what kind of effects on the rights and capabilities of children. Much more detailed research is necessary to shed light on this question.

19.4.3.2 Government Budgets[16]

The main question with regard to budgets and children is how the reforms have influenced government expenditure for education, health and other social sector items.[17] Table 19.18 shows trends in social sector spending. As percentage of GDP, India spends around 6 to 8 per cent on the social sector. In 1990–91, the share in GDP was 6.78 per cent. Only in 1998–99 was a higher level reached. Throughout the 1990s, social sector expenditure, in terms of percentage of GDP, was lower than that in the late 1980s. As percentage of aggregate government expenditure, India spends between 24 to 28 per cent on the social sector. The percentage started to increase in the middle of the 1990s. In terms of per capita real expenditure, social sector expenditure has continued to increase after 1993–94. Per capita expenditure has risen from Rs. 623 in 1990–91 to Rs. 959 in 2000–01, an increase of 54 per cent in 11 years.

16. The discussion is largely based on a study by Dev and Mooij (2002) on social sector budgets in India in the 1990s. This study defines the social sector as what comes under 'Social Services' and 'Rural Development' in the Indian budgets. Basically, this means health, education, water and sanitation, housing, anti-poverty programmes, employment programmes etc.

17. Another main question is, of course, whether, and to what extent children actually benefit from increases in government expenditure. The answer to this second question depends very much on the quality of the services, and whether increased expenditure goes together with quality improvements or not. This second issue is not taken up in this paper.

Almost all expenditure on the social sector is revenue expenditure, and on the whole this share has increased in the 1990s. This means very little money goes to investments in physical infrastructure, such as schools and health care centres.

Table 19.18

Social Sector (Social Services + Rural Development) Expenditure by Centre and States

Year	Social Sector Expenditure (Revenue and Capital)			
	As % of GDP	*As % of Agg. Pub. Exp. (Rev.+Capital)*	*Per Capita Exp. (in Rs.) In 1993–94 Prices*	*Revenue/Total Social Sector Expenditure (%)*
1987–88	7.74	25.29	562	93.4
1988–89	7.40	25.22	583	93.9
1989–90	7.64	25.19	633	94.6
1990–91	6.78	24.85	623	94.8
1991–92	6.58	24.28	599	94.4
1992–93	6.39	24.06	594	94.8
1993–94	6.46	24.58	623	95.4
1994–95	6.41	25.01	633	94.5
1995–96	6.40	25.95	675	95.3
1996–97	6.48	27.22	739	94.9
1997–98	6.60	26.95	789	95.3
1998–99	6.94	27.36	890	95.1
1999–2000(R)	7.55	27.69	1027	94.2
2000–01(B)	6.97	26.61	959	93.9

Note: R: revised; B: budget

Source: Based on Dev and Mooij (2002: Table 3), estimates based on data from *Indian Public Finance Statistics*, GOI, 1995 and 2000–01.

On the basis of this table, different arguments can be made. Advocates of the reforms can claim that the figures show that the reforms mean a reduced state intervention in certain sectors but an enhanced expenditure in the social sector. After all, after the mid-1990s, there has been an increase in social sector expenditure taken as a percentage of overall government expenditure. Opponents of the reforms, on the other hand, can claim that the social sector has suffered in the 1990s because, as a percentage of GDP, social sector expenditure in the 1990s was less than what it was in the late 1980s.

About 80 per cent of social sector expenditure is done by the state governments. There is a division of responsibilities, where the Centre is responsible for the all-India schemes (such as Operation Blackboard, the midday meal scheme, disease-related programmes, rural employment schemes), while the state governments have their own schemes and finance the departments, schools, hospitals, primary health care centres and other provision. Table 19.19 compares growth in social sector expenditure of the Centre with that of the aggregate states, in the 1980s and the 1990s. Both in the 1980s and in the 1990s, the annual trend growth has been higher in the Centre than in the states. The table also shows that, although social sector expenditure continued to increase in the 1990s (except for the states, taken as percentage of aggregate government expenditure), the annual trend growth rates were much higher in the 1980s than in the 1990s. So, although, by most indicators, social sector expenditure continued to increase in the 1990s, it was at a much lower pace than in the 1980s.

Table 19.19

Trend Growth Rates of Social Sector Expenditure

	1980–1990	*1992–2003*
Centre		
TGR as % GDP	8.93	1.34
TGR as % aggr. expenditure	5.41	0.82
TGR p.c. real expenditure	14.12	6.34
States		
TGR as % GSDP	4.34	0.85
TGR as % aggr. expenditure	2.46	–0.48
TGR p.c. real expenditure	9.29	5.44

Source: Dev and Mooij (forthcoming: Table 19.7).

A further disaggregation of social sector expenditure at the Central level shows that education expenditure has declined slightly in the early 1990s, but then increased from 0.25 per cent of GDP in 1992–93 to 0.36 per cent of GDP in 2000–01. Central expenditure on health and family welfare continued to fluctuate between 0.20 and 0.25 per cent of GDP (Dev and Mooij, 2002: Table 19.9). Table 19.20 gives information on changes within the education and health sectors. In the case of education, there was a clear shift away from secondary, adult and technical education, towards elementary education. This shift has not taken place in the states (Dev and Mooij, 2002: Table 19.21). In the case of health, the share of maternal and child health care has more than doubled. In short, the intra-sectoral allocations have moved clearly towards child-priority areas. In 1995–96, 3.8 per cent of GDP was spent on education (Centre and states), which is still much below the 6 per cent norm the Government of India formulated in its 1968 National Educational Policy.

Table 19.20

Intra-sectoral Allocation (%) in Education, Health and Rural Development: Central Government Expenditure

	1990-91	*1991-92*	*1992-93*	*1993-94*	*1994-95*	*1995-96*	*1996-97*	*1997-98*	*1998-99*	*1999-2000(R)*	*2000-01(B)*
					Education						
Education sector	100	100	100	100	100	100	100	100	100	100	100
Elementary	13.6	15.5	18.6	20.2	20.5	39.6	42.0	48.1	42.9	39.0	37.7
Secondary	23.5	24.4	25.0	25.6	24.1	19.9	19.0	15.0	15.5	14.4	14.3
University & higher	28.6	28.7	28.0	24.9	25.6	19.9	19.5	20.2	25.1	29.6	31.0
Adult	8.3	6.4	6.3	7.8	8.5	4.7	3.1	1.8	1.3	1.1	1.3
Technical	19.0	18.4	18.7	18.3	18.6	14.0	14.5	13.0	13.6	14.1	13.5
Others	7.0	6.6	3.4	3.2	2.7	1.9	1.9	1.9	1.6	1.8	2.2
					Health and Family Welfare						
Health & family welfare	100	100	100	100	100	100	100	100	100	100	100
Public health	13.0	12.9	16.6	16.6	18.0	17.7	19.7	18.9	16.4	14.1	14.8
Medical education	13.5	12.9	13.6	12.4	12.3	12.2	12.3	13.1	15.2	13.1	13.9
Rural family welf.	16.2	15.0	17.2	15.8	13.2	13.7	12.4	13.9	15.3	21.4	16.2
Maternal & child health	6.9	7.2	5.4	6.0	6.3	11.0	11.9	13.6	15.3	13.6	15.2
Other services and supplies	21.8	21.9	21.1	26.2	28.5	23.1	19.5	17.6	16.5	17.9	20.2
Others	28.6	30.1	26.1	23.0	21.7	22.3	24.2	22.9	21.3	19.7	19.6

Note: (1). All the data in this table refer to revised estimates; (2). Others in health & family welfare refer to Central government health schemes, hospitals & dispensaries, urban family welfare. Maternal & child heath was replaced by reproductive & child health in 1998–99.

Source: Dev and Mooij (2002: Table 12), based on Vol II, budget papers GoI,

In the 1990s, as a corollary of the reform process, the contribution of external aid to social sector expenditure has increased significantly. This is especially the case with regard to sectoral spending on children. The share of external aid in sectoral spending on children in the Union budget has increased from 0.5 per cent in 1990–91 to around 29 per cent in 1997–98. On average for the 1990s, out of every 100 rupees spent on children, around 20 rupees came from external aid (Haq, 2001).[18] The share of external aid is the highest in the health sector. More than 50 per cent of child health expenditure came from external sources. The main donors/lenders include international organisations such as World Bank, several organs of the United Nations and the British Department for International Development (DFID). The obvious disadvantage of this high share is that there is a risk that these programmes follow the demands of the foreign funders, both in substance and in organisation. Local ownership is compromised; departmental officers may be sidelined as the donors sometimes insist on implementation through a separate agency, and sustainability can become problematic when the donors withdraw. It is for that reason that Haq (2001: 32) is very critical and suggests it would be better not to tie 'the future of our children' to conditionalities imposed by the donors.

To sum up, there is no evidence of a significant decline in social sector expenditure in the 1990s. Central social sector expenditure has become more focused on child–priority areas. This may be the result of large donor contributions. Generally, the Centre has done better than the states. The decline in state allocations is worrisome. After all, the states have the main responsibility for social sector development. If we take allocations as a proxy for political commitment (which is what Prabhu (2001) does), the conclusion is that the commitment of the states to social development has declined during the reform period. In the area of health, the shift from the states towards the Centre is a cause for concern, as it means more emphasis on vertical disease-related interventions—which is what the Centre mainly does—and less on primary health care.

Finally, even though there is progress in certain respects, the expenditures on the social sector are still low. This becomes clear, for instance, when we compare the expenditure with some international norms. The United Nations Development Programme (UNDP) has proposed the following four ratios for comparing and monitoring social sector expenditure at the country level (UNDP, 1991).

---

18. To mention a few examples, the donors contributed substantially to the Integrated Child Development Programme (ICDS), Child Survival and Safe Motherhood, Reproductive and Child Health and the District Primary Education Programme.

- The Public Expenditure Ratio: The percentage of national income that goes into public expenditure. The recommendation is to keep this ratio around 25 per cent.
- The Social Allocation Ratio: The percentage of public expenditure earmarked for social services. This ratio, according to the UNDP, should be more than 40 per cent.
- The Social Priority Ratio: The percentage of social expenditure devoted to human priority concerns. This ratio has to be more than 50 per cent.
- The Human Expenditure Ratio: The percentage of national income devoted to human priority concerns. This ratio is the product of the above three ratios and the UNDP recommends that it should be about 5 per cent.

Table 19.21 gives these ratios for India in the late 1980s and the late 1990s. It is clear that there is progress, but the ratios are still far removed from the norms.

Table 19.21

Social Sector Ratios

	UNDP Norm	*Late 1980s*	*1998–99*
Public expenditure ratio	25	37*	25
Social allocation ratio	40	20	27
Social priority ratio	50	34	40
Human expenditure ratio	5	2.5	2.8

Note: Social priority ratio was taken as the share of social sector allocation to elementary education, water & sanitation, public health, maternal & child health and child nutrition.

* This is much higher than Dev and Mooij's (2002) calculation, and it may be that there is a difference in the methodologies used by the two sources.

Source: Based on UNDP (1991) and Dev and Mooij (2002).

19.4.4 Indirect Fallout

Perhaps the most important impact of the economic reform on welfare of children has to do with the intangible effects on people's mindsets and attitudes. This impact is visible in day-to-day life, although it is neither simple and straightforward, nor uniform across regions and social classes. Nevertheless, there is no doubt that in the past 10–15 years, social norms, public ideals and collective aspirations have changed, and that this is related to the reform process in one way or another. This paper discusses two such impacts, namely: 1) the changing ideas about the role of the state, and the emergence of a 'two-nation-state', and 2) cultural identities and subordination of women.

19.4.4.1 Ideas about the State and the Emergence of a 'Two–Nation–State'

In their assessment of the economic reforms in India, Corbridge and Harriss (2000: 169) make and important point, namely that the reforms "are not simply about the renegotiation of India's relationships with the global market-place, nor even are they about the relationships of private capital with the Indian state in the formal economy; the reforms are also about the reworking of the idea of the state itself and of the state's capacity to work on behalf of those who stand outside India's (expanding) social and economic elites." The question is what impact this 'reworking of the idea of the state' and its capacity to work for the marginalised sections of society will have on the long-term social commitment to work towards an improvement in the living conditions of poor people.

It is particularly in the areas of health and education that we may fear the consequences of this potentially declining commitment. Both sectors have experienced rapid privatisation in the past 10–15 years. With regard to health, while 40 per cent of the in-patients were treated in private hospitals in 1986–87, this percentage had risen to 55 per cent in 1995–96. Seventy-four (74) per cent of the rural out-patients were treated in private hospitals in 1986–87, as against 82 per cent in 1995–1996.[19] The figures are less extreme with regard to preventive care (immunisation, contraception) where a larger percentage of the population makes use of public sector facilities. Nevertheless, there is a clear trend towards the use of private sector facilities, which are generally more expensive. The government hospitals are becoming facilities of the last resort, accessed mainly by very poor people who have no other alternative.[20] The trend towards the private sector has been

19. Narayana (2003: Tables 19.1 and 19.2).

20. What comes under private care is, however, a mixed bag. It includes both quack-doctors as well as corporate hospitals, the importance of which is rising.

stimulated directly by the Centre and state governments and is part of the health reform policies.

With regard to education, the trend is also clearly in the direction of privatisation. The trend is stronger in urban than in rural areas, although also in villages, 'private schools are a flourishing business' (PROBE Report, 1999: 102). Although there is a lot of variation within the category of private schools, on average they are much more expensive than government schools. The PROBE team found that it is particularly this cost element that makes some poor parents decide not to send their children to a private school. Again, the trend towards privatisation has been stimulated by the government, by active encouragement of commercial investment in education (Srivastava, 2003: 74), but also indirectly by continuous neglect of government schools. The PROBE team reports that even in central Bihar, where poverty is endemic, "private schools can be found in many villages (...) due to the dysfunctional state of government schools" (PROBE Report, 1999: 102).

This privatisation of health and educational facilities does not only mean that less people are making use of public provisions, and that education and health care become more expensive. It is also likely to affect the quality of the public provisions in a negative way. At the micro-level, when better-off families do no longer make use of public health facilities and withdraw their children from government schools, the status of these provisions declines and the social pressure to provide good services diminishes. At the macro-level, the social support base for investment in public provisions is likely to be affected. The politically and economically influential middle and upper classes may lose interest in their quality and in financially contributing to these public services, when they themselves no longer make use of them. As these groups are the main tax payers, and are relatively influential in agenda setting and policy making, their loss of interest can easily translate in an overall neglect on the part of the state. The result may be a two–nation state, in which the richer parts of the population secure their social welfare through private channels, and the poorer sections have no choice but to resort to ever deteriorating public sector provisions.

19.4.4.2 Cultural Identities and Subordination of Women

One very worrisome trend briefly mentioned above is the decline in juvenile sex ratios (See Table 19.7). The 2001 Census showed that, while the overall sex ratio has gone up slightly between 1991 and 2001 (from 927 to 933), the juvenile sex ratio has gone further down, from 945 to 927. The first phenomenon indicates that the female death ratios have come down more than the male death ratios. The declining juvenile sex ratio is related to differences in girls' and boys' infant and child mortality rates, and, in certain regions to female foeticide.[21] Sex-determination of foetuses, as Sudha and Irudaya Raja (n.d.) report, is illegal, but the relevant legislation is full of loopholes and the number of clinics offering sex determination and instant abortus in case the foetus proves to be female has increased rapidly during the 1980s. "The first newspaper reports of private clinics offering sex selection techniques appeared in 1982–83, in cities such as Amritsar, Bombay, and Delhi. Within 2–3 years thereafter, the numbers of such clinics rose to several hundred in the larger cities, and several dozen in smaller towns in Maharashtra, UP, Punjab, and Gujarat states. (...) Remote districts that lacked basic amenities such as drinking water or electricity have been reported to have sex determination clinics; where refrigeration and cold chain facilities for vaccinations are not available but amniotic fluid samples are sent in ice packs to towns for testing (...)" (Sudha and Irudaya Raja, n.d.: 5).

A rather disconcerting phenomenon is that low juvenile sex ratios are not (cor)related to poverty and that the sex ratios do not increase with increasing prosperity. On the contrary. As Premi (2001: 1875) states, "All the states that have shown large declines in child sex ratio between 1991 and 2001—Punjab, Haryana, Himachal Pradesh, Gujarat, Maharashtra, Chandigarh and Delhi—are economically well-developed and have recorded a fairly high literacy rate." Relative female disadvantage is, hence, not a characteristic of economic underdevelopment, but rather the reverse. Upward economic mobility or

21. This last point is also stated by Mari Bhat (2002b), who is otherwise very cautious to draw conclusions about gender biases. This author states that "[t]he accelerated fall in the child sex ratio after 1981 seems to be largely due to the diffusion of prenatal sex selection techniques in regions with well-entrenched gender bias" (Mari Bhat, 2002b: 5244). See also Agnihotri (2003a).

prosperity seem to be positively associated with sex ratio differentials (Agnihotri, 2003b). This phenomenon is further explored by Nillisen and Harriss–White (forthcoming), who have correlated the probability of girl survival in two districts in Tamil Nadu with various social indicators. Their conclusion is that girl disadvantage is positively associated with increases in wealth, adult female literacy and landed property. The lowest juvenile sex ratio can be found among landed caste households. It is only 645, while the aggregate ratio of these two districts is 856.

Although declining juvenile sex ratios is not a new phenomenon, it is not inconceivable, as Nillisen and Harriss–White (forthcoming) also state, that the reforms have further contributed to this decline. This could be so because the reforms may reinforce the various motives behind a preference for sons as compared to daughters. Generally, the literature suggests that there are two kind of motives behind a preference for sons, and the regional variation in sex ratios.[22] First, sons are preferred to the extent that their future labour and income contribution to the household is more than that of daughters. This would explain some of the low sex ratios in the wheat-producing north of India, where traditionally women participate less in agricultural production.[23] Second, cultural factors, in particular the marriage system and the importance of dowry, would play an important role. Both explanations assume that daughters are seen as a liability, and that it is for that reason that female foetuses are aborted, or daughters are less well cared for than sons. Since the reforms affect employment patterns as well as cultural ambitions, it is plausible that they could indirectly affect the extent of son preference and girl survival chances.

Declining labour force participation of women and casualisation of female labour are well-known effects of structural adjustment programmes in many parts of the world, and have been highlighted in several studies on gender and structural adjustment.[24] The trend is also visible in India. Table 19.22 compares work participation rates of men

22. See Harriss–White (1999) for a review of some of the literature.

23. As Agnihotri (2003a) shows, the traditional north–south divide is breaking down, with the declining juvenile sex ratios in urban areas in south India.

24. See, for instance, Elson (1995).

and women, and illustrates that work participation of women has decreased more than that of men.

Table 19.22

Work Participation Rates (All Age Groups) (in percentages)

	Rural		*Urban*	
	Male	*Female*	*Male*	*Female*
1987–88	53.9	32.3	50.6	15.2
1993–94	55.3	32.8	52.1	15.5
1999–2000	53.1	29.9	51.8	13.9

Source: Chadha and Sahu (2002: Table 1), based on NSS data.

The quality of employment, as measured by the employment quality index, is considerably lower for women than for men, and has declined between 1987–88 and 1993–94 for both men and women (see Table 19.15), more or less to the same extent. Based on more recent extensive studies of women workers in various informal sectors, Jhabvala and Sinha (2002: 2037) conclude that in the era of liberalisation and globalisation, 'a decline in employment opportunities has seen a simultaneous "casualisation" and growing "feminisation" of the workforce—with concomitant ills of low wages and declining job security'. All these changes could have eroded the bargaining position and economic value of women within households even further, with negative effects on the position and relative survival chances of daughters.

Dowry has been one of the very important factors behind son preference. In fact, this was openly acknowledged in the early eighties, when sex determination clinics started to advertise with the slogan 'Better Rs. 500 today than Rs. 5,00,000 tomorrow'. As a result of protests from women's groups, the slogan was put to a stop, but the rationale still holds.[25] The importance of dowry has only increased during the last decades. Within one generation, the incidence of dowry has risen from 45 to 80 per cent of all marriages.[26] It has spread to

25. Sudha and Irudaya Raja (n.d.: 6).

26. Harriss–White (1999).

hierarchically 'lower' caste groups that did not practice dowry in the past. This sanskritisation, i.e., the process in which 'lower' caste groups adopt cultural practices of 'higher' caste groups, is sometimes seen as a concomitant of modernisation.[27] Another factor explaining the increasing incidence of dowry could be the spread of consumerism. With Sunder Rajan (1996), it could be argued that market development strengthens the dowry system as 'supply creates its own demand by seducing the customer into new forms of desire...[D]owry in contemporary India (is) significantly linked to the scenario of spreading consumerism through the market...Families can anticipate rapid upward social mobility in addition to (and because of) the actual price their sons fetch at the marriage market with the acquisition of such goods'.[28] If there is a relationship between market development, consumerism and dowry, we can expect that the reforms, with their impact on markets, lifestyles and consumption patterns, will have a devastating effect on the practice of dowry, and on girl survival chances.

It is, however, also important to note that scholars have warned against too simplistic explanations of excess girl child death. There are huge regional differences in India, not only in juvenile sex rations, but also in factors apparently correlated (Harriss-White, 1999). The issue is far from settled, but there is more than enough reason for concern about the declining juvenile sex ratios, and about the potentially negative fall-out of the reforms on the position of women, and on girl survival chances.

19.5 Conclusions and Research Questions

This paper started with a brief description of the various kinds of reforms that have been introduced in India generally. The third section of the paper proceeded with a short description of what happened to child welfare in India during the reform period. Altogether, there is no indication that the negative scenario that was depicted by UNICEF's *Adjustment with a Human Face* (Cornia *et al.*, 1987) has been reproduced in India. The picture is, in fact, quite mixed. Poverty figures

27. Nillisen and Harriss-White (forthcoming), Sudha and Irudaya Raja (n.d.).

28. Harriss-White (1999: 142).

(head count) have come down, but inequality has increased. Literacy rates and school enrolment have increased, and the rate of decline in illiteracy is higher in the 1990s than in the 1980s. Infant mortality rates have also continued to decline, but less so in the 1990s than in the 1980s. One particularly worrying aspect is the continuing decline of the juvenile sex ratio, indicating decreasing relative survival chances for girls as compared to boys. The level of government expenditure on social sector items, discussed in the fourth section of this paper, has not come down, although the pace of growth of social sector expenditure has been much lower in the 1990s than in the pre-reform period. With regard to education and health, the 1990s have witnessed a shift in spending patterns towards child priority areas. The financial support from international donors for child development programmes has multiplied in the 1990s. International donors, it seems, have taken the message from the UNICEF study very seriously. Although they do not want to give up on adjustment, they do want to make sure that children are not affected adversely.

It is impossible to establish simple and uniform causal relations between the reform process and aggregate trends in child welfare. The paper has, hence, proceeded in the fourth section with a discussion of a number of mechanisms through which reform policies could perhaps affect rights and capabilities of children. Four different kind of mechanisms were distinguished, namely: a) some sectoral policies may have a direct effect on children's rights and capabilities; b) economic policy changes may affect household livelihoods, and thereby indirectly the welfare of children in these households; c) some policies are likely to have an effect on the wider administrative and economic conditions (systems of governance; availability of government funds, etc.), which may impinge on the quality of government services and on child welfare; and d) the reforms may influence social norms, lifestyles and aspirations of people, with consequences for child welfare. Each of these mechanisms was elaborated and a number of relationships, linking (particular) reform (measures) with particular effects on child welfare (of particular groups of children) were discussed. Here I will highlight the most salient relationships and make some further research suggestions for each of them.

19.5.1 Reforms and Child Labour

The statistics of child labour do not suggest an overall increase in the 1990s. On the contrary, the incidence of child labour has declined in the 1990s. Nevertheless, and this is suggested by several authors,[29] it may well be that in particular pockets child labour has increased as a result of reform policies. Two different types of mechanisms may play a role. On the one hand, it may be that deteriorating livelihoods of particular groups of people (i.e., people who have become unemployed as a result of import liberalisation) have forced families to put their children to work. On the other hand, it may be that Indian industries, in order to survive in an increasingly competitive global environment, have to resort to the cheapest and most docile labour force, i.e., children.

So far, there are very few studies which prove empirically that particular instances of child labour are, indeed, related to recent economic policies.[30] More research would be useful to get a better idea of the relationship between reforms and child labour. Such studies could have three different components. First, the research could focus on the working children and their families, particularly in locations/sectors/industries in which child labour is a relatively new phenomenon. It needs to be investigated where these children came from (and what they used to do before), what their (or their families') motivation was to go for work, what their contribution is to overall household income and whether alternative household survival strategies exist. A second component could be research at the level of the firms, in order to understand the accumulative strategies of the entrepreneurs or (sub)contractors. This could be complemented with a more general investigation of the profitability of the sector in the world market. Such a study would be necessary to assess the validity of the pull–factor argument. A third component could be the investigation of firms that have decided to get rid of child labour. This could shed light on the conditions that made this local elimination of child labour possible and/or necessary (e.g. in the case of a looming international boycott). It may be that not only an occasional increase, but also the decrease of child

29. See, for instance, Gayathri and Chaudhri (2002), Gulrajani (1994), Raman (1997), Vidyasagar (1999) and Wazir (2002).

30. One of the rare empirical studies making this point is Swaminathan (1998).

labour in certain pockets or industries is related to the reforms policies, in direct or indirect ways.

19.5.2 Reforms, Privatisation of Education and Health Facilities and Poor Children's Access to Good Quality Services

The establishment of private educational and health facilities is not a new phenomenon that started with or after the reforms. Private institutions existed already long before 1991. There is, however, no doubt that the trend has intensified in the 1990s, that it is endorsed and promoted by the government, and that it fits in well with some of the ideological cornerstones of the reform process, namely that private initiative is to be encouraged and that profit-making institutions may work equally well or better than government institutions.

Given the abysmal level of some government schools and hospitals, it is probably often true that private institutions perform better than government institutions. There are, however, two major drawbacks related to: a) the higher costs, and therefore the in-built bias in favour of the better-off, and b) the indirect and possibly negative effects on the quality of government facilities. It is very likely that this quality will deteriorate even further because, when the relatively rich and politically more vocal and influential sections of the population do no longer use government facilities, they will no longer use their voice to demand good quality services, and will become less willing to contribute financially to them (as tax payers).

This scenario raises two more general and theoretical questions that could be taken up in further research. The first is: how is it possible that in a democratic country like India public social sector development could have become so neglected? Generally, it is assumed that in an electoral democracy with a free press, governments cannot afford to neglect the poor and their development. Politicians have to face the public once every five years (if not more often) and therefore have to show their commitment, if not compassion with the poor. The legitimacy of a political regime, and of the state generally, depends partly on what it does to improve the welfare and living conditions of the people. So, given India's democratic set-up, how is it possible that the government could neglect education and health care to the extent that it did? The second question is about the effect of the increasing dualism in health and education on the ability of the state to reach out to the poor. To what extent is India moving towards a two–nation state, in which the richer parts of the population secure their welfare through private channels, and do no longer take responsibility for social sector services in the general public interest?

19.5.3 Reforms, Consumerism, Dowry and the Girl Child

A very worrisome phenomenon is the declining juvenile sex ratio. Juvenile sex ratios decline already for decades in India, but it may be that the reforms have reinforced this trend. This is likely because the reforms have further casualised female labour and have decreased female work participation rates. It could well be that this has contributed to a further erosion of the bargaining position and economic value of women within households. Moreover, the reforms have brought a spurt in consumerism, something that may have exacerbated the phenomenon of dowry—one of the very important factors behind son preference.

These relationships are difficult to investigate. The observation of changing bargaining positions requires long-term intensive anthropological fieldwork, carried out by sensitive field workers. Dowry is officially illegal, but widely practised, and it would probably not be very difficult to list the size and composition of dowries of various social groups in particular localities. Since dowry is the result of a more or less public/family negotiation process, it is probably also possible to interview couples (or their family members) who married 10–15 years ago about the dowries given at the time of their marriage. The really difficult part of the research is, however, the collection of data about neglect of daughters, female infanticide and female foeticide. In contrast to dowry, these are not public phenomena. Dowry may be illegal, but it is never penalised. Female infanticide, however, if it becomes a publicly known fact, may lead to criminal prosecution. Midwives, mothers, doctors running sex-determination clinics and others involved are, hence, not likely to open up. The collection of information regarding the motivation and decision structure behind this neglect of girl children, female infanticide or foeticide is, hence, not easy. It requires not only sensitivity, but also a lot of local familiarity and trust. And even then, dilemmas remain, as it is hard to avoid that the women/mothers/midwives whose trust is needed are put at risk of criminal prosecution when they would cooperate in a research project. All this means that large-scale research is impossible, and that the only way to proceed, if at all, is by doing intensive studies in particular localities with the help of trusted local people or organisations, while securing anonymity as much as possible.

19.5.4 By Way of Conclusion

Reforms in India have not had such devastating effects on children as was feared by some at the start of the reform process on the basis of the earlier experiences. There is, however, also no reason to be complacent or satisfied with the achievements. Still almost half of the children is moderately or severely malnourished. Still about a quarter of the children does not go to school. Still, almost one-tenth of the children that are born alive does not reach the age of five years. Still, the government expenditures on education and health are much less than the UNDP and Indian norms. There is an urgent need to take children more seriously in priority setting and policy making. The paper has also argued that there are a number of ways in which the reforms, or some particular elements of the reforms, could have adverse effects on the rights and capabilities of (particular groups of) children. More fine-tuned and intensive research is necessary to understand the complex and caste-, class- or gender-specific effects of the reform process on children.

References

Acharya, Shankar (2002). "India: Crisis, reforms and growth in the nineties", *Working Paper* No. 139, Center for Research on Economic Development and Policy Reform, Stanford University.

Agnihotri, Satish B. (2003a). "Survival of the girl child. Tunnelling out of the chakravyuha", *Economic and Political Weekly* 38(41): 4351–4360.

———. (2003b). "Sex ratios and 'prosperity effect'. What do NSSO data reveal?" *Economic and Political Weekly* 38(41): 4381–4404.

Athreya, Venkatesh (2001). "Census 2001. Some progress, some concern", *Frontline*, April 27, pp. 107–110.

Baru, Rama V. (2001). "Health sector reforms and structural adjustment: A State-level analysis", in: Imrana Qadeer, Kasturi Sen and K.R. Nayar (eds) *Public Health and the Poverty of Reforms. The South Asian Experience*. New Delhi: Sage. pp. 211–234.

Bhaduri, Amit and Deepak Nayyar (1996). *The Intelligent Person's Guide to Liberalization*. New Delhi: Penguin Books.

Bhalotra, Sonia (2002). "Welfare implications of fiscal reform. The case of food subsidies in India", WIDER *Discussion Paper* No. 2002/32, United Nations University, World Institute for Development Economics Research.

Breman, Jan (1996). *Footloose Labour: Working in India's Informal Economy*. Cambridge: Cambridge University Press.

Chadha, G.K. and P.P. Sahu (2002). "Post-reform set-backs in rural employment. Issues that need further scrutiny", *Economic and Political Weekly* 37(21): 1998–2026.

Chelliah, Raja J. and R. Sudarshan (2001). *Income Poverty and Beyond. Human Development in India*. New Delhi: Social Science Press.

Chunkath, Sheela Rani and V.B, Athreya (1997). "Female infanticide in Tamil Nadu. Some evidence", *Economic and Political Weekly* 32(17): WS21–WS28.

Corbridge, Stuart and John Harriss (2000). *Reinventing India. Liberalization, Hindu Nationalism and Popular Democracy*. Cambridge: Polity Press.

Cornia, Giovanni Andrea, Richard Jolly and Frances Stewart (1987). *Adjustment with a Human Face*. Oxford: Oxford University Press.

Datt, Gaurav, Valerie Kozel and Martin Ravallion (2003). "A model–based assessment of India's progress in reducing poverty in the 1990s", *Economic and Political Weekly* 38(4): 355–361.

Deaton, Angus and Jean Dreze (2002). "Poverty and inequality in India. A re-examination", *Economic and Political Weekly* 37(36): 3729–3748.

Deshpande, Sudha (2002). "Girl child and food security in India", in Nira Ramachandran and Lionel Massün (eds.) *Coming to Grips with Rural Child Work. A Food Security Approach*. Institute for Human Development and United Nations World Food Security Programme, New Delhi. pp. 48–78.

Dev, Mahendra S. (2001). "Child labour in India: Dimensions, determinants and policies", in K.P. Kannan (ed.) *Economics of Child Labour*. New Delhi: Deep and Deep.

———. (2002). "Pro-poor growth in India: What do we know about the employment effects of growth 1980–2000?", *ODI Working Paper* No. 161, Overseas Development Institute, London.

———. (2003). "Right to food in India", Paper prepared for the project on *Right to Development in India* of the Centre for Development and Human Rights (CGHR), New Delhi.

———. (forthcoming). "The use of occupational data from NFHS: A study of female work participation and child labour", *Economic and Political Weekly.*

Dev, S. Mahendra and Jos Mooij (2002). "Social sector expenditures in the 1990s. Analysis of central and state budgets", *Economic and Political Weekly* 37(9): 853–866.

———. (forthcoming). "Patterns of social sector expenditures: Pre- and post-reform period", in R. Radhakrishna (ed.) *India Development Report 2004*. New Delhi: Oxford University Press.

Dev, S. Mahendra and C. Ravi (forthcoming). *Report on Food Security in India* written for the International Food Policy Research Institute, Washington.

Dreze, Jean and Amartya Sen (2002). *India: Development and Participation*. New Delhi: Oxford University Press.

Duggal, Ravi (2003). "Health and development in India. Moving towards rights to healthcare", Paper prepared for the *Right to Development Project* of the Centre for Development and Human Rights and FXB Centre, Harvard School of Public Health.

Elson, Diana (ed.) (1995). *Male Bias in the Development Process*. Manchester: Manchester University Press.

Gayathri, V. and D.P. Chaudhri (2002). "Introduction", in *Indian Journal of Labour Economics* (Special issues on Child Labour: Dimensions and Policy Options) 45(3): 443–450.

Ghose, Ajit K. (1999). "Current issues of employment policy in India", *Economic and Political Weekly* 34(36): 2592–2608.

Government of India (2002a). *National Human Development Report 2001*. Planning Commission, Government of India. Delhi: Oxford University Press.

———. (2002b). National Health Policy. Ministry of Health and Family Welfare, Government of India.

Gulrajani, Mohini (1994). "Child labour and the export sector in the third world: A case study of the Indian carpet industry", *Labour, Capital and Society* 27(2): 192–214.

Haq: Centre for Child Rights (2001). *India's Children and the Union Budget*. Chapter 1 Children's Budget. HAQ Centre for Child Rights, New Delhi.

Harriss-White, Barbara (1999). "Gender-cleansing: The paradox of development and deteriorating female life chances in Tamil Nadu", in: Rajeswari Sunder Rajan (ed.) *Signposts. Gender Issue in Post-Independence India*. New Delhi: Kali for Women. pp. 124–153.

———. (2003). *India Working. Essays on Society and Economy*. Cambridge: Cambridge University Press.

Hirway, Indira (2002). "Employment and unemployment situation in the 1990s. How good are the NSS data?", *Economic and Political Weekly* 37(21): 2027–2036.

Jenkins, Rob (1999). *Democratic Politics and Economic Reform in India*. Cambridge: Cambridge University Press.

Jhabvala, Renana and Shalini Sinha (2002). "Liberalisation and the women worker", *Economic and Political Weekly* 37(21): 2037–2044.

Johnson, Craig (2003). "Decentralisation in India: Poverty, politics and panchayats", *ODI Working Paper* No. 199, Overseas Development Institute, London.

Kothari, Smitu (1997). "Whose independence? The social impact of economic reform in India", *Journal of International Affairs* 51(1): 85–116.

Krishnan, T.N. (1999). "Access to health and the burden of treatment in India: An inter-state comparison", in: Mohan Rao (ed.) *Disinvesting in Health. The World Bank's Prescriptions for Health*. New Delhi: Sage. pp. 208–230.

Mahal, Ajay, Vivel Srivastava and Deepak Sanan (2000). "Decentralization and public sector delivery of health and education services: The Indian experience", ZEF *Discussion Paper* No. 20, Centre for Development Research, Bonn.

———. (2002a). "On the trail of 'Missing' Indian females. I. Search for clues", *Economic and Political Weekly* 37(51): 5105–5118.

Mari Bhat, P.N. (2002b). "On the trail of 'Missing' Indian females. II. Illusion and reality", *Economic and Political Weekly* 37(52): 5244–5263.

Mathew, George and Ramesh C. Nayak (1996). "Panchayats at work. What it means for the oppressed?", *Economic and Political Weekly* 31(27): 1765–1771.

Mooij, Jos (1999). "Real targeting: the case of food distribution in India", *Food Policy* 24: 49–69.

Mooij, Jos and S. Mahendra Dev (2002). "Social sector priorities. An analysis of budgets and expenditures in India in the 1990s", *IDS Working Paper* No. 164, Institute of Development Studies, Sussex.

Moore, Mick and James Putzel (2000). "Thinking strategically about politics and poverty", *IDS Working Paper* No. 101, Institute of Development Studies, Sussex.

Narayana, K.V. (2003). "Changing health care system", *Economic and Political Weekly* 38(12 and 13): 1230–1241.

NIEPA (2002). *India Education Report. A Profile of Basic Education*. Edited by R. Govinda, National Institute of Educational Planning and Administration. New Delhi: Oxford University Press.

Nillisen, Paul H.L. and Barbara Harriss-White (forthcoming). "Chapter 3-2: Life changes: development and female disadvantage", in: Barbara Harriss-White and S. Janakarajan (eds.) *Rural India Facing the 21st Century*. London: Anthem.

Panini, M.N. (1995). "The social logic of liberalization", *Sociological Bulletin* 44(1): 33–62.

Powis, Benjamin (2003). "Grass roots politics and 'second wave of decentralisation' in Andhra Pradesh", *Economic and Political Weekly* 38(26): 2617–2622.

Prabhu, Seeta (2001). *Economic Reform and Social Sector Development. A Study of Two Indian States*. New Delhi: Sage.

Premi, Mahendra K. (2001). "The missing girl child", *Economic and Political Weekly* 36(21): 1875–1880.

PROBE team (1999). *Public Report on Basic Education in India*. New Delhi: Oxford University Press.

Purohit, Brijesh C. (n.d.). "Structural adjustment and the health care sector in India. Some policy issues in financing", Queen Elizabeth House *Working Paper* Series No. 2, Oxford.

(Abjihit) Sen Committee (2002). *Report of the High Level Committee on Long-Term Grain Management*. Department of Food and Public Distribution, Ministry of Consumer Affairs, Food and Public Distribution, Government of India.

Raman, Vasanthi (1997). "Globalization and child labour", Paper presented in the seminar on *Globalisation and Democracy in the Third World*, Academy of Third World Studies, Jamai Millia Islamic Society, New Delhi, 7–8 October, 1997 (Abridged version available from: *http://revolutionarydemocracy.org/rdv4n1/childlab.htm*)

Reserve Bank of India (2002). *Handbook of Statistics on the Indian Economy*, RBI Mumbai.

RoyChowdhury, Supriya (forthcoming). "Labour and economic reforms: Disjointed critiques", in Jos Mooij (ed.) *The Politics of the Economic Reform Process in India*.

Sadgopal, Anil (2001). "Between the lines. Rights and wrongs in Education Bill", *The Times of India*, 28 November 2002.

———. (2002). "A convenient consensus. The political economy of the constitution (93rd Amendment) bill", *Frontline*, 4 January 2002.

Saleth, R. Maria (1993). "Structural adjustment and child welfare: Scenarios, strategies, and options", *IASSI Quarterly* 12(1&2): 137–152.

Sen, Amartya (1992). *Inequality Reexamined*. Oxford: Clarendon Press.

Shariff, Abusaleh and P.K. Ghosh (2000). "Indian education scene and public gap", *Economic and Political Weekly* 35(16): 1396–1406.

Srinivasan, T.N. (2003). "Indian economic reforms: A stocktaking", Paper presented at the Fourth Annual Conference on *Indian Economic Policy Reform*; the Center for Research on Economic Development and Policy Reform, Stanford University, June 6–7, 2003.

Srivastava, A.B.L. (2002). "Some significant features of literacy data of the 2001 census and projections of literacy rate for the population of age group 15+", Paper presented at Seminar on *Progress of Literacy in India: What the Census 2001 preveals*, NIEPA, New Delhi.

Srivastava, Ravi S. (2003). *The Right to Education in India*. Country Report for the Right to Development Project, Centre for Development and Human Rights New Delhi and Harvard Centre for Population and Development Studies.

Sudha, S. and S. Irudaya Raja (n.d.). "Intensifying masculinity of sex ratios in India: new evidence 1981–91", Forums Available from: *www.hsph.harvard.edu/Organizations/healthnet/SAsia/forums/foeticide/articles/sexratio.html*

Sunder Rajan, R. (1996). "The downed woman", Paper presented in *Modern Languages Conference*, Dec. 29-30. Washington.

Swaminathan, Madhura (1998). "Economic growth and the persistence of child labour: Evidence from an Indian city", *World Development* 26(8): 1513–28.

———. (2000). *Weakening Welfare. The Public Distribution of Food in India*. New Delhi: LeftWord Books.

———. (2001). "Errors of targeting. Public distribution of food in a Maharashtra village, 1995–2000", *Economic and Political Weekly*, June 30.

Tendler, Judith (1997). *Good Government in the Tropics*. Baltimore and London: John Hopkins University Press.

UNDP (1991). *Human Development Report 1991*. New York: Oxford University Press.

Vaidyanathan, A. (2001). "Quality, reliability of NSS data at stake", *The Hindu*, April 19.

Vidyasagar, R. (1999). "Overview of child labour in India", Paper presented at the workshop on *Needs Versus Rights: Social Policy From a Child-Centred Perspective*, Institute of Development Studies and Zakir Husain Centre for Educational Studies, JNU, New Delhi, July 28–30.

Virmani, Arvind and P.V. Rajeev (2002). "Excess food stocks, PDS and procurement policy", *Working Paper* No. 5/2002 –PC, Planning Commission India.

Wazir, Rekha (2002). "Eliminating child labour: Do NGO interventions add up to a strategy?", in *Indian Journal of Labour Economics* (Special issues on Child Labour: Dimensions and Policy Options) 45(3): 615–632.

White, Ben (1996). "Globalization and the child labour problem", *Journal of International Development* 8(6): 829–839.

White, Howard and Andrew Masters (n.d.). "Analysing the impact of macroeconomic and policy changes on child welfare outcomes", Background note for the *Children of the Millenium Project* (unpublished).

Williamson, John and Roberto Zagha (2002). "From the hindu rate of growth to the hindu rate of reform", *Working Paper* No. 144, Center for Research on Economic Development and Policy reform, Stanford University.

World Bank (1993). *World Development Report 1993: Investing in Health*. World Bank, Washington.

———. (2000). *Overview of Rural Decentralization*. (Vol. II Approaches to Rural Decentralization in Seven States.) World Bank, Washington.

20 Monitoring Poverty and Human Development Indicators*

A Framework

R.S. Deshpande and K.V. Raju

20.1 Need for a System of Poverty Monitoring

In the current phase of liberalisation, there is growing concern about the trends in poverty and the human face of reforms. Keeping in view the reform process, it is necessary to locate the impact of reforms on the poor, as fears are expressed that the poor as a group may be bypassed in the process of reforms. Poverty as a concept has been treated always as synonymous to under-nourishment and more often has been defined as the consumption level below a recommended balanced diet in terms of calories. For about three decades, barring a few exceptions, most of the studies used poverty line as given in the earlier works and updated it with the help of price deflators. One of the difficulties of such an approach is that poverty lines remained sensitive to price fluctuations and more attached to the income concept of poverty. Such exercises also presumed that price indices used are flawless in the methods of computation and the weights for CPI/WPI are updated frequently. But this view is now being challenged (Deaton and Tarozzi, 2000; Suryanarayana, 2000). It is more than accepted now that the official measure of poverty is essentially the income poverty concept based on per capita consumption expenditure and therefore, the debates as well as the policy interventions are tuned more to this measure of poverty.

* This is a fully revised version of the paper presented at the Workshop on Poverty and Human Development and Monitoring System, sponsored by Planning Department, Government of Karnataka on 2-3 February 2001. Authors wish to record their gratitude to the participants of the workshop for their comments and thanks to Mr. Abhijit Dasgupta for encouragement. Usual disclaimers apply.

The debate on poverty that serves as a strong background to the current thinking can be broadly classified into three phases. In the first phase, it was the argument between Dandekar on one side and V.K.R.V. Rao, Sukhatme and a few others holding contrary views on the other (see Krishnaswamy, 1996). The bone of contention was the intra-group differences in poverty and the method of computation of poverty. Some of the important issues discussed during that debate still hold ground and assume concurrent importance. One of the significant issues discussed during the debate related to the share of non-food consumption as an indicator of poverty (Rao and Vivekananda, 1982), thereby marking a simple but very pertinent point that poverty has a non-food angle too. The second phase of the poverty debate was marked by determinants of rural poverty and trends in poverty ratio. The literature pertaining to the search for determinants points towards the sectoral growth pattern, education levels, initial endowment, infrastructure and other important determinants of poverty across the states in the country (Ahluwalia, 1978; 2000 and Ravallion and Datt, 2000). This also features in the current debate, in the context of impact of liberalisation on poverty alleviation.

As regards the trends in income poverty estimates for India, there are substantial differences in perceptions available from the literature and a large part of this has to be attributed to the methodological fine-tuning. Ravallion and Datt (1996), Datt (1999) and Ravallion and Datt (2000) arrived at a time series of poverty estimates over a longer period. The trends indicate that rural poverty ratios stayed in the range of 45 to 63 per cent between 1951 to 1966 with an increasing trend. Subsequently, the poverty ratio declined at a faster rate till 1986–87 and thereafter remained in the neighbourhood of 40 per cent (Karanth and Deshpande, 2000). As regards urban poverty, the decline was marked only after 1973–74.[i] Tendulkar (in Chelliah and Sudarshan, 1999), in his analysis of trends in income poverty based on three points of time namely 1983, 1987–88, and 1993–94, records a decline in rural poverty. But at the same time points out to the wide inter-state variations and intricacies in the incidence of poverty across social groups (Tendulkar, 1999). The incidence and severity of poverty across social groups and sub-state level regional differences often eluded the attention of analysts.

Even with the income poverty angle, the location (numerical density) of poor and severity of poverty or deprivation in the groups of scheduled castes and scheduled tribes are quite clear (Karanth and Deshpande, 2000). This will become sharper if the quality of life parameters are considered.

The publication of the Human Development Report by UNDP during the nineties substantially changed the approach to studies on understanding of poverty. The current thinking therefore, focuses more on the indicators of quality of life. The concept of Human Development Index of UNDP in India is neither new nor novel. The writing of B.R. Ambedkar makes it quite clear that the concept was on the minds of Indian thinkers well before Independence. Following this, the recent initiatives taken by various state governments in bringing out similar reports at the state level, giving estimates of human development index (HDI) at desegregated levels, marked the third and current phase of the debate on poverty. In a gist, the third phase has extended the view of poverty beyond traditional understanding and brought forth quality of life into the current context.

Looking into the poverty debate and issues that featured during the last two decades among academia and policy sectors, a consensus is emerging to locate non-consumption indicators of poverty. The state-level experiments in arriving at HDI are quite praiseworthy and have brought out important dimensions of quality of life; the exercise of monitoring poverty and human development indicators assumed significant importance. Therefore, it is necessary to develop a proper system of poverty monitoring. The monitoring process should be quick and effective to introduce midcourse changes. Therefore, identification of proper indicators spanning various facets of quality of life becomes a pre-requisite. In addition to the mere location of such indicators, it is required that these should be amenable to monitoring at state and sub state level. There are a good number of studies suggesting various non-consumption poverty indicators and these could be effectively used for monitoring. Keeping this in view and the requirements of monitoring namely the framework, the frequency and the purpose of monitoring, we attempt here to set up such a frame.

The income poverty measures are neither easily amenable to calculations at sub-state level nor possible to monitor since consumption decisions are purely household-specific. It is clear that poverty as measured through consumption alone is not a clear measure of welfare. The problems with this approach from the perspective of monitoring are quite a few. First, the consumption surveys are not easily amenable to computations below state level. Second, the strict comparability across regions cannot be maintained. These indices look into only the consumption angle and therefore, closer to food insecurity and leave out the quality of life angle. In addition to these, there are a few data/survey-related problems (Vaidyanathan, 1986; Suryanarayana, 2000).[ii] More recently Abhijit Sen examined the NSS data set and argued that the data from the 55th round NSSO should help to bridge some of the shortcomings visible from the analysis of earlier data sets (Sen, 2000). Keeping these factors in view, it becomes essential to view the poverty issues from the perspective of quality of life indicators.

In the present paper, we take a view about the purpose and process of devising a monitoring system for such indicators. Our contention begins from two parallel standpoints: First, in the current scenario it is necessary to monitor poverty periodically and with effective parameters. Second, it will not be sufficient to only monitor the consumption poverty measures. Instead it goes beyond that and looks into quality of life indicators. Our basic material stems from the papers presented at a workshop on Poverty Monitoring held at the Institute for Social and Economic Change (see ISEC, 2001), which brought forth a large number of indicators, some of them amenable to measurement, whereas the others may have to be gathered through field surveys. In this paper we also take a review of the existing monitoring systems and suggest a few additions as well as setting up of the structure.

20.2 Issues Pertaining to Poverty Monitoring

Before getting into a proper system of poverty monitoring, we prefer to discuss the issues pertaining to this. Thirteen papers are prepared for this workshop and these can be broadly grouped into two groups. The first group has two papers from the income poverty angle, arguing the necessity of non-consumption poverty measures. Prof. Iyengar reviews some of the recent issues in the poverty debate and discusses various approaches of computation of poverty. He concludes the paper with a need to monitor poverty alleviation efforts since a large portion of budgetary resources is involved in the process of poverty alleviation. Keeping in view the rich experience and position that Prof. Iyengar holds in the academia, it will be essential to consider his views on a proper system of monitoring as the most pertinent. Another paper by Prof. Suryanarayana also argues about the utility of non-consumption anthropometric measures of poverty. He demonstrates the use of such measures by picking up some of the important indicators and the changes in such indicators during the recent past. These two papers, especially originating from two senior professors who have worked for more than three decades on income-poverty concept, serve as a landmark and underscore the need for using quality of life indicators of poverty. Thorat and his co-author on the other hand, bring forth the determinants of poverty to underscore the role of public spending and sectoral growth in poverty determination.

In the second group, the paper by Prof. Abu Saleh Shariff highlights various indicators both at the macro and micro levels and offers a comparison between the consumption measures of poverty as also the other indicators of quality of life. Prof. Shariff's contribution stems out of the countrywide survey undertaken under his guidance by NCAER. Thus, the second group of papers presented in the workshop covered the empirical evidence for the non-consumption measures of poverty. Prof. Shariff also concludes emphasising the need for monitoring the indicators that directly touch the quality of life. Though he did not suggest any measures, he hinted at initiating a specific survey for understanding the levels of deprivation among some social groups. The question of beneficiary selection in the anti-poverty programmes of the mid-70s had assumed quite an importance. Rao, Raju and Naidu address this issue and suggest quite a few indicators in order to understand the choice of the poor. This paper sets a tone to the requirement and necessity of understanding poverty indicators through non-consumption measures. Kaul *et al.*, Shobha Nambisan, Bhattacharjee and Sekhar, Usha Devi, Shankar Rao, Ganesh and Vijay Raghavachar and Keshava follow the lead. The paper by Kaul *et al.*, touches upon the wide span of indicators including health, demography and education. This team having worked earlier on the *Human Development Report of Karnataka* had an added advantage of defining the indicators to their finest use potential. Shobha Nambisan's paper systematically brings out the correct indicators relating to housing parameters. Quite often, these indicators get neglected and do not feature even in the discussions. The important aspect that gets underscored in Shobha Nambisan's paper is the conditions of living of the poor and it goes without saying that the poor can be easily identified more by the conditions of their living than by other factors. Bhattacharjee and Sekhar address the host of indicators from a demographic point of view and buttress their views with substantial empirical support from Karnataka. They also suggest a few indicators and methods to collect these. Education and literacy are important components in the Human Development Report. From the aggregate standpoint, a few indicators may not capture the depth of impact on poverty caused by this vital determinant. Usha Devi has ventured to bring out important aspects of education and education indicators pertaining to poverty. The paper by Shankar Rao takes a full view of the statistical system in Karnataka state and incorporates ways and means to enhance the system in order to capture the indicators of poverty in their sectors of origin. The paper by Vijay Raghavachar and Keshava initially includes discussion on the income poverty measures and then enlists systematically non-consumption indicators of poverty. They also give the sources of such data and the levels at which these data are available. This paper and the paper by Shankar Rao are quite exhaustive in their approach and have facilitated to arrive at a framework for poverty monitoring system for the state. The two papers dealing with the state income data by Ganesh and Ahalya Bhat have jointly concluded that the data collected for arriving at the state income will not be of any use for reaching towards the indicators of poverty.

As a synthesis, all these papers point out three important issues: (i) it is underscored in these papers that poverty cannot be totally understood through the measures of consumption that have prevailed in literature hitherto. The difficulties in getting estimates at sub-regional levels and in comparability have compounded the problems. The debate during the recent past has suggested that due care needs to be taken in order to arrive at poverty estimates through NSS data (Sen, 2000). In the current context however, it is also necessary to have a concurrent monitoring system set up to understand the changes without lapse of time. (ii) the monitoring process should not direct only towards the traditional measures of poverty but should incorporate the quality of life indicators as important components and determinants of poverty. (iii) the papers also suggest precautions that need to be taken and the agencies to be involved in the monitoring process. Thus, the papers are directed towards understanding poverty from the quality of human development indicators.

20.3 Basic Requirements for an Effective Monitoring System

Any monitoring system should function with ease in the existing administrative framework and satisfy four important requirements namely: (i) targetability (ii) flexibility (iii) result orientation (iv) feasibility of mid-course correction.

We have presently a monitoring system, which has a larger focus but is less effective. At the state government level, there is a monitoring system which was put in operation during the mid-eighties and known as Monthly Multi-level Monitoring Review Process. The process operates at three different levels and across the departments at the apex (state) level. The monthly multi-level review meetings support the Karnataka development programme, which is reviewed at the state level. Similar kinds of meetings are held at the *taluk* and district levels in each of the departments and the sum total is transferred to the divisional level and further to the state level. However, this system has a strong focus on monitoring the expenditure across the programmes/ departments rather than monitoring and analysing the results of the schemes. It does not provide any scope for mid-course corrections. In addition to this, no monitoring system has been put in place for the poverty alleviation programme.

Figure 20.1 is a clear picture of the purpose, levels and action points or actors for monitoring in the state. This system framework should be read with the indicators. The two things put together give us a blueprint of the monitoring system that should be set in the state under the auspices of the planning department. The committee on monitoring will essentially have the following important components for monitoring.

Figure 20.1

Monitoring Framework

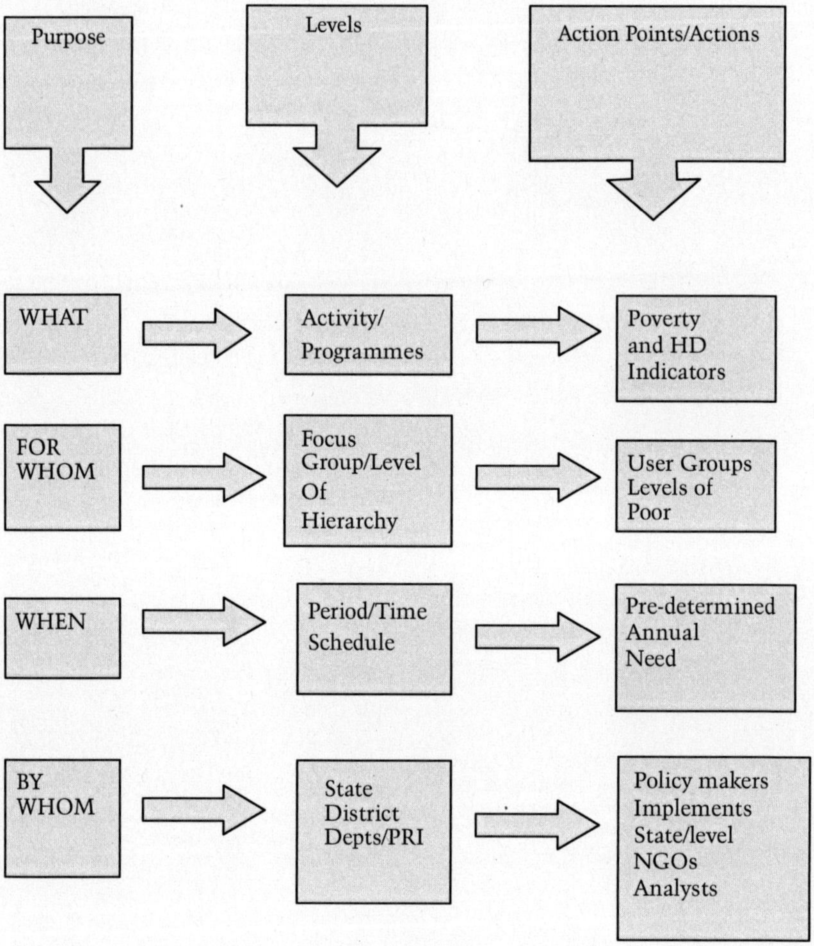

The list given below is not exhaustive and cannot be generalised for all the programmes and purposes but certainly helps to create a guideline for the purpose of monitoring. We can even go ahead by preparing a scorecard assigning rational weights to each of the components so that the programmes can be judged from the aggregate score obtained as a weighted average of the scores on this score card.

An effective monitoring system needs to have the following basic features:

a. Simple to operate and capable of producing data of acceptable accuracy with acceptable speed.
b. Appropriate to the purpose and targeted accordingly.
c. Flexible in application and adaptable to the needs of the project depending on its size and characteristics.
d. Monitoring should be internal, to minimise expenditure and coordination problems.
e. Monitoring procedure should be as consistent as possible (within existing staffing patterns, data collection, procedures).
f. It allows judgements to modify the operational plan for mid-course corrections, if needed.

20.3.1 Levels of Monitoring and Minimum Requirements

Monitoring is a management tool that facilitates continuous learning and provides quality information for arriving at decisions. The poverty alleviation programmes aim at reducing the poverty levels of the household and improve the livelihood of poor people. Monitoring poverty and human development indicators entails checking that the objectives with which the programmes were designed are successfully achieved. Monitoring thus generates information for analysis, keeps watch on the changes that take place in the physical system, assesses the conditions of the components of the process and improves thinking that will help to develop a warning system. It also helps in verifying whether assumptions made and parameters adopted in formulation of the operational plan for the system are realised during the actual operation. It facilitates the identification of the constraints so that timely remedial measures are taken. Monitoring is thus a valuable tool for improving efficiency of the management system.

The system diagram presented in Figure 20.2 has three levels of decision criteria, namely the spatial dimension, the time dimension, and the focus group dimension of poverty monitoring. In the spatial dimension of poverty monitoring, it is required to segregate indicators to be monitored at state, district, block and village levels. There are certain important indicators that need to be monitored even at the household level and should have a monitoring frequency, which is economically feasible. However, the decision about frequency can be taken only after thinking of the intensity of usefulness of such indicators in question. The group-specific monitoring is probably the most important component of the system of monitoring. The group-specific monitoring of poverty and human development indicators will not only help in economising the whole process of monitoring but it will also live up to the spirit of the exercise, namely concentrating on the target group in order to increase the welfare of those below the poverty line. Among components that need to be monitored, one can group five important groups at two levels. The first level involves basic need or absolute poverty indicators. Availability of food and access to food that directly convey the absolute poverty level are included here. This needs to be coupled with the existing as well as innovative safety net programmes. Among the existing safety net programmes and food distribution programmes, we have the public distribution system (PDS) and the targeted public distribution system (TPDS). There are a good number of studies analysing the PDS and its efficacy but probably, to the best of our knowledge, there is little work relating to monitoring such a system and giving a suitable monitoring framework. Presently, monitoring is usually done with the help of intra-departmental systems and hence, it is not quite effective. In addition to this, the departmental monitoring confines itself only to the financial sector. At the second level, we have more important indicators to monitor the human development indicators of poverty. These include health-related indicators, demographic indicators, literacy, quality of human capital related indicators, and finally basic infrastructure-related indicators. All these put together point towards the quality of human development for target groups and in sensitive areas. Therefore, any monitoring system should have first a decision about space, time or frequency and the identified social group. The second phase decisions relate to the choice of indicators from among the two groups mentioned earlier.

Figure 20.2

Three Levels of Decision Criterion and Focus Group Dimensions of Poverty Monitoring

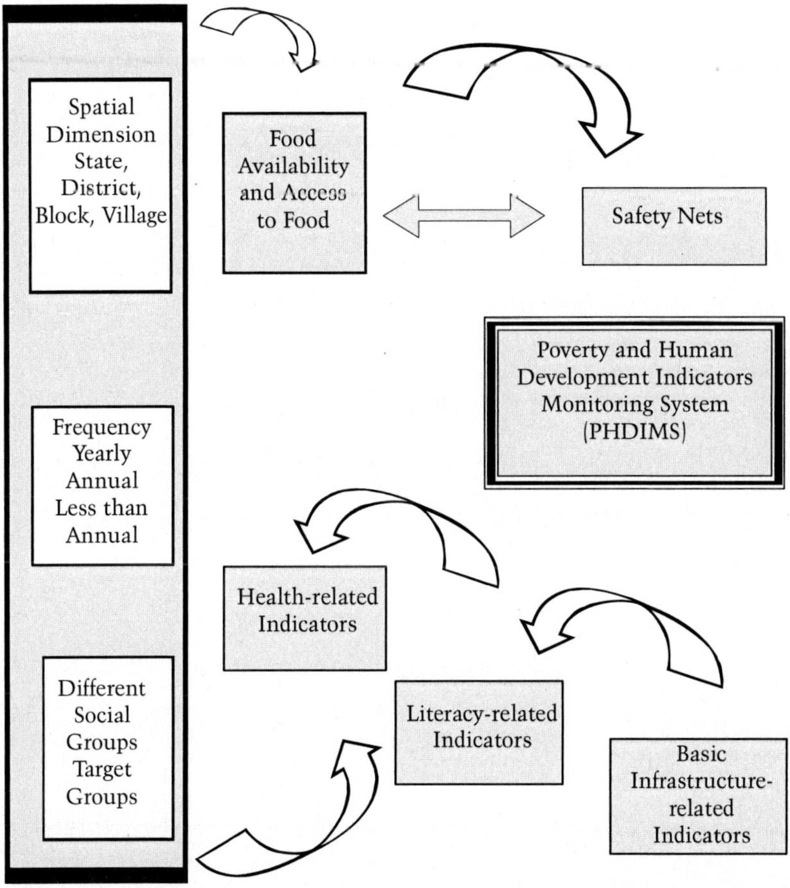

20.3.2 Span of Monitoring: Choice of Indicators and Frequency

The choice of programmes and indicators for monitoring will depend on quite a few factors. First it will be necessary to direct monitoring especially towards the identified groups and identified regions. Presently in Karnataka, we have a sizeable population of the poor. According to the latest full sample estimate given by Peter Lanjouw, the overall poverty ratio in Karnataka is in the neighbourhood of 30 per cent and a large proportion of them are concentrated in few regions.

Table 20.1

Poverty Incidence by Social Groups, 1993-94

Population Group	*Incidence of Poverty*		
	Urban	*Rural*	*Overall*
SC/ST	62.8	43.8	47.13
Other	35.7	27.4	28.00
Total	39.9	30.11	32.90

Source: Peter Lanjouw (2000).

Therefore, any monitoring system should have a focused approach towards the most deserving region or social group. This will not only reduce the extraneous expenditure but can also help in focusing directly on the problems of the poor. In the formulation of any monitoring system, we need to go through a process that involves three stages in monitoring *viz.*, focus of such monitoring, choice of indicators and the basic requirements for making the process effective. The span of monitoring system will be quite large and may cover a larger number of line departments and programmes. Therefore, it will require a perfect horizontal integration across various line departments and between the beneficiaries and the monitoring agency. Such integration is feasible only through the network of a decentralised administrative system put in place with the help of the 73rd Amendment. Local level institutions (*gram sabha*, *taluk panchayat* and *zilla panchayat*, or alternatively some NGOs, local non-governmental organisations) have to take charge of the programmes so that they are addressed to the region or location specific needs of the people.

Any monitoring system begins with identification, focus and design of the programme and leads to the concurrent modifications and future planning. Therefore, the span and spread of any monitoring system not only stretches across departments but also acquires depth in terms of self-sustenance of the process. The stages through which a monitoring system should be implemented are:

Stages in the Monitoring Process

- Identification of programmes/indicators for monitoring
- Objectives and focus of the process
- Designing of the tools for monitoring
- Reviewing the planned progress
- Identification of constraints
- Concurrent modifications
- Planning for future course of action

It can be seen that these stages are interdependent in terms of the work involvement, as well as the human power and financial allocations. More than that, the stages indicated above also have a circular flow. These stages can be fine-tuned keeping in view the focus of evaluation. Therefore, it is essential that monitoring is focused in view of the target group and has a specific purpose. In the present context, monitoring should be focused on the components presented below:

- The group of households for whom the poverty alleviation programmes are undertaken. (Target beneficiaries)
- The implementing agencies (state, district, *taluk* and *gram sabha*)—to monitor whether the planned results are being achieved and whether the strategy being employed to achieve these results is the appropriate one. It also helps in course correction.
- The government or other funding agencies, to ensure that the programme is moving towards meeting its objective, is building the necessary capacities and institutions, that it is cost effective and it merges with other development programmes of the government.

Monitoring exercise needs to be directed on the pre-determined indicators. The choice of the indicators is based on the end-users. For example, water users, or members of the watershed community, indicators that are easy to measure, but may not be scientifically precise, would suffice. On the other hand, to measure implications separately for families of very poor, poor, non-poor within the poor category along with specifically delineated characteristics, (as indicated in the papers presented in this Seminar) may be helpful on an annual basis. To the extent possible, indicators should be as objective as possible to reduce conflicts in interpretation. This becomes more important as the group of audience gets wider. Focus groups (BPL families) in itself can become important forces of change. Here we have tried to synthesise the indicators, frequency and the agency responsible for monitoring. This has been accomplished on the basis of the papers presented in the workshop.

Table 20.2

Monitoring of Poverty Indicators: Frequency, Level, Mode and Agency for Monitoring

Sl. No.	Indicator	Frequency	Level	Data Monitoring	Mode	Agency
1	Size of landholding	Quin	Village	Tal	Village records	DES
2	Ownership of consumer durable, Type of indebtedness, Expenditure survey	Quin	HH	Tal	Survey	PD/ DES
3	Household level calorie intake, Protein consumption, Composition of consumption	Quin	HH	Tal	Survey	PD/ DES
4	Literacy status of adult male, Literacy status of adult female, Schooling status, Enrolment	Dec	Ind	Tal/Vill	Survey/ Census	EDU
5	Employment and unemployment, Work status of children and child labour	Quin	Ind	Tal/Vill	Survey	Lab
6	Disability, Malnutrition, Incidence of anaemia	Yr	Ind/HH	Tal	Survey	HD/ SRS
7	Total fertility rate, Mortality rate, Causes of death	Once in 2 yrs	HH	Dist/Tal	Survey	HD/ SRS
8	Birth weights, Child malnutrition, Infant mortality rates, Life expectancy at birth	Once in 2 yrs	Ind/HH	Dist	Survey	HD/ SRS
9	Couple protection rate, Institutional delivery	Yr	HH	Tal	Survey	Hosp/ HD
9	Houseless population	Quin	HH	Dist	Census/ Survey	PD/ DES
10	Type of house (*kutcha*/*pucca*), Material for roof and walls, Number of rooms	Quin	HH	Vill	Census/ Survey	PD/ DES
11	Household amenities—toilets, electrification, cooking fuel, safe drinking water	Quin	HH/Vill	Vill	Census/ Survey	PD/ DES
12	Infrastructure availability	Dec	Vill	Vill/Tal	Vill Records	PD/ DES

Note: Quin=Quinquennial; Yr=Yearly; Dec=Decade; Dist=District, Tal=*Taluka*, Vill=Village; DES=Directorate of Statistics; PD=Planning Department, Ind=Individual; HH=Household; HD= Health Department; Hosp.=Hospital; EDU = Education Department; SRS = Sample Registration System.

Source: The indicators presented in the table are extracted from the papers prepared for the workshop (ISEC, 2001).

Among the indicators, we can make broadly three groups. The first group of indicators deals with the asset holding and consumption pattern. Land is taken as an important asset for understanding the base of poverty. We have not neglected the concept of income poverty and consumption of food as well as composition of food on similar lines as that of NSS surveys. These serve as the other important set of indicators. We suggest a state-level sample with district as a basic sampling unit for the purpose of these surveys. The second group of indicators includes the human resource level indicators that include literacy and related aspects. The health and demographic indicators form the second and third groups.

Indicators of Success: It may not always be possible to measure the results that have been achieved because they may be intangible or it may be too costly to measure them effectively. In such cases, indications that success is being achieved will make good proxies. Such indicators, however, must be chosen carefully so that they are reliable substitutes for direct measurement and are easy to measure in terms of time and effort.

Participatory Monitoring: In fact, it must be participatory to be effective. This means that each beneficiary is involved in identifying the indicators and in measuring them. Participation will ensure that those indicators will be chosen which are meaningful to the stakeholder. This helps to evolve region-specific and sub-group (of poor households) specific indicators. This also implies that the review of the indicators should be undertaken jointly by the focus groups, the implementing agency and the funding agency (government or others). Decisions to make any modifications in the programme being implemented must also be taken jointly based on the review.

20.3.3 Administrative Framework and Financial Implications

Any monitoring system will have three levels to operate, which begin at the purpose and focus of such monitoring, the regional or administrative levels of monitoring and action points or actors in this process. Therefore, the administrative framework for the process of monitoring will have to be centred at the planning department, since this department is entrusted with aggregate planning and allocation of resources across sectors in the state. Any planning process therefore, will have to take note of the situation of poverty in the state and plan for the efforts required for dealing with such situation. Therefore, the process of monitoring is best achieved from the department that directly controls the process and allocates resources, keeping in view the sector, the needs of the regions and the social classes concerned. However, this needs to be supported by various agencies and the non-governmental organisations, which directly deal with poverty and human development indicators. We suggest that a monitoring committee be set up under the planning department in order to monitor the progress and empirical collection of the data pertaining to the indicators. This committee can have representatives from various government departments concerned as well as NGOs and research organisations. The monitoring process contemplated here will have to go through a few phases, namely: identification of the target areas, choice of indicators and the process of collecting such indicators empirically. The agencies responsible for such indicators and analysis of such indicators should be planned and concurrently accomplished. Therefore, in our opinion, no separate administrative framework will be required and this can be achieved by relocating the duties and works of the existing line departments.

The monitoring committee suggested above should however, work in close collaboration with the Chief Secretary of the state or the Development Commissioner of the state, but the Chief Minister of the state should be the chairperson of such a committee. The committee can directly report to the Chief Minister through the Member Secretary who will be the Secretary of the planning department. The monitoring committee (set inside the planning department) should be free from all cumbersome procedures, in conducting measurement, surveys, consulting experts and taking quick decisions. If necessary, the government employees from other line departments can be drafted for facilitating the work of the committee. However, there is no need to create separate and full-fledged organisations for this purpose. If necessary, the human development cell and the monitoring committee can be interdependent but independent in their responsibilities and roles they play.

Some of the major components of an effective monitoring system are listed below.

20.3.4 Components of a Monitoring System

1. Organisational Capacity
   - i. Meetings (regular and productive, regular and unproductive, irregular and unproductive, and so on).
   - ii. Leadership (only project director can provide, others can take lead, nobody provides, and so on).
   - iii. Mid-course correction possibility incorporated in the design.
2. Financial Management
   - i. Finance (adequate funds, expenditure on time, inadequate funds, untimely disbursements).
   - ii. Availability and accessibility to beneficiaries (any time, non-availability, non-accessibility, including credit).
3. Linkages
   - i. Horizontal linkages (frequent cooperation with other agencies, non-availability, non-accessibility, not built, very difficult).
   - ii. Vertical linkages.
   - iii. Communication (widely known to all potential beneficiaries, known only to clerks concerned, known to local leaders, help desk is available).
   - iv. Contact with the authority (easy, difficult, with bribes).
4. Indicators of Success
   - i. Coverage of the intended target group.
   - ii. Incremental achievement in the immediately preceding period.
   - iii. Local-level flexibility and acceptance of the programme by the target group.
   - iv. Incremental income/employment.
5. Participation in the Programme
   - i. Participation and awareness at the time of planning.
   - ii. Organised as a group of beneficiaries.

iii. Possibility of mid-course correction.

iv. Stakeholder monitoring mechanism.

This can be developed further to arrive at a tool for easy collection of data and feedback to both higher and lower levels in a loop form. All local offices, at *taluk*, district, state cells/desks of poverty monitoring should have computers for easy feedback and easy access to any individual beneficiary. It may also be possible to design a format for collecting beneficiary level information: a) on annual basis, b) to sanction assistance (with list of attachments required), and c) set the process time (5 days, 10 days, maximum 15 days) at all levels. These things should reflect in the monitoring formats. It is necessary to understand what and why it takes more time to realise the results and how to reduce the time and cost delays. If human power is the only constraint then hiring NGOs or temporary staff can circumvent this. If the cumbersome procedures are hindering the smooth operations then it is needed to simplify them.

20.3.5 Developing Social Audit System

In addition to the monitoring committee suggested above at the state level, we also feel that there should be a process of social auditing system (SAS) set up at least at the *taluka* level. The SAS is the one which will involve three partners namely, the implementing agency, the representatives of the beneficiary groups and socially motivated individuals or organisations. The SAS should direct itself to understand the focus and spirit of the programme undertaken by the implementing agency. It also should look into the location of benefits accruable from the programme as well as the spillover effects of the benefits. The SAS will automatically require the beneficiaries to participate in the programme right from the first step involving planning for programme and through the implementation of the programme. As it will involve a larger number of representatives from the non-implementing agency, the SAS can be more effective in auditing the impact of the programme as well as plugging the leakage that usually dogs the implementation process. It is locally beneficial, easy to operate, socially acceptable, and politically correct. We can also think of including two representatives each from the three poverty groups (very poor, poor, non-poor).

Alternatively, the *gram panchayat*, *taluk panchayat* and *zilla panchayat*, each can have its own local committees to monitor this activity and send one/two pages statement to the higher authorities. If progress is not made (by the beneficiary), the committee has to provide reasons, and suggestions to improve. Otherwise, leaving the entire process of monitoring with the government departments may not make any significant change in the effectiveness of the programme.

20.4 Conclusion and Future Challenges

Poverty as measured through the consumption indicators is not easily amenable to monitoring. Moreover, the consumption-centred indicators do not measure squarely the concept of welfare. In the present economic scenario, it is not the consumption but the non-consumption measures that need to be monitored closely. The concept of entitlement developed by Amartya Sen becomes more prominent as an acknowledged step in clarifying the understanding of the concept of deprivation. Sen defines poverty as a person's ability to command food—indeed to command any commodity he wishes to acquire or retain—depends on the entitlement relation that govern possession and use in that society. It depends on what he owns, what exchange possibilities are offered to him, what is given to him free and what is taken away from him (Earlier work reproduced in Sen and Dreze, 1999: 154). Although we do not have strong empirical support for measuring entitlements, it will be quite useful in this context to approach poverty from the non-consumption point of view. An attempt is made here to look into the concept of non-consumption measures of deprivation and to set a scheme of monitoring these.

Any programme with a larger span of monitoring requires to be administered from the department that holds some control and has effective coordination with line departments in the state. Within the present administration, this can be effectively achieved only through the planning department or the Panchayat Raj department. Both the departments have an administrative set-up which has a close vertical integration as an essential component of any monitoring system. However, the first challenge faced in the monitoring system to be implemented through line departments is the confrontation with cross-cutting interests and multiplicity of task that each of the administrative agencies has to face. With the challenge of multiplicity of the task and given the manpower, it will be difficult to achieve an effective monitoring system unless full thought is given to the establishment of such a process in the state departments. The second important challenge comes from the lack of horizontal integration between various departments so that the inter-dependence helps in making the programme more effective and useful for the poor. The horizontal integration can be achieved by designating the responsibility of monitoring to a particular officer in each of the departments and having a second layer periodical check. The third and important constraint arises from the institutional form for monitoring the human development indicators. We have suggested above a committee at the planning department to take the administrative responsibility. This committee along with SAS can help in positive monitoring of the task. But the stability and responsibilities assigned to such institutions should be carefully looked into.

References

Ahluwalia, Montek, S (1978). "Rural poverty and agricultural performance in India", *Journal of Development Studies* 14(3): 298–323, April.

____ (2000). "Economic performance of states in post reform period", *Economic and Political Weekly* 35(19), May 6.

Chelliah, Raja J. and R. Sudarshan (1999). *Income-Poverty and Beyond Human Development in India*. New Delhi: Social Science Press.

Datt, Gaurav (1999). "Has poverty declined since economic reforms?", *Economic and Political Weekly* 34(50).

Datt, Gaurav and M. Ravallion (1998). "Why have some states performed better than others at reducing rural poverty?", *Economica* 65: 17–38.

Deaton, Augus and Alessandr Tarozzi (2000). *Prices and Poverty in India*. Research Program in Development Studies, Princeton University.

Deshpande, R.S. (2000). "Deprived castes and the process of economic reforms: An agrarian perspective", Dr. Ambedkar Memorial Lecture, Madras University, Chennai, February 10.

Dreze, Jean and Amartya Sen (1997). *Indian Development: Selected Regional Perspectives*. Delhi: Oxford University Press.

Eswaran, M. and A. Kotwal (1994). *Why Poverty Persists in India: A Framework For Understanding The Indian Economy*. New Delhi: Oxford University Press.

Fan, Shengen, Peter Hazell and Sukhadeo Thorat (1999). "Linkages between government spending, growth and poverty in rural India", *Research Report* 110, International Food Policy Research Institute, Washington.

Guhan, S. (1993). "Social security for the poor in the unorganised sector: A blueprint for India", in K.S. Parikh and R. Sudarshan (eds.), *Human Development and Structural Adjustment*. Chennai: Macmillan.

ISEC (2001). "Report of the workshop on poverty and human development monitoring system", Institute for Social and Economic Change, Bangalore, February 2–3.

Jalan, Bimal (ed, 1992). *The Indian Economy: Problems and Prospects*. Delhi: Pengin.

Karanth, G.K. and R.S. Deshpande (2000). "The pace of social and economic change in India: The question of poverty", Paper for Constitution Review Commission, Institute for Social and Economic Change, Bangalore.

Krueger, Anne O (1990). "Government failure and development", *The Journal of Economic Perspectives* 4(3): 9–13.

Krishnaswamy, K.S. (ed. 1996). *Poverty and Income Distribution*. Delhi: Oxford University Press.

Lanjouw, Peter (2000). "Poverty in Karnataka: Profiles and emerging issues", Note prepared for the Development Research Group, The World Bank, Washington.

Rao, Govinda M. (2000). "Poverty alleviation under fiscal decentralization", Paper presented at a conference in Honour of Raja Chelliah, Institute of Social and Economic Change, Bangalore, January 17.

Rao, V.M. and M. Vivekananda (1982a). "Calorie norm controversy", in *Economic and Political Weekly*, Feb. 13.

———. (1982b). "The poor as a social stratum—Some economic criteria for studying Poverty", in *Economic and Political Weekly* XVII(27), July 3.

Rao, V.M., V.J. Naidu and K.V. Raju (1998). "Choosing among the equals: Beneficiary selection for anti-poverty programmes", *Indian Journal of labour Economics* 41(2).

Rao, V.M. (2000). "Eradicating poverty: Some missing policy dimensions", Paper presented at a conference in Honour of Raja Chelliah, Institute of Social and Economic Change, Bangalore.

Rath, N. (1996). "Poverty in India revisited", *Indian Journal of Agricultural Economics* 51(1&2).

Ravallion, Martin and Gaurav Datt (1996). "How important to India's poor in the sectoral composition of economic growth?", *World Bank Economic Review* 10(1): 1–25.

———. (2000). "When is growth pro-poor? Evidence from the diverse experiences of India's states", *World Bank Discussion Paper*, World Bank, Washington D.C.

Sen, Abhijit (2000). "Estimates of consumer expenditure and its distribution: Statistical priorities after NSS 55th round", *Economic and Political Weekly*, 16th Dec.

Sen, Amartya and Jean Dreze (1999). *The Amartya Sen and Jean Dreze Omnibus*. New Delhi: Oxford University Press.

Shariff, A (1999). *India: Human Development Report*. New Delhi: Oxford University Press.

Suryanarayana, M.H. (2000). "How real is the decline in rural poverty", *Economic and Political Weekly* 35(25): 2129-2140 (June 17-23).

Tendulkar, Suresh (1999). "Trends in income poverty in India", in Raja J. Chelliah and R. Sudarshan (eds.), *Income-Poverty and Beyond Human Development in India*. New Delhi: Social Science Press. pp.13-52.

Thorat, S.K. and R.S. Deshpande (1999). "Caste and labour market discrimination", *The Indian Journal of Labour Economics* 42(4).

Vaidyanathan, A. (1986). "On the validity of NSS consumption data", *Economic and Political Weekly*, Review of Agriculture XXI(3).

World Bank (2000). "India policies to reduce poverty and accelerate sustainable development", *Report No.*19471, January 31.

———. (1975). *The Assault on World Poverty: Problems of Rural Development, Education and Health*. Baltimore: The John Hopkins University Press.

Annexure Table A-20.1

Monitoring of Poverty Indicators: Frequency, Level, Mode and Agency for Monitoring

Sl. No.	*Indicator*	*Frequency*	*Level*	*Data Monitoring*	*Mode*	*Agency*
I. Consumptive						
1	Cooking fuel,	Quin	HH/ Village	Village	Census/ Survey	PD/ DES
	Safe drinking water	Quin	HH	Village/ *Taluk*	Census/ Survey	DES
2	Ownership of consumer durable	Quin	HH	*Taluk*	Survey	DES
3	Household level calorie intake, Protein consumption, Composition of consumption	Quin	HH	*Taluk*	Survey	PD/ DES
II.	**Non-Consumptive**					
1	Size of landholding	Quin	Village	*Taluk*	Village Records	DES
2	Type of indebtedness, Expenditure survey	Quin	HH	*Taluk*	Survey	PD/ DES
3	Literacy status of adult male, Literacy status of adult female, Schooling status, Enrolment	Dec	Ind	*Taluk*/ Village	Survey/ Census	EDU
4	Social group of the household (SC/ST, women-headed, backward caste, OBC, forward caste)	Once in 2 yrs	HH	*Taluk*/ Village	Census/ Survey	DES
5	Casual labourers in the household (Adults and children, adults only, no casual labourers)	Yr	HH	*Taluk*/ Village	Census/ Survey	DES
6	Main occupation (Labour/ artisan, subsistence cultivation, Commercial cultivation, regular job)	Yr	HH	*Taluk*/ Village	Census/ Survey	DES
7	Type of indebtedness (Informal agency/consumption, informal agency/production co-ops, commercial bank)	Yr	HH	*Taluk*/ Village	Census/ Survey	DES
8	Preference for development assistance (Employment/PDS, IRDP schemes, TRYSEM/training, Loan/subsidy, more than 1lakh rupees)	Yr	HH	*Taluk*/ Village	Census/ Survey	DES
9	Migration from household (Casual work seasonal employment, Permanent job, Own enterprise)	Yr	HH	*Taluk*/ Village	Census/ Survey	DES
10	Employment	Quin	Ind	*Taluk*/ Village	Survey	Lab
11	Disability, Malnutrition, Incidence of anaemia	Yr	Ind/HH	*Taluk*	Survey	HD/ SRS

Contd...

...contd...

Sl. No.	*Indicator*	*Frequency*	*Level Data Monitoring*		*Mode*	*Agency*
12	Total fertility rate, Mortality rate, Causes of death	Once in 2 yrs	HH	Dist/Tal	Survey	HD/ SRS
13	Birth weights, Child malnutrition, Infant mortality rates, Life expectancy at birth	Once in 2 yrs	Ind/HH	Dist	Survey	HD/ SRS
14	Couple protection rate, Institutional delivery	Yr	HH	Tal	Survey	Hosp/ HD
15	Houseless population	Quin	Village	Dist	Census/ Survey	PD/ DES
16	Type of house (*kutcha/pucca*), Material for roof and walls, Number of rooms	Quin	HH	Village	Census/ Survey	PD/ DES
17	Household amenities—toilets, electrification	Quin	HH/ Village	Village	Census/ Survey	PD/ DES
18	Infrastructure availability	Dec	Village	Village/ *Taluk*	Village Records	PD/ DES

Note: Quin=Quinquennial; Yr=Yearly; Dec=Decade; Dist=District, Tal=*Taluka*, Vill=Village; DES=Directorate of Statistics; PD=Planning Department; Ind=Individual; HH=Household; HD= Health Department; Hosp.=Hospital; EDU = Education Department; SRS = Sample Registration System.

Source: The indicators presented in the table are extracted from the papers prepared for the workshop (ISEC, 2001).

Notes

i. The differences and discrepancies between the National Accounts Estimates and those of the NSS estimates were debated recently and the Expert Group appointed by the Planning Commission in 1993 accepted the NSS consumption data as better description of poverty. In calculating the poverty estimates for different states, the Expert Group recommended that the all-India calorie norms and the relevant consumption baskets at the country level be adopted uniformly for all the states. But this was not free of the intricate methodological problems. Guhan argued that the state level estimates of poverty do not reflect a true picture of poverty across states (Guhan, 1993). Therefore, the approach not only affects the time series picture but also makes the comparison difficult across states.

ii. It has been observed at the country level that decline in rural poverty was mainly during the phase of technological and institutional changes witnessed in the country after 1967–68. Ahluwalia (1978) related this decline in poverty with the agricultural performance across states in India. The relationship was estimated with the help of cross-section data across states. But probably the decline was a result of contribution by only those states, which had initial advantages in the process of development. While commenting on this aspect, Ravallion and Datt clearly indicated that the sectoral composition of growth really matters in the aggregate reduction of poverty and therefore, quality and location of growth become an important component of any poverty alleviation strategy. They also argued that the differences in the initial conditions covering rural development and human resource development induced the decline in rural poverty. In addition to this, analysts have indicated several factors associated with decline in poverty (Ravallion and Datt, 1996; Datt, 1999; Rath, 1996). Among the determinants irrigation, landlessness, agricultural output per hectare, non-farm product per person, state development expenditure, female literacy and urban–rural consumption ratio are the important determinants considered in various studies (Ravallion and Datt, 2000). All these exercises include quality of life indicators only incidentally.

21 Climate Change and Food Security

S.M. Jharwal

21.1 Introduction

Climate change is a change in the statistical distribution of weather over a long period of say decades to several centuries. The change may be limited to a specific region or may occur across the whole world. However, impact of climate change is inherently global in nature. This means that emission of greenhouse gages (GHGs) or pollution in any part of the world would affect the entire globe. The anthropogenic climate change (ACC) is generally known as global warming. Factors that can change climate include: (i) variations in solar radiation, (ii) deviations in earth's orbit, (iii) mountain building and continental drift, and (iv) changes in GHG concentrations. For the first time, United Nations Framework Convention on Climate Change (UNFCCC) was adopted in New York on May 9, 1992 and entered in to force on March 21, 1994 with its main goal expressed as "...stabilization of green house gas concentration in the atmosphere at a level that would prevent dangerous anthropogenic interference with the climate system..." The Kyoto Protocol or the United Nations Climate Change Conference (UNCCC) is an avenue through which member nations of UN are working to reduce GHGs. The protocol was initially adopted on December 11, 1997 in Kyoto, Japan and entered in to force on February 16, 2005. The second Kyoto meeting was in November 2006 when 6000 persons from 180 countries participated. As of November 2009 187 countries have signed and ratified the protocol. These countries account for about 64 per cent of the total emission estimated for 1990. Since then several initiatives were taken. Since the protocol had several issues to be decided, the Conference of Parties (CoP) attempted to resolve these issues in Hague in late 2000, but was unable to reach an agreement because of the difference of opinion between European Union (EU) on the one hand and USA, Canada and Japan on other. The latter group wanted less demanding and more flexible agreement. Another CoP was held in Bonn in 2001, followed by another meeting in Marrakesh also in 2001. The first meeting of the parties (MoP-1) to the Kyoto Protocol was held in Montreal in November-December 2005. CoP-13 was held in Bali in December 2007. Thereafter also meetings of various groups have been held or are yet to be held.

The fourth assessment report of the Intergovernmental Panel on Climate Change (IPCC), which was brought out in 2007, has created widespread awareness across the world on the scientific realities of human induced climate change. The report finds that, "warming of the climate system is unequivocal, as is now evident from observations of increases in global average air and ocean temperatures, widespread melting of snow and ice and rising global average sea level." The report also pointed out that most of the observed increase in global average temperatures since the mid-20th century is very likely due to the observed increase in GHG concentrations.

21.2 Greenhouse Gases and the Major Contributors

Carbon dioxide (CO_2) and Methane (CH_4) are the two major GHGs, which contribute to the global warming. The gases are emitted by variety of economic activities. Table 21.1 broadly provides a fair idea of the activities which causes global warming.

Table 21.1

Source-wise Contribution in Emission of Greenhouse Gases

Economic Activity	*Emission of GHG (Contribution in percentage)*	
	*Global**	*India*
Industrial process	19.4	8
Agriculture	30.9	28
Electric power generation	25.9	61 (combined)
Transportation	13.1	
Residential & commercial	7.9	
Waste disposal	2.5	2

Source: IIPC-2007 and India's Initial National Commission on Climate Change, 2004.

In absolute terms, as on 2007, the CO_2 emission, worldwide, stood at roughly 30 billion tonnes of which about half is absorbed in natural sinks of ocean, forests and soil. This means about 15 billion tonnes of CO_2 is released in to the atmosphere each year. Further, as per available estimates, the CO_2 has increased from 2184 billion tonnes in 1750 to about 2995 billion tonnes in 2007. Also, CO_2 is not the only GHG which has significantly risen, but CH_4 has also risen from 5569 to 13837 billion tonne during 1750 to 2005. Similarly, nitrous oxide (N_2O) is also reported to have increased from 2106 billion tonne to 2488 billion tonne during this period. Therefore, the effort at the global level is to restrain this increase to save the planet earth.

The per capita emission in the industrialised countries are as much as 10 times the average in the developing countries (Grubb, 2003). The countries which agreed to take quantified commitments for the first period (2008-2012) in Kyoto emitted 2 tonnes or more of carbon per capita in 1990. In 2005, top 20 emitters accounted for 80 per cent of the total GHG emissions. The top 10 emitters in 2005 included China (17%), USA (16%), European Union (11%), Indonesia (6%), India (5%), Russia (5%), Brazil (4%), Japan (3%), Canada (2%) and Mexico (2%). In terms of per capita tonne of carbon emission USA topped the list with (24.1), followed by Canada (23.2), Russia (14.9), Indonesia (12.9), EU and Japan (10.6), Brazil (10.0), Mexico (6.4), China (5.8) and India (2.1).

21.3 Effects of Climate Change

Because of the Climate change, cold days, cold nights and frosts have become much less frequent in most land areas. Heat waves have become more frequent. Frequency of heavy precipitation events has increased in most areas. Average temperatures have climbed by 1.4 degree fahrenheit (-17 degree celsius) around the world since 1880, much of this rise has been in recent decades (NASA Goddard Institute for Space Studies, GISS). The last two decades of 20th century were the hottest in the last 400 years and possibly the warmest for several millennia, according to a number of climate studies. According to the IPCC (2007), of the last 12 years, 11 years have been the warmest since 1850. Arctic is severely affected. The average temperature in Alaska,

Western Canada and Eastern Russia have risen twice the global average. (Multinational Arctic Climate Impact Assessment, ACIA (2000-2004).

Thus, arctic ice is rapidly disappearing. The region may have its first ice-free summer by 2040 or earlier. Glaciers and mountain snows are rapidly melting. For example, Montana's Glacier National Park now (2007) has only 27 glaciers as against 150 in 1910. Coral reefs, which are highly sensitive to small changes in water temperatures, suffered the worst bleaching in response to stress, as recorded in 1998, with some areas experiencing bleach rates of about 70 per cent. It is expected that such events will increase in frequency in the next 50 years.

Further, the global sea level has risen at an average of 1.8 mm per year. Since 1961 the rising sea level is a global threat, especially to the low-lying deltas, smaller Islands and coastal areas across the world. The implications are more serious since about 50 per cent of the world's population lives within 200 km of sea.

In the Indian context, the climate change and consequent rising temperatures are likely to provoke more frequent floods and droughts, spur disease and increase water scarcity. Himalayan glaciers are disappearing. It is estimated that by 2030, the glaciers would shrink from 5 lakh sq km to only about one lakh sq km (IPCC, 2007).

Such developments and events would seriously impact the agricultural sector in India. The productivity of cereals would decrease due to increase or sudden change in temperature. The decrease in water availability when in need would also affect the yield levels.

The Indo-Gangetic plains, which are the major contributors to the food grains basket in India, are likely to be affected adversely. Some global reports indicate a loss of 10-40 per cent in crop production by 2100. For instance, the year 2002-03 witnessed severe drought conditions and the food grains loss was 38 million tonnes over the preceding year's level of 213 million tonnes, which was almost 18 per cent decline. Rice production declined by 23 per cent and wheat by 9.6 per cent.

It is expected that the loss would be more during *rabi* season due to increase in temperature and reduced water availability. It is estimated that every 1°C increase in temperature during winter season would reduce wheat production by 4-5 million tonnes. Further, increased climate extremes are likely to result in wide fluctuations in agricultural production raising food security issues and import burden would suddenly increase. This problem is going to be compounded by new diseases due to the effect of temperature on pathogenic microbes and insects, affecting yield levels. Thus, to maintain increase in food grains, use of more inputs such as fertilisers, insecticides and water would be required. This would further result in higher emissions. However, the impact of increase in temperature is expected to be positive in Europe, North America, Russia and China and balance of trade in food grains would tilt towards them.

On the horticulture front, yield of major fruits would decline. For instance, due to lack of required chill, the yield of apples in Himachal Pradesh apart from wide fluctuation in yield level over the years, has shown a decline of almost 30 per cent during 1980-81 to 2000-01. Also, due to the increasing temperatures of sea and river water, fish breeding and overall harvest has been affected. There are instances of migration of aqua resources in several areas. Rise in the sea surface temperature by 2-2.25°C in May 1998 led to bleaching in 85 per cent coral reefs. There has been a situation of animal distress due to heat effects on reproduction. It is estimated that by 2020, a loss of about 1.5 million tonnes of milk shall be experienced if appropriate steps are not taken.

Low rainfall (droughts) and sudden precipitation (floods) are caused due to changes in climate which have taken place during the last century. An analysis of the production during the 4 drought years over the last 25 years shows that low rainfall significantly affects the production levels of wheat, rice, pulses, oilseeds and coarse cereals. However, by better management of seeds, water and other agricultural practices, the production in the case of wheat, pulses and oilseeds, could be maintained particularly during the *rabi* seasons. The impact is shown in Table 21.2.

Table 21.2

Rainfall Percentage and Loss in Production During the Drought Years

(Loss in Million Tonnes)

Crops/Year	*1987-88*		*2002-03*		*2004-05*		*2009-10**	
	Loss	*%age*	*Loss*	*%age*	*Loss*	*%age*	*Loss*	*%age*
Rice	3.7	6.1	21.52	23	5.4	6.1	11.19	11.13
Wheat	+1.55	+3.5	7.01	9.6	3.5	4.9	No	Loss
Coarse cereals	No	Loss	7.30	22.1	4.14	11.0	6.9	17.25
Pulses	0.75	6.4	2.24	16.75	1.78	11.9	No	Loss
Total food grains	8.56	5.7	38.1	17.9	14.83	6.9	16.28	6.9
Oilseeds	+1.38	+12.2	5.82	28.2	0.83	3.3	2.31	8.3
Sugarcane	+10.65	+5.7	53.52	18.6	No	Loss	10.35	3.6
Rainfall percentage	81		81		87		78.2	

Notes: *As per 3rd Advance Estimate; + is gain. Rest is loss.

It may be observed that the loss in food grain production ranged between 6-7 per cent in 3 of the 4 drought years, but it was as high as 18 per cent in 2002-03. The loss in rice production was still high at 23 per cent. In a drought year, coarse cereal production also declined substantially. Such a steep fall in production of food grains raises serious food security concerns.

21.4 Climate Change Commitments

As per the Kyoto Protocol, the participating nations committed themselves to tackling the issue of global warming and GHG emissions. The target agreed upon was an average reduction of 5.2 per cent by the industrialised countries from 1990 levels by the year 2012. According to the treaty, the signatory countries must fulfill their obligations of reduction of GHG emissions established for the first commitment period of 2008 to 2012. National limitations range from 8 per cent reductions for the EU and 7 per cent to UK, by 12.5 per cent for the USA (non-party), 6 per cent for Japan, Austria by 13 per cent, Denmark by 21 per cent, 0 per cent for Russia and permitted increases of 8 per cent for Australia, 10 per cent for Iceland, 13 per cent for Ireland, 15 per cent by Spain, 25 per cent by Greece and 27 per cent by Portugal. It needs to be noted here that the national emission targets exclude international aviation and shipping. Kyoto parties can use land, land-use change and forestry (LULUCF) in meeting the targets. LULUCF are also called sink activities. Changes in sinks and land use can affect the climate. Forest management, cropland management, grazing land management and revegetation are all eligible LULUCF activities under the protocol.

These targets apply to the four GHGs *viz.*, (i) CO_2, (ii) CH_4, (iii) N_2O and (iv) sulphur hexafluoride (SF_6). These are translated in to CO_2 equivalents for the purpose of emission reductions. These reduction targets are in addition to the industrial gases, chlorofluorocarbons (CFCs), which are dealt with under the 1987 Montreal Protocol on substances that deplete the ozone layer. Thus, a commitment on emissions by developing countries need not be a reduction, but rather limit emissions increase by a specified amount in future years.

21.5 Views on the Protocol

The Kyoto Protocol had only a slight effect on curbing global emissions growth (World Bank, 2010). Although, the treaty was negotiated in 1997, by 2005, energy related emissions had grown by 24 per cent. Further, the treaty had provided only a limited financial support to developing countries in reducing their emissions and adapting to climate change. On the climate justice front, the criticism has centred on the balance between the low emissions and high vulnerability of the developing world to climate change, compared to high emissions in the developed world. Some environmentalists have supported the Kyoto Protocol because they expect that the future emission reduction commitments may demand more stringent reductions. Some feel that the existing commitments are too weak. On the other hand, many economists think that the commitments are stronger than justified (Grubb, 2000). The authors in the Hartwell Paper brought out by London School of Economics and University of Oxford (2010), argued that after the failure of Copenhagen Summit (2009), the Kyoto Protocol crashed (2009) also which failed to produce any discernible real world reductions in emissions of GHGs in the last 15 years. It has also been commented that the Copenhagen Accord settles the ground to weaken the Kyoto Protocol as a multilateral treaty and as a legal document to make developed countries to accomplish their binding commitments on emissions reduction. Accordingly, the Article 3.1 of the Kyoto Protocol, have an agreement to reach a common global objective in emissions reduction through their emission allowances, reaching an aggregated amount and generating a compliance system within a legally binding system. The Copenhagen kills this methodology substituting it by a mechanism that does not establish any kind of bind and measurable commitment since it leaves countries free in terms of emission reduction objectives. The evaluation prepared by Climate Action Tracker states that the sum of commitments represents a global temperature increase of 3°C which is not sufficient to fulfill the basic objective established in the Accord. The objective presented varies between 11 per cent to 19 per cent over 1990-level which goes against the IPCC that established a reduction of at least 40 per cent to keep the increase in temperature within 2°C over that level.

21.6 What Next?

However, smaller groups such as Major Economies Forum (MEF), BASIC (Brazil, South Africa, India and China countries), G20 and others are also engaged in matters to effectively tackle the climate change. The focus is on monitoring, review and verification (MRV). As per Copenhagen Accord, industrialised countries will have to be brought under MRV. For the developing countries, supported mitigation measures are being considered for MRV. There are still outstanding issues on the mechanism for international consultation and analysis. Another issue will be related to adaptation, mitigation and finance. It also needs to be clearly understood as to whether the outcome of the climate negotiations will be in the form of a legally binding agreement, voluntary efforts or a schedules approach. The technology options, review of the renewable and efficiency deployment initatives will also be taken in the negotiations.

21.7 Efforts Being Made in India to Deal with Climate Change

As part of its commitment to countering climate change, India announced the National Action Plan on Climate Change (NAPCC) in

June 2008. There are eight National Missions which form the core of the plan, representing multipronged, long term and integrated strategies for achieving key goals in the context of climate change. The work on these Missions is in progress and specific strategies and action plans are being worked out.

21.7.1 Solar Mission

The Solar Mission was launched in January 2010. This is the first mission that has been launched by the Government. The aim is to significantly increase the share of solar energy in the total energy mix while recognising the need to expand the scope of other renewable and non-fossil options such as nuclear energy, wind energy and biomass.

21.7.2 Enhanced Energy Efficiency Mission

The launch of this mission awaits the passage of the amendment of the Energy Conservation Act of 2001. The Lok Sabha has passed the Bill, it awaits a nod from the Rajya Sabha. The mission aims to enhance energy efficiency. To this end, four new initiatives will be put in place including market based mechanism to enhance cost-effectiveness of improvements in energy efficiency in energy-intensive large industries and facilities, accelerating the shift to energy efficient appliances in designated sectors through innovative measure creating mechanisms that would help finance demand-side management programmes in all sectors by capturing future energy savings and developing fiscal instruments to promote energy efficiency. Thus, the mission seeks to upscale the efforts to unlock the market for energy efficiency on a public private partnership (PPP) basis, which is estimated to cost around Rs.74000 crore. This is expected to benefit the country and consumers.

21.7.3 Sustainable Habitat Mission

It aims to promote energy efficiency as an integral component of urban planning and urban renewal through the energy conservation building code, recycling of material and urban waste management, better urban planning, and promotion of urban public transport.

21.7.4 Water Mission

This mission aims to ensure integrated water resource management helping to conserve water, minimise wastage and ensure more equitable distribution both across and within states. The attempt will be to ensure that considerable share of the water needs of urban areas are met through recycling of waste water, and that the water requirements of coastal cities with inadequate alternative sources of water are met through adoption of new and appropriate technologies.

21.7.5 Sustaining the Himalayan Ecosystem

Work on some of its elements is already underway. It aims to evolve management measures for sustaining and safeguarding the Himalayan glacier and mountain ecosystem. Himalayas are a source of key perennial rivers. It will seek to understand, whether and the extent to which the Himalayan glaciers are in recession and how the problem could be addressed.

21.7.6 Green India Mission

The aim is to enhance ecosystem services including forests which serve as carbon sinks. Forests play an indispensable role in the preservation of ecological balance and maintenance of biodiversity. The national target of area under forest and tree cover is 33 per cent while the current area under forests is only 23 per cent.

21.7.7 Sustainable Agriculture Mission

This mission will devise strategies to make Indian agriculture more resilient to climate change. The strategy is to identify and develop new varieties of crops and especially thermal resistant crops and alternative cropping patterns, capable of withstanding extremes of weather, long dry spells, flooding and variable moisture availability. This will be supported by the convergence and integration of traditional knowledge and practice systems, water use efficiency measures, development of land in uncovered areas, treating soil for improving its productivity, using unexploited areas for agricultural activities, information technology, geospatial technologies, and biotechnology. New credit and insurance mechanisms will be devised to facilitate adoption of desired practices.

21.7.8 Strategic Knowledge for Climate Change Mission

This mission attempts to build India's capacity to study and ameliorate climate change. The Indian Network for Climate Change Assessment (INCCA), a network of Indian scientists and research organisations working on climate change is part of this effort. The aim is to enlist the global community in research and technology development and collaboration through mechanisms including open source platforms. It will ensure funding of high quality and focused research into various aspects of climate change. It will also have, on its research agenda, socioeconomic impacts of climate change including impact on health, demography, migration patterns, and livelihood of coastal communities.

21.8 Food Security Concerns

The effects of climate change, particularly on agricultural performance would severely influence the food security in the country. The consequences of climate change have been broadly brought out in the preceding sections. What emerges is that the productivity and production will be adversely affected in the case of food grains, oilseeds, fruits, milk, fish, etc. Widespread concerns are expressed about the food crisis and the rising prices of food products in various countries of the world. Particularly during drought and rain deficient years or when temperatures have fluctuated widely. Some analysts term this as global food crisis in those years and years that follow. India has also experienced subnormal monsoon for 4 years in the last 25 years, the impact of which had been seen on food grains and other food products. The emergent situation needs to be judged considering production, availability of various grains and their price trend.

21.9 Poverty and Hunger

It seems that in the immediate future the food grain availability is comfortable and the past experience shows that food crisis has been avoided by imports and better management and distribution of food grains. The country has also achieved a fair amount of self-sufficiency in food grain production and poverty levels have come down significantly.

However, a comparative status of agriculture in India, China and other groups of countries shows that in the scenario of falling share of agricultural production in total GDP and its share in overall growth raises serious doubts about food security in rural areas, when poverty ratio is still high in India. The position is shown in Table 21.3.

It is well recognised that low and stagnating incomes among the poor in the country leads to low purchasing power, which seriously affect the food and nutritional security of the households. Outcomes in terms of protein-energy malnutrition (PEM) also highlight this issue. According to National Family Health Survey (NFHS-2), in 1998-99, as much as 36 per cent of the adult population of India had a body mass index (BMI) below 18.5 (the cut-off for adult malnutrition). The position in 2005-06, as per NFHS-3, shows a small decline of 3 per cent to 33 per cent despite a decade of robust economic growth. Similarly, share of underweight children under-three in total child population had not fallen significantly, which was 47 per cent in 1998-99 and 46 per cent in 2004-05-2006.

Per capita food consumption in the world, especially of developing countries has improved from an average of 2280 kcal/person/day in the early 1960s to 2800 kcal/person/day by 2001-2003. While China's performance in this area is above world average, India still have to go a long way to even reach world average level of dietary energy, protein and fat consumption level.

Table 21.3

Share of Agriculture in GDP and Growth and Trends in Poverty

Region/Country	*Share of Agriculture in GDP (%)*		*Share of Agricultural Growth in overall Growth (%)*		*US$1a Day Poverty (%)*	
	1975	*2005*	*1975-1985*	*1995-2005*	*1981-1983*	*2004*
East Asia and the Pacific	32	13	20	7	58	9
China	32	13	21	6	64	10
South Asia	40	19	18	10	50	31
India	41	18	17	9	48	34

Source: World Bank, 2008.

Table 21.4

Dietary Energy, Protein and Fat Consumption Per Person/Day

	China	*India*	*USA*	*World*
Energy (Kcal/person/day)				
1979-1981	2330	2080	3180	2550
1989-1991	2680	2370	3460	2700
2001-2003	2940	2440	3770	2800
2002-2004	2930	2470	3760	-
Protein (g/person/day)				
1979-1981	54	51	99	67
1989-1991	65	57	107	72
2001-2003	82	57	114	75
2002-2004	91	63	133	-
Fat (g/person/day)				
1979-1981	33	33	128	59
1989-1991	53	41	138	68
2001-2003	90	52	156	78
2002-2004	91	51	144	-

Source: The State of Food and Agriculture (2007), FAO Food Security Statistics FAO.

Table 21.5

Percentage (%) and Number (Million) of Undernourishment in Total Population

Period	*China*	*India*	*USA*
1969-1971	46 (386.6)	39 (218.3)	<2.5
1979-1981	30 (304.0)	38 (261.3)	<2.5
1990-1992	16 (193.6)	25 (214.8)	<2.5
2001-2003 Provisional	12 (150.0)	20 (212.0)	<2.5
2002-2004 Preliminary	12 (153.7)	20 (209.5)	<2.5

Note: Figures in parentheses are number of undernourishment.

Source: Food Security Statistics, FAO.

As per the undernourishment data for 2002-2004 (preliminary) compiled by the FAO, around 12 per cent of the total population of China are undernourished. In case of India, during the corresponding period, 20 per cent of population are undernourished. In case of developed countries like USA, less than 2.5 per cent of the population are undernourished.

21.10 Global Hunger Index

One in seven people in the world (854 million) go to bed hungry every day. Poverty is the main cause for hunger, with undernourishment, hunger form a vicious circle which is often 'passed on' from generation to generation. The International Food Policy Research Institute (IFPRI) has developed the global hunger index (GHI). As hunger has many faces, a multidimensional approach is adopted to calculate GHI. The GHI

Table 21.6

Global Hunger Index in 118 Countries

Country	*GHI Rank*	*Global Hunger Index*	
		1990	*2008*
Mauritius	1	6.1	5
Libya	-	2.70	<5
Mexico	-	7.93	<5
China	15	12.77	7.1
Pakistan	61	25.73	21.7
India	66	32.5	23.7
Bangladesh	70	32.3	25.2
Burundi	86	32.6	38.3
Brazil	-	7.8	<5
Cuba	4	7.3	5.5
Indonesia	27	16.0	11.3
Kenya	55	23.5	19.9
Russian Federation	-	-	<5

Note: Countries with GHI of less than 5 are not included in the ranking.

Source: IFPRI

score varies between the best possible score of 0 and the worst possible score of 100. Higher score indicates greater hunger. Table 21.6 shows India's position in 118 countries.

21.11 Global Situation—Production and Consumption

Let us first consider the global situation. As per the assessment by FAO, the world cereal production in 2010 is forecast to reach 2279 million tonnes (including rice on a milled basis), 1 per cent up from last year's and close to the 2008 record. A reduction in wheat and rice is forecast due to reduced plantings in several major producing and exporting countries in response to reduced price prospects, while outputs of coarse grains are expected to rise. The increase expected for coarse grains largely reflects the recovery of maize crops in South America that were affected by drought in 2009 and expectations for a record maize crop in the United States. However, the closing stocks of rice and total cereals are estimated to be higher by about 1 per cent. The tradable stocks are also higher by 1 per cent in the case of cereals and more than 5 per cent for rice, which gives the required comfort to the importing countries. In the case of wheat, although the closing stocks are estimated to be lower by 1 per cent, the tradable quantity will be higher by about 1.2 per cent. Thus the food grain availability is expected to be better in the coming year. The position of production, stocks, trade and availability of cereals, wheat and rice at the global level is briefly given in Table 21.7.

Table 21.7

World Cereal Situation

(Million Tonnes)

Cereals	*2008-09*	*2009-10 Estimated*	*2010-11 Forecast*	*% change over 2009-10*
Production	2282.2	2253.1	2279.5	1.2
Trade	282.3	261.8	264.5	1.0
Consumption	2187.3	2223.4	2268.1	2.0
Stocks	510.4	528.1	532.8	0.9

Source: FAO.

Table 21.8

World Wheat Situation

(Million Tonnes)

Wheat	*2008-09*	*2009-10 Estimated*	*2010-11 Forecast*	*% change over 2009-10*
Production	683.8	682.4	676.5	-0.9
Trade	139.2	120.5	122.0	1.2
Consumption	648.6	662.8	675.0	1.8
Stocks	178.1	196.1	194.1	-1.0

Source: FAO.

Table 21.9

World Rice (Milled) Situation

(Million Tonnes)

Rice	*2006-07*	*2007-08*	*2008-09 Estimated*	*2009-10 Forecast*	*Change: 2009-10 Over 2008-09 (%)*
Production	428.7	440.2	458.0	455.5	-0.5
Trade	32.3	30.1	29.7	31.3	5.4
Consumption	427.1	435.7	444.5	453.9	2.1
Ending Stocks	104.6	110.6	124.2	125.3	0.9

Source: FAO.

21.12 Emerging Situation in India

In the recent past, India has emerged as a surplus producer. Unfortunately, the year 2009-10 has been a drought year due to sub-normal rainfall. The food grain production has declined both during *kharif* and *rabi* seasons. However, to ensure food security in the country, both the supply and demand sides are addressed. On the one hand, a fair price is assured to the farmers through a mechanism of minimum support prices and market intervention as and when prices of food grains and other edible products tend to fall below a specified level. Thus the farmers are encouraged to grow the required crops without incurring any loss. The Commission for Agricultural Costs and Prices (CACP), an expert body, based on a systematic analysis, recommends the prices to be offered by the government/procurement agencies. The prices so decided are enforced across the states through procurement by the designated agencies. Thus the system is made sustainable. The procured grains are stocked by Food Corporation of India (FCI) and other state agencies as "Central pool", out of which the grains are released, transported and distributed through network of godowns and fair price shops through the targeted public distribution system (TPDS). On an average, a total quantity of 23 million tonnes of rice and 19 million tonnes of wheat is distributed per annum out of the Central pool stocks. Further, a buffer stock of 4.0 million tonnes of wheat and 5.2 million tonnes of rice is also maintained at the beginning of respective marketing seasons to meet the food grain requirement, in the times of need. Almost about 45 per cent of the food grain consumption needs of the beneficiaries are met through TPDS. Further, of the total food grain requirement, about 25 per cent is provided through the TPDS. However, there is no legal binding on the government, in the present system, to provide a fixed quantity each month to the poor families. The system, more or less, is guided by the capacity, efficiency and commitment of various states for implementing the PDS. Considering the urgent needs of poor, it is being envisaged to enact a law by which the households below the poverty line (BPL) could be assured of a minimum quantity of food grains each month.

21.13 Demand–Supply Scenario

A comparative position of projected production and projected demand was worked out for 2011-12 and 2020. Although the year 2008-2009 displayed clearly that the production was more than the demand except for pulses and oilseeds, the year 2009-10 being a drought year witnessed a short fall of about 6 million tonnes of rice, 3 million tonnes of coarse cereals, 3 million tonnes of pulses, 25 million tonnes of oil seeds, as against the projected demand. This situation has brought the prices of food grains under pressure. The demand-supply balance sheets (Table 21.10) clearly bring out that the supply was just able to meet the demand. The year and stocks in the country were adequate to meet only about one month's requirement leaving little scope to control speculative tendency in the market.

Table 21.10

Demand/Supply Scenario

Crop	2008-09 Projected Demand	2008-09 Projected Production	2009-10@ Estimated Production	2011-12 Projected Demand	2011-12 Projected Production	2020 Projected Demand*
Rice	92.87	95.34(99.18)	89.31	98.79	104.21	111.90
Wheat	72.72	76.21(80.68)	80.98	77.36	83.61	79.90
Coarse cereals	35.90	34.57(40.03)	33.13	38.19	35.75	37.30
Pulses	17.51	14.43(14.57)	14.77	19.91	15.73	23.80
Food grains	219.00	220.55(234.47)	218.19	234.26	239.30	252.80
Sugarcane	275.91	296.88(285.03)	274.66	322.54	305.51	-
Oilseeds	47.43	26.32(27.72)	25.41	53.39	27.53	-

Note: *Based on GDP growth rate of 7 per cent and per capita GDP growth rate of 5.5 per cent as per *Report of NDC Sub-Group on Demand and Supply*.

*Figures in brackets are the actual production estimates.

@3rd Advance Estimate released on 12.5.2010.

(i) Projected production is based on the compound annual growth rate (CAGR) of 1.5 per cent for rice, 1.9 per cent for wheat, 1.12 per cent for coarse cereals, 0.24 per cent for pulses and 1.51 per cent for oilseeds observed between the Triennium Ending (TE) 1995-96 and TE (2006-07). Projected production also takes into account the targets of National Food Security Mission (NFSM).

(ii) Demand is based upon behaviouristic approach which takes into account the population growth, rate of growth of per capita disposable income at 4.8 per cent and expenditure elasticity at 0.55 per cent. Demand includes deed, feed and wastage.

Table 21.11

Demand and Supply Position of Rice (Estimated)

(Million Tonnes)

	2006-07	2007-08	2008-09	2009-10	2010-11
1. Opening stock with FCI	5.97	5.49	7.84	15.35	20.25
2. Production*	93.69	96.69	99.18	89.31	
3. Imports	0.00	0.00	0.00	0.00	
4. Total (1+2+3)	99.66	102.18	107.02	104.66	
5. Consumption	89.40	90.91	92.87	94.83	
6. Exports	4.78	6.30	1.89	1.56	
7. Total (5+6)	94.18	97.21	94.76	96.39	
8. Year-end balance (4-7)	5.48	4.97	12.28	14.52	
9. Stock available with@					
(i) FCI	5.49	7.86	15.35	20.25$	
(ii) Private (households & mills)	-0.01	-2.89	-3.07	-5.73	

Note: * Production figure for 2009-10 is 3rd advance estimates.

Consumption includes seed, feed, wastage and indirect consumption apart from household consumption.

@ Stock as on 30th September; $ Estimated; FCI – Food Corporation of India.

Source: Working group for 11th Plan and *Foodgrain Bulletin* of Department of Food and Public Distribution.

Table 21.12

Demand and Supply Position of Wheat (Estimated)

(Million Tonnes)

	2005-06	2006-07	2007-08	2008-09	2009-10	2010-11
1. Opening stock with FCI	4.07	2.01	4.70	5.80	13.40	16.10
2. Production	68.64	69.35	75.81	78.57	80.68	80.98
3. Imports	0.00	6.08	1.79	0.00	0.00	
4. Total (1+2+3)	72.71	77.44	82.30	84.37	94.08	97.08
5. Consumption	68.10	69.65	71.19	72.72	74.26	75.80
6. Exports	1.00	0.50	0.00	0.00	0.00	0.00
7. Total (5+6)	69.10	70.15	71.19	72.72	74.26	75.80
8. Year-end balance (4-7)	3.61	7.29	11.11	11.65	19.82	21.28
9. Stock available with@						
(i) FCI	2.01	4.70	5.80	13.40	16.10	18.50$
(ii) Private (households & mills)	1.60	2.59	5.31	-1.74	3.72	2.78

Note: * Production figure for 2008-09 is the estimated production during 2007-08 and for 2009-10 it is anticipated at lower than the current level by 15 million tonnes.

@Stocks as on April 1.

$Assuming offtake level of last year.

Source: Working group for 11th Plan and *Foodgrain Bulletin* of Department of Food and Public Distribution.

Table 21.13

Comparative Position of Procurement and offtake of Rice and Wheat

	2006-07		2007-08		2008-09		2009-10	
	Procure-ment	Offtake	Procure-ment	Offtake	Procure-ment	Offtake	Procure-ment	Offtake
Rice	25.10	25.06	28.74	25.23	33.68	24.62	29.70	27.38
Wheat	9.22	11.70	11.13	12.20	22.68	14.88	25.38	22.35
Total offtake (rice+wheat)	34.32	36.76	39.87	37.43	56.36	39.50	55.08	49.73

Source: *Foodgrain Bulletin* of Department of Food and Public Distribution.

What is visible during the last three years is that the government withdrew a substantial quantity from the market through higher procurement levels and market availability got reduced. This was mainly because of the attractive support prices offered by the government. This happened even in a drought year like 2009-10. The availability was further affected because the offtake (releases) was much less than the procurement in these years. As a result, prices came under strain despite the governments' capacity to release more of rice and wheat in the market. This raised several questions on effective food management system.

The rice balance sheet shows that the FCI had adequate stocks to intervene in the market through TPDS and open market sales, wherever required. However, the availability in the market is severely affected in 2009-10 due to high procurement of about 27.4 million tonnes from a crop which was lower by 10 million tonnes as compared to that of 2008-2009. Higher offtake/releases can be done in the backdrop of a good monsoon currently in progress in 2010 and larger area covered under paddy so far. In the case of wheat also, a similar situation prevails and the market intervention can be comfortably done to enhance the availability, which should enable the government to restrain any undue price increase during 2010-11 and 2011-12. The position which prevailed is evident from the above Tables 21.11, 21.12 and 21.13.

21.14 Steps Required for Enhancing Production

Considering the stagnation in yield levels in the major producing states and the continuous rise in demand, it would be essential to strengthen the production/supply side to ensure adequate food security on a sustainable basis. In this regard, *inter alia*, following measures are required to be taken:

(i) Invest more in water conservation and water saving technologies along with water harvesting and ground water recharge on a much larger scale, in a given timeframe. This would also address the problem of rainfed farming.

(ii) Utilise available ground water particularly in eastern India, *viz.*, Bihar, Eastern UP, Assam, West Bengal and Orissa by taking up a programme of dug wells/shallow tube wells with energisation. This will improve yield levels substantially.

(iii) Invest more in seed sector (both in research and multiplication) for developing drought/heat flood resistant varieties.

(iv) Invest more in land development and soil improvement (saline/alkaline land, use of gypsum, pyrite, land levelling etc.).

(v) Greater use of organic manure, compost and biofertilisers to maintain soil health and to improve water retention capacity.

(vi) Have a reliable system by which farmers can be assured of a minimum income (by appropriate insurance products and alternative crops and employment opportunities). Have a more dependable system for agri-insurance for prompt assessment of loss and disbursal of the amount.

(vii) A programme to cover additional 15 million hectare of *kharif* fallow lands during *rabi* season be taken up for producing wheat, *rabi* rice and pulses.

(viii) Interest on term loan for agriculture may be brought down to 6.5 per cent.

(ix) Invest more in command area development (through using the funds available under NREGA) for optimising the use of the additional irrigation potential created.

(x) Farm mechanisations to be expedited in view of increasing wage rates and shrinkage of labour availability for agricultural operations due to Mahatma Gandhi National Rural Employment Guarantee Act (MNREGA).

(xi) Have a targeted approach to provide required food items such as wheat, rice, coarse cereals, edible oils and sugar at fair price to the poor and put in place universal PDS in the areas which are chronically deficit and where normal trade does not function efficiently.

(xii) Take up R&D initative in the area of animal husbandry, aquaculture and horticulture to address the productivity losses due to the impact of climate change.

21.15 A Word About the Proposed Food Security Bill (2010)

In a situation of wide fluctuations in food grains production, uncertain availability situation resulting in to unreasonable price increase and also inefficient PDS in several parts of the country, the proposed Food Security Bill is the right initiative to meet the food grains need of the poor, although partly, by making it mandatory for the government to ensure provision of certain quantity of wheat and rice. However, there are several issues which need to be addressed and settled to see that the bill provides "food security" to the poor and vulnerable sections in real sense of the term:

(i) The first issue is as to why only wheat, rice and coarse cereals have been included. For ensuring food security for the poor, pulses, sugar and edible oils are also very crucial which are the important sources of energy/nutrition. As per available estimates, about 70 per cent of the total calorie intake is from wheat, rice, sugar and edible oils. Wheat and rice consumption taken together account for about 65 per cent of the total calorie intake by the poor in both rural and urban areas of this, about 41 per cent is met through TPDS.

(ii) The second, is the scale of ration, limited to 25 kg per family per month, adequate to ensure food security? As per the National Sample Survey Organisation's (NSSO) surveys, the per capita cereal consumption by the poor is relatively high. The scope of self-provisioning during harvest season also is limited since most of the poor are landless or have no adequate income to stock grains for future. Moreover, the price at which the cereals could be purchased even during the peak marketing season would be too high as compared to the price at which they would be provided cereals through the TPDS, will not motivate them to buy and stock. Hence at best, it can only be our presumption that the poor would make provisioning only for 3 months in a year. This would imply that they need to be provided cereals for at least equivalent to 9 months requirement. If a normal size of the family (poor) is taken as 5 persons, the monthly requirement per family per month would work out to 43 kg, if provision for 3 months is made by the family themselves. If the guarantee is to meet 100 per cent requirement, then the per family entitlement will be 68 kg per month. Therefore, 25 kg provision of cereals per family per month is on a lower side and the intended food security for the poor would get compromised. There is also a need to provide per capita monthly entitlement so that the bigger families of BPL household get their due.

(iii) The third issue is that the assessment of the BPL families is required to be notified by the Planning Commission for each of the state/UTs. While this may be all right for provisioning the requirement of each state, the actual number is bound to be different when the identification of such families is done. So what happens to the additional families who are genuinely poor? This needs to be addressed in an objective manner, otherwise the exclusion would take place based on social, political and other extraneous considerations.

(iv) The fourth issue is the State Food Security Allowance Fund (SFSAF), through which identified BPL families are proposed to be provided food security allowance in an event of non-supply of entitled food grains under the Bill. The question is how much allowance shall be provided? Will it be the difference between the market price and the TPDS price multiplied by the entitled quantity or would it be a fixed sum? What happens if the grains are not available in the market, and if available, at unreasonably high prices? In fact, the government would have to ensure continuous flow of grains specially in the far-flung, inaccessible, hilly tribal areas, etc., where there could be perpetual shortage. It needs to be provided in the Act itself.

(v) Lastly, (although there are other issues as well), it is not quite clear as to why in Section 1(2), it has been provided that the government may temporarily exclude all or any part of the territory of India from the operation of all or any of the provisions of the bill. Appropriately, the option should have been for both "inclusion" and "exclusion" because in a situation of "droughts" and "floods" which are often experienced in certain parts of the country, food security has to be ensured. Because of episodic events such as floods and droughts, need for "inclusion" would be often felt. In a drought situation, families at the margin often fall below the poverty line. Therefore, a suitable provision is required in the proposed bill so that certain areas/families excluded in normal situation could be included for the purpose of ensuring food security for them.

Notes and References

"Article 2". *The United Nations Framework Convention on Climate Change*. Retrieved 15 November 2005. "Such a level should be achieved within a time-frame sufficient to allow ecosystems to adapt naturally to climate change, to ensure that food production is not threatened and to enable economic development to proceed in a sustainable manner"

Borrador de Analisis de la Red del Tercer Mundo sobre el Acuredo de Copenhague, Enero 2010.

Briefing Paper : Cophenhagen Climate Deal – how to close the gap?

Comments on Copenhagen Accord (2010). "Summary", *South Centre Informal Note* 52, 18 January.

Dantwala, M.L. (1967). "Incentive and Disincentive in Indian Agriculture", *Indian Journal of Agriculture Economics* XVII(2) (April-June).

Depledge, J. (August 1999/August 2000). "Tracing the Origins of the Kyoto Protocol: An Article-by-Article Textual History", *UNFCCC Technical Paper*. Retrieved 2009-05-20.

Dessai, S. (2001). "The Climate Regime from The Hague to Marrakech: Saving or Sinking the Kyoto Protocol?", *Tyndall Centre Working Paper* 12, UK: Tyndall Centre. Retrieved 2010-05-05.

Ekardt, F. and A. von Hövel (2009). "Distributive Justice, Competitiveness, and Transnational Climate Protection", *Carbon & Climate Law Review* 3: 102–114.

G8 Summit (2007). "Breakthrough on climate protection", Heiligendamm. Retrieved 2007-06-07.

George, P.S. (1979). *Public Distribution of Foodgrains in Kerala, Income Distribution Implications and Effectiveness*. Washington: International Food Policy Research Institute, p.67.

Economic Times (various issues). Published from New Delhi.

Grubb, M. *et al*. (2009). "Climate Policy and Industrial Competitiveness: Ten Insights from Europe on the EU Emissions Trading System", *Climate Strategies*, 3 August. Retrieved 2010-04-14.

Grubb, M. (2003). "The Economics of the Kyoto Protocol", *World Economics* 4(3): 143-89, July-September.

———. (2000). "The Kyoto Protocol: An Economic Appraisal", *FEEM Working Paper* No. 30, SSRN, April. Retrieved 2010-04-02.

Global Cimate Change, NASA's Eyes on the Earth. NASA Jet Propulsion Laboratory, California Institute of Technology.

Gupta, Arvind (1977). *Public Distribution of Foodgrains in India* – Indian Institute of Management, Ahmedabad.

Gupta, S. *et al*. (2007). "Policies, Instruments, and Co-operative Arrangements", in: *Climate Change 2007: Mitigation*. Contribution of Working Group III to the Fourth Assessment Report of the Intergovernmental Panel on Climate Change (B. Metz *et al*. eds.). Cambridge, U.K., and New York, N.Y., U.S.A.: Cambridge University Press. Retrieved 2010-04-02.

IEA (2007). *World Energy Outlook 2007 Edition- China and India Insights*. International Energy Agency (IEA), Head of Communication and Information Office, Paris, France. pp. 600. Retrieved 2010-05-04.

IPCC (2007). *Climate Change 2007: Synthesis Report.* Contribution of Working Groups I, II and III to the *Fourth Assessment Report of the Intergovernmental Panel on Climate Change (Core Writing Team, R.K Pachauri and A. Reisinger (eds.)).* Geneva, Switzerland: IPCC. Retrieved 2010-05-28.

IPCC (2007). "Projected climate change and its impacts. Summary for Policymakers", *Climate Change 2007: Synthesis Report.* Contribution of Working Groups I, II and III to the Fourth Assessment Report of the Intergovernmental Panel on Climate Change (Core Writing Team *et al.* (eds.)". Cambridge, U.K., and New York, N.Y., U.S.A.: Cambridge University Press, Retrieved 2010-03-18.

Jharwal, S.M. (2010). "Rainfed Agiculture Need for Rainbow Revolution" *in* S. Singh and M.S. Rathore (eds.), *Rainfed Agricultural in India: Perspective and Challenges.* Jaipur: Rawat Publications.

———. (1998). *Public Distribution in India – Reassessed.* Delhi: Manak Publishers.

Jharwal, S.M., R.S. Deshpande, Vijay Paul Sharma, R.P.S Malik, Brajesh Jha and S.A Ansari (2007). *Glimpses of Indian Agriculture.* Vol. I: Macro Aspect. New Delhi: Academic Foundation.

Krishna, Raj *et al.* (1983). *Policy Modelling of a Dual Grain Market : The case of Wheat in India* – IFPRI, Research Report-38, pp.9-33. Washington.

Krishnana T.N. (1992). *Food Subsidy, Budget and Structural Adjustment.* Paper presented for pre-budget discussion with Finance Minister in January.

Kogan, Lawrence A. (2002). "The U.S. Response to the Kyoto Protocol – A Realistic Alternative?", *The Whitehead Journal of Diplomacy and International Relations* III(2), June. Retrieved 2001-10-20.

MNP (2007). "Greenhouse Gas Emissions of Countries in 2005 and Ranking of their Per Capita Emissions. Table 2.a. Top-20 Countries of Greenhouse Emissions in 2006 from Fossil Fuels and Cement Production", Netherlands Environment Agency. Retrieved 2010-05-01.

Nordhaus, W.D. and J.G. Boyer (2009). *Requiem for Kyoto: An Economic Analysis of the Kyoto Protocol.* Retrieved 2009-08-08.

Rao, V.M. (1992). Fixing Agricultural Prices : Issues and Experiences, *Economic and Political Weekly* XXVII(3): 639-645, March, 28.

Reutilinger (1987). "Food Security and Poverty in Developing Countries", in J. Price Gittinger *et al.* (ed.) *Food Policy – Integrating Supply, Distribution and Consumption*, World Bank, pp.205-214.

Science Insider (2010). "Do You Heart 'The Hartwell Paper'?", Retrieved 2010-05-12.

Sen, Amartya (1987). *Poverty and Entitlements* – Food Policy – Integrating Supply Distribution and Consumption, World Bank Publication – EDI services in Economic Development, pp.198-204.

———. (1982). *"Poverty and Famines"*, Published on behlaf of the ILO. Clarendon Press Oxford (U.K.).

Stern, N. (2007). *A Stern Review on the Economics of Climate Change* (pre-publication edition). Cambridge, U.K., and New York, U.S.A.: Cambridge University Press. Retrieved 2010-02-25.

Tyagi, D.S. (1990). *Managing India's Food Economy : Problems and Alternatives.*

UNFCCC (2009). "Kyoto Protocol: Status of Ratification". United Nations Framework Convention on Climate Change. Retrieved 2009-05-06.

———. (2006). *An Introduction to the Kyoto Protocol Compliance Mechanism.* Retrieved 2006-10-30.

Venugopal, K.R. (1992). *Deliverance from Hunger – The PDS in India.* New Delhi: Sage Publications.

Vyas, V.S. (1993). "New Economic Policy and Vulnerable Sections – Rationale for Public Intervention", *Economic & Political Weekly* 28(10), March 6.

Weyant, J.P. (ed.) (1999). "The Costs of the Kyoto Protocol: A Multi-Model Evaluation", *Energy Journal* (Special Issue), May. Retrieved 2009-08-08.

World Bank (2010). *World Development Report 2010: Development and Climate Change*. The International Bank for Reconstruction and Development. Washington DC:The World Bank, 20433. Retrieved 2010-04-06.

———. (2008). "Development and Climate Change: A Strategic Framework for the World Bank Group: Technical Report", The International Bank for Reconstruction and Development. Washington, DC: The World Bank. Retrieved 2010-04-03.

Section V

Governance

22 Budget Transparency, Accountability and Citizen Participation

The PROOF Campaign in Bangalore, 2002-03

Vinod Vyasulu

"Will you walk a little faster?" said a whiting to a snail,
There is a purpose close behind us, and he is treading on my tail.
See how eagerly the lobsters and the turtles all advance!
They are waiting on the shingle—will you come and join the dance?
Will you, wo'n't you, will you, wo'n't you will you join the dance?
Will you, wo'n't you, will you, wo'n't you, wo'n't you join the dance?

"You can really have no notion how delightful it will be
"When they take us up and throw us, with the lobsters, out to sea!"
But the snail replied "Too far, too far!" and gave a look askance—
Said he thanked the whiting kindly, but he would not join the dance.
Would not, could not, would not, could not would not join the dance.
Would not, could not, would not, could not, could not join the dance.

"What matters it how far we go?" his scaly friend replied.
"There is another shore, you know, upon the other side.
The further off from England the nearer is to France—
Then turn not pale, beloved snail, but come and join the dance.
Will you, wo'n't you, will you, wo'n't you, will you join the dance?
Will you, wo'n't you, will you, wo'n't you, wo'n't you join the dance?

"The Lobster Quadrille", Lewis Carroll

22.1 Introduction

Prof. V.M. Rao has been an inspiration to a whole generation of scholars in ISEC, where he spent the best part of his academic life. This generation includes younger colleagues like myself, who were not his students, but who have nevertheless benefitted from his encouragement when we were impatient, his erudition when we were rushing to conclusions, and his humanism when we were waxing eloquent on large issues. He would gently bring us back to the task on hand, and make us work our way through to the core of the issue on hand, all the while smiling and helping without intruding. Prof. Rao belongs to that rare breed of scholars who know what they could do, and knew how to leave alone what they could not. In all his work, he sought to take the insights of economic theory, interpreted in the light of painstakingly collected facts, to the realm of policy. In this essay written in tribute to one of Karnataka's homegrown scholars, I would like to detail a campaign that has the ingredients that Prof. Rao would have approved of—and hope that the lead given by this experience would prompt others in the groves of academe to engage the world around them.

This volume has the theme, "India's Development Initiatives During the 1990s". The 1990s were the decade of economic reforms, when India is supposed to have made a 'U' turn in economic policy. I will not enter that debate. It is enough to note also that the 1990s were also the decade of two fundamental constitutional amendments that gave local self government into India a constitutional status. The impact of these amendments is still being felt, and this paper deals with one specific instance of this particular initiative of the 1990s.

After the passing of the 74th Amendment of the Indian Constitution, there has been a belief that sharing of information and transparency in financial matters, such as government budgets, would both improve government accountability and nurture citizen participation in the public policy process. This is a big change in the basic norm of Indian governance, in which secrecy has been the norm.[1] It has also been recognised that there is, because of past experience, a great deal of cynicism and apathy on the part of citizens when it comes to practical issues of daily concern, like roads, schools, public health centres etc. In an effort to at least partially address this issue, several states, following upon the seminal and innovative work of the Mazdoor Kisan Sangharsh Sanghatan in Rajasthan, have passed laws on Right/ Freedom of Information. Karnataka is one of them.[2] A start in this

1. Vyasulu, Vinod (2002). "Transparency on Public Sector Finance and Public Financial Accountability in Karnataka", Paper submitted to the World Bank, June, unpublished.
2. Dey, Nikhil and Vinod Vyasulu (2003). "Setting the Rules of Engagement: The Right to Information in Karnataka", November, published in a special issue of the Press Trust of India journal.

direction has been made. The question is about how to move ahead now.

The implementation of the constitutional amendments has been half-hearted.[3] In rural India, there has been little participation by citizens in the *gram sabhas*, which are institutional mechanisms meant to facilitate citizen participation in issues of local governance. Prof. Rao has contributed deeply to our understanding of the rural scene in India. This paper takes his methods of work and research to the urban sector, which has been quite understudied in this country.

In urban India—and Bangalore—the ward committees in cities had not even been constituted. Why is there this divergence between sweeping legal changes, strongly held belief and widely documented reality? What has been missed out in the process of transformation now under way? Are there cases where the disclosure of financial information has been followed by active citizen participation in the budget process?

In Bangalore we have one such case, the PROOF campaign of 2002-2003.[4] What can we learn from this experience? Is citizen engagement with government meaningful at all?

---

3. Vyasulu, Vinod (2003). *Panchayats, Democracy and Development*. Jaipur: Rawat; "From Centralised Administration to Local Governance", lecture at the Institute of Advanced Studies, Bangalore, February 2003 unpublished.

4. A large number of people contributed to the PROOF campaign. Our thanks go to the BMP for partnering us in this endeavour. The mayor, the commissioner, the special commissioner, the additional commissioner, and many other officials gave generously of their time. The staff at FBAS provided excellent support. Without this co-operation from the BMP, the campaign would have had nowhere to go. This co-operation is all the sweeter because in the course of the campaign, there were honest differences of opinion. Sorting these out through discussion shows the maturity of the organisation, and the citizens it governs. The citizens of Bangalore, especially those who gave time in so many ways—through the PROOF Energy Centre, through community meetings, through participation in the development of indicators, in helping organise the public debates—there are so many ways. This was the other most important component of the PROOF campaign. Infosys provided the venue for the public debates, and its managing director chaired some of the sessions. A sumptuous lunch was provided to all who attended. We are grateful to Infosys for this support. There were many individuals who worked hard behind the scenes. Of them mention must be made of Prasad, Preetha Radhakrishnan, Vilasini Kumar, Seema Dargar and the many volunteers of Janaagraha who contributed time and effort selflessly. The best way of thinking all of then is to ensure that the spirit of disclosure, transparency, debate and partnership that the PROOF campaign stood for continues in our city, making it better in every way.

Considering the apathy of citizens and the widely prevalent belief that the local government was both corrupt and inefficient, this seemed utopian. If we took it up at all, it was because we believed that we had a new and different approach that had not been tried out before. We were not for confrontation. There has been enough experience with confrontative approaches in India, but little by way of specific improvements that followed. Trade unions may have won major victories for workers over the years, but many of these are also being reversed in the course of structural adjustment policies. The confrontative approach has been based on the belief that the system cannot be improved, it has to be replaced with a revolutionary alternative; and that has not happened, at least in India. On the other hand, many others working from different ideologies have managed to secure benefits and improvements for their constituents. Without taking a final position on this issue, it seems to be clear that some improvements in the system are possible. If these are attempted on a democratic basis, it is possible they will last. This does not mean better systems do not exist; it does mean that some sustained improvement is possible in the current system. It then becomes worthwhile to work with, and try to improve/change/strengthen the existing system democratically. The 73rd and 74th Amendments offer a unique opportunity for such efforts.

This paper presents the salient facts about the PROOF campaign, and reflects on the lessons it holds, in the tradition of Prof. Rao, not just for Bangalore, but for other cities in India as well. This is introspection by a partner in this campaign, but it does not claim to speak for the campaign.[5] Section 2 presents the facts as objectively as possible. Section 3 delves into some issues that cropped up in the course of the campaign in a personal manner—it may not represent the views or thinking of the other partners. It is meant only to share some personal experiences and reflections, in the hope that the debate on this subject may move ahead. Section 4 offers some conclusions.

---

5. Seema Dargar, an independent scholar, has documented this campaign. See "City government, Budget Analysis and People's Participation in India: The Experience of Bangalore", CBPS *occasional paper*, 2003.

22.2 Salient Facts about the PROOF Campaign

The PROOF (Public Record Of Operations and Finances) campaign was launched in July 2002 for a 10-month period by 4 independent, not-for-profit organisations in Bangalore.[6] The objective was that of building citizen confidence in the local city government (the Bangalore City Corporation, BMP by its Kannada initials), by facilitating public discussions around its quarterly financial performance. The idea was to create a space for constructive engagement between citizens and their local government.[7] We should be able to ask tough questions, get honest answers, and together work for common betterment.

The BMP had passed its budget in March 2002, and this was taken as given by the campaign. We did not ask if it was appropriate, as the elected body has its own legitimacy that must be respected in a democracy. We could, however, as citizens and tax payers, ask how the BMP performed in terms of its own targets and goals. What were the shortfalls, and what were the problems faced by the BMP in implementing its programmes approved in the budget? How could citizens of the city partner it in improving its functioning? Would transparency and accountability in this specific context enable and encourage citizen participation in the running of the city? We chose to ask the BMP for a disclosure of its quarterly financial performance. A simple format was prepared, and information was requested on revenue and expenditure; on assets and liabilities, and then for a management discussion and analysis for the past quarter. We would arrange for four public discussions, one for each quarter. This, we hoped would focus attention on issues of importance to the city, and led to gradual improvements through partnership between the BMP and citizens.

Our objective was not to find scapegoats and seek to punish them. Our aim was—and remains—that of improving the system of local governance. The way in which this is sought is through serious and continuous engagement. There are enough competent and honest people

6. The launch document gives details. Available on request from: *proof@vsnl.net*. The four organisations are: Centre for Budget and Policy Studies; Janaagraha; Public Affairs Centre and Voices, all based in Bangalore. See also, *www.janaagraha.org*

7. More detail is available in several articles in a special issue of *Voices*, November 2002.

in the BMP trying to work under difficult conditions. Janaagraha, one of the campaign partners, has been working with communities and the BMP at the local level, with elected corporators and citizens. As a result of this work, about four crore rupees of ward works requested by citizens were included in the budget for 2002-03. This showed that improvements are possible if we can work together to improve the entire system, not just parts of it. This will certainly call for changes, but these are changes that will be jointly agreed upon, with the pain of change being shared. This is the method that the PROOF campaign decided to work with. It extended Janaagraha's local level work to the entire city of Bangalore.

Most cities work with a single entry, cash book system of accounts. The BMP is the first city corporation in the country to develop and implement a fund based, double entry accrual system of accounts for itself. This is a bottom up method of financial accounting that is effectively computerised with special software developed for the purpose.[8] It was in the middle of the difficult organisational transition from the cash book single entry system of accounts to the new one. The supply side has been looked after—the data on financial performance is available in real time to the decision makers of the BMP.

If such an organisation has a poor public image, what was the reason for it? If this available data could be shared with citizens, who could also analyse it independently from their own point of view, it should add light to the prevailing situation in the city, and the interaction could throw up new ideas and solutions. We wanted a partnership in which we could engage in discussion and debate, through which we could together seek to improve city government. We would try this for a year, and review our experience to see what we had learnt. Future programmes would depend upon that. This, in essence, is PROOF.

---

8. Supported by the Bangalore Agenda Task Force, implemented by Messrs NCRCL Ltd., led by Murali, a chartered accountant. It involved more than 2,00,000 person hours of professional input from accountants and software engineers. Other municipalities can now learn from this system, called FBAS-Fund Based Accounting System.

This, we found, was an unusual initiative in citizen interaction with local government. We did not find any experience elsewhere on which we could draw. The weekly Tuesday afternoon meetings of the partners was where it all happened—discussions of strategy, decisions on what to do. As time went on, various other meetings came to be held, with citizens, with stakeholders in different areas, in many of which the concerned BMP officials took full part. That this has happened is encouraging; what impact it has had, it is perhaps too early to say. And finally, it should be citizens who decide if all this has been worthwhile, not the partners who launched the campaign.

The campaign's initial results exceeded completely the expectations of the partners who launched it. We had hoped for four public debates or discussions, one in each quarter. This we managed to do.[9] Each debate built on the other, and at the end we had a citizenry that was able to independently interact with the BMP on budget and related matters. Why and how did this happen? Was it due to factors unique to Bangalore, or was it simply the spirit of the times? Would it have happened anyway in Bangalore without the intervention we brought in through PROOF? Can it happen elsewhere—and under what conditions?

We found campaign work exploding around us. Citizens responded enthusiastically. With help from Voices, a partner in the campaign, citizens organised themselves into what has come to be called the PROOF Energy Centre (PEC). This centre took on a number of initiatives. It began to make demands on the campaign and its partners. Radio programmes—PROOF Puttanna—were aired on Akashvani every Wednesday evening, and we had to provide material. The idea was to inform citizens about PROOF and urge them to get involved. In the beginning, the partners somehow managed to find suitable material and this was aired live. Later, the PEC took over this function. Those who took part ranged from ordinary citizens to famous film stars. Programme were prepared in Voices, and a CD sent to Akashvani for broadcast.

9. Held in the Infosys J.N. Tata Conference Centre, on August 17, 2002, December 7, 2002, March 15, 2003 and May 17, 2003 before a carefully invited audience on each occasion.

In addition to the public discussions, there was a demand for a number of mini discussions in various parts of the city. We were unprepared for this. The PEC took over this chore. The PEC broke itself into sub-groups, with specific responsibilities. One was for building bridges between the BMP and citizens for regular interaction. Another was for arranging workshops to facilitate community analysis of the quarterly data. A third was ambitious: it wanted to work towards 'Namma Budget'—our budget. The PEC began to bring out a bi-weekly newsletter, first electronically, and then in print, called *Talk About PROOF*.

Another group of citizens decided to involve college students in the campaign. A number of activities were arranged—PROOF debates, skits etc. The response from both teachers and students was unbelievably enthusiastic.[10] While this took off after more then six months, it has laid the foundation for a corps of young people who should be able to sustain such efforts in the years to come.

In response to strong demand from citizens, we had to organise training in understanding municipal finances for them. We did, and the campaign prepared a manual and powerpoint presentation for this purpose.[11] Over 300 citizens went through this three hour session, often held on Saturdays. Again, in response to questions from both the BMP and citizens, we had to come up with performance indicators. Money is spent for a purpose, and is that purpose being achieved? How could we answer this question? And so we got into the development of performance indicators (PIs). In the areas of primary schools and public health, BMP officials, citizens, parents—stakeholders of all kinds—got together in a series of workshops to discuss the issues and develop indicators. This was massive exercise which strained our limited administrative resources to breaking point. But we survived.

---

10. Management students from Christ College in Bangalore have developed a simulation game, based on the facts of the city budget, using role play techniques, which can be used in the training process.

11. This material, in English and Kannada, is available with PROOF, and will be freely shared with others interested in such work. Contact *proof@vsnl.net* or *proof_voices@vsnl.com*

These indicators had to be simple. They had to build on available data, and they had to tell a story. A large number of output, outcome and efficiency indicators were agreed upon, and the BMP has agreed to begin using them for monitoring progress. In this process, other NGOs, with interests in these areas, have become its partners. And this exercise is growing. If this was not to gladden the hearts of citizens, what would?

Bangalore is a city of inequalities. These inequalities have been worsening over time, and therefore it was important that the work of the BMP reach the poor in the city. Many of the poor live in slums, and organisations working with slum dwellers wanted to analyse the budget from this point of view. Slum dwellers are citizens with the same rights as other middle class citizens. But they do not get basic services like drinking water and sanitation. Thus, a new line of work began—what do the poor contribute to taxes, as they pay indirect taxes? What do they contribute through the economic activities in the slum? Slums are places of jobs as well as residence, and thus contribute positively to the city economy. The city has norms for services—such as 40 litres of water per person per day. There should be a school within one kilometre. Do slum dwellers get this level of service? If not, why not? How can their demands—needs—be addressed? And so on and on.

How did this come to happen? What contributed to this 'success'? What were the campaign's limitations? If we are to continue, what should we build upon? What can other cities learn from our work? I turn to these issues in the next section. These, I emphasise, are my personal views.

22.3 Issues Emerged in the Course of Campaign

While it is not unusual for citizens' to launch such a campaign, it is unusual for the city government to partner it wholeheartedly. Why has the BMP participated so actively in the PROOF campaign? The BMP has to deal with many agencies and NGOs. There are many other demands on its time. That it chose to engage with PROOF in such earnestness and depth is remarkable. Was it because of the approach of engagement? Perhaps, as no one else worked this way? Was it because of the high profile of some of the persons involved? Perhaps; it is not possible for officials to turn a Nelson's eye to prominent citizens like Samuel Paul, Nandan Nilekani and Ramesh Ramanathan. Nilekani and Ramanathan are members of the Bangalore Agenda Task Force [BATF] set up by the Karnataka Chief Minister to make Bangalore a Singapore-like city, to which the agencies concerned with Bangalore were to report at intervals. Was it because PROOF showed that it was not a gleam in someone's eye that would shortly disappear, but a campaign that would last because citizens gathered around this banner? Perhaps. There could be many reasons. But the partnership had its ups and downs. I discuss below my personal version of two of these issues. What can we learn from this experience?

The partners had a bad time before the second public debate, when a difference of opinion with the BMP blew into the open over newspaper reports about a large loan the BMP was taking from the Housing and Urban Development Corporation—HUDCO. PROOF members heard about the 1000 crore loan that found no place in the BMP budget just before the second public debate. The partners were upset at what they considered an "unpleasant surprise" in a budgeting exercise. The Q2 figures did not show this loan. How could such a large loan be taken on an ad hoc basis? What about the past municipal bond loan of 125 crore? Why take such a huge loan before learning from the experience of bond loan and how it was used and managed? PROOF issued a hurried press note on this issue, asking for a public debate on this loan. Citizens were encouraged to demand information about the loan under the recently passed Karnataka Freedom of Information Act, and Rules notified under it. Many did just that.

Officials of the BMP were upset about both the PROOF campaign going to the press, and the campaign "organising opposition to the proposed loan" without knowing all the facts. They had issued public notices about the loan a month earlier. The elected body of the BMP and the state government had approved it. HUDCO was a public sector corporation that too had to follow strict governmental procedures. And all due procedures were followed. Why was PROOF making such a fuss without checking out the facts? BMP did take part in the second debate, in which the citizens were very vocal about their concerns, but left very unhappy with the process. They felt they were not consulted on the agenda and the date, and were not given a fair hearing. Further, they felt that citizens had a wrong notion of how democracy worked, because PROOF misled them. PROOF could not expect citizens to take over the running of the BMP, and for civil servants to accept this take over. Information would continue to be given as it pertained to public funds. But there was no point in the BMP participating in debates organised by a group that had little respect for the procedures of representative democracy.

This seemed a deadlock, and the end of the debates process. When PROOF asked for a date for the third public discussion, the BMP felt there was no point in senior officials participating in such proceedings. 'Hold your debates as you like; it is your privilege and your right', was the official attitude. The partners met the officials, but it seemed the end of the campaign so far as public debates with the BMP were concerned.

And it would have been the end of the PROOF campaign, if an important person like Nandan Nilekani, the Managing Director of Infosys, and the Chairman of the BATF, had not intervened. Nilekani is a cult figure and folk hero in Bangalore. The Infosys Conference Room was where the public discussions were held.[12] Nilekani, through the BATF, had encouraged the BMP to develop and move to the new fund based double entry accounting system. BMP could not ignore him. He organised a meeting of the commissioner and other senior officials, and the PROOF partners, to sort out the issue. It was a difficult meeting!

For the present it is enough to note that a problem arose, and that it was resolved after an apology was honestly tendered by the campaign co-ordinator, Ramesh Ramanathan, and graciously accepted by the BMP commissioner. The campaign accepted that the hurried resort to the press in this instance was a case of wrong judgement, but not mala fide intention, and all care would be taken to see it did not happen again. The requests of citizens for information was just that—not an organised campaign against the loan, but a request for a fact based discussion. A date for the Q3 debate was then set.

---

12. It is possible that some citizens came to the debate because of the opportunity to visit the Infosys campus!

It must also be noted that there was no response to the demands under the Freedom of Information Act, although the rules say that a reply must be given within a defined time span. The PROOF partners dropped the issue. Citizens probably forgot about it. What do we learn from this defining moment in the campaign? A compromise was made to keep the debates going. Did it in the final analysis help or hurt the campaign? I suspect we need to introspect much more on this experience.

There was a lot of thought, and a lot of agonising, on the communications strategy. An advertising firm, Fish Eye Creative Solutions, was roped in to help the campaign. The objective was to make a large number of Bangalore citizens aware about the PROOF campaign and to take an active part in it. The partners were aware that the kind of energy they had put in could not be indefinitely sustained unless citizens took over most of the activities. Training, for example, should be organised by citizens for citizens, with citizens serving as trainers. Communities should take the quarterly data and organise their own sessions for analysis, and they should also interact with the BMP on the results. For this, disaggregated data at the ward level becomes essential. It would have to be collected from the ward and divisional level offices of the MP, not the head office. Money is spent on a whole host of projects and services, but the aim is not expenditure, but service provision. How could budget figures be linked to service provision? There was much that needed to be done. How could we get citizens involved in all this? How could this need and urgency be conveyed to the average citizen, the Chinnappa or Sakamma of Bangalore?

After much discussion, in which hoardings, banners on buses and so on were debated, a poster campaign was agreed upon. The advertising consultant, after discussions with the partners, devised a one page handbill. The idea was to give it to citizens who had just paid a bill—in a restaurant, a super market etc.—and ask them if they would like to check the BMP bill as carefully. And it gave contact numbers for those who were interested to call. One side was in English, the other in Kannada. It should, at least, reach the literate in the IT city!

This was worked out by the end of the second public debate. If the handbill could be circulated before the third one, we hoped that the number of citizens who would know about, and take part in, PROOF, would dramatically increase.

Problems arose, and not only because of the lack of expertise on the part of some of the partners in such matters. When the handbills were tested in two localities—Indira Nagar and Malleshwaram—the response was very poor. After several thousand handbills had been distributed in Malleshwaram, there was only one phone call in response. Something was not right.

We never figured this out. A lakh handbills were printed, and by the time our internal discussions petered out, the third debate was on us. The handbills remain unused. Money was spent on this. But clearly we were in a hurry and we did not have clear cut ideas on what we were after. It is essential that we learn from this experience before embarking on a costly advertising type campaign again. Could it be that we were in too much of a hurry? Perhaps. For me the lesson is clear: on this subject I am ignorant, and I should not pretend I can contribute. It has to be left to those who know what they are doing. Collectively, we have to honestly introspect in depth. In a campaign that demands so much from the organisers, this is not easy in the daily rush of events. Strategy becomes a casualty!

While we had some significant success, in my opinion, on bringing together the BMP and different organisations, the BMP did not want PROOF to be acknowledged in the formal process. For example, it was the PROOF initiative with the performance indicators for primary schools of the BMP that led to the development of PIs that could be used for monitoring. PROOF got the Akshara Trust interested in working with these schools to put in place the PIs on an ongoing basis. PROOF even got the American Chamber of Commerce in Bangalore to agree to commit funds for this programme to be implemented. This was to be formalised in a memorandum of understanding (MoU) between these agencies and the BMP. But the BMP made it clear that PROOF should have no mention in the MoU. While we are happy that work has been promoted by us, why keep us out of the picture, especially if we can continue to play a role in the future? Have we conveyed an unintended message?

The same happened a second time. PROOF brought together the Confederation of Indian Industry and the BMP, with the CII agreeing to work with the BMP on the process of property tax collection in two wards of the city. Based on this experience, the implementation process in other wards would be toned up, so that tax revenues increase for the BMP through better collection. Here again an MoU is being signed without PROOF. Again, that work is proceeding is good. This is not a case of PROOF getting a reward. But not keeping PROOF in the picture may have long term consequences for the campaign. When Seema Dargar interviewed CII members about PROOF, they said it was simple CII co-operation with the BMP.

This is not about publicity or recognition. If PROOF has made a 'match', why should it be not acknowledged? Cannot PROOF continue to play an important role in these processes over a longer time span? Would not such recognition be important in citizen's continuing to be an active part of PROOF? I do not know the answers, but I think it is important for us to take this up with citizens and the BMP and resolve it to mutual satisfaction.

22.4 Conclusions

Where does the PROOF campaign go now? Do we need to continue in the same manner for another year? Or can we, having proved that engagement works, retreat to the background, and hope that the PEC takes on leadership? When will the citizens be ready for this? How can we raise funds for this campaign? How will we find answers to these questions?

PROOF enjoyed so much success in the first year for some specific reasons. First, the partners had among them credible organisations and some eminent personalities. The work of the BATF had led to the development of FBAS, so that the data we asked for was indeed available: in most cities this would not be true. The work of Janaagraha had already begun involving citizens in ward works of the BMP, and it was working very well. PROOF could build on this. Secondly, the approach of engagement, of partnership, removed any threat in the minds of officials of the BMP. At a time when the Karnataka Lok Ayukta was raiding offices for corruption, when the newspapers were full of such stories, here was a campaign that specifically went against the stream, acknowledging that there were good people in the BMP working under difficult conditions who should be strengthened. Not to partner the campaign in these circumstances would have been irrational—and counter-productive to the BMP. Thirdly, the specific focus—the BMP budget-captured the imagination of citizens as it offered something concrete in their day to day environment, with the hope that the efforts put in would bear fruit in a reasonable time. The BMP could respond because of FBAS. This was also an opportunity for direct information on citizen concerns. The fact that the public discussions did take place was welcome by all, and served to energise everyone. Fourthly, the enthusiastic response of citizens, which forced the partners to organise training etc., imparted a great deal of energy to the process. And finally, that it was a limited campaign for four quarters meant everyone had a chance to reconsider on the basis of experience.

There may be other specific conditions as well. When some distance has elapsed, and others have told this story, we can expect to get a better understanding of what happened in these momentous 10 months in Bangalore.

What about limitations or weaknesses or gaps? For an insider, this is difficult to grapple with, because I honestly think we succeeded way anything I expected. Yet, there is a niggling question. The BMP is an elected body. We dealt with the civil servants working in it. Our interaction with the elected representatives was formal and limited. If we are to continue, then this must be immediately dealt with. It is the elected representatives who bear the ultimate responsibility for the functioning of the BMP. It is to the elected representatives that the 74th Amendment delegates functions and funds. The civil servants work for the political masters. Maybe we got so far because we dealt with people who are like us, from the same broad stratum of society. But that is probably also our limitation. I leave it here for now.

PROOF has been spoken of in workshops from Mexico City to Hanoi in the past year. The World Bank's Annual Conference on Development Economics, to be held in Bangalore in May (21-23, 2003) has invited the partners to make a presentation in the Conference. There is thus enough material to supplement Seema's report. For those who want to look into nuances, there is enough material to inform—and confuse!

It is time to stop boasting. Humility in what we try is important, and we must end by accepting that it is the BMP and citizens who have made this campaign—perhaps with some catalytic help from the partners—and it is citizens who will take it forward. We end by saluting the spirit of Bangalore that made it all possible. We hope that Prof. Rao will use some time from his well earned retirement to push this exercise forward!

23

People, as they Perceive Themselves*

In Search of a 'Truly' Participative Research

G.K. Karanth and V. Ramaswamy

About 15 years ago, when one of us took the visiting scholar, Nick Hopkins, from the American University in Cairo to the village Rajapura (Magadi taluk, Bangalore district, Karnataka), almost every villager he met wanted to know to what 'caste' he belonged. Hopkins was pretending to be disappointed that none had queried him in terms of his 'class' or religious origin. Ten years later, Ruedi Baumgartner, NADEL-ETH, Zurich, was likewise disappointed that none asked him in Kodipalli (Srinivaspur taluk, Kolar district, Karnataka) of his caste, while almost everyone he met wanted to know about his income, and the money he was able to save after meeting all his needs!

23.1 Preamble

Social science research, especially of the 'applied' kind, generally tends to be an analysis of the impact or change in respect of any variable or a set of variables. The impact or change may be in terms of, say a new policy, education, increased or decreased income, or access to a facility. These changes are analysed in respect of, often repeated, attributes of people who

* The Swiss National Science Foundation, Swiss Agency for Development Cooperation and the NADEL-ETH, Zurich, sponsored the study, based on which this paper is written. We would like to acknowledge with gratitude the guidance by G.K. Kadekodi and S. Madheswaran to apply the statistical tests to measure association between variables and interpreting the meanings of the results. 'Errors', if any, that may creep into this analysis is entirely due our limited knowledge in that respect. Simon Charsley read an earlier version of the paper and gave critical comments. We have benefited also in many ways from Ms. Meera Murthy and K.G. Gayathri Devi in carrying out the study. We owe a special debt of gratitude to late Prof. M.N. Srinivas for his encouragement and the interest he showed in the progress of the study and in the writing up our analysis. To our research colleagues, Ruedi Baumgartner and Ruedi Hogger we remain thankful for many novel ideas and practice of participant research. It was a discussion of the outcome of our PRA with Prof. V.M. Rao, and the enthusiasm he showed that emboldened us to write up this paper. We do hope the contents meet his approval, and we feel it a privilege to offer this paper to a volume in his honour.

are 'respondents': e.g., age, sex, occupation and or income as reflective of class background. Thus, it has become almost a convention to appropriate these 'independent' variables, in terms of which the indicators are 'correlated' or 'cross-tabulated' for purposes of analysis. The findings are usually presented in the form of tables or graphs, if not both, with titles that are usually incorrect (e.g., 'sex-wise' or 'income-wise' fodder production)! Among the sociologists and social anthropologists, the most often found practice is to take 'caste-wise' and 'landownership-wise' as focus of analysis.

It is not our intention here to suggest that analysis of correlation between such independent variables and the observed features, as dependent variables, are merely conjectural in nature. Yet, it is necessary to recall that quantitative analysis of such 'correlations' or their qualitative explanations are, first and foremost suggestive of 'co-occurrence' of a set of phenomenon, although one tends often to mistake it as one 'determined' by the others. There are several measures of association, determinants, etc., yet analyses based on such measures tend to be mistaken as to what determines the other variable. Further, such analyses assume also that people, when their choices are made or behave one way or the other, are conscious of such 'independent' factors.

Ironic, further, it is when researchers claiming to be carrying out 'participatory' research too impute significance to such 'independent' variables, while the other key partners in such research—the people themselves—have little agency as participants to determine what these variables ought to be. While the specific objectives of a study may determine the different categories, the most often used are caste, size, class of landownership, gender, migrant status, etc. Whatever the category used, they are usually the ones identified by the researcher. Often they become so compelling in creating a sense of identity (e.g., forward castes, backward class and scheduled castes, etc.) for themselves, even though their day-to-day life may not have much to do with such labeling. In a few others, the people themselves may not identify with such categorisation; instead it is merely the researcher who has created them to order the data for purposes of analysis. Consequently, the responses received to a battery of questions could well be with an open mind, while our analysis of them could be in terms of what we, as researchers, consider as important.

Such research could hardly qualify to be truly participative in research. The authors of this paper joined a team of scholars during 1997-2000, in an effort to, among other objectives, convert conventional social science research as participative by taking back the findings of our research to the people with a view to sharing not only the findings but also our understanding of them and of their interpretations.[1] Individuals in a community are placed in a multiplicity of social roles and accordingly come to acquire multiple identities in such a way that specific social identities confer specific roles and obligations (Giddens, 1984). The individual actor thus acquires the skills or capacity to 'process social experience and devise the ways of coping with life' (quoted in Cleaver, 2000: 364). It is necessary therefore, we argue in this paper, to bring to the fore such roles and social experiences of people, as they have perceived them in any analysis than as researchers imposing our preferences upon their experiences for purposes of analyses. The paper has four other sections. Following these introductory statements, we present in Section 2 a brief background of the study as it was carried out in a village in Kolar district, Karnataka. Section 3 gives an outline of the categories that people chose to classify themselves. In Section 4, people's perceptions are compared with conventional categorisation. Section 5 brings together some of our conclusions.

23.2 A Brief Background of the Study

In a study carried out during 1994-1997, three conclusions among others were arrived at. First, rural livelihood systems (as they are emerging) depend increasingly on external resources. This weakens the necessity for village-based natural resource management and contributes to the unsustainability of its natural resource base. Second, the ongoing integration of village communities into an enlarged market economy does not further the more sustainable management of natural resources without an appropriate policy framework. Thirdly, effective village leadership in the past was perceived as the capability to organise people and to pool resources. With emerging patterns of leadership, the sustainable management of resources was lost priority in favour of taping efficiently the external resources from governmental or non-governmental sources. The

1. For a fuller account of this experience, and the rationale of the exercise, see Baumgartner *et al.* (2004a and 2004b).

study was carried out in Chinnaramannagaru Palli of Kadri *taluk*, Anantapur district in Andhra Pradesh.[2] The findings of the study were presented to an audience of multi-disciplinary background during which it was suggested that these conclusions could be validated in different field settings. Since such a validation was found possible within the scope of the research project, it was decided to undertake such a study.

The result was an attempt to repeat the study with some variations, in the village Kodipalli of Srinivaspur *taluk*, Kolar district of Karnataka. Selection of the village was based on the presence in it an NGO which had as its activities the promotion of women's self-help groups, watershed development, sustainable agriculture, etc. The other considerations were the size to be between 900-1200 acres in extent and 150 to 200 households. Since the research concerned natural resource management by the village communities, it was necessary to choose one that had the presence of tank, wastelands and other common property resources and preferably a forest. It was also considered that the village should be multi-caste in composition such that interests of different castes and classes could be examined. Further, there was a need that the chosen village will have a considerable history of migration of population. Finally, it was felt that such a village should not necessarily be on the roadside but fairly interior from the *taluk* headquarters or the nearest major town.[3]

On the district main road from Chintamani of Kolar district to Madanapalli of Chittoor in Andhra Pradesh, one finds travelling on a terrain that is plain on one side of the road and undulated landscape on the other. After about 19 kms from Chintamani, a road branches off to the left to take us to Kodipalli. The narrow road contours itself as the landscape develops in such a way that the traveller has a view of plains on the left of the road and undulated landscape on the right. The road winds itself to a small town called Gownipalli, the main marketing centre for villages of about 10 kms in different directions including Kodipalli. Gownipalli is also one of the large settlements bordering the neighbouring Andhra Pradesh, beyond which as a crow flies, about 40 kms in the north-western direction

2. See, Ramaswamy *et al.*, 1996.

3. For a detailed account of the process of selection of the village Kodipalli for the study, see Karanth and Ramaswamy (2005).

one may see C.R. Palli, a village in which a study had been carried out earlier.

Village Kodipalli has two hamlets namely, Dugganakunte and Gandhinagar. It is also the headquarters of a *panchayat* consisting of 10 villages and 2 hamlets as its constituencies.[4] Kodipalli thus forms a part of Srinivaspur *taluk samiti* and Kolar *zilla panchayat* from the point of view of the three-tier decentralised system of governance. The elected members in for the *gram panchayat* from Kodipalli are in such a way that at least one member is from a scheduled caste and the other, a scheduled tribe woman. The president of this *panchayat* can only be a woman from scheduled caste.[5] The factionalism that has been intensified in recent years as a result of elections to the *panchayat* is to be seen as an important milestone in the history of the village.

As one enters Kodipalli, she gets the view of a large tank on one side and of the village settlements on the other, the road winding itself through the settlement. Beyond the tank one can see also huge hillocks, which by definition is a forest but presenting itself as a vast tract of barren land. As has been the fate of many forests-by-definition, this forest too has no green cover, let alone the trees.

Depending on the season and performance of monsoon in a year, one gets to see varying extent of tank-bed either open or immersed under water. The tank has an area of 104 acres. Going by the accounts of the people, a third of the tank is increasingly dry, whose bed has now become a basis for seasonal activity for many an enterprising farmer of the village. One finds here brick-kilns at various stages of their completion. There has also been a gradual encroachment of the tank-bed by the farmers owning adjoining such areas. The tank is a part of system of tanks receiving water from the upper reaches and catering to the irrigation needs of two other villages which are situated on the other sides of the tank-bed: Gownipalli and Murrampalli.

4. The constituent villages are Kodipalli, Avaganapalli, Cheelepalli, Tummullapalli, Karipalli, Nakkalagadda, Murrampalli, Bypalli, Batlaguttalapalli and Kondamari.

5. As per the roster for the term beginning 1996.

Kodipalli is a multi-caste village. There are four numerically dominant castes: Reddis (also identified as Kapu Reddis, Kapus or Okkaligas),[6] Bheri Vaishyas, Nayakas and Bhovis. Kapus or Reddis have been the main land owning caste in the region who have also enjoyed dominance in the sphere of politics. Members of this caste too are by a majority living in nuclear families, with only about 15 per cent each who live in either joint or extended families. About 53 per cent of the households have either five or six persons living in them. Only two households (10.5 per cent) have more than seven persons, while about 16 per cent have three members living in them.

In terms of landownership, Okkaligas fare better than rest in the village (see Table 22.1). Indeed, it is by virtue of their population and landownership that Okkaligas enjoy dominance in the village. About 37 per cent of the households belonging to this caste own land between 5 to 10 acres, while 26 per cent have more than 10 acres. Less than a third of the caste households have lands below 5 acres, and one household is landless. Three households have been beneficiaries of land grants, although one of them now has some legal difficulties in establishing the claims over the land. Five out of the 19 households have benefited from land reforms either directly or indirectly. In relation to the numerical strengths of the castes, Okkaligas have a marginally greater share (26.3 per cent) in benefiting from land reforms than the rest.

Being an agricultural caste, members of this caste, one would anticipate, to be personally cultivating their lands. However, about a third of the households of Okkaligas in Kodipalli lease out part or all their lands to be cultivated by others, while about 15.8 (three households) have either leased in or are sharecropping with others in addition to cultivation of their own lands. Only two households have reported that rearing of buffaloes has improved since the time of their parents, while a majority reports it to have

6. The caste name Kapu or Kapu Reddi is typically Andhra in origin. Although part of Karnataka, Kodipalli and some adjoining villages on the Andhra-Karnataka border have more of Telugu-Andhra character than that of old Mysore. This is in keeping with the fact that the origin was part of Vijayanagara empire, and during the British rule under the Madras Presidency. Taking on the caste name similar to those in the culturally contiguous area is one of the ways by which broad basing of the castes take place. It is a process by which smaller endogamous caste units with similar cultural trait come together to claim a larger and substantial numerical strength by adopting a common name (See Karanth, 1997).

Table 23.1

Caste and Land Ownership

Caste	*Extent of Land Owned (In Per cent Figures)*						
	Landless	*Up to 1 Acre*	*1.01 to 2.50 Acres*	*2.51 to 5 Acres*	*5.01 to 10 Acres*	*10 Acres and above*	*Total (No.)*
Lingayat			100.00				1
Bhatraj			66.70	33.30			3
Bheri Vaishya	4.20	12.50	12.50	45.80	20.80	4.20	24
Okkaliga	5.30		5.30	26.30	36.80	26.30	19
Padmasali		25.00	25.00	50.00			4
Chakali		22.20	55.60	11.10	11.10		9
Dudekula				100.00			2
Nayaka		11.10	33.30	27.80	22.20	5.60	18
Tallabovi	15.80	31.60	42.10		5.30	5.30	19
Mannubovi		3.80	23.10	46.20	23.10	3.80	26
Chinnadasari		28.60	57.10	14.30			7
Koracha	11.10	11.10	44.40	22.20	11.10		9
Madiga	6.30		37.50	25.00	31.30		16
Christian	33.30	33.30	33.30				3
Total (No.)	8	19	48	46	30	9	160
%	5.00	11.90	30.00	28.80	18.80	5.60	100.00

Source: Based on field survey.

been the same.[7] However, a third of the households have reported that it has declined over a period. The largest decline, among Okkaligas, has been in regard to rearing of bullocks: 64 per cent of households report thus. In recent years, most farmers with large holding have tended to depend mainly upon mechanised tilling of lands, by hiring a power tiller.

Relative to other castes, Okkaligas are the largest users of the tanks in the village. Not a single farmer in this caste has reported to be cultivating lands without irrigation. About 58 per cent of Okkaliga landowners have tanks as a single source of irrigation for cultivation. Many among them have multiple sources of irrigation: tank and bore well (5.3 per cent), tank and open well (26.3 per cent), and tanks, wells and ponds (5.3 per cent).

A vast majority of Okkaligas has been living in the houses constructed by their ancestors, with or without some minor additions and repairs. Two households (10.5 per cent) have built houses more than 16 years ago.

7. "Same" does also mean that those who had no animal husbandry in the past do not have now too.

House construction among them has been a less important preoccupation considering the years since a house was built.

Bheri Vaishya as a caste is peculiar to the region. In the past they were known to have been traders by occupation in keeping with the title Vaishya as per the Varna scheme of stratification. The Bheri Vaishyas went from village to village or towns buying and selling the agricultural produce in small quantities. Like many other castes in the region, Bheri Vaishyas of Kodipalli too took to full time agriculture in recent years. They are distinguished from the Vaishyas in general by their use of a bullock to carry the load of things they bought and sold. The Vaishyas of the Varna scheme, in contrast, were known to be resident traders, largely in urban habitat.

As among most other castes, Bheri Vaishyas are, by a majority, living in nuclear families (70.1 per cent). Nearly 50 per cent of the households of this caste have families with a size of four to five persons, and about 21 per cent (five households) have six persons in a household. Four households have more than seven persons living in them. Half of Bheri Vaishya households in Kodipalli are small farmers, i.e., with 2.5 to 5.0 acres of land. In relation to other castes in the village, they are the only caste with a majority being small farmers. A quarter of the households owns less than 2.5 acres, while only one household owns more than 10 acres of land. None in their caste has been a beneficiary of land grants made from time to time, carving out the land from the village commons.

Out of the 24 households of this caste, nearly 59 per cent cultivate their own land, while about 25 per cent have been cultivating, besides their own, lands belonging to others. Four households (16.7 per cent) have not been cultivating their lands personally, but through others either by way of leasing out or through sharecropping. There has been a considerable decline in animal husbandry among them, particularly with respect to rearing of bullocks, buffaloes and sheep. None among the Bheri Vaishyas is landless. Only 4 out of the 24 households (16.7 per cent) do not have any irrigation source for cultivation, and they stand only next to Korachas in this respect. The rest of the castes in the village have much higher proportion of households without irrigation. Among those with irrigation source, a majority depends together on tanks and open wells. Only one household has a bore well, while the rest depend on tanks, wells and ponds.[8]

Eleven heads of the households of Bheri Vaishyas have not constructed their own living house during their lifetime, or do not have an own house built. The former lives in rented buildings. Among those who have built a house, a majority (20.8 per cent) did so about 16 years ago. 12.5 per cent built a house during the past five years, while 16.7 per cent built during the past one year.

Bhovi as a caste, in fact, constituted the single largest group in Kodipalli. But contrary to the broad-basing process referred to above, here the division based on endogamy, occupation and gods to be worshipped has divided them into two large groups. The Talla Bhovis specialise in rope making and live mainly in Kodipalli. Mannu Bhovis, on their part, distinguish themselves by their association with earthen work. The Telugu and Kannada term *mannu* refers to soil or earth. Almost all the Mannu Bhovis live in Dugganakunte, a hamlet which was established entirely for the habitation of the earthen workers from surrounding villages during the late 60s and early 70s. Talla Bhovi and Mannu Bhovi constituted 19 and 26 households respectively. In Karnataka, Bhovis of all denominations are classified as scheduled caste. Traditionally they called themselves as Oddas. Because the term Odda does not figure in the schedule of castes and because increasingly the term has come to acquire a negative meaning, they have preferred to call themselves as Bhovis. They now take it as an offence if referred to as Oddas.

The fourth numerically significant caste is Nayaka who call themselves also as Bedas. Until recently they were classified as a backward tribe and since early 1990s they have been accorded the status of scheduled tribes.

The other scheduled castes in the village are Koracha and Madigas; the latter having been an untouchable caste as per the erstwhile caste-based social order. There are also a few Muslims, known here as Dudekula, who

8. "Pond" as referred to here is stagnant water along the stream or canals from the tanks in the village. As such they are not a dependable source, for water in them is available only if the rains and run off in the streams/canals are good in any given area. Water has to be pumped out through irrigation pumpsets. Officially, such lands are not classified as "wet" lands.

traditionally were mattress makers. The Christian presence is seen among three households who, when situation demands, follow the faith of Christianity but retaining their Hindu or Muslim links.

At present, there are not many service castes inhabiting the village. Currently, there are nine households of washermen caste referred to as Chakali and four Padmasali, i.e., the weavers. There is a lone Lingayat household, a male member of which came to the village originally as a priest. Today besides being a priest, the family is also engaged in agriculture. Since about 4-5 years, the wife of the priest is working as a servant (*ayah*) in *anganwadi* (child care centre) in Kodipalli.

23.3 Categories that People Chose to Classify Themselves

The need to seek views on people, as they perceive themselves became evident when we asked a group of people to describe and classify the households in the village and one of its hamlets, as part of a PRA exercise. Our purpose was to assess the variation among people in regard to the use and maintenance of common pool resources: the village wood lot, tanks and ponds, and the grazing lands. Our initial invitation to them was to carry out a 'social mapping' of the households in terms of either landownership or castes, indicating those who use them and contribute voluntary labour for their upkeep. Although the village is multi-caste in its composition, there were two numerically dominant castes, the Kapu-Reddis and Bheri Vaishyas, besides many other service castes, which had tended to become autonomous of each other in the recent decades. The nature of inter-dependence between castes, significant under the rubric similar to the pan Indian Jajmani system, locally called *Marey,* had been disappearing; replaced by a market determined exchange of goods and services. Even though ownership of land was an important factor in differentiating people in terms of wealth, there had been market links that had enabled people to eke out a livelihood pattern not entirely dependent on land, at least the extent of land owned. Thus, there were households that owned less than an acre of land in the tank's command area whose dependence on the common pool resources was quite distinct in pattern than those who may have owned, say more than 10 acres of land and yet be as dependent, or otherwise on the resources as compared with a small or marginal farmer.

This had been our approach to the understanding of the resource use pattern.

The group of people who were taking part in the PRA exercise was of the view clearly that neither caste nor extent of land owned could explain the variation in the use pattern and contribution to the management of the common resources. Instead they argued that the nature and extent of their involvement and dependence on the market made a crucial difference. The group identified six categories into which the households in the village/ hamlet were classified. The criteria used by them could, as we have attempted in Section 4 below, be related to a blend of conventional academic categories such as landownership, caste, status and other factors with their own conceptions of how households carried on a livelihood. But this was the people's categorisation and, therefore, a special consideration for its analysis. Each of the categories is labeled in consultation with them, though the choice of English words is ours.

Little to sell or buy: These are households that have 'little to sell or buy' in the market. This group is made up of landless households or owning land, i.e., dry but in small size (less than 2.5 acres). They supplement their income by working as wage labourers, while for a majority it could be their only income. Some of them may have a milch animal of a local variety either to meet domestic dairy needs or sell dairy products in small quantities. Even if they have a need to depend on market, they have little to sell or can ill afford to buy. Their capability to deal in a market is therefore limited. Either they are ignorant of the market dynamics or lack the confidence. They can hardly afford to leave the village, for they have to eke a livelihood by keeping up their farm activities or working for others. In a way they are tied to their limited assets.

The group identified 36 households belonging to this category, who according to our data gathered through conventional method, make up 50 per cent of landless and about 12 per cent of those with less than 2.5 acres of land.

Sell less, buy more: This category is made up of households who own land mainly between 2.5 and 5 acres or some who may even own up to about 7 to 8 acres. A major portion of their land is dry while some may own land also in the tank command area, but in small sizes. The size of their households is also slightly big: more than five persons. They grow slightly less than what the household requires for consumption. It is for this reason that they sell small quantities of what is grown with a view to be able to buy their requirements from the market. In any case, they depend on the market to buy a wide range of commodities by selling what they produce. Indeed much of the commercial crops cultivated are meant mainly to be able to buy their day-to-day requirements. As such, they have very little scope for accumulation of capital.

The group identified 32 households as those belonging to this category. About 71 per cent of those with land between 1 to 5.00 acres belonged to this category.

Sell more, buy less: Households belonging to this category are an ideal which most farming households would aspire for. It consists of farming households, owning lands between 6 to 10 acres or more. The speciality of this group is that they have a favourable mix of dry and wet lands, often with multiple sources of irrigation (a plot of land in the tank's command and some with perennial water in wells close to the tank command and some more with a bore well). They also have a few fruit bearing trees (tamarind, mango, coconut, etc.) which provide income at different points of time in a year. Throughout the year there are several agricultural activities being carried out with the combination of domestic and hired labour, although their dependence on the latter is greater. Because there are several types of agricultural produce to be marketed throughout the year, there is constantly something or the other to be sold. The need to buy from the market is restricted to certain items that are not necessarily available from within the farmstead. These are, for instance, soaps and costumes, fruits and sweets, special vegetables. Of course, much of their buying activities in the market pertain to agricultural inputs: high yielding seeds, chemical fertilisers, pesticides, etc. For the purpose of selling, they may retain a broker or a middleman rather than indulging in direct selling in the local market. But, if the produce is being taken to places like Chintamani, Kolar or elsewhere, a young member from the family may be assigned the responsibility. Further, it is not uncommon for their dependence upon established commission agents for this purpose. These are also farmers who enjoy considerable credit-worthiness in the market, besides being able to lend money to many others with or without usury being involved. Often this enables them to be a patron in demand for many dependent households. Based on their recommendation, any other person would be eligible to a credit purchase of a commodity in the market or even an interest free loan for a short period.

If the size of the household is small, there is a likelihood of one or two trusted labourers entering into a sharecropping arrangement with them. It is also not uncommon for a few in this group to undertake lease farming, especially if they lack adequate underground water resources, in a plot of land from others to raise a commercial crop like tomato. But their preference would be to mortgage a plot of land rather than periodically leasing in.

53 households were identified to be belonging to this category. Thirty-six per cent of households with lands between 2.5 and 5.00 acres and 30 per cent with land between 5 and 10 acres belonged to this category.

Buy to sell: As the label indicates, these are households whose livelihood depends significantly on playing an active role in the market. These are people who buy finished products or agricultural produce and/or cattle, so as to, in turn, sell them elsewhere. The buying market is not necessarily one place: it could be within the village or from other villages or even the marketplace in Gownipalli. There is a small margin of profit if they buy a finished product and sell it. But for some the selling product is a value added commodity: e.g., the rope sold by the ropemakers, baskets by basketmakers, wooden or iron items by carpenters and smiths, textile by silk weavers and other things by different artisans. Some of them may graduate even to become professional brokers in the market without having to buy or sell anything, but facilitate the transactions involving such commodities. A common feature of those in this group are that they are resource poor, but known for their skills or being able to study market fluctuations.

Whatever resources they have, such as land, are inadequate to their livelihood. Because of their mobility and sensitivity to market fluctuations, they have an impressive income but which is highly unstable. A person may now be very rich but if the market is bad he (or exceptionally, she) may go through a lean phase. They are hard working and are keen to save and accumulate capital to enhance their resource base. Some who have taken avoidable risk have paid heavily and fallen low in esteem.

The group identified 14 households under this category. Twenty-one per cent of farmers, with land between 1 to 2.5 acres, and 50 per cent of those below 1.0 acre of land belonged to this category.

Resource poor, buy all: This is a section of the community which has very little resource of any kind: human resources, land or implements. Even if they do own some land, their ability to extract from it is limited, for, they have little to invest or no animals and/nor implements to work with. In any case, being resource poor they have to work as wage labourers whether in the village or elsewhere, on or off the farm. One day they may work as casual wage labourers, and the following day they may work as contract wage labourers engaged in road repair or house construction. Working for a wage is their main source of income. Often they work mainly with a view to buying what they need for a day or two.

Members of the community identified 19 households as belonging to this group. Forty-two per cent of them were made up of households with 1.0 to 2.5 acres, while another 21 per cent was made up of those with 2.5 to 5.0 acres. A majority in this category is drawn from the Madiga caste while a few are from Bheri Vaishya and Talla Bhovi caste. Interestingly, only 3 households among them were landless. While many in this group do own land, it needs to be recognised that from the point of view of the people either this resource is inadequate to support a household or the quality of land is not good enough to treat its owners as 'with land resource'. In any case, the land owned by them is not the one that enables them a role in the market other than having to buy their requirements. The group preferred to retain this category as a separate one, in addition to the first in this list. They were of the view that the two, apparently similar, but are different in nature.

Resource rich, buy more: This category of households consists of mixed background yet with a few common characteristics. They have a non-local orientation. Some are fond of the luxuries and entertainment available elsewhere, while others are in pursuit of a livelihood outside the village. A few others are aged and do not have adequate support from within the household. Yet others live in the past glory of their households and are unable to adjust with the changed circumstances by working hard as the fellow villagers. From time to time, some of them have even sold parcels of their land if not mortgaging them for small sums of money. In any case, a majority of them do not personally cultivate their land while a few even have left them fallow for a couple of years. To the extent they have fallen prey to their non-agrarian orientation and taken to bad ways (by local values), they are objects of ridicule if not of contempt to the fellow villagers. To the extent their resources are yielding returns, they enjoy limited creditworthiness, but the speculation is constantly ripe that it is not long before they sell their lands and leave the village.

Six households were identified to belong to this category. Four among them owned lands to the extent more than 5.0 acres.

23.4 People's Perceptions and Conventional Categorisation

With a view to comparing the categorisation made by the members of the community with what is most often used by sociologists and economists, we present below a comparison of the classification in terms of people's

Table 23.2

Landholding and People's Categorisation

	Little to Sell or Buy	*Sell less Buy more*	*Sell more Buy less*	*Buy to Sell*	*Resource rich Buy more*	*Resource Poor Buy all*	*Total*
Landless	4 (50.0)			1 (12.5)		3 (37.5)	8 (100.0)
Up to 1 ac	4 (21.1)	3 (15.8)	4 (21.1)	7 (36.8)		1 (5.3)	19 (100.0)
1.01 to 2.50 ac	14 (29.2)	13 (27.1)	9 (18.8)	3 (6.3)	1 (2.1)	8 (16.7)	48 (100.0)
2.51 to 5 ac	10 (21.7)	10 (21.7)	19 (41.3)	2 (4.3)	1 (2.2)	4 (8.7)	46 (100.0)
5.01 to 10 ac	3 (10.0)	5 (16.7)	16 (53.3)	1 (3.3)	2 (6.7)	3 (10.0)	30 (100.0)
10 ac and more	1 (11.1)	1 (11.1)	5 (55.6)		2 (22.2)		9 (100.0)
Total	36 (22.5)	32 (20.0)	53 (33.1)	14 (8.8)	6 (3.8)	19 (11.9)	160 (100.0)

Note: Figures in parentheses are percentages.
Source: Based on field survey.

categorisation *vis-à-vis* landownership and castes of people as collected through conventional methods.

Let us first recognise that each of these category identified by the people is only an ideal type. Thus, when we look at the economic background of the people, in terms of land owned by them, we notice that each of these categories consist of people who may not fit the popular images of them farmers. For instance, it is difficult to accept a large farmer, say with over 8 acres of land to have been classified by the local people as 'resource poor, and buy all' their needs from the market. For, the land owned by them may be so poor in quality that it could hardly be considered as a resource.

Table 22.2 shows that each of the category has one or the other landowning class of households representing it, although any one class is predominant amongst each of them. Thus, the category of households classified as 'Little to sell or buy' is made up of the 'landless' households by a majority (50 per cent) followed by 27 per cent with 2.5 to 5.0 acres of land.

The landless households in Kodipalli, by a majority, are grouped under the two similar categories: About 50 per cent in the 'Little to sell or buy' category and 37.5 per cent under 'Resource poor, buy all' category. The latter is distinct from the former by lacking in human resources as well. The one landless household classified as 'Buy to sell' type has a member who buys tender coconuts and other seasonal fruits and vegetables from villages in the surrounding areas to retail them in the town of Gownipalli.

The type 'Buy to sell' as identified by the participants in the PRA contains households from nearly all the class of large farmers (with more than 10 acres of land). However, the marginal and small farmers (up to 1.0 acre and between 1 to 2.5 acres, respectively) dominate this type. Taken as a whole, this type is made up by 50.0 per cent owning land up to 1.0 acre, followed by the households with 1.0 to 2.5 acres (21.4 per cent), and 14.3 per cent by those owning 2.5 to 5.0 acres. Many among these households, as we had studied them conventionally, do fit the description offered by the participants in the PRA. Members of the households grouped in this type earn a major portion of their income by engaging themselves as retailers of groceries and vegetables, milk vendors and as commission agents (brokers or middlemen) in the market. Inputs for agricultural purposes too are largely dependent on the market than mobilising them from within the farming household: seeds, manure, etc.

Households that are conventionally labeled as small farmers (lands between 1.0 to 2.5 acres in extent) are by a majority found to be classified as those with 'Little to sell or buy'. One may identify this group as the classic 'peasants' who pursue a subsistence livelihood. Their distribution diminishes gradually in proportion as one moves away from the more vulnerable categories towards the more dominant type such as the 'Resource rich, buy more'. The small farmers (1.0 to 2.5 acres) too are likewise found predominantly in the type labeled 'Sell more, buy less' (41.3 per cent), and an equal proportion (21.7 per cent) under 'Little to sell or buy' and 'Sell less, buy more'.

Large farmers, i.e., those with 5 to 10 acres, are mainly grouped as those who 'Sell more, buy less'. Only 10 per cent each among them are found among those with 'Little to sell or buy' and 'Resource poor, buy all'. A near fit is thus found among this class of farmers as well as among the very large farmers (10 acres or more). In the latter category, 55.6 per cent are classified as 'Sell more, buy less' and 22.2 per cent as 'Resource rich, buy more'. If a few households of this class of farmers have been grouped under any other but vulnerable types, it is because they have, by and large, given up cultivation of lands while taking to other pursuits.

Because the main focus of the study had been on the use and management of natural resources, we may now turn to analyse how the households as classified by the people are related to some of those issues. In our analysis, we had a concern for the challenges to mobilising collective action (Olson, 1965; Ostrom, 1990 and 1992). As has been the convention, we had proceeded to examine if members of certain castes, or members of households with varying extent of landownership had a tendency more or less to take part in collective action for the upkeep of common pool resources: land, tanks and the woodlot. Conclusions that had emerged from the analysis of variables such as caste and landownership had tended to be on the following lines: Castes that were traditionally considered to high in status had been less concerned about the maintenance of the natural resources, and extracting water without much concern for its regeneration or its need for other non-agricultural purposes. Landowners, even if they were dependent upon the tanks had not been showing any interest in either mobilising other people in the village or themselves contributing the conventional voluntary labour as in the past.[9]

Now that we had gathered fresh information concerning people's perception about themselves through a PRA, after we had presented the research findings to the members of the community, an attempt was made to examine how the behavioural pattern concerning natural resource management and use were 'associated' with the typologies offered by people and in contrast, if any, with the conventional categories that we had used. In this regard too, we had proceeded to prepare cross-tables to describe and analyse the pattern of distribution of frequencies in different cells in each of the tables that had been generated. Having been statistically uninitiated and reluctant to apply any statistical measures, we had tended to remain content in explaining the association or otherwise. Thanks largely to a suggestion from two of our colleagues, we applied Chi Square tests to data viewed both from the conventional pattern of variables (e.g., landownership) and the 'people suggested' categories as variables. The null hypotheses, as is usually formulated, was that the independent variable and the specific dependent variables have no association. The alternative hypotheses that may get accepted if the former is statistically rejected, for the benefit of others like who may be statistically uninitiated, would be that the two variables are associated. Rejection or acceptance was based on the statistical value to be at 5 per cent level of significance.

With respect of the different 'dependent variables' for which a test was carried out, the results are presented in Table 22.3. This test was carried out separately for the same set of data pertaining to a dependent variable, only viewed from two sets of independent variables, namely the conventional (landownership) and the people's perceived types (market dependence). While in respect of some dependent variables, both the sets of data were either statistically 'accepted' or 'rejected' the null hypotheses, there were some in regard to which one was 'accepted' while the other was 'rejected'.

---

9. For a detailed account of the findings of this study, see Karanth and Ramaswamy (2004 and 2005).

A few explanatory observations are to be made in regard to Table 22.3. First, for the purpose of demonstrating the utility of using 'people's variables' in any participative research, we have randomly picked a few of the 'dependent' variables and compared the results of statistical tests with those by using the 'conventional independent variable'. Given the field situation and the nature of data, we find that there are identical outcomes in respect of 5 out of 10 sets of 'dependent variables' (2 instances of both being accepted; and 3 instances of both being rejected). Whether or not the null hypotheses were accepted or rejected, the interpretations of the data would have made little difference, at least statistically. In other words, whether or not one used the conventional independent variable, or the people offered variable for an analysis of the behavioural patterns in respect of the five different dependent variables, there would have been little difference.

Table 23.3

Comparative Results of Statistical Measures of Association

Dependent Variables	*Results*	
	Conventional Variable	*People's Variable*
Variation in bullock rearing#	Accepted	Rejected
Variation in cow rearing	Accepted	Accepted
Variation in buffaloes rearing	Rejected	Rejected
Variation in sheep rearing	Accepted	Rejected
Reasons for increased animal husbandry	Accepted	Accepted
Reasons for reduced animal husbandry	Accepted	Rejected
Variation in use of FYM	Rejected	Rejected
Pattern of home grown food grains	Rejected	Accepted
Use of grazing land	Rejected	Rejected
Participate in tank works	Accepted	Rejected

Note: # 'Variation' refers to changes, if any, over a period of time in respect of, as in this case, bullock rearing. It could that the number of cattle heads reared has 'increased', 'declined' or has remained same, or there never had been any bullock rearing in the past or present. The same is applicable in the case of cows, buffaloes.

But of crucial importance is when there is a divergence in statistical measure of association with respect of one independent variable in contrast to the other, the wisdom guiding the choice of the independent variables could come under question. From Table 22.3, we find that the conventional independent variable was found to be statistically rejecting one null hypothesis. That is by rejecting the null hypotheses, the test was accepting an alternative hypothesis that the two variables (the conventional and a given independent variable) were found to be significant in their association. Four other cases of relationships were found to be accepted, thereby stating that the pairs of conventional variable and the specific dependent variable were associated in statistically insignificant manner. In contrast, the people's choice of a variable was being accepted in only one of the five instances of divergent results. This, incidentally, pertained to the pattern of dependence on homegrown food grains. By rejecting the null hypothesis that household dependence on the market has no association with the pattern of dependence on homegrown food grains, one has to accept the 'alternative hypothesis'. The latter is to be stated as prevalence of a significant association between the nature of market dependence and the pattern of homegrown food grains for consumption.

However, from the table above we find also that in respect of four dependent variables the null hypotheses of association with 'people's variables' were found to be rejected, while the conventional variables were accepting the hypotheses of association. Thus, had we confined merely to examine the relationship between landownership, and say people's participation in voluntary labour for tanks' upkeep, we would have perhaps not reflecting the view point of the people themselves. One of them could have argued with us over our finding, and stated that, instead of extent of land owned by households, it is how they are related to the market that may determine one contributing voluntary labour related to the upkeep of the tank! If one had been focusing on different class of landowners in an effort to mobilise collective action for the maintenance of this resource, he or she would have missed the role played by people's involvement with the market in varying manner!

Secondly, we find also that whether a null hypothesis is statistically and identically accepted or rejected, there is certainly a difference in the 'degree' in respect of the two independent variables. For, we are told that if the calculated Chi Square value is less than the critical value, greater is the degree of confidence with which a null hypothesis is accepted. This level is not necessarily identical between the two sets of variables, and we find the level of rejection is much less stronger in respect of the people's variable as compared to the conventional variable.

23.4 Conclusions

Although we have not presented the actual findings and analysis from the point of view of using the people's choice of independent variable, i.e., how they perceive themselves in relation to the market, we may sum up our understanding of the situation in the field. With respect to some of the key dimensions of natural resource use and management concerns, we find that the emergent class of households that have 'more to sell and less to buy' to be playing a crucial role. It is they who predominantly contribute their labour for upkeep of the resources, unlike the others who too may depend on the resources for their livelihood but remain 'free riders'. They are critical also because, as among a few others, in due course they are likely to be so intensively market oriented that they may encourage to lose interests (if not stakes) in the upkeep of common resources. But the purpose of this paper was not so much to highlight this role played by a class of people. Instead, it was to demonstrate the importance of taking into account non-conventional categories that may enrich the analysis. In the present case, we may have lost sight of this class of people had we depended entirely on the conventional variables such as 'landownership'. Such a choice, in addition, could hardly be loyal to the expressed goal of 'participative' character of research. While propagating the need for social researchers, especially concerned with development issues, to share the findings with the members of a rural community, Baumgartner *et al.* (2004a and 2004b) make a plea that even the research agenda should be participatively determined with active involvement of people and other stakeholders. This paper goes one step further to make a plea that, in addition to employing the conventional and academically popular categories one should be sensitive to people's own categories. There is much more to be gained, than the costs, of incorporating such participatory insights into any social research. Even if there may not be any serendipity pattern of discovery of facts and processes, there is certainly much scope for the analysis to be locally relevant and meaningful for both policies and academic interests.

No denying that the choice of the variables for analysis in any research is guided by the objectives and the nature of hypotheses, if any. In a truly participative research, we believe, the perceptions of people ought to be given importance as much as to what we may carry from our 'review of literature', or 'theoretical framework'. Having made thus a case for it, we should hasten also to point out to the limitations, for such limitations to a goal of giving 'agency' to the people cannot be overlooked.

a) *Contextual specificity of people's perception*: Concerns that members of a community may bring to the fore could often be misleading, for they are often in response to the current happenings or immediate past happenings. Had our study coincided with a fiercely fought election to a local *panchayat*, perhaps the concern for 'market dependence' may have been faded by identities of faction and party loyalties. Households could have been identified more in terms their support to a political party or faction leader! Likewise, if our study had been soon after a major inter-caste strife, if not violence, the categorisation could well have been in terms of castes rather than either landownership or their relationship with the market. The challenge, therefore, is to identify the more consistent and pervasive sets of issues that may differentiate people among themselves, or any other perceptions that should go into a participatory research. Finally, the perceptions are contextually specific also because the findings may not be easily comparable in another field settings.
b) *Diverse perceptions*: It was a chance that in our study we were able to come across a set of perceptions about households that were uniformly applicable to all the households or people in them. It is possible, that the perceptions could in turn be dependent on other factors, and what we had identified may not be of much use in conclusively explaining the variation in behavioural patterns.
c) *Contested perceptions*: Even if one succeeds in penetrating through the diverse perceptions, it was often a difficult challenge to overcome when one or the other was unwilling to submit to a given classification. For instance, as our PRA for this purpose was in progress there were quite a few persons who disagreed with their classification under 'resource rich, buy all' category while claiming that they would better fit the description as 'resource poor, buy all' category.

d) *Luxury of research for 'identification'*: Not all social research practice can afford the luxury of carrying out a PRA exercise as we did. Time and other resources are a major constraint. Further, had our research been any conventional in that sense, one may question if the results of our PRA exercise would have been the same had it been carried out at the very commencement of our research.

The list of limitations and challenges is only indicative and not meant to be exhaustive. We believe, despite such limitations, it is worth a try.

References

Baumgartner, Ruedi, G.S. Aurora, G.K. Karanth and V. Ramaswamy (2004a). "Participatory research on rural livelihoods: Promoting local ownership of research findings", in Baumgartner, Ruedi and Reudi Hogger (eds.) *In Search of Sustainable Livelihood Systems: Managing Resources and Change*. New Delhi: Sage Publications. pp. 331 – 350.

———. (2004b). "In dialogue with indigenous knowledge: Sharing research to promote empowerment of rural communities in India", in Bicker, Alan., Paul Sillitoe and Johan Pottier (eds.) *Investigating Local Knowledge: New Directions, New Approaches*. Hants: Ashgate. pp.207–231.

Cleaver, Francis (2000). "Moral ecological rationality, institutions and the management of common property resources", *Development and Change* 31: 361-83.

Giddens, A. (1984). *Constitution of Society: Outline of the Theory of Structuration*. Cambridge: Polity Press.

Karanth, G.K. (1997). "Caste after fifty years of Independence", *Review of Development and Change* II(2): 319-337.

Karanth, G.K., and V. Ramaswamy (2004). "From *Marey* to market: Changing faces of rural livelihood system", in R. Baumgartner and R. Hogger, *In Search of Sustainable Livelihoods Systems: Managing Resources and Change*. New Delhi: Sage Publications. pp.275-97.

———. (2005). "At loggerheads or towards sustainability? Changing rural livelihood system and natural resource management", (Social and Economic Change *Monograph Series*, No. 9). Bangalore: Institute for Social and Economic Change.

Nadkarni, M.V. and G.K. Karanth (1995). "Regularisation of encroached lands: Who are the main beneficiaries?", *Deccan Herald*, December 29.

Olson, Mancur (1965). *The Logic of Collective Action: Public Goods and the Theory of Groups*. Cambridge: Harvard University Press.

Ostrom, E. (1990). *Governing the Common: The Evolution of Institutions for Collective Action*. Cambridge: Cambridge University Press.

———. (1992). *Crafting Institutions for Self Governing Irrigation Systems*. San Francisco: ICS Press.

Ramaswamy, V., G.S Aurora, and G.K. Karanth (1996). "Rural livelihood systems and sustainable resource management: A report from an Andhra Pradesh village", Bangalore: Institute for Social and Economic Change. (*Mimeo*).

Wolf, Eric (1966). *Peasants*. New Jersey: Prentice Hall Inc.